EURAIL® GUIDE

How To Travel Europe And All The World By Train

By Kathryn Saltzman Muileman
and
Marvin L. Saltzman

Country Maps: Anton Muileman

EURAIL® GUIDE

Printed in the U.S.A.

by

Kathryn S. Muileman
and Marvin L. Saltzman

Library of Congress Catalog Number 72-83072
ISBN 0-912442-13-1
US ISSN 0085-0330

Published by
Eurail Guide Annual
27540 Pacific Coast Highway
Malibu, California 90265, U.S.A.

First Edition	1971	96 pages
Second Edition	1972	168 pages
Third Edition	1973	288 pages
Fourth Edition	1974	384 pages
Fifth Edition	1975	384 pages
Sixth Edition	1976	432 pages
Seventh Edition	1977	432 pages
Eighth Edition	1978	768 pages
Ninth Edition	1979	768 pages
Tenth Edition	1980	816 pages
Eleventh Edition	1981	816 pages
Twelfth Edition	1982	816 pages
Thirteenth Edition	1983	816 pages

DISTRIBUTED IN

U.S.A.

Argentina	France	Nicaragua
Australia	Greece	Northern Ireland
Austria	Guatemala	Norway
Belgium	Guyana	Panama
Belize	Holland	Paraguay
Bolivia	Honduras	Peru
Brazil	Hong Kong	Scotland
Canada	India	Singapore
Chile	Indonesia	South Africa
Colombia	Irish Rep.	Sultanate of Oman
Costa Rica	Israel	Sweden
Denmark	Italy	Switzerland
Dominican Rep.	Japan	Thailand
Ecuador	Luxembourg	Uruguay
El Salvador	Malaysia	Venezuela
England	Mexico	Wales
Finland	New Zealand	West Germany

IMPORTANT NOTES

Always--without exception—before commencing each journey doublecheck the departure and arrival times given in our book or in any timetable, as they are subject to change without prior notice. Changes will usually be minor and have no effect on the trips described in this book. We do not want you to miss a train or to be stranded.

Departure and arrival times in this book are given in 24-hour time. A departure at 1:10 PM is shown as 13:10. Midnight is 24:00. Time between Midnight and 1:00 AM is shown as 0:01 to 0:59.

All schedules shown are daily, unless designated otherwise.

Unless indicated otherwise, the departure and arrival times in our book are for the period of late May to late September. In most cases, these schedules change slightly during September-May.

Where we state that departures from a city are "at frequent times", this means at least once each hour between the 2 time periods indicated.

The schedules for one-day roundtrip excursions do not always reflect *all* the departure times from either the base-city or the destination-city. Only those departure times involved in making a one-day roundtrip are shown. On a particular route, there frequently are later departure times from the base-city and earlier departure times from the destination-city than are shown, none of which would be applicable to a one-day round-trip.

Many cities have 2 or more railstations. Wherever this is so, we note the name of the applicable railstation (in parenthesis) after the name of the city. For Austria, East Germany, Switzerland and West Germany, where no name is shown after the name of the city, the station is always "Hauptbahnhof".

The number appearing at the start of a schedule is the Thomas Cook Timetable number, such as the example below:

Bergen - Oslo 481

Dep. Bergen	7:20
Arr. Oslo	14:05

Every year hundreds of readers send us suggestions, each of which is checked and answered. Many are added to the next annually-revised edition. If you have discovered rail travel facts helpful to others, please send them to us.

TWO TABLES OF CONTENTS

The first Table of Contents lists 138 countries alphabetically.

The second Table of Contents lists these 138 countries by geographical areas (Eurailpass Europe, Britain, Eastern Europe, Middle East, Africa, etc.).

INDEX

An index of cities appears on pages 808-812.

TABLE OF CONTENTS #1

TABLE OF CONTENTS #2

TRAVELING SWITZERLAND'S RHONE VALLEY BETWEEN BERNE AND ISELLE

Chapter 1

THE JOY OF TRAIN TRAVEL

The least expensive, safest, most convenient, interesting and pleasant way to travel and really see the world is by train.

We accent "pleasant", because our book is about joyous adventure. Our goal is to make worldwide train travel easy and pleasurable.

When traveling by train, your departure is not delayed by weather, as it can be when traveling by airplane or automobile.

You leave and arrive in the center of a city, saving the time, effort and expense involved with going back and forth to distant airports. In fact, many high-speed trains actually get you from a hotel in one city to a hotel in another city faster than by airplane when the distance is 250-350 miles.

The cost of an uncomfortable and non-airconditioned 2-passenger mini car for 350 miles per day travel can come to as much as $65 (U.S.) per day—daily rental, very high taxes on the rental charge (as much as 20% in Sweden, 18% in Denmark, France, Greece and Holland), mileage charge, gasoline (often at $3.00 per gallon), insurance, servicing, overnight parking fee, substantial drop-off charge, etc.

By contrast, one can travel on high-speed, air-conditioned luxury trains with any of numerous bargain rail passes for $5-$10 per day. (See detailed list on our Inside Front Cover.)

In train travel, you reach thousands of interesting destinations not accessible by airplane. You eliminate the worries, frustrations and delays of socked-in airports, flat tires, the requirement to check-in early at airports, the interminable waiting for baggage to be unloaded, driving into the crowded streets of an unfamiliar city, coping with strange traffic laws and the many other problems, expenses and inconveniences connected with airplane and auto travel.

From London to Tokyo, you find at principal railstations a wide variety of services and goods: food, information on local tours, assistance in obtaining lodging, money exchange, waiting rooms where you can relax, shoe repair, etc.

If you plan your routes well, you will see an array of visual delights that airplane passengers never see: indescribable seashores, vineyards tinted by afternoon sunlight, castles that have been straddling their hilltops for centuries, raging rivers, breathtaking waterfalls, Alpine summits, remote villages founded before Christ, fjords, forests, lovely orchards and pastures—a feast of colorful pictures to enjoy long after the trip ends.

At the end of a train trip, you arrive at your destination relaxed and rested.

By selecting special luxury trains, you are able to enjoy not only great scenery en route and interesting destinations but also the added dimension of trains which in themselves are a worthwhile travel experience in the same way that leading steamships of the past were.

There is no waiting for the next city to have the use of lavatory facilities. Usually, a cup of coffee or bottle of beer is only a 2-minute walk away. During the trip you can get up from your seat, stretch, take a stroll through the train.

Only train travel affords the opportunity of meeting and conversing with the people in the area you are visiting and also with tourists from other parts of the world.

Since 1959, among the fellow passengers with whom we have shared train rides have been Amsterdam businessmen, students from California, Italian army officers, gregarious Yugoslav geologists, an Uruguayan cardiologist, North Dakota farmers, a Chinese woman doctor from Canada, a family from Brazil, a young Russian woman returning home from a trade fair in East Germany, and a professor of language from Boston.

Every year since the first Eurail® Guide in 1971, each annually-revised and expanded edition of our book has been the product of a large "family".

Our daughter Kathryn proposed the idea for Eurail® Guide when she was traveling Europe on a 3-month Eurailpass in 1970. We published our first annual edition in early 1971 as 96 pages, and the book has been growing ever since then.

Kathryn and I, in writing each new edition, are aided and abetted by Barbara, who uncovers errors, suggests improvements and causes endless revisions—the classic dissatisfied editor to whom authors become permanently indebted once the travail is over.

Kathryn has traveled at different seasons and has taken different routes than those Barbara and I have traveled, giving each edition a variety of experiences and strikingly different viewpoints. For one thing, no stranger has offered to carry my suitcases or take me to dinner.

Many others have provided information and assistance, for which we express our gratitude: Juergen Arnold, North American Assistant General Manager, German Federal Railroads . . . Walter Bruderer, North

American Public Relations Director, Swiss National Tourist Office . . . Peter Ueltschi, North American Railway Department, Swiss National Tourist Office . . . Andy Lazarus, A.J. Lazarus Associates . . . and Dagobert M. Scher, North American Assistant General Manager, French National Railroads.

Other important members of the Eurail® Guide family are the scores of readers who each Fall write us as we are preparing the next edition to tell us where they have traveled and describe their experiences.

Comments about your train journeys will be greatly appreciated. Write us what you liked and disliked . . . out-of-the-way places you visited and recommend . . . and anything else you believe would help other travelers plan future trips.

Send your notes to: Eurail Guide Annual, 27540 Pacific Coast Highway, Malibu, Cal. 90265, U.S.A.

In the following pages, we identify basic problems in train travel worldwide, show how these can be overcome, and tell you all you need to know in order to travel the world by train safely, economically and pleasantly.

(M.L.S.)

Postscript: Never plan to travel without finding out if the countries you are going to tour have low-price train passes.

And when those countries have train passes, make sure before you leave home to know if any pass you want to buy has to be purchased before you leave home or can be bought only after you arrive in the country you will be touring.

All of the train passes offered when this edition of Eurail® Guide went to press are described in our book.

Chapter 2

WHETHER TO EURAILPASS

Since 1959, Western European railroads have offered the travel bargain called Eurailpass, sold throughout the world except in Europe and North Africa.

Eurailpass and Eurail Youthpass entitle one to unlimited first or second-class train travel plus free or reduced fare on many buses and boats in these 16 countries: Austria, Belgium, Denmark, Finland, France, Greece, Holland, Irish Republic, Italy, Luxembourg, Norway, Portugal, Spain, Sweden, Switzerland and West Germany.

In Europe, first-class cars (and the first-class portion of mixed-class cars) are marked outside by a yellow line running above the windows.

Later in this chapter, we describe the separate Eurail Youthpass, good for unlimited *second-class* train space.

Neither Eurailpass nor Eurail Youthpass can be purchased after you arrive in Europe. Both are non-refundable if lost or stolen. If you present them to a Eurailpass office before they become valid, 85% of the purchase price will be refunded.

There are Eurail Aid Offices in several European cities (listed on the map that is given with each Eurailpass), where a lost Eurailpass or Eurail Youthpass can be replaced if the buyer has retained the purchase authentication slip.

Both passes become valid on the first day they are used, after first having been recorded at the ticket office of the station from where the first journey begins.

Prices in this chapter are U.S. dollars.

The phrase "unlimited travel" means exactly that. You can literally travel 24 hours a day for the entire period a pass is valid. Countless travelers have used 3 and 4 times the price of their pass, saving hundreds of dollars their itinerary would have cost if they had used ordinary tickets.

The bargain does not end there. Tickets for the fast Trans Europ Express, Inter-City and many of the TGV trains cost more than space on an ordinary, slower train on the same route, a supplemental charge ranging from $3.00(U.S.) to $18.00.

Eurailpass includes unlimited use of TEE, IC and TGV trains (described in Chapter 7) without having to pay any supplement. All of the TEE and many of the IC and TGV trains do require reservations. The $2.00(U.S.) fee per reservation must be paid when riding them, even when using a Eurailpass.

In addition to the money-saving feature, Eurailpass adds precious time to a travel schedule. Many travelers feel that never having to stand in a ticket-selling line when you have a Eurailpass or a Eurail Youthpass is enough reason to have the pass. It can take up to 30 minutes for purchasing each ticket along the way.

(With or without a pass, if reserved seats are required or desired it is necessary to allocate time for the separate Seat Reservation Line. More about reservations in Chaper 3.)

On the other hand, Eurailpass is not always an economy. Some European itineraries are less expensive using regular train tickets or using one or a combination of the many national and regional rail passes described in this book (France Vacances, GermanRail Tourist Card, Benelux Tourrail, etc.).

The only way to find out if a Eurailpass or the numerous other passes will save you money on your trip is to compare their price with the total prices of tickets for your particular itinerary.

There are over 100,000 miles of European train travel you can make with a pass. It is impossible for us to give you the fare and travel time for every possible trip in Europe.

However, we provide you in our Chapter 18 "Route Chart" a list of more than 700 train trips that most people touring the 16 Eurailpass countries might take, with the first-class fare and travel time for each of them.

If you are considering traveling the heavily-crowded second-class, compute second-class fares at two-thirds of the first-class fares shown. That will come close to actual second-class ticket prices.

The first step in using the Chapter 18 Route Chart is to make a list of your itinerary. It is advisable to schedule any part of your trip that is not in the 16 Eurailpass countries (such as England, Yugoslavia, etc.) either before or after the days you are touring the countries in which Eurailpass is valid so as to avoid consuming Eurailpass days and in order to buy the least expensive Eurailpass for your trip.

Next, consult the Route Chart and note the first-class fare for each leg of your trip that can be covered by Eurailpass or Eurail Youthpass.

Keep in mind that even though you purchase your Eurailpass weeks or months in advance of starting your trip, the Eurailpass validity period does not begin until the first day you actually use the pass.

It's a good idea to protect yourself from having your pass rendered partly or wholly invalid because the validity dates were entered incorrectly. The Eurailpass must be validated at the ticket office of the station at your first departure. At that time, the clerk writes on the pass both the first and last day it can be used. Before he does this, write a note with what you believe are the validity dates, show it to him, and ask him if he agrees with those dates. Only when he says your dates are correct, or explains why they are not, should you hand your pass to him for the dates to be entered on it.

Once the clerk has written any validity dates on the face of your Eurailpass, those dates cannot be changed, since any alteration of the dates invalidates the pass. That is why it is wise to have him agree on the correct dates *before* he writes anything.

If one fails to have the Eurailpass validated before boarding the first train ride, the train conductor can do so. However, there is a $3 fee for a post-departure validation.

After your Eurailpass or Eurail Youthpass has been validated, remove the "proof of purchase" stub from the 3-part pass. From then on, as you would do with a list of traveler's checks after purchasing them, keep that stub separate from the pass. It is this stub that is required for a replacement in case the pass itself is lost or stolen.

Both Eurailpass and Eurail Youthpass are accepted by those trains running between airports and cities: Amsterdam, Barcelona, East Berlin, Bilbao, Brussels, Dusseldorf, Frankfurt, Malaga, Munich, Paris, Vienna and Zurich.

The 1983 charge for Eurailpass is $260(U.S.) for 15 days, $330 for 21 days, $410 for one month, $560 for 2 months and $680 for 3 months. Children 4 to under 12 pay half-fare.

An average 21-day itinerary is $150-$250 more expensive with first-class tickets than with a Eurailpass. And, a Eurailpass gives you the convenience of not having to stand in time-consuming lines to purchase tickets.

Depending on the itinerary, it can be the least expensive formula to buy a combination of Eurailpass and train tickets. For example, when traveling by train over a 22-day period with a $40 ride on the last day, it saves $40 to buy a 21-day Eurailpass and a ticket for the 22nd day ($330 + $40 = $370) instead of buying a $410 one-month Eurailpass.

On the other hand, if the trip on the 22nd day is $81 or more, it will save money to buy a one-month Eurailpass even though it is being used only 22 days.

Depending on the circumstances, it can be worthwhile to have any length Eurailpass without using it all the days you are entitled to use it.

The Chapter 18 Route Chart makes it easy for you to compute the ticket price for your trip and then determine *whether* to buy a Eurailpass, which Eurailpass will save you the most money, and how to schedule your train trips so as to fit them into the validity period of your Eurailpass.

Figures in the Route Chart for travel time between 2 cities represent the longest time for each trip. In many instances, the time stated is for a night train and there is a shorter-time day train on which you could make the same journey. Or there may be 2 or more trains running during the day, one of which is a fast express which makes the trip in less time than indicated in the Route Chart.

Despite such differences in travel time, the Route Chart time, as a rule, will be no more than 10% greater than the fastest time between 2 cities.

The Eurail® Guide Route Chart is accurate enough to help you decide whether you want to make a particular trip in one day or break it up into 2 or more shorter trips.

EUROPE'S GREATEST TRAINS

Chapter 7 lists all of Europe's special, very fast TEE, IIC and TGV trains, indicating the itinerary and timetables for each. Seat reservations are mandatory for many of these trains and usually can be made 2 months in advance, some railroads taking reservations only one month before travel date.

The TGV takes only 4 hours 50 minutes to go from Paris to Marseille, traveling at a peak speed of 162 mph on some portions of that route. The running time for a regular train on that route is 7 hours, as noted in our Route Chart. A ticket on the Paris-Marseille TGV costs about $15(U.S.) more than on an ordinary train for the same trip.

The IIC train "Catalan" makes the Barcelona-Geneva run in 9½ hours versus the ordinary train time of 12 hours. A ticket on "Catalan" costs about $10(U.S.) more than a regular, slower train does.

These 2 examples illustrate a major Eurailpass bonus: being able to ride the all first-class TEE luxury, high-speed trains at no extra charge over the price you pay for your Eurailpass.

Conversely, the Eurail Youthpass (restricted to travel in second-class space) can be used for travel on TEE trains only if you pay the difference in fare. On "Aquitane", from Paris to Bordeaux, the extra fare for a passenger traveling with Eurail Youthpass comes to about $37(U.S.).

EURAIL YOUTHPASS

This pass is for unlimited *second-class* train travel in the same 16 countries which honor the first-class Eurailpass. In 1983, the $290(U.S.) price for a one-month Eurail Youthpass is a $120 savings compared to the $410 one-month Eurailpass. The $370 2-month Eurail Youthpass is a $190 savings compared to the $560 2-month Eurailpass.

Second-class space is very acceptable on trains in Austria, Belgium, Denmark, Finland, France, Holland, Irish Republic, Luxembourg, Norway, Sweden, Switzerland and West Germany.

The buyer of a Eurail Youthpass must prove he or she is under 26 years of age on the first day of using the pass.

Both Eurail Youthpass and Eurailpass can be purchased from a travel agent or directly from the following places:

U.S.A. and Canada

BEVERLY HILLS, CAL.
French National Railroads
9465 Wilshire Blvd.

BOSTON, MA.
German Federal Railroad
625 Statler Office Bldg.

CHICAGO, ILL.
CIT (Italian State Railways)
765 Route 83
Bensenville, Ill. 60106

French National Railroads
11 E. Adams St.

GermanRail
104 So. Michigan Ave.

CORAL GABLES, FLA.
French National Railroads
2121 Ponce de Leon Blvd. (33134)

DENVER, COL.
GermanRail
8000 E. Girard Ave. (80231)

HOUSTON, TEX.
German Federal Railroad
1121 Walker St. (77002)

SANTA MONICA, CAL.
GermanRail
520 Broadway (90401)

LOS ANGELES, CAL.
CIT (Italian State Railways)
5670 Wilshire Blvd. (90036)

MONTREAL, P.Q., CANADA
CIT (Italian State Railways)
2055 Peel St.

French National Railroads
1500 Stanley St. (H3A-1R3)

NEW YORK, N.Y.

CIT (Italian State Railways)
666 Fifth Ave.

French National Railroads
610 Fifth Ave. (10020)

German Federal Railroad
747 Third Ave. (10017)

Swiss Federal Railways
608 Fifth Ave.

SAN FRANCISCO, CAL.

French National Railroads
360 Post St. (94108)

GermanRail
1 Hallidie Plaza (94102)

Swiss National Tourist Office
250 Stockton St. (94108)

TORONTO, ONT., CANADA

GermanRail
1290 Bay St. (M5R 2C3)

VANCOUVER, B.C., CANADA

French National Railroads
409 Granville St. (B6C-1T2)

ELSEWHERE

AUSTRALIA: C.I.T. Australia (Sydney), Inter-Group Travel (Adelaide, Brisbane, Chadstone, Chatswood, Doncaster, Hobart, Melbourne, Perth, Sydney and Toowoomba), and the Commercial Banking Company of Sydney Ltd. (Sydney).

HONG KONG: American Express International Inc. and Lufthansa German Airlines.

INDONESIA: Pantravel and Travel & Tourism Service (Jakarta).

IRAN: Near East Tours (Teheran).

ISRAEL: European Wholesale Tour Representatives (Haifa).

JAPAN: Japan Travel Bureau (Fukuoka, Hiroshima, Kobe, Kyoto, Nagaya, Niigata, Osaka, Sapporo, Sendai, Tokyo and Yokohama).

LEBANON: Tabbath Comfort Travel (Beirut).

NEW ZEALAND: Thomas Cook (Auckland, Christchurch and Wellington).

PHILIPPINES: American Express International (Manila).

SINGAPORE: American Express International.

SOUTH AFRICA: Global Tours South Africa (Johannesburg), and World Travel Agency (Capetown and Johannesburg).

TAIWAN: American Express International (Taipei).

THAILAND: Dietheim International Transport Services (Bangkok).

SECOND-CLASS SPACE

The 3 price alternatives that passengers 26 or older have when traveling Eurailpass countries by train are: first-class tickets, Eurailpass, or second-class tickets.

Second-class tickets are very close to 66% of the first-class price. Therefore, the cost of the example itinerary using second-class tickets (and that precludes riding on any TEE trains) comes to about $350—more expensive than traveling first-class and TEE trains with a Eurailpass.

OTHER DISCOUNTS

There are alternative economies to use besides Eurailpass and Eurail Youthpass when traveling Europe by train. These are the special discount tickets, coupons, passes, etc. which various countries issue individually. Details on these appear in this book under the listing of each country.

Some of these discount tickets can be purchased outside Europe. Others may be purchased only in the issuing country itself. Since these regulations change frequently, it is suggested that you first contact the office nearest your residence. Those in the U.S. and Canada are listed here:

AUSTRIA

Austrian Federal Railways

200 E. Randolph Dr., Chicago, Ill. 60601
3440 Wilshire Blvd., Los Angeles, Cal. 90010
1010 Ouest Rue Sherbrooke, Montreal, Que. H3A 2R7
545 Fifth Ave., New York, N.Y. 10017
1007 N.W. 24th Ave., Portland, Ore. 97210
2 Bloor Street East, Toronto, Ont. M4W 1A8
736 Granville St., Vancouver, B.C. V6Z 1J2

BELGIUM

Belgian National Railroads

745 Fifth Ave., New York, N.Y. 10151
5801 Ave. Monkland, Montreal, P.Q. H4A 1G4

FRANCE

French National Railroads

9465 Wilshire Blvd., Beverly Hills, Cal. 90212
11 East Adams St., Chicago, Ill. 60603
2121 Ponce de Leon Blvd., Coral Gables, Fla. 33134
1500 Stanley St., Montreal, P.Q., Canada H3A-1R3
610 Fifth Ave., New York, N.Y. 10020
360 Post St., San Francisco, Cal. 94108
409 Granville St., Vancouver, B.C., Canada B6C-1T2

GREAT BRITAIN

BritRail Travel

333 No. Michigan Ave., Chicago, Ill. 60601
510 W. Sixth St., Los Angeles, Cal. 90014
630 Third Ave., New York, N.Y. 10017
55 Eglington Ave. East, Toronto, Ont. M4P 1G8, Canada
409 Granville St., Vancouver, B.C. V6C 1T2, Canada

GREECE

Greek National Tourist Organization

611 W. 6th St., Los Angeles, Cal. 90017
645 Fifth Ave., New York, N.Y. 10022

HOLLAND

Netherlands National Tourist Office

576 Fifth Ave., New York, N.Y. 10036
681 Market St., San Francisco, Cal. 94105
327 Bay St., Toronto, Ont., Canada M5H-2R2

IRELAND

Irish Tourist Board

230 No. Michigan Ave., Chicago, Ill. 60601
1880 Century Park East, Los Angeles, Cal. 90067
590 Fifth Ave., New York, N.Y. 10036
681 Market St., San Francisco, Cal. 94105
69 Yonge St., Toronto, Ont. M5E 1K3

ITALY

Italian State Railways

765 Route 83, Bensenville, Ill. 60106
5670 Wilshire Blvd., Los Angeles, Cal. 90036
2055 Peel St., Montreal, Que. 110
666 Fifth Ave., New York, N.Y. 10103
111 Richmond St. West, Toronto, Ont.

DENMARK, FINLAND, ICELAND, NORWAY, SWEDEN

Scandinavian National Tourist Offices

75 Rockefeller Plaza, New York, N.Y. 10019

POLAND

Polish Travel Bureau

500 Fifth Ave., New York, N.Y. 10036

SPAIN

Spanish National Tourist Office

845 N. Michigan Ave., Chicago, Ill. 60611
4800 The Galleria, 5085 Westheimer, Houston, Tex. 70056
665 Fifth Ave., New York, N.Y. 10022
Hypolita & St. George Sts., Saint Augustine, Fla. 32084
1 Hallidie Plaza, San Francisco, Cal. 94102
60 Bloor St. West, Toronto, Ont. M4W 1A1

SWITZERLAND

Swiss National Tourist Office

104 S. Michigan Ave., Chicago, Ill. 60603
608 Fifth Ave., New York, N.Y. 10020
250 Stockton St., San Francisco, Cal. 94108
P.O. Box 215, Commerce Court Postal Station, Toronto, Ont. M5L 1E8

WEST GERMANY

625 Statler Office Bldg., Boston, MA 02116
104 So. Michigan Ave., Chicago, IL 60603
8000 E. Girard Ave., Denver, Col. 80231
1121 Walker St., Houston, TX 77002
520 Broadway, Suite 320, Santa Monica, Cal. 90401
747 Third Ave., New York, N.Y. 10017
1 Hallidie Plaza, San Francisco, Cal. 94102
1290 Bay St., Toronto, Ont. M5R 2C3

EURAILPASS AND EURAIL YOUTHPASS BONUSES

In addition to unlimited train travel, the Eurailpass and Eurail Youthpass provide many free bonuses or reduced prices for boat trips, buses and private railways.

AUSTRIA Two rack railways: (1) Puchberg am Schneeberg-Hochschneeberg and (2) St. Wolfgang-Schafbergspitze. Two cruises: (1) Lake Wolfgang and (2) Danube, between Passau and Vienna. Reduction of 50% on Lake Constance ships.

BELGIUM Up to 50% reduction on Europabus lines.

DENMARK These ferry crossings: Aarhus-Kalundborg, Knudshoved-Halskov, Nyborg-Korsor, Fynshav-Bojden, Rodby Farge-Puttgarden, Helsingor-Helsingborg and Frederikshavn-Goteborg. Reduction of 20% on 4 boat trips: (1)Esberg-Harwich, (2)Esberg-Newcastle, (3)Esberg-Faero Islands, and (4)Copenhagen-Oslo.

FINLAND Three cruises: (1) Helsinki-Stockholm, (2) Turku-Stockholm, and (3) Turku-Aland Island-Stockholm.

FRANCE Irish Continental Line ferry crossings between LeHavre and Rosslare, also between Cherbourg and Rosslare. Port taxes are extra, payable in French francs. The Digne-Nice rail trip. Up to 50% reduction on Europabus lines.

GERMANY Two cruises: (1) Rhine (between Dusseldorf and Frankfurt), and (2) Mosel (between Trier and Koblenz). Eurail Youthpass holders must pay an extra charge on Express-steamers. One ferry crossing: Puttgarden to Rodby. Most of the Post/Railroad bus lines, including "Romantic Road" (Wiesbaden-Munich and vice versa) and "Castle Road" (Mannheim-Nurnberg and vice versa). Reduction of 50% on (1) Lubeck-Travemunde-Malmo ferry crossing, (2) cruises on Lake Constance, (3)the Freiburg(Breisgau)-Schauinsland private railroad, and (4)the Garmisch-Partenkirchen-Grainau-Zugspitze private railroad. A 20% reduction on some half-day and full-day excursions out of Munich operated by Oberbayern GmbH. A 10% reduction on Munich city sightseeing tours operated by Oberbayern.

GREECE The ferry crossing from Patras to Brindisi.

ITALY The ferry crossing from Brindisi to Patras. About 20% reduction on these 7 boat trips: (1) Naples-Palermo, (2) Naples-Malta, (3) Syracuse-Malta, (4) Genoa-Tunis, (5) Genoa-Alicante, (6) Genoa-Malaga, and (7) crossings to Sardinia. Reverse trips are subject to same reduction. A 30% reduction on the boat trip Venice-Piraeus-Haifa, and vice versa on the Adriatica Line.

WARNING !

Don't be diverted at the Patras or Brindisi railstations from Adriatica or Hellenic Mediterranean Lines (the only ferries that honor Eurailpass) to other ships that charge large fees after deceiving passengers into believing their ships accept Eurailpass, extorting the charges when it is too late for passengers to leave their ferry and go to the other docks. The proper lines charge pass holders $12(U.S.) between June 10 and September 30. Reservations are required when using Eurailpass or Eurail Youthpass.

IRELAND Irish Continental Line ferry crossings between Rosslare and both LeHavre and Cherbourg. Port taxes are extra, payable in Irish pounds.

NORWAY A 30% reduction on the boat trip between Kristiansand and Hirtshals.

SPAIN A 20% reduction on Transmediterranean ships that operate between Algeciras and Tangier, Barcelona, Valencia and Palmas de Mallorca.

SWEDEN These 5 boat trips: (1)Stockholm-Helsinki, (2)Stockholm-Turku, (3)Stockholm-Aland Islands-Turku, (4)Helsingborg-Helsingor, and (5)Goteborg-Frederikshavn. A 50% reduction on the ferry crossing between Malmo andLubeck-Travemunde.

SWITZERLAND Boats on the lakes of Geneva, Luzern, Thun, Brienz, Zurich, Neuchatel, Biel and Murten. Boats on the Rhine (Schaffhausen-Kreuzlingen) and on the Aare (Biel Bienne-Solothurn). A 50% reduction on Lake Constance boats Romanshorn-Friedrichshafen and Rorschach-Lindau.

INTER RAIL CARD

Unlimited second-class train travel for one month. (Example: January 14 to February 13.) Can be purchased only in Europe. Sold only to persons under 26 years old who prove they have resided in the issuing country at least 6 months. The bearer can travel half-fare in the issuing country and free on the railways of the other 20 countries. The validity period begins on the first day the card is issued, and that day must be within 2 months after the card is purchased. The card also allows these discounts on boat trips: 50% on Rhine cruises, 50% Lake Constance, 50% Stockholm-Helsinki and 30% Barcelona-Palma de Mallorca.

Must be paid for in the currency of the country that issues it. The 1983 price in French francs is 1,236FF.

Sold at most railstations in Austria, Belgium, Denmark, Finland, France, Great Britain, Greece, Holland, Hungary, Ireland, Italy, Luxembourg, Morocco, Norway, Portugal, Romania, Spain, Sweden, Switzerland, West Germany and Yugoslavia.

SENIOR INTER RAIL CARD

Sold only to persons 65 or older who prove they have resided in the issuing country for at least 6 months. Can be purchased only in Europe. Unlimited first or second-class train travel for one month. Has same bonuses as the Junior Inter Rail Card. The bearer travels half-fare in the issuing country and free on the railways of the other 16 countries.

Must be paid for in the currency of the country that issues it. The 1983 prices in French francs are: First-class 1,663FF. Second-class 1,109FF.

Sold at most railstations in Austria, Belgium, Denmark, Finland, France, Greece, Holland, Italy, Luxembourg, Norway, Portugal, Romania, Spain, Sweden, Switzerland, West Germany and Yugoslavia, plus the privately-owned Bern-Lotschberg Railway in Switzerland.

STUDENT TRAVEL DISCOUNTS

The ISIC (International Student Identity Card) is a passport to low-cost travel for fulltime students and anyone who graduates within the calendar year: lower air fares, tours, accommodations and travel books, plus reduced or free admission to many museums, theaters, cultural attractions, historical sites, etc. More than a million ISIC are issued every year.

It provides entry to special hotels and restaurants in Europe and Asia for low-cost lodging and meals. All intra-European student charter flights, trains and ships offer discounts of 50% or more to holders of this card.

Developed and regulated by the International Student Travel Conference, the card carries the owner's photo. In the U.S.A., it is available through Student Travel Services and hundreds of high schools and college/university campuses authorized by the Council on International Educational Exchange, with offices at:

205 E. 42nd St.
New York, NY 10017

1093 Broxton Ave.
Los Angeles, CA 90024

2511 Channing Way
Berkeley, CA 94704

312 Sutter St.
San Francisco, CA 94108

49, rue Pierre Charron
Paris 75008, France

In recent years, the fee for an ISIC has been $6.00(U.S.). The 1983 ISIC is valid from October 1, 1982 through December 31, 1983.

A free 68-page catalog detailing the services is available before purchasing the card. After buying the card, students receive with it a list of worldwide discounts and benefits.

Chapter 3

HOW TO PLAN A RAIL INTINERARY

There are 4 dimensions to every train tour: the number of days one can allot, interesting destinations, scenic routes, and riding on special trains that are in themselves an attractive travel experience.

Whenever time and budget permit, the minimum trip to Europe should be 23 days. That includes the day you fly away and the day you fly back. Out of the 21 remaining days, you can figure that what is left of your first day in Europe (after going from the airport to your hotel) is good for little more than recovering from the combination whammy of travel fatigue and time change. Very few people are immune to the temporary disablement of jet lag, and most travelers are well advised to go to bed and postpone any appreciable activity until the second day in Europe. That leaves only 20 active days for sightseeing, and it's difficult to really see even a fraction of Europe in that time.

We recommend staying a minimum of 2 or 3 nights in most cities you visit, with only occasional one-nighters mixed in the intinerary. Even the sturdiest develop a psychosis when they spend too many consecutive nights each in a different hotel room. Besides, if you travel mostly by day as we suggest in order to see the countryside and have some opportunity to visit with fellow passengers, you will arrive in a city late in the day. If you leave there the next morning, you certainly are not going to see much in that city.

On a 2-night basis, you can cover 10-11 different cities during your 21 full days in Europe. Reducing a trip to 14 days means reducing the number of cities where you stop to 5 or 6. If 14 days is your limit, the 15-day Eurailpass and some fast footwork will still let you have a happy tour and cover a great deal of Europe.

After deciding on the length of time one has to tour, the next stop in itinerary planning is to pick the places to be visited, and most people have several cities in mind, usually more than time, energy and distance will allow.

The common-sense approach is to consult a map and visualize from it what is practical and what is impractical in putting together a list of places to see. Part of this narrowing-down process depends of course on what interests you the most. Every hamlet in Europe has some art, but if it's the greatest masterpieces you want to see, you go to cities such as Paris and Florence, not to Avignon or Oslo. If your interest is Alpine scenery, you are going to concentrate on Zurich and Salzburg, not on Barcelona or Copenhagen.

Knowing the travel time between each point on your intinerary is essential unless you are indifferent to 15-hour journeys that bring you into a destination after Midnight. The timetables in this book give you that information on more than 9,000 different rail trips.

At this point, you have determined how many days you will be in Europe, where you want to go, and where you can go in that time. You should now consider the combination of using special trains along with the most rewarding routes.

For example, the journey from Paris to Marseille can be made on any one of a dozen ordinary trains instead of riding on a high-speed TGV. A traveler has the same choice on many railway routes all over the world, between riding a commonplace, slow train or having an encounter with extraordinary rail travel. All the information on "Europe's Greatest Trains" is provided in Chapter 7.

RESERVATIONS—HOTEL AND TRAIN

Once you have composed the elements of days, cities, trains and routes, you are ready to consider whether you want to reserve hotels in advance.

When traveling to places we haven't been either before or recently, we rely on recommendations by friends who enjoyed particular hotels recently and whose tastes are similar to ours. The "recently" qualification is important, because a hotel's quality changes from time to time. We do not recommend hotels or restaurants. Management of both change (and quality along with it) between our annually-revised editions. It is always best to consult a competent travel agent who has current input from clients recently returning.

As in most other things, there is a great deal of luck connected with traveling. We prefer to maximize the odds in favor of our comfort and security when we travel and, as most travel writers urge readers to do.

we reserve hotel space well in advance. We also reserve train seats whenever we want to be on a particular train on a certain date.

The objection to such reservations has a great deal of merit. It is that you cannot be a footloose, carefree vagabond, lingering where unexpected attractions are discovered and making impetuous detours as the spirit moves one or abruptly departing sooner than you had planned to do when someplace fails to come up to expectations.

The sturdier one is, physically and psychologically, the stronger that argument is. There is no question that for those of us forced by the circumstances of daily life to lead ordered routines, there are few lawful activities that offer as great an opportunity to achieve freedom from a structured existence as does traveling by train.

While not quite infinite, the random choices one can make spontaneously are considerable. The feature that many people find irresistible about European trains is how easily one can decide an hour after starting a ride to one destination to leave that train and head elsewhere. Depending on how strongly this motive moves you, how fundamentally lucky you are in most matters and what you are willing and able to endure, advance hotel reservations may not be important for you.

On the other hand, if you ever have played an entire night of poker without holding one winning hand, or if you arrived in Copenhagen on the opening day of a World Bank Conference (no room within 20 miles) and your next stop was Paris where the International Motor Salon opened on the day of your arrival and the largest ($250,000) horse race on the Continent was being run the next day (no room within 30 miles), and your next stop was Dijon where the first 2 hotels you phoned ahead to were sold-out even through nothing special was happening that October week in Dijon, you might want to weigh the whole proposition.

From May through early October, European and non-European tourists pack all classes of hotels in leading European cities. Trade shows and business conventions pick up the slack instantly in September, October, March and April. A hotel in Bordeaux (not Paris or Rome, mind you) wrote us on July 13 that it was booked for the 2 nights we had requested: October 2 and 3!

If you travel Europe without advance room reservations from March through October, it is wise to arrive in your destination city early in the day. Rooms available because of no-shows or last-minute cancellations frequently are taken before mid-afternoon.

Upon arriving without a hotel reservation, go at once to the tourist accomodations desk in the train station. For a fee of 50¢ to $1.00, one of its employees will phone hotels and do his best to find you a room that comes close to your specifications. In certain cities (Amsterdam, Bergen, Brussels, etc.), this convenient service is not offered at the station but can be found at the city tourist office, sometimes only across from the railstation, sometimes quite a distance from it.

In the peak Summer touring months you will find long lines and if, as is usually the case, your stay is brief, you will have to devote precious sightseeing time to obtaining a room.

When traveling in groups of 2 or more, this ploy is effective: one person remains at the station guarding the luggage while the other canvasses the area near the station to find a room. Many non-Europeans are unaware that stations even in the smallest cities have waiting rooms with comfortable, upholstered chairs. If you follow this system, be sure to use the shelter of these waiting rooms. All over Europe, you will find many hotels within a radius of 2 or 3 blocks from a railstation.

A third system has been used successfully by many—to stay in the suburbs and not even attempt to find a hotel room in major cities, provided the suburb is linked by train with the city you want to tour.

Pick a town of moderate size about 30-45 minutes train travel time away from a major Metropolis.

Your second consideration is whether to reserve train seats.

Reservations for seats on Europe's greatest trains (see Chapter 7) can be made 2 months in advance, and many Europeans grab spaces on them soon after they become reservable. Casual tourists discover a few days before they want to travel on a special train that it is completely sold-out.

Reservations are mandatory on many of the best trains. That is why we recommend reserving seats even before you arrive in the countries you plan to travel. The worldwide offices of French National Railroads, German Federal Railroad, Italian State Railways and Swiss Federal Railways will obtain seat reservations for special trains within their own countries and in many other (but not all) European countries. Their North American offices are listed in Chapter 2.

Before you pay for a Eurailpass, you or your travel agent should ask the seller to confirm that his or her office will obtain all the seat reservations in all the Eurailpass countries you plan to travel, on those trains which offer reserved seats. If the seller refuses to do this, check with other offices (listed in Chapter 2) that sell Eurailpass. Don't buy your Eurailpass until you find a seller who will obtain all your seat reservations,

It is advisable to have the office that issues you the Eurailpass cable your reservation requests to Europe. The fee for this is $1.00 to $2.00 per reservation. This can result in your obtaining seats which otherwise might have been sold to others if your request had been sent by mail.

If, on the other hand, you wait to reserve train space at each departure station, keep in mind that at most European stations you must get in one line for a ticket and in a different line for a seat reservation. If you have a Eurailpass (described in Chapter 2), you eliminate having to wait in the ticket line, often a long wait.

As a matter of fact, you face long waits in 5 different lines—and part of the trick of making the most of your limited time is to avoid standing in any, and hopefully all, of these lines: information, ticket purchase, seat reservation, hotel accommodation and baggage check-room.

We will cover how you can avoid needing information in the "Timetables" section of Chapter 4. If you use Eurailpass (Chapter 2), you never need to buy a ticket and therefore completely omit the time wasted standing in the ticket purchase line. The solution to the hotel accommodation line, of course, is to make those reservations before you leave home. The baggage check-room problem is discussed in Chapter 5.

There is a way to *reduce* the amount of time spent in either the ticket or seat reservation lines. These lines are far shorter Monday-Thursday than they are on the weekend, when the natives are traditionally restless, and in mid-morning, rather than during the lunch hours or at early evening in the height of the commuter rush hours. During the mid-June to mid-September tourist season, it is often advantageous to have the hotel concierge or the one who runs your pensione get your reservation for you from someone they know at the station.

Regardless whether you are originating a reservation or merely reconfirming a reservation for which a ticket has not been issued, be sure to do so as much in advance as possible, preferably upon your arrival in the departure city. Requirements for reservations vary from country to country and, within a country, from city to city. In Italy, for example, reservations cannot be made less than 2 hours before a departure in some cities. Milan requires 3 hours notice. Rome requires 5 hours notice.

Say your trip is New York to Paris, then train to Geneva and train from Geneva to Rome. Make the Paris-Geneva reservation your first day in Paris, and make the Geneva-Rome reservation a few minutes after you arrive at the Geneva depot.

This advice does not mean you *must* have seat reservations. They are *required* only on TEE and a few other trains. However, anyone traveling in peak tourist months without reserved space will probably make the trip standing in the aisle and being brushed-up against approximately every 30 seconds by passengers ambling up and down the corridor. Keep in mind that Europeans can, and do, reserve train seats 2 months in advance.

We rode a very ordinary train from Bordeaux to Tours on an

October Monday morning. It was completely sold-out.

If, as we urge you to do in Chapter 5, you eat your train meals in your compartment rather than in the train dining-room, there is something else you can and should do when you make your seat reservation. Specify the window seat. On most European trains these are the only seats that have a fold-out table. Moreover, you see the sights better from a window seat. In some compartments, the seats next to the sliding door also have a fold-out table.

Another variation in seat reservations is that on nearly all European trains you can reserve seats in a compartment in which smoking is either prohibited or permitted. Depending on what your preference is, this can make a great deal of difference in enjoying your trip.

And still another reservation to keep in mind is specifying on which *side* of the train you want to be seated. Often there is a decided sightseeing advantage on one side and a corresponding disadvantage on the alternate side. Obviously, if you are traveling along the Riviera, the view of the Mediterranean is 100 times better on the left side if you are traveling West, and on the right side if your route is going East.

After logic tells you which side of a train offers the best view, the first step is to inquire while making your seat reservation if there is seating on that side. If so, ask for seats accordingly.

Reservation clerks in many European cities speak little or no English. It will save you much time and insure against getting an incorrect reservation if you hand the clerk a note indicating your destination, departure time and day of departure. But be sure to follow the European custom of showing the day of the month first, followed by the number of the month. In Europe, July 8 is 8/7. If you wanted to take a train to Milan, leaving at 1:50 PM on July 8, your note would read "Milan—13:50—8/7".

Finally, here are 7 great tips to keep in mind. Having made a seat reservation, when you leave your compartment to go to the W.C., dining car or merely to stretch, leave some object on your seat—newspaper, hat, something—to inhibit seat-grabbers from settling down in your space during your absence. While it is true that the conductor will aid you in removing an interloper, finding the conductor, explaining the problem and using his intervention is somewhat more bothersome than simply preventing the event.

Do not waste time trying to make a seat reservation for a train trip within Belgium, Holland, Luxembourg or Switzerland. Those countries sell seat reservations only for rides going from them into another country. However, finding a seat on trains of those countries is not a problem except on peak travel days.

Next, on a business day even though the reservation clerk claims all seats on a certain train are taken, you can nevertheless occasionally hop aboard and find an empty seat. This is due to the custom of many European business men, when undecided as to which train they are taking or on which day they are making a trip, to make several advance reservations so as to cover all bases—and then forfeit their reservation fee on all trains other than the one they finally do take. This practice accounts for some seats being marked "reserved" which are not used.

If traveling without seat reservations, be careful you do not take a reserved seat while all the unreserved ones are being occupied.

Check the seat chart outside each compartment before you sit down. If the rightful owners claim your seat later, you may have to stand during the entire ride.

If the required advance time for making a seat reservation has run out, seek the conductor and, in your most charming manner, tell him what your destination is and ask him to help you find a seat. As a class, conductors are remarkably courteous and cooperative and many we have observed welcome the opportunity to use their authority constructively.

Never, never discard a train ticket until after your trip has been completed and you have left the arrival station. You will frequently ride a train for hours without being asked to show a ticket or pass. Then, after you get off the train you discover you are required to show your ticket or pass at the exit of the arrival station. If you have thrown yours away, you will end up having to buy a second one. Best bet is to always hold onto your ticket, whether or not a conductor checks it.

PREPARATION FOR AUTUMN TOURING

One thing that is nearly always overlooked in intinerary planning is to prepare in advance for one very important contingency connected with traveling off-season. If you travel Europe anytime after early September—and Fall is outstanding for touring Europe—you'll find that English-language city sightseeing tours are discontinued as the volume of American tourists decline, particularly in places such as Avignon, Verona, Rouen, Tours, etc.

Autumn travelers can solve that problem by taking advantage of the fact that nearly every city in Europe, even a hamlet such as Honfleur, has a tourist office which will give you a comprehensive folder that includes a fine city map, an interesting description of principal things to see and often a suggested 2 or 3-hour walking tour that allows a visitor to find on his own the worthwhile historic sites, museums, churches, palaces and all the other local highspots he would have been shown on the discontinued motorcoach sightseeing tour.

The only hitch is that by early September many city tourist offices run out of the current year's supply of these useful folders. To insure against the disappointment of arriving somewhere and finding that neither a city tour nor printed material to use in lieu of a tour is available, there is a precaution you can take.

In the early part of the year, write to the cities you plan to visit and ask them while their supply is still good to mail you a copy of all literature and tourist maps they have, and specify you want the English-language (or whatever your preference) version, since this material is usually printed in several languages.

Then, if you arrive in a town that Fall after the last bus tour of the season, you're all set to see the sights without a guide, and at your own leisurely pace.

Simply address your request to "Tourist Office". You'll be surprised how much this easy preparation will add to your travel enjoyment.

Chapter 4

DON'T MISS THE TRAIN!

MULTI-STATION CITIES

Determine beforehand whether your departure or transfer city has more than one railstation. If so, next make sure that the train on which you are going to continue your trip will depart from the same station at which you are arriving. The easiest way to do that is to consult Thomas Cook International Timetable. If you are making a transfer, then be certain that there is adequate time to get from one station to the other in the following European cities with more than one railstation:

Antwerp
Athens
Barcelona
Basle
Belfast
Belgrade
Berlin
Bilbao
Boulogne
Brussels
Bucharest
Budapest
Calais
Casablanca
Cologne
Como
Copenhagen
Dover
Dublin
Dunkerque
Essen
Exeter
Folkestone
Geneva
Genoa
Glasgow
Halsingborg
Hamburg
Harwich
Hendaye
Irun
Le Havre
Leningrad
Liege
Lisbon
Liverpool
Lodz
London
Lyon
Madrid
Malmo
Manchester
Marseille
Milan
Moscow
Munich
Naples
Newhaven
Oporto
Orleans
Oslo
Paris
Portsmouth
Prague
Ramsgate
Rome
Rotterdam
San Sebastian
Seville
Southampton
Stockholm
Tilbury
Tours
Turin
Venice
Vienna
Warsaw
Weymouth
Wiesbaden
Zurich

As can be seen from the preceding list, there are 70 European cities which have 2 or more railroad stations. Immediately upon *arriving* in any of these multi-station cities, find out from which station your train departs for your next destination. Do not rely on getting that information an hour or so before your departure from someone such as your hotel clerk or taxi or bus driver.

TIMETABLES

The venerable Thomas Cook Continental Timetable has been published since 1873 (except from 1939 to 1945). Its younger sibling, the Overseas Timetable, was started in 1981, prompted by the interest in train travel outside Europe that had been generated many years earlier by Eurail® Guide. Both timetables are published in England.

The Continental Timetable (European schedules) is supposed to be published the first day of each month but sometimes misses the mark. The Overseas Timetable, covering the rest of the world, is issued every other month, starting with January.

In addition to train, boat and bus schedules, these publications also provide information on types of food service and sleeping accommodations offered. Their extensive array of symbols for such services and other information are translated into ordinary language at the start of each edition, under "Explanation of Signs".

A key item that even many experienced users of Cooks have failed to note is Table #1000, which lists hundreds of resorts that are not situated on a railway in its timetables. This special list gives the nearest railstation to such resorts, and the distance from that station to the resort. Included in Table #1000 are such places as Delphi (121 miles by road from Athens), Ile de Levant (9 miles by ferry from Le Lavandou) and Offenbach am Main (6 miles by suburban railway from Frankfurt).

Summer European train schedules appear in the June, July, August and September "Continental Timetable" issues. The latter contains an advance Winter supplement. Similarly, the February through May issues contain an advance Summer service supplement.

Both publications can be obtained in North America at $16.95(U.S.) each, postage included, from Dept. "E", Forsyth Travel Library, P.O. Box 2975, Shawnee Mission, KS. 66201, or by telephoning Dept. "E" at (913) 384-0496 and charging the purchase against a Visa or Master Charge credit card at a service charge of $1.00. Add $2.00(U.S.) for postage on each copy of either timetable that is to be mailed to Canada. Cook's "Rail Map of Europe" costs $7.95(U.S.), postage included. FTL has an extensive list of travel publications, maps of all countries and hundreds of cities, atlases, etc.

Because many countries do not offer their own timetables, or run short of them, Cooks is valuable for carrying along on a trip as well as for studying at home while planning an itinerary. Numerous readers tell us that having a copy while touring allows them to make impromptu changes in travel plans on the spur of the moment.

As Cooks says in each edition, the services shown are subject to alteration, and travelers should re-check departure times upon arriving in each station. Our standard train travel procedure upon arriving anywhere is to first provide for shelter, when we have not made advance reservations. The second item we dispose of is deciding what train we are taking to the next city on our itinerary. Third, we make our seat reservation then and there for that departure. Having done this, we are now carefree for the balance of our time in that city.

A "European Timetable for Railway Enthusiasts" lists dozens of "fun railways" in Britain and on the European Continent, including many cable cars, rope railways, horse trams and steam-engine trains. It is published by Schweers + Wall, Lothringerstr. 66, D-5100 Aachen 1, West Germany.

The "Eurail Timetable-Horaire Eurail-Eurail Fahrplan" contains most connections between important cities in Western Europe. It is sold at major European railstations.

There are 3 other timetables, specialized and far more condensed than Cooks, that you may find useful. All are distributed free. They can be obtained from travel agents and those railroad offices which sell Eurailpass. One is the very useful 24-page mini-folder put out by French National Railroads, called "Les Trains d'Affairs" ("businessman's trains", not as romantic as it sounds!). Containing May-September schedules, it has timetables for many trains that connect French cities both with each other and with cities in other countries.

A second folder, 34 pages and also very tiny, issued by the French company that runs sleeper cars (Compagnie Internationale des Wagons-Lits), has 40 timetables of trains providing wagons-lits service throughout Europe, including Greece, Hungary, Turkey and Yugoslavia. It is published in both a Summer (June through September) and a Winter (October through May) edition.

The third is a 32-page pamphlet called "European Car Carrying Trains", issued by the German Federal Railroad. Highlighted in it is a list of 153 European trains that are equipped to carry one's auto while the motorist uses sleeper accommodations on the same train, plus a list of 21 other trains that only carry autos, while the motorist uses another train for his own transportation.

Europe's "Car-Sleeper Express Service" becomes more popular every year. You can either sleep in a couchette or sleeper on the same train that carries your auto, or you can ship your car ahead on an "Auto Express", take another train, and find your car waiting for you at your destination.

Started by French National Railroads in 1957, this service is now offered as well by Austria, Belgium, Britain, Holland, Italy, Spain and West Germany. It links cities in those countries and also in Portugal, Switzerland and Yugoslavia. In recent years, it has moved annually 500,000 people and more than 160,000 cars.

In most European countries, a Summer timetable goes into effect on the last Sunday of May, remaining in effect until and including the last Saturday in September. Outside Britain, Winter schedules usually start on the Sunday following the last Saturday of September and run until and including the Saturday preceding the last Sunday of March of the following year.

British timetables differ from the Continental pattern. Summer timetables for British rail service begin on the first Monday of May, and changes then occur usually on various dates first in October and then again in January.

Unless designated otherwise, the departure and arrival times given in this book are for the Summer tourist season and apply to trips that will be made from early April to late September.

TRAIN-SPLITTING

How can one fail to admire the superhuman efficiency of Europe's vast international rail systems? Thousands of trains daily transport millions upon millions of people and yet achieve a dependability factor that is nearly perfect. An important part of this remarkable capacity is the technique of avoiding unnecessary duplication of personnel and equipment by the methods of switching cars and timing transfers so that when one must take 2 or more trains to get from one place to another the time between each segment of a trip is very brief.

The foreign tourist is inclined to wrongly regard these positive factors as an undue bother when, actually, only a minimum effort and preparation is required in order to have the advantage of travel speed and flexibility along with reasonable ticket prices.

This is how simple it is to prevent a mix-up. Before you leave the station to go to the track, find out if the car in which you will be starting your journey is going all the way to your destination without being switched to some other train or if you must transfer from this train to another train en route to your destination.

If your car is to be switched to another train, find out the name of the city where the switching will occur, the time it will take place, and the name of the stop just prior to the switching point.

Next, you're at the correct track, your train is ready to board, and your last step is to get onto the correct car. Where a train originally consists of cars that are eventually going to different destinations, each car is clearly marked with the name of the city where it originated and the name of the city where it will terminate. Frequently, the sign will also designate, as the example below does, some of the cities en route where stops will be made.

VENEZIA
Bologna — Firenze
ROMA

This sign shows that the car began in Venice, stops at Bologna and Florence, and terminates in Rome. Next to the steps leading up into a car, either the numeral "1" or "2" appears, designating first-class or second-class seats. You may find an entirely first-class car coupled to an entirely second-class car, both cars marked with the same origin-destination sign. Or, a single car may be marked "1" at one end and "2" at the other end, indicating that part of this car is first-class and part is second-class.

A car change can occur while you are several cars away from your seat (and from your baggage, since it usually stays either in your compartment or at the end of your car). You may have so little time to get back to your car that you end up going one direction while your suitcases are heading, without you, for the place you had intended to go.

If you have determined in advance when and where your car is being switched and have also boarded the correct car, you are prepared for the change by being in your car when the change occurs. The following story illustrates the hazard we want you to avoid and may induce you to follow some practical recommendations we offer at the end of the vignette.

An officer in the U.S. Army Transportation Corps. who is an expert on both military and personal travel, Lt. Col. Will B. Allanson, wrote us about an experience he suffered when he was a novice: "I and my family had just arrived in France, for our first time in Europe, in the Summer of 1964. Within 5 days of our arrival, my boss asked me to make a business trip to an army installation in Germany. Thinking it would be nice to let the family catch an initial glimpse of Europe too, I bought tickets for them and off we went from Paris on a rapide headed for Frankfurt.

"At about 11:30, the train stopped at the little town of Bar-le-Duc. My children were beginning to get hungry, and there was no dining-car. Leaning out of the window of our car, the last car on the train, I spied a sandwich hawker up near the locomotive. I jogged up the track to him, bought some sandwiches and, not being certain how long the train would remain stopped, I boarded it near the locomotive. As I started walking through the train, heading back toward my car, the train started up.

"I got about as far as what had been the middle of the train . . . and there was no more train! It had been split.

"All I knew was that I was heading off towards an unknown direction, without my family, at approximately 80 mph.

"I had done just about everything wrong there was to do. First, of course, was leaving the car. Next, I had most of the travel money on me, leaving my wife practically penniless. But she had the trump—she had my ticket and my passport.

"Well, my wife was on her way to Frankfurt, heading Northeast, while I was heading due East to Nancy. I borrowed a timetable from the conductor and figured out that I could get off in Nancy and from there take another train to Metz. In Metz, I could then catch a train that would be following my wife's train by 2 hours.

"I did this and, in Metz, found my wife and kiddies (who had gotten off their train to wait for me) practically in a pool of tears. Other passengers in my wife's compartment were Frenchmen who, alarmed at my not returning, had guessed what had happened and urged my wife to get off in Metz and wait for me there."

This experience taught Col. Allanson these rules: Don't stray from your car while stopped in a station. When 2 or more people are traveling together, each should carry his own money, his own passport and his own ticket, or Eurailpass. On our travels, we divvy-up not only U.S. one-dollar bills and the currency of the country we're in, but we also carry separate traveler's checks in each name.

TRAIN-CHANGING

Frequently you will find that while you cannot take a train directly to some point, it is quite easy to get there by using a series of 2 or more trains. And in many cases the connections are very convenient, so that you change from one train to another with only a short waiting period at the transfer station. For example, there is no direct train from Zurich to popular Locarno, but the Zurich-Milan train arrives in Bellinzona at 12:43, and a train for Locarno departs Bellinzona 5 minutes later, at 12:48.

The track for the Bellinzona-Locarno train is next to the track on which you arrive from Zurich, making this change effortless. Even if the Zurich-Milan train is running a few minutes late—and you will be amazed how rarely trains in Western Europe are even slightly off schedule — your walk from one train to another on this connection is about 10 feet, and they will hold a local train such as the Bellinzona-Locarno one for you to make a train change when the principal train is running late.

On the other hand, international trains from eastern countries (Turkey, Greece, Yugoslavia, etc.) usually arrive late due to delays at border-crossings.

The problem in train-changing for which you should prepare, by being ready to step off the first train as soon as it pulls into the transfer station, is that if the transfer station is a large one you may find you are arriving on Track #2 and departing from Track #21, a considerable distance and invariably involving first descending into the underground walkway that connects all tracks, passing through it, and then climbing up the steps leading to your departure track. This transfer problem is compounded if your first train arrives late and the second train is an express train which cannot detain its scheduled departure time.

Normally, your first train will arrive on schedule, and you have more than enough time to make the change. However, it is best to inquire on board the first train from its conductor the number of the track on which you are arriving and the number of the track from which your departing train leaves and also to be ready at the exit door of your arriving train some minutes before it pulls into the transfer point.

The word for "track" in Europe is: Gleis (Austria, Germany and Switzerland), Spoor (Holland and Belgium, which also uses Voie), Spor (Norway), Spar (Sweden), Quai (France), Binario (Italy), Anden (Spain), Voie (Luxembourg), and Perron (Denmark).

Most train stops in Europe are efficiently very brief, 2 or 3 minutes. This is one of the reasons you can go from place to place so rapidly on European trains. Where a stop is fairly generous, say 20 minutes or more, it is often because some car on your train is being switched to another train and possibly also to another track in that station.

Unwary passengers are apt to get out of the train at a stop and wander away, discovering too late that their train has left without them! When we have the urge to stretch our legs, get some fresh air and look at the trackside activity, we never go more than a few feet away from the door of the train car. That way, if our car is being switched or the stop is merely a momentary one, we can jump back aboard.

Chapter 5

VALUABLE TRAIN TRAVEL TIPS

We have included in this chapter the many facts we wish we had known when we first traveled by train many years ago. They will make your journeys easier and happier.

DAY OR NIGHT

There are some advantages to traveling by night train. You can hop from one place to another without sacrificing daytime activities in either the departure city or the arrival city. Also, the holder of a Eurailpass (by going at night in a regular sitting compartment, not in an extra-fare couchette or sleeping compartment) can make a substantial contribution to a budget trip by dispensing with room rent.

On some trains the seats in the regular sitting compartments can be adjusted so that you can get your seat and the one facing you to either come together or nearly meet, and many who are fortunate enough to be in a compartment that is not full are able to stretch out, using the facing seat. This is the crafty technique for eliminating room rental at night that many students and other economy prone tourists have used successfully. However, if the seat opposite you has another passenger, both of you are going to spend the night sitting up.

The offsetting drawbacks to taking a night train, however, are considerable. The best way of meeting and conversing with Europeans and tourists from other parts of the world is to be on a train, but that opportunity is slim when you travel at night. And equally important, you miss the scenery en route.

Then, too, if you are in a generally excited state when you travel and don't sleep well on trains, that's another negative to weigh.

Train sleeping accommodations vary from one European country to another, but generally they consist of second-class Couchette, first-class Couchette, Tourist and first-class Wagons-Lit.

In second-class Couchette, you have one of the 6 berths in your compartment (2 vertical rows of 3 berths each). You are provided a blanket encased in a sheet-bag and a pillow. There is no way to tuck the blanket in, it just slides around during the night. You can stretch out, but you may not undress. First-Class Couchette is a berth in a compartment with 4 berths (2 rows of 2 berths each). Problem: the first-class Couchettes are so rare you not only won't find one, you probably will never meet someone who did!

Wagons-Lit are available in these 3 choices: Single (accommodating one passenger and comparable to the American railroad bedroom), Double (accommodating 2 persons, similar to the American double railroad bedroom), and Special (which accommodates one passenger and is similar to the American railroad duplex bedroom). There are very few Specials.

Tourist is a compartment accommodating 2 or 3 passengers and is second class.

All sleeping facilities cost a supplemental charge over and above a first or second-class ticket. And, these extra charges are *not* included in the Eurailpass. The supplemental charge for a single Wagons-Lit berth in a 2-berth compartment from Paris to Nice is about $50(U.S.) per person in 1981. The extra charge for either a first-class or second-class Couchette berth on this trip (and, strangely, on all overnight train trips in Western Europe) is $13(U.S.) per prson.

If you survive the intrusions of the customs officers and conductors, and the vibrations, and you don't mind missing the scenery and camaraderie that goes with daytime travel, you can absolutely count on being awakened sometime between 2:00 AM and 5:00 AM by the voice of a stationmaster bellowing over the public address system at some stations where your train stops along the way.

If we have not yet discouraged you from night travel, ponder this final fact: not one TEE train travels overnight. These marvelous luxury trains are all tucked-away in their station houses before Midnight, getting a good rest.

EATING ON TRAINS

Food in train dining cars is expensive, and the choice is limited. On many TEE trains the lunch is a fixed menu, very good and very caloric, and costs $15(U.S.) to $20 per person. On other trains, the food is adequate quality and also high-priced.

Both budget travelers and many of those who can afford the meals served on trains buy their food at a market or delicatessen (ah, those great French charcuteries!) before they get on the train—ranging from a hunk of cheese and some bread to a really sensational assortment of salads, meats, pates, fruits and wine.

Before we made the 12-hour ride from Copenhagen to Amsterdam, we bought a dozen, delicious smorre-brod sandwiches a block from the

Copenhagen station. The variety included shrimp, ham, chicken and beef, all garnished with tasty cucumbers, asparagus, tomatoes, etc. We ate some of them for lunch and the others for dinner that day. Total cost, 4 meals, 2 persons: $10 (U.S.). And we had the convenience of eating when we felt hungry rather than when we could get a table in the dining-car, where lunch and dinner for the 2 of us in that non-TEE dining-car would have cost us over $35.

On a trip from Dijon to Geneva, we feasted on 5 different salads and pates we bought for $6.00 in the supermarket at the big department store in Dijon where we shopped an hour before train time. On another trip, a charcuterie across from the station in Tours was the source for a delightful $5.00 assortment of meat, olives, salads, cheese, bread and custard that 2 of us had for lunch on the way to Rouen.

Some TEE trains such as the Paris to Brussels "Brabant" depart shortly before Noon and arrive in mid-afternoon. Others, like the Paris to Strasbourg "Kleber" start in late afternoon and cut across the dinner-hour. On many of these schedules, you must reserve a seat in the dining-car for the entire trip if you want lunch or dinner.

The meals are larger and heavier than we want, particularly at Noon, and the odor of cooked food for a whole trip is unpleasant to us. We much prefer on such 3-4 hour runs either to wait until we reach our destination and eat a late lunch (or dinner) after arriving there, or to bring our own food onto the train and eat when we are hungry and in our compartment.

If you find the features of "picnicking" attractive, you can ask your hotel or pensione to pack a lunch for you, or you can purchase food either at a store near the station, in a restaurant at the station, from a food market inside the station or, along the way, from vendors that push carts up and down the track at many station stops. Not only is the latter the most inferior food, but our experience is that the train always moves out just as the vendor rolls his cart toward our window.

You will find restaurants and food stores located in many principal railstations. Food stores in the Copenhagen, Stuttgart, Vienna and Zurich railstations offer meats, cheeses, salads, etc. that are excellent.

Whatever your source of bring-along food, don't forget the note in our chapter on "Reservations" to reserve the window-seat, with its convenient fold-out table.

If you want train food, make sure before you start the trip that the train you are taking has meal service. You can check this in the Eurail® Guide timetable footnotes and confirm it at the railstation.

BAGGAGE

The criticism we hear most often about rail travel in Europe concerns the problems of storing and handling suitcases. Don't count on being able to get a porter. Many small cities don't have them. Nearly all the large cities with porters have too few. Some stations provide self-service carts, but the stations which do so don't have enough of them at peak times.

An effective procedure if you travel in pairs is for one of you to guard your luggage while the other hurries toward the station to find a cart and returns to the track with it.

When boarding a train, you want to avoid the difficulty of hauling your luggage down the narrow corridors of several cars. Before your train arrives, examine the train diagram on the platform. Sequence of cars and the platform location for each car are shown for all long-distance trains. Then place yourself and your luggage at the correct site for boarding your car.

On some trains, there is a storage area for luggage at one or at both ends of the car. On most trains, you have to store your baggage on a rack above your seat. The racks are very high. Lifting a 30-pound (or heavier) weight above one's head can be a physical strain for the elderly, those who have a physical disability or even for an average healthy person who weighs less than 140 pounds—which covers most women.

In some compartments the seat construction is such that a small suitcase can be stored under the seats.

For these reasons, it is much better to travel with 2 small, relatively light-weight suitcases per person than with one monstrous case. The small ones are easier to lift, and there's a better chance of being able to store them on the floor under the seat.

Some trains have a baggage car. Using it is always inconvenient and, although the charge is fairly small, more expensive than having your cases with you in your own car or in your compartment. When your bag is in the baggage car, you don't have access to its contents. Also, you may have to wait up to 30 minutes for your cases to be unloaded if they happen to be in the rear of the baggage car.

Waiting for cases to be unloaded, in turn, delays you in getting to the room reservation desk at the tourist accommodation desk inside the depot—a delay that can cost you getting a decent room that night, since every minute counts in obtaining an available room during peak travel days. Waiting at the baggage car also delays you in getting into what is often a very long line for taxis.

We were riding on the crack Settebello, where it is mandatory to have your luggage in the baggage car. Shortly before arriving at the Milan destination, we strolled down the length of the train, passing through the baggage car as we did so. In the baggage car, a passenger was paying the porter several dollars.

When the train finally reached Milan, and we were outside the baggage car with 60 other people, trying to get our luggage, we then understood the transaction we had observed earlier. The suitcases of the tipping passenger had been placed in advance at the door of the baggage car so that these cases were the first to be unloaded. He had his suitcases a moment after the train stopped. It was 25 minutes later when the last suitcase had been unloaded.

In the interim, some passengers who were trying to make an imminent flight at the Milan airport became so frantic to get their luggage that they had climbed onto the baggage car and began fighting with the baggage clerk.

While some trains equipped with baggage cars require you to store your luggage in them, on other trains it is optional. When that is the case, always keep your luggage with you and avoid using the baggage car.

Another luggage problem is storing suitcases at a railroad station, both necessary and convenient when you want to avoid being burdened either upon arriving, while you search for lodging, or when departing if, as often happens, you must give up your room several hours before your train leaves and you want to sightsee in that interval. Very savvy travelers obtain a locker in the station the night before their departure so as to be sure of having the use of one the following morning.

Although there are baggage check-rooms at nearly all major rail-stations, using a check-room instead of a rental locker eats up precious time you could have used more pleasantly and productively because there frequently are long lines both when you leave your luggage and then again when you are claiming it. If you use check-rooms instead of rental lockers, be sure to leave yourself adequate time prior to your train's departure to retrieve your suitcases.

The most convenient and safest method of storing luggage is to place it in a 24-hour rental locker. Unfortunately, the lockers present their own set of problems. Several European stations we have checked-out have too few lockers. Every Summer, many travelers report this to be particularly true of Amsterdam.

Often during recent Summers in Amsterdam and other places, travelers lined up for hours waiting for a locker to become available. Furthermore, rental lockers in European stations are usually in 2 sizes. If you are carrying both a small and large case, you may find several small lockers available but not be able to locate one large locker. Again, we urge you to carry small suitcases.

Another wise maneuver is to have small change on hand for each destination. Remember, the lockers in each country are geared to the local coins. You cannot use a kroner for a locker in France, or a franc for one in Denmark !

CUSTOMS PROCEDURES AND DUTY-FREE PURCHASES

Items at "duty-free" shops in major airports are not always a bargain. Often, the merchandise in a duty-free shop is priced higher than in an ordinary store in the same city.

Only by comparison shopping can you be sure whether it is worthwhile buying at the duty-free shops.

Furthermore, upon returning to your home country you will often find that you must pay a duty on your "duty-free" purchases. "Duty-free" means only that the airport store from which you made a purchase did not have to pay a duty when it bought the article.

To know what can and cannot be brought back to the country of your residence and what the duty tax (if any) you will have to pay when returning home with articles purchased abroad, learn about your country's import regulations before you start your trip to another country.

Residents of the U.S.A. can obtain a copy of "Know Before You Go", a helpful booklet, by writing to: U. S. Customs Service, Custom Information Section, 6 World Trade Center, New York, N.Y. 10048.

Only a fool tries to smuggle through customs an article on which there is an embargo or to avoid paying duty for one which is subject to import tax. If caught, the penalty when entering the United States can be a combination of having the article seized, paying a penalty in the amount of the U.S. value, and criminal prosecution.

For example, in trying to avoid a $120 duty on a $1,000 piece of jade, you could lose the jade, be forced to pay a fine of $1,000 and go to jail.

It is almost a certainty that the salesperson who sells you any item of value or one which cannot legally be brought into your country will report your name and your purchase to your country's authorities in that country a few minutes after concluding the transaction. The informer receives a good reward for enabling the customs people at your home port to be expecting you.

To avoid delays and difficulty when you return to your home country, it is advisable before leaving home to register with your Customs

Service any major foreign-made items (cameras, watches, etc.) you take on your trip.

Always keep your sales slips, invoices or other evidence of purchase. These are essential when presenting a declaration upon re-entering your home country.

If you carry narcotic medicines or injection needles, have a statement from your physician about them.

Do not try to bring home fruits, vegetables or plants that cannot be cleared by your country's Agriculture Department. Without such clearance, it is a certainty such items will be confiscated.

AIRPORT-CITY RAIL CONNECTIONS

An increasing number of cities in Europe have fast rail service to and from their outlying airports: Amsterdam (6 minutes), Barcelona (11), Brussels (18), Dusseldorf (15), Frankfurt (16) London (50 minutes from Heathrow, 39 minutes from Gatwick), Malaga (20), Paris (20 minutes from De Gaulle, 47 minutes from Orly), Vienna (35) and Zurich (11).

LOST MONEY AND PASSPORTS

Having your money or passport stolen or losing them is certain to spoil your trip.

The best precaution is to carry little cash, have traveler's checks instead, and to keep the record of both your traveler's checks and passport number in a different location than you carry the checks and passport. Also guard your return airport ticket as closely as you guard cash, traveler's checks and passport.

Each year, approximately 3,000 U.S. passports are stolen and another 11,000 are lost. There is a big market for American and European passports in Latin America and Asia.

Here are the steps to take when your passport is taken or missing:

First, notify the police of the country in which you are traveling. At the moment you are without your passport, you are in that country illegally. Next, get a copy of the police report and take it to the local office of your country's consulate. Do not waste time going to your country's embassy. It is your consulate, not your embassy, that will assist you by issuing you a replacement passport.

Obtaining a replacement is expedited if you can provide the passport number. It frequently takes 3-4 business days (up to 6 or 7 days if weekends or holidays intervene) before the consulate receives a reply from a telegram sent to your country's capital, the procedure when you do not know your passport number.

If, in addition to the passport number, you also have a certified copy of your birth certificate or certificate of citizenship, the consulate usually can issue a new passport the same day without cabling your capital.

When your new passport is prepared, you must again provide 2 photos of yourself.

The trip delay, missed connections, taxis (to police, consulate, photographer, return trip to consulate, going to the airline to change your ticket), additional hotel days and various fees to your consulate can amount to a great expense.

OVERCOMING JET LAG

When your trip involves a 5-9 hour time change, many of the early days of your trip to another country can be drastically impaired.

There are ways you can greatly reduce the effects of "jet lag" and have more fun on your trip.

On the flight, drink a great deal of water to overcome dehydration resulting from cabin air conditioning. Do not drink alcoholic beverages. Eat very lightly. Dress comfortably by wearing loose clothing. Exercise as much as possible in flight.

Both SAS and Lufthansa have concise booklets which describe exercises that can be performed on a crowded airplane, while you are sitting. Do the motions involved in rowing a boat and picking apples from an overhead branch. Rise up and sit down repeatedly. Raise your knees to your elbows, alternately. Nod your head and turn it vigorously side to side. Turn your hands at the wrist while spreading and closing your fingers. Lift your heels up and place them down vigorously while placing pressure on your toes. With toes up, rotate your feet in large circles.

WHAT WEATHER TO EXPECT

These descriptions of weather patterns are helpful in planning what season is most comfortable for visiting the areas listed.

NORTH AMERICA AND EUROPE Spring is April-June, Summer July-September, Fall October-December. Winter January-March.

MEXICO AND CENTRAL AMERICA Very rainy May-October.

SOUTH AMERICA, AUSTRALIA AND NEW ZEALAND Spring is October-December, Summer January-March, Fall April-June, Winter July-September.

ASIA Year-round tropical heat in Hong Kong, India, Indonesia. Malaysia, Philippines, Singapore, Thailand, South Pacific islands, anywhere that is near the Equator. Typhoon season is June-September in Japan, August to mid-October in Taiwan. The monsoon months in India are June-August. The rainy season in most of Asia is May-September (June-November in the Philippines).

NORTH AFRICA Extremely hot, except December-February in Egypt.

MIDDLE EAST Israel has mild Mediterranean temperature year round. Iran, Iraq, Jordan, Lebanon and Syria have the same 4 seasons as North America and Europe.

LAST MINUTE CHECKLIST

Here are several important tips that can greatly increase the pleasure of your travel.

Carry as little luggage as possible. You will arrive at many railstations where it is a long walk from the train to the taxis (often requiring walking up and down stairs) and find there are neither porters nor carts.

If the luggage you take is a burden, bring along a folding cart of your own.

Take a container of drinking-water on any long trip. Most trains do not provide drinking-water.

Pack soft-ply toilet paper, wash-and-dry packets, and plastic bags. The bags are useful for storing left-over food items, wet soap and laundry that was not completely dry at the start of that day's journey.

When traveling in pairs, it is easier to pass a suitcase through the train window, into or from your compartment, than it is to carry luggage through the length of a crowded, narrow corridor. Unfortunately, the windows of many new air-conditioned train cars cannot be opened.

SIGNS—THE INTERNATIONAL LANGUAGE

The signs shown on next 3 pages appear in railstations and elsewhere all over the world. They help overcome language problems.

At the Train Station. It won't surprise you to learn that most every station is located in the center of town and is the focal point for all public transportation. A number of hotels are also in the immediate vicinity. What might surprise you is the number and variety of services available on the inside. You can find practically everything—from post office and telegraph bureau to barber and beauty shop, from bookstore and newsstand to gift shop, money exchange, and restaurants. But what will impress the foreign traveler most is the highly efficient information system with which almost every station overcomes the language barrier. Here's the most multilingual of visual aids you should look for . . .

Waiting Room

Telegram

Post office

Telephone

Ladies' Rest Room

Men's Rest Room

Drinking Water

Restaurant

Barber · Beauty Parlor

Bath

Smoking permitted

No smoking

Language. Don't worry. Europeans like to practice their conversational English, especially on trains. For detailed information, consult the English-speaking staff at tourist offices, information bureaus, and hotels. At the railroad stations, pictograms lead you not only to the information desk but to any other facility you may be looking for. There are also the highly visible and efficient timetables posted inside the railroad station for get-it-yourself train information. Once you acquire the knack of reading them (and we shall tell you how, later on), they will get you on the right train at the right time on the right track.

Information

Temporary Luggage Storage. At almost every large station you'll find coin-operated lockers. Else, use the special baggage storage indicated by a pictogram and/or the legend: CONSIGNE DES BAGGAGES . . . GEPAECKAUFBEWAHRUNG . . . CONSIGNA DE EQUIPAJES . . . DEPOSITO BAGAGLIO. You'll get a claim check which you have to present when you pick your luggage up again.

Baggage check room

Locker

Checking Your Luggage Through. Time and circumstances permitting, take your bulky luggage or bicycle along on your train, but not with you. Wherever international border crossings and train regulations don't stand in your way, avoid the hassle by checking your extra pieces through to your destination, to ride in the luggage-car. The right counter for this service is indicated by a pictogram.

Luggage registration office

Door-to-Door Luggage Service. If you really want to travel light in France or Germany—with a claim check instead of luggage—find out whether your train station in the city you're in is one of those which pick up your luggage where you're staying and deliver it at your next stay. If that's the case, the small service fee is worth every penny of it.

Baggage Claim

Border and Customs Control. Be in your seat. Immigration officials will inspect your passport and whatever visa or other required documents right in your compartment, while the train moves across border points. You will be asked whether you have anything to declare, but as a foreign tourist in transit, especially with a EURAILPASS or STUDENT-RAIL-PASS, you will be given the appropriate considerations.

Customs

Changing Money. A railroad station is a good place to exchange the bills and coins of one currency for another. Look for the sign where the action is: BUREAU DE CHANGE . . . GELDWECHSEL . . . WECHSELSTUBE . . . OFICINA DE CAMBIO . . . OFFICIO CAMBEIO . . . UFFICIO CAMBIO . . . or just follow the pertinent pictogram.

Currency exchange

Tickets

Which Ticket Window for What. At larger stations tickets for domestic and international travel are purchased at different windows. But as a EURAILPASS or STUDENT-RAILPASS holder, you have your ticket already. So all you'll really want is either the information or reservation window or desk—except in Spain, where you must get a boarding pass at the station before you can board a train.

Services for Businessmen. If you are combining pleasure with business, there are a number of TEE and Intercity trains on which you can hire a secretary, send telegrams or make telephone calls, make car-rental reservations ahead of arrival, or reserve a taxi to pick you up at your destination.

Rent-a-car

Taxi stand

Your Helpful Porter. You'll recognize him by his uniform or official badge. You can usually find one as your cab pulls up to the station. If not, look for him inside. Consult the proper pictogram to find the porters' room. You can rely on your porter to get you to the right track, train, and car. He will put you in a smoker or non-smoker, as you wish, will try his best to find a vacant window-seat, and will place your luggage into the overhead rack.

Call for porter

Washroom Facilities. You can freshen up in a "W.C." (Water Closet) at either end of your car. In most long distance trains next to the "WC" are separate Washrooms. And remember not to drink the tap water; it is not potable.

WC

Rest rooms

A Seat Reservation. Even though you can travel on a European train in most cases without a seat reservation, it's always nice to have a reserved seat—at a window, if possible, or where you want your lunch or dinner served (yes, advance reservations can be made on some TEE trains for meals to be served in your seat). EURAILPASS and STUDENT-RAILPASS holders must pay for seat reservations, but it's very little for a lot of convenience.

R

Reservation

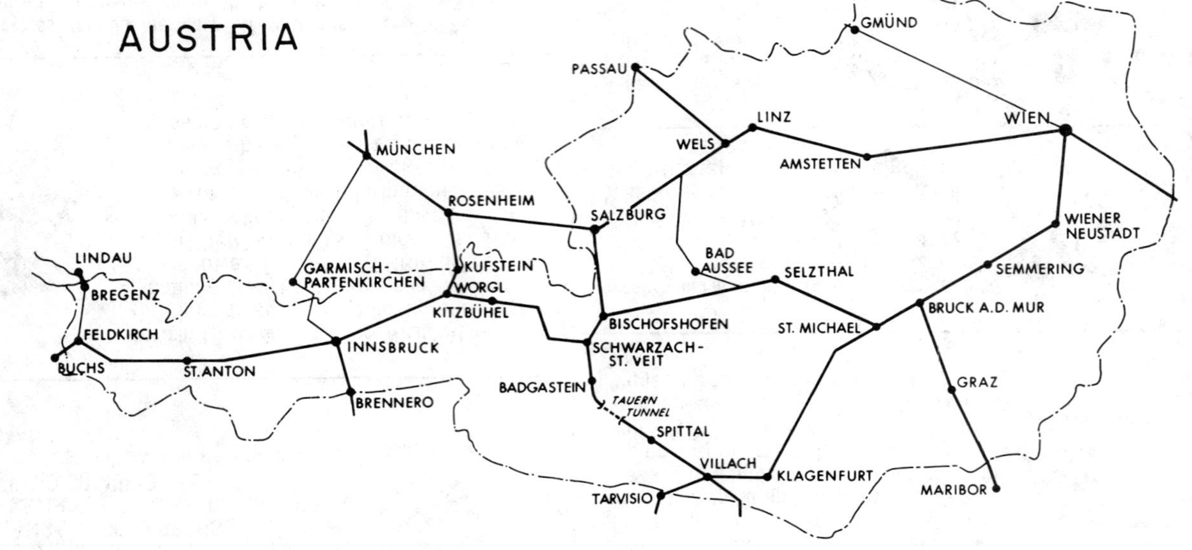
AUSTRIA
GMÜND
PASSAU
LINZ
WIEN
WELS
AMSTETTEN
MÜNCHEN
ROSENHEIM
SALZBURG
WIENER NEUSTADT
LINDAU
BAD AUSSEE
SELZTHAL
SEMMERING
GARMISCH-PARTENKIRCHEN
KUFSTEIN
WORGL
BREGENZ
BRUCK A.D. MUR
KITZBÜHEL
BISCHOFSHOFEN
ST. MICHAEL
FELDKIRCH
INNSBRUCK
SCHWARZACH-ST. VEIT
BUCHS
ST. ANTON
BADGASTEIN
GRAZ
BRENNERO
TAUERN TUNNEL
SPITTAL
VILLACH
KLAGENFURT
MARIBOR
TARVISIO

Chapter 6 EURAILPASS EUROPE

AUSTRIA

Austria's fast trains are: "Ex" (International Express Train "Expresszug"), "TS" (Long Distance Express Railcar "Triebwagenschnellzug") and "D" (all other express service). Except for passengers holding tickets issued outside Austria, these trains charge a supplement of 20 Austrian schillings. Special through tickets are required for "privilege trains", those which cross German or Italian borders without border formalities (customs, passport and currency control) when traveling from one part of Austria to another part of Austria. These trains do not allow passengers to board or leave the train in Germany or Italy.

The signs you will see at railstations in Austria are:

ABFAHRT	DEPARTURE
ANKUNFT	ARRIVAL
AUSGANG	EXIT
AUSKUNFT	INFORMATION
BAHNHOF	STATION
DAMEN	WOMEN
EINGANG	ENTRANCE
FAHRKARTEN-SCHALTER	TICKET OFFICE
FAHRPLAN	TIMETABLE
GARDEROBE	CHECKROOM
GLEIS	TRACK
HERREN	MEN
RAUCHER	SMOKING COMPARTMENT
RESERVIERSCHALTER	RESERVATIONS OFFICE
SCHLAFWAGEN	SLEEPING CAR
SPEISEWAGEN	RESTAURANT CAR
ZU DEN BAHNSTEIGEN	TO THE PLATFORMS

AUSTRIAN HOLIDAYS

A list of holidays is helpful because some trains will be noted later in this section as not running on holidays. Also, those trains which operate on holidays are filled, and it is necessary to make reservations for them long in advance.

January 1	New Year's Day
January 6	Epiphany
	Easter
	Easter Monday
May 1	May Day
	Ascension Day
	Whit Monday
	Corpus Christi Day
August 15	Assumption Day
October 26	National Holiday
November 1	All Saints Day
December 8	Immaculate Conception
December 25	Christmas Day
December 26	St. Stephen's Day

SUMMER TIME

Austria changes to Summer Time on the last Sunday of March and converts back to Standard Time on the last Sunday of September.

AUSTRIA TICKET

This pass provides unlimited travel on all Austrian railroads, buses (except municipal buses and trams), scheduled boats on Lake St. Wolfgang, and the Schaffberg and Schneeberg railways. Also, 50% discount on upstream Danube steamboats and scheduled boats on Lake Constance, 7%-50% discount on many aerial trams and chair lifts, and free admission to any one of the 10 casinos in Austria.

German Federal Railroads is the exclusive sales agent in North America. The pass can be obtained also at all railstations in Austria and at stations in major cities of West Germany and Switzerland. The first day of travel must be indicated when this pass is purchased. The 1983 prices are: First-class 9 days $140(U.S.), 16 days $200. Second-class 9 days $105, 16 days $150.

AUSTRIA'S YOUTH TICKET

Children under 6 not occupying a seaparate seat travel free. Passengers 6-23 can purchase the Second-class Austria Ticket at half-price.

AUSTRIA'S SENIOR CITIZEN HALF-FARE

Women 60 and over and men who are 65 and older can buy Austria Ticket at half-price after purchasing a Senior Citizen's Identification for $10(U.S.), available at all railstations and major post offices in Austria, and also at the Hauptbahnhof stations in Frankfurt, Munich and Zurich. The ID can also be obtained by mail by sending a travelers check in the amount of $10(U.S.) or equivalent, a photostat of the passport page which has a picture and states the holder's age, plus one passport-size photo to: OeBB-Verkaufsdirektion, Abt. IV/4, Gauernanngasse 2-4, A-1010 Wien, Austria.

AUSTRIA'S BUNDES-NETZKARTEN

Unlimited train travel in *all* of Austria. The 1983 prices are: First-class AS 1,950 for 9 days, AS 2,640 16 days, AS 4,200 one month. Second-class AS 1,300 9 days, AS 1,760 16 days, AS 2,800 one month.

AUSTRIA'S LAENDER-NETZKARTEN

Unlimited train travel in *only one province* of Austria. The 1983 prices are: First-class AS 780 for 9 days, AS 1,140 16 days, AS 1,740 one month. Second-class: AS 520 9 days, AS 760 16 days, AS 1,160 one month.

AUSTRIA'S KILOMETERBANK TICKET

May be used by 1-6 persons traveling together on trips of over 70 km. The 1983 prices are: First-class AS 2,250 for 2,000 km, AS 5,400 for 5,000 km, AS 10,500 for 10,000 km. Second-class costs AS 1,500 . . . AS 3,600 . . . and AS 7,000.

EURAILPASS BONUSES IN AUSTRIA

Two rack railways: (1) Puchberg am Schneeberg-Hochschneeberg and (2) St. Wolfgang-Schafbergspitze. Two cruises: (1) Lake Wolfgang and (2) Danube, between Passau and Vienna. Reduction of 50% on Lake Constance Ships.

ONE-DAY EXCURSIONS AND CITY-SIGHTSEEING

Here are 17 one-day rail trips that can be made comfortably from 4 major cities in Austria, returning to them in most cases before dinnertime. Notes are provided on what to see at each destination. The number below the name of each route is the Cook's timetable. The 4 base cities are Innsbruck, Linz, Salzburg and Vienna (Wien).

Innsbruck

Marvelous Winter resort. Gateway to many cable railway trips (Hungerburg, Hafelekar, Igls, Patscherkofel). See the 28 bronze statues around the enormous and magnificent tomb of Maximilian I in the 16th century Imperial Church (Hofkirche). Also the effigy of King Arthur there. The roof (2,657 gold plated tiles) on Goldenes Dachl, built in 1500. The Museum of Tyrolean Folk Art, considered the most important collection of costumes and rustic furniture in Austria. The 18th century Triumphal Arch. The paintings and furniture in the 18th century Hofburg Palace. The silver altar at the Silver Chapel.

Linz

The schloss (castle) where Emperor Fredrich III lived, with its Upper Austrian State Museum collections of prehistoric and Roman items. Martinskirche, one of Austria's oldest churches.

Salzburg

Do not miss seeing the most amusing place in Europe, the 17th century Hellbrun Palace. The 16th century 200-pipe barrel organ in the 12th century fortress, 500 feet above the town, Festung Hohensalzburg. The traditional Music Festival (last week of July until the end of August). The State Rooms in The Residenz, the 17th century city palace of Salzburg's archbishops. The painted ceilings in the 17th century Festspeilhaus. The collection of Mozart musical instruments and family memorabilia in the Mozart Museum, his birthplace. The vast musical library at Bibliotheca Mozartiana. St. Sebastian's Cemetery at Linzergasse 41. The 17th century Cathedral. The Universitatskirche. The Gothic cloister in the 9th century Benedictine Abbey of St. Peter. The Glockenspiel Tower (particularly at 7:00, 11:00 and 18:00 for the carillon concerts). The ancient marketplace, Alter Markt. The marble Angel Staircase in the 17th century Schloss Mirabell, and the marvelous gardens there. Take the cable car to the top (5,800 feet) of Untersberg for a breathtaking view of Salzburg and the Alps.

Vienna (Wien)

There is 35-minute train service from Vienna (Nord) to the city's Schwechat Airport (Flughafen) daily except Sundays and holidays at 5:15 and 5:51; also daily at 6:15 and hourly from 7:28 to 21:28 (also at 16:00 Monday-Friday, except holidays).

Rail service to Vienna (Nord) departs the Airport daily except Sundays and holidays at 5:28, 6:15 and 7:03; also daily at 6:38, 7:24 and hourly from 8:03 to 21:03 (also at 7:12 Monday-Friday, except holidays).

For a glimpse at the world's most beautiful horses and extraordinary riding skill, see the Spanish Riding School. The view from the top of the south steeple of Saint Stephen's Cathedral, or from the top of the Donauturm (Danube Tower), or from the hills in the Vienna Woods.

See the Opera House, the Art Gallery, the Museum of Natural History, the Burgtheater, the Rathaus (City Hall), and Prater, the amusement park. Take a boat ride on the Danube. See the crown jewels of the Holy Roman Empire and the Austrian Empire, in the Imperial Apartments at the Hofburg (Imperial Palace). The collection of great paintings (Titian, Rubens, etc.) and Egyptian, Greek, Etruscan and Roman antiquities at the Kunsthistorisches Museum. Do not miss visiting some of the 1,400 rooms in Schonbrunn Palace.

The superb collection of prehistoric objects, fossils and meteorites at the Naturhistoriches Museum. The many art museums in Belvedere Palace. The beautiful Austrian National Library at Josefplatz 1. Peterskirche. Karlskirche.

In the following timetables, where a city has more than one rail-station we have designated the particular station after the name of the city (in parentheses). **Where no station is designated for cities in Austria, Switzerland and West Germany, the station is "Hauptbahnhof".**

Innsbruck - Bregenz - Innsbruck 750

Dep. Innsbruck	6:48(1)	Dep. Bregenz	16:24	19:28(1)
Arr. Bregenz	10:29	Arr. Innsbruck	20:09	22:50

(1) Light refreshments.

Sights in Bregenz: The annual music festival (light opera and ballet on an unusual water stage in the lake) runs mid-July to mid-August. Take the funicular to the top (3,200 feet) of Pfander Mountain for a spectacular view of Bodensee, the town of Lindau and the Rhine.

Innsbruck - Kitzbuhl - Innsbruck 750

Dep. Innsbruck	7:03	8:40	11:00	12:21(1)	14:04
Arr. Kitzbuhl	8:14	10:33	12:13	13:36	15:08

Sights in Kitzbuhl: This is one of the major winter resorts in the Alps. Cable cars take you from Kitzbuhl to many mountaintops. The city has one museum, some old churches.

Dep. Kitzbuhl	12:38	14:09(2)	16:03(1)	17:25	18:57(3)
Arr. Innsbruck	13:44	15:28	17:21	19:12	20:12

(1) Meal service. (2) Light refreshments. (3) Plus other departures from Kitzbuhl at 19:48(1), 21:45(1) and 22:50.

Innsbruck - Mayrhofen - Innsbruck 758

Dep. Innsbruck	8:55	9:06	11:20	12:55	14:12
Arr. Jenbach	9:18	9:45	11:42	13:30	14:33

Change to bus or to a narrow-gauge train.

730

Dep. Jenbach	9:43	10:40(1)	12:35(2)	13:45(3)	15:35(1)
Arr. Mayrhofen	60-70 minutes later				

Sights in Mayrhofen: This is a popular Winter resort, with horse sleighs.

730

Dep. Mayrhofen	12:35(1)	13:30(4)	14:45(5)	14:50(6)	15:45(7+10)
Arr. Jenbach	13:43	14:28	15:48	15:50	16:47

Change from bus or narrow-gauge train to another train.

758

Dep. Jenbach	14:01	14:43	16:06	16:12	17:08
Arr. Innsbruck	40 minutes later				

(1) Steam train. (2) Train. Sat. and Sun. only. (3) Train. Daily, except Sundays and holidays. (4) Bus. Daily, except Sundays and holidays. (5) Bus. Sat. and Sun. only. (6) Bus. Mon.-Fri., except holidays. (7) Train. Daily. (8) Bus. Daily. (9) Train. Sat. only. (10) Plus other departures from Mayrhofen at 18:35(8) and 19:40(9).

Innsbruck - Munich - Innsbruck 758

Dep. Innsbruck	7:40	8:55(1)	9:01(2)	11:20(3)	12:08(4)
Arr. Munich	10:05	11:03	11:16	13:50	13:54

Sights in Munich: The works of Durer, El Greco, Raphael, Holbein, Rembrandt and many other great painters at Alte Pinakothek. Frauenkirche Cathedral, and the view from its north tower . . . and then later see the view of Frauenkirche from the top of Neues Rathaus (City Hall). The paintings of Cezanne, Gauguin, Renoir and other impressionists at the Haus der Kunst. Wittelsbach Fountain. The fine exhibits and planetarium at Deutsches Museum, considered the best scientific museum in the world. The view of the Alps from the top of

Peterskirche. The best collection of tapestries and wood carvings in Germany, at the Bavarian National Museum. Munich's most famous beer palace, Hofbrauhaus. The Schatzkammer in the Residenz palace, and the flower gardens in the park north of it. The decorations in Asamkirche. Schack Gallery. Theatinerkirche. At Schloss Nymphenburger: the porcelain in the showrooms of Nyphenburger Porzellan Manufaktur and in the Residenzmuseum, the enormous Festsaal, and the park outside the castle.

Dep. Munich	15:38(4)	16:26(3)	16:55(1)	19:20(2)	20:08(6)
Arr. Innsbruck	17:26	18:36	19:00	21:30	22:37

(1) Meal service. (2) Runs from late May to late September. (3) Light refreshments. (4) TEE. Reservation required. Meal service. (5) Fri. only.

Innsbruck - Zell am See - Salzburg - Innsbruck

This is one of the most scenic rides in Austria, as well as a trip to an interesting destination. Exceptionally beautiful views of gorges, lakes, mountains and rivers.

750

Dep. Innsbruck	7:03(1+3)	7:35(2)	8:40(1)	9:35(2+4)
Dep. Zell-am-See	9:02	-0-	11:35	-0-
Arr. Salzburg	10:32	9:36	13:32	11:36

Sights in Salzburg: See notes about city-sightseeing in Salzburg at the start of this section.

Dep. Salzburg	13:35(1+3)	14:25(1)	16:19(2)	17:22(1+3+5)
Dep. Zell-am-See	15:09	16:25	-0-	18:57
Arr. Innsbruck	17:21	19:12	18:20	20:55

(1) Of the 2 routes between Innsbruck and Salzburg, this train takes the more interesting one (via Zell-am-See), one of the most scenic rail trips in Austria. (2) Via Rosenheim. Special ticket required for car that does not take up or set down passengers in Germany. Meal service. (3) Meal service. (4) Plus another departure from Innsbruck at 11:35(2). (5) Plus other departures from Salzburg at 18:19(2), 19:22(1+3) and 20:19(2).

Linz - Munich - Linz

61

Dep. Linz	9:54(1)	Dep. Munich	17:20(1)
Arr. Munich	13:34	Arr. Linz	20:42

(1) Meal service.

Sights in Munich: See notes about city-sightseeing in Munich earlier in this section, under "Innsbruck-Munich".

Linz - Salzburg - Linz 750

Dep. Linz	8:00	8:54(1)	9:29(2)	9:54(1)	10:54(1+3)
Arr. Salzburg	9:50	10:15	11:06	11:30	12:10

Sights in Salzburg: See notes about city-sightseeing in Salzburg at the start of this section.

Dep. Salzburg	11:57(1)	12:40(2)	14:40(1)	16:40(1)	17:40(1+4)
Arr. Linz	13:25	14:01	16:01	18:01	19:01

(1) Meal service. (2) Light refreshments. (3) Plus other departures from Linz at 11:54(1), 12:05 and 12:54(1). (4) Plus other departures from Salzburg at 17:50, 18:40(2), 19:17(1), 19:40(1), 20:40(2) and 21:10(2).

Linz - Vienna - Linz 750

Most of these trains have meal service or light refreshments.

Dep. Linz	Frequent times from 6:38 to 21:08
Arr. Vienna (Westbf.)	2-2½ hours later

Sights in Vienna: See notes about city-sightseeing in Vienna at the start of this section.

Dep. Vienna (Westbf.)	Frequent times from 7:00 to 22:00
Arr. Linz	2-2½ hours later

Salzburg - Zell am See - Innsbruck - Salzburg

This is one of the most scenic rides in Austria, as well as a trip to an interesting destination. Exceptionally beautiful views of gorges, lakes. mountains and rivers.

750

Dep. Salzburg	8:42(1)	10:19(2)	11:25(1)	12:14(2)
Dep. Zell-am-See	10:29	-0-	13:17	-0-
Arr. Innsbruck	12:40	12:25	15:28	14:12

Sights in Innsbruck: See notes about city-sightseeing in Innsbruck at the start of this section.

Dep. Innsbruck	15:35(2)	16:25(1)	17:35(2)	21:08(1)
Dep. Zell-am-See	-0-	18:51	-0-	23:31
Arr. Salzburg	17:36	20:31	19:36	1:25

(1) Of the 2 routes between Salzburg and Innsbruck, this train takes the most interesting one (via Zell-am-See), one of the most scenic rail trips in Austria. (2) Via Rosenheim. Special ticket required for car that does not take up or set down passengers in Germany. Meal service.

Salzburg - Linz - Salzburg 750

Most of these trains have meal service or light refreshments.

Dep. Salzburg	Frequent times from 6:40 to 21:10
Arr. Linz	80 minutes later

Sights in Linz: See notes about city-sightseeing in Linz at the start of this section.

Dep. Linz	Frequent times from 8:00 to 21:59
Arr. Salzburg	80 minutes later

Salzburg - Munich - Salzburg 684

Dep. Salzburg	7:08	7:55	8:22	8:47	9:45	10:12
Arr. Munich	9:18	9:42	10:14	10:52	11:47	12:18

Sights in Munich: See notes about city-sightseeing in Munich earlier in this section, under "Innsbruck-Munich".

Dep. Munch	Frequent times from 12:22 to 23:36
Arr. Salzburg	2-2½ hours later

Salzburg - Vienna - Salzburg 750

Dep. Salzburg	6:40(1)	7:40(1)	8:40	9:40(1)	10:40(1)
Arr. Vienna (Westbf.)	3¼ hours later				

Sights in Vienna: See notes about city-sightseeing in Vienna at the start of this section.

Dep. Vienna (Westbf.)	13:00(1)	14:00(1)	15:00(1)	16:00(1)	17:00(1+3)
Arr. Salzburg	3¼ hours later				

(1) Meal service. (2) Light refreshments. (3) Plus other departures from Vienna at 18:00, 19:00(2), 20:00(1) and 21:00(2).

Vienna - Baden - Vienna

A local tram runs at frequent time from the center of Vienna to Baden and v.v.

Sights in Baden: Famous since the 1st century for the curative powers of its hot sulphur springs. See the Baroque Trinity Column. Try your luck in the Casino in Kurpark. Visit the house where Beethoven lived, at 10 Rathausgasse, open daily except Thursdays, May-September, 9:00-11:00 and 15:00-17:00.

Vienna - Graz - Vienna	762			
Dep Vienna (Sudbf.)	7:00(1)	8:00(2)	10:00(1)	12:00(1)
Arr. Graz	9:35	10:44	12:35	14:35

Sights in Graz: From the main square (Hauptplatz)with its many markets of vegetables, fruits and flowers, go to the arcades with shops in the 17th century Luegghaus. Then to the City Hall (Rathaus)to see the city's symbol, a carved white panther. Follow Neutorgasse to the Joanneum (State Museum of Styria), one of the world's oldest museums, to see its archaeological collection, library, paintings and exhibits of Styrian crafts (9:00-12:00 daily, 14:30-17:00 Monday, Wednesday and Friday).

Continue on Landhausgasse and Herrengasse to the splendid Renaissance Landhaus. Next door, in the Styrian Armory (Zeughaus)is an exhibit of 17th century armor said to be the best and largest (30,000 weapons)collection in Europe (same hours as the Joanneum).

Walk on Opernring to the outstanding Opera House and then through marvelous Stadtpark with its fantastic double-spiral Gothic staircase and cross the Glacis to visit the city's oldest church, 13th century Leekirche, the Church of the Teutonic Order. Pass the castle and see the Diocesan Museum and Treasury in the 15th century Cathedral. Across a narrow street is the 17th century Mausoleum of Emperor Ferdinand II (11:00-12:00 and 14:00-15:00 from May to September, only 11:00-12:00 the rest of the year).

Don't miss the folk dance by carved wood figures performing at 11:00 and 18:00 on the ancient clock in Glockenspielplatz. See the exhibits of regional costumes, tools, folk art, etc. in the Volkskundemuseum (Folk Art Museum of Styria) open Monday, Wednesday and Friday 14:30-17:00.

Take the tram to Eggenberg to see the hunting museum in the 17th century castle there. Go to the top of Castle Hill (Schlossberg)by foot or funicular for a great view of Graz and tour the Bell Tower and Clock Tower, where the big hands show the hour and the small hands the minutes.

Drink Schilcher, the local rosé wine, and Steiermark beer. Local food specialties to sample are: Steierische Wurzelfleisch (pork shoulder), Sulmtaler Krainer (smoked pork sausage)and Steierische Brettljause (a dish of bacon, sausage, cheese, peppers and tomatoes served on a wooden platter).

Take a local bus to nearby Stubing, which has the largest open-air museum in Austria (ancient wood churches, peasants' homes). Another tour goes to Koflach, where a stud farm that is an auxiliary of Vienna's Spanish Riding School has been breeding thoroughbred horses since 1798,

A 2½-hour motorcoach sightseeing tour of Graz starts from in front of the Opera House weekdays at 10:00, June through September.

Dep. Graz	12:20(1)	14:20	16:20(1)	17:05(1+3+4)
Arr. Vienna (Sudbf.)	15:05	17:05	19:05	20:05

(1) Meal service. (2) Light refreshments. (3) Change trains in Bruck an der Mur. (4) Plus other departures from Graz at 18:20 and 19:40(1+3).

Vienna - Linz - Vienna 750

Most of these trains have meal service or light refreshments.

Dep. Vienna (Westbf.)	Frequent times from 7:00 to 23:00
Arr. Linz	2 hours later

Sights in Linz: See notes about city-sightseeing in Linz at the start of this section.

Dep. Linz	Frequent times from 6:42 to 21:08
Arr. Vienna (Westbf.)	2 hours later

Vienna - Melk - Vienna Train Ride + Danube Boat Trip

Train 750

Dep. Vienna (Westbf.)	9:05	12:20
Arr. Melk	10:01	13:23

Danube Steamship 740

Dep. Melk	15:20(1)
Arr. Vienna (Reichsbrucke)	20:15

(1) Runs from early May to late September.

Sights in Melk: Walk from the railstation up the hill to the abbey. See the library there and, from the terrace of the abbey, a splendid view of the Danube. For the return trip to Vienna by boat, go to the main river dock, not to the dock below the abbey.

Vienna - Salzburg - Vienna 750

Dep. Vienna (Westbf.)	7:00(1)	8:00(1)	9:00(1)	10:00(1)
Arr. Salzburg	10:15	11:30	12:10	13:25

Sights in Salzburg: See notes about city-sightseeing in Salzburg at the start of this section.

Dep. Salzburg	14:40(1)	16:40(1)	17:40(1)	18:40(2+3)
Arr. Vienna (Westbf.)	17:55	19:55	20:55	21:55

(1) Meal service. (2) Light refreshments. (3) Plus another departure from Salzburg at 19:40(1).

SCENIC RAIL TRIPS

Gmunden - Bad Aussee

There is fine lake scenery on this portion of a circle trip that starts and ends in Salzburg.

750

Dep. Salzburg	9:55	11:57(1)
Arr. Attnang Puchheim	10:50	12:45
Change trains.		
760		
Dep. Attnang Puchheim	10:57	12:52
Dep. Gmunden	11:16	13:10
Arr. Bad Ausee	12:52	14:40
Arr. Stainach Irdning	13:33	15:30
Change trains.		
745		
Dep. Stainach Irdning	13:37(2)	16:22(2)
Arr. Salzburg	17:10	19:07

(1) Meal service. (2) Change trains in Bischofshofen.

Innsbruck - Brennero 758

The beautiful mountain scenery here can be seen either on an easy one-day roundtrip from Innsbruck or as a portion of the Innsbruck-Verona route. For the first way:

Dep. Innsbruck	9:05	9:35	10:40	13:15	14:17
Arr. Brennero	9:54	10:11	11:22	14:05	15:07
		*	*	*	
Dep. Brennero	10:20	11:32(1)	12:35	14:41	16:08
Arr. Innsbruck	11:02	12:05	13:28	15:30	16:56

(1) TEE. Reservation required.

Here is the schedule for going from Innsbruck to Italy:

381

Dep. Innsbruck	6:38(1)	10:00(2)	10:40	16:05
Dep. Brennero	7:40(1+3)	10:56	11:42	17:06
Arr. Verona	11:25	14:25	15:27	20:59

(1) Runs from late May to late September. (2) Meal service. (3) Light refreshments.

Innsbruck - Buchs 750

The excellent mountain scenery here can be seen either on an easy one-day roundtrip from Innsbruck or as a portion of the Innsbruck-Zurich route. For the first way:

Dep. Innsbruck	6:22(1)	8:55(1)	12:30(2)
Arr. Buchs	9:36	12:01	15:05
	*	*	*
Dep. Buchs	10:51(2)	12:48(2)	17:48
Arr. Innsbruck	13:24	15:27	20:55

(1) Light refreshments. (2) Meal service.

Here is the schedule for going from Innsbruck to Switzerland.

268

Dep. Innsbruck	6:22(1)	8:55(1+2)	12:30(3)	14:22(3)
Dep. Sargans	10:34	12:46	15:34	17:34
Arr. Zurich	11:33	13:47	16:33	18:33

(1) Light refreshments. (2) Change trains in Sargans. (3) Meal service.

Innsbruck - Bruck an der Mur - Vienna

This indirect route from Innsbruck to Vienna, traveling south of the main line (via Linz), offers excellent mountain scenery.

750			
Dep. Innsbruck	7:03(1)	8:40	11:00(1)
Arr. Bischofshofen	9:46	12:42	14:05
Change trains.			
745			
Dep. Bischofshofen	10:05(1)	12:50	14:23
Arr. Bruck an der Mur	13:11	16:13	18:22
Change trains.			
762			
Dep. Bruck an der Mur	14:58	16:58(1)	18:58
Arr. Vienna (Sudbf.)	17:05	19:05	21:05

(1) Meal service.

Innsbruck - Garmisch - Zugspitz

The outstanding mountain scenery here can be seen either on an easy one-day roundtrip from Innsbruck or as a portion of the Innsbruck-Munich route. For the first way:

756

Dep. Innsbruck	6:33	7:32	9:00	10:45	11:45
Arr. Garmisch	8:27	9:02	10:24	12:22	13:24

Change trains.

The following schedule allows one to ride one cable railway to the summit of Zugspitz and ride a different cable railway en route back to Garmisch.

693

Dep. Garmisch	9:00	10:00	11:00	13:00	14:00
Arr. Eibsee	9:37	10:37	11:37	13:37	14:37
Change to cable railway.					
Dep. Eibsee	9:45(1)	10:45	11:45	13:45	14:45
Arr. Zugspitz	10 minutes later				

(1) Every 30 minutes to 17:45.

Use a different cable railway in returning to Garmisch.

Dep. Zugspitz	10:15(1)	11:15	12:15	14:15	15:15
Arr. Sceefernerhaus	10:19	11:19	12:19	14:19	15:19

(1) There are also departures from Zugspitz at 45 minutes after each hour.

Change to train.

* * *

693

Dep. Sceefernerhaus	10:25	11:25	12:25	14:25	15:25
Arr. Garmisch	11:45	12:45	13:45	15:45	16:45

Change trains.

756

Dep. Garmisch	-0-	13:28	15:27	16:24(1)	17:31
Arr. Innsbruck	-0-	15:01	16:53	17:46	19:10

(1) Meal service.

Here is the schedule for continuing on from Garmisch to Munich.

683

Dep. Garmisch	12:30	13:34	14:34	15:34	16:34(1)
Arr. Munich	13:58	14:55	15:55	17:13	17:55

(1) Plus other departures from Garmisch at 17:34, 18:34 and 20:11.

Innsbruck - Salzburg - Innsbruck

The good gorge, lake, river and mountain scenery on this route can be seen either on an easy one-day roundtrip from Innsbruck or as a portion of the Innsbruck-Vienna route.

For the first way, see details earlier in this section, under the "Innsbruck-Zell am See-Salzburg-Innsbruck" one-day excursion.

Innsbruck - Vienna 750

Here are the schedules for going across Austria. All of these trains require a special ticket and have meal service.

Dep. Innsbruck	7:35	9:35	11:35	13:35	15:35
Arr. Vienna (Westbf.)	12:55	14:55	16:55	18:55	20:55

Linz - Vienna

Great Danube River scenery on this 10-hour 297km (180-mile) cruise that is covered by Eurailpass.

740

Dep. Linz	10:00(1)	Dep. Vienna (Reichsbrucke)	8:00(1)
Arr. Vienna (Reichsbrucke)	20:10	Arr. Linz	24:00

(1) Runs daily from early May to late Sept.

Salzburg - Zell am See - Innsbruck

Exceptionally beautiful views of gorges, lakes, mountains and rivers on one of the most scenic rides in Austria. Schedules for this trip appear earlier in this section under both "Salzburg-Innsbruck" and "Innsbruck-Salzburg" one-day excursions.

Salzburg - Villach - Salzburg

The excellent gorge and mountain scenery on this ride can be seen either on an easy one-day roundtrip from Salzburg or as a portion of the Salzburg-Venice route. For the first way:

759

Dep. Salzburg	7:50(1)	10:03(1)	11:05(2+3)	11:36(1)
Arr. Villach	10:50	13:28	14:33	15:00

* * *

Dep. Villach	12:15(3)	14:45(1)	15:21(2+3)	16:05(1+5)
Arr. Salzburg	15:50	18:05	18:46	19:07

(1) Meal service. (2) Runs from late May to late September. (3) Light refreshments. (4) Daily, except Saturday. (5) Plus other departures at 17:08(1), 18:50 and 21:12(4).

Here is the schedule for going from Salzburg to Italy:

75

Dep. Salzburg 14:00
Arr. Villach 17:17

Change trains. Be sure to be in a car marked "Venice S.L." when you depart Villach.

Dep. Villach 18:28(1)
Arr. Venice (S.L.) 23:40

(1) Meal service.

The very scenic Klagenfurt-Udine-Trieste portion of the Vienna-Trieste route is described at the end of this section. A departure from Salzburg can connect with that trip at Villach. Complete schedules appear under the "Vienna-Trieste" trip.

Selzthal - Hieflau This portion of the easy one-day Linz-Selzthal-Amstetten-Linz circle trip affords fine gorge mountain scenery.

755			
Dep. Linz	7:40	9:49	14:33
Arr. Selzthal	9:23	11:59	16:30
Change trains.			
754			
Dep. Selzthal	10:05	14:47	17:02
Dep. Hieflau	10:53	15:33	17:47
Arr. Amstetten	12:52	17:42	19:21
Change trains.			
750			
Dep. Amstetten	14:02	17:58	19:27(1)
Arr. Linz	14:58	18:59	20:10

The same trip can be made in reverse, using this schedule:

750			
Dep. Linz	7:39(2)	10:08	12:15
Arr. Amstetten	8:20	11:01	13:09
Change trains.			
754			
Dep. Amstetten	9:12	11:35	14:43(3)
Dep. Hiefflau	10:54	13:46	16:48
Arr. Selzthal	11:38	14:20	17:35
Change trains.			
755			
Dep. Selzthal	13:55(4)	15:26	19:02
Arr. Linz	15:37	17:15	20:32

(1) Runs from late May to late September. (2) Light refreshments. (3) Daily, except Sundays and holidays. (4) Meal service.

Vienna - Bruck an der Mur - Innsbruck

This indirect route from Vienna to Innsbruck, traveling south of the main line (via Linz), offers excellent mountain scenery.

762			
Dep. Vienna (Sudbf.)	7:00(1)	8:00(2)	10:00(1)
Arr. Bruck an der Mur	8:57	10:07	11:57
Change trains.			
745			
Dep. Bruck an der Mur	9:01	10:04	13:43
Arr. Bischofshofen	11:55	14:08	17:00
Change trains.			
750			
Dep. Bischofshofen	12:24(2)	14:20(1)	17:15
Arr. Innsbruck	15:28	17:21	20:12

(1) Meal service. (2) Light refreshments.

Vienna - Klagenfurt - Udine - Trieste

The marvelous farm and lake scenery on this route includes seeing Worthersee, a lake fed by warm springs that is very popular for swimming and boating, and the beautiful coastline from Udine to Trieste. The great Worthersee resort area is open June through mid-September. Even if you don't stop there, at least watch for that area a few minutes before the stop at Klagenfurt. An early departure from Vienna is recommended in order to be able to see the Adriatic shore approaching Trieste in the afternoon sunlight, as we have done.

The comfortable local train from Udine hurtles downhill too fast to permit picture-taking, but you will have a memory of that truly beautiful scene forever. Be certain to have a seat on the right-hand side of the train for the best possible view.

Not only is Trieste a worthwhile one-day stopover, it is also ideal as a base for several short rail trips into Yugoslavia such as Villa Opicina, Sezana, Pivka, Postojna and Ljubljana. It is also easy to make a one-day excursion to see the sights in Udine while staying in Trieste.

47		388	
Dep. Vienna (Sudbf.)	7:55(1)	Dep. Udine	15:32
Arr. Klagenfurt	12:04	Arr. Trieste	16:43
Arr. Villach	12:33		
Dep. Villach	12:40	(1) Meal service.	
Arr. Udine	15:07		
Change trains.			

Sights in Trieste: Miramare Castle, Maximilian and Charlotte's lovely seaside palace. Charlotte returned here after their tragic brief time as rulers of Mexico, made insane by Maximilian's death. You will enjoy Trieste's Piazza della Liberta, reminiscent of St. Mark's in Venice. See the 17th century Castello di San Giusto. The 14th century Cathedral of San Giusto. The ruins of a Roman amphitheater. The Civic Museum of History and Art. The Giant Grotto.

If you are originating from Salzburg rather than Vienna, the Udine-Trieste route can be seen by making a connection in Villach, shown here:

759		388	
Dep. Salzburg	7:50	Dep. Udine	15:32
Arr. Villach	10:50	Arr. Trieste	16:43
Change trains.			
47			
Dep. Villach	12:38		
Arr. Udine	15:07		
Change trains.			

Now for the one-day excursion to Udine:

Trieste - Udine Trieste

388			
Dep. Trieste	7:15	9:38	12:22
Arr. Udine	8:36	11:28	13:27

Sights in Udine: The collection of paintings in the Civic Museum and Gallery, a 20-minute walk from the railstation. Do they still have in Room 32 Vollett's "Crepuscolo" and Cormaldi's "La Donna e lo Specchio" ? Tiepolo's paintings are featured in both the Bishop's Palace and the Cathedral. Visit Piazza della Liberta.

Dep. Udine	10:58	13:10	15:32	18:45	20:54	21:47
Arr. Trieste	11:57	14:20	16:43	19:55	22:30	22:50

INTERNATIONAL ROUTES FROM AUSTRIA

The Austrian gateways for travel to West Germany (and on to Copenhagen) are both Innsbruck and Salzburg. Vienna is the access point for travel to Poland and Czechoslovakia (and on to Russia), Hungary, Romania and Yugoslavia (and on to Bulgaria, Greece and Turkey). Innsbruck, Salzburg and Vienna are also starting points for trips to Italy. Innsbruck is also the gateway to Switzerland (and on to Belgium, France, Holland and Luxembourg).

Innsbruck - Munich 758

Dep. Innsbruck	7:38	8:57	9:05(1)	11:07(2+6)
Arr. Munich	10:05	11:03	11:27	13:25

(1)Runs from late May to late September. (2)Light refreshments. (3)TEE. Reservation required. Meal service. (4)Meal service. (5)Runs from mid-July to late September. (6)Plus other departures at 12:08(3), 12:26(1+4), 14:12(2), 15:00(5), 18:38(1), 19:12(1+2), 20:00(4) and 23:35(1).

Salzburg - Munich

Arrive at the Salzburg railstation sufficiently in advance of departure time to complete the German Customs clearance that takes place before boarding the train.

684

Dep. Salzburg	Frequent times from 5:12 to 21:32
Arr. Munich	2 hours later

Vienna - Prague

	746	747
Dep. Vienna (Mitte)	9:30(1)	21:30(2)
Arr. Prague (Main)	15:02	5:12(3)

(1)Meal service. (2)Carries sleeping car. Departs from Vienna's Subbahnhof railstation. (3)Arrives at Prague's Hlavni (Main) railstation.

Vienna - Warsaw (or Kiev) - Moscow

	748	48
Dep. Vienna (Sudbf.)	19:20(1)	21:30(2)
Arr. Warsaw (Gdanska)	-0-	11:49(3)
Arr. Kiev	5:17(3)	-0-
Arr. Moscow (Byel.)	17:30(4)	10:06(4)

(1)Carries sleeping car from late May to late September. (2)Carries sleeping car. (3)Day 2. (4)Day 3.

Vienna - Budapest and Bucharest

	798	42 + 798	32 + 798
Dep. Vienna (Westbf.)	7:45(1+2)	10:20(3)	16:24
Arr. Budapest (Deli)	11:15	-0-	-0-
Arr. Budapest (Keleti)	-0-	14:25	20:30
Dep. Budapest (Keleti)	-0-	16:15(1)	21:30(4)
Arr. Bucharest (Nord)	-0-	8:25	13:30

(1) Runs late May to late Sept. (2) Departs from Vienna's Sudbahnhof railstation. (3) Meal service. (4) Carries sleeping car.

Vienna - Belgrade and Athens 65

Dep. Vienna (Sudbf.)	18:55(1)	22:50
Arr. Belgrade	6:52(2)	13:19(2)
Change trains.		
Dep. Belgrade	8:30(2+5)	13:55(2+6)
Arr. Athens	7:55(3)	14:35(3)

(1) Carries sleeping car. Also has couchettes. (2) Day 2. (3) Day 3. (4) Has couchettes. (5) Has couchettes, which are replaced with sleeping cars on Thurs. and Sun. from late May to late Sept. Meal service. (6) Has couchettes. Meal service on Day 3.

Vienna - Belgrade and Istanbul 65

Dep. Vienna (Sudbf.) 22:50
During Summer Time, set your watch back one hour.
Arr. Belgrade 6:15 Day 2
Change trains.
65
Dep. Belgrade 9:05(1) Day 2
All year, set your watch forward 2 hours.
Dep. Kapikule 4:50(2) Day 3
Arr. Istanbul 10:45 Day 3

(1) Reservation required. Has couchettes. (2) Meal service.

Innsbruck - Verona and Milan 381

Dep. Innsbruck	1:42(1)	6:38	10:00(3)	17:29(4)
Arr. Verona (P.N.)	6:00	11:25	14:25	21:13(4)
Change trains.				
Dep. Verona (P.N.)	6:40	11:56(2)	14:51	21:24(4)
Arr. Milan	8:35	13:45	16:35	22:50

(1) Carries sleeping car. Also has couchettes. (2) Light refreshments. (3) Meal service. (4) TEE. Direct train. No train change in Verona. Reservation required. Meal service.

Innsbruck - Verona - Bologna - Florence - Rome 381

Dep. Innsbruck	1:42(1)	10:00(2)	16:05	18:54(1)	21:48(5)
Arr. Verona	6:00	14:25	20:59	0:14	2:38
Dep. Verona	6:20	14:41(2)	21:35(3)	0:37(1)	2:58(5)
Arr. Bologna	7:47	16:06	23:37	1:56	4:24
Dep. Bologna	8:17	16:24(2)	1:26(3)	2:20(1)	4:40(5)
Arr. Florence	9:38	17:44(2)	2:50(3)	3:47(1)	6:07(5)
Arr. Rome (Ter.)	13:18	21:12	6:30(4)	7:58	10:15

(1) Carries sleeping car. Also has couchettes. (2) Meal service. (3) Carries sleeping car. (4) Arrives at Rome's Tiburtina railstation. (5) Runs from mid-June to mid-September. Has couchettes.

Salzburg - Vienna 75 + 759

Dep. Salzburg	1:00(1)	7:50(2)	14:00(3)
Arr. Villach	4:05	10:50	17:17
Change trains.			
Dep. Villach	4:45	12:38	18:28(2)
Arr. Venice (S.L.)	9:37	16:57(4)	23:40

(1) Carries sleeping car. Also has couchettes. (2) Meal service. (3) Runs from late May to late September. (4) Change trains at Venice's Mestre railstation before taking 4-minute ride to Venice's Santa Lucia railstation.

Vienna - Venice 763

Dep. Vienna (Sudbf.)	7:55(1)	13:00(1)	21:00(2)	23:00(2)
Arr. Venice (S.L.)	16:57	23:40	5:58	9:37

(1) Meal service. (2) Carries sleeping car. Also has couchettes.

Innsbruck - Zurich 268

There is marvelous Alpine scenery on this route. About 2½ hours before reaching Zurich, the train passes through one of Europe's longest rail tunnels, the 6.3-mile long Arlberg.

Dep. Innsbruck	4:13(1)	6:22(2)	8:55(2+3)	12:30(4+5)
Arr. Zurich	8:33	11:33	13:47	16:33

(1) Carries sleeping car. Also has couchettes. (2) Light refreshments. (3) Change trains in Sargans. (4) Meal service. (5) Plus other departures from Innsbruck at 14:22(4), 16:25(4) and 17:46(4).

BENELUX

(BELGIUM, NETHERLANDS and LUXEMBOURG)

There is 11-minute train service from Amsterdam (RAI)and 7-minute train service from Amsterdam (Zuid)to the city's Schiphol Airport every 14-16 minutes from 5:39 to 0:10. Same schedules from the Airport to Amsterdam. Tram No. 4 goes from Amsterdam (Central)to the RAI railstation and v.v.

There is 18-minute train service from Brussels (Central)and 15-minute train service from Brussels (Nord)to that city's National Airport every 20-30 minutes until 23:08. Same schedules (until 23:37) for the trip from the Airport to Brussels. Bus service is available in the evening when rail transportation is not operating.

The signs you will see at railstations in Belgium, Holland and Luxembourg are:

	BELGIUM and LUXEMBOURG	HOLLAND
Arrival	Arrivee	Aankomst
Departure	Depart	Vertrek
Exit	Sortie	Uitgang
Information	Renseignements	Inlichtingen
Luggage Check-Room	Consignee	Hetbagagedepot
Men	Messieurs	Heren
Restaurant Car	Wagon-Restaurant	Restauratie-Wagen
Sleeping Car	Wagon-Lit	Slaapcoupe
Smoking Compartment	Fumeurs	Rokers
Station	Gare	Station
Timetable	Horaire	Spoorboekje
Track	Quai	Spoor
Women	Dames	Dames

SUMMER TIME

Belgium, Holland and Luxembourg change to Summer Time on the last Sunday of March and convert back to Standard Time on the last Sunday of September.

HOLLAND HOLIDAYS

January 1	New Year's Day	May 1	Labor Day
	Good Friday		Ascension Day
	Easter		Whit Monday
	Easter Monday	December 25	Christmas Day
April 30	Queen's Birthday	December 26	Boxing Day

BENELUX

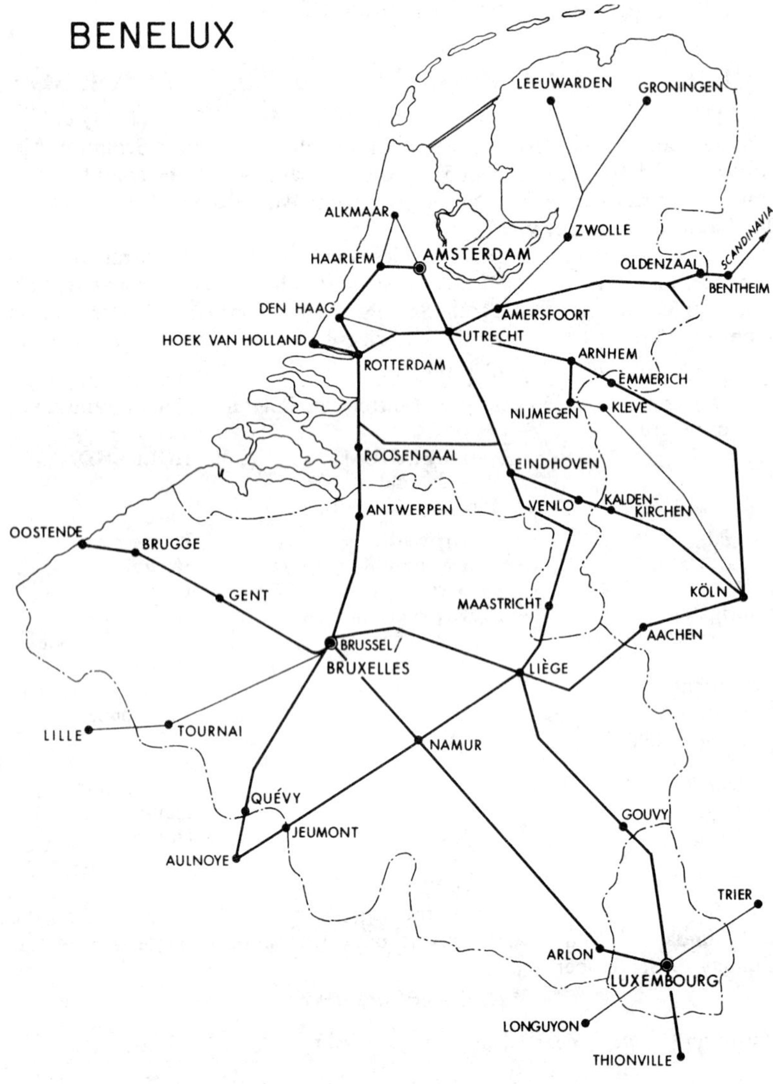

LEEUWARDEN
GRONINGEN
ALKMAAR
ZWOLLE
SCANDINAVIA
HAARLEM
AMSTERDAM
OLDENZAAL
BENTHEIM
DEN HAAG
AMERSFOORT
HOEK VAN HOLLAND
UTRECHT
ROTTERDAM
ARNHEM
EMMERICH
NIJMEGEN
KLEVE
ROOSENDAAL
EINDHOVEN
VENLO
KALDEN-
KIRCHEN
ANTWERPEN
OOSTENDE
BRUGGE
GENT
MAASTRICHT
KÖLN
AACHEN
BRUSSEL/
BRUXELLES
LIÈGE
LILLE
TOURNAI
NAMUR
QUÉVY
JEUMONT
AULNOYE
GOUVY
TRIER
ARLON
LUXEMBOURG
LONGUYON
THIONVILLE

BELGIAN HOLIDAYS

A list of holidays is helpful because some trains will be noted later in this section as not running on holidays. Also, those trains which operate on holidays are filled, and it is necessary to make reservations for them long in advance.

January 1	New Year's Day
	Easter
	Easter Monday
May 1	Labor Day
	Ascension Day
	Whit Monday
July 21	Independence Day
August 15	Assumption Day
November 1	All Saints Day
November 11	Armistice Day (World War I)
November 15	Dynasty Day
December 25	Christmas Day
December 26	Boxing Day

NOTE: When any holiday falls on a Sunday, the following day is also a holiday.

LUXEMBOURG HOLIDAYS

January 1	New Year's Day
	Shrove Monday
	Easter
	Easter Monday
May 1	Labor Day
	Ascension Day
	Whit Monday
June 23	National Holiday
August 15	Assumption Day
December 25	Christmas Day
December 26	Boxing Day

EURAILPASS BONUSES

There are no Eurailpass bonuses in Belgium, Holland and Luxembourg.

BENELUX TOURRAIL

This pass is for 8 days of unlimited travel (out of any 16-day period from 10 days before Easter until October 31) on all the lines of Belgium, Holland and Luxembourg. Sold at the railstations of all 3 countries. The 1982 prices for first-class were 3,650 Belgian francs for adults 26 and over, 2,740FB for persons 12-25, and 1,830FB for children 4-11.

For second-class: 2,430FB, 1,830FB and 1,230FB. Children under 4 travel free when not occupying a separate seat.

BENELUX JUNIOR TOURRAIL

For persons up to 25 years old. Valid April 1-October 31 and December 15-31. Eight days of unlimited train travel out of any 16-day period. Priced in Dutch guilders. First-class: 183g. Second-class: 122g.

BELGIAN TOURRAIL

Unlimited train travel in Belgium for either any 5 days out of a 16-day period or for any 8 days out of a 16-day period from 15 days before Easter until September 31 and from December 15 through December 31. The 1982 prices for 5 days first-class were: 1,820FB for adults 26 and over, 1,330FB for persons 12-25 years old, and 920FB for children 6-11. The 5-day second-class prices were: 1,210FB, 910FB and 610FB.

The 1982 prices for 8-day first-class were: 2,400FB, 1,800FB and 1,200FB. The 8-day second-class prices were: 1,600FB, 1,200FB and 800FB.

BELGIAN 16-DAY CARD

Unlimited train travel for 16 consecutive days. First-class: 3,180BF. Second-class: 2,120BF.

BELGIAN HALF-FARE CARD

Entitles the traveler to unlimited train travel at half-fare for one month. The 1982 prices were: first-class 620FB, second-class 410FB.

ONE-DAY HOLLAND TOURS

Netherlands Railways offers during the Spring and Summer months more than 30 one-day excursions from Amsterdam to interesting destinations. Eurailpass holders pay only for the non-rail portions of these trips and for admission fees.

One example is the day-trip that starts with a train ride from Amsterdam to Rotterdam, entrance to Blijdorp Zoo, a boat ride in the harbor, and the train ride back to Amsterdam.

HOLLAND RETURN

On a same-day roundtrip, the charge for the return ride is 2 guilders, if the return departure is at 20:00 or later.

On a roundtrip that begins with a Saturday train departure, if the return train ride is made anytime the next day, the charge for the return ride on Sunday is 1.50g.

HOLLAND'S ROVER TICKETS

These rail passes are sold in 5 versions. All are available in Holland at railstations and accredited travel agencies. The buyer must provide a passport-size photo or passport number. Prices listed here are valid through September 30, 1983. Children 4 to under 10 travel at 40% discount. Children under 4 travel free.

One-Day Rover One day of unlimited train travel. In 1983, first-class costs 68.50 guilders. Second-class: 45.50g.

3-Day Rover Three consecutive days of unlimited train travel. In 1983, first-class costs 99g. Second-class: 66g.

7-Day Rover Seven consecutive days of unlimited train travel. In 1983, first-class costs 133g. Second-class 91.50g.

One-Month Rover One month of unlimited train travel. In 1983, first-class costs 490g. Second-class 330g.

Multirover One day of unlimited train travel. Valid for 2-6 people. Cannot be used from 24:00 Sunday to 9:00 Monday. In 1983, first-class costs 96g for 2 persons, 114.50g for 3, 132.50g for 4, 151g for 5, and 169g for 6. Second-class: 64g for 2 persons, 76.50g for 3, 88.50g for 4, 101g for 5, and 113g for 6.

HOLLAND'S FAMILY CARD (GEZINSTOERKAART)

Unlimited train travel any 4 days in a 9-day period for parents and any number of their children under 18 years old. A passport photo of one of the parents is required. Valid only during June, July and August. Sold at railstations. In 1983, first-class costs 180g, second-class 130g.

LUXEMBOURG'S CARTES D'ABONNEMENT

Unlimited train and bus travel. Prices charged in 1983 are shown.

One-Day Carte Second-class only. Not valid for journeys departing from or arriving at border stations.146 Luxembourg francs.

5-Day Carte Valid any 5 days within a 15-day period for either first or second-class. 413FL.

One-Month Carte Second-class only. Valid from first to last day of one calendar month. 1,100FL.

LUXEMBOURG'S SENIOR CITIZEN HALF-FARE

Presentation of identity card or passport required. People over 65 receive 50% discount on both first and second-class tickets. Not valid for journeys departing from or arriving at border stations.

LUXEMBOURG'S RETURN TRIP DISCOUNT

Check on the discount offered and conditions for both weekend and holiday return tickets.

ONE-DAY EXCURSIONS AND CITY-SIGHTSEEING

Here are 39 one-day rail trips that can be made comfortably from 3 major Benelux cities, returning to them in most cases before dinner time. (Five of these trips offer, in addition to interesting destinations, scenic fields of flowers in bloom mid March through May.) Notes are provided on what to see at each destination. The number below the name of each route is the Cook's timetable.

Details on 3 other rail trips recommended for exceptional scenery and schedules for international connections conclude this section.

The 3 base cities are: Amsterdam, Brussels and Luxembourg City.

Amsterdam

Your city-sightseeing in Amsterdam should include the Rijksmuseum collection of Rembrandt paintings, Rembrandt's house and, near it, the Flea Market. Anne Frank's house at Prisengracht 263. The Tropical Museum, with its display of Indonesian and Far Eastern art and anthropology. The Amsterdam Historical and Jewish Historical Museum. A 75-minute ride in a glass-roofed canal boat, starting at the piers in front of Central Railstation or at Stadhouderskade, near the Rijksmuseum. Royal Palace. The Tower of Tears. The attic church of the Amstelkring Museum. Mint Tower. The Maritime Museum. Free samples when ending the tour of Heineken Brewery, Monday-Friday starting at 10:00.

Brussels

There is rail service between the center of Brussels (Central and Nord station) and the city's airport every 20-30 minutes until 23:08.

Sightseeing starts in Grand Place, the ornate town square with many gilded buildings. Inside Hotel de Ville (Town Hall), there is a tapestry museum. Next to it is a reproduction of a 17th century brewery. See the 15th century Notre Dame des Victoires church and the 17th century Flemish houses in nearby Place du Grand Sablon.

The marvelous Place Parc de Bruxeles gardens and lakes. The Royal Palace, at one end of this park, is open 9:30-16:00 every day. The Belgian Parliament is located at the other end of the park.

One of the world's best collections of 15th and 16th century Flemish and Dutch paintings (Rubens, Brueghel, Bosch) is exhibited at the Museum of Ancient Art on Rue de la Regence. See the impressive array of African art in The Central Africa Museum.

See the view from the Palais de Justice. The Law Courts. The tapestries in the 13th century Cathedral of St. Michael. The Museum of Modern Art. The Brussels City Museum. The Museum of Arms and Armor. The Postal Museum. The Royal Greenhouses. The Brueghel Museum, in the house where the painter lived his last 6 years. The Railway Museum, on the mezzanine of Brussels' Nord railstation. A bus can be taken 10 miles to Waterloo.

Luxembourg City

The Citadel, with its 53 forts connected by 16 miles of tunnels. Fish Market, site of the city's oldest buildings. The National Museum. The Palace. City Hall. The old quarter of Pfaffenthal, with its medieval buildings. The Fort of Three Acorns. Malakoff Tower. The Church of St. Michael. The Three Towers, marking the outer limits of the town in 1050. Notre Dame Cathedral. The 4th century Chapel of St. Quirinus, one of the oldest shrines in Christendom. The Museum of History and Art. General Patton's grave in the U.S. Military Cemetery, 3 miles away, at Hamm.

In the following timetables, where a city has more than one rail-station we have designated the particular station after the name of the city (in parentheses).

ONE-DAY EXCURSIONS AND CITY-SIGHTSEEING

On day trips from Amsterdam that we have designated "H-L", you will see in the area between Haarlem and Leiden, from mid-March through May, fields of tulips, narcissus, crocus and other bulb flowers in bloom. The region is known as the "Champs de Fleurs" (Fields of Flowers).

Amsterdam - Alkmaar - Amsterdam

224

Dep. Amsterdam twice each hour.
Arr. Alkmaar 32-50 minutes later.

Sights in Alkmaar: The Friday Cheese Market, from the end of April until the end of September, 10:00-12:00. The organ at St. Lawrence Church. City Hall.

Dep. Alkmaar twice each hour until 23:44.
Arr. Amsterdam 32-50 minutes later.

Amsterdam - Alkmaar - Haarlem - Amsterdam

It is easy to visit both Alkmaar and Haarlem in a single day-trip.

224 + 223

Dep. Amsterdam twice each hour.
Arr. Alkmaar 32-50 minutes later.
Dep. Alkmaar twice each hour.
Arr. Haarlem 10-20 minutes later.

Dep. Haarlem twice each hour.
Arrive Amsterdam 14-18 minutes later.

Sights in Haarlem: Frans Hals Museum at 62 Groot Heiligland (note the address, that is the only mark outside the building!) St. Bavo, Holland's most beautiful church, with its Muller organ. The World Clock at 88 Wagenweg. Teyler's Museum at 16 Spaarne, for 16th to 20th century Dutch, Italian and French paintings.

Amsterdam- Antwerp - Amsterdam 223

Dep. Amsterdam	7:24(1+2)	7:48(2)	8:26(2)	8:53(3+4+6)
Arr. Roosendaal	9:09	9:35	10:09	-0-
Change trains.				
214				
Dep. Roosendaal	9:12	9:43	10:12	-0-
Arr. Antwerp (Cent.)	9:39	-0-	10:39	-0-
Arr. Antwerp (Ber.)	9:46	10:09	10:46	10:55

Sights in Antwerp: Visit a diamond firm to watch the cutting of diamonds. The Cathedral, open only in the afternoon. Flemish, Italian, French, Dutch and German masterpieces in the Gallery of Fine Arts. Rubens House, with many of his paintings. The 16th century printing shop in the Plantin-Moretus Museum. The Marine Museum. The Mayer van den Bergh Museum. The Open-Air Museum of Sculpture. The Folk-lore Museum. Town Hall. Guild Houses. Vieille Bourse. The Rockox Mansion. The view of Antwerp from the 24th floor of Torengebouw.

214				
Dep. Antwerp (Ber.)	14:08(4)	14:44(2)	15:44(2+4)	16:44(2+4+7)
Dep. Antwerp (Cent.)	-0-	14:53(2)	15:53(2+4)	16:53(2+4+8)
Arr. Roosendaal	-0-	15:20	-0-	-0-
Change trains.				
223				
Dep. Roosendaal	-0-	15:23(2)	-0-	-0-
Arr. Amsterdam	16:32	17:05	18:05	19:05

(1) Daily, except Sundays and holidays. (2) Light refreshments. (3) TEE. Reservation required. Meal service. (4) No train change in Roosendaal. (5) Meal service. (6) Plus frequent other departures from Amsterdam 9:26 - 20:29. (7) Plus frequent other departures from Antwerp (Berchem) 17:45 - 21:45. (8) Plus frequent other departures from Antwerp (Cent.) 17:53 - 21:54.

Amsterdam - Brussels - Amsterdam

214

Dep. Amsterdam	7:48(1+2)	8:26(2)	8:53(1+3)	9:16(2)
Arr. Roosendaal	-0-	10:09	-0-	11:09
Change trains.				
Dep. Roosendaal	-0-	10:12	-0-	11:12
Arr. Brussels (Nord)	10:42	11:15	11:26	12:15
Arr. Brussels (Central)	-0-	11:19	-0-	12:19
Arr. Brussels (Midi)	10:49	11:23	11:33	12:23

Sights in Brussels: See notes about city-sightseeing in Brussels at the start of this section.

Dep. Brussels (Midi)	13:27(1)	14:09(2)	15:09(2)	16:09(5)
Dep. Brussels (Central)	-0-	14:13	15:13	16:13
Dep. Brussels (Nord)	13:35	14:17	15:17	16:17
Arr. Roosendaal	-0-	15:20	16:20	17:20
Change trains.				
Dep. Roosendaal	-0-	15:23	16:23	17:23
Arr. Amsterdam	16:30	17:05	18:05	19:05

(1)No train change in Roosendaal. (2)Light refreshments. (3)TEE. Reservation required. Light refreshments or meal service. (4)Runs from late June to early September. (5)Plus other departures from Brussels (Midi) at 17:02(2), 18:09(2), 18:31(2), 19:09(2), 19:44(4), 20:09(2), 20:15(1+3) and 20:11(2).

Amsterdam - Delft - Amsterdam

222

Dep. Amsterdam (RAI)	Frequent times from 5:39 to 0:10
Dep. Amsterdam (Zuid)	Frequent times from 5:43 to 0:14
Arr. Delft	55 minutes later

Sights in Delft: The 14th century New Church, where members of the Dutch royal family are buried. The Mausoleum of William the Silent. Prinsenhof Museum. Tetar van Elven Museum, containing the works of Vermeer and Pieter de Hoogh. Old Church. The Grain Market. Town Hall. The Old Delft Canal. The Delft Pottery Factory.

Dep. Delft	Frequent times from 5:28 to 23:22
Arr. Amsterdam (Zuid)	50 minutes later
Arr. Amsterdam (RAI)	3 minutes after arriving at Zud railstation

More frequent returns to Amsterdam are possible by taking a local bus from Delft to Den Haag (H.S.). This is a 9km (5½ mile) ride. Trains leave Den Haag 2-3 times each hour for the 45-minute ride from Den Haag to Amsterdam.

Amsterdam - Den Haag - Amsterdam 223

Dep. Amsterdam 2-3 times each hour from 6:26 to 23:41
Arr. Den Haag about 45 minutes later

Sights in Den Haag: Binnenhof, a complex of palaces and courtyards, including Holland's parliament, the Hall of Knights, and Gevangenpoort, Holland's 14th century prison. Mauritshuis, a great art gallery. The Gemeentemuseum. The Peace Palace. The Hidden Church, at 38 Molenstraat. The Mesdag Museum. The Costume Museum. Municipal Museum. The miniature city of Madurodam, with everything on a scale of 1/25th life size.

Dep. Den Haag 2-3 times each hour until 23:20
Arr. Amsterdam about 45 minutes later

Amsterdam - Den Haag + Utrecht - Amsterdam (H-L)

It is possible to visit both Den Haag and Utrecht in one day.

223

Dep. Amsterdam frequent departures from 6:26 to 23:41
Arr. Den Haag (H.S.) about 45 minutes later

225

Dep. Den Haag Frequent times from 5:55 to 22:02
Arr. Utrecht about 40 minutes later

Sights in Utrecht: The 13th century Dom Cathedral, and the view from the top of its 465 steps. The museum of mechanical instruments, at 38 Lange Nieuwstraat. The Netherlands Railway Museum, at 6 Van Oldenberneveltlaan. The 11th century St. Peter's Church. The paintings at The Central Museum, 1 Agnietenstraat.

227

Dep. Utrecht Frequent times from 7:01 to 23:01
Arr. Amsterdam 30 minutes later

For those who prefer the direct trip to Utrecht and to have more time there, refer to notes later in this section under "Amsterdam-Utrecht".

Amsterdam - Gouda - Amsterdam 222a

Dep. Amsterdam 8:21 9:21 10:21 11:21 12:21 13:21
Arr. Gouda 51 minutes later.

Sights in Gouda: Stained-glass in Sint Janskerk. The 15th century Town Hall. The famous Thursday cheese market.

Dep. Gouda 20 minutes after each hour, from 9:20 to 23:20
Arr. Amsterdam 51 minutes later

Amsterdam - Haarlem - Amsterdam 223

Dep. Amsterdam twice each hour from 6:26 to 23:41
Arr. Haarlem 14 minutes later

Sights in Haarlem: The Frans Hals Museum at 62 Groot Heiligland (note the address, that is the only mark outside the building !). St. Bavo, Holland's most beautiful church, with its Muller organ. The World Clock at 88 Wagenweg. Teyler's Museum at 16 Spaarme, for 16th to 20th century Dutch, Italian and French paintings.

Dep. Haarlem	twice each hour from 9:20 to 23:50
Arr. Amsterdam	14 minutes later

Amsterdam - Hoorn - Amsterdam Suburban train service.

Dep. Amsterdam	Frequent times	Dep. Hoorn	Frequent times
Arr. Hoorn	35 minutes later	Arr. Amsterdam	35 minutes later

Sights in Hoorn: The full-scale enactment of 17th century trades and crafts in Hoorn's "Old Dutch Market" takes place in the Rodesteen Square on Wednesdays mid-June to mid-August: folk dances and stalls with basket weaving, net mending and the making of wood shoes.

Daily from mid-June to mid-August (plus Saturdays and Sundays from mid-August through mid-September), a steam train with antique coaches operates between Hoorn and Medemblik.

See Hoorn's 17th century mansions and warehouses. The collection of paintings and antiques in the West Friesian Museum. The 17th century Weighhouse. The 16th century Hospital of St. John. The 2 medieval churches: Noorderkerk and Oosterkerk. The 16th century St. Mary Tower and East Gate, remains of the original fortification. The 17th century almshouse, St. Pietershof.

Amsterdam - Leiden - Amsterdam 223

Dep. Amsterdam	Twice each hour from 6:26 to 23:41
Arr. Leiden	33 minutes later

Sights in Leiden: Pieterskerk, the church where the Pilgrim fathers worshipped for 10 years before setting sail for America in 1620. The University. The Royal Arms Museum. The National Museum of Antiquities. The Municipal Museum. The National Ethnicological Museum.

Dep. Leiden	twice each hour until 23:32
Arr. Amsterdam	33 minutes later

Amsterdam - Maastricht - Amsterdam 227

Most of these trains have light refreshments.

Dep. Amsterdam (Cent.)	8:00(1)	9:30	10:30	11:30
Arr. Maastricht	10:40	12:03	13:03	14:03

Sights in Maastricht: The 6th century St. Servatius Church, oldest church in Holland, where Charlemagne occasionally attended mass. The carved wood columns of the choir in the 10th century Basilica of Our Gracious Lady. The many 17th and 18th century houses in the Stokstraat Quarter. A bus departs from the railstation for the short trip to the Mount

St. Peter caves, consisting of 200 miles of labyrinths where people hid during a Spanish invasion in 1570 and where residents sought safety during World War II. It was originally a sandstone quarry, worked from Roman times until the end of the 19th century.

Dep. Maastricht	13:28	14:28	15:28	15:53(2)
Arr. Amsterdam (Cent.)	16:00	17:00	18:00	18:30

(1)From late May to late September: daily. From late September to late May: daily, except Sundays and holidays. (2)Plus other departures from Maastricht at frequent times from 16:28 to 21:28.

Amsterdam - Paris - Amsterdam 214

Dep. Amsterdam (Cent.)	7:00(1)	7:48(2)	8:53(3)
Arr. Paris (Nord)	12:52	13:52	14:11

* * *

Dep. Paris (Nord)	15:18(4)	16:46(1)	17:41(3)
Arr. Amsterdam (Cent.)	21:33	22:38	22:45

(1)Runs from late June to early September. (2)Daily. Light refreshments. (3)TEE. Reservation required. Light refreshments or meal service. (4)Meal service.

Sights in Paris: As indicated above, it is possible to make a one-day roundtrip from Amsterdam to Paris, although leaving only enough time in Paris to stroll the Champs Elysee from Place Concorde to the Arch of Triumph before having to board the train for the ride back to Amsterdam.

Amsterdam - Rotterdam - Amsterdam (H-L) 223

Dep. Amsterdam	Frequent times from 5:48 to 23:26
Arr. Rotterdam (Cent.)	60 minutes later

Sights in Rotterdam: The view from the top of the 365-foot high Euromast. Nearby, Heineken's Brewery (Crookswigksingle 50). The fantastic collection of 15th to 19th century Flemish and Dutch paintings and a wing of modern sculpture and art (Van Gogh and Kandinsky to the present day) in the Boymans-van Beuningen Museum (Mathenesserlaan 18-20). Devices used by smugglers to defraud customs, at the Profesor van der Poel Tax Museum (Parklaan 14).

The collection of globes, ships and atlases in the Maritime Museum (Burgemeester's Jacobplein 8). The 75-minute boat trip in the harbor, one of the world's largest ports, departing every 45 minutes from Willemsplein Landing. Stroll through the noteworthy Lijnbaan shopping center. Hear a free lunchtime concert every day at De Doelen, an enormous complex of music and congress halls, just across from Central Station.

Unwind in the 10,000-acre Zuiderpark, Plaswijck Park, Zuiderparkgordel, Het Park, and the Kralingse Bos (woods). See the wide variety of trees in Arboretum Trompenburg. Visit Blijdrop Zoo. See the many statues located throughout the city, particularly Mastroianni's "Kiss", at the Central Railroad Station.

The collection of folk art of primitive cultures from the non-Western world at the Museum of Geography and Ethnology (Willemskade 25). Complete 17th, 18th and 19th-century interiors at the Rotterdam Historical Museum in the Schielandhus. Many art galleries, including Lijnbaan Centrum (Lijnbaan 165) and Kunstzaal (Zuidplein 120). Nearby, Delfshaven, the port from which the Puritans started their voyage to the New World, sailing from there on July 22, 1620, before boarding the Mayflower off the English coast. That group spent its last night praying in Delfshaven's Reformed Church, now called Pelgrimvaderskerk (Pilgrim Fathers' Church). A stained-glass window and a plaque there commemorate the Pilgrims' sailing.

The Netherlands Tourist Information Bureau (look for its "VVV" sign) has offices all over Holland. The main office in Rotterdam features a "Lunchtime Tour" daily except Sunday (12:00-14:00) that includes visiting Delfshaven, the "De Dubbelde Palmboom" Museum (with everyday objects used centuries ago in Rotterdam), and a pewter workshop in the Sack Carriers guildhouse, plus a typical Dutch lunch, all at a little over 8 Guilders.

Dep. Rotterdam (Cent.)	Frequent times from 5:32 to 23:03
Arr. Amsterdam	60 minutes later

Amsterdam - Rotterdam + Den Haag - Amsterdam (H-L)

This circle trip allows seeing only a few of the sights in Rotterdam (see notes in preceding listing) and in Den Haag (see notes earlier in this section), but one can see something of both Rotterdam and Den Haag in this one-day trip.

222	
Dep. Amsterdam (RAI)	Frequent times from 5:39 to 0:45
Arr. Rotterdam (Cent.)	65 minutes later
222 + 223	
Dep. Rotterdam (Cent.)	Frequent times from 4:35 to 23:09
Arr. Den Haag (Hbf.)	16 minutes later
222 + 223	
Dep. Den Haag (Hbf.)	Frequent times from 4:54 to 23:32
Arr. Amsterdam (RAI)	35 minutes later

Amsterdam - Utrecht - Amsterdam (H-L) 235

Dep. Amsterdam	Frequent times from 6:23 to 23:32
Arr. Utrecht	about 36 minutes later

For sights in Utrecht, see notes earlier in this section under "Amsterdam - Den Haag + Utrecht - Amsterdam".

Dep. Utrecht	3-4 times each hour until 0:04
Arr. Amsterdam	about 36 minutes later

Brussels - Amsterdam - Brussels 214

Dep. Brussels (Midi)	6:18	7:09(1)	8:09(1+2)	9:09(1+6)
Dep. Brussels (Cent.)	4 minutes after departing Midi station			
Dep. Brussels (Nord)	4 minutes after departing Central station			
Arr. Amsterdam	9:43	10:04	11:04	12:04

Sights in Amsterdam: See notes about city-sightseeing in Amsterdam at the start of this section.

Dep. Amsterdam	13:26(1)	14:26	15:26(1)	16:26(1+7)
Arr. Brussels (Nord)	16:14	17:22	18:15	19:15
Arr. Brussels (Cent.)	4 minutes after arriving Nord station			
Arr. Brussels (Midi)	4 minutes after arriving Central station			

(1) Light refreshments. (2) Saturdays and Sundays only. (3) TEE. Reservation required. Meal service if specified when reserving seat. (4) Daily, except Sundays and holidays. (5) Daily, except Saturdays. (6) Plus other departures from Brussels at 9:55(3+4) and 10:09(1). (7) Plus other departures from Amsterdam at 17:26(1), 17:55(3+5), 18:26(1), 19:26(1) and 20:29.

Brussels - Antwerp - Brussels 214

Dep. Brussels (Midi)	Frequent times from 6:18 to 23:14
Dep. Brussels (Central)	4 minutes later
Dep. Brussels (Nord)	4 minutes later
Arr. Antwerp (Central)	45 minutes after departing Brussels (Midi)

Sights in Antwerp: See notes about city-sightseeing in Antwerp earlier in this section under "Amsterdam - Antwerp - Amsterdam".

Dep. Antwerp (Central)	Frequent times from 6:37 to 23:43
Arr. Brussels (Nord)	40 minutes later
Arr. Brussels (Central)	4 minutes later
Arr. Brussels (Midi)	4 minutes later

Brussels - Bruges - Brussels 206

Dep. Brussels (Nord)	7:58	8:17	8:51	9:50	10:48	11:25
Dep. Brussels (Cent.)	6 minutes after departing Nord station					
Dep. Brussels (Midi)	5 minutes after departing Central station					
Arr. Bruges	9:12	9:25	9:57	10:57	11:57	12:36

Sights in Bruges: The relic (displayed on Fridays) brought from the Second Crusade to Bruges in 1150, at the 12th century Basilica of the Holy Blood. Also there, a fine display of gold, silver and copper artwork. See the lace, pottery, gold pieces, musical instruments and weapons in the 15th century mansion that houses the Gruuthuse Museum.

The black slate and gilded brass 16th century effigies in the Church of Our Lady. Behind the Church, the Dutch masterpieces at the Groeninge museum (open daily 9:30-12:00 and 14:00-17:00. The artwork at the Memling Museum, in a section of the 13th century Hospital of St. John (open 9:00-12:30 and 14:00-18:00 in Summer, 9:00-12:00 and 14:00-16:00 the rest of the year). Paintings and silverwork at the Archer's Guild of St. Sebastian.

The famous 47-bell carillon in the city's main square, Markt. The Tourist Office is in the nearby Government Palace. Canal boats leave from several docks for half-hour cruises with English-language guides.

Dep. Bruges	Frequent times from 6:24 to 23:08
Arr. Brussels (Midi)	One hour later
Arr. Brussels (Cent.)	10 minutes after arriving Midi station
Arr. Brussels (Nord)	3 minutes after arriving Central station

Brussels - Cologne (Koln) - Brussels

206

Dep. Brussels (Midi)	6:35(2)	8:12	10:10(1)
Dep. Brussels (Cent.)	4 minutes after departing Midi station		
Dep. Brussels (Nord)	5 minutes after departing Central station		
Arr. Cologne (Hbf.)	9:17	10:39	12:48

Sights in Cologne: The Cathedral, above all, that took 600 years to build. The view of Cologne from the top of the Cathedral. The Dionysos Mosaic, on the side of the Cathedral. The luxury shops on Hohestrasse. The Wallraf-Richartz Museum, with its collection of Cologne masters. The 15th century Gurzenich. The Zoo. The Roman-German Museum. The Metropolitan Historical Museum. Old Town Hall. Praetorium, with its 1st-4th century Roman Palace ruins. The 3rd century Roman Tower. St. Pantaleon Church. St. Andreas Church. Relics and treasures in the Golden Room of the Church of St. Ursula.

Dep. Cologne	13:21(2)	15:08(2)	17:06(1+3)
Arr. Brussels (Nord)	15:48	17:46	19:47
Arr. Brussels (Cent.)	-0-	17:51	19:52
Arr. Brussels (Midi)	15:55	17:56	19:57

(1) Meal service. (2) Light refreshments. (3) Runs from late May to late September. (4) Plus other departures from Cologne at 18:18(1), 20:20(2) and 20:50(3).

Brussels - Gent - Brussels 206

Dep. Brussels (Nord)	8:51	9:50	10:48	11:15
Dep. Brussels (Cent.)	4 minutes after departing Nord station			
Dep. Brussels (Midi)	5 minutes after departing Central station			
Arr. Gent (St. Pieters)	9:30	10:30	11:30	12:04

Sights in Gent: The superior collection of paintings at the Fine Arts Museum. The collection of furniture at the Museum of Decorative Arts. The reproductions of medieval Gent homes, ironwork, costumes and weapons at the Byloke Museum. The fantastic altarpiece in St. Bavo's Cathedral. See the foreboding dungeons and torture chambers in the 12th century Gravensteen (Castle of the Counts), modeled 8 centuries ago on forts visited by Philip of Alsace when he led Crusaders in Syria. Sint Jorishof, built in 1228 and operated as a hotel since the 15th century. It is believe to be the oldest hotel in Europe, with 70 rooms in the original building.

Dep. Gent (St. Pieters)	36 minutes after each hour until 23:36
Arr. Brussels (Midi)	30 minutes later
Arr. Brussels (Cent.)	12 minutes after arriving Midi station
Arr. Brussels (Nord)	3 minutes after arriving Central station

Brussels - Liege - Brussels 206

Dep. Brussels (Midi)	Frequent times from 6:36 to 22:36
Dep. Brussels (Central)	5 minutes later
Dep. Brussels (Nord)	6 minutes later
Arr. Liege (Guillemins)	72 minutes after departing Brussels (Midi)

Sights in Liege: The wonderful collection of illuminated manuscripts, ancient Roman pottery, tapestries, medieval sculpture and ancient coins in the Musee Curtius (do not miss seeing the enormous twin fireplaces in the large hall on the second floor). In a building at the rear of the Curtius is the Musee du Verre, which has an incredible collection of ancient Egyptian and Roman glassware. See the exhibit of very beautiful guns in the Musee d'Armes, on nearby Quai de Maestricht. The clocks, tapestries, wood paneling, chandeliers, leather covered walls, porcelain, kitchen utensils and furniture in the Musee d'Ansembourg. The collection of impressionist and expressionist paintings (Courbet, Corot, Chagall, Gauguin and Picasso)at the Musee des Beaux-Arts. The Aquarium.

See the columned courtyard at the Palais des Princes-Eveques. Stroll La Roture, the city's old quarter. Visit the colorful Sunday market at La Batte.

Dep. Liege (Guillemins)	Frequent times from 6:21 to 22:42
Arr. Brussels (Nord)	60-70 minutes later
Arr. Brussels (Central)	6 minutes later
Arr. Brussels (Midi)	3 minutes later

Brussels - Luxembourg - Brussels

216

Dep. Brussels (Midi)	7:19(1)	8:18	8:40(4)	
Dep. Brussels (Cent.)	-0-	8:22	8:44	
Dep. Brussels (Nord)	7:27(1)	8:28	8:50	
Dep. Brussels (Q.L.)	7:37(1)	8:40	9:00	
Arr. Luxembourg	9:49	11:15	11:53	

Sights in Luxembourg: See notes about city-sightseeing in Luxembourg at the start of this section.

Dep. Luxembourg	12:08(1)	14:35(2)	15:22	16:59(1+5)
Arr. Brussels (Q.L.)	14:15	17:02	18:02	19:15
Arr. Brussels (Nord)	14:25	17:12	18:13	19:25
Arr. Brussels (Cent.)	-0-	17:24	18:18	-0-
Arr. Brussels (Midi)	14:34	17:28	18:22	19:33

(1) Meal service. (2) Monday-Friday, except holidays. (3) Daily, except Sundays and holidays. (4) Plus other departures (from all 4 Brussels railstations), leaving Midi station at 10:40 and 12:40(3). (5) Plus other departures from Luxembourg at 17:30, 17:59 and 20:16(2).

Brussels - Namur - Brussels

216

Dep. Brussels (Midi)	40 minutes after each hour (8:40-22:40)
Dep. Brussels (Central)	4 minutes later
Dep. Brussels (Nord)	6 minutes later
Arr. Namur	One hour after leaving Brussels (Midi)

Sights in Namur: The silver art in Sisters of Our Lady Convent. The fortress. The baroque 18th century Cathedral. The Diocesan Museum. The extremely elegant Casino, featuring gastronomic feasts.

Dep. Namur	25 minutes after each hour until 22:25
Arr. Brussels (Nord)	47 minutes later
Arr. Brussels (Central)	6 minutes later
Arr. Brussels (Midi)	4 minutes later

Brussels - Paris - Brussels

106

Dep. Brussels (Midi)	6:42(1+2)	7:30(1+3)	8:15	10:06(4+5)
Arr. Paris (Nord)	9:10	10:05	11:18	12:52

Sights in Paris: As indicated here, it is possible to make a one-day roundtrip from Brussels to Paris, but not enough time to see even a fraction of the sights there. There is sufficient time to stroll the Champs Elysee from Place Concorde to the Arch of Triumph and to sit at a sidewalk cafe and watch the Parisians. For complete notes on city-sightseeing in Paris, see the start of the section on France, later in this chapter.

Dep. Paris (Nord)	15:19(4)	17:41(1)	18:41(1+2)	19:27(6+8)
Arr. Brussels (Midi)	18:17	20:08	21:07	22:30

(1) TEE. Reservation required. Meal service. (2) Monday-Friday, except holidays. Runs from early September to late June. (3) Daily, except Sundays (4) Light refreshments. (5) Runs from late June to early September. (6) Meal service. (7) Daily, except Saturdays. (8) Plus another departure from Paris at 20:28(1+7).

Brussels - Tournai - Brussels 201

Dep. Brussels (Nord)	8:04	9:08	10:08	11:08(1)
Dep. Brussels (Midi)	8:18	9:18	10:18	11:18
Arr. Tournai	9:25	10:25	11:25	12:25

Sights in Tournai: One of Belgium's leading art towns.

Dep. Tournai	12:27	13:27(2)	14:27	15:27	16:24(4)
Arr. Brussels (Midi)	13:33	14:33	15:33	16:35	17:35

Arr. Brussels (Nord) 11 minutes after arriving at Midi station

(1) Daily, except Sundays and holidays. (2) Daily, except Saturday. (3) Monday-Friday, except holidays. (4) Plus other departures from Tournai at 17:27, 18:27, 19:27, 20:21(3), 21:23(2) and 22:35(3).

Luxembourg - Basle - Luxembourg 176

Dep. Luxembourg	5:40(1)	7:55(1)	10:00(2)
Arr. Basle (S.B.B.)	10:06	12:30	13:39

Sights in Basle: Superb Holbein, Delacroix, Gaugin, Matisse, Ingres, Courbet and Van Gogh paintings in the Kunstmuseum on St. Alban Graben. The collection of 18th century clothing, ceramics and watches in the Kirschgarten. The Historical Museum in the Franciscan church in Barfusserplatz. Shop on Freiestrasse. See the 16th century Town Hall. The fishmarket. The 15th century New University. Take a boat excursion from the pier in the back of Hotel Three Kings. See the view of the city from the Wettstein Bridge. Visit Munsterplatz.

Dep. Basle (S.B.B.)	13:20(2)	16:25(2)
Arr. Luxembourg	16:49	20:06

(1) Daily, except Sundays and holidays. (2) Meal service.

Luxembourg - Bonn - Luxembourg 625

625

Dep. Luxembourg	5:40	
Arr. Trier	6:22	

Change trains.

623

Dep. Trier	7:19(1)	8:20
Arr. Bonn	9:16	10:50

(1) Monday-Friday only.

623

Dep. Bonn	16:45	18:29(1)
Arr. Trier	18:58	20:32

Change trains.

625

Dep. Trier	21:33	21:33
Arr. Luxembourg	22:15	22:15

Sights in Bonn: The government buildings in the capital of West Germany. Beethoven's birthplace. The University, in the Electors' Castle. Collegiate Church and Cloister. Poffelsdorf Castle. Jesu Church. The Rhineland Museum. The 13th century Remegius Church. The view from the Alte Zoll.

Luxembourg - Brussels - Luxembourg

216

Dep. Luxembourg	7:01(1)	8:23	9:20(2)	10:19(1)
Arr. Brussels (Q.L.)	9:18	11:02	11:42	13:02
Arr. Brussels (Nord)	9:28	11:12	11:52	13:12
Arr. Brussels (Cent.)	9:32	11:18	-0-	13:18
Arr. Brussels (Midi)	9:36	11:22	12:02	13:22

Sights in Brussels: See notes about city-sightseeing in Brussels at the start of this section.

Dep. Brussels (Midi)	13:40(3)	13:57(2+4)	15:57(2)	16:39(6)
Dep. Brussels (Cent.)	13:44(3)	14:01(2+4)	-0-	16:43(6)
Dep. Brussels (Nord)	13:50(3)	14:06(2+4)	15:45(2)	16:49(6)
Dep. Brussels (Q.L.)	14:00(3)	14:16(2+4)	15:56(2)	17:00(6)
Arr. Luxembourg	16:55	16:34	18:08	19:49

(1) Daily, except Sundays and holidays. (2) Meal service. (3) Change trains in Arlon. (4) Monday-Friday, except holidays. (5) Light refreshments. (6) Plus other departures (from all 4 Brussels stations), leaving Midi station at 18:20(2), 18:58(4), 19:40 and 22:26(5).

Luxembourg - Clervaux - Luxembourg

The best view (from the viaduct) as you depart Luxembourg City is from the left-hand side of the train.

217

Dep. Luxembourg	6:05(1)	9:27	10:00	12:08
Arr. Clervaux	7:07	10:28	11:10	12:59

Sights in Clervaux: The Benedictine Abbey of St. Maurice. De Lannoi Castle, with its Museum and the World War II U.S. Army tank that is a monument of the "Battle of the Bulge". The Castle is open 10:00-17:00 June through September (13:00-17:00 on Sundays and bank holidays the rest of the year).

Dep. Clervaux	12:48	17:15	19:54
Arr. Luxembourg	13:52	18:05	20:46

(1) Daily, except Sundays and holidays.

Luxembourg - Cologne (Koln) or Dusseldorf - Luxembourg

625		634		
Dep. Luxembourg	5:40	Dep. Dusseldorf	15:30	17:30
Arr. Trier	7:43	Arr. Cologne	15:53	17:52
Change trains.		Change trains.		
623		623		
Dep. Trier	8:20	Dep. Cologne		18:35
Arr. Cologne	11:12	Arr. Trier		21:25
Change trains.		Change trains.		
634		625		
Dep. Cologne	11:18	Dep. Trier		21:33
Arr. Dusseldorf	11:43	Arr. Luxembourg		22:15

(1)Monday-Friday.

Sights in Cologne: See notes about city sightseeing in Cologne earlier in this section, under "Brussels - Cologne" one-day roundtrip.

Sights in Dusseldorf: Many sensational modern buildings. The Paul Klee collection at Kunstammlung Nordhein-Westfallen. The Goethe Museum, with its first editions, paintings and over 30,000 manuscripts. The Aquarium at the Museumbunker am Zoo. Hofgarten. The Fine Arts Museum. Jagerhof Castle.

Luxembourg - Frankfurt - Luxembourg

625		662	
Dep. Luxembourg	5:40	Dep. Frankfurt	18:29(1)
Arr. Koblenz	7:43	Arr. Koblenz	19:56
Change trains.		Change trains.	
662		625	
Dep. Koblenz	7:57(1)	Dep. Koblenz	20:10
Arr. Frankfurt	9:26	Arr. Luxembourg	22:15

(1)Supplement charged. Meal service.

Sights in Frankfurt: Goethe's House. Goethe's Museum. The Zoo. The emperor's coronation hall in the Romer complex at medieval Romerberg square. The wonderful doors in the 13th century Leonhardskirche. The 13th century chapel of Saalhof in the remains of the palace of Frederick Barbarossa. Cloth Hall. The Botanical Garden. The pews and murals in the Cathedral of St. Bartholomew. The Church of St. Nicholas.

Luxembourg - Koblenz - Luxembourg

625

Dep. Luxembourg	5:40	9:40	
Arr. Trier	6:22	10:22	
Arr. Koblenz	7:43	11:43	

Sights in Koblenz: Old Town. St. Castor's Church. The Middle Rhine Museum.

Dep. Koblenz	12:10	15:10	20:10
Dep. Trier	13:33	16:33	21:33
Arr. Luxembourg	14:15	17:15	22:15

Luxembourg - Liege - Luxembourg

217

Dep. Luxembourg	6:05(1)	9:27
Arr. Liege (Guillemins)	9:54	12:03

Sights in Liege: See notes about sightseeing in Liege earlier in this section, under "Brussels-Liege".

Dep. Liege (Guillemins)	15:23	18:20
Arr. Luxembourg	18:05	20:46

(1) Daily, except Sundays and holidays.

Luxembourg - Mainz - Luxembourg

625

Dep. Luxembourg	5:40
Arr. Koblenz	7:43

Change trains.

662

Dep. Koblenz	8:22
Arr. Mainz	9:19

662

Dep. Mainz	18:39
Arr. Koblenz	19:34

Change trains.

625

Dep. Koblenz	20:10
Arr. Luxembourg	22:15

Sights in Mainz: The art collection in the Cathedral. The Museum of the Central Rhineland. The rare books in the World Museum of Printing in the Romischer Kaiser. The restored Baroque mansions on the Schillerplatz and Schillerstrasse, in the Kirschgarten. Old Town. The sculptures in the Diocesan Museum.

Luxembourg - Metz - Luxembourg

176

Dep. Luxembourg 6:18(1) 7:55(2) 10:00 10:33(2) 12:50(4)
Arr. Metz 50 minutes later

Sights in Metz: The oldest church in France, the 4th century Pierre-aux-Nonains. The largest stained-glass windows in the world, in the 16th century Cathedral of Saint Etienne. The Cathedral was formed by the joining of two 12th century churches into a single building. Its contemporary Marc Chagall and Jacques Villon stained-glass are exceptional. There are Gallo-Roman antiquities in the city's Museum. Walk across the 13th century Porte des Allemands (Gate of the Germans).

Dep. Metz 11:12 13:56 16:05 19:22 20:01(3+4)
Arr. Luxembourg 50 minutes later

(1)Sunday and holidays only. (2)Daily, except Sundays and holidays. (3)Change trains in Thionville. (4)Plus another departure from Metz at 23:01.

Luxembourg - Paris - Luxembourg

177

Dep. Luxembourg 5:40(1+2) 6:44(3) 7:55(1)
Arr. Paris (Est) 9:23 11:25 11:52

Sights in Paris: As indicated above, it is possible to make a one-day roundtrip from Luxembourg to Paris, although leaving only enough time in Paris to stroll the Champs Elysee from Place Concorde to the Arch of Triumph before having to board a train for the ride back to Luxembourg. For complete notes on city-sightseeing in Paris, see the start of the section on France, later in this chapter.

Dep. Paris (Est) 17:15(4) 18:52(3) 19:50(2+5)
Arr. Luxembourg 20:48 23:29 23:50

(1)Daily, except Sundays and holidays. (2)Tray meal service. (3)Light refreshments. (4)Supplement charged. Meal service. (5)Daily, except Saturday.

Luxembourg - Saarbrucken - Luxembourg

625		623	
Dep. Luxembourg	9:40	Dep. Saarbrucken	16:09(1)
Arr. Trier	10:22	Arr. Trier	17:19
Change trains.		Change trains.	
623		625	
Dep. Trier	11:33	Dep. Trier	19:21(2)
Arr. Saarbrucken	12:43	Arr. Luxembourg	20:21

(1) Daily, except Sat. (2) Plus another departure from Trier at 21:33.

Sights in Saarbrucken: The Electors' Palace. Ludwigskirche. The Saarland Museum. The City Hall.

Luxembourg - Strasbourg - Luxembourg

176		
Dep. Luxembourg	7:55(1)	10:00(2)
Arr. Strasbourg	10:58	12:08

Sights in Strasbourg: The famous astronomical clock in the Cathedral. The Alsatian Museum at 23 Quai St. Nicholas. Place Kleber. The Chateau des Rohan museums of archaeology, fine arts and decorative arts.

Dep. Strasbourg	14:39(2)	17:57(2)
Arr. Luxembourg	16:49	20:06

(1) Daily, except Sundays and holidays. (2) Meal service.

Luxembourg - Trier - Luxembourg

625		
Dep. Luxembourg	9:40	12:40
Arr. Trier	10:22	13:22

Sights in Trier: There are more Roman monuments here than in any other German city: the 4th century Porta Nigra gate, 2nd and 4th century baths, a 1st century amphitheater, and a 4th century basilica with its throne room of Roman emperors.

See the "Holy Coat of Trier", said to be Christ's robe, in the Romanesque Cathedral, started in the 6th century. Roman and medieval relics in the Municipal Museum. Peter's Fountain in the market square and, nearby, the 17th century Electoral Palace and 18th century Kasselstatt Palace.

Dep. Trier	13:33	15:36(1)	16:33	17:40(2+4)
Arr. Luxembourg	14:15	16:30	17:15	18:35

(1) Daily, except Sundays and holidays. (2) Sundays and holidays only. (3) Monday-Friday, except holidays. (4) Plus other departures from Trier at 18:29(3), 19:21 and 21:33.

SCENIC RAIL TRIPS

Most of the scenic rail trips of the Benelux countries are in Holland, and all of those are included in the list of one-day roundtrips from Amsterdam preceding this section. They are the train rides between Amsterdam and Delft, Den Haag, Leiden, Rotterdam and Utrecht. The scenery on these trips is best from mid-March through May: fields of tulips, narcissus, crocus and other bulb flowers in bloom. The region is known as "Champs de Fleurs" (Fields of Flowers).

Three other scenic trips in the Benelux countries are listed below. All are noteworthy for beautiful river scenery.

Liege - Jemelle

This fine farm and river scenery can be seen by taking an indirect route from Brussels to Luxembourg.

206				
Dep. Brussels (Midi)	8:12	10:10(1)	11:10(2)	12:10(1)
Dep. Brussels (Cent.)	4 minutes after departing Midi station			
Dep. Brussels (Nord)	6 minutes after departing Central station			
Arr. Liege (Guillemins)	9:14	11:18	12:22	13:17
Change trains.				
218				
Dep. Liege (Guillemins)	9:48	11:48	12:48(2)	13:48
Arr. Namur	10:33	12:33	13:33	14:33
Change trains.				
216				
Dep. Namur	11:41	13:03(1)	13:41(2)	14:41
Dep. Jemelle	12:25	-0-	14:23	15:29(3)
Arr. Luxembourg	13:50	14:44	16:05	16:55

(1) Meal service. (2) Daily, except Sundays and holidays from Namur to Luxembourg. (3) Change trains in Arlon.

Luxembourg - Liege

Excellent farm and river scenery on this easy one-day roundtrip.

217		
Dep. Luxembourg	6:05(1)	9:27
Arr. Liege (Guillemins)	9:54	12:03
*	*	*
Dep. Liege (Guillemins)	15:23	18:20
Arr. Luxembourg	18:05	20:46

(1) Daily, except Sundays and holidays.

Namur - Dinant

This is a spur off the Brussels-Luxembourg route. The great farm and river scenery here can be seen either by breaking-up the ride from Brussels to Luxembourg (or vice versa), or as an easy one-day roundtrip from Brussels.

For the first way:

216		
Dep. Brussels (Midi)	8:15	
Dep. Brussels (Central)	8:19	
Dep. Brussels (Nord)	8:24	
Arr. Namur	9:10	
Change trains.		
215		
Dep. Namur	9:45	
Arr. Dinant	10:23	
Change trains.		
Dep. Dinant	11:31(1)	13:39
Arr. Namur	12:09	14:17
Change trains.		
216		
Dep. Namur	13:03	14:41
Arr. Luxembourg	14:44	16:55

216	
Dep. Luxembourg	10:05(2)
Arr. Namur	12:20
Change trains.	
215	
Dep. Namur	12:47
Arr. Dinant	13:27
Change trains.	
Dep. Dinant	13:39
Arr. Namur	14:17
Change trains.	
216	
Dep. Namur	14:25
Arr. Brussels (Nord)	15:12
Arr. Brussels (Central)	15:18
Arr. Brussels (Midi)	15:22

(1) Monday-Friday, except holidays. (2) Daily, except Sundays and holidays.

Here is the Brussels one-day roundtrip:

216	
Dep. Brussels (Midi)	10:40
Dep. Brussels (Cent.)	10:44
Dep. Brussels (Nord)	10:50
Arr. Namur	11:38
Change trains.	
215	
Dep. Namur	12:45
Arr. Dinant	13:26

215	
Dep. Dinant	13:39
Arr. Namur	14:18
Change trains.	
216	
Dep. Namur	14:25
Arr. Brussels (Nord)	15:12
Arr. Brussels (Cent.)	15:18
Arr. Brussels (Midi)	15:22

INTERNATIONAL ROUTES FROM BELGIUM

The Belgian gateway for rail travel to London, Amsterdam, Basle (and on to Zurich and Milan), Cologne (and on to Hamburg and Copenhagen) and Paris (and on to Madrid) is Brussels. (Notes on the route to London appear in Chapter 10.)

Brussels - Amsterdam

214

Dep. Brussels (Midi)	Frequent times from 6:18 to 21:09
Dep. Brussels (Cent.)	4 minutes after departing Midi station
Dep. Brussels (Nord)	4 minutes after departing Central station
Arr. Amsterdam	3 hours later.

Brussels - Basle

These trains depart one hour earlier from late September to early April.

63

Dep. Brussels (Midi)	7:19(1)	12:12(1)	15:37(1)	18:20(1)	22:26(2)
Dep. Brussels (Nord)	7:27(1)	12:20(1)	15:45(1)	18:30(1)	22:35(2)
Dep. Brussels (Q.L.)	7:37(1)	12:30(1)	15:56(1)	18:40(1)	-0-
Arr. Basle	13:39	18:25	22:03	1:12	5:20

(1) Meal service. (2) Carries sleeping car. Also has couchettes.

Brussels - Cologne (Koln)

206

Dep. Brussels (Midi)	6:36(1)	7:32(1)	8:12	10:10(2+6)
Dep. Brussels (Cent.)	6:40(1)	-0-	8:16	10:15(2)
Dep. Brussels (Nord)	6:44(1)	7:41(1)	8:22	10:20(2)
Arr. Cologne	9:17	10:19	10:32	12:48

(1) Light refreshments. (2) Meal service. (3) Reservation required. (4) Runs from late May to late September daily except Sundays and holidays. (5) Runs from late June to late August. (6) Plus other departures from Midi station at 12:10(2), 15:10(1), 16:01(1), 18:10(2), 18:27 (2+3), 18:52(4), 20:10(2) and 22:33(1+3).

Brussels - Luxembourg

216

Dep. Brussels (Midi)	-0-	8:18(1)	8:40(2)	10:40(6)
Dep. Brussels (Cent.)	-0-	8:22(1)	8:44(2)	10:44
Dep. Brussels (Nord)	6:36	8:28(1)	8:50(2)	10:50
Dep. Brussels (Q.L.)	6:46	8:40(1)	9:00(2)	11:00
Arr. Luxembourg	9:43	11:15	11:53	13:42

(1) Meal service. (2) Change trains in Arlon. (3) Daily, except Sundays and holidays. (4) Monday-Friday, except holidays. (5) Light refreshments. (6) Plus other departures from Brussels' Midi station at 12:12(1), 12:40(3), 13:40(2), 13:57(1+4), 14:40(4), 15:37(1), 16:11(4), 16:39, 18:20(1), 18:58(4), 19:40 and 22:26(5).

Brussels - Paris

106

Dep. Brussels (Midi)	0:32(1)	6:41(2+3+4)	7:30(2+5+11)
Arr. Paris (Nord)	6:42	9:10	10:05

(1) Has couchettes. (2) TEE. Reservation required. Meal service. (3) Monday-Friday, except holidays. (4) Runs from early September to late June. (5) Daily, except Sundays and holidays. (6) Runs from late June to early September. (7) Light refreshments. (8) Meal service. (9) Supplement charged. (10) Daily, except Saturday. (11) Plus other departures at 8:15, 10:06(6+7), 11:03(8), 11:43(2), 14:07(7), 16:08(7), 17:17(2), 17:53(8+9), 18:38(2+3+4), 19:15(8)and 20:42(2+10).

INTERNATIONAL ROUTES FROM HOLLAND

The Dutch gateway for rail travel to London, Basle (and on to Zurich and Milan), Cologne, Hamburg (and on to Copenhagen) and Paris (and on to Madrid) is Amsterdam. (Notes on the route to London appear in Chapter 9.)

Amsterdam - Brussels

214

Dep. Amsterdam	Frequent times from 6:26 to 20:26
Arr. Brussels (Nord)	3 hours later
Arr. Brussels (Cent.)	4 minutes after departing Nord station
Arr. Brussels (Midi)	4 minutes after departing Central station

Amsterdam - Cologne (Koln) - Basle

68

Many castles are seen in the Koblenz-Mainz area as the train travels alongside the Rhine River.

Dep. Amsterdam	7:49(1)	8:38(2)	14:49	19:49(3)
Arr. Cologne	10:46(1)	12:00(2)	18:38	23:39(3)
Arr. Basle (Bad Bf.)	15:25	17:26	0:35	5:28

(1) TEE. Reservation required. Meal service. (2) Meal service. (3) Carries sleeping car. Also has couchettes.

Amsterdam - Hamburg - Copenhagen

67

Dep. Amsterdam	8:01	17:00(1+2)	18:01	20:01(3)
Arr. Hamburg	14:04	22:49	23:21	2:12
Dep. Hamburg	14:15	-0-	-0-	2:21
Arr. Copenhagen	20:09	-0-	-0-	8:09(4)

(1) Daily, except Saturday. (2) Meal service. (3) Has couchettes. (4) Arrives 9:09 from late September to late March.

Amsterdam - Luxembourg

63

Dep. Amsterdam	11:51(1)
Arr. Maastricht	14:32
Arr. Luxembourg	18:05

(1) Runs all year. From late September to late May, change trains at Maastricht. Light refreshments until 14:32.

Amsterdam - Paris

76

Dep. Amsterdam	6:57(1)	7:50(2)	8:50(3)	10:55(4)	15:55(2+6)
Arr. Paris (Nord)	12:52	13:54	14:11	17:00	22:06

(1) Runs from late June to early September. Light refreshments. (2) Meal service. (3) TEE. Reservation required. Meal service. (4) Light refreshments. (5) Daily, except Saturday. (6) Plus another departure from Amsterdam at 17:53(3+5).

INTERNATIONAL ROUTES FROM LUXEMBOURG

Luxembourg City is a gateway for rail travel to London, Amsterdam, Basle (and on to Zurich and Milan), Brussels, Cologne, Koblenz (and on to Frankfurt), and Paris. (Notes on the routes from Amsterdam, Brussels and Paris to London appear in Chapter 10.)

Luxembourg - Amsterdam

63

Dep. Luxembourg	12:08(1)
Arr. Maastricht	15:21
Arr. Amsterdam	18:03

(1) Runs all year. Change trains at Maastricht from late September to late May.

Luxembourg - Basle

176

Dep. Luxembourg	1:18(1)	5:40(2)	7:55(2)	10:00(3)	14:54(3+4)
Arr. Basle (SNCF)	5:20	10:06	12:30	13:39	18:25

(1) Carries sleeping car. Also has couchettes. (2) Daily, except Sundays and holidays. (3) Meal service. (4) Plus other departures from Luxembourg at 18:26(3) and 21:14.

Luxembourg - Brussels

216

Dep. Luxembourg	4:57(1)	7:01(2)	8:23	9:20(3+7)
Arr. Brussels (Q.L.)	7:18	9:18	11:02	11:42
Arr. Brussels (Nord)	7:28	9:28	11:12	11:52
Arr. Brussels (Cent.)	-0-	9:32	11:18	-0-
Arr. Brussels (Midi)	7:37	9:36	11:22	12:02

(1) Light refreshments. (2) Daily, except Sundays and holidays. (3) Meal service. (4) Does not stop at Brussel's Central station. (5) Change trains in Arlon. (6) Monday-Friday, except holidays. (7) Plus other departures from Luxembourg at 10:19(2), 12:08(3+4), 15:20, 16:59(3+4), 17:30-(3), 17:59(5), 19:21(6), 20:00(5) and 20:16(3).

Luxembourg - Cologne

625

Dep. Luxembourg	7:16(1)	9:40	15:40
Arr. Trier	8:10	10:22	16:22

Change trains.

623

Dep. Trier	9:50(2)	12:50(2)	17:32(2)
Arr. Cologne	12:42	15:45	20:23

(1) Monday-Friday, except holidays. (2) Light refreshments.

Luxembourg - Paris

177

Dep. Luxembourg	5:40(1+2)	6:44(3)	7:55(1)	17:18(3+5)
Arr. Paris (Est)	9:23	11:25	11:52	21:53

(1) Daily, except Sundays and holidays. (2) Specify meal required when reserving first-class seat. (3) Light refreshments. (4) Supplement charged. (5) Plus another departure from Luxembourg at 17:27(2+4).

FRANCE

French rail tickets purchased in France are valid for travel any day within 2 months from the date of purchase.

Before boarding a train, passengers are required to validate tickets purchases in France, in one of the many orange-colored machines located at the entrance to the platforms. Tickets are spot-checked on the trains. A person holding a non-validated ticket is subject to a fine.

Train tickets obtained before arrival in France are valid for 6 months, and it is not required that a ticket purchased outside France be validated.

The signs you will see at railstations in France are:

ARRIVEE	ARRIVAL
CONSIGNE	CHECKROOM
DAMES	WOMEN
DEPART	DEPARTURE
ENTREE	ENTRANCE
FUMEURS	SMOKING COMPARTMENT
GARE	STATION
HORAIRE	TIMETABLE
MESSIEURS	MEN
QUAI	PLATFORM
RENSEIGNEMENTS	INFORMATION
SORTIE	EXIT
VOIE	TRACK
WAGON-LIT	SLEEPING CAR
WAGON-RESTAURANT	RESTAURANT CAR

SUMMER TIME

France changes to Summer Time on the last Sunday of March and converts back to Standard Time on the last Sunday of September.

EURAILPASS BONUSES

Ferry crossings on the Irish Continental Line between Le Havre (France) and Rosslare (Ireland) 21 hours, or between Cherbourg (France) and Rosslare 17 hours. Port taxes and cabin accommodations are not covered.

The bus (7-franc charge) that transports passengers from Le Havre railstation to the boat pier takes people on a first-come-first-served basis. When the bus is filled, people left at the railstation must take a taxi to the pier.

On arrival in Ireland, the bus service there (taking passengers from Rosslare pier to the Rosslare railstation) accommodates all passengers, and at no charge.

Europabus Line #241, Paris to Nice, via Avallon, Lyon and Grenoble. (and vice versa).

FRENCH HOLIDAYS

A list of holidays is helpful because some trains will be noted later in this section as not running on holidays. Also, those trains which operate on holidays are filled, and it is necessary to make reservations for them long in advance.

January 1	New Year's Day		Pentecost
	Easter		Pentecost Monday
	Easter Monday	July 14	National Day (Bastille Day)
May 1	Labor Day		
May 8	Victory Day (World War II)	August 15	Assumption Day
		November 1	All Saints' Day
	Ascension Day	November 11	Armistice Day (World War I)
	Joan of Arc Day		
		December 25	Christmas Day

FRANCE VACANCES

This pass for unlimited train travel is restricted to persons living outside France and its territories.

The first-class prices in 1983 are $170(U.S.) for 7 days, $220 for 15 days, and $345 for one month. For children under 12: $105, $135 and $205. With the 7 or 15-day first-class France Vacances, each pass holder also receives one day of free car rental and 100 kilometers. With the one-month pass this bonus is 2 days of free car rental and 200 kilometers. Car rental is available in 23 cities.

The second-class prices in 1983 are $115 for 7 days, $150 for 15 days, and $230 for one month. For children under 12: $70, $90 and $130.

Both first and second-class passes provide free train transportation between Paris and its airports. The 7-day pass also provides 4 days of subway and bus travel in Paris. The 15-day and one-month passes also provide 7 days of subway and bus travel in Paris.

France Vacances can be purchased from travel agents or from offices of French National Railroad.

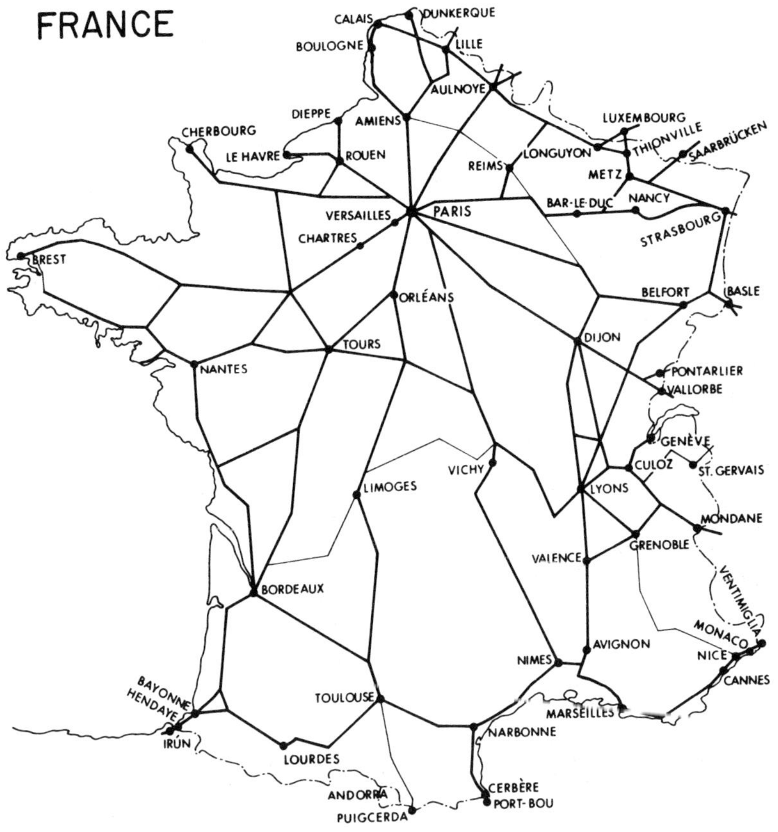
FRANCE
CALAIS
DUNKERQUE
BOULOGNE
LILLE
AULNOYE
DIEPPE
AMIENS
CHERBOURG
LE HAVRE
ROUEN
LUXEMBOURG
THIONVILLE
SAARBRÜCKEN
REIMS
LONGUYON
METZ
BAR-LE-DUC
NANCY
VERSAILLES
PARIS
STRASBOURG
CHARTRES
BREST
BELFORT
BASLE
ORLÉANS
DIJON
TOURS
NANTES
PONTARLIER
VALLORBE
GENÈVE
CULOZ
ST. GERVAIS
VICHY
LYONS
LIMOGES
MONDANE
GRENOBLE
VALENCE
VENTIMIGLIA
BORDEAUX
MONACO
AVIGNON
NICE
NIMES
CANNES
BAYONNE
HENDAYE
TOULOUSE
MARSEILLES
NARBONNE
IRÚN
LOURDES
CERBÈRE
ANDORRA
PORT-BOU
PUIGCERDA

WORLD'S FASTEST TRAINS

Since 1981, France has operated the world's fastest trains, the "Trains à Grande Vitesse", which have run at 237 miles per hour and are operated at the top speed of 160mph. The usual composition is 386 seats: 111 in first-class, 275 in second-class.

Reservations are required. Although normal fares are charged at off-peak times, a supplement is charged for those TGV that run at the busiest times. Each TGV has a bar. Meals are brought to seats in some of the first-class cars.

The 1982 service (Paris-Lyon, Paris-Dijon and Paris-Geneva) was expanded in 1983 to include Paris-Marseilles, Paris-Montpelier and Paris-Annecy-Grenoble. A TGV service Paris-Lausanne (with cross-platform transfer in Lausanne for trains to Milan) is scheduled to begin in 1984. Details on TGV schedules appear in Chapter 7.

ONE-DAY EXCURSIONS AND CITY-SIGHTSEEING

Here are 42 one-day rail trips that can be made comfortably from Avignon, Lyon, Nice and Paris, returning to those cities in most cases before dinnertime. Notes are provided on what to see and do at each destination. The number below the name of each route is the Cook's timetable.

Paris

There is rail service from the center of Paris (Nord station) to Charles-de-Gaulle Airport every 15 minutes from 5:30 to 23:30. The rail service from that airport to Paris is every 15 minutes from 5:15 to 24:00.

Rail service is also available between 5 Paris stations and Orly Airport at frequent times from 5:30 to 22:30 (Blvd. Victor, Invalides, Quai d'Orsay, Austerlitz and Pont de Rungis). There is bus service between Pont de Rungis and Orly from 6:15 to 23:15.

Bus service connects these Paris railstations:

(1) From Austerlitz to Est, Nord and St. Lazare. (2) From Lyon to Est, Nord and St. Lazare. (3) From Nord to Lyon and Austerlitz. (4) From Est to Lyon and Austerlitz.

Your city sightseeing in Paris should include: the Montmartre area and Sacre Coeur. Eiffel Tower. Place Concorde. The Arch of Triumph. The stained-glass at St. Chapelle. Norte Dame Cathedral. Napoleon's Tomb. The Louvre. Luxembourg Palace. Strolling the Champs Elysee. Visit Galleries Lafayette, the most beautiful department store building in the world. The Musee of the Renaissance, in the 16th century Chateau d'Ecouen Castle, with its antique tapestries, ceramics, arms, furniture, outstanding carved white fireplace and painted ceilings. Open daily except Tuesdays 9:45-12:30 and 14:00-17:15.

Marvelous costumes in the Musee de la Mode et du Costume, 10 Ave. Pierre Premier de Serbie. Open daily except Monday 10:00-17:40.

The large poster collection in the Musee de l'Affiche, 18 Rue de Paradis. Open daily except Tuesdays 12:00-18:00.

The Tiepolo ceilings, fantastic staircase, excellent paintings (Rembrandt, Reynolds, Manet, Monet and many other Impressionists) in the Musee Jacquemart-Andre, 12 Rue Louis-Boilly. Open daily except Monday 13:30-17:30.

Paintings and engravings illustrating the history of Paris, along with 17th and 18th century furniture, in the Musee Carnavalet, 23 Rue de Sevigne. Open daily except Monday 10:00-17:40.

The collection of opera costumes, scores and photos in the Museum at the Opera. Open daily except Sunday 10:00-17:00 and during intermissions of performances.

Near the Opera, at 25 Boulevard des Capucines, is the Musee Cognac-Jay, which has an exhibit of lorgnettes, snuff boxes, letter openers and sewing kits, all of them in porcelain, precious metals and jewels. Open daily except Monday and Tuesday 10:00-17:40.

Information about tours sponsored by the Department of Historical Monuments (botanical gardens, the Latin Quarter, churches that are architecturally interesting, private homes) can be obtained at the Caisse Nationale des Monuments Historiques, at 62 Rue Saint-Antoine.

See if you can look through the windows of Fauchon's (finest foods in the world), 26 Place de la Madeleine, and not salivate. There are 2 Fauchon's. One sells extremely fancy produce (green beans from Kenya, kiwis from New Zealand, breadfruit from Martinique, mangoes from northern Egypt) and canned foods. It also has a wine-liquor section and a delicatessen section with incredible items produced by a staff of 20 cooks: whole glazed ducks decorated with peaches, $50-a-pound fresh foie gras, eggplant stuffed with ground mutton and boiled eggs in watercress sauce, 6 different kinds of ham, snails, countless salads and every conceivable tidbit.

Across the street from that store is a second Fauchon's. This one, staffed with 20 bakers, offers snacks, beverages and countless sweets. Every year, it sells 18 tons of chocolates, 8 tons of marrons glace and 15 tons of candied fruits (whole melons, strawberries, oranges, prunes). Its prices for chocolates are $14 to $16 a pound. The candied fruits are $12 a pound.

For Americans, Fauchon's has all of its 120 salespeople take English-language lessons 3 times a week. (Its total staff numbers 240.) The store stocks such American items as Aunt Jemima's pancake mix, Sarah Lee cheesecake and Fritos. At Thanksgiving, Fauchon's features cans of cranberry sauce and pumpkin pie filling.

Avignon

This walled city, the tourist capital of Provence, can be entered through 14 different gates. You can obtain a city map or a personal guide at the Syndicat d'Initiative (41 Cours Jean-Jaures). During the 14th century, Avignon was briefly the world headquarters of the Catholic Church when it was unsafe for a series of French popes to be in Rome. Take the one-hour tour of the Palace of the Popes. Outside the Palace you can board a trackless 2-car train pulled by a gasoline-powered locomotive and climb to the top of the hill overlooking the Palace for a view of the city and the Rhone Valley. See the primitive art in the museum in the 14th century Petit Palais. The sculptures in the Lapidary Museum, housed in the 17th century Jesuit Church. The collection of ironwork in the Calvet Museum on Rue Joseph Vernet. See the view of Avignon from Villeneuve-les-Avignon, on the other side of the Rhone River.

All-day bus tours from Avignon to many interesting places in this area can be taken from in front of the railstation. One tour includes Roman ruins at St. Remy, the village of Les Baux (sculptured during the Middle Ages from the top of a stone hill), and the Roman theatre in Arles.

Lyon

Occasionally, 2 trains depart from the same track at Lyon's Perrache railstation, heading in opposite directions. Be sure to stand at the correct end (North or South) of the track in order to board the train you want to ride. Check the departure signs at the underground passageway. Do not rely merely on a track number when departing from Perrache railstation !

Next to the North passageway of Track "A" is a take-out restaurant, handy for provisioning your trip.

A metropolitan train connects Lyon's Brotteaux and Perrache railstations. The ride is 15 minutes.

Try to keep from eating at the spectacular Nouvelle Les Halles food market: 65 tantalizing stalls of meat, poultry, fish, produce, cheese, bread, pastry, coffee, tea, spices, wine and candy, plus small restaurants and a florist. Open 7:00-19:00 Monday-Saturday and 7:00-12:00 on Sunday.

Here, you can buy pheasants in plumage, partridges, wild ducks, quail, snipe, frog legs, 4 varieties of oysters, shrimp, eel, cod and sole. There are goose, duck and game pates. Do not fail to sample the 3 Lyon specialties: Morteau de Jesu (pork meat in a pig's foot casing), the peppery pink and white salami, and the garlicky Lyon sausage.

The wine here is magnificent. It has been said that Lyon has 3 rivers: the Rhone, the Saone, and the Beaujolais.

Stroll for a few hours through the winding streets of the 3-block wide half-mile long ancient section (Vieux Lyon) and see the magnificent 15th century Renaissance mansions. Much information is available in the booklet "Guide du Vieux Lyon" sold everywhere in the city.

See the Historical Museum and International Marionette Museum in Lyon's largest Renaissance structure, Hotel de Gadagne. Also in the old town: The tableau of the Cathedral clock at 12:00, 13:00 14:00 and 15:00. The Roman ruins on the hill atop which the Basilica of Notre Dame de Fourviere is located.

In the modern area, take Bus #13 from the railstation, through the main shopping streets, to the Place de la Croix Rousse and then walk to Place des Terreaux to see City Hall, the 19th century Opera House and The Fine Arts Museum. Do not miss seeing the Italian fountain with its 4 bronze horses, sculptured by the same Bartholdi who created the Statue of Liberty.

Window-shop around Place Bellecour and along Quai des Celestins. Nearby, see the nearly 2,000-year old collection of Oriental and European silks and velvets in the Musee Historique des Tissus (34 Rue de la Charite). Next door to it, there is a good collection of silver objects, kitchen utensils, furniture, tapestries and enamels in The Museum of Decorative Arts. Also visit The Museum of Printing and Banking (13 Rue de la Poullaillerie) and The Museum of Medicine in Hotel-Dieu on Rue de l'Hopital.

Nice

It is a 15-minute walk South from the railstation to the hotels and casinos along the beach, where boats can be hired. Watch the International Set cavort, and remember that you are now a member of it. Visit the Matisse Museum and the antique shops.

In the following timetables, where a city has more than one railstation we have designated the particular station after the name of the city (in parentheses).

Avignon - Arles - Avignon 151

Dep. Avignon	9:28	12:09	14:51		
Arr. Arles	20 minutes later				

Sights in Arles: The ancient Roman cemetery, Alyscamps, that contains 400,000 sarcophagi, hand-carved granite caskets. The 21,000-seat Roman arena. The Forum, built during Augustus' rule. The Thermae, from Constantine's era. The 12th century Cloister in the marvelous Romanesque Church of Saint-Trophime.

Dep. Arles	12:34	14:54	16:00(1)	17:57	18:36(2)
Arr. Avignon	20 minutes later				

(1)Runs from late June to mid-September. (2)Plus other departures from Arles at 20:14, 22:15 and 22:38.

Avignon - Lyon - Avignon 151

Dep. Avignon	6:57(1)	8:19(2)	10:47(2)	12:55(2)
Arr. Lyon (Perrache)	9:08	10:20	12:45	14:56

Sights in Lyon: See notes about sightseeing in Lyon at the start of this section.

Dep. Lyon (Perrache)	12:18	14:07(2)	17:07(2)	18:14(3)
Arr. Avignon	14:46	16:05	19:04	21:10

(1)Light refreshments. (2)Meal service. (3)Plus other departures from Lyon at 18:43(1), 20:55(1) and 23:55.

Avignon - Marseille - Avignon 150 + 151

Dep. Avignon	7:42	11:56(1+2)	12:09(3)	13:54(3)
Arr. Marseille (St. Ch.)	60 minutes later			

Sights in Marseille: Fancy shops on Canebiere, the main street. The dungeon from which the Count of Monte Cristo escaped, at Chateau d'If.

Dep. Marseille (St. Ch.)	13:58(1)	14:38(3)	15:09(1+5)	16:37(1+5+7)
Arr. Avignon	60 minutes later			

(1)TGV. Reservation required. Meal service or light refreshments. (2)Supplement charged Monday-Friday. (3)Meal service. (4)Light refreshments. (5)Supplement charged daily except Saturday. (6)Supplement charged only on Friday and Sunday. (7)Plus other departures from Marseilles at 17:10(3), 17:41(1+6), 17:43(4), 20:30, 21:49, 22:35, 22:59 and 23:59.

Avignon - Monte Carlo - Avignon 151

Dep. Avignon	6:20
Arr. Monte Carlo	11:06

Sights in Monte Carlo: The glittering Casino, built in 1865. There is a 12-franc charge to stroll through the huge gaming room, the Salon des Ameriques, where the minimum bet is 10 francs. See the marble pillars in the gilded Hotel de Paris (erected in 1863) and its lovely gardens, next to the Casino. The outstanding Oceanographic Museum and the beautiful Aquarium. The old city, with its Prince's Palace, Palace Museum (Napoleonic items), the collection of dolls in the National Museum, the Museum of Anthropology in the Exotic Garden, and the Zoological Gardens. The changing of the guard at the Palace, daily at 11:55. The array of pleasure boats in the harbor.

Dep. Monte Carlo	18:06	19:21	19:47
Arr. Avignon	22:42	0:04	1:11

Avignon - Nice - Avignon 151

Dep. Avignon	6:31	7:00	9:30(1)
Arr. Nice	10:33	10:57	13:43

It is a 15-minute walk South from the railstation to the hotels and casinos along the beach.

Sights in Nice: See notes about sightseeing in Nice at the start of this section.

Dep. Nice	14:41(1)	16:25(1)	18:40	20:00
Arr. Avignon	18:12	20:32	22:44	0:04

(1) Meal service.

Avignon - Nimes -Avignon 162

Dep. Avignon	7:48	9:39	11:52(1)	12:15	12:52(2+3)
Arr. Nimes	30 minutes later				

Sights in Nimes: Many Roman ruins in excellent condition, such as the 1st century amphitheater (seating 24,000 people) in the center of the city, used in recent years for bullfights to entertain Spanish migrant workers. The construction of the arena was done by fitting large stones together without the use of mortar.

Also see the beautiful 1st century rectangular temple, Maison Carree, and its collection of Roman sculptures. The view of Nimes from the oldest Roman building, Tour Magne, on a hill outside the city. A few miles away is the enormous Pont du Gard Roman aqueduct.

Visit the collection of Iron Age and Roman objects in the Archaeological Museum. Stroll through the 18th century Garden of the Fountain

Dep. Nimes	12:00	14:25	15:14	16:02(2)	17:04(1+4)
Arr. Avignon	30 minutes later				

(1)TGV. Reservation required. Supplement charged. (2)Runs from late June to mid-September. (3)Plus other departures from Avignon at 13:51(1) and 14:04. (4)Plus other departures from Nimes at frequent times from 17:46 to 22:31.

Lyon - Annecy - Lyon

En route, the train splits. Some cars go to Annecy, others to Grenoble. Be sure to sit in a car marked "Annecy".

167

Dep. Lyon (Perrache)	7:28	10:18	12:12
Arr. Annecy	9:28	12:20	14:50

Sights in Annecy: This is a beautiful lake resort. See the 12th century Island Palace. The shops in the old quarter.

Dep. Annecy	14:15	16:06	19:57
Arr. Lyon (Perrache)	16:44	18:20	22:17

Lyon - Dijon - Lyon

151

Dep. Lyon (Perrache)	5:50	6:33(1)	9:12(2)	12:57(3)
Arr. Dijon	7:33	9:29	10:52	14:28

Sights in Dijon: Town Hall, formerly the palace of those swashbuckling dukes of Burgundy and now one of the richest museums in France. The Church of Notre Dame. The 13th century Cathedral of St. Benigne archaeological museum. The Palace of Justice. The Magnin Museum. The 14th century Chartreuse de Champmol, with its famous chapel portrait and Moses Fountain. Rude Museum. Don't fail to have lunch in Dijon, France's food and wine capital.

Dep. Dijon	12:10(3)	15:47(3)	16:57(3)	19:20(2+4)
Arr. Lyon (Perrache)	13:54	17:42	18:39	20:52

(1)Change trains in Chagny on Saturday and Sunday. (2)Light refreshments. (3)Meal service. (4)Plus another departure from Dijon at 21:55.

Lyon - Grenoble - Lyon 154

Dep. Lyon (Perrache)	7:21(1)	8:03	11:03(1+2)	12:15
Arr. Grenoble	8:46	9:32	12:28	13:42

Sights in Grenoble: The very rich (Utrillo, Picasso, Ruben) art museum in the 16th century Palace of Justice. Take the cable car ride up to Guy Pape Park for a marvelous view of the city below and the fields surrounding Grenoble. While at the top, visit the military museum in the 19th century fort, the Bastille, and the Auto Museum. Walk back to Grenoble, downhill, through the Jardine des Dauphines.

Dep. Grenoble	11:32(3)	12:50	13:26	16:03(5)
Arr. Lyon (Perrache)	13:21	14:21	14:50(2)	17:36

(1) Daily, except Sundays and holidays. (2) Depart/Arrive Lyon's Brotteaux railstation. (3) Meal service. (4) Daily, except Saturday. (5) Plus other departures from Grenoble at 16:40, 17:04, 18:24(2+4), 19:18(1) and 21.09.

Lyon - Marseille - Lyon 151

Dep. Lyon (Perrache)	7:11(1)	9:58(1)	11:50(1)
Arr. Marseille (St. Ch.)	10:33	13:10	14:54

Sights in Marseille: See notes about sightseeing in Marseille earlier in this section, under "Avignon-Marseille".

Dep. Marseille (St. Ch.)	14:38(1)	15:16(2)	17:10(1)	17:43(3+4)
Arr. Lyon (Perrache)	17:51	18:37	20:34	21:57

(1) Meal service. (2) Runs from late June to mid-September. (3) Light refreshments. (4) Plus departures from Marseille at 19:22(1), 21:25(2), 21:38 and 21:49.

Lyon - Tours - Lyon 128

Dep. Lyon (Perrache)	6:48(1)	9:28(1)
Arr. St. Pierre des Corps	11:32	14:19

Change to suburban train waiting for transfer.

Dep. St. Pierre des Corps	11:33	14:20
Arr. Tours	11:38	14:25

Sights in Tours: The fine collection of paintings in the Musee des Beaux-Arts. Much of the old city was destroyed in the 1944 bombings which forced German occupiers to retreat and resulted in liberation.

Dep. Tours by suburban train	15:53	18:21
Arr. St. Pierre des Corps	15:58	18:26

Change to train waiting for transfer.

Dep. St. Pierre des Corps	15:59(1)	18:27(1)
Arr. Lyon (Perrache)	20:36	23:04

(1) Light refreshments.

Lyon - Vienne - Lyon 151

Dep. Lyon(Perrache) 7:11 9:15 12:18 14:23
Arr. Vienne 20 minutes later

Sights in Vienne: Many good Roman ruins. The Temple of Augustus and Livia, a large amphitheater, and the pyramid which once marked the center of a Roman coliseum. Ancient jewels and bronze and ceramic relics on exhibit at the Museum of Fine Arts. Try to dine at one of the world's most famous restaurants, Pyramide, open daily except Tuesday and closed November through mid-December.

Dep. Vienne 14:29 17:59 18:16(1) 21:36 22:32
Arr. Lyon (Perrache) 20 minutes later
(1)Runs from late June to mid-September.

Nice - Cannes (and Grasse) - Nice 151

Dep. Nice Frequent times from 5:47 to 23:20
Arr. Cannes 40 minutes later

Sights in Cannes: Stroll along Promenade de la Croisette to see the beautiful beach and splendid yachts, all the way to the Palm Beach Casino. Take boat rides on the Bay of Cannes or to the St. Honorat and St. Marguerite islands. On the latter, you can visit the prison that held the Man in the Iron Mask. There is also a short boat trip to Lerins, where the 5th century Monastery of the Cistercians is located. It is said that St. Patrick began his evangelical tour of Europe from there. Visit the 10th century castle, Castrum Canois, on a mountain that overlooks Cannes. It houses the Museum of Mediterranean Civilization.

La Napoule is a few miles west of Cannes. The attraction there is the Chateau de la Napoule Art Foundation, one of the finest art galleries on the Riviera, open daily except Tuesday, with guided tours in the afternoon.

Sights in Grasse: Take the 50-minute bus ride from Cannes' rail-station to nearby Grasse, the perfume capital of France. Many of the 35 perfume factories there are open to visitors. One of them, Parfumerie Fragonard, is only a 5-minute walk from the Grasse bus terminal. Near it is a Perfume Museum. The nearby hillsides are covered with wild-flowers and jasmine every Spring.

Dep. Cannes Frequent times from 7:31 to 23:54
Arr. Nice 40 minutes later

Nice - Marseille - Nice
151

Dep. Nice	6:52(1)	8:45(2)	10:30(1)	11:20(2)
Arr. Marseille (St. Ch.)	9:16	11:38	13:10	13:38

Sights in Marseille: See notes about sightseeing in Marseille earlier in this section under "Avignon-Marseille".

Dep. Marseille (St. Ch.)	13:22	15:03(3)	15:17	16:49(2+4+5)
Arr. Nice	16:03	17:30	18:12	19:04

(1) Light refreshments. (2) Meal service. (3) Runs from late June to mid-September. (4) Supplement charged. (5) Plus other departures from Marseille at 17:25(3), 18:34, 19:25(1), 20:17 and 22:00(2).

Nice - Monte Carlo - Nice
151

Dep. Nice	Frequent times from 7:05 to 0:19
Arr. Monte Carlo	30 minutes later

Sights in Monte Carlo: See notes about sightseeing in Monte Carlo earlier in this section, under "Avignon-Monte Carlo".

Dep. Monte Carlo	Frequent times from 5:19 to 23:22
Arr. Nice	30 minutes later

Nice - Saint Raphael - Nice 151

Dep. Nice	Frequent times from 5:47 to 22:27
Arr. St. Raphael	60 minutes later

Sights in Saint Raphael: An excellent Riviera beach resort. There is a gambling casino to fill the nighttime hours. Good golfing, hiking and sailing here.

Dep. St. Raphael	Frequent times from 6:15 to 23:30
Arr. Nice	60 minutes later

Paris - Amsterdam - Paris 10-B

Dep. Paris (Nord)	7:22(1)+(2)	Dep. Amsterdam	18:01(1)+(3)
Arr. Amsterdam	12:30	Arr. Paris (Nord)	23:09

(1) TEE. Reservation required. Meal service. (2) Daily, except Sundays. (3) Daily, except Saturdays.

Sights in Amsterdam: As indicated above, it is possible to make a one-day roundtrip from Paris to Amsterdam, although leaving only enough time in Amsterdam for no more than minimal sightseeing. Best bet: take a 75-minute ride in a glass-roofed canal boat, starting at the piers in front of Central Railstation before having to board the train for the ride back to Paris.

Paris - Bayeux - Paris 122

Dep. Paris (St. Lazare)	7:08(1)	9:02
Arr. Bayeux	9:34	11:45

Sights in Bayeux: The world-famous 235-foot long tapestry, made in 1077, depicting in 58 scenes the Norman conquest of England. The view of a magnificent seascape from Notre Dame's high center tower.

Dep. Bayeux	14:56(2)	15:17(3)	17:01(4)	18:23(5+6)
Arr. Paris (St. Lazare)	17:10	18:35	19:58	20:37

(1)Late June to mid-September: runs daily. Mid-September to late June: runs daily except Sundays and holidays. (2)Runs only from mid-September to late June, daily except Sundays and holidays.
(3) Runs from late June to mid-September. (4) Sundays and holidays only. (5) Daily, except Sundays and holidays. Supplement charged. Meal service. (6)Plus other departures from Bayeux at 20:53(4), 21:10(4) and 21:28.

Paris - Bayeux - Caen - Paris 122

As shown below, it is possible to combine a visit from Paris to both Bayeux and Caen in one day.

Dep. Paris (St. Lazare)	7:08(1)	Dep. Bayeux	13:47	14:57(2+3)
Arr. Bayeux	9:30	Arr. Caen	14:11	15:14

Sights in Bayeux: See notes about sightseeing in Bayeux in the listing preceding this.

Sights in Caen: Although much was destroyed here during the 1944 Normandy invasion battle, numerous historical buildings have been preserved. Hotel d' Escoville, the "Chateau". The 11th century Abbaye aux Hommes and Abbaye aux Dames. The Museum. The church of Saint Sauveur. The Palace of Justice. For lunch, try these regional specialties: tripes, berlingots, cider, Calvados.

Dep. Caen	17:55(2)	18:42(2+4)	19:25(5)	19:40(5+6)
Arr. Paris (St. Lazare)	20:00	20:37	21:57	22:03

(1)Daily except Sunday from mid-September to late June. Daily from late June to mid-September. Meal service, except Sundays and holidays. (2)Daily, except Sundays and holidays. (3)Runs from mid-September to late June. (4)Supplement charged. Tray meal service. (5)Sundays and holidays only. (6)Plus other departures from Caen at 20:01(2), 21:15(5)and 21:46.

Here are schedules for having more time in Caen.

Dep. Paris (St. Laz.)	7:08(1)	8:06	9:02	9:17
Arr. Caen	9:00	10:12	11:25	12:16

* * *

Dep. Caen	12:03(2)	13:46(3)	14:35(2)	15:16(1+7)
Arr. Paris (St. Laz.)	13:58	15:46	16:37	17:10

(1)Late June to mid-September: daily. Mid-September to late June: daily except Sundays and holidays. (2)Meal service. (3)Daily, except Sundays and holidays. (4)Runs from late June to mid-September. (5)Sundays and holidays only. (6)Runs from mid-September to late June. (7)Plus other departures from Caen at 15:46(4), 16:15(3), 16:27(5+6), 17:24(5), 17:54(3), 18:42(2+3), 18:56(5), 19:27(5), 19:40(5), 21:46 and 21:54(5).

Paris - Blois - Paris
136

Dep. Paris (Aust.)	7:05	9:06	10:15(2)	12:06(1)
Arr. Blois	8:46	11:04	11:54	13:43

Sights in Blois: Two fine Chateaux: Chambord and Bracieux (Herbault-en-Sologne). St. Louis Cathedral. Church of Saint Nicolas. Church of Saint Vincent. Church of Saint Saturin, and its curious cemetery. The Alluye Manor. The Castle of Blois. For lunch, try regional specialties: Rillettes, Loire fish, great wines and cheeses.

Dep. Blois	13:52(2)	16:18	17:04(1)	17:57(3+4)
Arr. Paris (Aust.)	15:33	18:16	18:54	19:45

(1)Meal service. (2)Daily, except Sundays and holidays. (3)Runs from late June to mid-September. (4)Plus other departures from Blois at 18:48, 19:44 and 21:35(1).

Paris - Blois - Tours - Paris 136

As shown below, it is possible to combine a visit from Paris to both Blois and Tours in one day.

Dep. Paris (Aust.)	7:05	Dep. Blois	11:55(1)
Arr. Blois	8:46	Arr. Tours	12:27

(1)Daily, except Sundays and holidays.

Sights in Blois: See notes in preceding listing.

Sights in Tours: Take a 90-minute walk from the Tours railstation up Boulevard Heurteloup to Rue Nationale, then turn right and go up one side of Rue Nationale to the bridge, come back on the other side of Rue Nationale, cross Boulevard Heurteloup, go one block further, turn left onto Rue de Bordeaux, taking it directly back to the railstation. There are several good restaurants on Rue Nationale and on Boulevard Heurteloup.

Dep. Tours	15:37	16:17(1)	16:47(2)	17:19(3)	18:16(7)
Arr. Paris (Aust.)	18:13	18:40	19:00	19:24	20:33

(1)Runs from late June to mid-September. (2)Runs from late May to late September. Light refreshments. (3)Runs from late June to early September. (4)Daily except Saturday. (5)Meal service. (6)Supplement charged. (7)Plus other departures from Tours at 19:28(4+5+6), 19:38(5+6) and 20:56(1+5).

Paris - Tours - Paris 136

Here are schedules for having more time in Tours than when combining a trip from Paris to both Blois and Tours.

Dep. Paris (Aust.)	7:05	7:50(1)	8:04(2)	9:09(2+8)	
Arr. Tours	9:22	9:31	10:01	11:11	
		*	*	*	
Dep. Tours	13:13(5)	14:10(4)	16:47(4+6)	17:19(6)	18:16(5+9)
Arr. Paris (Aust.)	15:33	16:16	19:00	19:24	20:30

(1)TEE. Reservation required. Meal service. Runs from early September to late June, daily except Sundays and holidays. (2)Meal service. (3)Runs from late June to mid-September. (4)Light refreshments. (5)Daily, except Sundays and holidays. (6)Runs from late June to early September. (7)Supplement charged. (8)Plus other departures from Paris at 10:00(3+4), 11:24(2) and 12:06(2). (9)Plus other departures from Tours at 19:05, 19:28(2+7) and 20:56(2).

Paris - Bordeaux - Paris 136

Dep. Paris (Austerlitz)	7:50(1+2)	8:04(3)	9:00(3)	
Arr. Bordeaux (St. Jean)	11:53	12:56	13:23	
	*	*	*	
Dep. Bordeaux (St. Jean)	14:05(4)	16:04(3)	16:58(5)	17:44(1+6+7)
Arr. Paris (Austerlitz)	19:00	20:57	21:38	21:46

(1)TEE. Reservation required. Meal service. (2)Runs from early September to early July, daily except Sundays and holidays. (3)Meal service. (4)Runs from late May to late September. Meal service. (5)Supplement charged. Meal service. (6)Runs from early September to early July, daily except Saturday. (7)Plus other departures from Bordeaux at 17:52(3) and 19:10(3).

Sights in Bordeaux: Information about tours of the port and an excellent city map for making a walking tour of Bordeaux are available at the Tourist Office, 12 Cours du 30 Juillet. The opera, parks, hotels, Roman ruins and 18th century mansions are in the northern sector of the city. Museums, churches and fine shops are in the southern part of Bordeaux.

See the Maritime Museum, on the Quai de la Douane. Wonderful Louis XV houses on Rue Fernand Philippart. The modern stained-glass in the 14th century St. Michel Church on Place Dubourg. The view of

Bordeaux from the top of that church's tower. The large 15th century belltower, Grosse Cloche. The 13th century Gothic St. Andre's Cathedral. The art in the Musee des Beaux Arts, open daily except Tuesday 10:00-12:00 and 14:00-18:00.

The fans with mother of pearl, ivory and silver handles (plus Medieval furniture, costumes and ceramics) in the Musee des Arts Decoratifs at 39 Rue Bouffard, open 14:00-18:00 daily except Tuesday.

Do not miss seeing the array of fruits, cheeses, wild game and many exotic foods at the market on Place des Grands Hommes. The fantastic carved plants and the swan boat in the Jardin Public. The Maison des Vins at 1 Cours du 30 Juillet, where you can obtain information on visiting nearby famous wineries.

See the lovely 18th century Opera House. The Grand Theatre. The Museum of Painting and Sculpture. The Numismatic Museum. The Museum of Old Bordeaux. The Bonie Museum of Far Eastern Art.

Paris - Brussels - Paris 106

Dep. Paris (Nord)	6:42(1+2)	7:19(1+3)	7:49(4)	9:08(5+11)
Arr. Brussels (Midi)	9:11	9:48	10:50	12:02

Sights in Brussels: The gilded buildings in Grand Place. Town Hall. The Law Courts. The Royal Palace. The tapestries in the 13th century Cathedral of St. Michael. Flemish paintings in the Museum of Ancient Art. The Museum of Modern Art. The Central Africa Museum. The Brussels City Museum. The Museum of Arms and Armour. The Postal Museum. The Brewery Museum. The Royal Greenhouses. The Brueghel Museum, in the house where the painter lived his last 6 years. The view from the Palais de Justice. The Railway Museum on the mezzanine of Brussels' Nord railstation. A bus takes you 10 miles to Waterloo.

Dep. Brussels (Midi)	14:07(4)	16:08(4+6)	17:17(1+7+12)
Arr. Paris (Nord)	17:00	18:56	19:46

(1)TEE. Reservation required. Meal service. (2)Runs Monday-Friday except holidays from early September to late June. (3)Daily, except Sunday. (4)Light refreshments. (5)Saturday all year. Also Sunday from late June to late September. (6)Supplement charged. (7)Specify meals required when reserving seat. (8)Meal service. (9)Runs from late June to early September, Monday-Friday except holidays. (10)Daily, except Saturday. (11)Plus another departure from Paris at 10:25(8). (12)Plus other departures from Brussels at 17:53(6+8), 18:38(1+2), 19:15(8) and 20:42(1+7).

Paris - Chantilly - Paris

SNCF Timetable #B-27

Dep. Paris (Nord)	Frequent times from 4:55 to 0:45
Arr. Chantilly	30-40 minutes later

Sights in Chantilly: The 16th and 18th century chateaus (closed in Winter), the later ones regarded by many as the most beautiful houses in France. The collection of paitings by Delacroix, Fouquet, Ingres, Rembrandt and others in the Museum. The racetrack. The spectacle of the Tuesday and Saturday fox hunts.

Dep. Chantilly Frequent times from 4:41 to 19:22
Arr. Paris (Nord) 30-40 minutes later

Paris - Chartres - Paris

	123	125	126
Dep. Paris (Montpar.)	11:10	10:50	12:58
Arr. Chartres	55 minutes later		

Sights in Chartres: The main attraction is the magnificent 13th century Cathedral, third largest in the world, exceeded in size only by St. Peter's and Canterbury. Its stained-glass is unrivalled. Other sights: The Former Collegiate Church. The Church of Saint Aignan. The Church of Saint Martin-au-Val. The Church of Saint Foy.

	125	125	126	125
Dep. Chartres	14:10	17:28	18:26	20:49
Arr. Paris (Montpar.)	55 minutes later			

Paris - Cologne (Koln) - Paris 62

Dep. Paris (Nord)	7:30(1)	Dep. Cologne (Hbf.)	16:35(1)
Arr. Cologne (Hbf.)	12:40	Arr. Paris (Nord)	21:50

(1) Meal service.

Sights in Cologne: The Cathedral, above all, that took 600 years to build. The view of Cologne from the top of the Cathedral. The Dionysos Mosaic, on the side of the Cathedral. The luxury shops on Hohestrasse. The Wallraf-Richartz Museum, with its collection of Cologne masters. The 15th century Gurzenich. The Zoo. The Roman-German Museum. The Metropolitan Historical Museum. Old Town Hall. Praetorium, with its 1st-4th century Roman Palace ruins. The 3rd century Roman Tower. St. Pantaleon Church. St. Andreas Church. Relics and treasures in the Golden Room of the Church of St. Ursula.

Paris - Compeigne - Paris 106

Dep. Paris (Nord) 7:49 12:14
Arr. Compeigne 45 minutes later

Sights in Compeigne: Town Hall. Vivenel Museum. Hotel Dieu. The 7th century Beauregard Tower. The "Clairere de l'Armistice" in Compeigne Forest, where Marshal Foch signed the 1918 armistice for France.

Dep. Compeigne	10:31	13:08	19:03	20:10(1)	21:54(2)
Arr. Paris (Nord)	45 minutes later				

(1) Sundays and holidays only. (2) Daily, except Saturday.

Paris - Dijon - Paris 151 + 157

Dep. Paris (Lyon)	6:36(1+2)	7:50(3)	8:30	9:43(3)
Arr. Dijon	8:57	10:12	11:03	12:07

Sights in Dijon: See notes about sightseeing in Dijon earlier in this section, under "Lyon-Dijon".

Dep. Dijon	14:48	15:58	16:42(3)	17:20(6+9)
Arr. Paris (Lyon)	17:00	18:50(5)	19:10	21:24

(1)TGV. Supplement charged. Meal service. (2)Daily, except Sundays and holidays. (3)Meal service. (4)Runs from late August to early July. Operates Monday-Friday. (5)Arrives at Paris-Bercy. (6)Light refreshments. (7)TEE. Reservation required. Light refreshments. (8)Plus another departure from Paris at 12:08(1+4). (9)Plus other departures from Dijon at 18:45, 20:25(3) and 21:01(7).

Paris - Evreux - Paris 122

Dep. Paris (St. Laz.)	8:06	9:17	10:52(1)	11:50(2+3+4)
Arr. Evreux	9:03	10:30	11:50	12:46

Sights in Evreux: The Cathedral of Notre Dame, a jumble of architectural styles due to having been built over a period of 6 centuries—from the 11th to the 17th. Goldsmith work in the Church of Saint Taurin. The ancient Eveche. The tower of The Clock. For lunch, try the Norman cuisine.

Dep. Evreux	13:20	14:52(2)	15:42	17:12(5+9)
Arr. Paris (St. Laz.)	14:15	15:46	16:37	18:17

(1)Daily, except Saturday. (2)Daily, except Sundays and holidays. (3)Does not run on Friday from late June to mid-September. (4)Meal service. (5)Runs from late June to mid-September. (6)Runs from mid-September to late June. (7)Light refreshments. (8)Sundays only. (9)Plus other departures from Evreux at 17:40(6+7), 19:06(2), 19:25(8), 22:53(2) and 23:08(8).

Paris - Fontainebleau - Paris

SCNF Timetable #B-50

Dep. Paris (Lyon)	Frequent times from 6:02 to 0:47
Arr. Fontainebleau-Avon	30-40 minutes later

Take the 10-minute bus ride from the railstation to the palace, open 8:00 to sunset, daily except Tuesdays.

Sights in Fontainebleau: It is advisable to plan on an entire day here for seeing the magnificent 16th century palace that many kings of France occupied, and the parks and gardens surrounding it. Guided tours of the palace 10:00-12:30 and 14:00-18:00. Many visitors bring a picnic lunch.

Dep. Fontainebleau-Avon	Frequent times from 5:19 to 22:10
Arr. Paris (Lyon)	30-40 minutes later

Paris - Mt. St. Michel - Caen - Paris

From early July to the end of August, there is a direct train on Saturdays. Depart Paris (Montparnasse) at 7:00. Arrive Pontorson at 11:28. Board the bus for Mt. St. Michel. At the end of the day of sightseeing, take the bus from Mt. St. Michel to the Pontorson railstation. Depart Pontorson at 19:10. Arrive at Paris' St. Lazare railstation at 23:50.

The schedules below are for the less direct route.

122		118	
Dep. Paris (St. Lazare)	9:02	Dep. Pontorson	19:16(1)
Arr. Lison	12:14	Arr. Caen	21:29
Change trains.		Change trains.	
118		122	
Dep. Lison	14:48	Dep. Caen	21:46
Arr. Pontorson		Arr. Paris (St. Lazare)	23:52
(Mt. St. Michel)	16:31		

(1) Daily, except Saturday.

Sights in Mt. St. Michel: It is a 10-minute bus ride from the Pontorson railstation to the medieval splendor of the walled town of Mont-Saint-Michel, where there are several hotels. The rushing tides that attract more than 1,400,000 tourists here every year occur 36 hours after the new and full moon, with the fastest tides occurring near March 21 and September 23.

Also worth seeing are the buttressed walls, vaulted halls and colonnaded cloister in the 8th century abbey, which has 90 steps visitors must climb.

One-hour guided tours of the abbey are offered. Those in English-language are conducted daily except Thursday at 10:30, 14:30 and, if a group of at least 15 people is mustered, also at 16:00. Visitors are not allowed to walk through the abbey unescorted.

Columns measuring 16 feet in circumference in a semicircular room called the Crypte des Gros-Piliers support the choir of the sanctuary above that room. Other pillars, in the 115-foot long Knights' Hall, should be seen. A bronze statue of St. Michel, raising his sword to slay a dragon, sits at the top of the main spire of the church, 500 feet above the sea. The mountain is illuminated from nightfall until 23:00.

Do not fail to eat the special omelette made here.

Visitors can see dioramas of this mountain's history and collections of ancient clocks in both the Musee Historique (open all year) and in the Musee Historical du Mont (open from March 1 to November 30).

The last bus from Mt. St. Michel to Pontorson leaves at 18:10, well in advance of the train departures from Pontorson to Paris.

Paris - Limoges - Paris 138

Dep. Paris (Aust.)	6:28(1)	7:41(2+3)	9:38(1)	
Arr. Limoges	10:24	10:39	13:08	

Sights in Limoges: Tours of the porcelain and enamel factories, free by applying to the Syndicat de la Porcelain, 7 Rue du General Cerez. The Adrien Dubouche Museum, with its great collection of ceramics. The Municipal Museum, to see its display of china made in Limoges from the 12th century to the present. The Cathedral of Saint Etienne.

Dep. Limoges	14:34(1)	17:05(1+4)	18:04(1)	19:38(5+7)
Arr. Paris (Aust.)	18:00	20:24	21:26	23:03

(1) Meal service. (2) Supplement charged. Meal service. (3) Daily, except Sundays and holidays. (4) Supplement charged. Runs Monday-Friday, except holidays. (5) Sundays and holidays only. (6) Daily, except Saturday. (7) Plus another departure from Limoges at 20:52(2+6).

Paris - Lyon - Paris 150

All of these trains are TGV and have meal service, unless designated otherwise.

Dep. Paris (Lyon)	6:15(1)	7:15(2+3)	8:15(4+13)
Arr. Lyon (Brot.)	8:54	10:07	10:53

Sights in Lyon: See notes about sightseeing in Lyon at the start of this section.

Dep. Lyon (Brot.)	14:00(4+6)	15:00(2+6)	16:00(6+7+14)
Arr. Paris (Lyon)	16:42	17:42	18:40

(1) Mon.-Fri. Supplement charged every day. (2) Daily. (3) Supplement charged Mon.-Fri. (4) Daily, except Sun. and holidays. (5) Supplement charged on Sat. and Sun. (6) Light refreshments. (7) Daily, except Sat, (8) Supplement charged every day. (9) Supplement charged on Fri. and Sun. (10) Supplement charged only on Sun. (11) Runs only on Sun. (12) Supplement charged every day except Sat. (13) Plus other departures from Paris at 9:15(2+5+6), 11:15(3+7) and 12:15(4). (14) Plus other departures from Lyon at 17:00(2+6+9), 18:00(2+8), 19:00(2+9), 20:00(2+10) and 21:00(6+11).

Paris - Nancy - Paris 172

Dep. Paris (Est)	6:45(1+2)	7:45(3+4)	8:35(2)	11:00(5+6)
Arr. Nancy	9:33	10:26	11:54	13:32

Sights in Nancy: The Ducal Palace, with its museum of this city's 2,000-year history. The Church of the Cordeliers. The 14th century Porte de la Craffe, oldest monument in Nancy. The wrought-iron grillwork and fountains in Place Stanislas. Lovely 18th century houses on Place de la Carriere.

Dep. Nancy	14:30(7)	17:13(7)	18:29(5+8)	18:53(9+10)
Arr. Paris (Est)	17:20	20:11	21:08	22:04

(1) Daily, except Sundays and holidays. (2) Meal service. (3) Supplement charged. (4) Specify meal required when reserving first-class seat. (5) TEE. Reservation required. Meal service. (6) Daily, except Sundays and holidays. Runs from early September to late June. (7) Light refreshments. (8) Daily. Runs from early September to mid-July. (9) Light refreshments daily. Tray meal service Monday-Friday, except holidays, and only from early September to late June. (10) Plus other departures from Nancy at 19:45(3+7) and 20:33(3+4).

Paris - Reims - Paris 177

Dep. Paris (Est)	7:16(1)	8:03(2)	11:06	12:47(2)
Arr. Reims	1½ hours later			

Sights in Reims: The 13th century Cathedral of Notre Dame. Seeing champagne processed. The public is invited to visit the Taitinger and Pommery caves. The Porte Mars 13th century Arch. Saint Remi Basilica. The Church of St. Jacquet. The museum at the Church of St. Denis.

Dep. Reims	12:24(2)	17:57(1)	18:10(3)	18:55(4+5)
Arr. Paris (Est)	1½ hours later			

(1) Light refreshments. (2) Daily, except Sundays and holidays. (3) Monday-Thursday. (4) Fridays only. (5) Plus another departure from Reims at 20:24(1).

Paris - Rouen - Paris 120

Dep. Paris (St. Laz.)	7:45(1+2+3)	8:15(3)	9:15	12:00(3)
Arr. Rouen (Rive Dr.)	8:53	9:46	10:26	13:37

Sights in Rouen: Walk out of the railstation and then down Rue de Jeanne D'Arc about 1½ miles. Turn right onto Rue de la Grosse Horloge and continue a short distance to the remodeled ancient, large central market, Vieux Marche, the place where Joan of Arc was tied to a stake and burned. This is now the Church of St. Joan, built in 1977. It is in the shape of an upside-down boat and has magnificent stained-glass windows that were saved from the Church of Saint-Vincent, bombed during World War II. Try the regional specialty (terrine of duck) in one of the nearby restaurants.

Then, go back along Rue de la Gross Horloge (crossing Rue de Jeanne D'Arc). Straight ahead is the gigantic, ornate clock for which the street was named. The clock presents a spectacle of moving figures when each hour strikes.

Past the famous clock is the Cathedral, with its renowned Carillon of 56 bells. Nearby, see the sculptures on the doors of the Church of Saint-Maclou and the macabre scenes on the portals of the Cloisters of Saint-Maclou.

Visit the remains of an 11th century building that was either a Jewish school or a synagogue, below the Palace of Justice. See the Hebrew graffiti written on the walls there more than 900 years ago, the elaborate carved columns and the 2 inverted Lions of Judah.

Other sights: The stained-glass windows in the Church of St. Godard and the Church of St. Patrice. From Rouen, it is an easy bus trip to either the colorful harbor at Honfleur or to Giverny, to visit the home and spectacular garden of painter Claude Monet.

Dep. Rouen (Rive Dr.)	12:55(2+3)	14:07(3)	14:54	18:03(5)
Arr. Paris (St. Laz.)	14:04	15:37	16:05	19:12

(1)Supplement charged. (2)Specify meal required when reserving first-class seat. (3)Daily, except Sundays and holidays. (4)Sundays and holidays only. (5)Plus other departures from Rouen at 18:47(1+2+3), 19:38, 21:11(3) and 22:02(4).

Paris - Strasbourg - Paris 172

This ride is along the Marne, with clear views of the area near famous World War I battlefields.

Dep. Paris (Est)	6:45(1+2)	7:45(3)	8:35(2)	11:00(4+5)
Arr. Strasbourg	10:52	11:42	13:40	14:45

Sights in Strasbourg: Stroll down Rue du Bain-aux-Plantes, an alley where herbs were once sold. See, smell and taste the brown bread at the almost 300-year old bakery, Boulangerie Winckelsass. Visit the 3 good museums in Chateau des Rohan: the collection of Monet, Renoir, El Greco, Goya and Tintoretto in the Art Gallery; the relics in the Archaeological Museum; and the display of clocks, ironwork, earthenware and porcelain in the Museum of Decorative Arts.

Rooms dating from the early 17th century (furnished with marvelous utensils, stoves, wooden molds and pottery from the same era) at the Musee Alsacien, 23 Quai St. Nicholas. Wonderful Alsatian art in the Musee de l'Oeuvre Notre Dame.

On Rue de la Rape, see the city's majestic Cathedral and its famous astronomical clock, alive with figures appearing and disappearing on the hour and quarter hours. In Summer, a fabulous sound-and-light show is presented inside the Cathedral: illuminated stained-glass windows, bells tolling, organ music.

Walk around Place Kleber. Sample the world's best pate de foie gras.

Dep. Strasbourg	15:48(6)	17:13(4+7)	17:16(6)	18:23(8+9)
Arr. Paris (Est)	20:10	21:08	22:04	22:24

(1)Daily, except Sundays and holidays. (2)Meal service. (3)Supplement charged. Specify meal required when reserving seat. (4)TEE. Reservation required. Meal service. (5)Daily, except Sundays and holidays. Does not run from late June to late August. (6)Light refreshments.

(7) Daily, except Saturday. Does not run from mid-July to late August. (8) Light refreshments. Supplement charged. (9) Plus another departure from Strasbourg at 19:17(3).

Paris - Tours - Paris

This one-day excursion appears earlier in this section, immediately following "Paris-Blois-Tours-Paris".

Paris - Trouville and Deauville - Paris

127

Dep. Paris (St. Laz.)	6:50(1+2)	7:55(3)	8:40(4)	10:26(2+6)
Arr. Trou Deau	8:47	9:52	10:54	12:14

Sights in Trouville: There is no chance of obtaining hotel rooms here in Summer without advance reservation. One of France's most beautiful swimming beaches. A gambling casino. Marvelous seafood.

Sights in Deauville: One of France's most beautiful swimming beaches. Two racetracks. Lovely gardens. To explore the Norman countryside, you can rent a car at the Deauville railstation.

Dep. Trou Deau	13:10(2)	15:47(2)	17:22(2+3)	17:47(1+2+7)
Arr. Paris (St. Laz.)	15:07	17:40	19:50	19:39

(1) Daily, except Sundays and holidays. (2) Runs from late June to mid-September. (3) Sundays and holidays only. (4) From late June to mid-September: daily. From mid-September to late June: Saturdays and Sundays only. (5) Sundays only. Supplement charged. (6) Plus another departure from Paris at 12:15(1+2). (7) Plus other departures from Trou Deau at 18:58(3), 19:22(1+2), 20:00(3) and 20:56(5).

Paris - Troyes - Paris 171

Dep. Paris (Est)	6:55(1+2)	7:03(1)	8:37(3+4)	9:07(1+2+7)
Arr. Troyes	8:22	9:09	10:11	10:36

Sights in Troyes: The Cathedral of St. Paul and St. Peter. The mansions of Voluisant, Autry, des Ursins and Marisy. The Museum of Fine Arts, with its solid collection of 17th-18th century paintings and 13th-14th century sculptures.

Dep. Troyes	12:30(1)	16:35(2)	17:33(5)	19:07(3+8)
Arr. Paris (Est)	14:20	18:09	19:38	21:12

(1) Daily, except Sundays and holidays. (2) Light refreshments. (3) Sundays and holidays only. (4) Meal service. (5) Daily, except Saturday. (6) Supplement charged. (7) Plus another departure from Paris at 11:55. (8) Plus other departures from Troyes at 19:26(1), 20:30(3), 20:58(2+3+6) and 21:57(4).

Paris - Versailles - Paris

SCNF Timetable #B-37

Dep. Paris (Invalides)	Frequent times from 5:47 to 23:52
Arr. Versailles	30 minutes later

Sights in Versailles: The fabulous palace where Louis XVI lived like a king, and the elegant gardens there. The palace is open daily, except Monday. Guided tours are offered from 10:00 to 17:00. Visitors can purchase a book there which makes it possible to see and appreciate the palace interior without a guide.

Dep. Versailles	Frequent times from 5:13 to 23:19
Arr. Paris (Invalides)	30 minutes later

SCENIC RAIL TRIPS

Chamonix - Vallorcine - Chamonix

Good mountain scenery on this short ride. It is easy to combine this with the one-day roundtrip from Geneva to Chamonix, described in the Switzerland section of this chapter.

285

Dep. Chamonix	6:07	7:38	8:19	9:48	12:15	13:11	14:43
Arr. Vallorcine	30 minutes later						

* * *

Dep. Vallorcine	7:05	8:54	11:03	13:11	14:52	16:38	18:06(1)
Arr. Chamonix	30 minutes later						

(1) Plus another departure from Vallorcine at 19:28.

Grenoble - Marseille - Grenoble

Fine mountain scenery on this easy one-day roundtrip.

154

Dep. Grenoble	5:48(1)	Dep. Marseille (St. Ch.)	13:20	18:03
Arr. Veynes	7:45	Arr. Veynes	16:04	20:59
Change trains.		Change trains.		
Dep. Veynes	7:55	Dep. Veynes	16:14	21:15(1)
Arr. Marseille (St. Ch.)	10:38	Arr. Grenoble	18:04	23:05

(1) Runs from early July to early September.

Limoges - Toulouse - Limoges

Recommended for mountain scenery. This can be seen either as an easy one-day roundtrip between Limoges and Toulouse or as a portion of the route from Paris to Toulouse.

138			
Dep. Limoges	10:40(1)	13:13(2)	16:57(3)
Arr. Toulouse (Mat.)	13:48	16:59	20:22
	*	*	*
Dep. Toulouse (Mat.)	14:32(2)	17:44(4)	
Arr. Limoges	17:59	20:50	

(1)Supplement charged. Runs daily, except Sundays and holidays. Meal service. (2)Light refreshments. (3)Meal service. (4)Runs daily. Meal service. Supplement charged, except on Saturday.

Here is the schedule for the Paris-Toulouse route:

138			
Dep. Paris (Aust.)	7:41(1+2)	9:36(3)	13:21(4)
Dep. Limoges	10:39(1+2)	13:13(3)	16:56(4)
Arr. Toulouse (Mat.)	13:48	16:53	20:32

(1)Supplement charged. (2)Daily, except Sundays and holidays. Meal service. (3)Light refreshments. (4)Meal service.

Lyon - Geneva 155

The Amberieu-Geneva portion of this trip is noted for scenic gorges.

Dep. Lyon (Perrache)	7:05	9:43	14:13	16:09
Dep. Lyon (Brotteaux)	7:14	9:51	14:21	16:17
Dep. Amberieu	7:41	10:15	-0-	16:41
Arr. Geneva (Cornavin)	9:25	11:45	16:05	18:08

Marseille - Grenoble - Marseille

Excellent mountain scenery on this easy one-day roundtrip.

154	
Dep. Marseille (St. Ch.)	7:56
Arr. Veynes	10:51
Change trains.	
Dep. Veynes	11:08
Arr. Grenoble	13:04

* * *

Dep. Grenoble	13:56	17:49
Arr. Veynes	15:52	19:52
Change trains.		
Dep. Veynes	16:00	19:58(1)
Arr. Marseille (St. Ch.)	18:44	22:42

(1)Early July to mid-September: daily. Mid-September to early July: Saturday and Sunday only.

Marseille - Nimes - La Bastide - Clermont Ferrand 148a

The train follows a beautiful river valley between La Bastide and Clermont Ferrand.

Dep. Marseille	7:28(1)	12:12(2)
Dep. Nimes	8:53	13:47
Dep. La Bastide	11:08	15:51
Arr. Clermont Ferrand	14:14	18:47

Dep. Clermont Ferrand	8:40(1)	12:51(2)
Dep. La Bastide	11:50	15:52
Arr. Nimes	13:46	17:45
Arr. Marseille	15:12	19:08

(1)Runs from late June to early September. (2)Meal service.

Marseille - Genoa 356

Dep. Marseille (St. Ch.)	5:22	6:00	8:00	13:22(3)
Arr. Ventimiglia	9:00	9:45	11:40	17:00
Change trains.				
Dep. Ventimiglia	9:40(1)	10:20(2)	12:30	17:43(2)
Arr. Genoa (P.P.)	12:37	12:59	15:35	20:50

(1)Meal service. (2)Light refreshments. (3)Direct train to Genoa. No train change in Ventimiglia.

Narbonne - Carcassone **Carcassone - Narbonne**

Outstanding farm and vineyard scenery. Easy to make as a one-day roundtrip or can be covered in the short route from Narbonne to Toulouse and Bordeaux.

	139	139	139	138	139
Dep. Narbonne	8:39	10:14	11:59	12:50	15:23(1)
Arr. Carcassone	40-45 minutes later				

Sights in Carcassone: The most interesting walled city in France and Europe's best preserved relic of the Middle Ages. It is actually double-walled. The inner wall, built by the Romans in the 2nd century, bears 29 towers. The 13th century French outer wall has 17 towers and barbicans (fortified castles).

Nearby are the ruins of 5 other walls, to the South, erected by France in medieval days as additional protection from attack by the Spaniards.

As you stand on the walkways at the top of the French wall, it is easy to imagine yourself shooting arrows through the narrow slits or dropping oil on the marauders below.

Inside the Basilica of St. Nazare are many stone carvings depicting scenes from the fort's history, magnificent stained-glass windows, and the rectangular tombstone of Bishop Radulph.

139

Dep. Carcassone	9:52	11:03	12:55	13:28(1)	15:04(2)
Arr. Narbonne	40-45 minutes later				

(1)Runs from late June to mid-September. (2)Plus other departures from Carcassone at 17:55 and 19:31.

Sights in Narbonne: The Cloister adjacent to the Palace of the Archbishops. The choir of the incomplete Cathedral of Saint-Just.

Here is the schedule for the Narbonne-Bordeaux route:

139

Dep. Narbonne	8:40	10:13	11:59
Arr. Carcassone	9:11	10:47	12:39
Arr. Toulouse (Matabiau)	9:58	11:38	13:44
Arr. Bordeaux (St. Jean)	12:10	13:55	16:38

Nice - Digne - Nice 185

This is a very scenic line that is operated only from late May to late September. An easy one-day roundtrip, this is also the route from Nice to Geneva.

Dep. Nice (C.P.)	8:20	Dep. Digne	16:30
Arr. Digne	11:45	Arr. Nice (C.P.)	19:50

Sights in Digne: The 15th century Cathedral of Saint Jerome. Many fruit orchards. Digne is famed for the lavender cultivated here.

Paris - Torino (and Rome)

The Culoz-Modane portion of this trip offers outstanding lake and mountain scenery. On this route, the train goes through the 8.5-mile long Mont Cenis Tunnel, constructed in 1871.

152

Dep. Paris (Lyon)	8:23(1)	Dep. Rome (Termini)	0:25(1)
Dep. Culoz	13:57	Dep. Torino (P.N.)	11:45
Arr. Modane	16:06	Dep. Modane	14:02
Arr. Torino (P.N.)	18:10	Arr. Culoz	16:02
Arr. Rome (Termini)	7:22(Day 2)	Arr. Paris (Lyon)	21:38

(1) Meal service.

Toulouse - Limoges - Toulouse

Recommended for mountain scenery. This route can be seen either as an easy one-day roundtrip between Toulouse and Limoges or as a portion of the ride from Toulouse to Paris.

138

Dep. Toulouse (Mat.)	5:46	7:43(1)	10:21(2)	
Arr. Limoges	9:11	10:47	14:22	
	*	*	*	
Dep. Limoges	10:39(3)	13:13(2)	16:56(2)	20:26(4)
Arr. Toulouse (Mat.)	13:48	16:53	20:32	23:43

(1)TEE. Reservation required. Meal service. Daily, except Sundays and holidays. (2)Meal service. (3)Daily, except Sundays and holidays. Supplement charged. Meal service. (4)Daily, except Friday and Saturday.

Here is the schedule for the Toulouse-Paris ride:

Dep. Toulouse (Mat.)	7:43(1)+(2)	10:27(3)	14:32(3)	17:44(4)
Dep. Limoges	10:49(1)+(2)	14:33(3)	18:05(3)	20:52(1)
Arr. Paris (Aust.)	13:47	18:00	21:25	23:48

(1)TEE. Reservation required. Meal service. (2)Daily, except Sundays and holidays. (3)Meal service. (4)Supplement charged, except on Saturday. Meal service.

INTERNATIONAL ROUTES FROM FRANCE

The French gateway for rail travel to London, Amsterdam, Bern (and on to Zurich and Vienna), Brussels, Cologne, Geneva and Madrid is Paris. (Notes on the route to London appear in Chapter 9.) From Marseille, there is rail service to Barcelona and Genoa (and on to Florence, Milan, Rome and Venice). From Paris, there are trains to Torino and Genoa.

Nice - Marseille - Avignon - Nimes - Narbonne - Barcelona	162			
Dep. Nice	-0-	22:18(1)	-0-	-0-
Dep. Marseille	-0-	1:16(1)	5:58	7:15(3)
Dep. Avignon	1:56	-0-	-0-	7:48(4+7)
Dep. Nimes	2:28(1)	2:45(1)	7:07	8:35(3)
Arr. Narbonne	4:05	4:37	8:34	10:12
Change trains.				
Dep. Narbonne	4:18	4:42	9:06	10:32
Arr. Port Bou	5:56	6:05	10:51	13:00
Change trains.				
Dep. Port Bou	7:10(2)	7:10(2)	11:15	13:45
Arr. Barcelona (Cent.)	9:39	9:39	14:05	15:55

(1)Has couchettes. (2)Light refreshments. (3)Meal service to Narbonne. (4)Local train to Nímes. (5)Runs from late June to mid-September. (6)Supplement charged. Meal service. Arrives Barcelona at 21:16. (7)Plus other departures from Avignon at 15:50(6) and 16:12.

Marseille - Nice - Genoa - Milan	356			
Dep. Marseille (St. Ch.)	-0-	5:25(1)	6:00(2)	8:00(8)
Dep. Nice	6:20	8:20	8:57	10:45(9)
Arr. Genoa (P.P.)	10:35	12:37	12:59	15:35
Arr. Milan (Cent.)	12:48	14:58	14:58	18:05

(1) Meal service. (2) Light refreshments. (3) Does not go to Genoa.
(1)Meal service. (2)Light refreshments. (3)Does not go to Genoa.
(4)Carries sleeping car. Also has couchetes. (5)Has couchettes. (6)Runs from late May to late September. (7)Adjustment note. (8)Plus other departures frm Marseille at 10:48(3), 13:22(2), 16:49(1), 17:25(4) and 19:25(5). (9)Plus other departures frm Nice at 13:18, 14:13(3), 16:18(2), 17:55(6), 19:06(1), 20:27(4) and 22:48(5).

Paris - Amsterdam	106			
Dep. Paris (Nord)	7:19(1+2)	7:49(3)	10:27(4)	15:19(3+7)
Arr. Amsterdam	12:30	14:13	16:30	21:33

(1)TEE. Reservation required. Meal service. (2)Daily, except Sunday. (3)Light refreshments. (4)Meal service. (5)Supplement charged. (6)Runs from mid-June to early September. Has couchettes. (7)Plus other departures from Paris at 16:46(5), 17:41(1) and 23:35(6).

Paris - Bern

56

Dep. Paris (Lyon)	7:41(1)	17:00(2)	23:49(3)
Arr. Bern	13:45	23:06	7:05

(1)Light refreshments. (2)Meal service. (3)Has couchettes.

Paris - Bordeaux - Lisbon

28

Dep. Paris (Austerlitz)	8:59(1)
Dep. Bordeaux	13:27
Dep. Bayonne	15:14
Dep. Irun	17:40
Dep. San Sebastian	18:05
Dep. Salamanca	1:05
Set your watch back one hour.	
Arr. Lisbon (S. Apol.)	9:55

(1)Reservation required. Supplement charged. Carries sleeping car Irun-Lisbon. Has couchettes Paris-Lisbon. Meal service Irun-Lisbon. The long stop in Hendaye is for changing the wheels on the couchette cars to conform with the wider track in Spain.

Paris - Brussels

106

Dep. Paris (Nord)	6:42(1)	7:19(1+3)	7:49(4)	9:07(5+10)
Arr. Brussels (Midi)	9:11	9:48	10:50	12:02

(1)TEE. Reservation required. Meal service. (2)Monday-Friday, except holidays. Runs September through June. (3)Daily, except Sunday. (4)Light refreshments. (5)Saturday all year plus Sunday from late June to late September. (6)Meal service. (7)Supplement charged. (8)Daily, except Saturday. (9)Has couchettes. (10)Plus other departures from Paris at 10:25(6), 11:37(1), 12:56(6), 15:18(4), 15:46(4+7), 17:41(1), 18:41(1+2), 19:27(6), 20:30(1+8) and 23:15(9).

Paris - Cologne (Koln)

62

Dep. Paris (Nord)	7:30(1)	12:56(2+3)	17:10(2)	17:45(3+4+6)
Arr. Cologne	12:41	18:48	22:33	22:49

(1)Meal service. (2)Light refreshments. (3)Supplement charged (4)Daily, from late June to early September. Monday-Friday from early September to late June. Meal service. (5)Carries sleeping car. Also has couchettes. (6)Plus other departures from Paris at 21:34(5)and 23:10(1+5).

Paris - Geneva

	152			
Dep. Paris (Lyon)	7:45(1)	17:00(2)	19:12(1)	23:02(3)
Arr. Geneva (Corn.)	12:00	23:01	23:27	7:25

(1)TGV. Meal service. Reservation required. Supplement charged on certain days. (2)Meal service. (3)Has couchettes.

Paris - Bordeaux - Madrid

	422		
Dep. Paris (Aust.)	6:45(1+2)	14:00(4+5)	18:02(6+10)
Dep. Bordeaux (St. J.)	11:30(1+3)	18:35(4+5)	22:18(5+11)
Arr. Madrid (Cham.)	21:52	8:34	10:05

(1)Reservation required. Meal service. (2)Runs daily, except Sundays and holidays. (3)Daily. (4)Carries sleeping car. (5)Has couchettes. (6)Reservation required. Supplement charged. Meal service. Has couchettes. (7)Meal service. (8)Supplement charged. (9)Runs from late June to late September. (10)Plus other departures from Paris at 20:00(4+5+7+8), 21:55(5) and 22:50(8). (11)Plus another departure from Bordeaux at 3:52(5+9).

Paris - Torino - Genoa

	16	24
Dep. Paris (Lyon)	18:50(1+2)	20:39(1+3)
Arr. Torino (P.N.)	3:01	5:40
Arr. Genoa (P.P.)	4:59	8:10

(1) Carries sleeping car. Also has couchettes. (2) Meal service. (3) Light refreshments.

THE FERRY-CROSSING TO IRELAND

Cherbourg - Rosslare **Le Havre - Rosslare**

1022

These times are for the period April 1 to September 30.

Dep. Cherbourg	21:00(1)		Dep. Le Havre	18:00(2)
Arr. Rosslare	14:00 Day 2		Arr. Rosslare	14:00 Day 2

(1)Tuesdays and Saturdays only. (2)Daily, except Tuesday and Saturday.

GREECE

The signs you will see at railstations in Greece are:

ANDRON	MEN
EISODHOS	ENTRANCE
EXODHOS	EXIT
GRAPHEION TON EISTIRON	TICKET OFFICE
GYNAIKON	WOMEN
IMATOPHYLAKION	CHECKROOM
PLIROPHORIA	INFORMATION
STATHMO	STATION

GREEK HOLIDAYS

January 1	New Year's Day		Easter Monday
January 6	Epiphany	May 1	Labor Day
	Ash Monday		Holy Spirit Day
March 25	Independence Day	August 15	Virgin Mary's Day
	Good Friday	October 28	National Day
	Good Saturday	December 25	Christmas Day
	Easter	December 26	Additional Holiday

SUMMER TIME

Greece changes to Summer Time on the last Sunday of March and converts back to Standard Time on the last Sunday of September.

GREECE'S TRAIN PASS

Greek Touring Card Unlimited second-class train travel. Can be purchased only in Greece. The 1983 prices are: 10 days $40(U.S.), 20 days $55, 30 days $80.

EURAILPASS BONUSES IN GREECE

See details on the Patras-Brindisi ferry-boat trip on page 146.

ONE-DAY EXCURSIONS AND CITY-SIGHTSEEING

Here are 6 one-day rail trips that can be made comfortably from Athens and Thessaloniki, returning to them in most cases before dinner-time. Notes are provided on what to see and do at each destination. The number below the name of each route is the Cook's timetable.

Details on 2 longer rail trips in Greece follow the one-day excursions. Schedules for international connections conclude this section.

GREECE

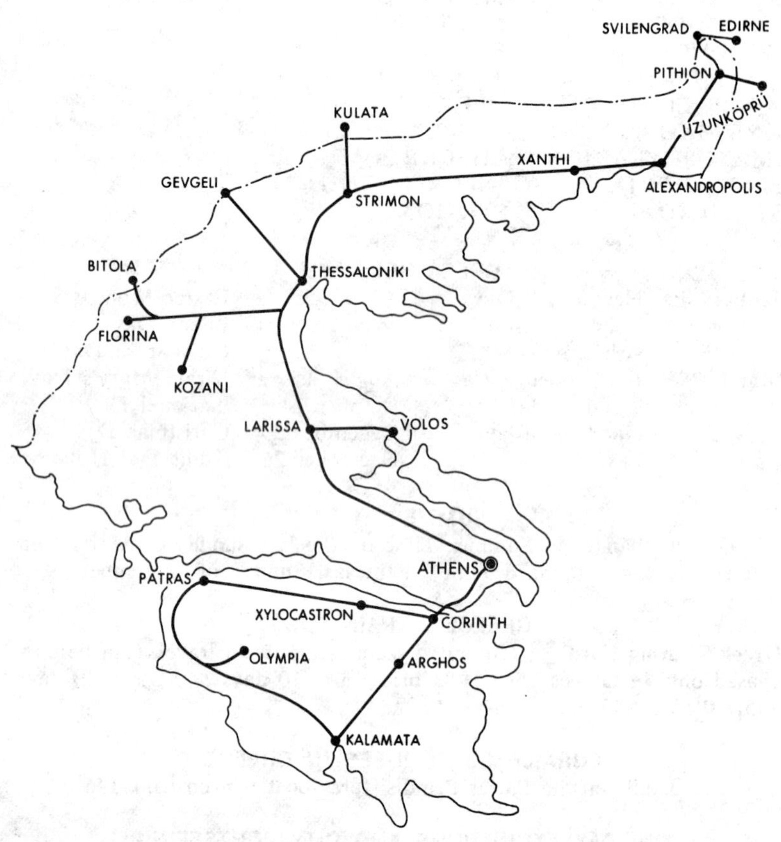
SVILENGRAD
EDIRNE
PITHION
UZUNKÖPRÜ
KULATA
XANTHI
ALEXANDROPOLIS
GEVGELI
STRIMON
BITOLA
THESSALONIKI
FLORINA
KOZANI
LARISSA
VOLOS
ATHENS
PATRAS
XYLOCASTRON
CORINTH
OLYMPIA
ARGHOS
KALAMATA

Athens

From 7:30 to sunset, and from 21:00 to 24:00 on nights of a full moon, visit the Parthenon, the elegant temple of the Wingless Victory and the Erechtheion at the ancient Acropolis. Then walk northwest to the partly restored ancient Agora to see the best preserved Doric temple in Athens, the Hephaistos, also known as the Thesseion.

Also near the Acropolis are: The old theater of Dionyssos. The gravestones and sculptures in Kerameikos, the city's ancient cemetery. The Corinthia-style columns of the Temple of Olympian Zeus. Hadrian's Arch. The all-marble Athenian Stadium, where the Olympic Games were revived in 1896. The Clock of Kyrrestos, showing the prevailing wind on each of its 8 sides, standing in Aerides Square, named for the function of the clock. The Roman Forum.

Walk downhill to the Monastiraki area, where the daily "Flea Market" is held. See the view of Athens from the white chapel of Agios Georgios on the Hill of Lycabettus, climbed either by foot or by cable car.

Athens' best-known museums are the National Archaeological Museum, The Acropolis Museum, the Byzantine Museum (for its collection of icons), the Museum of Greek Popular Art, the Museum of the Ancient Agora excavations in the Stoa (ancient commercial community) at Attalos, and the fantastic Benaki Museum in central Athens.

The 28 exhibit rooms at the Benaki, arranged chronologically, cover the entire spectrum of Greek culture from the early Bronze Age to the start of the 20th century: gold, ornaments, jewelry, portraits, statues, embroidery, icons, rare 17th and 18th century bibles, and 8 centuries (10th to 18th) of Islamic art that includes ceramics, textiles and wood carvings. Located on Queen Sofias Avenue, opposite the National Garden, the Benaki is open daily except Tuesday 8:00 to 14:00.

There are sound-and-light performances in English at Pnyx Hill every night at 21:00. When it ends, cross the road and see native dances of Greece, performed nightly at 22:15 on the Hill of Filopappos.

For Greek arts and handicrafts (ceramics, hand-woven fabrics, alabaster articles, embroideries, hand-carved wood furniture), shop on the streets around Syntagma Square, the center of the city.

Athens - Arghos - Athens

Sit on the right-hand side of the train en route to Arghos in order to see best the view of the canal that connects the Aegean and Ionian Seas, about 80 minutes after leaving Athens. The train crosses a 108-foot long bridge, 200 feet above the water. It is a short walk or inexpensive taxi ride from the Arghos railstation to the town center.

898

Dep. Athens	7:20(1+2)	9:43(1)
Arr. Arghos	9:50	12:35

Sights in Arghos: The Museum, with its archaeological exhibits. From there, it is a 15-minute walk to the ancient theater, carved into the hillside, and to some Roman ruins. A 5-mile taxi ride to the 800 B.C. ruins of Tiryns is well worth the small fare. At the birthplace of Hercules you will see the ruins of Greece's oldest recognizable temple: underground galleries polished for many centuries by the woolly backs of innumerable sheep who sought shelter there during storms. Massive Cyclopean walls.

Dep. Arghos	12:40(1)	14:38(1)	17:14(1)	19:03(1+2)
Arr. Athens	15:41	17:41	20:13	21:36

(1) Light refreshments. (2) Supplement charged.

Athens - Corinth - Athens

Watch 80 minutes after departing Athens for the same view described above, under "Athens-Arghos". The arrival in Corinth is in the "modern" Corinth, built after the 1858 earthquake.

898

Dep. Athens	7:20(1)+(2)	8:36(1)+(2)	9:43(1)	10:22(3)	12:01(1)
Arr. Corinth	8:54	10:11	11:27	12:13	13:52

Sights in Corinth: The 2500-year old Temple of Apollo. The Kato Pirini Fountain. The rostrum from which St. Paul preached Christianity to the Corinthians.

Dep. Corinth	12:14(1)	13:10(1)	13:52(1)	15:48(1)	16:39(3)+(4)
Arr. Athens	13:59	14:46	15:44	17:40	18:34

(1) Light refreshments. (2) Supplement charged. (3) Meal service. (4) Plus other departures from Corinth at 18:23(1), 19:30(3), 19:58(1+2) and 21:03(1+2).

Athens - Kalamata - Athens

898

Dep. Athens	7:20(1)	Dep. Kalamata	15:30(1)
Arr. Kalamata	13:28	Arr. Athens	21:35

(1) Supplement charged. Light refreshments.

Sights in Kalamata: The exhibits at the Museum in the Kyriakos mansion, ranging from Stone Age weapons to Venetian mirrors and coins as well as relics from the 1821 War of Independence. The Byzantine-style Church of Aghii Apostoli. The splendid view from the Frankish castle and, descending from there, see the handmade silk articles at the Convent. Aghios Haralambos, one of the finest Byzantine churches in the area, is a short distance east of the Convent. Stroll along the seafront.

Athens - Olympia

898			897		
Dep. Athens	8:36(1)	10:22(2)	Dep. Olympia	7:25	10:36(5)
Arr. Pirghos	13:52	17:10	Arr. Pirghos	8:08	11:12
Change trains.			Change trains.		
897			898		
Dep. Pirghos	14:04	18:12	Dep. Pirghos	9:12(3)	11:35(2)
Arr. Olympia	14:45	18:48	Arr. Athens	14:46	18:34

(1)Supplement charged. Light refreshments. (2)Meal service. (3)Light refreshments. (4)Supplement charged. (5)Plus other departures from Olympia at 13:27 and 16:31 (Pirghos at 14:57(2) and 17:17(4)).

Sights in Olympia: The first Olympic Games (776 B.C.) were held here and continued here every 4 years for the next 12 centuries. See the Stadium. The fine Olympic Museum, with its marvelous Hermes of Praxiteles sculpture. The temples of Hera and Zeus.

Athens - Patras - Athens 898

Dep. Athens	6:39(1)	8:36(2)	Dep. Patras	17:02(1)	18:58(2)
Arr. Patras	10:58	12:15	Arr. Athens	21:20	22:39

(1) Meal service. (2) Supplement charged. Light refreshments.

Sights in Patras: Cross the street in front of the railstation to the park. Then walk from the Trion Fountain along Ayiou Nikulauo to the steps that ascend to the Patras Acropolis for a fine view of Patras, the surrounding mountains and the port, third largest of Greece.

After descending the steps, go to the left along Georgiou Street to the old Roman Theater, the Odeon.

Another walk from the Trion Fountain is to the Archaeological Museum to see its collection of exhibits from the Mycenean, Geometric, Archaic and Roman periods. Also worth seeing are the Venetian castle and Greece's largest church, St. Andrews's.

Athens - Piraeus 892a

Subway trains depart every few minutes from the southbound section of a combined north-and-south platform at Athens' Omonia Square railstation for the 20-minute ride to Piraeus. Be certain, at the same platform, you are not boarding the northbound train for Kifissia. There is also ordinary train service from Athens to Piraeus.

Sights in Piraeus: One of the largest ports on the Mediterranean, from here ships sail daily to almost all the Aegean islands and to many other Greek ports. The 2 small adjoining ports of Zea and Mikrolimano are for pleasure craft. Bus #20 (the bus terminal is to the left of the railstation) goes to these ports.

See the neo-classical style Municipal Theater and the exhibits in the Archaeological Museum and the Maritime Museum. Plays are performed at the open-air Theater of Kastella in the Summer.

Athens - Thessaloniki 891

Dep. Athens (Larissa)	7:05(1)	8:00(2)	14:10(1)	19:30(3+8)
Arr. Thessaloniki	14:35	15:50	22:05	4:13

Sights in Thessaloniki: Second largest city in Greece. See the ruins of the Roman Baths, north of the Church of Agios Demetrios. The Roman Market and Theater. Nymphaion, the ancient circular building. The Arch of Galerius. The unique mosaics in the 4th century Rotunda, at the intersection of Agiou Georgiou and Filippou streets.

The 2 surviving early Christian churches: the 4th century Ahiropiitos and the 5th century Osios David. The 15th century White Tower. The collection of pre-historic to Byzantine items in the Archaeological Museum on YMCA Square. Articles from the past 3 centuries at the Folklore and Ethnological Museum, 68 Vasilisais Olgas.

Dep. Thessaloniki	8:00(1)	9:00(4+5)	13:52(6)	14:55(4+5+9)
Arr. Athens (Larrissa)	15:00	17:00	21:35	22:55

(1)Supplement charged. Light refreshments. (2)Reservation required. Supplement charged. Meal service. (3)Reservation required. Meal service. Has couchettes. (4)Meal service. (5)Supplement charged. (6)Light refreshments. (7)Carries sleeping car. Also has couchettes. (8)Plus other departures from Athens at 21:40(3) and 23:05(3+7). (9)Plus other departures from Thessaloniki at 21:50(7) and 23:45(3).

Thessaloniki - Kavala - Thessaloniki 893

Dep. Thessaloniki	6:23(1)	9:25(1)	15:00(1)	16:22(1)	23:14(2)
Arr. Drama	10:22	13:49	18:38	21:05	2:15

Change to bus for 22-mile ride to Kavala.

Dep. Drama	N/A	N/A	N/A	N/A	N/A
Arr. Kavala	N/A	N/A	N/A	N/A	N/A

* * *

Dep. Kavala	N/A	N/A	N/A	N/A	N/A
Arr. Drama	N/A	N/A	N/A	N/A	N/A

Change to train.

Dep. Drama	6:53	9:56(1)	15:59(1)	3:32(2)
Arr. Thessaloniki	11:24	13:27	20:10	7:24

Sights in Kavala: The view from the Byzantine Fort. The colossal 16th century aqueduct, Kamares. Imaret, the group of Moslem buildings constructed a short time prior to the 1821 War of Independence. The ancient relics in the Archaeological Museum. Beautiful beaches. Walk to the lighthouse, especially in the evening, when the fishing boats are leaving the harbor. See the view from the Church of the Prophet Elias. Take the 80-minute ferry-boat ride to the island of Thassos to see its marble ruins.

SCENIC TRIPS IN GREECE

Thessaloniki - Katerini - Athens

About one hour after departing Katerini, you can see on the right side of the train 9000-foot high Mt. Olympus, home of the ancient Greek gods. Thirty minutes later, the train passes through Tembi Valley and goes along Pinios River. From Domokos to Tithorea, the train winds along Mt. Orthrys and Mt. Iti, provding a panoramic view of many valleys and high mountains and, at one point, of the sea in the distance.

891			
Dep. Thessaloniki	5:45(1)	9:00(2)	13:52(3)
Arr. Katerini	6:05(4)	10:20(4)	15:12(4)
Arr. Athens	14:22	17:00	21:35

(1)Meal service. (2)Supplement charged. Meal service. (3)Light refreshments. (4)Estimated.

Athens - Pirghos

Most of this trip is alongside the sea, through green fields of citrus and olive trees. Between Athens and Corinth, the train goes across the bridge spanning Korinthos Canal, which separates northern Greece from Peloponesia.

898	
Dep. Athens	8:36
Arr. Corinth	10:11
Arr. Pirghos	13:52
Change trains.	

897	
Dep. Pirghos	14:04
Arr. Olympia	14:45
Sightsee in Olympia.	
Dep. Olympia	16:31
Arr. Pirghos	17:12
Change trains.	
898	
Dep. Pirghos	17:17
Arr. Athens	23:39

INTERNATIONAL ROUTES FROM GREECE

Athens is Greece's gateway to Italy and Yugoslavia (and on to Western Europe) as well as to Turkey (and on to the Middle East).

Athens - Belgrade + Munich or Venice

	65	65	40
Dep. Athens	8:00(1+2+3)	19:30(1+2)	21:40(1)
Set your watch back one hour from late September to early April, 2 hours from early April to late September.			
Arr. Belgrade	5:40(4)	16:12(4)	18:20(4)
Dep. Belgrade	6:17(1+2+3)	16:50(1+2)	19:20(6)
Arr. Munich	23:30	10:14(5)	-0-
Arr. Venice (S.L.)	-0-	-0-	11:30(5)

(1)Meal service. Has couchettes. (2)Reservation required. (3)Supplement charged. (4)Day 2. (5)Day 3. (6)Carries sleeping car. Also has couchettes.

Athens - Patras - Brindisi

The Patras-Brindisi boat trip is covered by Eurailpass and Eurail Youthpass—but only if you go on Adriatica/Hellenic Mediterranean Lines. WARNING: The employees of other lines intimate that their ships honor the 2 passes and then charge fees after the boat leaves the pier.

With or without a Eurailpass or Eurail Youthpass, a reservation theoretically can be made on day of departure or day before departure—but it is very unlikely that space will be available (particularly during July and August) unless a reservation is made many weeks in advance of departure date.

Those gambling on making a reservation after arriving in Patras can make application January 1-June 9 and October 1-December 31 only at the Adriatica/Hellenic Mediterranean Lines embarkation office, located at Othonos Amalias 8.

From June 10 to September 30, those without advance reservations can apply also to any Patras travel agency that displays in its window the green badge "Eurail Information - Eurailpass".

Holders of advance reservations must go at all times directly to the A/HM Lines embarkation office to have their tickets checked, settle port taxes due and obtain the required Embarkation Ticket. That office is open 9:00-13:30 and 16:00-22:00.

Advance reservations before you start your trip, at $1.50(U.S.) each, can be made at any office that issues Eurailpass (see pages 22-23) or at travel agencies in countries where Eurailpass is sold. There is also a

$12(U.S.) surcharge, in addition to the reservation fee, for travel from June 10 to September 30.

Another fee is charged for such special accommodations as aircraft type seats, pullman berths and cabins. There is also a port tax of 180 Drachmas that is not covered by Eurailpass and must be paid in Drachmas.

Passengers without advance reservations must obtain the Embarkation Ticket at least 2 hours prior to the ship's departure time. The ships reserve the right to cancel a reservation when that is not done and to give the space to a standby passenger.

898					
Dep. Athens	6:39(1)	8:36(2)	10:22(1)	13:10(2)	15:42(1)
Arr. Patras	10:58	12:15	14:56	17:00	19:56

For sightseeing in Patras, see notes on page 147.

Walk to Patras Harbor.

For sailing dates, check Cook's Table #1440.

Dep. Patras Harbor	17:00(3)	22:00(4)
Arr. Brindisi	8:00(5)	17:00(5)

(1) Meal service. (2) Supplement charged. Light refreshments. (3) Runs from early June to late September. (4) Runs all year. (5) Day 2.

Athens - Istanbul

900		
Dep. Athens	23:05	(second-class only)
Arr. Istanbul	9:45	Day 3

IBERIAN PENINSULA (SPAIN AND PORTUGAL)

Spain and Portugal have the broadest gauge railroad tracks in Western Europe (5′ 6″ versus 4′ 8½″ in France and the other Western European countries). It is therefore necessary in most crossings from Spain into France (at Irun/Hendaye, Port Bou/Cerbere, or La Tour-de-Carol) to change trains. A few trains running between Spain and France are adaptable to either gauge.

Many Spanish train tickets include the price of a lunch or dinner. It is wise to determine this in advance of a trip.

For most Spanish trains, it is necessary to reserve a seat and have one's ticket stamped with the train number and departure date. Even when traveling on a Eurailpass, an endorsed ticket should be obtained for trains requiring them. Do not discard a ticket during the journey. Frequently, the ticket is collected at the termination of a ride. If it is not presented at the destination railstation, the passenger must purchase a second ticket. It is wise to retain rail tickets all over the world so as to avoid having to pay twice for one journey.

Every year, some tourists using Eurailpass report being ejected from a Spanish train either just before its departure or at a station en route to their destination for failing to obtain the required endorsed tickets.

A person using a Eurailpass has been indoctrinated with the idea that he or she need not have either a ticket or (when riding an ordinary train) a seat reservation. This is confirmed on all of one's travels in Europe outside Spain.

Unaware of the Spanish Railway regulation, the passenger blithely steps aboard a train in Spain without having the ticket and seat reservation required there — and a ticket can be obtained without charge upon presenting the Eurailpass.

If the train is not exceptionally crowded that day and the conductor appears before the train departs, the passenger is told to get off the train, go back into the railstation, and obtain the required endorsed ticket. Frequently, the notice to do this is given so close to the departure time that the train leaves before the passenger is able to return to it.

If the train departs before the conductor has discovered the omission of an endorsed ticket, often the passenger is forced to leave the train at the next stop to obtain a ticket. If that stop is typically brief, the train leaves that station before the passenger is able to return to the train.

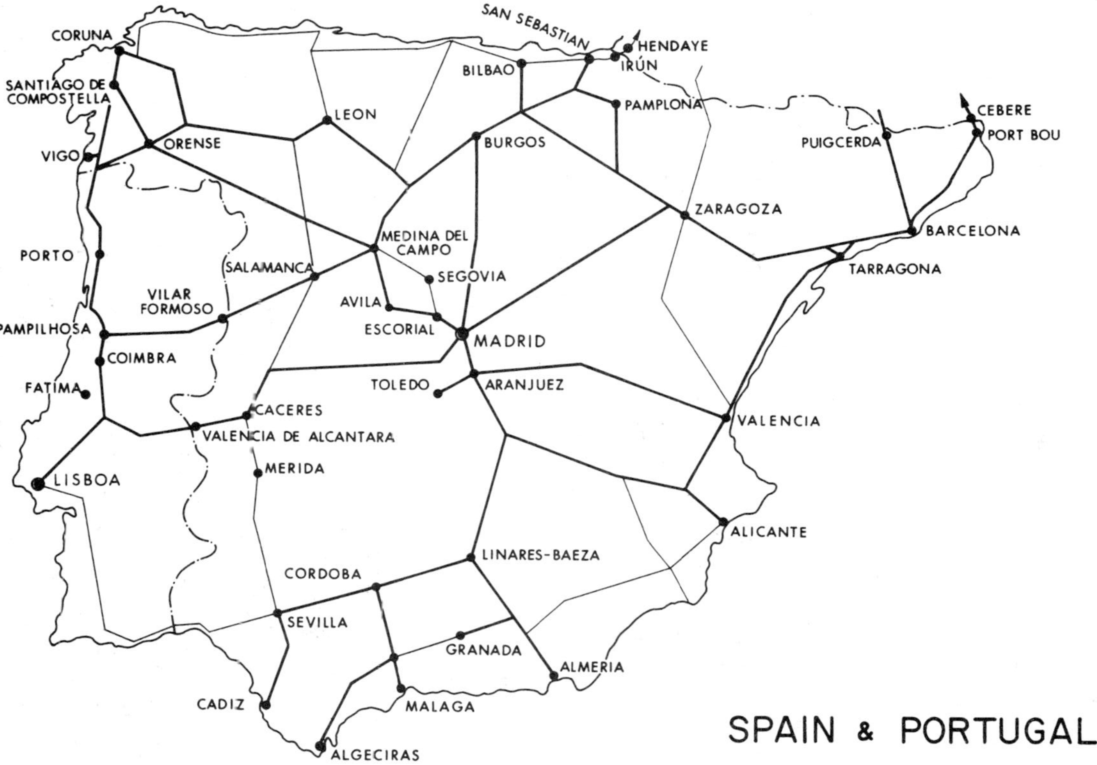
CORUNA
SAN SEBASTIAN
HENDAYE
IRÚN
BILBAO
SANTIAGO DE COMPOSTELLA
PAMPLONA
CEBERE
PORT BOU
LEON
PUIGCERDA
VIGO
ORENSE
BURGOS
ZARAGOZA
BARCELONA
MEDINA DEL CAMPO
PORTO
SALAMANCA
TARRAGONA
SEGOVIA
VILAR FORMOSO
AVILA
ESCORIAL
PAMPILHOSA
MADRID
COIMBRA
TOLEDO
ARANJUEZ
FATIMA
CACERES
VALENCIA
VALENCIA DE ALCANTARA
MERIDA
LISBOA
ALICANTE
LINARES-BAEZA
CORDOBA
SEVILLA
GRANADA
ALMERIA
CADIZ
MALAGA
ALGECIRAS
SPAIN & PORTUGAL

The justification for the Spanish ticket-and-reservation requirement is that Spain's first-class fares are substantially lower than those of other countries. For example, the charge for the 8-hour Madrid-Barcelona run is about 60% of what French National Railroads charges for the 7-hour trip from Paris to Avignon or what Norwegian State Railways charges for the 8½-hour Bergen-Oslo trip. The demand for Spain's limited number of express train seats far exceeds the supply. Only by issuing endorsed tickets can they control the situation.

The Spanish name for Spanish National Railways is "Red Nacional de los Ferrocarriles Espanoles." Abbreviation: RENFE. Reservations can be made at RENFE offices both in the major railstations and at numerous locations outside the station, as well as at various travel agencies in Spanish cities.

Making train reservations in Spain is very easy. More than 90% of the stations in Spain are hooked-up with a computer in Madrid, making it usually possible to arrange at one time all of your reservations for train trips in Spain. Reservations can be made as much as 2 months in advance. Timetable information can be obtained at offices of RENFE and at Spanish travel agencies.

Tell the clerk at the train information window your departure date, train number (which you can find in the railstation on the list of departures) and/or departure time, destination and number of seats required.

You will be handed a form which you then take to a ticket window, where you will be handed a seat reservation computer card. It will show either an exact seat number or the symbol "SR" ("Seat Reserved") under the column "Asiento".

If it is marked "SR", the conductor will tell you which seat to occupy after you board the car designated on the reservation computer card.

Do not board a Spanish non-local train without a seat reservation!

To ride without a Eurailpass on Spanish trains classified "Rap", one must pay a supplement. A higher supplement must be paid when riding a train classified "Talgo", "E.L.T." or "T.E.R.", all of which are air-conditioned.

A Eurailpass entitles the bearer to ride these special trains without having to pay their supplemental charges, the same as when riding Trans-Europ Express trains.

First-class sleeping cars in Spain have single-berth and 2-berth compartments. Second-class sleeping cars have 3-berth tourist compartments, except the Barcelona Talgo, which has tourist compartments with 4 berths. There is a supplemental charge for air-conditioned sleeping cars. Neither berths nor this supplement are covered by Eurailpass. Some

Spanish trains have second-class couchette cars, with 6-berth compartments, as are also available in other Western European countries.

First-Class sleeping cars in Portugal have single-berth compartments. Second-class Portuguese sleeping cars have 2-berth compartments. The Sud Express also provides second-class 3-berth compartments.

In order to avoid waiting in the wrong line for Spanish tickets and seat reservations, take note of these signs you will find in large Spanish railstations:

TRENES DE SALIDA INMEDIATE (trains ready to depart),
VENTA PARA HOY (trains leaving later in the day), and
VENTA ANTICIPADA (for trains leaving on a future day).

Other railstation signs:

A LOS ANDENNES	TO THE PLATFORMS (TRACKS)
CABALLEROS	MEN
COCHE-CAMA	SLEEPING CAR
COCHE-LITERA	COUCHETTES
COCHE-RESTAURANTE	RESTAURANT CAR
ENTRADA	ENTRANCE
ESTACION	STATION
HORARIOS DE TRENES	TIMETABLES
LA CONSIGNA	LUGGAGE CHECK-ROOM
LARGO RECORRIDO	LONG DISTANCE
LLEGADA	ARRIVAL
SALIDA	DEPARTURE (EXIT)
SENORAS	WOMEN
TREN CON SUPLEMENTO	TRAIN WITH SURCHARGE

Signs you will find in Portuguese railstations:

CARRUAGEM-CAMA	SLEEPING CAR
CARRUAGEM-RESTAURANTE	RESTAURANT CAR
CHEGADA	ARRIVAL
ESTACAO	STATION
HOMENS	MEN
HORARIO DOS CAMINHOS	TIMETABLES
PARTIDA	DEPARTURE
PLATAFORMA	PLATFORM (TRACK)
SAIDA	EXIT
SENHORAS	WOMEN

SPANISH HOLIDAYS

A list of holidays is helpful because some trains will be noted later in this section as not running on holidays. Also, those trains which operate on holidays are filled, and it is necessary to make reservations for them long in advance.

January 1	New Year's Day
January 6	Epiphany
March 19	Saint Joseph's Day
	Maundy Thursday
	Good Friday
	Easter
	Easter Monday (Barcelona)
April 1	Victory Day
May 1	St. Joseph Artisan Day
	Ascension Day
	Corpus Christi Day
June 29	St. Peter and St. Paul
July 18	National Holiday
July 25	Saint James' Day
August 15	Assumption Day
October 12	Columbus Day
November 1	All Saints Day
December 8	Immaculate Conception
December 25	Christmas Day

PORTUGUESE HOLIDAYS

The main public holidays in Portugal are:

January 1	New Year's Day
	Shrove Tuesday
	Good Friday
	Easter
June 10	Day of The Race (Portuguese National Day)
	Saint Anthony's Day (Lisbon)
August 15	Assumption of Our Lady
October 5	Anniversary of the Proclamation of the Portuguese Republic
November 1	All Saints Day
December 1	Restoration of Independence
December 8	Immaculate Conception
December 25	Christmas

SUMMER TIME

Portugal is one hour earlier than Spain all year. Portugal is on the same time as England nearly all year, except for a few weeks in the Spring and Fall. Both Portugal and Spain change to Summer Time on the last Sunday of March and convert back to Standard Time on the last Sunday of September. During Summer Time, when it is 12:00 in England, it is 12:00 in Portugal and 13:00 in Spain.

PORTUGAL'S TRAIN PASSES

All of the following are sold only in Portugal. Children under 4 travel free.

Tourist Ticket Unlimited train travel for any class. The 1983 prices are: 7 days 3,820 escudos, 14 days 6,100 escudos, 21 days 8,710 escudos.

Kilometric Ticket Valid for 3 months, covering up to 3,000 km of travel. The 1983 prices for first-class are: 10,015 escudos for express trains, 7,155 escudos for other trains. Second-class: 6,680 and 4,770.

Senior Citizen Discount Persons 65 or older pay half-fare.

Family Ticket For 3 or more persons. Valid only for trips of more than 149 km. Passports and documents proving family relationship must be presented. One person must pay full fare. Half-fare for others who are over 12 years old. One-quarter fare for children 4-11. Children under 4 travel free.

Group Ticket For 10 or more persons, a 20% discount for trips of more than 99 km. One free ticket for a group of 15-50 people. Two free tickets for a group of more than 50.

SPAIN'S TRAIN PASSES

All of the following are sold only in Spain.

Chequetren 1983 prices: 15,000 pesetas of train travel costs 12,750 pesetas, while 20,000 pesetas of train travel costs 17,000 pesetas.

Senior Citizen Discount For persons 65 or older. Must first purchase a "Tarjeta Dorada" (Gold Card) for 25 pesetas at any railstation or Renfe ticket office. Proof of age (Passport, etc.) required. With the Gold Card, there is a 50% discount for trips of more than 100 kilometers (60 miles).

Roundtrip Discount A 25% discount on trips of more than 100 kilometers. Not valid approximately 60 holidays in every year.

EURAILPASS BONUSES

There are no Eurailpass bonuses in Spain or Portugal.

ONE-DAY EXCURSIONS AND CITY SIGHTSEEING

Here are 39 one-day rail trips that can be made comfortably from 7 major Spanish and Portuguese cities, returning to them in most cases before dinnertime. Notes are provided on what to see at each destination. The number below the name of each route is the Cook's timetable.

This section concludes with details on 12 rail trips recommended for exceptional scenery plus 6 trips to/from Madrid, the schedules for 2 other major routes (Barcelona-Valencia and Lisbon-Seville), and the international rail connections from Portugal and Spain.

The 7 base cities are: Barcelona, Lisbon, Madrid, San Sebastian. Seville, Tarragona and Valencia.

Barcelona

There is rail service between the center of Barcelona (Sants station) and the city's airport every 15 minutes from 6:00 to 22:45. The rail service from the airport to the city is every 15 minutes from 6:30 to 23:15. There is bus service from the city to the airport at 23:15, 23:45, 00:15 and 00:45. Bus service from the airport to the city is offered at 23:45, 00:15, 00:45 and 1:15.

Local trains, not requiring seat reservations, depart from Barcelona's underground Paseo de Gracia and Sants railstations. Faster express trains, requiring seat reservations, also depart from Paseo de Gracia and from Sants, as well as from Barcelona's Termino station.

Your sightseeing here can be divided into covering 4 separate areas of Barcelona. In the Gothic Quarter: The cloisters in the 14th century Cathedral (La Seu), the Episcopal Palace, Palacio de la Generalidad, many elegant 14th and 15th century palaces, the Federico Mares Museum. The Picasso Museum.

In the Montjuich area: the Museum of Catalan Art in the National Palace, the collection of El Greco, Velasquez and Rembrandt paintings at the Archaeological Museum in Palacio Real, handicrafts and architecture representing every region of Spain in the Spanish Village.

In the Tibidado area: Pedralbes Palace, Pedralbes Monastery, the Picasso Museum, and the view all the way to Montserrat and the Pyrenees.

In the modern city center: Stroll the mile-long Ramblas, from Plaza de Cataluna to Plaza Puerta de la Paz, with its Columbus monument at the waterfront. You will enjoy seeing the numerous stalls selling hundreds of varieties of birds, the many stands with flowers and plants, the very large central food market, cafes offering tapas (the local and varied between-meal snacks), and at least half the population of Barcelona.

Another rewarding walk, in the opposite direction, is along beautiful Paseo de Gracia, from Plaza de Cataluna to Avenida del Generalismo Franco (also called "Diagonal", its original name), to see luxury shops, decorative sidewalks designed by Dali, and several buildings created by Barcelona's most radical and inventive architect, Antonio Gaudi.

In Plaza Gaudi, you must see the uncompleted and absolutely unique church, La Sagrada Familia, the architect's most important work. It was started in 1884. Because of lack of funds, Barcelonians believe construction will not be finished for another century.

What has been constructed is well worth seeing: the 4 lofty towers (nearly 300 feet tall), the Nativity and Passion facades with the Tree of Life supported by the central arch, and the wrought-iron plants in the side chapels of the completed crypt.

Although public transportation is not available to the Gaudi-designed park, Parque Guell, we suggest you take a taxi there to see it and for the view of Barcelona from its elevated plaza. The paths in this park are decorated with concrete pillars that imitate trees and vines. Also see the colorful undulating bench surfaced with broken ceramic pieces, on the plaza. And the gigantic tiled frog fountain on the steps leading down from the park's plaza.

Lisbon

Santa Apolonia is Lisbon's railstation for departure to Madrid and beyond (to France and the rest of Europe). It has currency exchange (9:00-21:00) and hotel reservation services (9:30-17:30).

See the beautiful Avenida de Liberdade. The Tower of Belem (monument to Portugal's sailors). The view from the bi-cultural St. George's Castle, built by the Visigoths in the 5th century and by the Moors in the 9th century. The Palace of Queluz.

Largo das Portas do Sol (Sun Gateway), one of the 7 gates into the ancient Arab City. Santa Cruz quarter. Alfama Quarter. Salazar Bridge. The lovely Praco de Rossio. The Gulbenkiam Museum. The marvelous collection of tapestries, jewelry, ceramics, and Dutch, Spanish and Italian paintings in the Ancient Art Museum.

Edward VII Park. The Zoological Garden. The Botanical Garden. The Museum of Modern Art. The Municipal Museum. The greatest collection in the world of royal coaches, at Praca Afonso de Albuquerque. The Flea Market. The Military Museum.

The Maritime Museum, in the West wing of Hieronymite Monastery. Jeronimo's Church. The Cathedral. House of Facets, its front entirely faced with dark stones that have been cut into diamond-like facets.

Madrid

There is train service connecting Madrid's Chamartin and Atocha stations, and Eurailpass can be used on it. At Chamartin, look for the track marked "Linea de Atocha y Guadalajara". At Atocha, go to the separate small station, a short walk from the main station.

The Prado Museum, with its breathtaking collection of great paintings. Puerta del Sol. The Goya Pantheon. Plaza Mayor. San Miguel Basilica. San Isidor Cathedral. The Royal Palace, including: State Apartments and Chapel, Apartments of Queen Maria Cristina of Hapsburg, the Private Apartments, Royal Pharmacy, Armory, Carriage Museum, Library, Numismatic Museum and Music Museum.

Descalzas Reales Convent. The Archaeological Museum. The Folk Museum. The Americas Museum. The Bullfighting Museum. Retiro

Park. University City. Plaza de Espana, with its stone monument to Cervantes. The Royal Tapestry Factory.

For the best food in Spain, and it is moderately priced, dine at Restaurante Botin, at Calle de Cuchilleros 17. Every dish is marvelous. Their specialties are roast suckling pig and roast baby lamb. These and many other foods are cooked there by oak wood in the original 16th century tiled oven. Botin is run by a young and very handsome gentleman, Antonio Gonzalez Jr. His family has operated Botin for 80 years.

San Sebastian

Excellent beaches. The Goya and El Greco collection at San Sebastian Picture Gallery. Sta. Maria Church. San Telmo Museum. The Oceanographic museum in Sea Palace. The picturesque fishing village nearby. Mount Urgull.

Seville

The city of Don Juan and Carmen. You must not miss seeing Corpus Christi Cathedral, largest Gothic cathedral in the world and the site of Columbus' tomb.

The 14th century Alcazar Palace with its magnificent chambers, particularly the room where foreign ambassadors were received. Its colorful mosaics and tiles, delicate wrought-iron and carved wood ceilings are spellbinding. You can see nearby Segovia from the tower of Isabella's castle. Allow time to stroll through the elaborate gardens there: bronze and marble statues, lovely fountains and the extraordinary Pavillion of Carlos V.

On one side of the Alcazar is a university, formerly Antigua Fabrica de Tobacos, the tobacco factory Bizet immortalized in his opera, Carmen. On the other side of the Alcazar is Barrio de Santa Cruz, with its ancient buildings and narrow streets. Once a refuge for Jews fleeing the Inquisition, now it is a fashionable residential section of Seville.

You can enjoy spending many hours in Maria Luisa Park, seeing the beautiful buildings, gardens, pools and fountains there. Particularly noteworthy is the magnificent Plaza de Espana.

Other notable sights in Seville: The 12th century La Giralda Tower, a minaret when the Moors ruled here. The 12-sided Tower of Gold. Meander along the city's cobbled streets to see many picturesque homes.

The only way to reach the 200 BC Roman ruins called Italica (a few miles outside Seville) is by auto. Schedule at least one hour to see the third largest arena in Europe (after Rome and Nimes) and many excellent mosaic floors of what had been the houses of those who lived here 2,100 years ago.

Valencia

The Holy Grail, the chalice used at the Last Supper, in the 13th century Cathedral. The great art collection in the Convent of Pio V.

The Orange Court at the 15th century Lonja del Mercado. The Arenas, Pinedo y Saler and Nazaret beaches. The scent of the vast surrounding orange groves, perfuming the night.

* * *

RESERVATIONS ARE STRONGLY ADVISED ON ALL SPANISH TRAINS.

* * *

In the following timetables, where a city has more than one railstation we have designated the particular station under the name of the city (in parentheses).

Barcelona - Blanes - Barcelona 424

Go to the "Estacion de Cercanias" (suburban section of Barcelona's Termino railstation) to board the train for Blanes. Seat reservations are not required for this ride. Board well before departure time to avoid standing for 1½ hours.

Take a bus or taxi from Blanes' railstation to the center of the village. It is a half-mile walk there from the station.

Dep. Barcelona (Ter.)	Frequent times from 5:45 to 21:45
Arr. Blanes	60 minutes later

Sights in Blanes: Stroll the waterfront. See the Aquarium and Botanical Garden, near the location of the daily fish auction, at 17:00. Daily boat excursions go from Blanes to Tossa and Lloret.

Dep. Blanes	Frequent times from 6:10 to 21:40
Arr. Barcelona (Ter.)	60 minutes later

Barcelona - Gerona - Barcelona 424

Dep. Barcelona (Ter.)	7:45(1)	9:00(1)	10:02(2)	10:31(1+3+4)
Arr. Gerona	9:01	11:04	11:08	11:49

Sights in Gerona: The magnificent 14th century Cathedral. The Provincial Archaeological Museum. The 12th century Arab Baths. Sobreportes, the ancient gate. Narrow 17th century streets.

Dep. Gerona	11:45	12:21(1)	13:15(1)	14:40(1+5)
Arr. Barcelona (Ter.)	13:11	14:05	15:05	15:55

(1) Second-class only. (2) Supplement charged. (3) Depart/Arrive Barcelona's Paseo de Gracia railstation. (4) Plus other departures from Barcelona at 10:45(1) and 13:05(1). (5) Plus other departures from Gerona at 15:45(1), 17:20(1), 18:43(1), 20:11(2), 20:45(2+3), 20:50(1) and 22:13(1).

Barcelona - Lerida - Barcelona

It is advisable to make a reservation for this ride well in advance of departure datc. Although departures are from other stations, go to Triunfo station to make this reservation. On boarding, find a seat on the left-hand side so as to have a good view of the restored 13th century hilltop Seo Antiqua Cathedral before the arrival in Lerida.

412			
Dep. Barcelona (Ter.)	-0-	8:35	12:15(1)
Dep. Barcelona (P. de G.)	-0-	-0-	12:23(1)
Dep. Barcelona (Sants)	8:00(1)	-0-	12:30(1)
Arr. Lerida	9:55	11:35	15:03

Sights in Lerida: The Archaeological Museum, in the Antiguo Hospital de Santa Maria, where the tourist office is located. A walking tour is easy with the city map available there. See the old Byzantine-Gothic-Moorish 13th century Cathedral. The Palacio de la Paheria. Stroll the maze of narrow streets in the interesting old section on the right bank of the Segre River, and visit the 12th century Alcazaba (castle).

Dep. Lerida	14:48(1)	17:57(1)	19:23(1)	20:12(1)
Arr. Barcelona (Sants)	17:21	-0-	21:28	22:13
Arr. Barcelona (P. de G.)	17:28	-0-	-0-	22:21
Arr. Barcelona (Ter.)	17:37	20:59	-0-	22:30

(1)Reservation required. Supplement charged. Meal service.

Barcelona - Montserrat - Barcelona

0000					
Dep. Barcelona (P. de Espana)	9:10	11:10	13:10	15:10	17:10
Arr. Montserrat	10:09	12:09	14:09	16:09	18:09

Sights in Montserrat: The 9th century Monastery, still occupied by hundreds of Benedictine monks, is 3700 feet above a valley. It ranks with Zaragoza and Santiago de Compostela as one of the most important pilgrimage sites in Spain. See the Grotto of the Virgin, the Mirador, the Chapel of San Miguel and the Chapel of Santa Cecilia. Then take a funicular to the Grotto of San Juan Garin and an aerial tram to the 4,000-foot-high Hermitage of San Jeronimo, from where you will have a view of the Eastern Pyrenees.

Dep. Montserrat	11:41	13:41	15:41	17:41	19:41
Arr. Barcelona (P. de Espana)	12:40	14:40	16:40	18:40	20:40

Barcelona - Sitges - Barcelona

425

Many local trains run from Termino, Paseo de Gracia and Sants stations to Sitges, a 30-minute trip.

Sights in Sitges: The 18th century furnishings at Casa Llopis. Antique dolls collected from every part of Europe, in the Lola Anglada Museum. El Greco paintings at the Cau Ferrat Museum.

Barcelona - Tarragona - Barcelona

425

Many local trains run from Termino, Paseo de Gracia and Sants stations to Tarragona, a 90-minute trip.

Sights in Tarragona: Relics of pre-Roman, Roman, Visigothic and Moorish cultures.

It is a short, but severely uphill, walk from the railstation to the long promenade, Balcon del Mediterraneo, from which there is a marvelous view of the sea. Two strolling streets start at each end of the "balcony". The first is Rambla del Generalismo. The other is Rambla de San Carlos.

We suggest you rest a while at one of the many sidewalk cafes on either Rambla. Then, start your walking tour of Tarragona by going 2 blocks from the "balcony", down Rambla de San Carlos to where it intersects with San Augustin. Turn right (the street name changes to "Mayor") and walk one-quarter mile to the 12th century Cathedral, worth seeing for its large and architecturally unique Cloisters, influenced by Roman, Gothic and Moorish styles.

Next, return to Rambla de San Carlos and turn right. Walk down it 2 blocks until it intersects with Abalto. Turn right and walk uphill, alongside the Roman wall.

You will then be on the semi-circular Paseo Arqueologico walk, from which there are excellent views of the countryside surrounding Tarragona.

At the end of this walk, bear to the right and come downhill on Avenida de la Victoria for 5 minutes until you reach Plaza del Rey. There, you can visit both the museum in the 1st century B.C. Pretorio and also the marvelous mosaics and ancient coins in the Archaeological Museum.

Across from Plaza del Rey is the Roman Amphitheater. Having completed a circle, you will again be at Balcon del Mediterraneo, and it is all downhill to return to the railstation.

Granada - Malaga - Granada

Between Bobadilla and Malaga, the train travels through the spectacular El Chorro gorge.

439

Dep. Granada	8:30(1)	Dep. Malaga	18:35(1)
Arr. Bobadilla	10:21	Arr. Bobadilla	19:34
Change trains.		Change trains.	
Dep. Bobadilla	10:29(1)	Dep. Bobadilla	19:55(1)
Arr. Malaga	11:30	Arr. Granada	21:52

(1) Reservation required. Supplement charged.

Sights in Malaga: Winter sun. The 9th century Alcazaba Moslem palace and the ruins of Gibralfaro Castle, 2 fortresses which made Malaga a major stronghold in the Middle Ages. The Fine Arts Museum. Sagrario, an unusual rectangular church that was originally a mosque. The Cathedral.

Lisbon - Coimbra - Lisbon

445

Dep. Lisbon (S. Apol.)	8:25(1)	8:50(2)	11:35(3)	14:25(1)
Arr. Coimbra	10:24	11:16	14:03	16:32

Sights in Coimbra: Almedina Gate. The Cathedral and the Cloisters. The Machado do Castro Museum. The 13th century University. Try the local food specialty, roasted suckling pig (leitao).

Dep. Coimbra	11:11(2)	13:34(2)	15:59(1)	16:37(4)
Arr. Lisbon (S. Apol.)	13:40	16:10	18:10	20:02

(1) First-class only. Reservation required. Light refreshments. (2) Light refreshments. (3) Meal service. (4) Plus other departures from Coimbra at 17:13, 18:26(1), 19:12, 20:26(2) and 22:31(1).

Lisbon - Estoril and Cascais - Lisbon

443

Dep. Lisbon (Cais do Sodre)	Every 15-20 minutes
Arr. Estoril	28 minutes later
Arr. Cascais	4 minutes after departing Estoril

Sights in Estoril: Portugal's major beach resort. Try your luck in the Casino.

Sights in Cascais: Bloodless bullfights on Summer Sundays. Surf fishing.

Dep. Cascais	Every 15-20 minutes
Dep. Estoril	4 minutes later
Arr. Lisbon (Cais do Sodre)	28 minutes after departing Estoril

Lisbon - Figueira da Foz 449

Dep. Lisbon (Rossio)	7:40	Dep. Figueira da Foz	18:32
Arr. Figueira da Foz	11:38	Arr. Lisbon (Rossio)	23:00

Sights in Figueira da Foz: The Casa do Paco Museum, with what is said to be the world's greatest collection of Delft tiles. Try your luck in the Casino Oceano.

Lisbon - Porto (Oporto) - Lisbon

445

Dep. Lisbon (S. Apol.)	7:25(1)	8:25(1)	8:55(2)	11:00(1)
Arr. Porto (Campanha)	10:25	11:45	13:00	14:00

Sights in Porto: The more than 80 wine stores occupying all of the Vila Nova de Gaia quarter. The 12th century Cathedral. Soares dos Reis Museum. The 3 great bridges: Dom Louis, Dona Maria and Ponte da Arrabida. Portugal's oldest chapel, Sao Martinho de Cedofeita. The gilded woodcarvings in the Church of San Francisco. The Church of the Clerigos, with its 10-story tower. The city's many beautiful gardens.

Dep. Porto (Campanha)	14:25(1)	15:30(3)	16:10	17:00(1+4)
Arr. Lisbon (S. Apol.)	18:10	19:45	22:10	20:35

(1) First-class only. Reservation required. Supplement charged. Meal service or light refreshments. (2) Light refreshments. (3) Daily, except Saturday. (4) Plus other departures from Porto at 18:45(2), 20:15(1) and 21:15(1).

Lisbon - Setubal - Lisbon

The start and the end of this trip are a 30-minute ferry boat ride.

450

Dep. Lisbon (T. de Paco Pier)	6:40	8:10	11:45(1)
Arr. Barreiro (Pier)	7:10	8:40	12:15
Change to train.			
Dep. Barreiro (Stn.)	7:15	8:50	12:20
Arr. Setubal	8:05	9:15	12:53

Sights in Setubal: The paintings in the Town Museum. Next to it, the lovely Church of Jesus. The view from Saint Philip's Castle, while having lunch there. Many sardine canneries, some of them open to the public. The Maritime Museum. Take an inexpensive taxi ride to the nearby (5½ miles) Palmela Castle.

Dep. Setubal	12:08	15:10	21:25
Arr. Barreiro (Stn.)	12:37	15:55	21:55
Change to boat.			
Dep. Barreiro (Pier)	12:50	16:00	22:10
Arr. Lisbon (T. de Paco Pier)	13:20	16:30	22:40

(1) Daily, except Sundays and holidays.

Lisbon - Sintra - Queluz

	443
Dep. Lisbon	Frequent times
Arr. Sintra	41 minutes later

Sights in Sintra: Take the "Sintra-Vila" bus from the railstation to the city's tourist office, where guide books and maps are available. Use inexpensive taxis to see the view from the 19th century Palacio de Pena, the Moorish Castle, the Palacio Real and the marvelous gardens at the Palacio de Monserrate.

Dep. Sintra	Frequent times
Arr. Queluz	20 minutes later

Sights in Queluz: The beautiful gardens, monument to Maria I and exquisite restaurant at the 18th century Palacio de Queluz.

Dep. Queluz	Frequent times
Arr. Lisbon	21 minutes later

Madrid - Aranjuez - Madrid

	416	433	416	438
Dep. Madrid (Atocha)	7:28	9:00(1+2)	9:45(1)	9:55(2)
Arr. Aranjuez	40-50 minutes later			

Sights in Aranjuez: The Museum of Royal Robes and the luxurious interiors of the Porcelain Room and Throne Room in the Palacio Real. The magnificent furnishings at the Casa del Labrador. The Pastere and Island gardens. The collection of royal ships in the Casa de Marinos.

	433	438	416	416
Dep. Aranjuez	13:23(1)	15:48	16:39	20:14(1+4)
Arr. Madrid (Atocha)	-0-	-0-	17:32	20:57
Arr. Madrid (Cham.)	14:14	16:55	-0-	-0-

(1) Light refreshments. (2) Departs from Madrid's Chamartin station. (3) Reservation required. Supplement charged. (4) Plus other departures from Aranjuez at (#433) 20:47(1) and (#438) 21:08(1+3).

Madrid - Avila - Madrid

	422	420	422	422
Dep. Madrid (Norte)	-0-	8:05(2)	-0-	-0-
Dep Madrid (Atocha-Apeadero)	-0-	-0-	8:30	-0-
Dep. Madrid (Chamartin)	7:55(1)	-0-	8:43	10:00(1)
Arr. Avila	9:37	10:30	10:29	11:42

Sights in Avila: There are bus and inexpensive taxi services from Avila's railstation to the city center, about one mile from the station. Take a stroll on the 1½-mile long 11th century walls that circle Avila to see best the 88 semi-circular towers and more than 2,300 battlements (11:00-13:00 and 16:15-18:00, closed weekday afternoons from October through April).

Also see the El Greco painting and the enormous (nearly 200 pounds) silver monstrance in the fortress Cathedral. The baroque 17th century Convent of St. Teresa. The Basilica of St. Vincent.

	422	422	422	420
Dep. Avila	13:39(1)	14:37(1)	15:37	18:42(1+3)
Arr. Madrid (Chamartin)	15:23	16:21	17:22	-0-
Arr. Madrid (Atocha-Apeadero)	-0-	-0-	17:37	-0-
Arr. Madrid (Norte)	-0-	-0-	-0-	20:09

(1)Reservation required. Supplement charged. Meal service or light refreshments. (2)Plus another departure from Madrid(Norte) at (#420) 9:40(1), arriving Avila at 11:26. (3)Plus other departures from Avila at (#420)19:30(1), (#422)19:48, (#418)20:03 and (#422)21:31.

Madrid - Burgos - Madrid

427

Dep. Madrid (Cham.)	9:20	12:10(1)	12:35
Arr. Burgos	13:43	15:59	16:26

Sights in Burgos: The many interesting chapels in the magnificent 13th century Cathedral of Santa Maria, where the remains are of Spain's greatest hero, El Cid, and those of his wife. The Archaeological Museum. Stroll 15 minutes on Paseo del Espolon, from the 14th century Arch of Santa Maria to the statue of El Cid.

To see the Royal Monastery of Las Huelgas, only a few minutes outside Burgos, take a bus from Plaza de Jose Antonio.

Dep. Burgos	17:35	18:37(2)
Arr. Madrid (Cham.)	22:18	21:52

(1)Runs from late June to late September. (2)Reservation required. Supplement charged. Meal service.

Madrid - Cuenca - Madrid 433

Dep. Madrid (Cham.)	9:00(1)	10:45(2)	Dep. Cuenca	14:52(2)	19:01(1)
Arr. Cuenca	11:40	14:42	Arr. Madrid (Cham.)	19:02	21:40

(1)Reservation required. Supplement charged. Light refreshments.
(2)Second-class only.

Sights in Cuenca: The old houses hanging from sheer cliffs in this 15th century setting. The best modern art museum in Spain, Museo de Arte Abstracto. Marvelous strolling down the winding lanes and narrow footpaths. Wonderful El Greco paintings and 15th and 16th century altarpieces in the cathedral. A few steps away from the Cathedral, the collection of coins, statues and Roman mosaics at the Archaeological Museum in a restored 14th century granary. Paleolithic red paintings of bison, wild boars, horses and archers at La Pena del Escrito National Monument. The Tourist Information Office at Calderon de la Barca 28 is only a 5-minute walk from the railstation.

Madrid - Escorial - Madrid

	420	422	422
Dep. Madrid (Norte)	8:15	-0-	-0-
Dep. Madrid (Atoche-Apeadero)	-0-	8:30	13:25
Dep. Madrid (Cham.)	-0-	8:43	13:39
Arr. Escorial	9:04	9:29	14:24

* * *

	420	422	422	422
Dep. Escorial	12:25	16:31	20:41	22:24
Arr. Madrid (Chamartin)	-0-	17:22	21:31	23:14
Arr. Madrid (Atocha-Apeadero)	-0-	17:37	21:46	23:29
Arr. Madrid (Norte)	13:15	-0-	-0-	-0-

Sights in Escorial: Burial place of Spanish kings and queens. The Royal Monastery of San Lorenzo del Escorial. This enormous granite fortress (300 rooms) has more than 1,600 paintings (many of the finest Velasquez and El Greco) and murals, and it houses the Charter Hall Royal Library, containing 60,000 volumes. See the Phillip II Apartments, the Basilica, the Throne Room, Apartments of the Bourbon kings, the Royal Pantheon, Whispering Hall and Casita del Principe. Don't miss seeing the famous cross by Benvenuto Cellini and paintings by El Greco, Ribera and Velasquez in the church.

Do not fail to see the circular, domed Royal Pantheon, crypt for most of the Spanish kings since the 17th century. Thirty feet underground, it contains 26 marble coffins, in 5 tiers, and is illuminated by Italian baroque candelabra.

In planning a visit here, keep in mind that this enormous 16th century building covers 8 acres. It is open 10:00-13:00 and 15:30-18:30 (18:00 in Winter).

Also visit the nearby monumental Valley of the Fallen, memorializing those who died in Spain's civil war. A 492-foot-high cross of concrete faced with stone marks this crypt. You can ride to the top of it in an elevator.

Madrid - Salamanca - Madrid

420

Dep. Madrid (Norte)	8:05	9:40(1)
Arr. Salamanca	12:41	13:09

Sights in Salamanca: The Convent of San Sebastian. The House of Shells. The 15th and 16th century houses around the beautiful Plaza Mayor. The oldest university in Spain. The church and cloister at St. Stephens Monastery.

Dep. Salamanca	15:35	17:39(1)
Arr. Madrid (Norte)	20:04	21:05

(1) Reservation required. Supplement charged. Meal service.

Madrid - Segovia - Madrid

Frequent departures can be made from Madrid's Chamartin, Atocha, Recoletos and Nuevos Ministerios railstations. A ticket is about $1.00 (U.S.). En route, you can see El Escorial, the enormous granite fortress, and also the gigantic cross that marks Franco's Spanish Civil War monument, the Valley of the Fallen.

419

Dep. Madrid (Atocha-Apea.)	7:05	8:35	10:05	11:05	12:39	
Dep. Madrid (Chamartin)	7:19	8:48	10:19	11:19	12:53	
Arr. Segovia	9:15	10:43	12:19	13:14	14:47	
	*	*	*			
Dep. Segovia	13:15	14:48	16:40	17:40	18:40	19:40(1)
Arr. Madrid (Chamartin)	14:59	16:32	18:29	19:26	20:27	21:36
Arr. Madrid (Atocha-Apea.)	12 minutes after arriving Chamartin					

(1) Plus another departure from Segovia at 21:24.

Sights in Segovia: The bus which meets the train goes uphill from the railstation to the main square, Plaza de Franco. Seen on the way is the half-mile long ancient Roman aqueduct, 7 stories high in some places.

A 40-minute stroll from the Plaza includes seeing San Martin Church along Calle de la Juderia Vieja (Old Ghetto), leading to the rear of the immense 16th century Cathedral and, from there, to Alcazar, Isabella's fairy-tale castle, next to the Eresma River.

Across the Eresma is Vera Cruz, where you will find the 13th Century Church of the Knights Templar and the 15th Century Parral Monastery.

Madrid - Toledo - Madrid

Seat reservations are not required or obtainable for this ride. Board well before departure time to avoid standing for 90 minutes. The walk from Toledo's railstation to the center of the city is long. It is best to take a bus or taxi.

438a

Dep. Madrid (Atocha)	8:11	9:15	10:00	12:16	14:10
Arr. Toledo	9:41	10:44	11:19	13:35	15:31

Sights in Toledo: The most spectacular Cathedral in Spain (750 stained-glass windows, priceless church clothing, jeweled ornaments, hundreds of tapestries, and paintings by Goya, El Greco, Velasquez, Tintoretto, Murillo and Titian). The house of El Greco, with a superb collection of his paintings. The 15th century Palace of the Duchess of Lerma. The Church of Santo Tome, containing El Greco's "Burial of the Count of Orgaz". The Sefardi Museum in the 14th century El Transito Synagogue. The Provincial Museum of Archaeology and Fine Arts in the 16th century Hospital de Santa Cruz. The Army Museum in the Alcazar (fortress).

The Museum of Santa Cruz. Cristo de la Luz, the church first built in the 11th century as a Mosque (on the site of the ruins of a Visigothic church). It was then converted into a Catholic church in the 12th century. The works of Spain's leading modern sculptor, in the Vitorio Macho Museum.

Dep. Toledo	11:55	13:36	14:25	16:25	18:25(1)
Arr. Madrid (Atocha)	13:20	15:00	15:50	17:50	19:55

(1) Plus other departures from Toledo at 20:05, 20:41 and 22:00.

Madrid - Valladolid - Madrid 422

Dep. Madrid (Atocha-Apeadero)	-0-	8:30	-0-
Dep. Madrid (Chamartin)	8:00(1)	8:43	10:00(2)
Arr. Valladolid	10:56	11:45	12:55

Sights in Valladolid: The National Museum of (Wood) Sculpture in San Gregorio College, founded in the 15th century by the confessor to Isabella. The adjacent Church of San Pablo. The Cathedral. Cervantes' House, where he spent the last years of his life. Simancas Castle, 7 miles from Valladolid. Charles V converted the castle into a storehouse for state records. It holds 8,000,000 documents that provide a history of Spanish administration from the 16th through the 20th century.

Dep. Valladolid	14:15	18:28	20:11
Arr. Madrid (Chamartin)	17:22	21:31	23:14
Arr. Madrid (Atocha-Apeadero)	15 minutes later		

(1) Reservation required. Supplement charged. Meal service or light refreshments. (2) Light refreshments.

Madrid - Zaragoza - Madrid

412

Dep. Madrid (Cham.)	8:35(1)	11:10(2)
Arr. Zaragoza	13:17	15:00

Dep. Zaragoza	18:29(2)
Arr. Madrid (Cham.)	22:08

(1) Light refreshments. (2) Reservation required. Supplement charged. Meal service.

Sights in Zaragoza: The Tapestry Museum in the Cathedral. The Exchange. Aljaferia, an 11th century Moorish palace. The Basilica de Pilar. The Goya and El Greco paintings at the Museo de Pintura.

San Sebastian - Bayonne - San Sebastian

422

Dep. San Sebastian (Amara)	7:40	9:14
Arr. Hendaye	8:15	9:50

Change trains.

136

Dep. Hendaye	8:50(1+2)	11:20(1+2+3)
Arr. Bayonne	9:31	12:01

Sights in Bayonne: The Cote Basque's leading port and private yacht harbor. The Cathedral. The Basque Museum. The Museum Bonnat. Chateau-Vieux.

136

Dep. Bayonne	11:35	13:19(4)	15:14(5)	15:58(2+6)
Arr. Irun	12:41	14:17	16:08	17:03

Change trains.

422

Dep. Irun	12:40	14:55(1)	16:30	17:50
Arr. San Sebastian (Amara)	30 minutes later			

(1) Reservation required. Supplement charged. (2) Light refreshments. (3) Runs from late May to late September. (4) Daily, except Sundays and holidays. (5) Meal service. (6) Plus other departures from Bayonne at 18:01 and 20:34(2).

San Sebastian - Bilbao - San Sebastian 417

Dep. San Sebastian (Amara)	7:00	11:35
Arr. Bilbao (Achuri)	10:16	14:54

Sights in Bilbao: The Fine Arts Museum. The Biscay Historical Museum. The Begona Sanctuary.

Dep. Bilbao (Achuri)	15:10	18:00
Arr. San Sebastian (Amara)	18:28	21:18

San Sebastian - Burgos - San Sebastian 422

Dep. San Sebastian (Norte)	8:48(1)	9:22	10:30(2)
Arr. Burgos	11:59	13:47	14:49

Sights in Burgos: The Cathedral of Santa Maria, with the remains of Spain's greatest hero, El Cid, and many interesting chapels. The Archaeological Museum. Santa Maria Arch. To see the Royal Monastery of Las Huelgas, only a few minutes outside Burgos, take a bus from the Plaza de Jose Antonio.

Dep. Burgos	16:05(2)	17:04	17:52(1+4)
Arr. San Sebastian (Norte)	19:58	20:49	21:04

(1) Reservation required. Supplement charged (2) Runs from late June to late September. (3) Meal service. (4) Plus other departures from Burgos at 18:27(1+3) and 21:47(1+3).

San Sebastian - Pamplona - San Sebastian 423

Dep. San Sebastian (Norte)	9:43(1)	Dep. Pamplona	17:15(1)
Arr. Pamplona	12:06	Arr. San Sebastian (Norte)	19:18

(1) Reservation required. Supplement charged. Meal service.

Sights in Pamplona: The 14th century Gothic Cathedral, with its cloisters and Diocesan Museum. The Navarre Museum. The running of the bulls through the city's streets, every year between July 6 and July 15.

Seville - Cadiz - Seville 416

Dep. Seville (S. Ber.)	7:05(1)	7:42(2)	9:08(3)	10:45(2)
Arr. Cadiz	9:30	9:48	10:42	12:35

Sights in Cadiz: The African environment. The Fine Arts Museum. The Museum of Archaeology and Art. The Cathedral, with its monumental Silver Tabernacle, decorated with almost 1,000,000 jewels. The Historical Museum.

Dep. Cadiz	13:45	15:10(2)	18:15(3)	18:30(2+4)
Arr. Seville (S. Ber.)	15:03	17:05	19:54	20:35

(1) Meal service. (2) Second-class only. (3) Reservation required. Supplement charged. (4) Plus other departures from Cadiz at 20:15(2) and 21:35(1).

Seville - Cordoba - Seville 416

Dep. Seville (P.A.)	6:42(1)	8:05(2)	8:10(1)	10:30(1)	10:54(3+4)
Arr. Cordoba	8:46	9:20	10:12	12:19	12:41

Sights in Cordoba: The array of marble, jasper, onyx and granite on the 80 marble columns in the 8th century Mosque, built on top of what was first a Roman temple and later a Catholic church, before the Moors seized Cordoba.

Following the recapture of the city by the Spaniards and in the conversion of the building to a church again, most of the original 1,000 marble columns were removed to provide space for a nave and a high altar.

Called "Mezquita", its interior is illuminated by 4,000 bronze and copper lamps. Its ceiling is carved cedar.

The 6:42 and 8:05 departures are preferable because the Mosque is closed from 12:00 to 16:00, and the Alcazar is closed from 12:00 to 17:00.

Also see the 14th century Synagogue. The Fine Arts Museum. The Museum of Julio Romero de Torres. The Museum of Cordoban art, with its Bullfight Museum. The Provincial Archaeological Museum, one of the most important archaeological collections in Spain. The Roman Bridge, built in the time of Emperor Augustus. The Alcazar.

Dep. Cordoba	13:57(2)	15:20(1)	17:14(4)	18:07(2)	18:30(1+5)
Arr. Seville (P.A.)	15:17	17:07	18:56(3)	19:26	20:26

(1) Second-class only. (2) Reservation required. Supplement charged. Meal service or light refreshments. (3) Departs/Arrives Seville's S. Bernardo station. (4) Light refreshments. (5) Plus other departures from Cordoba at 19:39(2+3) and 20:46(1).

Seville - Granada - Seville 439

Dep. Seville (S. Bernardo)	8:10(1)	Dep. Granada	17:45
Arr. Bobadilla	10:25	Arr. Bobadilla	19:32
Change trains.		Change trains.	
Dep. Bobadilla	10:40	Dep. Bobadilla	19:50(1)
Arr. Granada	12:31	Arr. Seville (S. Bernardo)	22:00

(1) Reservation required. Supplement charged.

Sights in Granada: The crypts of Ferdinand and Isabella in the Cathedral's Royal Chapel. The indescribable palace of The Alhambra (The Court of Myrtle Trees, Hall of Ambassadors, King's Chamber, Hall of Two Sisters, Court of Lions, the gardens, and the Towers). The Fine Arts Museum and Hispano-Moorish Museum in Charles V's Palace. The 14th century Generalife, Summer Palace of the Moorish caliphs. The Royal Hospital. The Moorish Baths. Casa Castril.

Seville - Jerez - Seville 416

Dep. Seville (S.B.)	7:05(1)	7:42(2)	9:08(3)	10:45(2)	14:05(2)
Arr. Jerez	8:30	9:06	10:03	11:52	16:14

Sights in Jerez: A 3,000-year old city, famous for its horses, beautiful women and sherry wine. Its renowned Andalusian horses, bred from Spanish mares and stallions which the Moorish invaders brought here more than 1,500 years ago, do not date as far back as the wine does.

Phoenicians started the vineyards here in 1100 B.C. Later Romans began the vinting of sherry. Many of the best wineries offer tours that conclude with tasting.

See the annual September Wine Festival. Its opening ceremony takes place on the steps that lead into the 17th century Collegiate Church of Santa Maria. Next to it is the 11th century Moorish fort, the Alcazar. Also visit the 15th century San Dionisio Church. See the exhibit of Punic, Roman and Arabic pottery, tombstones, household implements and statues in the Archaeological Museum that occupies 2 small rooms inside Chapter House on tiny Plaza de la Asuncion, across from San Dionisio Church. Look for the 7th century BC Corinthian helmet, believed to be the oldest Greek artifact ever found in Spain.

Dep. Jerez	14:25(2)	15:53(2)	18:50(3)	21:08(2)	22:32(1)
Arr. Seville (S.B.)	15:36	17:05	19:51	22:35	23:50

(1) Meal service. (2) Second-class only. (3) Reservation required. Supplement charged.

Seville - Merida 448

Dep. Seville (P.A.)	7:30(1)	Dep. Merida	16:28(2)	18:15(2)
Arr. Merida	11:06	Arr. Seville (P.A.)	21:24	22:05

(1) Reservation required. Supplement charged. (2) Second-class only.

Sights in Merida: During the 400 years this city was ruled by Romans, the population was 100,000—nearly 3 times today's population. Come here to see the 2,000-year old antiquities. The longest bridge ever built by Romans (82 arches, more than half a mile long), Puente Romano. The mosaic floors in the restored, large 9th century fort. covering 2 city blocks. The 6,000-seat theater (where plays are still performed) and 14,000-seat amphitheater. Trojan's Arch. The Temple of Diana.

The collection of statues, coins, tombstones, pottery and tools at the Archaeological Museum in the 17th century Santa Clara Church.

Seville - Malaga (via Cordoba) - Seville 416

Dep. Seville (P.A.)	6:42(1)	Dep. Malaga	14:50(3)	17:10(2)
Arr. Cordoba	8:46	Arr. Cordoba	17:04	20:48
Change trains.		Change trains.		
Dep. Cordoba	9:02(2)	Dep. Cordoba	18:30(1)	20:52(1)
Arr. Malaga	12:34	Arr. Seville (P.A.)	20:26	22:48

(1)Second-class only. (2)Light refreshments. (3)Reservation required. Supplement charged.

Sights in Malaga: Winter sun. The 9th century Alcazaba Moslem palace and the ruins of Gibralfaro Castle, 2 fortresses which made Malaga a major stronghold in the Middle Ages. The Fine Arts Museum. Sagrario, an unusual rectangular church that was originally a mosque. The Cathedral.

The second route from Seville to Malaga follows:

Seville - Malaga (via Bobadilla) - Seville 439

Dep. Seville (S. Bernardo)	8:10(1)	
Arr. Bobadilla	10:25	
Change trains.		
Dep. Bobadilla	10:32	
Arr. Malaga	11:28	
* * *		
Dep. Malaga	13:47(2)	18:35(2)
Arr. Bobadilla	15:07	19:34
Change trains.		
Dep. Bobadilla	15:23(2)	19:49(1)
Arr. Seville (S. Bernardo)	18:35	22:05

(1)Reservation required. Supplement charged. (2)Second-class only.

Seville - Torremolinos - Seville 439

Dep. Seville (S.B.) 8:10(1) See "Seville-Malaga" schedule above.
Arr. Malaga 11:28
(1)Reservation required. Supplement charged.

Change to electric train (Malaga-Fuengirola). 435

Dep. Malaga Every 30 minutes from 6:00 to 22:30
Arr. Torremolinos 25 minutes later

Sights in Torremolinos: Characters from all over the world, on and around this resort's 5-mile beach.

Dep. Torremolinos Every 30 minutes from 7:29 to 23:59
Arr. Malaga 25 minutes later

Change trains. 439

Dep. Malaga See preceding "Seville-Malaga-Seville" schedules.
Arr. Seville 4-5 hours later

Tarragona - Tortosa - Tarragona 425

Dep. Tarragona	7:26(1)	8:19(2+3)	10:41(1)	11:33(2+4)
Arr. Tortosa	8:41	9:04	11:37	12:35

Sights in Tortosa: St. Louis College, founded in 1554 by Charles V for Moors converting to Christianity. The Cathedral. The Bishop's Palace.

Dep. Tortosa	14:47(2+3)	16:20(2+4)	18:14(2+3)	20:26(1)
Arr. Tarragona	15:37	17:21	19:00	21:19

(1) Second-class only. (2) Reservation required. Supplement charged. (3) Meal service. (4) Runs from late May to late September.

Valencia - Alicante - Valencia 426

Dep. Valencia (Ter.)	7:00(1)	8:40(2)	Dep. Alicante (Ter.)	17:01(2)	19:50(1)
Arr. Alicante (Ter.)	9:58	11:28	Arr. Valencia (Ter.)	19:55	23:00

(1) Light refreshments. (2) Reservation required. Supplement charged. Light refreshments.

Sights in Alicante: The avenue lined with date palms, part of the complete African atmosphere. The huge Moorish castle. Take the 26-mile bus trip to Elche to see the only palm forest in Europe.

Valencia - Cuenca - Valencia 433

Dep. Valencia (Ter.)	8:34(1)	Dep. Cuenca	15:02	17:57(1)
Arr. Cuenca	11:39	Arr. Valenica (Ter.)	19:16	20:44

(1) Reservation required. Supplement charged. Light refreshments.

Sights in Cuenca: See notes about city-sightseeing in Cuenca earlier in this section, under "Madrid-Cuenca".

Valencia - Murcia - Valencia 426

Dep. Valencia (Ter.)	8:35(1)	Dep. Murcia	15:55(1)
Arr. Murcia	12:45	Arr. Valencia (Ter.)	20:04

(1) Reservation required. Supplement charged. Light refreshments.

Sights in Murcia: The Moorish granary. The 14th century Gothic-Romanesque Cathedral. Glass, pottery and leather factories.

Valencia - Tarragona - Valencia 425

Dep. Valencia (Ter.)	5:43(1)	6:04(1)	8:15(1)	9:25(2)
Arr. Tarragona	9:58	10:26	12:49	12:58

Sights in Tarragona: See notes about sightseeing in Tarragona earlier in this chapter, under "Barcelona-Tarragona".

Dep. Tarragona	13:18(2)	16:56(1)	18:12(2)	18:19(1)	21:58(1)
Arr. Valencia (Ter.)	16:28	21:26	21:43	22:23	2:11

(1) Light refreshments. (2) Reservation required. Supplement charged. Meal service or light refreshments.

SCENIC RAIL TRIPS

Here are 11 exceptionally scenic rail trips.

Barcelona - Massanet - Blanes - Barcelona

Fine coastline and mountain scenery on this easy one-day circle excursion from Barcelona.

424

(Via Granollers)				
Dep. Barcelona (Ter.)	7:45(1)	8:46(1+2+3)	10:31(1)	13:05(4)
Arr. Massanet	8:34	9:53	11:22	14:08
	*	*	*	
(Via Mataro)				
Dep. Massanet	9:57	12:53	13:53	14:53(5)
Arr. Blanes	10:12	13:08	14:08	15:08
Arr. Barcelona (Ter.)	11:36	14:20	15:20	16:36

(1)Reservation required. Supplement charged. (2)Departs from Barcelona's Paseo de Gracia railstation. (3)Meal service. (4)Second-class only. (5)Plus other departures from Massanet at 16:53, 17:53, 19:53 and 21:27.

Barcelona - Madrid 412

Many ancient towns, castles, mountains and gorges to see on this route.

Dep. Barcelona (Ter.)	-0-	10:25(2)	14:15(2+6)	-0-
Dep. Barcelona (P. de G.)	-0-	10:33(2)	14:23(2+7)	-0-
Dep. Barcelona (Sants)	8:20(1)	10:41(2)	14:30(2)	19:40(3+8)
Arr. Madrid (Cham.)	18:25	19:17	22:08	7:48

(1)Light refreshments. (2)Reservation required. Supplement charged. Meal service. (3)Has couchettes. Light refreshments. (4)Carries sleeping cars (some air-conditiond). Also has couchettes. (5)Carries sleeping car. Also has couchettes. (6)Plus another departure from Termino station at 22:00(2+4). (7)Plus another departure from Paseo de Gracia station at 22:10(2+4) and 22:20(2+5). (8)Plus other departures from Sants station at 22:19(2+4) and 22:29(2+5).

Barcelona - Puigcerda 428 + 147

There is beautiful Pyrenees mountain scenery on this portion of the Barcelona-Toulouse route. As shown below, this trip also can be made as a one-day excursion from Barcelona.

Dep. Barcelona (Sants)	9:26	13:51		
Dep. Barcelona (P. de Cat.)	9:32	13:57		
Arr. Puigcerda	13:08	17:12		
Arr. La Tour-de-Carol	13:15	17:19		
Change trains.				
Dep. La Tour-de-Carol	13:46	17:20(1)	17:45(2)	19:05(1)
Arr. Toulouse	16:40	20:40	20:48	22:17

(1) Runs from late June to early September. (2) Runs from early September to late June. Operates daily, except Sundays and holidays.

The easy one-day excursion follows:

Dep. Barcelona (Sants)	5:51	6:39	-0-	9:26	11:56
Dep. Barcelona (P. Cat.)	5:57	6:44	7:05(1)	9:32	12:01
Arr. Puigcerda	9:47	10:19	12:07	13:08	15:58
	*	*	*		
Dep. Puigcerda	12:15	13:52	14:10	16:45	18:24
Arr. Barcelona (P. Cat.)	15:34	17:21	18:45(1)	20:35	22:08
Arr. Barcelona (Cent.)	15:41	17:28	-0-	20:43	22:15

(1) Barcelona's Termino railstation.

Barcelona - Tarragona

This trip is noted for excellent scenery along the Mediterranean coastline. City-sightseeing notes for both Barcelona and Tarragona appear earlier in this section. Complete schedules can be found under one-day excursions.

Cordoba - Malaga - Cordoba 416

Scenic gorges can be seen on this trip, an easy one-day excursion from Cordoba. See notes earlier in this section (under Seville-Cordoba-Seville excursion) for city sightseeing in Cordoba.

Dep. Cordoba	8:10(1)	9:02
Arr. Malaga	11:28	12:34

Sights in Malaga: The 9th century Alcazaba Moslem palace and the ruins of Gibralfaro Castle, 2 fortresses which made Malaga a major stronghold in the Middle Ages. The Fine Arts Museum. Sagrario, an unusual rectangular church that was originally a mosque. The Cathedral.

Dep. Malaga	14:50(1+2)	17:10(3)	18:25	22:00(1+2)
Arr. Cordoba	17:04	20:48	22:00	1:22

(1) Reservation required. Supplement charged. (2) Meal service. (3) Light refreshments.

Granada - Moreda - Almeria - Granada

Excellent mountain scenery on this trip.

426		441			
Dep. Granada	9:50(1)	Dep. Almeria	6:10(2)	11:25	13:45(1)
Arr. Moreda	11:09	Arr. Moreda	8:46	14:02	15:28
Change trains.		Change trains.			
441		426			
Dep. Moreda	15:39	Dep. Moreda	8:54(2)	16:52(3)	17:31(1)
Arr. Almeria	18:00	Arr. Granada	10:18	18:20	18:52

(1) Reservation required. Supplement charged. Light refreshments. (2) Second-class only. (3) Light refreshments.

Leon - Oviedo - Leon

Very good mountain scenery. Sights in Leon: The stained-glass windows in the Cathedral and the 11th century Church of San Isidoro.

418				
Dep. Leon	6:55(2)	15:04(1)		
Arr. Oviedo	10:06	17:34		
		*	*	*
Dep. Oviedo	12:38(2)	14:45(1)	16:20(2)	19:11(2)
Arr. Leon	15:41	17:07	19:54	22:25

(1) Reservation required. Supplement charged. Meal service. (2) Second-class only.

The best daytime connections between Madrid and Leon are:

418				
Dep. Madrid (Chamartin)	8:44(1)	10:00(2)	Dep. Leon	17:09(2)
Arr. Leon	13:48	15:04	Arr. Madrid (Chamartin)	21:37

(1) Reservation required. Supplement charged. Meal service. (2) Second-class only.

Leon - Monforte - Vigo

The Leon-Monforte portion of this route is recommended for mountain scenery and can be made as an easy one-day roundtrip, as this schedule indicates.

421					
Dep. Leon	7:41(1)	8:30(2)	Dep. Vigo	9:25(3)	13:05(1)
Arr. Monforte	11:33	12:56	Arr. Monforte	12:03	16:15
Dep. Monforte	12:04	14:40	Dep. Monforte	12:07	16:30
Arr. Vigo	15:25	18:23	Arr. Leon	15:34	20:49

(1) Light refreshments. (2) Change trains at Monforte. (3) Reservation required. Supplement charged. Meal service.

Vigo - Santiago de Compostela - Vigo

A worthwhile extension of the Leon-Vigo scenic trip is to continue on from Vigo to Santiago de Compostela.

For detailed notes on the marvelous attraction in Santiago de Compostela, please refer to the "Madrid-Santiago" schedule, later in this section, under "The Madrid Routes".

413

Dep. Vigo	7:00	8:57	12:25	13:55	15:40	18:10(1)	19:55
Arr. Santiago	2 hours later						
		*	*	*			
Dep. Santiago	7:50	10:13	11:04(1)	11:35	16:10	18:57	20:30
Arr. Vigo	2 hours later						

(1) Reservation required. Supplement charged.

Lisbon - Porto - Vigo **Vigo - Porto - Lisbon**

We recommend breaking this trip by staying overnight in Porto.

445

Dep. Lisbon (S. Apol.)	7:25(1)	8:25(1)	8:55(2)	11:00(1+5)
Arr. Porto (Campanha)	10:25	11:45	13:00	14:00

Change trains.

447a

Dep. Porto (Campanha)	7:37	14:08	18:09
Set your watch forward one hour.			
Arr. Vigo	13:30	19:21	23:13

Sights in Porto: See notes about sightseeing in Porto earlier in this section, under the "Lisbon-Porto" one-day excursion.

447a

Dep. Vigo	7:20	13:50	20:25
Set your watch back one hour.			
Arr. Porto (Campanha)	10:35	16:51	23:55

Change trains.

445

Dep. Porto (Campanha)	11:50(2)	0:25(4)	7:15(1)	8:15(1+6)
Arr. Lisbon (S. Apol.)	16:10	6:50	10:15	11:35

(1) First-class only. Reservation required. Supplement charged. Meal service or light refreshments. (2) Light refreshments. (3) Meal service. (4) Carries sleeping car. Light refreshments. Trip takes 6-6½ hours. (5) Plus other departures from Lisbon at 11:35(3), 14:25(1), 15:30, 17:00(1), 19:00(2), 20:15(1), 21:15(1) and 0:25(4). (6) Plus other departures from Porto at 9:25(2), 11:00(1), 14:35(1), 15:30, 17:00(1), 18:45(3), 20:15(1) and 21:15(1).

Madrid - Barcelona

Many ancient towns, castles, mountains and gorges to see on this route.

412

Dep. Madrid (Cham.)	8:35(1)	11:10(2+3)	14:35(2+3+6)
Arr. Barcelona (Sants)	18:46	19:42	22:13
Arr. Barcelona (P. de G.)	-0-	19:50	22:21
Arr. Barcelona (Ter.)	-0-	20:00	22:30

(1)Light refreshments. (2)Supplement charged. Reservation required. (3)Meal service. (4)Has couchettes. (5)Carries sleeping car. Also has couchettes. (6)Plus other departures from Madrid at 20:10(1+4), 21:40(2+3+5) and 22:40(2+5).

Porto - Regua

Good river scenery on this easy one-day roundtrip.

447

Dep. Porto (S. Bento)	7:45	10:45	14:10
Dep. Porto (Campanha)	8:00	10:55	14:24
Arr. Regua	10:09	13:07	16:48
	*	*	*
Dep. Regua	11:15	16:05	21:11
Arr. Porto (Campanha)	13:20	18:21	23:24
Arr. Porto (S. Bento)	13:30	18:38	23:32

Santander - Palencia

This trip offers fine mountain views crossing the Cordillera Cantabrica. Santander's seashore is a major Summer resort.

419

Dep. Santander	7:58	14:55(1)	Dep. Palencia	12:30	16:24(2)
Arr. Palencia	12:08	17:47	Arr. Santander	16:19	20:22

(1)Reservation required. Supplement charged. Light refreshments. (2)Plus another departure from Palencia at 18:58(1).

THE MAJORCA ONE-DAY RAIL TRIP

This narrow-gauge, easy one-day trip goes through olive groves before tunneling through a mountain and emerging high above Soller. At the tunnel exit, the train stops for 10 minutes to allow passengers to enjoy the view before the train spirals downhill to Soller. A quaint tram makes the short ride from Soller to the seaside Puerto de Soller.

Palma - Soller	437				
Dep. Palma	8:00	10:40	13:00	15:15	
Arr. Soller	55 minutes later				
	*	*	*		
Dep. Soller	9:15	11:50	14:10	18:20	21:00(1)
Arr. Palma	55 minutes later				

(1)Sundays only.

THE TRIP TO ANDORRA

La Tour-de-Carol to Sant Julia de Loria

428			
Dep. Barcelona (P. Cat.)		9:26(1)	13:51(1)
Arr. La Tour-de-Carol		13:15	17:19
Change to bus. 192			
Dep. La Tour-de-Carol		13:30(2)	17:45(3)
Arr. Andorra la Vella		15:30	20:00
Arr. Sant Julia de Loria		15:45	20:20
	*	*	*
Dep. Sant Julia de Loria	7:00(4)	8:00(2)	13:45(3)
Dep. Andorra la Vella	7:15(4)	8:15(2)	14:00(3)
Arr. La Tour-de-Carol	10:00	10:55	17:10
Change to train.			
428			
Dep. La Tour-de-Carol	-0-	13:45(1)	18:20(1)
Arr. Barcelona (P. Cat.)	-0-	17:29	22:20

(1)All year. (2)Runs from December 1 to March 1. (3)Runs from July 1 to September 30. (4)Runs from April 1 to November 30, weather permitting.

THE MADRID ROUTES

Madrid is the hub of the Iberian Peninsula, with spokes going from it to the major cities of Spain and Portugal: Barcelona, Bilbao, Cordoba, Lisbon, San Sebastian, Santiago de Compostela, Seville and Valencia.

Where city sightseeing notes are not indicated in the following schedules, they can be found at the beginning of this section.

Here are the schedules for reaching those cities from Madrid:

Madrid - Barcelona

Covered under the description of scenic trips, earlier in this section.

Madrid - Bilbao

422

Dep. Madrid (Cham.)	7:55(1)	10:00(1+2)	12:35(3+6)
Arr. Miranda de Ebro	13:16	15:18(2)	18:14
Change trains.			
Dep. Miranda de Ebro	13:30	15:21(1)	18:35
Arr. Bilbao (Norte)	15:23	16:56	20:38

Sights in Bilbao: This is the largest Basque city. A major port and industrial city.

Dep. Bilbao (Norte)	8:00(1+2)	10:15	15:43(1+2+7)
Arr. Miranda de Ebro	9:43(2)	12:04	17:17(2)
Change trains.			
Dep. Miranda de Ebro	9:55(1)	12:25(3)	17:32(1)
Arr. Madrid (Cham.)	15:13	17:48	21:58

(1)Reservation required. Supplement charged. Meal service. (2)Direct train. No change in Miranda. (3)Meal service. (4)Reservation required. Supplement charged. Carries air-conditioned sleeping car. Also has couchettes. (5)Adjustment footnote. (6)Plus other departures from Madrid at 15:15(1+2), 22:35(4) and 23:35(2+4). (7)Plus another departure from Bilbao at 22:50(2+4).

Madrid - Lisbon

448

Dep. Madrid (Atocha)	10:15(1+2)	23:05(1+3)
Set your watch back one hour.		
Arr. Lisbon (S. Apolonia)	19:05	9:35

* * *

Dep. Lisbon (S. Apolonia)	7:30(1+2)	21:00(1+3)
Set your watch forward one hour.		
Arr. Madrid (Atocha)	18:38	9:00

(1) Reservation required. Supplement charged. (2) Meal service. (3) Carries air-conditioned sleeping car. Also has couchettes. Light refreshments.

Madrid - San Sebastian 422

Dep. Madrid (Cham.)	8:00(1+2)	12:10(3)	12:30(2)	15:20(1+2+6)
Arr. San Sebastian	15:39	19:58	20:44	21:33

* * *

Dep. San Sebastian	8:48(1)	9:22(2)	10:30(3)	15:13(1+2+7)
Arr. Madrid (Cham.)	16:29	17:48	19:03	21:58

(1) Reservation required. Supplement charged. (2) Meal service. (3) Runs from late June to late September. (4) Carries air-conditioned sleeping car. (5) Has couchettes. (6) Plus other departures from Madrid at 18:08(1+2), 22:05(4+5) and 22:35(4+5). (7) Plus other departures from San Sebastian at 22:42(4+5), 23:02(4+5) and 2:19(1+2+5).

Madrid - Santiago de Compostela

There is a good circle trip: Madrid-Santiago-Vigo-Porto-Lisbon-Madrid.

420

Dep. Madrid (Norte)	12:45(1)	21:25(2)
Arr. Santiago	21:06	7:57

Dep. Santiago	11:39(1)	22:47(2)
Arr. Madrid (Norte)	20:09	9:21

(1) Reservation required. Supplement charged. Meal service. (2) Carries air-conditioned sleeping car. Also has couchettes. Meal service.

Sights in Santiago de Compostela: One of the 3 most sacred places in Christendom, ranking equally with Jerusalem and Rome since 812. It is believed that this is the repository of St. James (Santiago), a cousin of Jesus, son of Mary's sister, and the first follower of Jesus to attain martyrdom.

After witnessing the crucifixion, James came to Spain in 44, converted 9 Iberians to Christianity, was visited at Zaragoza by the Virgin Mary, returned to the Holy Land, and was beheaded there by King Herod Agrippa.

The legend which has generated the pilgrimage to Santiago de Compostela for the past 1100 years is that, after the decapitation in Jerusalem, his body was disinterred and found to have the head intact. The body was brought to Spain's West Coast in A.D. 44.

Eight centuries later, a hermit saw a bright star (stela) over a vacant field (compo). Excavations were conducted, and the remains of James were found. Since that event, pilgrims have come to this shrine by horse and in vehicles, as well as on foot (from as far as Scandinavia) to pray and meditate here.

You would stop here to see the majestic Cathedral built in the 12th century.

See its beautiful Baroque sculptured Obradoire facade. The carved Romanesque 12th century Door of Glory. Touch the grooves left in the central pillar by the fingers of millions of pilgrims over the centuries.

Visit the Archaeological Museum in its basement, the art pieces in its Treasury, the collection of tapestries with designs by Goya and Rubens in the many halls of the Cathedral's Tapestry Museum.

Also see the gigantic 6-foot tall, 118-pound brass censer in the Library of the Cathedral.

In the early pilgrimage years, it was difficult for priests to tolerate the odor of worshippers from afar who had gone unbathed for weeks and months. The censer here is called Botafumeiro (smoke-thrower).

A custom that originated in the early days of pilgrimages here is perpetuated today. On feast days, this censer is brought into the Cathedral, filled with incense, hung by ropes from the dome 104 feet above the floor, and swung in an arc, barely passing over the heads of people standing in the Cathedral.

It is easy to explore Santiago de Compostela on foot. See the marvelous view of the town from Alameda Park. Santa Maria del Sar, one of the more than 40 churches here, is a splendid example of 12th century Romanesque architecture.

Madrid - Seville 416

Dep. Madrid (Atocha)	8:45(1)	9:45(2)	14:30(1+7)
Arr. Seville (P. de Armas)	15:17	-0-	-0-
Arr. Seville (S. Ber.)	-0-	18:56	20.55
*	*	*	
Dep. Seville (S. Ber.)	-0-	10:54(2)	15:12(1+8)
Dep. Seville (P. de Armas)	8:05(1)	-0-	-0-
Arr. Madrid (Atocha)	14:42	21:03	21:42

(1)Reservation required. Supplement charged. Meal service or light refreshments. (2)Light refreshments. (3)Carries air-conditioned sleeping car. Also has couchettes. (4)Meal service. (5)Departs from Seville's Plaza de Armas station. (6)Departs from Seville's San Bernardo station. (7)Plus other departures from Madrid at 21:20(3+4) and 23:00(3). (8)Plus other departures from Seville at 23:00(3+5)and 24:00(3+4+6).

Madrid - Valencia 438

Dep. Madrid (Chamartin)	7:00(1)	12:00(2)	16:30(1+5)
Dep. Madrid (Atocha)	7:11(1)	12:11(2)	16:41(1+6)
Arr. Valencia (Ter.)	11:47	16:47	21:17

* * *

Dep. Valencia (Ter.)	6:00(1)	12:00(2)	16:30(1+7)
Arr. Madrid (Atocha)	10:38	16:38	21:08
Arr. Madrid (Chamartin)	11 minutes later		

(1)Supplement charged. Light refreshments. (2)Reservation required. Supplement charged that includes meal. (3)Carries air-conditioned sleeping car. Also has couchettes. (4)Arrives only at Madrid's Chamartin station. (5)Plus other departures from Madrid Chamartin at 18:30(2) and 23:00(3). (6)Plus another departure from Madrid Atocha at 18:41(2). (7)Plus other departures from Valencia at 18:30(2) and 23:00(3+4).

Barcelona - Valencia
425

Dep. Barcelona (Termino)	7:00(1)	9:15(2+9)	-0-
Dep. Barcelona (P. de G.)	7:08(1)	9:23(2)	10:09(3+10)
Dep. Barcelona (Sants)	7:14(1)	9:30(2)	10:17(3+11)
Arr. Valencia (Termino)	11:05	13:55	15:13

* * *

Dep. Valencia (Termino)	1:28(5)	5:43(4)	6:04(4+12)
Arr. Barcelona (Sants)	7:43	11:41	12:17
Arr. Barcelona (P. de G.)	-0-	-0-	-0-
Arr. Barcelona (Termino)	-0-	-0-	-0-

(1)Reservation required. Supplement charged. Meal service or light refreshments. (2)Scond-class only. (3)Runs from late May to late September. (4)Light refreshments. (5)Has couchettes. (6)Arrives at Barcelona's Sants, Paseo de Gracia and Termino stations. (7)Arrives at only Barcelona's Sants station. (8)Arrives at Barcelona's Sants and Paseo de Gracia stations. (9)Plus other departures from Barcelona (Termino)at 11:10(2). (10)Plus another departure from Barcelona Paseo de Gracia at 11:58(1). (11)Plus other departures from Barcelona Sants at 12:07(1), 15:15(4), 16:43(4), 16:59(1), 20:10(4+5) and 21:40(5). (12)Plus other departures from Valencia at 7:10(2+6), 8:15(4+7), 9:25(1+4+7), 12:30(1+8), 13:40(1+3+8), 16:14(1+6) and 18:15(2+6).

INTERNATIONAL ROUTES FROM PORTUGAL

The route to southern Spain is Lisbon-Seville.

The 2 routes to France and beyond are Lisbon-Madrid (covered in the preceding section under "The Madrid Routes" and Lisbon-Hendaye on the "Sud Express' which goes north of Madrid, via Pampilhosa and Medina del Campo.

Lisbon - Seville 448

Dep. Lisbon (S. Apol.)	7:35	0:10	-0-
Arr. Badajoz	13:40	6:45	-0-
Set your watch forward one hour.			
Change trains.			
Dep. Badajoz	15:35(1)	7:30(2)	9:15(1)
Arr. Seville (P.A.)	21:28	12:17	16:25

(1)Second-class only. (2)Supplement charged. Reservation required.

Lisbon - Hendaye - Bordeaux - Paris 28

Dep. Lisbon (S. Apol.)	16:20(1)
Dep. Vilar Formoso	23:02
Set your watch forward. one hour.	
Arr. Salamanca	4:06
Arr. San Sebastian	11:32
Arr. Irun	11:58
Arr. Hendaye	12:17
Arr. Bayonne	14:18
Arr. Bordeaux	16:00
Arr. Paris (Austerlitz)	20:54

(1)Reservation required. Supplement charged. Carries sleeping car to Hendaye. Has couchettes from Lisbon to Paris. Meal service Lisbon-Hendaye. The 80-minute stop in Hendaye is for changing the bogies on the couchette cars to conform with the narrower track in France. Departs 2 hours earlier from late September to late May.

INTERNATIONAL ROUTES FROM SPAIN

Reservations for travel from Spain to other countries on night trains are complex, taking often as long as one month to obtain. Normally, day trains are not such a problem. When traveling by train from another country to Spain, if you want to travel later from Spain back into France and/or beyond France, it is advisable to book the trip out of Spain before you enter Spain.

If this is not possible, then we suggest that immediately after you clear Spanish customs (leaving France) that you go as soon as possible to the reservation booth in the Spanish arrival city to reserve space for your train trip back into France.

The Spanish gateway for rail travel to London, Paris, Brussels and Amsterdam is Madrid. (Notes on the route to London, via Paris, appear in Chapter 8).

From Barcelona, there is rail service to southwestern France (via Toulouse) and to southeastern France (Avignon, Marseille and Nice), from where there are connections to Italy, Austria and Switzerland (and on to Germany and Denmark).

Seville - Lisbon 448

Dep. Seville (P.A.)	8:15(1)	Dep. Badajoz	19:25
Arr. Badajoz	15:05	Arr. Entroncamento	21:59
Set your watch back one hour.		Change trains.	
Change trains.		Dep. Entroncamento	22:23
		Arr. Lisbon (S. Apol.)	23:35

(1) Second-class only. Reservation required and supplement charged from Merida to Badajoz.

Madrid - Lisbon

Schedules for this trip appear earlier in this section, under "The Madrid Routes".

Madrid - Paris 422

Dep. Madrid (Cham.)	8:00(1+2)	12:35(1+3)	15:15(1+2+7)
Arr. Paris (Aust.)	23:40	7:51	7:15

(1) Direct train to Paris. No train change in Hendaye. (2) Reservation required. Supplement charged. Meal service. (3) Meal service. Has couchettes. (4) Inclusive ticket covers sleeping facility (sleeping car or couchette). (5) Change trains in Hendaye. (6) Carries air-conditioned sleeping car. Also has couchettes. (7) Plus other departures from Madrid at 18:08(1+2+3), 19:40(1+2+4), 22:05(5+6) and 22:35(5+6).

Barcelona - Toulouse - Paris 428 + 147 + 138

Dep. Barcelona (Sants)	9:26(1)	13:51(1)	-0-
Dep. Barcelona (P. Cat.)	9:32(1)	13:57(1)	-0-
Arr. La Tour-de-Carol	13:15	17:15	-0-
Change trains.			
Dep. La Tour-de-Carol	13:46	17:45(3+4+5)	19:05(3+5+6)
Arr. Toulouse (Mat.)	16:40	20:48(3)	22:17(3)
Change trains.			
Dep. Toulouse (Mat.)	17:44(2)	21:43(4+5)	22:48(5+6)
Arr. Paris (Aust.)	23:52	6:28	6:45

(1) Second-class only. (2) Daily. Reservation required. Supplement charged except on Saturday. Meal service. (3) Direct train to Paris. No train change in Toulouse. (4) Daily, except Sunday. Operates from early September to late June. (5) Has couchettes. (6) Daily from late June to early September. Runs Sundays all year.

Barcelona - Avignon - Geneva 11a

This train requires reservation, charges a supplement, is air-conditioned and has meal service.

Dep. Barcelona (Ter.)	10:02	Dep. Avignon	15:29
Arr. Avignon	15:27	Arr. Geneva (Corn.)	19:44

Barcelona - Narbonne - Avignon - Marseille - Nice - Genoa - Rome

	11a	162	424
Dep. Barcelona (Ter.)	10:02(1)	15:00	19:00
Arr. Cerbere	12:30(1)	18:06	21:40
Change trains.			
	11a	162	162
Dep. Cerbere	12:35(1)	18:45(3)	23:40(4+5)
Arr. Narbonne	13:36(1)	20:02(3)	1:20(4)
Change trains.			
	11a	162	78
Dep. Narbonne	13:38(1)	20:19(3)	1:53(4+5)
Arr. Avignon	15:27	22:32(3)	-0-
Change trains.			
	151	151	78
Dep. Avignon	16:08	22:47(3)	-0-
Arr. Marseille (St. Ch.)	17:14	23:51	4:55(4)
Change trains.			
Dep. Marseille (St. Ch.)	17:25(2)	-0-	5.22(4+5)
Arr. Nice	20:09	-0-	8:05(4)
	151		78
Dep. Nice	20:27	-0-	8:20(4+6)
Arr. Genoa (P.P.)	0:20	-0-	12:37(4+6)
Arr. Rome (Ter.)	-0-	-0-	20:05

(1) Direct train to Avignon. Reservation required. Supplement charged. Meal service. Air-conditioned. (2) Meal service Marseille-Nice. (3) Direct train to Marseille. Meal service. (4) Direct train to Rome. (5) Carries sleeping car. Also has couchettes. (6) Meal service.

REPUBLIC OF IRELAND

SUMMER TIME

Ireland changes to Summer Time on the last Sunday of March and converts back to Standard Time on the last Sunday of October.

EURAILPASS BONUSES IN IRELAND

Ferry crossings between Rosslare (Ireland) and Le Havre (France) 21 hours, or Cherbourg (France) 17 hours. Neither port taxes nor cabin accommodations are covered by Eurailpass or Eurail Youthpass.

IRISH TRAIN PASSES

Rambler Pass Unlimited travel in the Irish Republic. Sold at rail and bus stations throughout Ireland and also at CIE Tours, 590 Fifth Ave., New York, N.Y. 10036. The 1983 prices for only rail *or* bus are: 8 days £40, 15 days £58. For both rail *and* bus: 8 days £50, 15 days £72. Children under 16 pay half-fare.

Youth Rambler Pass Available to persons 14-26 years old. Must be purchased from CIE Tours before arriving in Ireland. Covers *both* rail and bus travel. The 1982 prices were: 8 days $65(U.S.), 15 days $87, 30 days $113.

Overlander Pass Covers train and bus travel to Northern Ireland as well as in the Irish Republic. Sold only in Ireland, at the CIE offices in Dublin and Limerick City. The 1983 prices: 15 days £82. Children under 15 pay half-fare.

ONE-DAY EXCURSIONS AND CITY SIGHTSEEING

Here are 5 one-day rail trips that can be made comfortably from Belfast, Cork, Dublin, Galway and Limerick, returning to them in most cases before dinnertime. Notes are provided on what to see at each destination. The number below the name of each route is the Cook's timetable.

Dublin - Belfast 613

Dep. Dublin (Con.)	8:00(1+2)	10:30(3)	11:00(1+2)	13:00(1+5)
Arr. Belfast (Cent.)	10:20	12:50	13:10	15:20

* * *

Dep. Belfast (Cent.)	8:00(1+2)	10:15(2+3)	11:00(1+2)	15:00(1+2+6)
Arr. Dublin (Con.)	10:10	12:40	13:15	17:15

(1)Daily, except Sundays and holidays. (2)Meal service. (3)Sundays and holidays only. Light refreshments. (4)Daily. (5)Plus other departures from Dublin at 15:00(1+2), 18:10(2+4) and 20:00(1). (6)Plus other departures from Belfast at 17:10(1) and 18:00(2+4).

Sights in **Dublin:** Capital of the Irish Republic. See the outstanding Bronze Age gold ornaments, the 8th century Ardagh chalice and the 12th century Cross of Cong, in the National Museum, open Tuesday-Saturday 10:00-17:00 and Sunday 14:00-17:00. The collection of paintings (Rubens, Rembrandt, Goya) at the National Gallery, open Monday-Saturday 10:00-18:00 and Sunday 14:00-17:00. The 8th century Book of Kells, a richly illuminated bible regarded as one of the most beautiful books ever made, on view in the Old Library of Trinity College.

The pulpit from which Jonathan Swift preached, at the 12th century St. Patrick's Cathedral, and a performance of the young boys' choir there. The collection of oriental manuscripts at Chester Beatty Library. The Zoo, in the 1,760-acre Phoenix Park. The 13th century Dublin Castle. Leinster House. The restored 12th century Christ Church Cathedral.

The 18th century mansions on St. Stephen's Green. Window-shop on Grafton Street. Stroll on O'Connell Street. See the historic General Post Office, site of the 1916 uprising. The Georgian houses on Parnell Square. The house where George Bernard Shaw was born. Take a tour of the facilities of the Irish Sweepstakes. A tour of Guinness's Brewery.

Sights in **Belfast:** This is the capital of Northern Ireland. A major port. See Queen's University. The collection of antique locomotives and train cars in the Transport Museum.

Dublin - Cork - Dublin

The train ride to Ireland's lush southern area.

615

Dep. Dublin (Heu.)	7:30(1)	8:30(1+2)	10:05(3+7)
Arr. Cork (Kent)	10:30	12:10	13:50
	*	*	*
Dep. Cork (Kent)	7:30(1)	9:00(6)	11:25(1+8)
Arr. Dublin (Heu.)	10:32	12:50	15:15

(1)Daily, except Sundays and holidays. Meal service. (2)Change trains in Mallow. (3)Daily. Meal service. (4)Sundays and holidays only. Meal service or light refreshments. (5)Daily. (6)Daily, except Saturday. Meal service. (7)Plus other departures from Dublin at 12:55(1), 14:25(3), 17:30(1), 18:30(4), 18:45(1), 19:15(1) and 21:00(5). (8)Plus other departures from Cork at 14:25(1), 15:05(4), 17:35(1), 18:00(4) and 18:45(5).

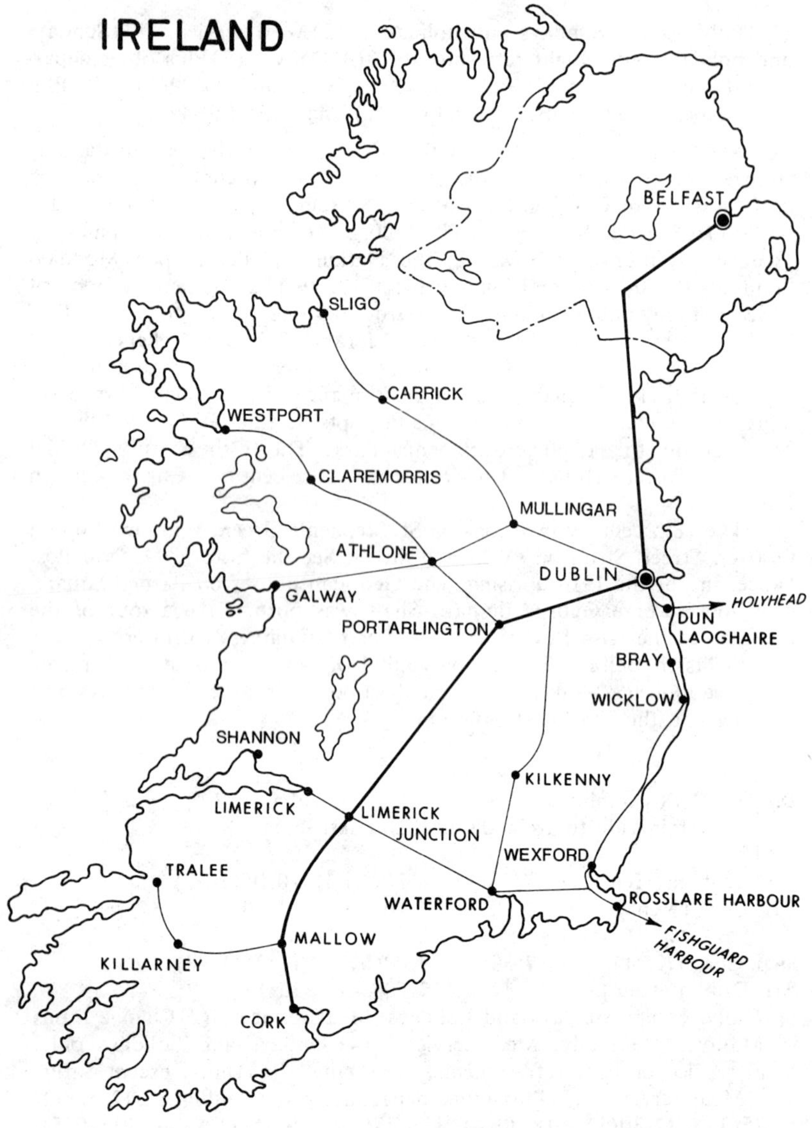
IRELAND
BELFAST
SLIGO
CARRICK
WESTPORT
CLAREMORRIS
MULLINGAR
ATHLONE
DUBLIN
GALWAY
HOLYHEAD
DUN
LAOGHAIRE
PORTARLINGTON
BRAY
WICKLOW
SHANNON
KILKENNY
LIMERICK
LIMERICK
JUNCTION
WEXFORD
TRALEE
WATERFORD
ROSSLARE HARBOUR
FISHGUARD
HARBOUR
MALLOW
KILLARNEY
CORK

Cork - Killarney - Tralee 616a

Beautiful scenery throughout this fertile area.

Dep. Cork	10:55(1)	12:50(2)	15:40(2+3+4+8)
Arr. Mallow	11:25	-0- (2)	-0- (2)
Change trains.			
Dep. Mallow	11:39(1)	-0-	-0-
Dep. Killarney	12:34	14:30	17:17
Arr. Tralee	13:10	15:15	17:55

* * *

Dep. Tralee	7:45(4+5)	8:00(2+4+5)	9:50(2+3+9)
Dep. Killarney	8:16	8:34(2)	10:25(2)
Arr. Mallow	9:11	-0- (2)	-0- (2)
Change trains.			
Dep. Mallow	9:18	9:40	11:43
Arr. Cork	30 minutes later		

(1)Daily. Meal service. Only light refreshments on Sundays and holidays. (2)Direct train. (3)Daily, except Sundays and holidays. (4)Meal service. (5)Sundays and holidays only. (6)Light refreshments. (7)Daily. Light refreshments. (8)Plus another departure from Cork at 20:35(2+5). (9)Plus other departures from Tralee at 14:30(5) and 17:20(7).

Sights in Killarney: It is 85 miles from Shannon Airport. See the sculpture by Seamus Murphy, called The Shy Woman of Kerry. The marvelous garden and the exhibit of early crafts and housing at Muckross House, a 19th century mansion on the outskirts of Killarney, Shop here for linens, glassware and crocheted women's clothing. Take the 112-mile, all-day "Ring of Kerry" bus sightseeing trip, a popular excursion. You will see many lakes and mountains.

Dublin - Galway 614

Beautiful lakes in this area.

Dep. Dublin (Heu.)	8:46(1+2)	9:55(3+4)	11:42(1+3)	14:37(1+3+6)
Arr. Galway	11:00	13:05	13:55	16:50

Sights in Galway: The 14th century St. Nicholas' Church. The ruins of a 13th century Franciscan friary. The 13th century town walls.

Dep. Galway	7:50(1+2)	9:25(2+4)	11:35(1+2)	15:10(1+3+7)
Arr. Dublin (Heu.)	10:40	12:25	14:30	18:05

(1)Monday-Saturday, except holidays. (2)Meal service. (3)Light refreshments. (4)Sundays only. (5)Departs from Dublin's Connolly station. (6)Plus other departures from Dublin at 18:15(2+4), 18:35(1+2) and 20:15(1+5). (7)Plus other departures from Galway at 18:05(1+3) and 18:50(3+4).

Dublin - Limerick 616

There is bus service between Limerick and Shannon Airport.

Dep. Dublin (Heuston)	7:30(1)	8:30(2)	9:35(3+4+5+7)
Arr. Limerick Junction	9:20	10:37	-0- (5)
Change trains.			
Dep. Limerick Junction	9:25	10:40	-0-
Arr. Limerick	9:55	11:15	12:35

* * *

Dep. Limerick	7:45(1+5)	8:05(1)	9:15(3+5+6+8)
Arr. Limerick Junction	-0- (5)	8:35	-0- (5)
Change trains.			
Dep. Limerick Junction	-0-	8:42	-0-
Arr. Dublin (Heuston)	10:20	10:32	12:35

(1) Monday-Saturday, except holidays. Meal service. (2) Daily. Meal service. (3) Sunday only. (4) Meal service. (5) Direct train. No train change in Limerick Junction. (6) Light refreshments. (7) Plus other departures from Dublin at 10:05(2), 12:55(1), 14:25(1), 14:40(3), 17:45(1), 18:05(3+6), 18:45(1) and 19:15(3+6). (8) Plus other departures from Limerick at 9:45(1), 10:05(3+4), 12:20(1), 15:10(1), 15:45(3+6), 15:55(1), 17:45(3+5+6), 18:15(1), 19:05(1) and 19:30(3).

THE FERRY-CROSSING TO FRANCE

Rosslare to Le Havre or Cherbourg

1022 (No sailings on December 24 and 25.)

Dep. Rosslare	17:00(1)	17:00(3)
Arr. Le Havre	15:00(2)	-0-
Arr. Cherbourg	-0-	11:00(2)

(1) Operates Wednesday, Friday and Sunday from October 1 to March 31. Daily except Monday and Friday from April 1 to September 30. (2) One hour earlier from late September to late October . (3) Operates Monday and Friday from April 1 to September 30.

RAIL CONNECTIONS WITH ENGLAND

See page 440.

ITALY

Italy has 3 types of fast trains: Rapido, Direttissimo (Express) and Diretto. Passengers using individual tickets (not traveling with first-class passes or Eurailpass) must pay a supplemental charge when riding on Rapido trains. Seats should be reserved in advance for all 3 types.

Sleeping-car service is offered by Wagon-Lits Company in first-class compartments, second-class compartments, first-class couchette and second-class couchette. All of these should be reserved in advance.

Food service on Italian trains ranges from FM (full meals served in restaurant car) to TM (tray meals served at one's seat) and S (snacks, sandwiches, fruit, candy and beverages sold by a strolling vendor). Few Italian trains offer full meal service.

The signs you will see at railstations in Italy are:

ARRIVI	ARRIVAL
BINARIO	TRACK
CARROZA RISTORANTE	RESTAURANT CAR
DEPOSITO	CHECKROOM
DONNE	WOMEN
ORARIO FERROVIARIO	TIMETABLE
PARTENZE	DEPARTURE
SCOMPARTIMENTO PER FUMATORI	SMOKING COMPARTMENT
STAZIONE FERROVIARIO	RAILSTATION
UOMINI	MEN
USCITA	EXIT
VAGONE LETTO	SLEEPING CAR

ITALIAN HOLIDAYS

A list of holidays is helpful because some trains will be noted later in this section as not running on holidays. Also, those trains which operate on holidays are filled, and it is necessary to make reservations for them long in advance.

January 1	New Year's Day
January 6	Epiphany
	Easter
	Easter Monday
April 25	Liberation Day
May 1	Labor Day
	Proclamation of the Republic (First Monday in June)
August 15	Assumption Day
	Victory Day (World War I) (First Monday in November)
December 8	Immaculate Conception
December 25	Christmas Day
December 26	St. Stephen's Day

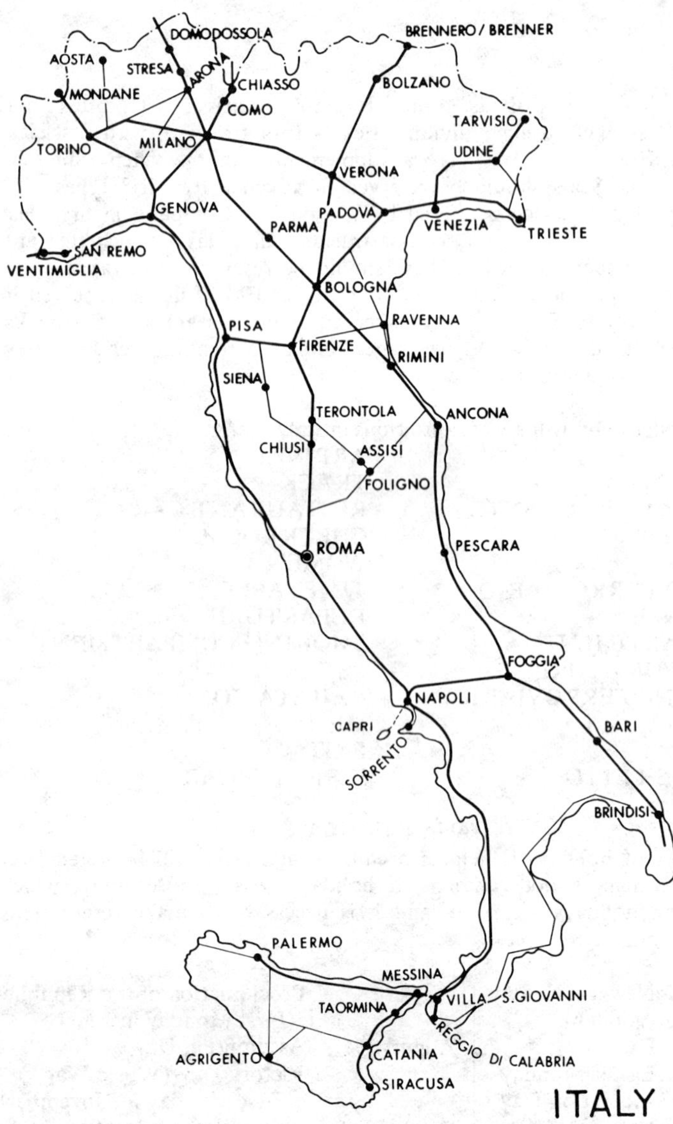
DOMODOSSOLA
BRENNERO / BRENNER
AOSTA
STRESA
ARONA
CHIASSO
BOLZANO
MONDANE
COMO
TARVISIO
TORINO
MILANO
UDINE
VERONA
GENOVA
PADOVA
VENEZIA
TRIESTE
PARMA
SAN REMO
VENTIMIGLIA
BOLOGNA
RAVENNA
PISA
FIRENZE
RIMINI
SIENA
TERONTOLA
ANCONA
CHIUSI
ASSISI
FOLIGNO
ROMA
PESCARA
FOGGIA
NAPOLI
CAPRI
BARI
SORRENTO
BRINDISI
PALERMO
MESSINA
TAORMINA
VILLA
S.GIOVANNI
REGGIO DI CALABRIA
AGRIGENTO
CATANIA
SIRACUSA

ITALY

SUMMER TIME

Italy changes to Summer Time on the last Sunday of March and converts back to Standard Time on the last Sunday of September. Many Italian trains and international trains originating or terminating in Italy have different schedules during Summer Time than they do the balance of the year.

EURAILPASS BONUSES IN ITALY

The Brindisi-Patras boat trip is covered by Eurailpass and Eurail Youthpass — but only if you go on Adriatica/Hellenic Mediterranean Lines. WARNING: The employees of other lines intimate that their ships honor the 2 passes and then charge fees after the boat leaves the pier.

With or without a Eurailpass or Eurail Youthpass, a reservation theoretically can be made on day of departure or day before departure—but it is very unlikely that space will be available (particularly during July and August) unless a reservation is made many weeks in advance of departures date.

Those gambling on making a reservation after arriving in Brindisi can make application January 1-June 9 and October 1-December 31 only at the Adriatica-Hellenic Mediterranean Lines embarkation office, located at Maritime Station, a 15-minute walk from Brindisi's Central railstation, along Corso Umberto and Corso Garibaldi. Taxis are available at the railstation.

From June 10 to September 30, those without advance reservations can apply also to any Brindisi travel agency that displays in its window the green badge "Eurail Information-Eurailpass".

Holders of advance reservations must go at all times directly to the A/HM Lines embarkation office to have their tickets checked, settle port taxes due and obtain the required Embarkation Ticket. That office is open 8:30-13:00 and 15:30-22:30.

Advance reservations before you start your trip, at $1.50(U.S.) each, can be made at any office that issues Eurailpass (see pages 22-23) or at travel agencies in countries where Eurailpass is sold. There is also a $12(U.S.) surcharge, in addition to the reservation fee, for travel from June 10 to September 30.

Another fee is charged for such special accommodations as aircraft type seats, pullman berths and cabins. There is also a port tax of 4,000 Lira that is not covered by Eurailpass and must be paid in Lira.

Passengers with advance reservation must obtain the Embarkation Ticket at least 2 hours prior to the ship's departure time. The ships reserve the right to cancel a reservation when that is not done and to give the space to a standby passenger.

The trains from northern Italy to Brindisi, timed to connect with the ferry departures are frequently late. For that reason, it is advisable to arrive Brindisi the day before a ferry departure to Patras.

For Eurailpass holders, there is about a 20% reduction from the fare for these 7 boat trips: (1) Naples-Palermo, (2) Naples-Malta, (3) Syracuse-Malta, (4) Genoa-Tunis, (5) Genoa-Alicante, (6) Genoa-Malaga, and (7) crossings to Sardinia. Reverse trips are subject to the same reduction. There is a 30% reduction from the fare for the Venice-Piraeus-Haifa boat trip, and vice versa.

Brindisi - Patras - Athens

For sailing dates, see Cook's Table #1440.

Dep. Brindisi Harbor	20:00(1)	22:30(2)
Dep. Patras	13:00	18:00
Walk to Patras railstation.		
898		
Dep. Patras	13:47(3)	18:58(4)
Arr. Athens	19:01	23:06

(1)Runs from mid-June to late September. (2)Runs all year. (3)Meal service. (4)Supplement charged. Light refreshments.

ITALIAN RAIL PASSES

Italian Tourist Ticket. (Biglitteo Turistico di Libera Circolazione). Offers unlimited travel on all Italian trains, including TEE trains, including free seat reservations. Sleeper and couchette services are not included. Available at travel agencies worldwide outside Italy. The 1983 prices for first-class are: 8 days $114(U.S.), 15 days $139, 21 days $166, and 30 days $202. Second-class: 8 days $72, 15 days $87, 21 days $102, and 30 days $127. The 15, 21 and 30-day tickets can be extended to double their initial period. Half-fare for children 4-12 years old.

Kilometric Ticket. Permits travel up to a maximum of 20 single trips totaling 3,000kms (1,875 miles) within a 2-month period. Can be used by more than one person at a time, to a maximum of 5 persons. When a child travels on this ticket, only half the mileage used is counted. Available before you leave home at both the offices of Italian State Railways and from travel agents worldwide. Also available in Italy at all railstations and from Italian travel agencies. Can be used on TEE and Rapido trains if a supplement is paid when the reservation is made. The 1983 prices are: $140(U.S.) for first-class, $79 for second-class.

Family Ticket. Allows 30% reduction on train ticket prices when used by at least 4 passengers (father, mother and 2 children, for example). This ticket can be purchased only at railstations in Italy.

ONE-DAY EXCURSIONS AND CITY SIGHTSEEING

Comprehensive maps which make it easy to find the worthwhile sights in an Italian city can be obtained in most cities there in offices marked "Azienda Autonoma di Turismo" or "Ente Provinciale di Turismo", located on a principal street.

Here are 60 one-day rail trips that can be made comfortably from Bologna, Florence, Genoa, Messina, Milan, Naples, Palermo and Rome, returning to those cities in most cases before dinnertime. Notes are provided on what to see and do at each destination. The number below the name of each route is the Cook's timetable.

Bologna

See the dissection theater in the ancient medical school. The fantastic inlaid wood panels in the Chorus at San Domenico Church. (Be sure to turn on the electric lights there in order to get a good look at the marvelous woodwork.) The Church of San Petronio. The Art Gallery. Neptune's Fountain, where Piazza Maggiore and Piazza Nettuno connect.

The 2 leaning towers in Piazza di Porto Ravegnana: the 330-foot high Asinelli and the 165-foot tall Garisenda. After climbing the 486 steps of the Asinelli, there is a splendid view from the top of it. Visit the churches on Santo Stefano. The Municipal Archaeological Museum. The Communale, Podesta, Mercanzia, Re Anzio and Bevilacqua palaces. Try the marvelous Bolognese food.

Genoa

The house where Columbus was born. St. Lawrence Cathedral. Do not fail to walk down the 15th century streets near the waterfront, too narrow for a tour bus and unfortunately not seen by many visitors to Genoa. The incredible Monumental Cemetery, with its vast number of dramatic statues of many of the people buried there. The landscaped hillside with colorful plants painting a flowering tapestry of Columbus' fleet: the Nina, the Pinta and the Santa Maria.

Florence (Firenze)

The 14th century Cathedral of Santa Maria del Fiore is where most visitors begin sightseeing in Florence. Ascend its 292-foot high belltower for a great view of the city. Across from the Cathedral, see the magnificent sculptured bronze Ghiberti doors ("Gates of Paradise" was Michelangelo's description) on the octagonal Baptistry of San Giovanni.

There is much more to see, in 2 different directions from the Cathedral-Baptistry complex. Facing the Baptistry, you proceed North on Via Ricasoli to visit Area #1. You go South, toward the Arno River, for the sightseeing in Area #2.

Area #1: See the breathtaking marble floors, walls and crypts at the Medici Chapel. The street behind the Chapel is lined with vendors. On the other side of the street is an enormous food market where game with colorful furs and feathers make an unusual display.

An easy walk from the Chapel is the Academia, housing the stupendous statue of David. Nearby is the Fra Angelico Museum in the Church of San Marco, with its interesting frescoes and monk's cells.

Across the street from the Academia, you can board a city bus for the 20-minute ride uphill to the village of Fiesole, where there are Etruscan ruins, a Roman amphitheater, a 13th century Cathedral, the Convent of St. Francis, and a splendid view of Florence.

Area #2: The Piazza della Signoria and, next to it, the thousands of great art treasures in the 29 exhibit rooms of the Palazzo degli Uffizi. Nearby is the Franciscan Church of Santa Croce, where Michelangelo, Machiavelli, Rossini and Galileo are buried. Also see the sculptures at the Bargello Museum, in a 13th century palace.

Next, cross to the other side of the Arno River, over the Ponte Vecchio (lined with tiny jewelry shops) to visit the outstanding paintings, statues, tapestries and furniture in the 28 exhibit rooms and galleries of the Palazzo Pitti.

Milan

The Duomo Cathedral, holding more than 20,000 people, begun in 1386 and taking 5 centuries to complete. There are more than 3,000 statues on its exterior. Then go through the incredibly beautiful shopping arcade, The Galleries, to La Scala. One of the world's greatest theaters, accommodating 3,600 people, it was first constructed in 1776. Its opera museum is open daily except Sundays 9:00-12:00 and 14:00-18:00.

Exhibited in the museum are old paintings and engravings of the opera house before its destruction by bombs in 1943 and its reconstruction in 1946, portraits of many famous singers, several of Verdi's pianos and such other Verdi memorabilia as his manuscripts and death mask.

Opposite La Scala, behind a statue of da Vinci, is the 16th century Palazzo Marino, now the City Hall. Just past the gate (Porta Nuova) at the end of Via Manzoni are the Museum of Natural History, the Zoo and the Planetarium.

See da Vinci's "Last Supper" at Santa Maria delle Grazie. It can be viewed Tuesday-Saturday 9:00-13:30 and 14:00-18:30, and on Sunday 9:00-15:00. Do not fail to see the enormous and elaborate crypts at the Monumental Cemetery. Visit the Palazzo Dugnani, on Via Manin, to see the Tiepolo ceiling fresco there.

It is a short taxi ride from the Dugnani to the enormous Castello Sforzesco, which has a vast collection of paintings (including Michelangelo's last work, the Rondanini Pieta) and exhibits of harpischords, wrought iron, tapestries and ceramics. The Castle is open daily except Monday 9:30-12:00 and 14:30-17:00.

See the collection of sculpture, Flemish and Persian tapestries, paintings, scientific instruments, glass and armor at Museo Poldi-Pezzoli, at 12 Via Manzoni, open Tuesday-Sunday 9:30-12:30 and 14:30-17:30. Many great paintings (Raphael, Tiepolo, Canaletto) are exhibited in the Accademia di Brera on Via Brera, open Tuesday-Saturday 9:00-14:00, and on Sunday 9:00-13:00.

Both the Modern Art Gallery at 16 Via Palestra and the Archaeological Museum at 15 Corso Magenta are open Wednesday-Saturday 9:30-12:30 and 14:30-17:30, and on Sunday 9:30-13:00. There are marvelous paintings by Raphael, Caravaggi and Botticelli in the Ambrosian Library, open daily except Saturdays, Sundays and holidays 10:00-12:00 and 15:00-17:00, and on Saturdays, Sundays and holidays 15:00-17:00.

Gourmets will want to visit the fantastic food store called Peck's, at No. 9 Via Spadari, opened in 1892 by a Czechoslovak named Franz Peck. It is the Italian equivalent of Fauchon's, described under "Paris" in the section of this chapter on France.

What you will see at Peck's are: large wedges of parmigiano and reggiano cheese, Italian wines, roasts, loins, saddles and breasts of white veal, caviar, numerous cold seafood salads, mussels, langouste, squid, lobster, celery remoulade, pates, head cheese, scampi, sturgeon, hot vegetable dishes (baked fennel, baby zucchini, asparagus milanese), roasted quail skewered with sausages and wrapped in bacon, tripe in tomato sauce, a wide range of pasta (green ravioli al forno, tortellini, ravioli alla contadina), paella with saffron rice, white mushrooms in oil, many sausages and many fish (herring, smoked salmon, smoked eels, smoked trout).

If that is not enough, across the street from Peck's is a famous pork store, La Bottega del Maiale, with an enormous display of whole baby pigs, pork parts (loins, ears, fillets, tongue, liver) and such sausages as sopresa Calabra, salame Toscana, coppa, cacciatorini, stagionata, capocolla and finocchiona.

Next door to the pork store is Peschere Spadari, a great fish store, selling nearly everything that swims: scampi, Channel sole, mackerel, scampi, squid, mussels. A short distance down the street, at No. 1 Via Speroni, is a large cheese store.

Naples

The view from Certosa de San Martino monastary and, inside, its National Museum. The 13th century Castel Nuovo. The National Library. The Archaeological Museum, with its great Grecian and Roman sculptures. The Capodimonte Gallery. The Teatro San Carlo, home of Neapolitan opera. Scores of palaces.

Rome

St. Peter's, the most wonderful work by man in all the world. The Vatican. Capitoline Hill. The Roman Forum. Palatine Hill. The Imperial Fora. Marcellus Theatre. The Jewish Synagogue. The Temple of Avesta.

Aventine Hill. St. Paul's Gate. The view of Rome from the Borghese Gardens. The Protestant cemetery, with the graves of Keats and Shelley. The Colosseum. The Arch of Constantine. The Basilica of St. Paul Outside the Walls. Michelangelo's statue of Moses in the Church of St. Peter in Chains. The Pantheon. The mosaics at the Baths of Caracella.

In the following timetables, where a city has more than one railstation we have designated the particular station after the name of the city (in parentheses).

Bologna - Florence - Bologna

Exceptional mountain scenery on this easy one-day roundtrip.

The train goes through the 11.5-mile long Apennine Tunnel, Italy's longest tunnel.

374 + 398

Dep. Bologna — Frequent times from 1:26 to 22:53
Arr. Florence — 70 minutes later.

Sights in Florence: See notes about city-sightseeing in Florence at the start of this section.

Dep. Florence — Frequent times from 0:25 to 22:58
Arr. Bologna — 70 minutes later.

Bologna - Milan - Bologna 374

Dep. Bologna — Frequent times from 2:01 to 21:07
Arr. Milan (Centrale) — 2 hours later

Sights in Milan: See notes about city-sightseeing in Milan at the start of this section.

Dep. Milan (Centrale) — Frequent times from 0:30 to 23:10
Arr. Bologna — 2 hours later.

Bologna - Parma - Bologna 374

Dep. Bologna	7:26	8:16	11:05	13:23
Arr. Parma	65 minutes later			

Sights in Parma: Corregio's fresco of the Assumption at the Cathdral. The 5-story red marble Baptistry, one of Italy's finest buildings. Italy's most modern museum, in the Palazzo della Pilotta. Also in the Palazzo, more than 40,000 rare manuscripts in the Pallatine Library and the collection of Etruscan, Roman, medieval and Renaissance works of art in the National Museum of Former Ages.

Dep. Parma	13:14	14:38	16:02	16:59(1)
Arr. Bologna	65 minutes later			

(1) Plus other departures at 18:16, 19:41, 20:56, 21:30 and 22:54.

Bologna - Pisa - Bologna

374

Dep. Bologna	6:18	7:22(1)	9:13(1)	10:23
Arr. Florence (S.M.N.)	7:52	8:47	10:33	11:41
Change trains.				
364				
Dep. Florence (S.M.N.)	8:36	9:37	11:15	12:00
Arr. Pisa	10:00	10:36	12:30	13:10

(1) Light refreshments.

The #1 Bus at the railstation takes you to the Piazza del Duomo in 10 minutes.

Sights in Pisa: The Piazza del Duomo, with 4 major attractions. Walk up the spiral stairs of the Leaning Tower to its roof and see the view from there. A few feet from the base of the Tower is the majestic 11th century striped marble Cathedral. Key features of it are the magnificent bronze entrance doors and, inside, paintings, statues, mosaics, a fantastic pulpit, and Galileo's lamp.

While watching the lamp swing, Galileo timed each arc by his pulse and observed that every swing, long or short, took the same time span. By that, he postulated "the isochronism of the pendular movement".

Next, walk the short distance from the Cathedral to the beautiful, enormous 11th century circular marble Baptistry to see its font and its 6 columns of porphyry, marble and oriental granite. Three of the columns rest on carved lions. Biblical scenes are carved on each panel.

A very short walk from the Baptistry is a large building with a cemetery in its central court. Each section of the building exhibits many frescoes. See the 50-foot by 19-foot "Triumph of Death" in the North Gallery.

An hour before the train from Bologna reaches Pisa, it stops 2 minutes in Campiglia Marittima, which has a large statue of a mongrel dog at its railstation, the dog appearing to watch the procession of coming and going trains.

Lampo ("flash of lightning") liked train travel as much as we do. He learned the train schedules and took a trip every day—more than 3,000 train trips.

Owned by the assistant stationmaster, Lampo escorted his master's daughter to school every morning. For that reason, he made short rail trips on schooldays, longer journeys on weekends. Always, he would go only such distances and make the necessary connections so as to return home every day before dawn.

Prior to Lampo's death in 1961 (under a freight train), he had become known not only by every trainman in Italy but by Italy's public as well, through reports of his love of train travel on Italian television and in Italy's newspapers.

Local railway workers say only a person with a printed timetable could have equaled the dog's feat, when he once went past his stop on a certain trip and then managed to return home by taking a complex series of connecting trains to get back to Campiglia Marittima.

Dep. Pisa	Frequent times to 22:28.
Arr. Florence (S.M.N.)	70-80 minutes later.
Change trains.	
374	
Dep. Florence (S.M.N.)	Frequent times to 0:25
Arr. Bologna	3-3½ hours after departing Pisa

Bologna - Ravenna - Bologna 379

Dep. Bologna	6:13	8:25	9:05(2)	11:06(1)	12:42(2)
Arr. Ravenna	7:47	9:40	11:24	12:13	14:08

Sights in Ravenna: The marvelous 5th century monuments, the Mausoleum of Galla Placidia and the Orthodox Baptistery. Just behind the Mausoleum, see the mosaics at the Church of San Vitale. Great mosaics also in Sant'Appollinare Nuovo Church, where it is helpful to use binoculars or even an opera glass in order to see those mosaics that are at the top of the walls. See the ivory pulpit in the Archbishop's Palace. Dante's Tomb. The Museum of Antiquities. The exhibits at the Academy of Fine Arts.

Dep. Ravenna	13:00	14:30	16:14(2)	17:51	18:44(2+3)
Arr. Bologna	14:45	15:45	18:21	19:20	20:30

(1) Runs from late June to mid-September. (2) Change trains in Castel-Bolognese. (3) Plus another departure from Ravenna at 20:47(2).

Bologna - Siena - Bologna 374 + 363

Dep. Bologna	6:18	10:14(1)	10:23(2)
Arr. Florence	7:52	11:34	11:41
Change trains.			
Dep. Florence	8:00	11:40	12:15(3)
Arr. Siena	9:38	13:21	14:31

(1) Light refreshments. (2) Meal service. (3) Daily, except Sundays and holidays. Change trains in Empoli.

Sights in Siena: The pervasive color, named for Siena, that dominates this hill town. The view of Italy's most unique square, Piazza del Campo, from the top of the Mangia Tower of the Palazzo Publico (with its marvelous 14th century murals) or from a window of the Palazzo Piccolomini (open 9:00-13:00, except Sundays), where records in unbelievable calligraphy going back to the 12th century are exhibited with 15th century costumes and fine frescoes.

Also see the Pisano sculpture and mosaic floors at the Cathedral, on Piazza del Duomo. The paneled Duccio Crucifixion in the Museum of the Cathedral. Climb from there to the top of Facciatone, the skeleton for a new cathedral whose construction ceased when the Black Death of 1348 ravished Siena.

Pinacoteca, the art museum, on a street that is down from the Cathedral. Fontebranda, the old fountain with 3 arches. The ancient houses along Via degli Archi, Vicolo della Fortuna, and Vicolo delle Scotto, all of these streets radiating out from the Piazza del Campo.

363

Dep. Siena	13:28	15:43	17:14(1)	19:32
Arr. Florence	15:19	17:28	19:10	21:24

Change trains.

374

Dep. Florence	16:28(2)	18:18(3)	19:21(3)	22:18
Arr. Bologna	17:57	19:46	20:39	0:02

(1) Change trains in Empoli. (2) Light refreshments. (3) Meal service.

Bologna - Venice - Bologna 389

Dep. Bologna	5:58	8:08	11:11
Arr. Venice (S.L.)	8:15	10:30	13:50

Sights in Venice: After the obligatory gondola ride, start with standing at either end of Piazza San Marco and try to cope with the enormity and beauty of the most impressive square in the world. Then visit St. Mark's Cathedral, the most wonderful Byzantine structure in Europe. Next door, see the Doge's Palace. Then relax at one of the outdoor cafes on St. Mark's Square and take in the wonder of it all while waiting for the figures on the enormous 15th century clock to emerge and strike the bell. For another view of St. Mark's Square and the entire Lagoon, go to the top of the Bell Tower. Walk through the colorful, narrow streets of shops to Rialto Bridge and, standing there, watch the canal traffic. Then cross over the Bridge and walk a short distance to the extraordinary fish market, which should be seen before Noon. It is a short and inexpensive boat ride to the island of Murano to watch glass-blowing and visit the Glassworks Museum in Palazzo Giustiniani. Among the score of churches to see in Venice are: San Giuliano, Santa Maria Formosa, Santa Maria dei Miracoli, San Giovanni e Paolo, San Francesco della Vigna, San Zaccaria, Santo Stefano, Santa Maria Gloriosa dei Frari, Santa Maria del Carmine, San Sebastiano, Madonna dell'Orto and Santi Apostoli. There are 5 synagogues. A 15-minute boat ride takes you to the Lido, Venice's beach resort and site of its gambling casino.

A 3-minute boat ride takes you to the beautiful, white Church of Santa Maria della Salute, built on more than one million wood pilings.

Dep. Venice (S.L.)	14:04	15:06	16:25(1)	17:05	18:28(2)
Arr. Bologna	16:24	17:28	18:51	19:17	20:39

(1) Meal service. (2) Plus other departures at 19:55, 20:50 and 22:42.

Bologna - Verona - Bologna

381

Dep. Bologna	8:18	11:16	12:20(1)	13:00
Arr. Verona	10:00	13:12	13:48	14:33

Sights in Verona: The large and excellently preserved first century Arena. Then take Via Mazzini (Verona's main shopping street) to Piazza della Herbe (Herb Square), where you will find a marvelous display of fruits, vegetables, live pet birds, and dead game birds. Only a few minutes walk from there, the Veronese marble lobby of the Hotel Due Torri is worth seeing. At Piazza dei Signori are the tombs of the Della Scala family, once rulers of Verona. La Scala Opera House in Milan is named after them. See the paintings in the Church of Sant'-Anastasia. Visit the Cathedral and the Museum of Art in Castelvecchio, on Corso Cavour. The main attraction in Verona, since Shakespeare, has always been Juliet's balcony, at Via Cappelo 17-25.

Dep. Verona	13:19	14:15	14:41	15:07	15:41(2)
Arr. Bologna	1½-2 hours later				

(1) Light refreshments. (2) Plus other departures from Verona at 16:43, 18:45, 19:22 and 21:35.

Florence - Arezzo - Florence

374

Dep. Florence	8:02	9:48(1)	10:23(1)	11:44(1)
Arr. Arezzo	70-75 minutes later			

Sights in Arezzo: The 15th century frescoes in the Church of San Francesco. The carvings on the facade of the 11th century Church of Santa Maria della Pieve. Behind Pieve, the marvelous Piazza Grande, with its palaces. There are many other fine palaces on Corso Italia.

The musical scale was invented in the 10th century by Guido of Arezzo. The Piazza Guido Monaco is named for him.

See the 16th century stained-glass in the Cathedral. The collection of Etruscan and Roman artwork in the Archaeological Museum at the Convent. The enormous fortress, Medicea, built in the 16th century by the Medicis. A library and museum is maintained in the home where Petrarch was born.

Dep. Arezzo	12:08(2)	13:33(2)	14:03(1)	15:08(2)	16:55(2+3)
Arr. Florence	70-75 minutes later				

(1) Light refreshments. (2) Meal service. (3) Plus other departures at 17:58(2), 18:47(1), 20:50, 21:40 and 23:02.

Florence - Assisi - Florence 374

Dep. Florence (S.M.N.)	7:08	9:48(1)	11:44(1)
Arr. Terontola	8:37	11:20	13:16
Change trains. 378			
Dep. Terontola	8:41	11:25	13:21
Arr. Assisi	9:59	12:38	14:34

Sights in Assisi: St. Francis' tomb in the 13th century Basilica on the Hill of Paradise, and the many outstanding paintings there. St. Claire's Church. The medieval Castle. Piazza del Commune. The upper and lower churches at the Convent of St. Francis, with their many frescos. Prison Hermitage. The 16th century Church of Santa Maria degli Angeli. The 12th century Cathedral of St. Ruffino. The 14th century La Rocca Maggiore fortress.

Dep. Assisi	13:00	14:01	16:30(2)	18:21	19:34(4)
Arr. Terontola	14:09	15:22	-0- (2)	19:40	21:04
Change trains. 374					
Dep. Terontola	14:38(1)	16:29(3)	-0-	20:18	21:17
Arr. Florence (S.M.N.)	16:18	18:08	19:50	22:06	22:48

(1) Light refreshments. (2) Direct train. No train change in Terontola. (3) Meal service. (4) Plus another departure from Assisi at 21:31.

Florence - Bologna - Florence

Exceptional mountain scenery on this easy one-day roundtrip.

The train goes through the 11.5-mile long Apennine Tunnel, Italy's longest tunnel.

374

Dep. Florence	Frequent times from 5:46 to 22:58
Arr. Bologna	80 minutes later

Sights in Bologna: See notes about city-sightseeing in Bologna at the start of this section.

Dep. Bologna	Frequent times to 23:23
Arr. Florence	80 minutes later

Florence - Livorno - Florence 358a

Dep. Florence	12:00	Dep. Livorno	17:37
Arr. Livorno	13:32	Arr. Florence	19:10

Sights in Livorno: The old and new forts, both from the 16th century. The marble statue of Ferdinand. Tacca's 17th century bronze statues of "The Four Moors". Villas once occupied by Shelley and Byron. The paintings and the Communal Library, both in the Civic Museum. Italy's Naval Academy.

Florence - Milan - Florence 374

Dep. Florence (S.M.N.)	5:46	6:45(1)	9:15	10:42(2)
Arr. Milan (Centrale)	9:50	9:55	13:40	13:55

Sights in Milan: See notes about sightseeing in Milan at the start of this section.

Dep. Milan (Centrale)	14:20(3)	16:50(2)	16:55	17:15(4+7)
Arr. Florence (S.M.N.)	18:46	20:08	21:09	21:43

(1) Daily, except Sundays and holidays. First-class only. Supplement charged. (2) TEE. Reservation required. Meal service. (3) Meal service. (4) Runs from early July to mid-September. (5) Light refreshments. (6) Monday-Friday, except holidays. (7) Plus other departures from Milan at 19:35, 19:40(3), 19:50(5) and 20:40(6).

Florence - Padua - Florence 389

Dep. Florence (S.M.N.)	6:25	9:56(1)	10:50
Arr. Padua	9:52	12:53	14:00

Sights in Padua: The 13th century university on the Via 8 Febraio. Scrovegni Chapel. The Church of Eremitani. The Basilica of Sant'Antonio, with several statues by Donatello.

Dep. Padua	13:17(2)	14:39(2)	15:45	17:21(3+4)
Arr. Florence (S.M.N.)	17:03	18:46	19:30	20:32

(1) Meal service. (2) Change trains in Bologna. (3) Meal service. (4) Plus other departures from Padua at 17:41, 19:04(2), 20:35(2) and 21:28.

Florence - Parma - Florence

374

Dep. Florence (S.M.N.)	5:46(1)	6:25	9:15
Arr. Bologna	-0-	7:50	10:46
Change trains.			
Dep. Bologna	-0-	8:10	11:05
Arr. Parma	8:28	9:16	12:11

Sights in Parma: See notes about city-sightseeing in Parma earlier in this section, under "Bologna-Parma".

Dep. Parma	13:22	14:39(1)	16:03(1+3)	19:44(4)
Arr. Bologna	14:33	-0- (1)	-0- (1)	20:53
Change trains.				
Dep. Bologna	14:55(2)	-0-	-0-	21:13
Arr. Florence (S.M.N.)	16:09	17:22	18:46	22:39

(1) Direct train. No train change in Bologna. (2) Light refreshments. (3) Meal service. (4) Plus another departure from Parma at 21:32(1+2).

Florence - Perugia - Florence

374

Dep. Florence (S.M.N.)	7:06	8:02	9:38(1)	11:42(1)
Arr. Terontola	8:33	9:35	11:07	13:13
Change trains.				
378				
Dep. Terontola	8:40	9:56	11:15	13:18
Arr. Perugia	9:28	10:40	12:03	14:05

Sights in Perugia: The Municipal Palace, to see the magnificent carved and inlaid wood panels in the Library, the chapel of the Stock Exchange, and the great paintings in the National Gallery (Pinacoteca). On display to the left of the main door of the Stock Exchange chapel is the white onyx ring with which the Virgin Mary was married. Also visit the 13th century Church of San Ercolano. Galleng Palace, with its Foreign University. Stroll along Maesta della Volte, Via dei Priori (to the Oratory of San Bernardino), Via Bagliona and Corso Vannucci, the main street.

Dep. Perugia	13:26	14:34	17:00(2)	18:53	20:13(3)
Arr. Terontola	14:09	15:22	-0-	19:40	21:04
Change trains.					
374					
Dep. Terontola	14:42(1)	16:29(1)	-0-	20:18	21:17
Arr. Florence (S.M.N.)	16:19	18:06	19:50	22:04	22:48

(1) Light refreshments. (2) No train change in Terontola. (3) Plus another departure at 22:02.

Florence - Pisa - Florence

364

Dep. Florence	Frequent times from 6:10 to 14:00.
Arr. Pisa	1-1½ hours later.

Sights in Pisa: See notes about city-sightseeing in Pisa earlier in this section, under "Bologna-Pisa".

Dep. Pisa	Frequent times to 24:00.
Arr. Florence	1-1½ hours later.

Florence - Ravenna - Florence

397

Dep. Florence (S.M.N.)	6:42	8:15	
Arr. Ravenna	10:12	11:10	

Sights in Ravenna: See notes about city-sightseeing in Ravenna earlier in this section, under "Bologna-Ravenna".

Dep. Ravenna	15:57	17:23	18:44(1)
Arr. Florence (S.M.N.)	19:04	20:47	21:57

(1) Change trains 3 times en route to Florence.

Florence - Rimini - Florence

358a

Dep. Florence	7:14	Dep. Rimini	19:27
Arr. Rimini	10:32	Arr. Florence	22:37

Sights in Rimini: Malatesta Temple. Sigismondo's Castle. The Bridge of Tiberius over the Marecchia River. The Arch of Augustus. Frescos in St. Augustin's Church. Remains of the Roman amphitheater.

Florence - Siena - Florence

363

Dep. Florence	8:00	9:40(1)	11:40
Arr. Siena	9:43	11:18	13:24

Sights in Siena: See notes about city-sightseeing in Siena earlier in this section, under "Bologna-Siena".

Dep. Siena	13:28	15:43(2)	17:17(2)	19:35	21:22	22:47
Arr. Florence	15:18	17:44	19:16	21:18	22:58	0:35

(1) Sundays and holidays only. (2) Change trains in Empoli.

Florence - Verona - Florence

374

Dep. Florence (S.M.N.)	6:25	9:16(1)	9:56
Arr. Bologna	7:50	10:53	11:23

Change trains.

381

Dep. Bologna	8:18	11:16	12:20
Arr. Verona	10:00	13:12	13:48

Sights in Verona: See notes about city-sightseeing in Verona earlier in this section under "Bologna-Verona".

Dep. Verona	15:05	18:45	19:22
Arr. Bologna	16:56	20:27	21:51

Change trains.

374

Dep. Bologna	17:16	21:13	22:07
Arr. Florence (S.M.N.)	18:46	22:37	23:58

(1) Departs from Florence's Campo di Marte station.

Genoa - Bologna - Genoa

357a

Dep. Genoa (Brignole)	6:32		Dep. Bologna	17:50
Arr. Bologna	11:14		Arr. Genoa (Brignole)	22:50

(1) No meal service.

Sights in Bologna: See notes about city-sightseeing in Bologna at the start of this section.

Genoa - Cremona - Genoa

359

Dep. Genoa (P.P.)	9:15	10:50
Arr. Milan (Centrale)	10:50	12:40

Change trains.

366

Dep. Milan (Centrale)	12:05	14:10
Arr. Cremona	13:15	15:19

Sights in Cremona: One of Italy's most impressive squares, the Piazza del Commune, with its octagonal Baptistry, 12th century Duomo Cathedral, Loggia de Militi, and the Gothic Torrazzo (tallest bell tower in Italy). Cremona is where the art of violin-making reached its apex, with the works of Amati, Stradivari and Guarneri. It is possible to watch young violin makers following that great tradition by visiting La Scuola Internazionale de Liuteria, in a renovated 16th century palace. At the City Museum every day at 11:00, an outstanding violin made by Stradivari is played by the museum curator. Located near the Liuteria are many shops which will make a special violin to order. On view at the City Hall are 2 original Stradivari, 2 Amatis and a Sacconi.

Dep. Cremona	16:02	17:40(1)	18:25	19:27
Arr. Milan (Centrale)	17:18	20:03	20:40	20:57

Change trains.

359

Dep. Milan (Centrale)	17:52	20:30(2+3)	21:55(2+4)	22:25
Arr. Genoa (P.P.)	20:07	22:04	23:23	0:29

(1)Change trains in Codogno. (2)Reservation required. (3)Meal service. (4)Light refreshments.

Genoa - Milan - Genoa 359

Dep. Genoa (P.P.)	6:37	8:00(1+2)	8:03	8:53(3)	9:15(4+5)
Arr. Milan (Cent.)	8:20	9:25	10:20	10:44	10:50

Sights in Milan: See notes about sightseeing in Milan at the start of this section.

Dep. Milan (Cent.)	14:15	15:05	15:50	16:45(3)	17:52(6)
Arr. Genoa (P.P.)	16:00	17:04	18:13	18:49	20:07

(1)Reservation required. (2)First-class only. (3)Light refreshments. (4)Meal service. (5)Plus other departures from Genoa at 10:52(3)and 11:48(4). (6)Plus other departures from Milan at 18:25(1), 18:35(1), 19:45, 20:30(1+4), 21:55(1+2+3) and 22:25.

Genoa - Parma - Genoa 357a

Dep. Genoa (Brignole)	6:32	Dep. Parma	18:59
Arr. Parma	10:05	Arr. Genoa (Brignole)	22:50

Sights in Parma: See notes about city-sightseeing in Parma earlier in this section, under "Bologna-Parma".

Genoa - Pisa - Genoa 355

Exceptional mountain and Mediterranean coastline scenery on this ride.

Dep. Genoa (P.P.)	6:47	7:47(1)	8:14(2)	8:45(5)
Arr. Pisa (Cent.)	10:02	10:09	10:31	11:53

Sights in Pisa: See notes about city-sightseeing in Pisa earlier in this section, under "Bologna-Pisa".

Dep. Pisa (Cent.)	14:45(2)	15:45(2)	17:14(3)	18:07(1+6)
Arr. Genoa (P.P.)	17:35	18:05	20:15	20:27

(1)Runs from late May to late September. (2)Meal service. (3)Light refreshments. (4)Reservation required. (5)Plus other departures from Genoa at 9:59(2+4) and 11:45(2). (6)Plus other departures from Pisa at 18:55(2), 19:45(2+4), 20:48, 21:38(2+4) and 22:26.

Genoa - San Remo - Genoa 356

Dep. Genoa (P.P.)	5:58	6:58	8:30(1)	8:45(2+4)
Arr. San Remo	8:29	9:43	10:16	11:32

Sights in San Remo: Bathing beauties (and uglies) on the largest of the Italian Riviera beach resorts.

Dep. San Remo	13:00	13:42	15:27	18:08(2+5)
Arr. Genoa (P.P.)	15:35	17:22	18:10	20:50

(1)Reservation required. Supplement charged. Meal service. (2)Light refreshments. (3)Runs from late May to early September. (4)Plus other departures from Genoa at 9:30(3), 10:00 and 11:40. (5)Plus other departures from San Remo at 19:27(3), 20:08(1) and 22:05.

Genoa - Torino - Genoa

355

Dep. Genoa (P.P.)	7:30	8:15	10:40	12:10	
Arr. Torino (P.N.)	9:40	10:38	12:48	14:40	

Sights in Torino: The beautiful Piazza Carlo Felice park, near the railstation. Piazza San Carlo, considered second only to St. Mark's in Venice. The imposing Palazzo Madama, with its enormous marble staircase and Royal Armory, in Piazza Castello. The museum in Palazzo Carignano, including the third most important (after London and Cairo) Egyptian collection in the world. The university in Piazzo Carlo, where Erasmus of Rotterdam earned his doctorate in 1506. The view from the top of Mole Antonelliana, on Via Montebello. Parco del Valentino, with its splendid gardens and buildings. Frescos in the Castello del Valentino. The Church of the Great Mother of God, patterned after Rome's Pantheon. In the black and white marble Chapel of the Holy Shroud, the urn holding what is believed to be the shroud placed on Jesus when he was taken from the cross. The Auto Museum on Corso Unita d'Italia, with models going back to 1893.

Dep. Torino (P.N.)	12:22	13:40(2)	15:18	16:35(3)	16:52(4)
Arr. Genoa (P.P.)	14:15	15:36	17:17	18:29	19:18

(1) Runs early June to late September. (2) Light refreshments. (3) Reservation required. Meal service. (4) Plus other departures at 18:55, 19:45(1), 21:10, 21:45 and 23:05.

Milan - Bologna - Milan

374

Dep. Milan (Cent.)	5:55	7:00(1)	7:55(2)	8:00(3+7)
Arr. Bologna	8:36	9:52	10:16	10:46

Sights in Bologna: See notes about city-sightseeing in Bologna at the start of this section.

Dep. Bologna	12:00(4)	12:30(1)	13:23	14:01(8)
Arr. Milan (Cent.)	13:55	15:20	16:00	16:42

(1) Light refreshments. (2) Meal service. (3) Runs from late May to late September. (4) TEE. Reservation required. Meal service. (5) Runs from late June to late August. (6) Reservation required. Meal service. (7) Plus other departures from Milan at 8:10(4), 8:30(5), 9:15 and 9:30(4). (8) Plus other departures from Bologna at 15:00(2), 15:46(4), 15:52(3), 16:07, 17:12(4), 17:21(1), 18:20(1+6), 18:49, 19:08(3), 19:32(5), 19:58(2), 20:09(3), 20:51(2), 21:07, 21:50(4) and 22:08.

Milan - Como - Milan

	277	368	277	368	277
Dep. Milan (Cent.)	7:10	-0-	9:10	-0-	13:10
Dep. Milan (P.Gar.)	-0-	8:25	-0-	10:20	-0-
Arr. Como (S.G.)	7:49	9:22	9:50	11:20	13:50

Sights in Como: Take Bus No. 4, marked "Piazza Cavour", from the railstation to reach both the lakeshore and the cable car which ascends the 2300-foot high Mount Brunate in 7 minutes. At the peak. there is a wonderful view of Lake Como and the Alps.

Dep. Como (S.G.)	Frequent times from 10:54 to 23:01
Arr. Milan (Cent.)	40 minutes later

Milan - Cremona - Milan 366

Dep. Milan (Cent.)	6:35	8:25(1)	9:05(2)	12:05	14:10
Arr. Cremona	8:02	9:37	11:16	13:14	15:20

Sights in Cremona: See notes about city-sightseeing in Cremona earlier in the section, under "Genoa-Cremona".

Dep. Cremona	12:23	13:21	14:14(1)	16:02	17:40(3+4)
Arr. Milan (Cent.)	13:45	15:17(2)	15:30(1)	17:18	20:03

(1)Saturday and Sunday only. Depart/Arrive Milan's Lambrate station. (2)Depart/Arrive Milan's Porta Garibaldi station. (3)Change trains in Codogno. (4)Plus other departures from Cremona at 18:25 and 19:27.

Milan - Florence - Milan 374

Dep. Milan (Cent.)	6:48(1+2)	7:00(2)	7:55(3)	8:10(4)
Arr. Florence (S.M.N.)	10:33	11:34	11:41	11:17

Sights in Florence: See notes about city-sightseeing in Florence at the start of this section.

Dep. Florence (S.M.N.)	14:23(4)	15:24(2)	16:55(3+5)	18:18(3+6)
Arr. Milan (Cent.)	17:40	20:20	20:30	22:45

(1)Departs from Milan's Lambrate station. (2)Light refreshments. (3)Meal service. (4)TEE. Reservation required. Meal service. (5)Reservation required. (6)Plus other departures from Florence at 19:21(3), 19:41 and 20:34(4).

Milan - Genoa - Milan 359

Dep. Milan (Cent.)	6:40(1)	7:08	9:00	10:50(2+3+7)
Arr. Genoa (P.P.)	8:15	8:55	10:55	12:20

Sights in Genoa: See notes about city-sightseeing in Genoa at the start of this section.

Dep. Genoa (P.P.)	14:00	14:37(2+3)	14:52	16:00(8)
Arr. Milan (Cent.)	1½-2 hours later			

(1)Reservation required. Meal service. (2)Reservation required. First-class only. (3)Light refreshments. (4)Runs from late May to late September. (5)Meal service. (6)Supplement charged. (7)Plus other departures from Milan at 11:00 and 12:15(5). (8)Plus other departures from Genoa at 16:32(5), 17:42(6), 18:37(4), 19:34, 21:20(3), 21:55(1) and 22:45.

Milan - Locarno - Milan

The Camedo-Locarno portion of this trip is one of the 5 most scenic rail trips in Europe, with outstanding mountain, gorge and river scenery.

251

Dep. Milan (Cent.)	-0-	7:05	-0-	10:05
Dep. Milan (P. Gar.)	6:38	-0-	9:05	-0-
Arr. Domodossola	8:58	8:50	11:25	11:50

Change trains. Walk outside the Domodossola railstation and go to the underground track in order to board the Centovalli narrow-gauge local railway.

252

Dep. Domodossola	9:05(1)	10:05(1)	-0-	12:05(1)
Dep. Camedo	10:08(1)	11:08(1)	-0-	13:05(1)
Arr. Locarno	40 minutes later			

Sights in Locarno: Stroll the gardens along the shore of lake Maggiore and take the funicular ride to the church high above the village for a fine view of Locarno and lake Maggiore.

Dep. Locarno	11:05(1)	13:00(1)	15:00	16:20(2+6)
Dep. Camedo	11:46(1)	13:42(1)	15:42	17:10
Arr. Domodossola	12:44	14:43	16:43	18:25

Change trains. Walk from underground Centovailli track, up to the main Domodossola railstation.

251

Dep. Domodossola	14:04	15:28	17:37	19:32(3)
Arr. Milan (P. Gar.)	-0-	-0-	-0-	-0-
Arr. Milan (Cent.)	16:00	17:00	19:05	21:00(4)

(1)Light refreshments. (2)Change trains in Camedo. (3)TEE. Reservation required. Light refreshments. (4)Arrives at Milan's Centrale station. (5)Arrives at Milan's Garibaldi station. (6)Plus other departures from Locarno at 17:20(1+4) and 18:40(5).

Milan - Lugano - Milan

277

Dep. Milan (Cent.)	7:49(1)	9:10(1)	11:10(1)	13:10(2)
Arr. Lugano	8:47	10:40	12:40	14:40

Sights in Lugano: Take the cable car from the railstation to Piazza Cioccaro. Walk downhill from there to the city center, Piazza Riforma. Take one of the many boat trips on the lake. Also the cogwheel train to the 5300-foot top of Mt. Generoso and the chair-lift to the slightly higher top of Mt. Lema. Stroll the shore of lovely Lake Lugano. See the collection of over 400 masterpieces (Rubens, Goya, Durer) in the gallery of the La Villa Favorita mansion.

Visit in nearby Melide the Swissminiatur Model Village, a Swiss version of Holland's Madurodam. On the same 1:25 scale as Madurodam, there are excellent reproductions of castles, churches, farmhouses, town squares, etc., in a beautifully landscaped garden setting. Open mid-March to the end of October 8:00-18:00 (until 22:00 during July and August). The entry fee is reduced one Swiss Franc if you are carrying a copy of Eurail® Guide.

Dep. Lugano	14:13	16:13	17:29	18:13	20:13(4)
Arr. Milan (Cent.)	1½ hours later				

(1) Meal service. (2) Light refreshments. (3) Arrives at Milan's Lambrate station. (4) Plus other departures from Lugano at 22:06, 22:13 and 0:07(3).

Milan - Torino - Milan

354

Dep. Milan (Cent.)	7:00(1)	-0-	-0-	10:20(1)	11:20(3)
Dep. Milan (P.Gar.)	-0-	8:00	9:10(2)	-0-	-0-
Arr. Torino (P.N.)	8:30	10:08	11:10	11:48	12:55

Sights in Torino: See notes about city-sightseeing in Torino earlier in this section, under "Genoa-Torino".

Dep. Torino (P.N.)	12:30	13:30	14:30(2)	15:30	16:30(1+4)
Arr. Milan (P.Gar.)	-0-	-0-	-0-	17:15	-0-
Arr. Milan (Cent.)	14:25	15:20	16:20	-0-	18:00

(1) Reservation required. Supplement charged. (2) Light refreshments. (3) Plus another departure from Milan's Garibaldi station at 12:20. (4) Plus other departures from Torino at 17:30(2), 18:30, 19:30, 20:10, 21:03, 21:40(1) and 22:40.

Milan - Venice - Milan

390

Dep. Milan (Cent.)	5:55	6:55(1)	7:20	8:10	8:40(2+6)
Arr. Venice (S.L.)	9:44	9:52	11:00	11:38	11:50

Sights in Venice: See notes about city-sightseeing in Venice earlier in this section, under "Bologna-Venice".

Dep. Venice (S.L.)	12:55	14:00(1)	15:00	16:05(3)	17:35(4+7)
Arr. Milan (Cent.)	16:35	16:50	18:38	19:35	21:10

(1) Reservation required. First-class only. Meal service. (2) Runs from early June to late September. (3) Light refreshments. (4) Meal service. (5) Sundays and holidays only, from mid-July to early September. (6) Plus other departures from Milan at 9:10 and 9:35(1). (7) Plus other departures from Venice at 18:15(2+4), 18:35(1), 18:58(5), 19:20, 20:35(1) and 20:40.

Milan - Verona - Milan

390

Dep. Milan (Cent.)	7:20	8:10	8:40(1)	9:10	9:35(2+7)
Arr. Verona (P.N.)	9:10	9:55	10:10	10:56	11:09

Sights in Verona: See notes about city-sightseeing in Verona earlier in this section, under "Bologna-Verona".

Dep. Verona (P.N.)	12:50	14:51	15:24(2)	16:41	17:45(8)
Arr. Milan (Cent.)	1½ hours later				

(1) Runs from late May to late September. (2) Reservation required. Supplement charged. First-class only. (3) Meal service. (4) Light refreshments. (5) TEE. Reservation required. Meal service. (6) Adjustment footnote. (7) Plus other departures from Milan at 11:25(3), 12:15 and 13:00(4). (8) Plus other departures from Verona at 19:23(4), 19:56, 20:12(2+3), 21:24(5), 21:30, 22:00(2) and 22:32.

Naples - Pompeii - Naples 401

This trip is not covered by Eurailpass.

Dep. Naples (F.S.)	Frequent times from 4:53 to 22:54
Arr. Pompeii	30 minutes later

A travolator connection provides transportation from Naples' Central station to Naples' F.S. station.

Sights in Pompeii: See where 20,000 people were living and how they lived 1900 years ago when this city was buried in a few minutes under a volcanic rain of ashes from nearby (still active) Vesuvius, when it was young and strong.

Dep. Pompeii	Frequent times from 4:43 to 22:49
Arr. Naples (F.S.)	30 minutes later

Naples - Rome - Naples 392

Dep. Naples (Cent.)	5:30	6:00	7:00	8:00(4)
Arr. Rome (Ter.)	8:15	8:30	9:25	11:05

Sights in Rome: See notes about city-sightseeing in Rome at the start of this section.

Dep. Rome (Ter.)	13:30	14:30(1)	15:30	16:00(1+2+5)
Arr. Naples (Cent.)	15:52	17:18	18:02	18:10

(1) Meal service. (2) Reservation required. (3) Light refreshments. (4) Plus another departure from Naples at 9:00(3). (5) Plus other departures from Rome at 16:30(2+3), 17:00, 17:30, 19:00(3), 19:30(1+2), 20:00, 20:30 and 21:30.

Rome - Anzio - Rome

380

Dep. Rome (Ter.)	8:05	9:45	12:43	13:20(1)	14:07
Arr. Anzio	50-60 minutes later				

Sights in Anzio: This has been a beach resort since ancient times. Many Americans visit the nearby military cemeteries, holding those killed in the January 22, 1944 Allied invasion.

Dep. Anzio	9:29	13:04	15:03	16:14	18:14(2)
Arr. Rome (Ter.)	50-60 minutes later				

(1) Daily, except Sundays and holidays. (2) Plus other departures from Anzio at 20:08, 21:14 and 23:04.

Rome - Assisi - Rome

395

Dep. Rome (Ter.)	7:05(1)	8:17	9:25(2)	10:33(2)
Arr. Foligno	8:53	10:23	12:34	13:37

(1) Reservation required. (2) Change trains in Orte, en route to Foligno. Change trains in Foligno.

378

Dep. Foligno	9:15	10:50	12:38	13:43
Arr. Assisi	9:31	11:09	12:56	14:01

Sights in Assisi: See notes about city-sightseeing in Assisi earlier in this section, under "Florence-Assisi".

378

Dep. Assisi	12:40	15:22(1)	18:22(1)	20:08(1+2)
Arr. Rome (Ter.)	15:20	18:07	21:20	22:38

(1) Change trains in Foligno. (2) Reservation required from Foligno to Rome.

Rome - Florence (Firenze) - Rome 374

Dep. Rome (Termini)	5:42(1)	6:40(2)	7:50(3)	8:05(2+6)
Arr. Florence (S.M.N.)	9:05	9:46	10:37	11:17

Sights in Florence: See notes about city-sightseeing in Florence at the start of this section.

Dep. Florence (S.M.N.)	13:30	14:25(2+4)	14:57(2)	15:11(3+7)
Arr. Rome (Termini)	17:05	17:13	18:50	17:46

(1) Depart/Arrive Rome's Tiburtina station. (2) Meal service. (3) TEE. Reservation required. Meal service. (4) First-class only. Reservation required. (5) Light refreshments. (6) Plus other departures from Rome at 9:25(2) and 11:27(3). (7) Plus other departures from Florence at 15:51(5), 16:19(2), 16:43(2), 17:18(1), 17:54(2), 18:56(2), 20:18(3), 20:42(2) and 21:21.

Rome - Naples - Rome

392

Dep. Rome (Ter.)	6:30(1)	7:00(2)	7:30	8:00(7)
Arr. Naples (Cent.)	9:05	9:00(3)	10:25	10:40

Sights in Naples: See notes about city-sightseeing in Naples at the start of this section.

Dep. Naples (Cent.)	12:30(4)	13:00(5+6)	13:30(6)	14:00(4+5+8)
Arr. Rome (Ter.)	15:00	15:15	15:50	16:05

(1) Depart/Arrive Rome's Tiburtina station. (2) First-class only. Reservation required. Meal service. (3) Arrive/Depart Naple's Mergellina station. (4) Meal service. (5) Reservation required. (6) Light refreshments. (7) Plus other departures from Rome at 8:30(6), 9:30 and 12:05(2+3). (8) Plus other departures from Naples at 14:30, 15:30, 16:11(2+3), 17:00, 17:30, 18:30(6), 19:12(3+4+5), 19:30, 20:00, 20:30(1) and 21:00.

Rome - Orvieto - Rome

374

Dep. Rome (Ter.)	7:20(1)	10:33(2)	12:20(1)
Arr. Orvieto	8:39	12:11	13:33

Sights in Orvieto: The gold mosaics, marble pieces, bronze canopies, Fra Angelico and Luca Signorelli frescoes, and rose window in the 13th century Cathedral.

Dep. Orvieto	13:19(1)	14:27(1)	15:53	17:35(2+4)
Arr. Rome (Ter.)	14:45	15:52(3)	17:05	18:55

(1) Light refreshments. (2) Meal service. (3) Arrives at Rome's Tiburtina station. (4) Plus other departures from Orvieto at 18:18(1) and 21:21(2).

Rome - Perugia - Rome

395

Dep. Rome (Termini)	7:05(1)	8:17	9:25(2)	10:33(2)
Arr. Foligno	8:53	10:23	12:34	13:37

Change trains.

378

Dep. Foligno	9:10	10:50	12:42	13:43
Arr. Perugia	9:55	11:34	13:35	14:31

Sights in Perugia: See notes about city-sightseeing in Perugia earlier in this section, under "Florence-Perugia".

Dep. Perugia	12:13(3)	14:58	17:52	19:38
Arr. Foligno	-0-	15:37	18:40	20:25

Change trains.

395

Dep. Foligno	-0-	15:42	19:10	20:55(1)
Arr. Rome (Termini)	15:20	18:07	21:20	22:38

(1)Reservation required. (2)Change train in Orte. (3)Direct train. No train change in Foligno.

Rome - Pescara - Rome

376

Exceptional mountain scenery on this ride.

Dep. Rome (Termini)	7:00(1)	8:02
Arr. Pescara (Cent.)	10:30	11:59

Sights in Pescara: A nice beach resort on the Adriatic coast.

Dep. Pescara (Cent.)	13:17	14:14	16:15(1)	18:03	20:25
Arr. Rome (Termini)	17:52	21:01(2)	19:45	22:12	23:54

(1)Reservation required. (2)Arrives at Rome's Tiburtina station.

Rome - Pisa - Rome

355

Dep. Rome (Ter.)	6:40	7:25(1+2)	8:15	10:40(2)	12:05(2)
Arr. Pisa	11:20	10:38	12:31	14:35	15:38

Sights in Pisa: See notes about city-sightseeing in Pisa earlier in this section, under "Bologna-Pisa".

Dep. Pisa	14:37(2)	15:47(2)	16:42	18:38(4)	19:42(5)
Arr. Rome (Ter.)	18:40	20:05	21:06	22:25	23:45

(1)Reservation required. (2)Meal service. (3)Arrives at Rome's Tiburtina station. (4)Light refreshments. (5)Plus another departure from Pisa at 20:43(1+2).

Rome - Pompeii - Rome

392

Dep. Rome (Ter.)	8:30(1)	Dep. Pompeii	16:16 17:52(1)
Arr. Pompeii	11:29	Arr. Rome (Ter.)	19:58 20:52

(1) Light refreshments.

Sights in Pompeii: See notes about sightseeing in Pompeii earlier in this section, under "Naples-Pompeii".

Rome - Spoleto - Rome

395

Dep. Rome (Ter.)	7:10(1)	8:12	9:32(2)	10:33(2)
Arr. Spoleto	8:34	10:03	12:12	13:08

Sights in Spoleto: Roman ruins. The enormous 14th century Rocca (fortress). The central mosaic, magnificent Lippi fresco, and 8 rose windows in the Cathedral. The 14th century arched bridge that holds the aqueduct which still supplies Spoleto its water.

Dep. Spoleto	11:11(2)	13:28	16:07	19:30	21:11(1)
Arr. Rome (Ter.)	13:48	15:20	18:07	21:18	22:38

(1) Reservation required. (2) Change trains in Orte.

Rome - Siena - Rome

374

Dep. Rome (Ter.)	7:20	9:25
Arr. Chiusi	9:09	11:22

Change trains.

363

Dep. Chiusi	9:15	11:34
Arr. Siena	10:59	13:12

Sights in Siena: See notes about city-sightseeing in Siena earlier in this section, under "Bologna-Siena".

Dep. Siena	13:47	14:58	16:49	17:30	19:34
Arr. Chiusi	15:18	16:37	18:34	19:15	21:27

Change trains.

374

Dep. Chiusi	15:27	17:09(1)	18:39(1)	19:45(1)	21:32
Arr. Rome (Ter.)	17:05	18:50	20:07	21:12	22:58

(1) Meal service.

THE TRAIN ROUTES TO THE TOE OF ITALY

Here are the 2 rail routes to Southern Italy: along the Adriatic and Ionian seacoasts from Pescara to Reggio di Calabria, and along the Tyrrhenian seacoast from Naples to Reggio di Calabria.

Pescara - Foggia - Barletta - Bari - Brindisi - Taranto - Catanzaro - Reggio di Calabria

393

Dep. Pescara	10:53	13:10(1)	15:19(2+3)	17:10(4)	18:00(5+7)
Arr. Foggia	13:52	15:37	17:37	19:56	20:22
Arr. Barletta	14:28	-0-	18:17	20:42	21:04
Arr. Bari	16:05	17:01	18:55	21:15	21:41
Dep. Bari	16:30	17:15	19:48	22:03	21:55
Arr. Brindisi	18:23	18:37	21:15	23:58	23:15

(1)Runs from late June to mid-September. (2)TEE. Reservation required. Meal service. (3)Change trains in Bari. (4)Light refreshments. (5)Reservation required. Meal service. (6)Carries sleeping car. Also has couchettes. (7)Plus other departures from Pescara at 0:58, 2:36(6), 3:00, 3:24(6) and 4:45(6).

Change trains.

400

Dep. Brindisi	3:50	4:30	6:10	6:55	8:57	11:01(1)
Arr. Taranto	4:50	5:42	7:33	8:35	9:51	12:23

(1)Plus other departures from Brindisi at 12:40, 14:33, 17:29, 21:02 and 22:44.

Change trains.

407

Dep. Taranto	5:09	8:12	9:57(1)	11:20(2+4)
Arr. Catanzaro	11:18	15:29	13:40	16:32
Arr. Reggio (Cent.)	15:56	19:39	16:08	21:37

(1) Reservation required. (2) Change trains at Crotone, en route to Catanzaro. (3) Has couchettes. (4) Plus other departures from Taranto at 16:54 and 22:30(3).

Reggio di Calabria - Catanzaro - Taranto - Brindisi - Bari - Barletta - Foggia - Pescara

407

Dep. Reggio (Cent.)	6:22	6:53	10:52	15:16(1)	22:36(2)
Dep. Catanzaro	9:11	12:30	15:52	17:39	1:28
Arr. Taranto	12:55	18:44	21:20	21:32	6:18

(1) Reservation required. (2) Has couchettes.

Change trains.

400

Dep. Taranto	6:47	7:50	9:24	11:52	13:05(1)
Arr. Brindisi	8:28	8:42	10:42	13:15	14:21

(1) Plus other departures from Taranto at 14:29, 15:45, 19:36, 21:23 and 23:58.

Change trains.

393

Dep. Brindisi	9:41(1)	10:54(2)	12:03(3)	15:28	16:45(5)
Arr. Bari	11:16(1)	12:10(2)	13:31(4)	16:53	18:18
Dep. Bari	11:40(1)	12:37(2)	13:52(4)	17:14	18:38
Dep. Barletta	12:27(1)	-0-	14:28(4)	17:50	19:20
Arr. Foggia	13:13(1)	13:55(2)	15:07(4)	18:37	20:04
Arr. Pescara	16:07	16:40	17:33	21:54	22:43

(1) Light refreshments. (2) Runs from late June to mid-September. (3) Reservation required. (4) Meal service. (5) Plus other departures from Brindisi at 17:55, 18:52 and 19:26.

Sights in **Bari:** The Picture Gallery. The Archaeological Museum. The relics of St. Nicholas, in the 11th century Basilica of S. Nicola. The rebuilt Norman castle. The 12th century Romanesque Cathedral. Much wine, olive oil and almonds in this area.

Sights in **Barletta:** The 13th century S. Sepolcro Church. The Norman castle. The 12th century Gothic Cathedral.

Sights in **Brindisi:** Many Crusaders set out from here for Jerusalem. See the Roman column that marks the end of the Appian Way. The Civic Museum in the 11th century circular S. Giovanni al Sepolcro Church. Frederick II's 13th century castle. The rebuilt 11th century Cathedral.

Sights in **Catanzaro:** The Baroque S. Domenico Church. The paintings in the Museum.

Sights in **Foggia:** Much wool has been marketed here for centuries. See the ancient records of sheep tax at the Library. The city has an Art Gallery, a Museum and a Cathedral.

Sights in **Pescara:** See notes about sightseeing in Pescara earlier in this section, under "Rome-Pescara-Rome".

Sights in **Reggio di Calabria:** A very popular tourist resort. Founded by the Greeks in 720 B.C. See the fine archaeological collection in the Museo Nazionale della Magna Grecia. The reconstructed Romanesque-Byzantine Cathedral. There are many Greek and Roman ruins in this area.

Sights in **Taranto:** The 15th century Aragonese castle. The 14th century S. Domenico Maggiore Church. The exhibit of Greek vases and statues in the Museo Nazionale. The early 19th century Arsenal. The 11th century S. Cataldo Cathedral.

Rome - Naples - Villa San Giovanni - Reggio di Calabria

	398	398	398	392
Dep. Rome (Ter.)	-0-	-0-	-0-	7:00(4)
Dep. Rome (Tib.)	0:52(1)	1:22(3)	3:10(1)	-0-
Dep. Naples (Cent.)	3:26(2)	4:00(2)	5:51(1)	-0-
Arr. V.S. Giovanni	9:22	10:20	11:57	14:15
Arr. Reggio di Cal.	10:10	11:00	12:43	14:49

	392	392	392	392
Dep. Rome (Ter.)	8:30(3)	12:05(4)	-0-	15:30
Dep. Rome (Tib.)	-0-	-0-	13:56(5)	-0-
Dep. Naples (Cent.)	11:06(3)	-0-	16:22(5)	18:15
Arr. V.S. Giovanni	17:25	19:20	22:16	1:10
Arr. Reggio di Cal.	18:18	19:57	22:44	1:44

	392	392	392	398
Dep. Rome (Ter.)	17:00	19:00(5)	20:00(7)	-0-
Dep. Rome (Tib.)	-0-	-0-	-0-	21:02(5)
Dep. Naples (Cent.)	-0-	21:46(5)	22:35	23:31(2)
Arr. V.S. Giovanni	2:25	3:34	3:58	5:57
Arr. Reggio di Cal.	3:06	4:15	4:33	6:44

(1)Carries sleeping car. Also has couchettes. (2)Departs from Naples' Campi Flegrei station. (3)Runs from early July to mid-September. Has couchettes. (4)Reservation required. Supplement charged. Meal service. (5)Light refreshments. (6)Has couchettes. (7)Plus other departures from Rome(Termini) at (#392)22:00(6) and (#398)23:18(6).

Reggio di Calabria - Villa San Giovanni - Naples - Rome

	392	392	392	392
Dep. Reggio di Cal.	1:10	6:58(1)	10:22(2)	11:24(1)
Dep. V.S. Giovanni	2:05	7:30(1)	11:00(2)	12:08(1)
Dep. Naples (Cent.)	8:38(1)	13:30(1)	-0-	18:30(1)
Arr. Rome (Tib.)	-0-	-0-	-0-	-0-
Arr. Rome (Ter.)	11:50	15:50	18:00	20:52

	392	392	398	392
Dep. Reggio di Cal.	12:58(3)	13:21(1)	14:18(5)	14:51(7)
Dep. V.S. Giovanni	13:40(3)	13:50(1)	15:02(5)	15:23(7)
Dep. Naples (Cent.)	-0-	21:59(1)	21:25(6)	21:37(7)
Arr. Rome (Tib.)	-0-	-0-	-0-	-0-
Arr. Rome (Ter.)	21:10	0:24(4)	23:42(4)	0:04(4)

	398	392	398	398
Dep. Reggio di Cal.	14:59	15:26(8)	16:37(9)	19:34(10+11)
Dep. V.S. Giovanni	15:52	16:20(8)	17:24(9)	20:18(10)
Dep. Naples (Cent.)	22:20(6)	-0-	23:40(6)	2:34(6)
Arr. Rome (Tib.)	0:43	-0-	2:05	5:02
Arr. Rome (Ter.)	-0-	1:03(4)	-0-	-0-

(1) Light refreshments. (2) Reservation required. Supplement charged. Meal service. (3) Reservation required in first-class. Meal service. (4) Arrives at Rome's Ostiense station. (5) Runs from early July to mid-September. Has couchettes. (6) Arrives/Departs Naple's Campi Flegrei station. (7) Runs from late June to mid-September. Has couchettes. (8) Has couchettes. Light refreshments. (9) Carries sleeping car. Also has couchettes. (10) Has couchettes. (11) Plus other departures from Reggio at 20:07(10), 20:55, 21:56(10) and 22:49(9).

TRAIN RIDES TO SICILY

Rome - Naples - Messina - Catania - Siracusa - Palermo

This trip includes a 35-minute ride on the ferry boat between Villa S. Giovanni and Messina (Maritima).

	398	398	60	60
Dep. Rome (Ter.)	7:00(1)	9:00(2)	10:30(1)	17:00(3)
Dep. Rome (Tib.)	3:00	3:22(1)	4:33(1+2)	5:34(2)
Dep. Naples (C. Fleg.)	5:27	5:51	-0-	-0-
Dep. Naples (Cent.)	-0-	-0-	7:17(3)	8:30(3)
Arr. Messina (Marit.)	12:50	13:25	14:20	16:00
Arr. Catania	15:09	15:48	-0-	18:42
Arr. Siracusa	16:52	17:16	-0-	20:00
Arr. Palermo	17:36	17:57	18:45	-0-

	392	392	392	392
Dep. Rome (Ter.)	7:00(4)	8:30(3)	12:05(4)	17:00(5+9)
Dep. Naples (P. Gar.)	9:16(4)	-0-	14:00(4)	19:45(5+6)
Dep. Naples (Cent.)	-0-	11:06(3)	-0-	-0-
Arr. Messina (Marit.)	15:20	18:50	20:35	3:45
Arr. Catania	17:18	21:02	22:13	-0-
Arr. Siracusa	18:31	22:42	23:18	-0-
Arr. Palermo	19:05	23:14	23:53	8:25

(1)Carries sleeping car. Also has couchettes. (2)Departs from Rome's Ostiense station. (3)Light refreshments. (4)Reservation required. Supplement charged. Meal service. (5)Has couchettes. (6)Departs from Naples' Campi Flegrei station. (7)Departs from Rome's Termini station. (8)Departs from Rome's Tiburtina station. (9)Plus other departures from Rome at (#392)20:00(1+7), (#392)21:02(3+5+8), (#392)-22:00(1+7) and (#398)23:18(1+7).

Palermo - Siracusa - Catania - Messina - Naples - Rome

This trip includes a 35-minute ride on the ferry boat between Messina (Maritima) and Villa San Giovanni.

	392	392	392	398
Dep. Palermo	6:25(1)	6:40(2)	8:52(3)	10:07
Dep. Siracusa	6:58(1)	7:23(2)	9:18(3)	10:16
Dep. Catania	8:08(1)	8:46(2)	10:30(3)	11:54
Dep. Messina (Marit.)	9:50(1)	10:50(2)	12:25(3)	14:20
Arr. Naples (Cent.)	-0-	18:18	-0-	22:20(4)
Arr. Naples (P. Gar.)	15:55	-0-	18:55	-0-
Arr. Rome (Ter.)	18:00	20:52	21:10	0:43(5)

	392	398	60	392
Dep. Palermo	-0-	11:48(6)	13:02(6)	14:20(6+9)
Dep. Siracusa	11:22(2+6)	12:06(6)	-0-	14:41(6+10)
Dep.Catania	12:52(2+6)	13:44(6)	-0-	16:20(6)
Dep. Messina (Marit.)	15:00(2+6)	16:05(6)	17:30(2+6)	18:45(6)
Arr. Naples (Cent.)	22:46(4)	23:40(4)	0:55	2:34(4)
Arr. Naples (P. Gar.)	-0-	-0-	-0-	-0-
Arr. Rome (Ter.)	1:03(7)	2:05	3:39(7)	5:02

(1)Reservation required. Supplement charged. Meal service. (2)Light refreshments. (3)Reservation required in first-class. Meal service. (4)Arrives at Naples' Campi Flegrei station. (5)Arrives at Rome's Tiburtina station. (6)Carries sleeping car. Also has couchettes. (7)Arrives at Rome's Ostiense station. (8)Has couchettes. (9)Plus other departures from Palermo at 15:08(8), 18:00(6) and 19:06(6). (10)Plus other departures from Siracusa at 17:35(8) and 20:42(6). (11)Plus other departures from Catania at 17:56(8), 19:20(6) and 22:28(6).

Sights in **Messina:** The Cathedral and the Annunciata dei Catalani Church, both rebuilt in the 12th century by Norman occupiers. The beautiful astronomical clock in the modern Bell Tower, next to the Cathedral. The art in the Museo Nazionale. The Botanical Gardens.

Sights in **Catania:** Founded 729 B.C. by Greek settlers. Now a very busy seaport and a popular Winter beach resort. Whatever could happen to a city happened here in the 16th and 17th centuries: famines, civil wars, epidemics, pirate raids, earthquakes, and the eruption of Mt. Etna in 1693, after which Catania was almost completely rebuilt. The dark gray color of the city results from the use of volcanic matter in constructing buildings.

See the Greek and Roman theaters, aqueducts and baths. The excellent collection of art and archaeological relics in the Civic Museum of the 13th century Castello Ursino. The tomb of the composer Vincenzo Bellini in the rebuilt 11th century Cathedral, also containing relics of St. Agatha. Sicily's largest church, San Nicolo. Next to it, the Benedictine San Nicolo Monastery, started in the 14th century.

The medieval manuscripts in the library of the University. The royal chapel, Collegiata. The 18th century palaces circling the Piazza del Duomo, with its Elephan Fountain. The museum at the birthplace of Bellini. The Astronomical Observatory.

Sights in **Siracusa:** Settled by Greeks in 734 B.C., 5 years after the founding of nearby Catania. An earthquake that destroyed much of Catania leveled Siracusa in 1693, after which Siracusa was rebuilt.

A comprehensive tour of Siracusa starts by visiting on the hill of Neapolis the Roman Amphitheater (which held 15,000 people attending gladiator fights), constructed during the reign of Augustus, before the birth of Christ. This structure was severely stripped in 1526 for the building of the city's defensive walls.

Above the Amphitheater is the 600-foot-long alter of Hieron II, where 450 oxen were simultaneously sacrificed on pagan religious days. Nearby is an ancient quarry in which the cave called "the ear of Dionysius" is located. Next to it is the 5th century B.C. Greek Theater, where Plato and Aeschylus performed. Behind the Theater is the "Grotto of the Nymphs". Five miles further, on the hill of Epipoli overlooking Siracusa, is the Castle of Euryalus, the mightiest and most complete fortress of Greek times.

Returning downhill, along Corso Gelone, you come to the ruins of the Roman Forum, at Piazzale Marconi. Go along Corso Umberto I and cross the Ponte Nuovo to reach the island of Ortygia. There. in Piazza Pancali, are the remains of the Temple of Apollo, which the conquering Arabs turned into a mosque. Other sights in Ortygia are the 16th century Santa Maria dei Miracoli church, the 15th century arch (Porta Marina), the Maniace Castle, and the 13th century Bellomo Palace, which houses a museum of medieval and modern art.

Other sights: the 17th century Palazzo del Municipo (Town Hall), the 18th century Palazzo Benevantano del Bosco, The National Archaeological Museum, which has one of the most important collections (Greek, Roman and Byzantine) of sarcophagi, pottery, coins and bronzes in Italy. Its most famous treasure is the 2nd century B.C. Venus Landolina sculpture.

The ancient Cathedral is dominated by the Doric columns of the original Temple of Minerva, where many works of art are exhibited.

Sights in **Palermo:** The capital of Sicily. Severely damaged by bombs in July of 1943. See the fine archaeological collection in the Museo Nazionale, on Via Roma. South of it, tombs of important Sicilians, in the San Domenico Church. The 800-year old Cathedral and, next to it, The Archepiscopal Palace, both on Vittorio Emanuele. Nearby, the marvelous Oriental garden at the Church of San Giovanni degli Eremiti. The Risorgimento Museum, at Piazza San Domenico.

La Vucceria, the all-day outdoor market, on a small, twisting street. Sicilian pastries, cheeses and many exotic foods such as fried lungs and spleen, sea urchins, and pork sausage encased in the skin of a pig's foot are among the local delicacies sold there.

The statues of former Spanish rulers in the Quattro Canti (Four Corners), a small octagonal piazza. The Palace of the Norman Kings. Teatro Massimo, an enormous opera house. The 12th century Royal Palace. Martorana Church. The Cuba and Zisa palaces. The catacombs under the Convent of the Capuchin Friars.

Take the #9 bus to see the famous Norman Cathedral and Cloister in Monreale, 5 miles away. Take the #14 or #77 bus to the bathing beach, Mondello. There are half-day bus excursions and local train service to Segesta and Selinunte, sites of substantial Greek ruins.

There is hydrofoil service in the Spring and Summer to 2 interesting islands. Ustica's Blue Grotto attracts many visitors. The Archaeological Museum on Lipari is worthwhile. From Lipari, there is boat service to other nearby islands: Alicudi, Filicudi, Salina, Stromboli and Vulcano. Passenger ships run from Palermo to Tunisia.

It is a short drive to see the excellent mosaics in the 12th century Cathedral at Monreale.

TRAIN ROUTES IN SICILY
(including One-Day Excursions)

Messina - Milazzo - Palermo
405

Dep. Massina (Cent.)	4:28	5:30	6:17	8:10(1)	8:45(3)
Arr. Milazzo	4:56	5:58	6:57	8:48	9:30
Arr. Palermo	8:25	9:09	10:00	11:39	13:12

Sights in **Milazzo:** Founded 7 centuries before Christ. An important naval victory over the Carthaginians was won by the Romans in Milazzo's bay more than 2,200 years ago. See the 13th century Norman castle and the 16th century Spanish walls at the old town, on a hill above the modern city.

Sights in **Palermo:** See notes about sightseeing in Palermo earlier in this section, under "Naples-Messina-Palermo".

Dep. Palermo	6:25(2)	6:40	8:55(2)	10:00	11:40(4)
Dep. Milazzo	8:49(2)	9:33	11:16(2)	12:40	14:35(5)
Arr. Messina (Cent.)	9:25	10:09	11:53	13:13	15:20

(1)Light refreshments. (2)Reservation required. (3)Plus other departures from Messina at 9:45, 11:03, 12:20, 13:40, 14:12, 14:59, 15:57, 19:40 and 20:55(2). (4)Plus other departures from Palermo at 13:02, 14:20, 15:08, 18:00 and 19:06. (5)Plus other departures from Milazzo at 14:03, 15:59, 17:11, 18:11, 18:43, 19:30, 20:49 and 22:01.

Messina - Taormina - Catania - Siracusa 406

Dep. Messina (Cent.)	5:38	8:50	9:48	12:14	13:40	14:08(3)
Arr. Taormina	6:18	9:38	10:25	13:10	14:19	14:46
Arr. Catania	7:12	10:44	11:28	14:18	15:11	15:41
Dep. Catania	7:44	10:56	11:40	14:23	15:24	15:51
Arr. Siracusa	9:15	12:30	13:16	15:46	16:50	17:15

(1)Reservation required in first-class. (2)Adjustment footnote. (3)Plus other departures from Messina at 16:00(1), 16:52, 19:38 and 20:58(1).

Sights in **Taormina:** A year-around resort, with very mild Winter weather, consisting mainly of 3 streets, each on a different level, connected to each other by many stairways, all on one side of Mont Venere. One funicular provides access to the beaches below the little town (4,000 population).

Stroll and shop for pottery, embroidery and carved wood figures along Corso Umberto, the main street. See the 3rd century Roman theater, facing Mt. Etna. The medieval great halls in the 15th century Palazzo Corvaja. The 14th century Palace of the Duke of St. Stephen. The 13th century Cathedral.

Sights in **Catania:** See notes about sightseeing in Catania earlier in this section, under "Palermo-Siracusa-Catania-Naples".

Sights in **Siracusa:** See notes about sightseeing in Siracusa earlier in this section, under "Palermo-Siracusa-Catania-Naples".

Dep. Siracusa	6:58(1+2)	7:23	9:18(1)	10:16	11:22(4)
Arr. Catania	8:04	8:34	10:26	11:34	12:40
Dep. Catania	8:08(1+2)	8:46	10:30(1)	11:54	12:52
Arr. Taormina	8:41	9:27	11:10	12:43	13:32
Arr. Messina (Cent.)	9:25	10:09	11:50	13:34	14:20

(1) Reservation required. (2) First-class only. (3) Change trains in Catania. (4) Plus other departures from Siracusa at 12:06, 14:41, 15:24(3), 17:35 and 20:42.

Palermo - Agrigento 410

Dep. Palermo	5:40	8:11	9:32	12:28	14:26	16:38	20:48
Arr. Agrigento	8:30	11:30	12:45	15:28	17:16	19:37	23:38

Sights in Agrigento: Founded by Greeks in 581 B.C. See the extremely fine Greek ruins: 7 Doric temples, many aqueducts and cemeteries. The 14th century Cathedral. The 13th century churches: S. Nicola, Santa Maria dei Greci and S. Spirito. Baroque palaces. There is an especially good Archaeological Museum here.

Dep. Agrigento	5:22	8:53	12:51	14:37	17:03	19:24(1+3)
Arr. Palermo	8:08	11:04	15:32	18:16	19:30	22:04

(1) Daily, except Sundays and holidays. (2) Sundays and holidays only. (3) Plus another departure from Agrigento at 20:40(2).

Palermo - Caltanisetta 409

Dep. Palermo	6:29	8:45	12:08	14:08	16:38(1)
Arr. Caltan. (Xirbi)	8:54	10:43	14:42	16:24	18:57

(1) Plus other departures at 19:20 and 20:48.

Sights in Caltanisetta: The Greek, Arabic and Norman ruins at the Pietrarossa Castle. The excellent archaeological collection in the Civic Museum. The Baroque Cathedral and Palazzo Moncada.

Dep. Caltan. (Xirbi)	6:56	8:29	9:40	14:17	17:43(1)
Arr. Palermo	9:17	10:27	11:49	16:35	19:53

(1) Plus other departures from Caltanisetta at 19:34 and 21:40.

Palermo - Catania 409

Dep. Palermo	6:29	8:45	12:08(1)	14:08(1)	16:38(1)	19:20
Arr. Catania	11:05	12:48	17:24	18:51	21:33	23:36

Sights in Catania: See notes about sightseeing in Catania earlier in this section, under "Naples-Messina-Catania".

Dep. Catania	6:25	7:10(1)	11:05(1)	15:32	19:17
Arr. Palermo	10:27	11:36	16:35	19:53	0:03

(1) Change trains in Caltanisetta Xirbi.

Palermo - Trapani
405

Dep. Palermo	5:21	7:02	9:08	10:25	12:21	13:44(1)
Arr. Trapani	2½ hours later					

(1) Plus other departures at 14:05, 16:54, 18:50, 20:55 and 23:30.

Sights in Trapani: A major Carthaginian and Roman naval base in the 3rd century B.C. See the outstanding 14th century Santuario dell' Annunziata, rebuilt in the 18th century. The 14th century Santo Agostino Church. The excellent sculptures and paintings in the Museo Nazionale Pepoli. The 17th century Cathedral. The Baroque Palazzo della Giudecca. The 15th century Santa Maria di Gesu Church.

Dep. Trapani	4:55	5:19	6:18	7:40	10:55	12:00(1)
Arr. Palermo	2½ hours later					

(1) Plus other departures at 14:15, 16:23, 17:40 and 19:55.

Agrigento - Caltanisetta 409

Dep. Agrigento	4:15	8:32	9:56	12:31(1)
Arr. Caltanisetta (Cent.)	6:00	10:21	11:53	14:36
Arr. Caltanisetta (Xirbi)	10 minutes after arriving Centrale station			

Sights in Caltanisetta: See notes about sightseeing in Caltanisetta earlier in this section, under "Palermo-Caltanisetta".

Dep. Caltanisetta (Xirbi)	9:38	11:06	16:41	0:12
Dep. Caltanisetta (Cent.)	9:56	11:48	17:05	0:23
Arr. Agrigento	11:42	14:22	19:24	1:46

(1) Plus other departures from Agrigento at 14:05, 16:06 and 19:40.

Catania - Caltanisetta 409

Dep. Catania	6:26	7:10	7:52	11:01	13:35(1)
Arr. Caltanisetta (Xirbi)	8:49	9:34	11:00	13:08	16:31

Sights in Caltanisetta: See notes about sightseeing in Caltanisetta earlier in this section, under "Palermo-Caltanisetta".

Dep. Caltanisetta (Xirbi)	6:11	8:54	10:35	12:04	14:50(2)
Arr. Catania	8:23	11:02	13:00	14:35	17:24

(1) Plus other departures from Catania at 15:32, 19:17 and 21:52.
(2) Plus other departures from Caltanisetta at 16:32, 19:14 and 21:39.

THE MALTA CRUISE

Reggio di Calabria, Catania and Siracusa are gateways for the boat trip to Malta.

1427

Dep. Reggio	8:30(1)	Dep. Malta	8:45(2)
Dep. Catania	13:00	Arr. Siracusa	14:00
Dep. Siracusa	16:30	Arr. Catania	17:45
Arr. Malta	21:30	Arr. Reggio	22:00

(1) Sundays, Tuesdays and Fridays. (2) Mondays, Wednesdays and Saturdays.

SCENIC RAIL TRIPS

Arona - Brig

There is beautiful lake and mountain scenery on this portion of the Milan-Lausanne route.

251

Dep. Milan (Cent.)	7:05	9:00(1)	10:05	11:05(4)
Dep. Arona	7:59	-0-	10:54	12:00
Arr. Brig	9:37	11:04	12:37(2)	13:37
Arr. Lausanne	11:26	12:32	14:26	15:26

(1) Supplement charged. (2) Light refreshments. (3) TEE. Reservation required. (4) Plus other departures from Milan at 12:35, 14:55(2+3), 15:00 and 17:15.

Bologna - Florence

374 + 398

Excellent mountain scenery on this ride.

The train goes through the 11.5-mile long Apennine Tunnel, Italy's longest tunnel.

Complete schedules appear earlier in this section, under "Bologna-Florence" and "Florence-Bologna" one-day excursions.

Bolzano - Brennero

Exceptional mountain scenery on this portion of the route from Verona to Innsbruck and on to Munich.

Verona - Innsbruck - Munich 381

Dep. Verona (P.N.)	8:26(1)	9:04
Dep. Bolzano	10:04	11:17(2)
Arr. Fortezza	10:42	12:12
Dep. Brennero	11:37	13:05
Arr. Innsbruck	12:10	13:59
Arr. Munich (Hbf.)	14:03	16:25

(1) TEE. Reservation required. Meal service. (2) Light refreshments.

Fortezza - Dobbiaco

Very good mountain scenery on this spur off the Bolzano-Brennero route, appearing above. The following schedule shows how the Verona-Innsbruck-Munich trip can accommodate this en route detour.

381		383		
Dep. Verona (P.N.)	9:04	Dep. Dobbiaco	14:36	18:30
Arr. Fortezza	12:12	Arr. Fortezza	15:50	19:55
Change trains.		Change trains.		
383		381		
Dep. Fortezza	12:44	Dep. Fortezza	17:09	21:38
Arr. Dobbiaco	14:06	Arr. Innsbruck	19:00	23:27
		Arr. Munich (Hbf.)	21:26	1:37(1)

(1) Arrives at Munich's Ost station.

Torino - Cuneo - Breil - Nice 370

There is spectacular scenery on the 74-mile-long Cuneo-Nice rail route through the Roya Valley and the Alps, a service that first became operational in 1928. Severe damage during World War II caused it to be closed in 1940, and it was not re-opened until the Winter of 1979.

An outstanding feat of engineering, this line is a succession of very high viaducts, bridges and 60 tunnels that span 27 miles of this route, interspersed with sections that look down into deep valleys. This route has attracted many tourists.

Dep. Torino (P.N.)	8:35(1)	8:54(2)	13:52
Arr. Fossano	9:19(1)	10:12(2)	14:51
Change trains.			
Dep. Fossano	9:21(1)	10:14(2)	14:53
Arr. Cuneo	9:39(1)	10:37	15:18
Change trains.			
Dep. Cuneo	9:43(1)	10:42	16:06(3)
Arr. Breil	11:08	12:17	17:56(3)
Change trains.			
Dep. Breil	11:15	12:33	18:14(3)
Arr. Nice	12:18	13:39	19:22

(1)Direct train to Nice. No train changes en route. (2)Direct train to Cuneo. No train change in Fossano. (3)Direct train to Nice. No train change in Breil.

The magnificent Cuneo-Breil scenery can also be seen on an easy one-day roundtrip from Torino.

Torino - Cuneo - Torino 370

Dep. Torino (P.N.)	8:35	12:26(1)	Dep. Breil	12:12(2)	16:49(2)
Arr. Breil	11:02	15:03	Arr. Torino (P.N.)	15:10	19:50

(1)Departs from Torino's Porta Susa station. (2)Change trains in Cuneo.

Another route for viewing the breathtaking Cuneo-Breil scenery is a one-day roundtrip from Genoa.

Genoa - Torino - Cuneo - Ventimiglia - Genoa and v.v.

355		356	
Dep. Genoa (P.P.)	10:05	Dep. Genoa (P.P.)	11:40
Arr. Torino (P.N.)	12:21	Arr. Ventimiglia	14:55
Change trains.		Change trains.	
370		370	
Dep. Torino (P.N.)	12:40(1)	Dep. Ventimiglia	16:39(1)
Arr. Cuneo	13:53(1)	Dep. Cuneo	18:24(1)
Arr. Ventimiglia	16:10	Arr. Torino (P.N.)	19:50
Change trains.		Change trains.	
356		355	
Dep. Ventimiglia	17:43(2)	Dep. Torino (P.N.)	21:10
Arr. Genoa (P.P.)	20:50	Arr. Genoa (P.P.)	23:55

(1)Change trains in Cuneo. (2)Light refreshments.

Sights in Cuneo: The 10th century Cathedral. The 13th century Church of San Francesco. The Marvelous viaduct over the Stura di Demonte. The Civic Museum in the 18th century Palazzo Audiffredi. The 18th century Town Hall.

Brindisi - Taranto - Reggio

Splendid coastline scenery on this trip.

400		
Dep. Brindisi	6:09	8:53
Arr. Taranto	7:33	9:52

Change trains.

407			
Dep. Taranto	8:12	10:01(1)	10:27(2)
Arr. Reggio (Cent.)	19:35	16:08	21:22

(1)Reservation required. Supplement charged. (2)Change trains in Crotone at 15:20.

Genoa - Pisa

There is exceptional mountain and Mediterranean coastline scenery on this ride. Complete schedules appear earlier in this section under the "Genoa-Pisa" one-day excursion.

Genoa - Nice - Cannes - Marseille

A close look at more than 100 miles of outstanding seashore resorts along the Mediterranean's Ligure coastline: the Savona and San Remo beaches (on the Italian Riviera) and the Monaco, Nice, Antibes, Cannes and St. Raphael beaches (on the French Riviera).

151				
Dep. Genoa (P.P.)	6:58(1)	8:23(2)	8:45(3)	10:00(4+7)
Arr. Nice	11:39	11:16	13:35(3)	15:08
Dep. Nice	12:33(1)	12:20(2)	13:55(3)	15:10(4)
Arr. Cannes	12:57(1)	11:43	14:20	15:51(4)
Dep. Cannes	13:00	11:45(2)	14:23	16:52(5)
Arr. Marseille (St. Ch.)	14:52	13:38	16:20	19:05

(1)Runs from late June to late August. Change trains in Cannes. (2)Supplement charged. Meal service. (3)Change trains in Nice. (4)Change trains in Cannes. (5)Meal service. (6)Light refreshments. (7)Plus another departure from Genoa at 13:24(6).

Milan - Locarno

The great gorge, mountain and river scenery is on the portion of this route from Domodossola to Locarno by a narrow-gauge local train. This Centovalli (one hundred valley) ride is one of the 5 most outstanding scenic rail trips in Europe. Complete schedules appear earlier in this section under the "Milan-Locarno" one-day excursion.

Milan - Genoa

Views of marble quarries, mountains, farms and the Mediterranean coast, all in 1½ hours. An easy one-day roundtrip. See schedules earlier in this section, under one-day excursions.

Milan - Zurich

This is one of the 5 most outstanding scenic rail trips in Europe. A feast of beautiful farms, lakes, mountains, rivers and vineyards. You go through the 9.3-mile long Gotthard Tunnel. Before it was opened to traffic in 1882, there was no direct rail route from Italy to eastern Switzerland through the Alps.

Prior to entering the Gotthard, the train goes through the beautiful Ticino Valley.

Immediately upon exiting the first of a series of 9 tunnels, you first see the small, white Wassen Church on your right, 170 feet below the track. The next time the church comes into view, after exiting tunnel #4. the church is to your left and nearly level with the track. Later, after exiting tunnel #6, you have a third view of the church, again to your left, this time nearly 230 feet above the track, but you will see it there only if you look far ahead and before being alongside the church. (The train is in the Kirchberg Tunnel when it is directly alongside the church.)

The turns inside 3 semi-circular tunnels in this area (Leggistein. Wattinger and Pfaffensprung) are engineered so well that there is no sensation of the curves that the train is making inside those tunnels.

Try this interesting experiment: make a pendulum of any object, holding the top of a weighted string, chain or handkerchief against the inner face of a train window (a left-hand window when inside Leggistein, and a right-hand window when inside Wattinger and Pfaffensprung). As the train goes around a curve, the weighted bottom will move away from the window.

The Mediterranean climate on the Italian end of the tunnel is usually much warmer than the Alpine temperature on the Swiss end. The train makes 3% gradients at 45-50 miles per hour.

277

Dep. Milan (Cent.)	7:49(1)	9:10(2)	11:10(2)	13:10(1+4)
Arr. Zurich (Hbf.)	11:50	13:50	15:50	17:50

(1)Light refreshments. (2)Meal service. (3)TEE. Reservation required. Meal service. (4)Plus other departures from Milan at 15:10(2) and 16:50(3).

Milan - Sondrio - Tirano - St. Moritz - Chur - Zurich

This is an alternate route from Milan to Zurich. Between Milan and Tirano, you will see many rivers and lakes. The descent from St. Moritz to Chur is spectacular.

357			
Dep. Milan (Cent.)	6:35(1)	9:15(3)	12:00(3)
Arr. Sondrio	9:32	-0-	-0-
Change trains.			
Dep. Sondrio	9:42(2)	-0-	-0-
Arr. Tirano	10:18	12:22	14:41
Change trains.			
304			
Dep. Tirano	10:30	12:30	14:47(4)
Arr. St. Moritz	13:08	15:02	17:00(4)
Change trains.			
269			
Dep. St. Moritz	14:08(5)	15:20	18:08(6)
Arr. Chur	16:13	18:33	20:13
Change trains.			
268			
Dep. Chur	16:24	19:16(6)	20:24(6)
Arr. Zurich (Hbf.)	17:47	20:47	21:47

(1)Departs from Milan's Garibaldi station. (2)Daily, except Sunday and Monday. (3)Direct train. No train change in Sondrio. (4)Direct train. No train change in St. Moritz. Light refreshments. (5)Runs from mid-June to late September. (6)Light refreshments.

Naples - Brindisi

Very good mountain scenery on this route.

400				
Dep. Naples (Cent.)	5:30(1)	8:50(2)	12:15	
Arr. Taranto	10:39	14:18	19:20	
Change trains.				
Dep. Taranto	11:46	15:45	19:36	
Arr. Brindisi	13:13	16:57	20:44	
	*	*	*	
Dep. Brindisi	6:10	8:57	11:01	14:33
Arr. Taranto	7:33	9:51	12:23	15:58
Change trains.				
Dep. Taranto	7:52(1)	9:37(3)	12:35	16:10(1)
Arr. Naples (Cent.)	12:40	18:18	19:15	20:40

(1)Reservation required. Supplement charged. (2)Change trains in Salerno. (3)Change trains in Potenza and Salerno.

Naples - Siracusa

Wonderful Mediterranean coastline scenery on this trip. See details earlier in this section, under "Train Rides To Southern Italy".

Naples - Sorrento

Excellent Mediterranean coastline scenery on this ride.

401

Dep. Naples (Circumvesuviana) and Naples (F.S.) at one or 2 times per hour from 4:53 until 22:54 for the 60 minute ride to Sorrento.

Dep. Sorrento at one or 2 times every hour from 4:23 to 22:29 for the ride back to Naples. (There are stops in both directions at Pompeii.) A travolator provides transportation between Naples' F.S. station and Naples' Centrale station.

Naples - Taranto

Very good mountain scenery on this route.

396

Dep. Naples (P. Gar.)	7:13(1)	10:10(1)
Arr. Bari	11:12	14:32

Change trains.

407

Dep. Bari	13:04	15:25
Arr. Taranto	14:49	16:41

407

Dep. Taranto	7:54	13:10
Arr. Bari	9:26	14:34

Change trains.

396

Dep. Bari	11:40(2)	15:37(1)
Arr. Naples (P. Gar.)	17:55(3)	20:01

(1)Reservation required. Supplement charged. (2)Change trains in Foggia. (3)Arrives at Naples' Centrale station.

Pisa - Genoa

Exceptional mountain and Mediterranean coastline scenery on this ride. Complete schedules appear earlier in this section under the "Genoa-Pisa" one-day excursion.

Reggio - Taranto - Brindisi

Excellent coastline scenery on this ride, which allows a sightseeing stopover in Taranto.

407

Dep. Reggio (Cent.)	6:24
Arr. Taranto	12:53

400

Dep. Taranto	13:00	14:29	15:45
Arr. Brindisi	14:16	15:43	16:57

Sights in Taranto: See description earlier in this section, under "Reggio di Calabria - Pescara".

Rimini - Pescara - Brindisi

The excellent scenery on this route includes olive groves, vineyards and superb beaches on the Adriatic coastline. This can be broken into a 2-day trip by stopping in Pescara one night and then continuing on to

Brindisi the next day. Also, this trip can be extended by continuing on from Brindisi to Reggio, a ride that offers fine coastline scenery (see schedules later in this section under "Taranto-Reggio".

393

Dep. Rimini	6:50	9:57(1)	12:37(2)
Arr. Pescara (Cent.)	10:43	13:06	15:16
Dep. Pescara (Cent.)	10:53	13:10(1)	15:19(2)
Arr. Brindisi	18:23	18:37	21:15

(1) Runs from late June to mid-September. (2) TEE. Reservation required. Meal service. Change trains in Bari.

Rome - Pescara

Excellent mountain scenery on this trip. Complete schedules appear earlier in this section under the "Rome-Pescara" one-day excursion.

Torino - Paris

The Modane-Culoz portion of this trip offers outstanding lake and mountain scenery.

152

Dep. Torino (P.N.)	11:35	Dep. Culoz	16:07(1)
Dep. Modane	14:02	Arr. Paris (Lyon)	21:41

(1) Meal service.

Udine - Trieste

This portion of the Venice-Trieste ride has excellent scenery of the Adriatic coastline. Have a seat on the right-hand side for best viewing. The schedules allow a sightseeing stopover in Udine.

389

Dep. Venice (S. Lucia)	6:50(1)	9:48	11:32	13:05	14:00	15:32
Arr. Udine	8:52	11:32	13:25	15:04	15:58	17:22

Change trains.

388

Dep. Udine	9:00	10:08	10:59	13:18	15:32	18:44
Arr. Trieste	10:16	11:36	11:57	14:29	16:43	19:55

(1) Meal service.

Udine - Villach

This portion of the Venice-Vienna trip offers fine mountain scenery.

389

Dep. Venice (S. Lucia)	6:50(1)	13:05(1)
Dep. Udine	9:14	15:08
Arr. Villach	12:00	17:34
Arr. Vienna (Sudbf.)	18:05	22:25

(1) Meal service.

INTERNATIONAL ROUTES FROM ITALY

The primary Italian gateway for rail travel to Switzerland, western West Germany, Luxembourg, Belgium, Holland and northeastern France (Paris) is Milan.

A secondary gateway for rail travel from Italy to Switzerland is from Torino, via Aosta, to either Brig or Geneva.

There is rail service to southern France (Nice, Marseille and Avignon), Paris, and to Spain from Genoa.

The gateways for travel to Austria, eastern West Germany and Denmark are Verona and Venice.

Venice is also the starting point for trips to Yugoslavia, Czechoslovakia, East Germany and the rest of Eastern Europe (Bulgaria, Greece, Romania, Hungary, Poland and Russia).

Milan - Zurich

277

Dep. Milan (Cent.)	1:30(1)	4:28(1+2+3)	7:10(4)	9:10(5+7)
Arr. Zurich (Hbf.)	6:15	9:50	11:50	13:50

(1)Has couchettes. (2)Carries sleeping car. (3)Departs from Milan's Lambrate station. (4)Light refreshments. (5)Meal service. (6)TEE. Reservation required. Meal service. (7)Plus other departures at 11:00(5), 13:10(4), 15:10(5), 16:50(6) and 18:40(5).

Milan - Luzern - Basle

277

Dep. Milan (Cent.)	7:10(1)	9:20(1+2)	11:20(1+2)	13:10(1+7)
Arr. Luzern	11:37	13:37	15:37	17:37
Arr. Basle (S.B.B.)	12:53	14:53	16:53	18:53

(1)Meal service. (2)Supplement charged. (3)Runs from late May to late October. (4)Light refreshments. (5)Carries sleeping car. (6)Has couchettes. (7)Plus other departures from Milan at 15:10(1), 17:55(1+3), 18:05(4), 22:55(5+6) and 1:30(6).

Torino - Aosta Gateways to Switzerland

(1) Via San Bernardo Tunnel

Torino - Aosta - Martigny - Brig or Lausanne

362

Dep. Torino (P.N.)	6:37	12:35
Arr. Aosta	8:51	14:40

Change to bus.

337

Dep. Aosta (P. Narbonne)	10:00(1)	16:25
Arr. Martigny (CFF)	N/A(2)	N/A(2)

(1)Runs from late June to mid-September. (2)Times not available in 1981.

Change to train.

251

Dep. Martigny	12:43	19:13
Arr. Brig	13:38	20:28

OR

Dep. Martigny	12:57	18:59
Arr. Lausanne	13:52	19:46

(2) Via Mt. Blanc Tunnel

Torino - Aosta - Chamonix - Geneva

362			
Dep. Torino (P.N.)	6:37	8:54	12:35
Arr. Aosta	8:51	11:50	14:36
Change to bus.			
191			
Dep. Aosta	N/A(1)	N/A(1)	N/A(1)
Arr. Chamonix	2½ hours later		
(1) Two departures per day in Winter. Six per day in July and August.			
Change to train.			
167			
Dep. Chamonix	11:19	15:29	17:10
Arr. St. Gervais	11:55	16:05	17:46
Change trains (1)			
Dep. St. Gervais	12:20	16:15	17:56
Arr. La-Roche-sur-Foron	13:13	17:02	18:53
Change trains (1)			
158			
Dep. La-Roche-sur-Foron	13:20	17:15	19:07
Arr. Annemasse	13:40	17:34	19:27
Change trains (1)			
Dep. Annemasse	14:04	17:40	20:23
Arr. Geneva (Eaux-Vives)	8 minutes later		

(1) All of the Chamonix-Geneva train changes are cross-platform, each taking less than one minute.

ROUTES TO OTHER COUNTRIES

Genoa - Nice - Cannes - Marseille - Avignon

151

Dep. Genoa (P.P.)	8:23(1+2)	8:45(2)	10:00	13:24(4+9)
Arr. Nice	11:16(2)	13:36(2)	15:08	18:22(4+6)
Arr. Cannes	11:43(2)	14:20(2)	15:51	19:11
Change trains.				
Dep. Cannes	11:45	14:23	16:57(4+5)	19:16(4+6)
Arr. Marseille	13:38	16:20	19:05	21:28(4)
Change trains.				
Dep. Marseille	13:58(3)	16:37(3)	19:22(5)	21:38
Arr. Avignon	14:55	17:34	20:32	22:44

(1)Reservation required. Supplement charged. Meal service. (2)Direct train to Marseille. No train change in Cannes. (3)TGV. Supplement charged on certain days. Light refreshments. (4)Direct train to Avignon. No train change in Marseille. (5)Meal service. (6)Light refreshments from Cannes to Marseille. (7)Goes only to Nice. (8)Goes only to Marseille. (9)Plus other departures from Genoa at 15:29(2), 16:17(7) and 17:45(2+8).

Genoa - Torino - Paris

	24	16
Dep. Genoa (P.P.)	21:25(1+2)	23:43(1+3)
Dep. Torino (P.N.)	23:38	1:42
Arr. Paris (Lyon)	9:00	10:06

(1)Carries sleeping car. Also has couchettes. (2)Light refreshments on Day 2 from 6:06 to 9:00. (3)Meal service on Day 2 from 5:01 to 10:06.

Rome - Venice - Budapest - Kiev - Moscow

89

Dep. Rome (Ter.)	12:20(1)	
Dep. Venice (S. Lucia)	21:22(1)	
Arr. Budapest (East)	14:45(2)	Day 2
Arr. Kiev	19:25(2)	Day 3
Arr. Moscow (Kiev)	7:15	Day 4

(1)Carries sleeping car daily except Saturday from Rome and Venice. No service on Thursday in Winter from Rome or Venice. (2)Carries sleeping car daily from Budapest and Kiev.

Verona - Innsbruck - Munich

381

Dep. Verona (P.N.)	3:35(1)	4:00	5:34	8:23(2+8)
Arr. Innsbruck	8:41	10:13	11:02	12:05
Arr. Munich (Hbf.)	11:16	-0-	13:50	13:54

(1)Runs from mid-June to mid-September. (2)TEE. Reservation required. Meal service. (3)Light refreshments. (4)Goes only to Innsbruck. (5)Meal service. (6)Arrives at Munich's Ost station. (7)Carries sleeping car. Also has couchettes. (8)Plus other departures from Verona at 9:04(3), 13:40(4), 14:00(3), 15:00, 18:30(3+6) and 23:58(7).

Venice - Belgrade (Beograd)

390

Dep. Venice (S. Lucia)	8:07(1)	16:55(2)
Arr. Belgrade	22:10	7:44

(1)Departs from Venice's Mestre station. Meal service. (2)Carries sleeping car. Also has couchettes.

Venice - Salzburg

389

Dep. Venice (S. Lucia)	6:50(1)	11:30	13:05	20:04
Arr. Villach (Hbf.)	12:00	16:54	17:34	0:57

Change trains.

759

Dep. Villach (Hbf.)	12:15(2)	17:08(1)	18:50	2:37(3)
Arr. Salzburg	15:50	20:18	23:35	5:46

(1)Meal service. (2)Light refreshments. (3)Carries sleeping car. Also has couchettes.

Venice - Vienna (Wien)

389

Dep. Venice (S. Lucia)	6:50(1)	13:05	20:14(2)	23:20(2)
Arr. Vienna (Sudbf.)	18:05	22:25	6:52	9:10

(1)Meal service. (2)Carries sleeping car. Also has couchettes. Has coach cars only from late June to early September.

SCANDINAVIA (Denmark, Finland, Norway, Sweden)

SCANDINAVIAN RAIL PASS

Unlimited train travel throughout Denmark, Finland, Norway and Sweden. Can be purchased only at railstations in Scandinavia. The 1983 prices are quoted in Danish krone. First-class: 1,500DK for 21 days. Second-class: 1,000DK for 21 days. Half-price for children 4-12 years old.

SUMMER TIME

Denmark, Finland, Norway and Sweden change to Summer Time on the last Sunday of March and convert back to Standard Time on the last Sunday of September. Finland is one hour ahead of Denmark, Norway and Sweden all year.

MIDNIGHT SUN CALENDAR

An average June day has over 17 hours of daylight in Copenhagen and almost 19 in Helsinki, Oslo and Stockholm. Above the Arctic Circle, the whole disc of the sun remains visible throughout the night for periods of 30 to 120 days, depending how far north a city is. Some of the best vantage points are:

NORWAY		SWEDEN	
Green Harbor	April 21-Aug. 22	Bjorkliden	May 26-July 19
North Cape	May 14-July 30	Abisko	May 31-July 14
Hammerfest	May 17-July 28	Kiruna	May 31-July 14
Tromso	May 21-July 23	Gallivare	June 2-July 12
Harstad	May 26-July 19	Boden	June 4-July 10
Narvik	May 26-July 19		
Svolvaer	May 26-July 19	FINLAND	
Bodo	June 5-July 9	Utsjoki	May 22-July 24
Trondheim	June 8-July 6	Kilpisjarvi	May 27-July 18
Andalsnes	June 5-July 3	Pallastunturi	May 30-July 15

Gallivare, Kiruna and Abisko are on the rail route from Boden to Narvik. Andalsnes, Trondheim and Bodo can be reached by train service from Oslo. Trondheim also can be reached by rail from Stockholm.

NORWAY SWEDEN DENMARK

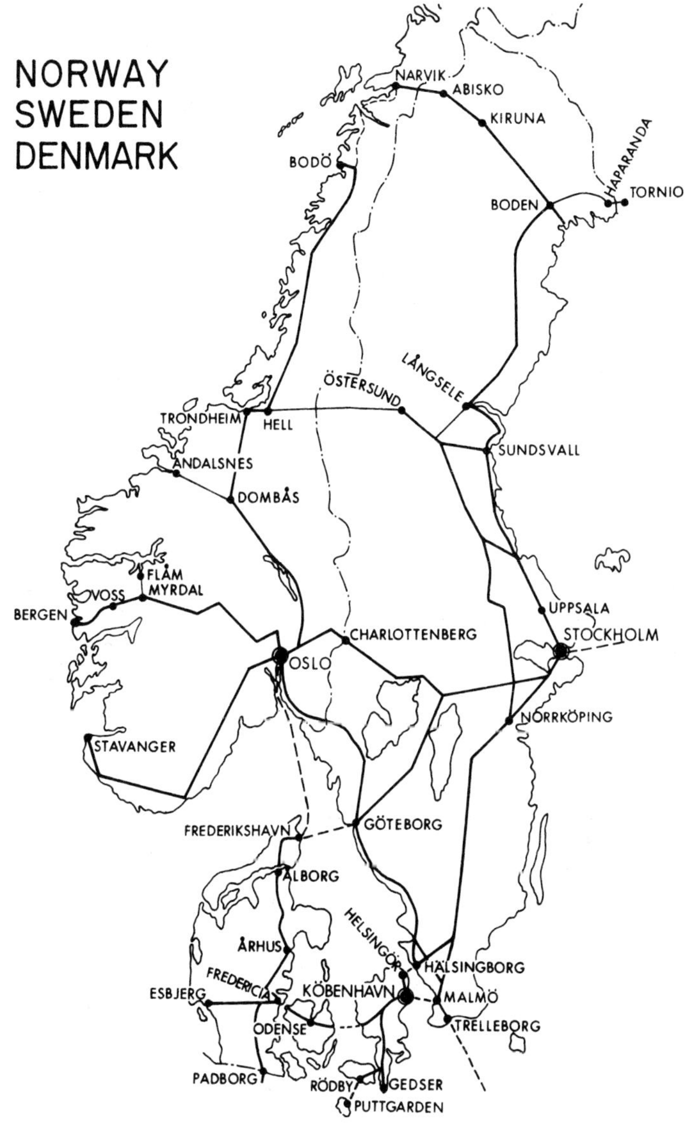

DENMARK

Denmark's 2 categories of fast trains are "IC" (Intercity Trains) and "L" (Lightning Trains). Reservations are required for "IC" and "L" trains that journey via the Great Belt ferries that cross from Nyborg to Korsor and vice versa. This is the route connecting the island where Copenhagen is located with the rest of Denmark, to Odense and Frederikshavn for ferry service to southern Norway, and to Esbjerg for ferry service to England.

The signs you will see at railstations in Denmark are:

AFGANG	DEPARTURE
ANKOMST	ARRIVAL
BANEGARDEN	RAILSTATION
BILLETKONTORET	TICKET OFFICE
DAMER	WOMEN
GARDROBEN	CHECKROOM
HERRER	MEN
INDANG	ENTRANCE
KOREPLAN	TIMETABLE
LYNTOG	FAST INTERCITY TRAIN
OPLYSNING	INFORMATION
PLADSBESTILLINGEN	RESERVATIONS
PERRON	TRACK
RYGEKUPE	SMOKING COMPARTMENT
SOVEVOGN	SLEEPING CAR
SPISEVOGN	RESTAURANT CAR
TIL PERRONERNE	TO THE PLATFORMS
TOG AFGAR	DEPARTURE TIMETABLE
TOG ANKOMMER	ARRIVAL TIMETABLE
UDANG	EXIT

DANISH HOLIDAYS

A list of holidays is helpful because some trains will be noted later in this section as not running on holidays. Also, those trains which operate on holidays are filled, and it is necessary to make reservations for them long in advance.

January 1	New Year's Day
	Maundy Thursday
	Good Friday
	Easter
	Easter Monday
	Prayer Day (4th Fri. after Easter)
	Ascension Day
June 5	Constitution Day (from Noon)
	Whit Sunday
	Whit Monday
December 24	(From Noon)
December 25	Christmas Day
December 26	Boxing Day

EURAILPASS BONUSES IN DENMARK

These ferry crossings: Aarhus-Kalundborg, Knudshoved-Halskov, Nyborg-Korsor, Fynshav-Bojden, Rodby Faerge-Puttgarden, Helsingor-Helsingborg and Frederikshavn-Goteborg.

Reduction of 20% on 4 boat trips: (1) Esbjerg-Harwich, (2) Esbjerg-Newcastle, (3) Esbjerg-Faeroe Islands, and (4) Copenhagen-Oslo.

DENMARK'S TRAIN PASSES

All of Denmark's passes must be purchased in Denmark.

One-Month Ticket Unlimited travel on trains and ferries for one month. The 1983 prices are: first-class 1,420DK, second-class 1,120DK. Half-price for children 4-11 years old.

Take Five Ticket Unlimited travel on trains and ferries for any 5 days within a 17-day period. The 1982 prices were: first-class 630DK, second-class 480DK. Half-price for children 4-12 years old.

Landsrabatkort (National Rebate Card) Gives 50% discount on train and ferry tickets. The 1982 prices were: 850DK for one year, 550DK for half-year. Half-price for children 4-11.

Senior Ticket Roundtrip tickets at 50% discount for people over 65 after obtaining a free ID card, available at all main railstations. Not valid Friday 14:00-Saturday 14:00 or Sunday 14:00-24:00.

Group Ticket Three persons or more (need not be related) obtain 20%-50% discount, depending on size of the group.

ONE-DAY EXCURSIONS AND CITY-SIGHTSEEING

Here are 13 one-day rail trips that can be made comfortably from Copenhagen, returning there in most cases before dinnertime. Notes are provided on what to see at each destination.

Copenhagen

City tours start from Town Hall Square, in front of the Palace Hotel. To get to the Mermaid or Amalienborg Castle on your own, take bus #1 or #6. For brewery visits, take bus #6 to Carlsberg, or take bus #1 to Tuborg.

Also see Thorvaldsen Museum, with his sculptures and tomb. Tivoli Gardens. Christiansborg Palace, where the Danish Parliament meets. The Danish Resistance Museum. The Zoo. Windowshop in the walking area, Stroget.

The vast collection in the National Museum reflecting Danish life from the Ice Age to today, open daily except Monday. From mid-June to mid-September: 10:00-16:00. From mid-September to mid-June: 11:00-15:00 Tuesday-Friday and 12:00-16:00 on Saturday and Sunday.

An exhibit of superb French Impressionists and also Egyptian, Greek, Roman and French sculptures at Glyptotek (behind Tivoli Gardens), open daily except Monday. From May through September: 10:00-16:00. From October through April: 12:00-15:00 (10:00-16:00 on Sunday).

The Toy Museum is open all year Wednesday-Sunday 10:00-16:00. There is a good collection of weapons and uniforms in the Royal Arsenal. From May through September: 13:00-16:00 on weekdays, 10:00-16:00 on Sunday. From October through April: 13:00-15:00 on weekdays, 11:00-16:00 on Sunday.

The City Museum, at 59 Vesterbrogade. The view from the top of Town Hall's 350-foot-high tower. Borsen, the oldest stock exchange in the world, still functioning.

The gilded spiral staircase of the Old Saviour's Church (Vor Frelsers Kirke), and the view at the top, from its tower. Regensen, a residential university since 1623. The marble statues by Thorvaldsen of Christ and the Apostles in Our Lady's Church (Vor Frue Kirke).

The picturesque buildings along Nyhavn Canal. The line of foreign naval ships along Langelinie Promenade.

The crown jewels and other possessions of Danish monarchs in the museum at Rosenborg Palace, particularly the pearl-encrusted saddle of Christian IV. Nearby, the 25-acre Botanical Garden and the National Art Gallery. The Frilandsmuseet open-air museum of Danish houses and farms. The collection of modern art at the Louisiana Museum, 20 minutes away, in nearby Humlebaek, open daily 10:00-17:00.

In the following timetables, where a city has more than one rail-station we have designated the particular station after the name of the city (in parentheses).

Copenhagen - Alborg - Copenhagen 452

Dep. Copenhagen	7:15(1)	9:00
Arr. Alborg	12:58	15:43

Sights in Alborg: This thousand-year old town is the most important in the north Jutland area. Many medieval houses, down the lanes winding off the modern boulevards. The early 15th century Monastery of the Holy Ghost. The early 16th century Aalborghus Castle. The outstanding Jens Bang House. The 12th century St. Botolph Cathedral.

Dep. Alborg	13:00	14:30	15:30	16:10(2+3)
Arr. Copenhagen	20:13	21:01	22:13	21:56

(1) Daily, except Sundays and holidays. (2) Daily, except Saturday. (3) Plus another departure at 17:30(1).

Copenhagen - Aarhus - Copenhagen

There are 2 ways to make this trip. The first is by train between Copenhagen and Kalundborg, then by boat between Kalundborg and Aarhus. The boat has a smorgasbord cafeteria, and the scenery on the cruise is good.

The second way to Aarhus, entirely by train, is via Fredericia.

It makes an interesting day to go to Aarhus by the combination of train and boat via Kalundborg and return to Copenhagen by train via Fredericia.

Boat - via Kalundborg	460	
Dep. Copenhagen (H.)	7:30(1)	10:02
Arr. Kalundborg	8:52	11:23
Change to boat.		
Dep. Kalundborg	9:00	11:35
Arr. Aarhus (Stn.)	12:18	14:58

* * *

Dep. Aarhus (Stn.)	15:13	19:47(2)
Arr. Kalundborg	18:20	23:15
Change to train.		
Dep. Kalundborg	18:28	23:21
Arr. Copenhagen (H.)	19:49	0:42

(1) Daily from mid-June to late August. Daily except Sundays and holidays from late August to mid-June. (2) Daily from mid-June to late August. Daily except Saturdays from late August to mid-June.

Sights in Aarhus: Board the train at the pier and take it to Aarhus' railstation. See the completely furnished medieval houses at the open-air museum (Den Gamle By) in the Botanical Gardens. The 12th century Cathedral. The ancient University. Take bus #6 from the railstation to see the great collection of primitive relics in the Prehistoric Museum at Moesgaard, open daily in Summer 10:00-17:00. It is closed Mondays in Winter.

Train - via Fredericia 452

All of these trains require reservation (unless otherwise designated) and have light refreshments.

Dep. Copenhagen (H.)	6:00	7:00	7:15(1)	9:00
Arr. Aarhus	10:57	11:57	11:27	13:57

* * *

Dep. Aarhus	13:15	15:15	16:15	17:15(4)
Arr. Copenhagen (H.)	18:13	20:03	21:13	22:13

(1) Daily, except Sundays and holidays. (2) Daily, except Saturday. (3) Sundays and holidays only. (4) Plus other departures from Aarhus at 17:45(2), 19:15 and 20:15(3).

Copenhagen - Alborg - Aarhus - Copenhagen 452

It is possible to visit both Alborg and Aarhus in one day by using the following schedule. All of these trains require reservation (unless otherwise designated) and have light refreshments.

Dep. Copenhagen (H.)	6:00	
Arr. Aarhus	10:57	
Sightsee in Aarhus.		
Dep. Aarhus	13:05	14:05
Arr. Alborg	14:43	15:43
Sightsee in Alborg.		
Dep. Alborg	16:10(1)	17:30
Arr. Copenhagen (H.)	21:57	0:13

(1) Daily, except Saturdays.

Copenhagen - Helsingborg - Copenhagen

	465	465	465	466
Dep. Copenhagen (H.)	7:34	8:19(1)	9:34	10:00(7)
Arr. Helsingborg	8:50	9:35	10:50	11:20

Sights in Helsingborg: Stained-glass windows, depicting the city's 900 years of history, in the Radhuset (Town Hall). Karnan, the 14th century fort with walls up to 15 feet thick, one of the best preserved Medieval buildings in Scandinavia. To reach it, take the elevator at the left of The Terrace, from the Main Square.

See the view of the Sound from Rosengarden, and the beautiful roses there. The Municipal Museum. The magnificent pulpit in the 15th century Mariakyrkan (Church of St. Mary). The handsome Concert Hall in Stadsbiblioteket (Town Library). The bronze statue in Hamntoget (Harbor Square).

	466	465	465	465
Dep. Helsingborg	13:35(4)	14:20(5)	16:05(5)	18:35(5+8)
Arr. Copenhagen (H.)	14:51	15:37	17:21	19:51

(1) Runs from late June to early September. (2) Daily, except Saturday. (3) Runs from late May to late September. (4) Light refreshments. (5) Reservation required. (6) Meal service. (7) Plus other departures from Copenhagen at (#465) 11:19(1+2), (#466) 12:34(5) and (#465) 13:19(3+6). (8) Plus other departures from Helsingborg at (#466) 19:35(4), (#465) 20:20(1), (#466) 21:35(4) and (#466) 22:05(2).

Copenhagen - Helsingor - Copenhagen 455

Dep. Copenhagen (Central)	Frequent times from 6:08 to 0:38
Arr. Helsingor	40-50 minutes later

Sights in Helsingor: Kronborg Castle (of Shakespeare's Hamlet). The stained-glass, depicting the town's history, in the Council Chamber of the Radhus (Town Hall). If time allows you to visit only Helsingor or Hillerod (described in the next listing), do not choose Helsingor. Fredericksborg Castle at Hillerod is by far the more interesting of the 2.

Dep. Helsingor	Frequent times from 5:50 to 0:02
Arr. Copenhagen (Central)	40-50 minutes later

Copenhagen - Hillerod - Copenhagen

This is an excellent one-day trip by local commuter train on which Eurailpass is valid. We recommend leaving Copenhagen (Central) at 8:42 or 9:42 for the 40-minute ride. It is a 25-minute walk from the Hillerod railstation, through the village, past the lake and market square, to Fredericksborg Castle and its National Historic Museum of both worldwide art and Danish history. You could spend many days enjoying its contents. A full morning will fly by.

The Castle is open 10:00-17:00 May through September, 10:00-16:00 in October, and 11:00-16:00 November through March.

Market days in Hillerod are Monday, Thursday and Saturday (9:00-13:00).

You can eat lunch at the Castle's restaurant or in the village on your walk back to the railstation, for departures to Copenhagen every hour at 17 minutes past the hour.

If you depart Hillerod at 13:17 or 14:17, there is time to stop in Humlebaek to see the Louisiana Museum of Modern Art on the return trip to Copenhagen.

Copenhagen - Malmo - Copenhagen 1203b

This ferry-boat ride to Sweden's West Coast is popular and can be made with Eurailpass. A recommended roundtrip is to go to Malmo on the conventional 90-minute ferry and than return to Copenhagen on the 40-minute hydrofoil ride.

The hydrofoil, which requires a small additional charge if you are using a Eurailpass, leaves Copenhagen (Havnegade) and Malmo hourly from 7:00 to 24:00.

Here is the schedule for the slower ferry-boat:

Dep. Tuborg Havn*	7:15(1)	9:00(2)	10:45	12:30(2)	14:15(3)
Arr. Malmo (Har.)	90 minute later				

* There is bus service between Copenhagen's Svanemollen bus terminal and Tuborg Havn for most sailings to and from Malmo.

Sights in Malmo: The Art, Archaeology, Military, Technical and Carriage Museums, all in the Castle. Town Hall. St. Peter's Church. The Sailor's House (3 Fiskehamnsgatan). The 17th and 18th century houses on Lilla Torg (Small Square).

Dep. Malmo (Har.)	5:30(1)	9:00	10:45(2)	12:30	14:15(2+4)
Arr. Tuborg Havn	90 minutes later				

(1) Monday-Friday, except holidays. (2) Daily, except Sundays and holidays. (3) Plus other departures from Copenhagen's Tuborg Havn at 16:00(2), 17:45, 19:30(2) and 21:15. (4) Plus other departures from Malmo at 16:00, 17:45(2), 19:30 and 21:15(2).

Copenhagen - Odense - Copenhagen 453

En route, the train drives onto a ferry for the 65-minute boat ride between Korsor and Nyborg. Passengers can leave the train and stroll on the boat for fine views of the shoreline.

All of these trains require reservation (unless otherwise designated) and have light refreshments.

Dep. Copenhagen (H.)	7:00	8:00	9:00	10:00	11:00
Arr. Odense	9:55	10:55	11:55	12:55	13:55

Sights in Odense: The home of Hans Christian Andersen, now a museum, on Hans Jensenstraede. Another Andersen Museum is at Munkemollestraede 3. Also see the National Railway Museum in the Dannebrogsgade. The 13th century Cathedral of St. Knud.

Dep. Odense	Frequent times from 10:16 to 22:16
Arr. Copenhagen (H.)	3 hours later

Copehagen - Roskilde - Copenhagen

	460	456	460	456	456
Dep. Copenhagen (H.)	7:30(1)	9:10(2)	9:55	11:10(2)	12:10(5)
Arr. Roskilde	20 minutes later				

Sights in Roskilde: The 40 tombs of Denmark's kings and queens, 500-year old clock, and the post on which such royalty as Peter the Great and the 20th century Duke of Windsor marked their heights (some of them with humorous exaggeration), all in the red brick Cathedral. Open for tours weekdays April-September 9:00-17:45 and October-March 10:00-15:45. Also on Sundays and holidays 12:30-17:45 June-August and 12:30-15:45 September-May.

Also see the exhibits in the Viking Ship Museum. Open 9:00-18:00 June-August, 9:00-17:00 September and October, 10:00-16:00 November-March, and 9:00-17:00 April and May.

	456	456	460	456	456
Dep. Roskilde	10:38	11:38	12:07	12:38	14:38(6)
Arr. Copenhagen (H.)	20 minutes later				

(1) From mid-June to late August: daily. From late August to mid-June: daily except Sundays and holidays. (2) Daily, except Sundays and holidays. (3) From late May to late August: daily. From late August to late May: daily except Saturday. (4) Daily, except Saturday. (5) Plus other depar-

tures from Copenhagen at (#456)14:10 and (#460)14:55(3). (6)Plus other departures from Roskilde at (#456)17:02, (#460)17:07(3), (#456)18:38, (#460)19:27, (#456)19:48, (#456)20:38, (#456)21:38(4) and (#456)23:38.

Copenhagen - Vordingborg - Copenhagen

456

Dep. Copenhagen (H.)	6:43(1)	9:10(2)	11:10(2)	12:10	14:10
Arr. Vordingborg	8:06	10:39	12:39	13:39	15:39

Sights in Vordingborg: An interesting old town.

Dep. Vordingborg	10:32(2)	11:37	13:32	15:55	17:32(4)
Arr. Copenhagen (H.)	11:59	12:59	14:59	17:25	18:59

(1)Light refreshments. (2)Daily, except Sundays and holidays. (3)Daily, except Saturday. (4)Plus other departures from Vordingborg at 19:32, 20:32(3) and 22:35.

SCENIC RAIL TRIPS

Odense - Fredericia - Odense

There is fine coastline scenery on this easy one-day roundtrip. This can also be seen as a portion of the Copenhagen-Frederickshavn route.

453

All of these trains require reservation.

Dep. Odense	57 Minutes after each hour, from 7:57 to 23:57
Arr. Fredericia	39 minutes later.

* * *

Dep. Fredericia	35 minutes after each hour, from 7:35 to 20:35
Arr. Odense	39 minutes later.

INTERNATIONAL ROUTES FROM DENMARK

Copenhagen is the gateway for travel from Denmark, Norway and Sweden to Western Europe, starting with its connections to Berlin and Hamburg, and then on from those cities to the rest of Western Europe.

Copenhagen - Berlin 769

Dep. Copenhagen (H.)	6:43(1)	23:10
Arr. Berlin (Ost)	15:51	8:05
Arr. Berlin (Fried.)	16:09	8:26
Arr. Berlin (Zoo)	16:35	8:52

(1) Light refreshments from 12:36 to 15:51.

Copenhagen - Hamburg
648

Dep. Copenhagen (H.)	7:20	9:25(1+2)	10:15(3)	13:20(7)
Arr. Hamburg (Hbf.)	12:27	15:02	15:07	18:26
Arr. Hamburg (Altona)	12:46	-0-	-0-	-0-

(1) Runs from late May to late September. (2) Light refreshments. (3) Supplement charged. (4) Runs from mid-June to early September. (5) Carries sleeping car. Also has couchettes. (6) Has couchettes. (7) Plus other departures from Copenhagen at 15:15(4), 16:45(1+2), 17:45, 21:10(5), 22:15(6) and 23:45(5).

Copenhagen - Oslo
466

Dep. Copenhagen (H.)	1:05(1)	10:00	12:34(2)	20:49(3+4+5)
Arr. Oslo (Cent.)	13:19	19:55	22:05	6:46

(1) Runs from mid-June to early September. Has couchettes. (2) Reservation required. Meal service. (3) Runs from late June to early September. (4) Carries sleeping car. Also has couchettes. (5) Plus another departure from Copenhagen at 23:00(4).

Copenhagen - Stockholm
465

Dep. Copenhagen (H.)	7:34(1)	8:19(2+3)	9:34(4+10)
Arr. Stockholm (Cent.)	15:47	17:17	18:28

(1) Meal service. (2) Runs from late June to early September. (3) Light refreshments. (4) Light refreshments all year. Meal service from late June to early September. (5) Daily, except Saturday. (6) Runs from late May to late September. (7) Reservation required. (8) From late May to late September: daily. From late September to late May: daily, except Saturday. (9) Carries sleeping car. Also has couchettes. (10) Plus other departures from Copenhagen at 11:19(1+2+5), 13:19(1+6), 15:19(1+7), 21:19(8+9), 23:19(9) and 1:05(2).

FINLAND

Travel on Finnish trains titled "Rap" requires payment of a small supplement. The tracks in Finland are constructed with the wide Russian gauge of 5′ 0″. This makes for spacious cars. The rail service extends as far north as Lapland. Service is maintained during severe Winter weather.

All major Finnish name express trains are equipped with radiotelephones for passengers to use. Long-distance express trains, stopping only at main railstations, are called Erikoispikajuna and Pikajuna. Both charge supplemental fares. Local trains, stopping at all stations, are called Henkilojuna. Finland's national timetable is called Suomen Kulkuneuvot.

The signs you will see at railstations in Finland are:

AIKATAULUT	TIMETABLE
LAHTO	DEPARTURE
LAITURILTA	TRACK
LIPPULUUKKU	TICKET OFFICE
MAKUUVAUNU	SLEEPING CAR
MATKALIPPUJEN	RESERVATIONS
MIEHILLE	MEN
NAISILLE	WOMEN
NEUVONTATOIMIST	INFORMATION
ODOTUSSALI	CHECKROOM
RAUTATIEASEMALLE	RAILSTATION
RAVINTOLAVAUNU	RESTAURANT CAR
SAAPUMINEN	ARRIVAL
SISAAN	ENTRANCE
TUPAKOITSEVILLE	SMOKING COMPARTMENT
ULOS	EXIT

FINLAND'S TRAIN PASSES

Finnrailpass Unlimited rail travel. Cannot be purchased in Finland. Sales agents in North America are: German Federal Railways (offices listed on page 26) and Holiday Tours of America (1290 Ave. of the Americas, New York, N.Y. 10019). The 1983 first-class prices are $90(U.S.) for 8 days, $132 for 15 days, $177 for 22 days. Second-class: $60 for 8 days, $88 for 15 days, $118 for 22 days.

65 Card Available at railstations. Buyer must pay about $1.50(U.S.) and provide photo. Allows persons over 65 to purchase up to 6 tickets for trips of at least 48 miles at half-fare.

Return Ticket Allows 10%15% discount. For trips over 45 miles, allows up to one month to make the return trip

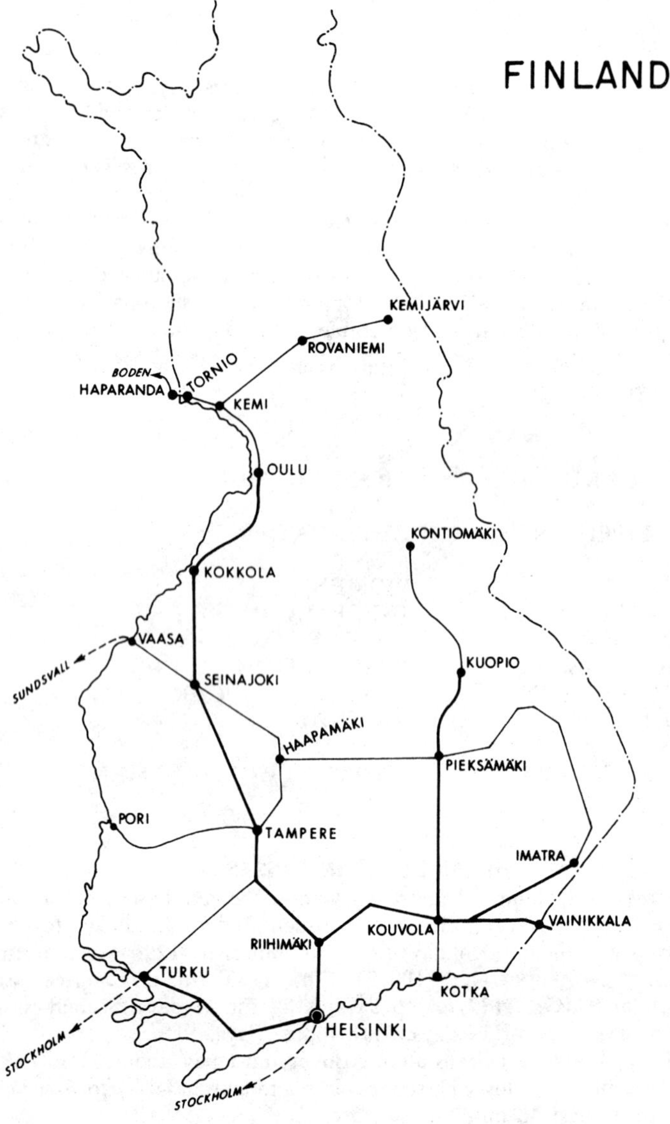
FINLAND
KEMIJÄRVI
ROVANIEMI
BODEN
TORNIO
HAPARANDA
KEMI
OULU
KONTIOMÄKI
KOKKOLA
VAASA
SUNDSVALL
KUOPIO
SEINAJOKI
HAAPAMÄKI
PIEKSÄMÄKI
PORI
TAMPERE
IMATRA
VAINIKKALA
KOUVOLA
RIIHIMÄKI
TURKU
KOTKA
HELSINKI
STOCKHOLM
STOCKHOLM

FINNISH HOLIDAYS

A list of holidays is helpful because some trains will be noted later in this section as not running on holidays. Also, those trains which operate on holidays are filled, and it is necessary to make reservations for them long in advance.

January 1	New Year's Day		Midsummer's Day (Saturday nearest to June 24)
	Epiphany	June 21	Finnish Flag Day
	Good Friday		All Saint's Day
	Easter	December 6	Independence Day
	Easter Monday	December 25	Christmas Day
	Ascension Day	December 26	Boxing Day
May 1	Labor Day		

EURAILPASS BONUSES IN FINLAND

These cruises: Helsinki-Stockholm, Turku-Stockholm, and Turku-Aland Islands-Stockholm.

ONE-DAY EXCURSIONS AND CITY-SIGHTSEEING

Here are 6 one-day rail trips that can be made comfortably from Helsinki, returning there in most cases before dinnertime. Notes are provided on what to see at each destination. The number below the name of each route is the Cook's timetable.

Helsinki

Helsinki's single most inspiring sight is Temppeliaukio Church, known since its 1969 dedication as the "Rock Church". This fantastic structure was quarried on its site, out of the bedrock in the middle of one of the oldest residential districts of Helsinki. Because the area occupied by worshipers is below the street level, all that can be seen as you walk toward the church is a low rock wall and the massive (70-foot diameter) copper dome.

Also see the large tubular steel sculpture, symbolizing music, in Sibelius Park. Tapiola, the model "new town". Finlandia Hall. The National Museum. The floral cemetery. The onion towers on the Greek Orthodox Uspenski Cathedral.

You should visit Market Square, before Noon, to see the flowers, fish and mountains of berries. The Town Hall. The Empress Stone obelisk. (Ferries from a pier near the obelisk go every hour to the island Suomenlinna Fortress.) See the impressive columns of Parliament House. The University Library and the Cathedral, in Senate Square.

The paintings and sculptures in the National Art Gallery. The National Theater. The Elaintarhantie shopping complex, opposite the railstation. The Botanical Gardens. The Linnanmaki amusement center.

The collection of Finnish wood houses at the open-air Museum of Seurasaari. The Ateneum Art Gallery. The Gallen-Kallela Museum. The art and furniture at the Helsinki Municipal Museum. Old-fashioned and modern farm tools and implements in the Agricultural Museum. The Military Museum. Take the #6 tram to Arabia and see the original site of Helsinki, Old Town.

Helsinki - Hameenlinna - Helsinki 492

Dep. Helsinki	6:10	10:00(1)	14:00
Arr. Hameenlinna	7:36	11:16	15:15

Sights in Hameenlinna: The medieval castle. Ahvenisto Tower. The Art Museum. The City Museum.

Dep. Hameenlinna	14:15(1)	19:45(1)	22:22(1)
Arr. Helsinki	15:30	21:00	23:30

(1) Meal service.

Helsinki - Hanko - Helsinki 493

A beautiful ride through woods and along lakes.

Dep. Helsinki	7:32(1)	9:10(2)	12:40(1)
Arr. Karjaa	8:40	10:20	13:50

Change to local train.
000

Dep. Karjaa	8:55	10:30	14:00
Arr. Hanko	9:50	11:25	14:55

Sights in Hanko: Take a 2-hour cruise, leaving from the eastern harbor, operating June through September. There is good fishing here. See the statue dedicated to the many Finns who disembarked from here to migrate to the United States between 1880 and 1930. Dance or try your luck at the Casino.

Dep. Hanko	15:50	17:50	21:15
Arr. Karjaa	16:45	18:45	22:10

Change to standard train.

Dep. Karjaa	17:20(1)	19:10(1)+(3)	22:20(1)
Arr. Helsinki	18:27	20:22	23:32

(1) Light refreshments. (2) Meal service. (3) Daily, except Saturday.

Helsinki - Lahti - Helsinki 498

Dep. Helsinki	7:05(1)	9:25(2)	10:30(2)	13:10(2)
Arr. Lahti	8:34	10:52	11:57	14:37

Sights in Lahti: The Art Gallery. The Ethnographic Museum. The Radio Museum. See the view from the top of the ski-jump, elevators operating June-September 10:00-19:30.

Dep. Lahti	11:27(2)	12:04(2+3)	15:03(2)	18:00(2)	18:47(2+5)
Arr. Helsinki	12:55	13:30	16:30	19:30	20:30

(1)Daily from early June to late August. Daily, except Sundays and holidays,from late August to early June. (2)Meal service. (3)Reservation required. Supplement charged. (4)Daily from early June to late August. Daily, except Saturday, from late August to early June. (5)Plus other departures from Lahti at 21:03(2+3) and 21:17(2+4).

Helsinki - Riihimaki - Helsinki

	497	498	497	498	497	498
Dep. Helsinki	8:00	9:25	10:00	10:30	11:00	13:10
Arr. Riihimaki	50 minutes later					

Sights in Riihimaki: The wood-working mills of H. G. Paloheimo. The glass factories of Riihimaen Lasi Oy. The Museum Peltosaari. The Municipal Museum.

	498	497	497	498	497	497
Dep. Riihimaki	12:05	12:10	13:10	15:41	16:03	17:41(1)
Arr. Helsinki	50 minutes later					

(1)Plus other departures from Riihimaki at frequent times from 18:40 to 22:00.

Helsinki - Tampere - Helsinki

All of these trains have meal service, unless designated otherwise.

497

Dep. Helsinki	8:00	9:05	10:00	11:00(1)
Arr. Tampere	10:10	11:15	12:10	13:07

Sights in Tampere: The aquarium, planetarium, children's zoo, amusement park, observation tower and planetarium at the Sarkanniemi Recreation Center. The more than 30,000 objects exhibited in the Hame Museum, particularly the handwoven rugs and tapestries. Many excellent artworks, frescoes and the altarpiece in the Cathedral, completed in 1907. The fine modern architecture of Kaleva Church. The National history Museum. The Haihara Doll Museum. The largest church bells in Finland, at the Orthodox Church.

See a performance at Tampere's Summer Theater in Pyynikki Park, from a seat in the unique bowl-shaped auditorium that rotates 360 degrees. Everyone sitting in the last row at the beginning of a performance also has a front-row seat during the show.

Dep. Tampere	11:40(1)	14:45	16:15	17:40	18:45(4)
Arr. Helsinki	14:00	16:55	18:30	19:55	21:00

(1)Light refreshments. (2)Daily, except Saturday. (3)Sundays only. No food service. (4)Plus other departures from Tampere at 19:20(1), 20:30(2) and 21:50(3).

Helsinki - Turku - Helsinki 493

All of these trains have light refreshments.

Dep. Helsinki	7:32	9:10	12:40
Arr. Turku (Stn.)	10:10	11:51	15:20

Sights in Turku: The Museum and the marvelous Banquet Hall in the 13th century Castle, a short walk from the Silja Line railstation, only a few minutes ride past the Main railstation. The 13th century Cathedral. See the 2 old sailing ships from St. Martins Bridge: Sigyn and Soumen Joutsen. Qwensel House, the oldest residence in Turku, now housing the Apothecary Museum. The handicrafts center, a complex of 17 charming 18th century houses, on Luostarinmaki (Cloister Hill).

Dep. Turku (Stn.)	12:15	15:45	17:20(1)	20:56
Arr. Helsinki	14:55	18:27	20:22	23:32

(1) Daily, except Saturday.

INTERNATIONAL ROUTES FROM FINLAND

Helsinki is the gateway both to Russia (Leningrad, and on to Moscow) and Western Scandinavia (Stockholm, and on to Oslo and Copenhagen). Oulu is the starting point for trips to northern Sweden (Boden) and northern Norway (Narvik).

Helsinki - Leningrad 495

Dep. Helsinki	12:00(1)	Arr. Leningrad	20:05

(1) Reservation required. Meal service.

Helsinki - Moscow 855

Dep. Helsinki	17:00(1)	Arr. Moscow	9:30

(1) Carries sleeping car. Also has couchettes. Meal service halt in Viborg at 22:44.

Helsinki - Stockholm 493 + 1233

Dep. Helsinki	7:32(1)	16:02(2)	18:02(1)
Arr. Turku (Harbor)	10:20	19:08	20:55

Walk to Abo Pier.

The price for the cruise across the Bay of Bothnia on the comfortable and pleasant Silja Line ships is about $44(U.S.). This passage is covered by Eurailpass. The fare for a sleeping cabin is not covered by Eurailpass. Food on the ship is varied and delicious. We recommend the daytime sailing in order to see the thousands of tiny islands on the ride through this extremely interesting archipelago. During the daytime cruise, there is a good smorgasbord for both lunch and dinner. A small band plays music in a delightful bar area. Movies are shown in a small theater. There is a duty-free shop on board. The ships ferry autos.

Dep. Turku (Abo)	10:30(3)	19:30	21:30
Arr. Stockholm (Vartan)	20:30	8:00	7:00

(1) Light refreshments. (2) Meal service. (3) From late April to the end of August: daily. From the first of September to late April: daily, except Monday.

Helsinki - Oulu - Haparanda - Boden - Narvik 492

Dep. Helsinki	22:00(1+2)	23:05(3+4)	7:00(1)	10:00(1+7)
Arr. Oulu	7:40	8:38	14:28	18:07

Sights in Oulu: The Art Museum. The Zoological Museum.

Dep. Oulu	8:00(1)	-0-	-0-	-0-
Arr. Kemi	9:15	-0-	-0-	-0-

Change trains.

496

Dep. Kemi 9:20

Set your watch back one hour.

Arr. Haparanda 8:55

Change trains.

Dep. Haparanda 10:20

Arr. Boden 12:55

Change trains.

We recommend stopping-over in Boden for the night so as to travel Boden-Narvik during the daylight hours in order to be able to see the fine mountain scenery on that route. You cross the Arctic Circle going from Boden to Narvik.

476

Dep. Boden	15:05(1)	6:48(4)	10:14
Arr. Narvik	22:20	14:10	17:32

(1) Meal service. (2) Carries sleeping car. (3) From late May to late August: Sunday to Friday. From late August to late May: Friday only. (4) Light refreshments. (5) Reservation required. (6) Runs daily from late June to early September. (7) Plus another departure from Helsinki to Oulu at 16:00(1+5).

NORWAY

Norway has the most number of scenic rail trips of any Scandinavian country. Its trains are classified Expresstog (express trains stopping only at main railstations), Hurtigtog (fast), and Persontog (slow, local trains, usually stopping at all railstations).

Norwegian State Railways has one coach on the Oslo-Bergen and Bergen-Oslo runs (and is adding similar service on other long-distance routes) designed for conveying handicapped persons and other passengers requiring special care, such as mothers traveling with young children.

These special cars have a compartment accommodating 2 wheel chairs that are lifted aboard. An 8-seat compartment in these cars, equipped for mothers and their infants, is provided with a baby-chair, bottle heater, and other equipment helpful when caring for small children. This compartment is adjacent to a space with fitted toilets and a diaper-changing table. The car also has oxygen tanks, a stretcher and a small wheel chair for handicapped persons to use in moving about inside the train.

From Dombas and on north, you are in the land of the Midnight Sun. (See "Midnight Sun Calendar" at the start of the Scandinavia section.)

The signs you will see at railstations in Norway are:

ANKOMST	ARRIVAL
AVGANG	DEPARTURE
BANESTASJONEN	RAILSTATION
BILLETLUKEN	TICKET OFFICE
DAMER	WOMEN
GARDEROBEN	CHECKROOM
HERRER	MEN
INFORMASJON	INFORMATION
INGANG	ENTRANCE
RESERVASJONSLUKEN	RESERVATIONS
ROKERE	SMOKING COMPARTMENT
SOVEVOGN	SLEEPING CAR
SPISEVOGN	RESTAURANT CAR
SPOR	TRACK
TIL PLATTFORMENTE	TO THE PLATFORMS
TOGTABELL	TIMETABLE
UTGANG	EXIT
VEKSLIGSKONTOR	CURRENCY EXCHANGE
VINDUSPLASS	WINDOW SEAT

NORWEGIAN HOLIDAYS

A list of holidays is helpful because some trains will be noted later in this section as not running on holidays. Also, those trains which operate on holidays are filled, and it is necessary to make reservations for them long in advance.

January 1	New Year's Day		Ascension Day
	Maundy Thursday	May 17	Constitution Day
	Good Friday		Whit Monday
	Easter	December 25	Christmas Day
	Easter Monday	December 26	St. Stephen's Day
May 1	Labor Day		

EURAILPASS BONUSES

A 30% reduction on the fares of the Steamship Company KDS for the cruise between Kristiansand and Hirtshals.

NORWAY'S TRAIN PASSES

All of Norway's passes must be purchased in Norway.

Norwegian Bargain Rail Pass Sold at all Norwegian railstations. Available in 2 versions. Both are valid for 7 days and allow unlimited stopover. Cannot be used on Friday, Sunday or a major holiday. The 1982 prices were quoted in Norwegian Krone. For a one-way ticket not exceeding 470 miles, the price was 200NK. For unlimited mileage: 280NK.

Family Reduction One adult pays full fare. Other family members traveling with that adult, including children up to 25 years old, pay half-fare. Minimum journey is 90 miles.

Senior Citizen Discount A person over 67 and the spouse (even if younger) can buy tickets at half-fare. Must obtain an ID card, available at railstations.

ONE-DAY EXCURSIONS AND CITY-SIGHTSEEING

Here are 5 one-day rail trips that can be made comfortably from Oslo, returning there at or shortly after dinnertime. Notes are provided on what to see at each destination. The number below the name of each route is the Cook's timetable.

In the following timetables, where a city has more than one railstation, we have designated the particular station after the name of the city (in parentheses).

Oslo

Walk from the railstation, up Karl Johansgate, to the Royal Palace. En route, you will pass the National Theater. Behind it is the underground suburban train station. See the massive mural, in the post World War II City Hall, commemorating the Nazi occupation of Norway. From the pier behind City Hall, take a 4-minute boat ride to Bygdoy to see the 4 interesting museums there: Viking ships, the balsa Kon Tiki raft, Amundsen's polar expedition ship Fram, and the 80.000 exhibits in the Norwegian Folk Museum.

Later, see the bronze and granite sculptures of Gustav Vigeland in Frogner Park. Also the Vigeland Museum at Nobelsgate 32. The Munch Museum. The Historical Museum. The National Gallery. Oslo Cathedral. The Museum of Applied Art. Gamle Aker Church. The 14th century Akershus Fortress. The Sonja Henie-Nils Onstad collection of modern paintings at Henie-Onstad Art Center. The Ski Museum at Holmenkollen. Take the trolley to the Merchant Marine Academy at Sjomannsskolen.

Take Bus #36 from Town Hall Square for a one-hour ride to Sundvollen. Beautiful Tyri Fjord scenery.

Oslo - Goteborg - Oslo

487

Dep. Oslo (Sent.)	7:40(1)	Dep. Goteborg	17:25(2)
Arr. Goteborg	12:18	Arr. Oslo (East)	22:05

(1) Reservation required. Meal service. (2) Meal service.

Sights in Goteborg: A great seaport. The one-hour sightseeing bus tour leaves from Stora Teatern. There are one-hour boat trips covering the 7-mile harbor and its canals, leaving from Kungsportsbron. See the view of the harbor and city from the Sailor's Tower near the Maritime Museum at Gamla Varvsparken. The Liseberg amusement park. The magnificent City Theater and Concert House.

Oslo - Hamar - Oslo

Be sure to sit on the right-hand side for the best view of the fantastic scenery along the western shore of Lake Mjosa, Norway's largest lake (75 miles long).

483

Dep. Oslo (Sent.)	7:13(1+2)	9:13(2)	10:00(3)
Arr. Hamar	8:49	11:02	11:41

Sights in Hamar: The enormous outdoor Hedmark Museum complex of more than 40 buildings, most of them from the 18th and 19th centures, brought here from other places. One of the buildings is a house built in 1871 in North Dakota, U.S.A., by a Norwegian emigrant. Also visit the 7½-acre Railway Museum, open May-September, to see many early coaches and locomotives as well as Norway's first railstation.

Dep. Hamar	11:50(2)	14:25(3)	17:43(3)	19:50(2+5)
Arr. Oslo (Sent.)	13:38	16:08	19:38	21:38

(1) Reservation required. (2) Light refreshments. (3) Meal service. (4) Sundays and holidays only.

Oslo - Lillehammer - Oslo

483

Dep. Oslo (Sent.)	7:13(1)	10:00(2)	Dep. Lillehammer	13:36(2)	14:07(3+4)
Arr. Lillehammer	7:37	12:37	Arr. Oslo (Sent.)	16:08	16:38

(1) Reservation required. Light refreshments. (2) Meal service. (3) Daily, except Sundays and holidays. (4) Plus other departures from Lillehammer at 16:40(2) and 19:44(1).

Sights in Lillehammer: The Sandvig collection of more than 100 old buildings and craftwork demonstration at the 100-acre open-air Maihaugen Museum, open daily 11:00-19:00 from late June to early August and 11:00-14:00 the rest of the year. See the "White Swan" paddle-wheel steamboat, Skibladner, at the city's dock.

Oslo - Vinstra - Oslo

483

Dep. Oslo (Sent.)	7:13(1+2)	10:00(3)
Arr. Vinstra	10:35	13:56

Sights in Vinstra: A mountain resort. Home of the legendary Peer Gynt. See the memorial over his grave in the village church. Cross-country skiing is popular here.

Dep. Vinstra	12:31(3)	12:59(1+3)	15:22(3)	18:41(1+2)
Arr. Oslo (Sent.)	16:08	16:38	19:38	22:11

(1) Reservation required. (2) Light refreshments. (3) Meal service.

(THE NEXT SCHEDULE IS TO BE READ ON PAGE 264, UNDER "OSLO NORDAGUTU-OSLO")

Here are schedules for taking a different route in returning to Oslo from Nordagutu, by making it a circle trip, via Kongsberg.

Nordagutu - Kongsberg - Oslo 482

Dep. Nordagutu	14:05	16:22(1)	20:03(2)
Dep. Kongsberg	14:55	17:10	20:42
Arr. Oslo (West)	16:23	18:35	21:55

(1) Light refreshments. (2) Reservation required. Meal service.

THE FJORD TRAIN ROUTE

Oslo - Drammen - Tonsberg - Sandefjord - Larvik - Skien - Nordagutu - Oslo

This one-day excursion offers great views of several fjords (starting with the Oslofjord), wooded countryside, and lovely lakes. As the schedules indicate, stops can be made for sightseeing in several of the towns on this route.

488			
Dep. Oslo (West)	7:30(1)	9:30(1)	11:30(1)
Arr. Drammen	8:00	10:00	12:00
Arr. Tonsberg	8:56	10:56	12:56
Arr. Sandefjord	9:18	11:18	13:18
Arr. Larvik	9:37	11:37	13:37
Arr. Skien	10:20	12:20	14:20
Dep. Skien	-0-	13:30	15:27
Arr. Nordagutu	-0-	14:00	16:02
	*	*	*
Dep. Nordagutu	10:05(1)	14:03(1)	20:04
Arr. Skien	10:35	14:35	20:30
Dep. Skien	10:40	14:40	20:40
Dep. Larvik	11:23	15:23	21:23
Dep. Sandefjord	11:40	15:40	21:40
Dep. Tonsberg	12:03	16:03	22:03
Dep. Drammen	13:00	17:00	23:00
Arr. Oslo (West)	13:35	17:35	23:35

(1) Light refreshments.

Sights in **Drammen:** The activity along the busy docks. Many attractive old buildings. Watching the Drommensfjorden meet the Drammen River.

Sights in **Tonsberg:** Norway's oldest town. See today's whaling ships and the ruins of an ancient Viking castle, Tonsberghus. Also, the Vestfold Museum, the 12th century St. Michael's Church, the 12th century Sem Church, and the 13th century Royal Castle.

Sights in **Sandefjord:** The main port for Norway's whaling ships. See the whaling monument in the square. The Whaling Museum. Nearby are the mouth of the Oslofjorden and the head of the Sandefjorden.

Sights in **Larvik:** The Museum. The fjord.

Sights in **Skien:** The large sawmill operations. The meeting of Skien River and Lake Hjelle.

SCENIC RAIL TRIPS

Bergen to Oslo . . . The Stalheim-Flam Detour

Indisputably, the most scenic rail route in Europe. There are 2 alternative ways to make this detour, adding either one or 2 days to the trip between Bergen and Oslo. After describing the sights to see in Bergen, we detail both directions for this splendid journey: Bergen-Oslo and Oslo-Bergen.

Bergen

Visit Torget, a fish market that has been operating for 9 centuries (weekdays: 8:30-15:00). See Bergenhus Fortress, with its 13th century Hakon Hall. The 12th century Mariakirken (St. Mary's Church). Europe's most modern aquarium and the collection of 19th century houses in Gamle Bergen (Old Bergen). Edvard Grieg's home in Troldhaugen. Take the 5-minute funicular ride to the top of Mt. Floien. See the Hanseatic Museum. The Maritime Museum. The Arts and Crafts Museum. Take the cable car to the top of Mt. Ulriken. It's only 22 minutes for the bus ride and short walk to see the 13th century Fana Church and Fantoft, the old stave church.

Bergen to Oslo

There are train departures from Bergen to Voss at 7:20 (reservation required), 8:35 (not a through train to Oslo) and 9:45, arriving Voss at 8:36, 10:05 or 11:03. If you are eliminating the Stalheim-Flam detour and going direct to Oslo, the 7:20 departure arrives Oslo at 14:05. The 9:45 departure arrives Oslo at 17:40. (Cook's Table #481.) The first 40 minutes of this ride are along the lovely Sorfjorden.

The complete Bergen-Oslo line was opened in 1909 as the only year-round land transportation between Norway's 2 largest cities. It was electrified in 1964. Terrain and climate both caused construction problems which prior to then had never been encountered in building a railway line. The 300-mile length of track must pass through 200 tunnels and 18 miles of snow sheds in addition to also crossing more than 300 bridges.

Travelers are frustrated by the interruptions of viewing the scenery caused by the many snow sheds. However, it would be impossible for the trains to operate daily year round and stick to a strict timetable if it were not for these structures.

You omit the 63-minute Voss-Myrdal portion of the main line route when taking the Voss-Stalheim-Flam-Myrdal detour we have been recommending since 1971.

Upon arriving Voss at 8:36, 10:05 or 11:03, you leave the train and continue on to Stalheim by the bus waiting at the Voss railstation. The one-hour bus ride from Voss to Stalheim passes (on your left) the spectacular Tvinde waterfall. You arrive Stalheim at 10:00, 11:00 or 12:00.

At Stalheim there is only a Norwegian village museum and a hotel. But what an elegant place Stalheim Hotel is, managed superbly by handsome Reidar Chris Thomassen. There is a view here of such magnificence that Kaiser Wilhelm II came to Stalheim annually for 25 years to look at it. Then there is a smorgasbord lunch that alone makes taking a trip from anywhere in the world to this Scandinavian oasis worthwhile. We always allow 2½ hours for this outstanding meal.

The land here has been farmed since 400 A.D. Some facility for food and lodging has existed here since 1647 when mail was carried by Norway's "pony express" from Bergen to Oslo, and Stalheim was one of the stations for changing horses and riders, right up until 1900.

An inn was operated at Stalheim before 1700. The first hotel here, constructed in 1885, burned in 1900. A second hotel, built in 1901, met the same fate in 1902. Another hotel, constructed and used first in Voss, was moved to Stalheim in 1906, enlarged in 1912, and burned down in 1959.

The present Stalheim Hotel was built in the Winter of 1959-1960 and enlarged in 1967 to its present capacity of 130 units, ranging from single rooms to doubles and then suites consisting of a double room plus sitting-room with fireplace. Stalheim can accommodate 219 guests, and it is filled nearly every day in its April-September operation.

The terrace of the hotel provides a view over the Naro, Brekke and Jordal valleys, the Sivle and Stalheim waterfalls, and the conical peak of Mt. Jordal.

Two mounds on the right-hand side of the hotel's terrace date from 800 A.D. These were opened in 1890, revealing the remains of a woman who had been buried with her frying-pan, loom, bronze brooches and bracelets—and the remains of a man, with his sword, axes and other utensils.

These relics were given to the museum in Bergen. The mounds have been reconstructed, and photos of the relics are displayed in the hotel's entrance hall.

Of those who start lunch at Stalheim at 12:30, few finish before 14:30. The remainder of the afternoon can be used enjoying the after-lunch euphoria in the spacious main lobby or on the large terrace. A leisurely stroll through the Open Air Museum on the hill behind the hotel is an enjoyable way to fill part of the afternoon and prepare oneself for dinner.

A walk down the narrow country road in September when delicious and accessible wild raspberries are in profusion is another pleasant diversion.

The hotel will arrange a tour of the ancient village museum. Kaare Tonneberg, the owner of Stalheim, gives an excellent commentary on the old log buildings, the lives that were led in them, the white mansion of the landowner who built it in 1726, and the contents of all the structures.

These objects dramatize the contrasting life-style between the rich and the poor of that era. Among the contents are antique Norwegian furniture, arms, glass, silver, pewter and brass, some of which are also displayed in the hotel lobby.

If your schedule does not allow staying overnight at Stalheim, from mid-June to mid-August a boat leaves Gudvangen (only a 30-minute bus ride from Stalheim) at 20:05 for a cruise along the Sognefjord, all in Midnight Sun daylight, arriving Flam at 21:45. This is one of the most scenic fjord trips in Norway.

To get the most out of the Stalheim-Flam detour, remain at Stalheim for an excellent dinner that night and have the enormous "cold table" breakfast the next morning. The traditional Norse breakfast (cereals, fruits, fish, cold and hot meats, salads, cheeses, breads and beverages) originated in the days when a farmer doing heavy physical work in sub-freezing temperatures had to be sustained by one meal from dawn until sunset.

We tourists are fortunate that most Norwegian hotels have perpetuated this eating tradition long after most of the people in Norway have come to work in heated factories or offices 7 hours a day !

You can leave Stalheim by bus on Day 2 at 10:15 to connect with the Gudvangen-Flam boat ride on the Sognefjord, starting at 11:10 for arrival in Flam at 13:30. Snacks and beverages are available on the boat, or you can have lunch after you reach Flam at either the excellent Hotel Fretheim or the fine Heimly Pensjonat.

Short strolls from either of these bring you to the foot of several interesting waterfalls, or you can swim in Fretheim's heated pool.

On the morning of the following day, take the ride on the 12½-mile "Flam Line" railroad to Myrdal (Cook's Table 481a) to connect with the train that left Bergen at 9:50, and then continue from Myrdal to Oslo. The "Flam Line" is one of the 5 most beautiful train rides in Europe.

Departing Flam at 10:15, this 45-minute ride goes along the Aurlandsfjord, a branch of the Sognefjord. Watch for sturdy, wild mountain goats that often cluster on huge granite boulders only a few feet from the track.

This railway has the greatest incline of any Norwegian track, 5.5 percent at one stretch. The descent is so steep that the train takes a longer time to go downhill than it does to go up. It has 5 different braking systems, any one of which is sufficient to stop the train.

Along one stretch the mountainside is so steep that the train has to go through reverse tunnels, and the track in one particular short distance must go on 3 different levels on one side of the Kjosfossen Gorge and 2 levels on the other side of the Gorge. There are 20 tunnels with a combined length of 3.7 miles in the 12½-mile route.

Over the finest scenic sections, the train proceeds slowly or stops in order for passengers to have the best possible views of magnificent scenery and of a road built in 1895 to supply materials for building the railway. This road has 21 hairpin bends.

Along another stretch, the train crosses a 110-yard-long embankment and stops there for several minutes so that passengers can get off and walk closer to an enormous, raging waterfall that cascades close to the train. Its force is marvelous to see and hear.

Arrival in Myrdal at 10:56 is timed to transfer to the Oslo-Bergen train that connects with "Flam Line" in Myrdal at 12:02.

The first stop en route from Myrdal to Oslo is at Finse, highest elevation (4,267 feet) of the entire Bergen-Oslo line. Workers are stationed permanently at Finse to fight snow on the tracks 9 months out of the year and repair the snow sheds during the 3-month Spring-Summer-Autumn there.

Between Finse and Oslo, the scenery changes from glacier to ski resorts, waterfalls, and then beautiful valley farms and fast-moving rivers. You arrive Oslo at 17:40.

If time does not permit going to Stalheim, you can leave Bergen (June, July and August, reservation required) bv fiord boat at 8:00. Arrive Flam at 13:50. Depart on the "Flam Line" train at 14:55 or also (late May to late August only) at 15:25. Arrive Myrdal at 15:36 or 16:10. Connect in Myrdal with the train that departed Bergen at 15:05. Depart Myrdal on that train at 17:10 (reservation required). Arrive Oslo at 22:00.

Despite the late arrival, you will see all of the interesting scenery between Myrdal and Oslo in daylight if you are taking this trip in Summer.

Oslo to Bergen 481

Depart Oslo (Sentrum) at 7:30, 10:05 or 15:45. If you eliminate the Myrdal-Flam-Stalheim-Voss detour, you arrive Bergen at 14:10, 18:30 or 22:30. The 7:30 and 15:45 Oslo departures require reservation and have meal service.

If you take the detour we recommend, depart Oslo at 7:30 or 10:05. The 15:45 train does not stop at Myrdal.

The 7:30 and 10:05 Oslo departures arrive Myrdal at 12:10 and 15:52. Change trains. "Flam Line" departs Myrdal at 12:15 and also at 16:20 (late May to late August), 17:12 and 19:00(daily, except Friday) for the splendid 40-minute ride to Flam. Spend the night in Flam.

On the morning of Day 2, leave Flam Pier at 8:45 for the boat trip on Sognefjord. Arrive Gudvangen at 10:45. Take a bus to Stalheim for the great Smorgasbord lunch there. Either the same day or (if you stay overnight in Stalheim) the next day, go by bus from Stalheim to Voss, and then by train from Voss to Bergen.

Dep. Voss	8:40(1)	12:54(2+3)	16:58(3)	19:10	21:12(2+3)
Arr. Bergen	10:10	14:10	18:30	20:55	22:30

(1)Daily, except Sundays and holidays. (2)Reservation required. (3)Light refreshments.

Hotel Grand Terminus is a 2-minute walk from the Bergen railstation.

If time does not permit going to Stalheim on Day 2, you can depart Flam by fjord boat at 15:15 (June, July and August, reservation required), arriving Bergen at 21:15 the same day.

Oslo - Dombas - Andalsnes 483

This 71-mile "Rauma Line" detour off the "Dovre Line" (Oslo to Trondheim) is, mile for mile, one of the 5 greatest scenic rides in Europe.

Even for one who is not going further north than Dombas, the 2-day roundtrip is well worth the time involved. There is no question that the route is worth seeing twice, and from 2 perspectives.

Be sure to obtain a free brochure at Oslo's Sentrum railstation before beginning the trip. We would enjoy riding "Rauma Line" every day of our lives. Depart Oslo (Sentrum) at 10:00. Arrive Andalsnes at 17:00. In the Summer, you can read a newspaper there by sunlight at Midnight.

Soon after the train leaves Dombas it crosses the granite Jora Bridge, which spans a 120-foot deep gorge. At Bjorli, the Romsdal Valley comes into view, and you will see (at least in late Spring and early Summer) unmatched foaming torrents of thawed-glacier water, rushing at 80 miles an hour down vertical mountain slopes and through the boulder-strewn Rauma River bed.

The descent from Bjorli involves a double spiral through 2 circular mountain tunnels — first the 1,550-yard-long Stavem Tunnel, then through the 500-yard-long Kylling Tunnel.

Between these 2 tunnels, at Verma railstation, there is a monument that commemorates the opening of the Rauma Line by King Haakon in 1924. Along the opposite side of the Rauma River are small, well-kept farms, lush from the benefit of the warmth of the Gulf Stream, which keeps temperatures moderate along most of the coast of Norway.

The train next crosses Kylling Bridge, 200 feet above a thundering run of the Rauma River through a steep, narrow gorge. You are now approaching the valley floor.

Near Flatmark, you cross Foss Bridge and see Bridal Veil, best known of the numerous waterfalls on this route. At Marstein railstation, the sun is visible only 7 months of the year due to the combination of the tall surrounding mountains and the arc of the sun at this latitude.

After passing along the glaciated foot of the majestic Romsdalshorn Mountain, whose peak rivals the Matterhorn as a climber's challenge, one can see on the left the highest vertical rock face in northern Europe, the "Troll's Wall" (Trollveggen), which is 3,000 feet in height.

The "Rauma Line" reaches sea level in the Romsdall Valley before ending at Andalsnes (population 2,500) on the shore of Isfjord, at the head of the Romsdallfjord.

There is a bus connection between Andalsnes and Alesund. At Alesund, one can make flights to Oslo, Bergen or Trondheim, or make coastal express boat trips to Bergen or Trondheim.

The Rauma River is fished by sportsmen for salmon and trout.

To return to Oslo, depart Andalsnes at 10:00, daily except Sundays and holidays. Change trains in Dombas. Depart Dombas at 12:07 (reservation required). Arrive Oslo at 16:35. Or, depart Andalsnes on a through train at 12:00. Arrive Oslo at 19:30. The Oslo-Andalsnes-Oslo roundtrip can be made without stopping overnight in Andalsnes. There is a night departure from Andalsnes at 23:00, arriving Oslo the next morning at 7:20. What a shame, to take this ride at night !

The only overnight lodging we know of in Andalsnes is at the excellent 65-room Grand Hotel Bellevue. Advance room reservations are recommended.

There is a 2-hour bus/ferry connection from Andalsnes to Molde, Norway's "town of roses" located on a fjord and surrounded by 87 beautiful snowcapped peaks. In Molde, see the many ancient wood buildings from the 11th century. The Romsdal Museum, largest Norwegian provincial museum. The floral decorations in the modern concrete and glass Town Hall. The view of the Norwegian Sea and the countryside from the Varden Restaurant, 1300 feet above the town. An International Jazz Festival (music, art, poetry and theatrical events) has been held in Molde the first week of August every year since 1960.

Take the Eide bus 18 miles to visit the grottos and caves at the Troll's Church and the waterfall against a marble mountain.

Oslo - Andalsnes - Trondheim - Bodo - Narvik

This is a marvelous 5-day rail trip up Norway's Gulfstream-warmed coastline. Keep in mind when reading the timetables that there is constant daylight on this route during June and July.

A transplanted herd of gigantic musk oxen live along the Dombas-Trondheim route, Day 2 of this journey. On one of our trips, we saw a mother and baby grazing on a grassy slope near the train track.

The scenery of forests, rich valleys, waterfalls, rivers and farms is lovely almost all the way to the crossing of the Arctic Circle, on the route from Trondheim to Bodo.

Passengers are given a brochure with details about the Arctic Circle trip. Announcements during the ride over a public address system alert passengers to approaching points of interest. A steward or hostess is on board to provide information. After reaching the stone monument that marks the Arctic Circle, the train stops there for 5 minutes, allowing passengers adequate time to take photographs.

We were fortunate that it was snowing on our first crossing of the Arctic Circle, one June, giving the trip the feeling of a polar environment. A few hours later, as the train's route came close to the coastline, and when we were considerably north of the Arctic Circle, it was sunny and warm. There was then no sensation of being so far north, nor was there in Narvik the next day by which time you are 700 miles above the Arctic Circle.

The northernmost rail service from Oslo is to Bodo. Train service from Narvik is across northern Norway, to Sweden. Passage from Bodo to Narvik is via an all-day bus trip through beautiful countryside and includes 3 ferry-boat crossings.

Here are the schedules for a recommended rail trip from Oslo to Narvik, and then to Stockholm. On the trip from Narvik to Boden, you cross the Arctic Circle again, although without the interesting ceremony that is presented on the Trondheim-Bodo ride.

Day 1
483

Dep. Oslo (Sent.)	10:00(1)
Arr Andalsnes	17:10

Day 2 (Bus trip to Dombas)
483

Dep. Andalsnes	15:20
Arr. Dombas	17:30
Change to train.	
Dep. Dombas	18:53(2)
Arr. Trondheim	21:35

Day 3 In Trondheim

Day 4
489

Dep. Trondheim	8:15(3)
Cross the Arctic Circle	17:15
Arr. Bodo	19:30

Day 5 Bus trip to Narvik.

Dep. Bodo	7:50(4)
Arr. Narvik	15:00

(1) Daily all year. Meal service. (2) Runs from mid-June to mid-August. daily except Saturday. Plus another departure from Bodo at 19:38(1). (3) Reservation required. Meal service. (4) Food available at occasional stops.

Keep in mind that during June, July and August the Midnight Sun allows you to see all the scenery to Trondheim, despite the 21:35 arrival time there. The light is not blinding, but you can read a newspaper at 24:00.

Sights in Trondheim: This is the gateway for northern cruises. See the old Nidaros Cathedral. The 18th century rococo Striftsgarden royal residence. The Bishop's Palace.

Sight in Narvik: The second (after Murmansk) most northern rail passenger terminus in the world. Founded in 1901 at the western tip of Ofot Fjord to provide an ice-free port for the mid-Winter export of iron ore from Swedish mines which cannot ship via the frozen Bay of Bothnia during Winter.

For the most breathtaking view of Midnight Sun sky, fjords, mountains and the town of Narvik, take the 10-minute walk from Grand Hotel Royal to the base of the cable that lifts you 2,000 feet in 13 minutes to the top of Mt. Fagernesfjell.

Food and beverages are sold in the Fjellsheimen restaurant on the peak, an ideal site for taking spectacular photos and watching the sun revolve clockwise around the horizon.

A crucial British-German naval battle (commemorated at a small museum in the center of town) was fought in Narvik's fjords during World War II. Destroyed in 1940, Narvik was completely rebuilt after the war.

Narvik - Boden - Stockholm 476

The way to see most of the Narvik-Stockholm route during what are the average person's awake hours is to take the 6:00 departure from Narvik, spend the night in Boden, and take the 6:45 departure from Boden the next day.

Day 6

Dep. Narvik	5:45(1)	9:20(7)	15:00(2+6+10+13)
Arr. Boden	13:00	17:56	22:00
Dep. Boden	13:20(1)	18:15(8)	22:19(2+6+14)
Arr. Langsele	20:10(1)	0:53(3)	5:13(3+9)
Arr. Stockholm	7:20(3)	8:20(3)	13:15(3)

(1) Change trains in Langsele. (2) Carries sleeping car. Also has couchettes. (3) Day 7 of the Oslo-Narvik-Boden-Stockholm trip. (4) From late June to early September: daily. From mid-September to late June: Saturday and Sunday only. (5) Reservation required. (6) Meal service. (7) Footnotes 4+5+6. (8) Footnotes 2+4+5+6. (9) Stops only to leave passengers off train. (10) Change trains in Boden. (11) Daily, except Saturdays and holidays. (12) Daily, except Sundays and day after a holiday. (13) Plus another departure from Narvik at 15:50(10+11). (14) Plus another departure from Boden at 6:40(3+5+6+10+12).

Oslo - Kritiansand - Stavanger 482

There is excellent mountain scenery between Kristiansand and Stavanger.

Dep. Oslo (West)	8:05(1)	10:05(2)	22:30(3)
Arr. Kristiansand	12:55	15:50	4:00
Arr. Stavanger	16:17	19:50	7:40

Sights in Stavanger: Many old streets and houses in this 1100-year old town. See the market of fruits, vegetables, flowers and fish. The 11th century Cathedral. Outside the city, see the prehistoric Viste Cave. Try a deep-sea fishing trip.

Dep. Stavanger	8:40(4)	13:40(1)	22:00(3)
Arr. Kristiansand	12:15	16:55(1)	1:27
Arr. Oslo (West)	18:35	21:55	7:15

(1) Reservation required. Meal service Oslo-Kristiansand and v.v. (2) Reservation required. Light refreshments. (3) Daily, except Saturday. Reservation required. Carries sleeping car. (4) Light refreshments.

Here is the schedule for the short coastline roundtrip, returning to Oslo at the end of the day:

488

Dep. Oslo (West)	9:30(1)
Arr. Drammen	10:00
Arr. Larvik	11:37
Arr. Nordagutu	14:00

482

Dep. Nordagutu	14:05(1)	16:17(1)	20:03(2)
Arr. Oslo (West)	16:20	18:16	21:50

(1) Light refreshments. (2) Reservation required. Meal service.

Stavanger - Kristiansand - Stavanger 482

From Stavanger, it is an easy one-day roundtrip to see the fine mountain scenery en route to Kristiansand.

Dep. Stavanger	8:44(1)
Arr. Kristiansand	12:20

Dep. Kristiansand	13:05(2)	16:15(1)
Arr. Stavanger	16:17	19:50

(1) Light refreshments. (2) Reservation required. Meal service.

Voss - Granvin

This spur off the Bergen-Oslo route affords great farm, mountain and river scenery. It is an easy one-day roundtrip.

481

Dep. Bergen	8:35	12:50(1)
Arr. Voss	10:05	14:36

Change trains.

485

Dep. Voss	10:20	14:45
Arr. Granvin	11:10	15:35

485

Dep. Granvin	11:55	15:55
Arr. Voss	12:45	16:45

Change trains.

481

Dep. Voss	12:54(3)	16:58(4)
Arr. Bergen	14:10	18:30

(1) Daily, except Sundays and holidays. (2) Adjustment footnotes. (3) Reservation required. Light refreshments. (4) Light refreshments.

INTERNATIONAL ROUTES FROM NORWAY

Bergen is Norway's starting point for cruises to England and Holland. Oslo is the gateway for rail trips to Sweden (Stockholm, and on to Finland) and Denmark (Copenhagen, and on to Germany and the rest of Western Europe).

Bergen - Newcastle 1107

Dep. Bergen	11:00(1)	13:00(2)	16:00(3)	19:00(4)
Arr. Newcastle (Tyne)	9:00	12:30	11:30	14:30

(1)Runs from mid-September to mid-October. Wednesday only. (2)From late May to mid-September: Tuesday. From late May to mid-October: Friday. (3)Runs from mid-September to mid-October: Monday only. (4)Runs from late May to mid-September: Sunday only.

Bergen - Amsterdam 1107

These boat schedules are early July to early September.

Dep. Bergen	15:00(1)	17:00(2)
Dep. Stavanger	21:00(1)	-0-
Arr. Amsterdam (Suezhaven)	19:00(3)	20:00(3)

(1)Thursday only. (2)Tuesday only. (3)Day 2.

Narvik - Boden - Stockholm

Schedules for this trip appear earlier in this section, under "Scenic Rail Trips".

Narvik - Boden - Haparanda - Kemi - Oulu - Helsinki

476		
Dep. Narvik	5:45	15:00
Arr. Boden	13:00	22:00
Change trains.		
496		
Dep. Boden	15:15	8:30
Arr. Haparanda	17:49	11:00
Change trains.		

496		
Dep. Haparanda	18:03(1)	12:18
Set your watch forward one hour.		
Arr. Kemi	21:45	14:10
Change trains.		
492		
Dep. Kemi	22:10(2)	14:29(3)
Dep. Oulu	23:40(2)	16:00(3)
Arr. Helsinki	8:55	23:30

(1)Change trains in Tornio. (2)Carries sleeping car. Light refreshments. (3)Meal service.

This is the way to see all of the Narvik-Helsinki route during what are the average person's awake hours: take the 5:45 departure from Boden, Narvik, spend that night in Boden, take the 8:30 departure from Boden, spend that night in Oulu, and on Day 3 depart Oulu at either 7:00 or 12:15, arriving Helsinki the afternoon or night of Day 3.

Oslo - Stockholm

471

Dep. Oslo (Sent.)	8:40(1)	12:55(2)	15:55(1+3)	22:55(3+4)
Arr. Stockholm	15:00	21:55	22:30	8:00

(1) Reservation required. Meal service. (2) Change trains in both Karlstad and also Hallsberg. (3) From late May to late September: daily. From late September to late May: daily, except Saturday. (4) Reservation required. Carries sleeping car all year. Has couchettes only from late June to early September.

Oslo - Copenhagen

466

Dep. Oslo (Sent.)	7:40(1)	11:00(2)	20:00(3+4)	22:40(4)
Arr. Copenhagen (H.)	17:21	20:51	6:11	9:07

(1) Meal service. (2) Light refreshments. (3) Runs from late June to early September. (4) Carries sleeping car. Also has couchettes.

SWEDEN

In Sweden, passengers not holding reserved seats, and who board a train in which reserved seats are required, are charged twice the reservation fee on board the train.

The signs you will see at railstations in Sweden are:

ANKOMST	ARRIVAL
AVGANG	DEPARTURE
BILJETTLUCKAN	TICKET OFFICE
DAMER	WOMEN
GARDEROBEN	CHECKROOM
HERRAR	MEN
JARNVAGSSTATIONEN	RAILWAY STATION
INGANG	ENTRANCE
INFORMATIONSDISKEN	INFORMATION
LIGGPLATSVAGN	COUCHETTE CAR
PLATSBILJETTER	RESERVATIONS
RESTAURANGVAGN	RESTAURANT CAR
SOVVAGN	SLEEPING CAR
SPAR	TRACK
TILL SPAREN	TO THE PLATFORMS
UTGANG	EXIT
VAXELKONTORET	CURRENCY EXCHANGE

SWEDISH HOLIDAYS

A list of holidays is helpful because some trains will be noted later in this section as not running on holidays. Also, those trains which operate on holidays are filled, and it is necessary to make reservations for them long in advance.

January 1	New Year's Day
	Epiphany
	Good Friday
	Easter
	Easter Monday
May 1	Labor Day
	Ascension Day
	Whit Monday
	Midsummer Day
	All Saints' Day
December 25	Christmas Day
December 26	Boxing Day

EURAILPASS BONUSES IN SWEDEN

These boat trips: Goteborg-Fredrickshavn, Helsingborg-Helsingor, Stockholm-Helsinki, Stockholm-Turku and Stockholm-Aland Islands-Turku. There is also a 50% reduction of the fares of the ferry between Malmo and Lubeck-Travemunde (West Germany).

SWEDEN'S TRAIN PASSES

All of Sweden's passes must be purchased in Sweden.

Family Reduction Allowed for 3 or more relatives traveling together. A 40% discount for adults, 70% discount for children 6-21.

Senior Citizen Discount Persons over 65 can buy first or second-class tickets at 40% discount irrespective of distance traveled. but not accepted on Easter, Christmas or weekends in June, July and August.

Lagpriskort Valid one year. Allows 45% discount on ticket prices. Sold at railstations. Photo required. Prices are quoted in Swedish krone. The 1982 prices were: 180SK for first-class, 110SK for second-class.

ONE-DAY EXCURSIONS AND CITY SIGHTSEEING

Here are 9 one-day rail trips that can be made comfortably from Stockholm and Goteborg, returning to them in most cases before dinnertime. Notes are provided on what to see at each destination. The number below the name of each route is the Cook's timetable.

Goteborg

A great seaport. The one-hour sightseeing bus tour leaves from Stora Teatern. There are one-hour boat trips covering the 7-mile harbor and its canals, leaving from Kungsportsbron. See the view of the harbor and city from the Sailor's Tower near the Maritime Museum at Gamla Varvsparken. The Liseberg amusement park. The magnificent City Theater, Concert House and Art Museum, all in the large square, Gotaplatsen. Antikhallarna, Scandinavia's largest permanent antiques and collectors market.

The view from Ramberget, highest point on the Hisingen side of Goteborg. The Botanical Garden. The 7:00 fish auction, weekdays, at Scandinavia's largest fish market. The 17th century Elfsborg Fortress. The Museum, located in the city's oldest (1643) building. The view of the harbor and city from the top of Sjomanjtornet, a 193-foot high tower. The Slottsskogen Zoo.

Stockholm

Bus connections to the city's airport are available at a terminal across the street from the Central railstation. Stockholm's subways depart from the same level as the Tourist Information Office in Central railstation. A Tourist Ticket, good for rides on both buses and subways, is sold for 2 periods: one day and 3 days. These can be purchased at the Tourist Information Office in Central railstation.

Bus #47 can be taken from across the street from Central railstation to the Wasa Museum, where the 17th century battleship is on exhibit. This ancient ship sank in Stockholm harbor at the moment she set forth on her first voyage as flagship of the Swedish Navy and rested in 100 feet of water from 1628 until it was raised in 1956, restored and turned into a museum.

Also see the historic and art treasures in Chapel Royal, the king's silver throne in the Hall of State, the palace museum, and the Bernadotte and Festival suites, all in the Royal Palace. Changing of the guard is Wednesday and Saturday at 12:00, Sunday at 13:00, every day at 12:00 during July and August.

Other sights: the 13th century Cathedral, across from the Palace. The tall old houses and Stock Exchange on Stortorget, the city's oldest square. The outdoor museum of life in early Stockholm and the zoo, at Skansen, an amusement park. The collection of Carl Milles statues at Millesgarden.

Do not miss seeing the Golden Hall, Blue Hall, Prince's Gallery, Terrace and the view from the Tower, all at Town Hall. You can obtain maps, literature and advice at the Stockholm Tourist Association, in Sweden House at Hamngatan 27, in the central business-shopping district. The casino connected to the restaurant (Centalens Restaurang) at the Central Railstation.

Goteborg - Kalmar - Goteborg 467

Dep. Goteborg	7:55(1)	Dep. Kalmar	17:40(2)
Arr. Kalmar	13:20	Arr. Goteborg	22:53

(1) Daily, except Sundays and holidays. (2) Daily, except Saturdays.

Sights in Kalmar: The moat, courts and towers of the Castle. A bus trip to the nearby glassworks.

Stockholm - Eskilstuna - Stockholm

Swedish State Railways Timetable #65

Dep. Stockholm	8:02(1)	8:17(2)	10:02	10:30(1)	12:30
Arr. Eskilstuna	9:40	11:15	11:40	13:15	15:15

Sights in Eskilstuna: The 6 Rademacher Forges that are more than 300 years old, on display in the center of town. Eskilstuna is the capital of Sweden's steel industry. Also see the wooden Fors Church and the statue of the 10th century English missionary, Saint Eskil, for whom the town was named in 1659, one year after Reinhold Rademacher built the forges which launched the local industry.

The Zoo and Amusement Park. The 12th century church. The wonderful collection of Scandinavian art in the Art Museum. Take a local bus 8 miles to Sundbyholm Castle. Shop for gold, iron and copper souvenirs.

Dep. Eskilstuna	14:33(1)	14:33(3)	16:33	18:33(1)	20:20(4)
Arr. Stockholm	16:13	17:42	18:13	20:13	21:58

(1) Monday-Friday, except holidays. (2) Daily except Saturday, Good Friday, May 1, Ascension Day, Whit Monday and the day before Midsummer Day. (3) Daily except Saturdays and holidays. Via Vasteras. (4) Sundays only, except Easter and the last 2 Sundays of December.

Stockholm - Gavle - Stockholm 476 + 478

Dep. Stockholm (Cent.)	8:15(1)	10:15	12:15(2)	
Arr. Gavle	2 hours later			

Sights in Gavle: The Swedish Railway Museum.

Dep. Gavle	11:11(1)	13:50(2)	15:50	17:50(3+5)
Arr. Stockholm (Cent.)	2 hours later			

(1) Reservation required. Meal service. (2) Mon.-Fri., except holidays. (3) Light refreshments. (4) Daily, except Sat. (5) Plus other departures from Gavle at 19:50(1), 20:34(1) and 21:58(4).

Stockholm - Goteborg - Stockholm 469

All of these trains require reservation and have meal service, unless otherwise designated.

Dep. Stockholm (C.)	6:05(1)	7:35(2)	8:05	9:05(1)
Arr. Goteborg	10:45	11:50	12:45	13:45

Sights in Goteborg: See notes about sightseeing in Goteborg at the start of this section.

Dep. Goteborg	13:15	14:15(3)	15:15	16:15(3+6)
Arr. Stockholm (C.)	17:55	18:55	19:55	20:55

(1) Daily, except Sundays and holidays. (2) Runs Monday-Friday from early August to late June. (3) Daily, except Saturday. (4) Runs from early August to late June. (5) From late June to early August: Sunday only. From early August to late June: daily, except Saturday. (6) Plus other departures from Goteborg at 16:50(3+4), 17:15 and 18:15(5).

Stockholm - Malmo - Stockholm 465

Dep. Stockholm (Cent.)	6:13(1+2)	7:13(1+3)	8:13(1)
Arr. Malmo (Cent.)	13:00	14:03	14:55

Sights in Malmo: See notes about sightseeing in Malmo earlier in this chapter, in the "Denmark" section, under "Copehagen-Malmo".

Dep. Malmo (Cent.)	14:56(3+4)	16:00(1)	17:00(1+3+5)
Arr. Stockholm (Cent.)	21:47	22:47	23:16

(1) Reservation required. Meal service. (2) Daily, except Sundays and holidays. (3) Change trains in Hassleholm. (4) Meal service. (5) Mon.-Friday.

Stockholm - Mora - Stockholm 480

Dep. Stockholm (Central)	8:28
Arr. Mora	13:03

Dep. Mora	14:50(1)	18:50(2)
Arr. Stockholm (Central)	19:23	23:40

(1) Reservation required. (2) Daily, except Saturday.

Sights in Mora: The outdoor museum of 40 timber buildings, some 600 years old. The collection of Anders Zorn, Sweden's most famous painter.

Stockholm - Norrkoping - Stockholm 465

All of these trains require reservation and have meal service, unless otherwise designated.

Dep. Stockholm (C.)	7:13	8:13	9:13	10:13(4)
Arr. Norrkoping	2 hours later			

Sights in Norrkoping: The amazing collection of more than 25,000 cactus plants in beautiful Karl Johans Park. Take the short sightseeing trip by boat, from the pier at the end of this park. See the 3,000-year old Bronze Age carvings and also the display of roses in Himmelstalund Park, to the right of the railstation. On the other side of the railstation, visit the ruins of Johannisborg Fort. See the Lindo Canal.

Hear the bell-chiming at 13:00 in front of the Radhuset (Council House). See Hedvigs Kyrka, the German Church.

Dep. Norrkoping	12:50	13:50(1)	14:50	15:50(2+5)
Arr. Stockholm (C.)	2 hours later			

(1) Reservation not required. (2) Daily, except Sundays and holidays. (3) Daily, except Saturday. (4) Plus other departures from Stockholm at 11:13 and 12:13. (5) Plus other departures from Norrkoping at 16:20(1), 16:50, 17:50(1+3), 18:50, 19:50(1), 20:50 and 21:19.

Stockholm - Rattvik - Stockholm 480

Dep. Stockholm (Cent.)	8:28
Arr. Rattvik	12:33

Dep. Rattvik	15:19(1)	19:19(2)
Arr. Stockholm (Cent.)	19:23	23:40

(1) Reservation required. (2) Daily, except Saturday.

Sights in Rattvik: The rustic arts museum.

Stockholm - Uppsala - Stockholm 478

Dep. Stockholm (Cent.)	8:10(1)	10:10	12:10(2)	14:10(3)
Arr. Uppsala	40-50 minutes later			

Sights in Uppsala: The largest church in Scandinavia, Uppsala Cathedral, a short walk from the railstation. Sweden's largest library, Carolina Rediviva, with more than 20,000 hand-illuminated medieval manuscripts, including the only book in existence that is written in pure Gothic, the famous Codex Argentus, the 5th century Silver Bible. The Great Hall of State in the old red Castle, open 11:00-16:00 from mid-May to mid-September. Take a bus marked "Gamla Uppsala" for a 2-mile ride to see relics of heathen worship going back to the 5th century.

	478	476	478	478
Dep. Uppsala	12:21(1+4)	12:49(1+3+5)	14:49(2)	16:49(7)
Arr. Stockholm (Cent.)	40-50 minutes later			

(1) Reservation required. (2) Monday-Friday, except holidays. (3) Light refreshments. (4) Meal service. (5) Daily, except Sundays and holidays. (6) Daily, except Saturday. (7) Plus other departures at 18:49(3), 20:55(1+4), 21:56(1+4) and 23:22(6).

SCENIC RAIL TRIPS

Ostersund - Trondheim

There is fine mountain scenery on this portion of the Stockholm-Trondheim route.

478	
Dep. Stockholm (Cent.)	22:10(1)
Dep. Ostersund	7:37
Arr. Trondheim	12:35

(1) Carries sleeping car. Also has couchettes.

INTERNATIONAL ROUTES FROM SWEDEN

Stockholm is the gateway for rail trips to northern Norway (Trondheim and Narvik) and to northern Finland (Oulu), as well as by boat to Helsinki (and on to Leningrad). It is also the gateway for travel to southern Norway (Oslo, and on to Bergen or Stavanger). Malmo is the starting point for rail travel to Denmark (Copehagen, and on to Germany and the rest of Western Europe).

Stockholm - Trondheim

478		
Dep. Stockholm (Cent.)	7:40(1)	22:10(2)
Arr. Storlien	16:47	-0-
Change to bus.		
Dep. Storlien	17:10	-0-
Arr. Trondheim	19:45	12:35

(1) Reservation required. Meal service 7:40-14:06. (2) Carries sleeping car. Also has couchettes. Direct train. No change to bus in Storlien.

Stockholm - Copenhagen

465

All of these trains require reservation and have meal service, unless otherwise designated.

Dep. Stockholm (C.)	7:13	9:13	11:13	12:43(1+2+8)
Arr. Copenhagen (H.)	15:37	17:21	19:51	21:36

(1)Runs from late June to early September. (2)Reservation not required. (3)Saturday only. (4)Daily, except Saturday. (5)Carries sleeping car. Also has couchettes. (6)Runs from mid-June to early September. (7)Carries sleeping car. Light refreshments. (8)Plus other departures from Stockholm at 15:13(2+3), 15:43(4+5), 17:43(2+5+6), 21:13(2+4+7) and 23:13(2+5).

Stockholm - Helsinki (Boat and Train)

The price for the cruise across the Bay of Bothnia on the comfortable and pleasant Silja Line ships is about $44(U.S.). This passage is covered by Eurailpass. The fare for a sleeping cabin is not covered by Eurailpass. Food on the ship is varied and delicious. We recommend the daytime sailing in order to see the thousands of tiny islands on the ride through this extremely interesting archipelago. During the daytime cruise, there is a good smorgasbord for both lunch and dinner. A small band plays music in a delightful bar area. Movies are shown in a small theater. There is a duty-free shop on board. The ships ferry autos.

1233 Boat

Dep. Stockholm (Vartan)	8:30(1)	19:30	21:30
Arr. Turku (Abo)	20:15	8:00	8:45

Walk to either railstation.

493

Dep. Turku (Harbor)	20:30(2)	8:35(3)	-0-
Dep. Turku (Stn.)	20:46	8:47(3)	10:15(4)
Arr. Helsinki	23:32	11:35	13:05

(1)Daily during June, July and August. (2)Light refreshments. (3)Meal service. (4)From late May to late August: daily. From late August to late May: daily, except Sundays and holidays. Meal service.

Stockholm - Narvik 476

The most scenic portion of this trip is from Boden to Narvik, best seen on the 16:55 or 20:10 departures from Stockholm.

Dep. Stockholm (Cent.)	8:10(1)	16:55(5)	20:10(6)	22:10(7)
Arr. Boden	23:02(2)	7:00	9:55	14:45
Dep. Boden	2:23(3)	7:13	10:10	15:05
Arr. Kiruna	6:29(2)	10:44	13:55	19:00
Dep. Kiruna	6:50(4)	11:00(4)	14:10	19:20
Arr. Narvik (Day 2)	10:24	14:00	17:03	22:20

(1) Reservation required. Meal service until 12:55. (2) Change trains. (3) Daily, except Sundays and holidays. (4) Light refreshments. (5) Carries sleeping car. Also has couchettes. Meal service 17:00-21:55. (6) From late June to early September: daily. From early September to late June: Thursday and Friday only. Reservation required. Carries sleeping car. Also has couchettes. Meal service until 13:55 on Day 2. (7) Carries sleeping car. Also has couchettes. Change trains in Langsele at 7:19 on Day 2.

Stockholm - Oslo 471

Dep. Stockholm (Cent.)	7:00(1+2)	15:55(1+3+4)	23:10(4+5)
Arr. Oslo (Sent.)	13:25	22:08	7:55

(1) Reservation required. (2) Meal service 7:00-10:54. Light refreshments 11:32-13:25. (3) Meal service 15:55-19:49. Light refreshments 20:00-22:08. (4) From late May to late September: daily. From late September to late May: daily, except Saturday. (5) Carries sleeping car all year. Has couchettes only from late June to early September. Departs Stockholm one hour earlier on Saturday.

Stockholm - Oulu - Helsinki

476

Dep. Stockholm (Cent.)	17:40(1)
Arr. Boden	8:12

Change trains.

496

Dep. Boden	8:30(2)
Arr. Haparanda	11:00

Change trains.

496

Dep. Haparanda	12:18(2)

Set your watch forward one hour.

Arr. Kemi	14:10

Change trains.

492

Dep. Kemi	14:29(2)
Arr. Oulu	15:47
Dep. Oulu	16:00(2+3)
Arr. Helsinki	23:30

(1) From late June to early September: daily. From early September to late June: daily, except Saturday. Carries sleeping car. Also has couchettes. (2) Daily. (3) Meal service.

SWITZERLAND

The signs you will see at railstations in Switzerland are those you would see in France, Germany or Italy, depending on the section. French is the language south and southwest of Bern. Italian is dominant in the southeast corner of the country. Elsewhere, the prevailing language is German. There are free timetables at the railstations.

A traveler with a confirmed flight reservation for a departure from Zurich's or Geneva's airport can check bags at a special counter in the railstation at nearly 100 Swiss cities. Unencumbered with luggage, the passenger using "Fly Luggage Service" rides a train from places such as Bern, Locarno and Luzern directly to the airport, checks-in at the airport's "Express" counter, boards the airplane, and claims the luggage at the end of the flight. The time required for baggage deposit in advance of train departure varies from one Swiss railstation to another. Be sure to obtain that information before departure day.

SWISS TRAIN PASSES

Must be purchased before arriving in Switzerland.

Swiss Holiday Card. Good for unlimited travel on trains, lake steamers and postal buses. Also provides discounts up to 50% on many extremely scenic and very expensive privately-owned mountain railroads and aerial cable cars that are not covered by Eurailpass.

The 1983 first-class prices are: $77(U.S.) for 4 days, $103 for 8 days, $129 for 15 days, and $182 for one month. Second-class: $56 for 4 days, $71 for 8 days, $93 for 15 days, and $129 for one month. Half-fare for children 6 to under 16.

Half-Fare Travel Card Honored on both first and second-class space, allowing purchase of tickets at 50% discount: 15 days $27(U.S.), one month $35.

Senior Citizen Half-Fare Travel Card May be purchased by women over 62 and men over 65. The 1983 price is $52(U.S.). In addition to 50% discount on tickets, this card also entitles the bearer to reduced prices at participating Swiss hotels. Valid for one year.

Junior Half-Fare Travel Card For persons 16-26 years old. The 1983 price for one month is $16(U.S.).

SUMMER TIME

Switzerland changes to Summer Time on the last Sunday of March and converts back to Standard Time on the last Sunday of September.

EURAILPASS BONUSES IN SWITZERLAND

Boat trips on the Rhine from Schaffhausen to Kreuzlingen and also on the Aare from Biel/Bienne to Solothurn and on the lakes of Biel, Brienz, Geneva, Luzern, Murten, Neuchatel, Thun and Zurich.

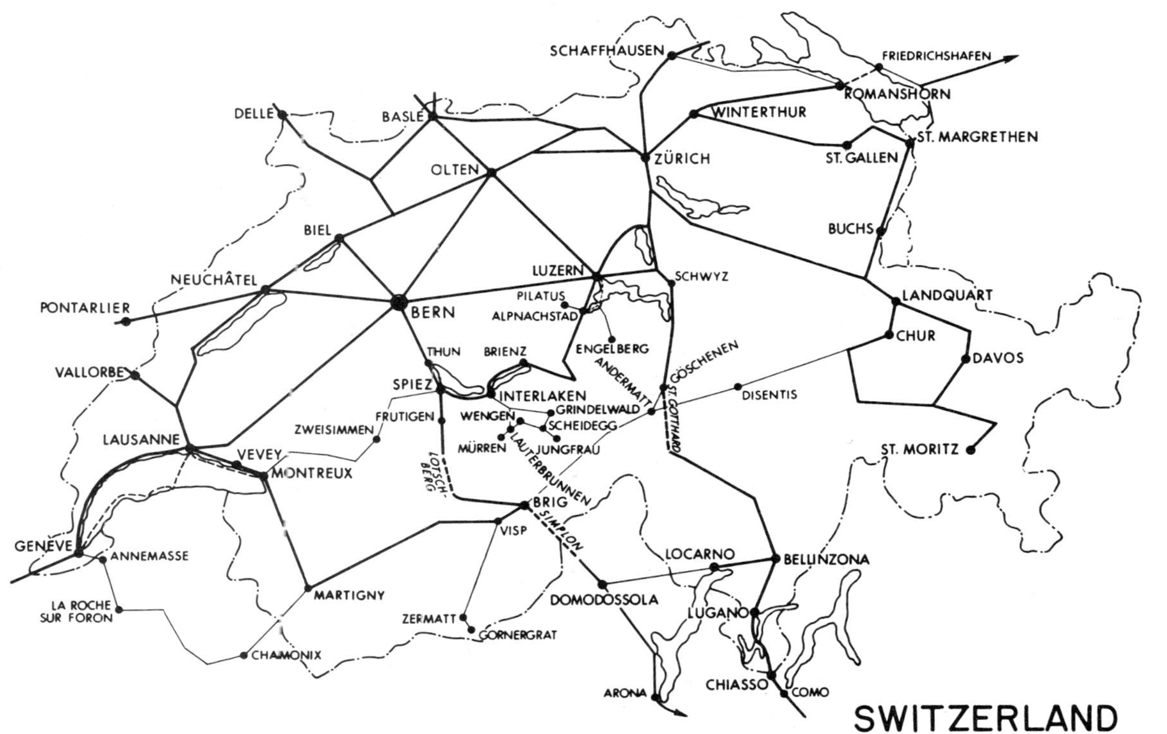
SCHAFFHAUSEN
FRIEDRICHSHAFEN
ROMANSHORN
WINTERTHUR
DELLE
BASLE
ST. MARGRETHEN
ST. GALLEN
ZÜRICH
OLTEN
BUCHS
BIEL
LUZERN
SCHWYZ
NEUCHÂTEL
PILATUS
LANDQUART
PONTARLIER
BERN
ALPNACHSTAD
CHUR
ENGELBERG
THUN
BRIENZ
GÖSCHENEN
DAVOS
VALLORBE
ANDERMATT
SPIEZ
INTERLAKEN
ST. GOTTHARD
DISENTIS
FRUTIGEN
WENGEN
GRINDELWALD
SCHEIDEGG
ZWEISIMMEN
LAUSANNE
MÜRREN
JUNGFRAU
ST. MORITZ
VEVEY
LÖTSCH-BERG
MONTREUX
LAUTERBRUNNEN
BRIG
VISP
SIMPLON
GENEVE
ANNEMASSE
LOCARNO
BELLINZONA
MARTIGNY
DOMODOSSOLA
LA ROCHE SUR FORON
ZERMATT
LUGANO
GORNERGRAT
CHAMONIX
ARONA
CHIASSO
COMO
SWITZERLAND

SWISS HOLIDAYS

A list of holidays is helpful because some trains will be noted latei in this section as not running on holidays. Also, those trains which operate on holidays are filled, and it is necessary to make reservations for them long in advance.

January 1	New Year's Day		Ascension Day
	Good Friday		Whit Monday
	Easter	August 1	National Independence Day
	Easter Monday	December 25	Christmas Day

ONE-DAY EXCURSIONS AND CITY-SIGHTSEEING

Here are 56 one-day rail trips that can be made comfortably from 6 major cities in Switzerland, returning to them in most cases before dinnertime. Notes are provided on what to see at each destination. The number below the name of each route is the Cook's timetable. The 6 base cities are: Basle, Bern, Geneva, Interlaken, Luzern and Zurich.

When no station is designated for cities in Austria, Switzerland and West Germany, the station is "Hauptbahnhof".

Basle

The superb Holbein, Delacroix, Gauguin, Matisse, Ingres, Courbet and Van Gogh paintings in the Kunstmuseum. The Historical Museum in the Franciscan Church in Barfusserplatz. The Municipal Casino. The collection of 18th century clothing, ceramics and watches in the Kirschgarten mansion. Shop on Freiestrasse. See the 16th century Town Hall. The fishmarket. The 15th century New University. Take a boat excursion from the pier in the back of the Hotel Three Kings. See the view of the city from the Wettstein Bridge. The beautiful Munsterplatz.

Munster, the 13th century Cathedral. The more than 100,000 rarities from every continent (particularly those from New Guinea and the South Seas) in the Ethnological Museum at Augustinerstrasse 2. In the same complex, the extraordinary geological section at the Museum of Natural History.

The Jewish Museum of Switzerland, at Kornhausgasse 18, where Theodore Herzl presided over the first Zionist Congress, in 1897. The Zoo, Switzerland's largest, is a short stroll from the SNCF and SBB railstations. Or, take Trolleys #4 and #7 from the stations.

Bern

The comic antics of the denizens of the Bear Pit. How they love figs ! The performance every hour of the clock tower, the Zytglockenturm. The nearby old arcaded streets. Lunch on the terrace of the Casino restaurant and the view from there of the River Aare. The Art Museum, with the largest Klee collection in the world. The Cathedral.

One of the world's largest stamp collections, at the Swiss PTTT Museum. The statue honoring the world postal system. The view of the Alps from the terrace of the Federal Palace, and the nearby open-air flower and produce market (Tuesday and Saturday mornings). The Swiss Alpine Museum. The Natural History Museum. Prison Tower. Holy Ghost Church. The Botanical Gardens. The many window-boxes with flowering geraniums throughout the streets in the city center.

Geneva

Walk from the railstation, down Rue du Mont Blanc, to the shore of Lake Leman. See the monument to international Protestantism and the fabulous clock of living flowers and plants in the park across the lake. It is on that side of the lake you will find the city's old narrow streets and, in St. Peter's Cathedral, the pulpit from which Calvin preached. See the view from the top of the Cathedral's North Tower. In modern Geneva: Palais des Nations, today the European headquarters of the United Nations Organization. The chinaware collection in the Ariana Museum.

The Art and History Museum, 2 rue Charles-Galland, Bus #1 from the railstation, has an archaeological collection, paintings, decorative art and sculptures, open 10:00-12:00 (except Monday) and 14:00-18:00 daily. The National History Museum, 11 route de Malagnou, one of the most modern museums in Europe, open daily 10:00-12:00 and 14:00-17:00 (except Monday), Bus #5 from the railstation. Nearby, at 15 route de Malagnou, is the Watch and Clock Museum, open daily 10:00-12:00 (except Monday) and 14:00-16:00, also Bus #5 from the railstation.

The Voltaire Museum, 25 rue des Delices, open Monday-Friday 14:00-17:00, Bus #6 from the railstation. The world-famous Davidoff's Cigar Store on rue de Rive, open Monday-Friday 8:00-19:00 and Saturday 8:00-18:30, where the No. 2 coronas sold for $6.60(U.S.) each in 1982. Also in stock there: enormous ebony and mahogany humidors.

Luzern

Walk across the 14th and 15th century bridges spanning the Reuss River and see the 120 paintings on the ceiling of Kappelbrucke depicting Luzern's history and the 45 "Dance of Death" paintings inside the Spreuerbrucke. See the immense 30-foot high, 42-foot long Lion of Luzern, carved in 1821 into a sandstone cliff at what is now the entrance to the Glacier Gardens outdoor museum. The lion commemorates the bravery of those Swiss soldiers who defended Marie Antoinette during the French Revolution. The Glacier Museum, in operation since 1872, is well worth visiting. You will see there the absolute proof that palm trees once grew here, when this area was tropical. The old railway cars, locomotives, trolley cars, buses and autos at the Swiss National Transport Museum, the largest museum of its kind in Europe. The exhibit of model railways, nearby. The Art Museum, near the railstation. The August music festival. The giant (12,000 square foot) canvas Grand Panorama, depicting war in Winter.

Zurich

Here is a great 2-hour walk: Upon arriving at the main Zurich railstation, take the escalator down one level and enjoy a snack or meal in Shopville, the enormous underground shopping center beneath Bahnhof Platz, the square in front of the station. Come up from Shopville on the other side of Bahnhof Platz. Walk one mile down one side of Bahnhofstrasse, lined with smart stores. When this city's Fifth Avenue ends at the shore of Lake Zurich, take in the lakeside promenade before returning to the railstation by walking along the opposite side of Bahnhofstrasse that you walked earlier. Upon returning to the station, go all the way through it, cross Museumstrasse, and visit the National Museum. Other sights: The Bellevue Platz amusement center. The paintings and sculptures at the Kunsthaus. African and Asian art at the Rietberg Museum. Kunstgewerbemuseum. The Museum of Applied Arts (handicrafts, architecture and industrial design).

The 5 Chagall stained-glass windows (red, blue and green) in the 13th century Fraumunsterkirche. The great toy museum on the top floor of the marvelous Franz Carl Weber Toy Shop, on Bahnhofstrasse.

A cruise on Lake Zurich is covered by Eurailpass. Board the boat at the lake end of Bahnhofstrasse.

There is rail service from Zurich's Hauptbahnhof railstation to the Zurich airport and v.v. every 24-30 minutes from 5:30 to 23:00.

Basle - Baden Baden - Basle	664			
Dep. Basle (S.S.B.)	8:08(1)	10:08(1)	11:12(2)	12:08(1)+(3)
Dep. Basle (Bad. Bf.)	5 minutes later			
Arr. Baden Baden	9:35	11:35	13:11	13:37

Sights in Baden Baden: Praised for its hot salt springs since the Romans discovered the curative water in this area nearly 2,000 years ago. The illnesses treated here include rheumatism, abnormal blood pressure, metabolic disturbances, respiratory ailments, and problems caused by lack of physical exercise.

Nearly 300 prominent European families once had their permanent homes here. Fantastic landscape. The Oos Valley has been called the most beautiful valley in the world. Exotic trees include the Japanese maple, American tulip, East Asian ginkgo, Chinese trumpet, magnolia and fig. The colors of many deciduous trees make Autumn glorious here.

See the Louis XIII and Louis XIV decor of the halls in the casino. The fancy boutique shops. Exhibitions of international art in the Staatliche Kunsthalle (City Art Gallery).

Motorized vehicles are not permitted in the core area of Baden Baden. There is a constant schedule of balls, fashion shows and concerts.

Food specialties here are Grunkernsuppe (a vegetable soup), game pate, pike dumplings, Blaufelchen (a kind of whitefish from Lake Constance), raspberry schnapps and kirsch with smoked bacon, bread baked with charcoal, and pate of truffled goose-liver from nearby Strasbourg.

Dep. Baden Baden	13:15(1)	14:02(4)	14:49(5)	16:15(1+6)
Arr. Basle (Bad Bf.)	14:39	15:25	16:28	17:39
Arr. Basle (S.B.B.)	10 minutes later			

(1) Supplement charged. Meal service. (2) Light refreshments. (3) Daily, except Saturday. (4) TEE. Reservation required. Meal service. (5) Meal service. (6) Plus other departures from Baden Baden at 16:50(2), 18:15(1+3), 19:50(2), 21:00, 22:16(1), 23:07 and 23:35.

Basle - Bern - Basle 260

All of these trains have light refreshments.

Dep. Basle (S.B.B.)	6:56	7:46	8:56	9:46	10:56(1)
Arr. Bern	8:09	9:09	10:09	11:09	12:09

Sights in Bern: See notes about sightseeing in Bern at the start of this section.

Dep. Bern	11:45	12:45	13:45	14:45	15:45(2)
Arr. Basle (S.B.B.)	13:08	13:58	15:08	15:58	17:08

(1) Plus other departures from Basle at 11:46, 12:56 and 13:46. (2) Plus other departures from Bern at frequent times from 16:45 to 22:41.

Basle - Interlaken - Basle 260

All of these trains have light refreshments.

Dep. Basle (S.B.B.)	6:56	7:46	8:56	9:46(1)
Arr. Interlaken (West)	9:27	10:15	11:27	12:15
Arr. Interlaken (Ost)	5 minutes later			

Sights in Interlaken: A fine Summer resort and health spa. Take the funicular to Heimwehfluh for a marvelous view of the mountains.

Dep. Interlaken (Ost)	12:24	13:24	14:34	15:24(2)
Dep. Interlaken (West)	5 minutes later			
Arr. Basle (S.B.B.)	15:08	15:58	17:08	17:58

(1) Plus other departures from Basle at frequent times from 10:56 to 20:56. (2) Plus other departures from Interlaken at 16:34, 17:24 and 18:34.

Basle - Luxembourg - Basle 176

Dep. Basle (SNCF)	5:03	8:21(1)
Arr. Luxembourg	9:05	11:56

Sights in Luxembourg: See notes about sightseeing in Luxembourg on page 82.

Dep. Luxembourg	14:54(2)	18:26(1)	21:14
Arr. Basle (SNCF)	18:25	22:03	1:28

(1) Meal service. (2) Supplement charged. Meal service.

Basle - Luzern - Basle 277

Most of these trains have meal service or light refreshments.

Dep. Basle (S.B.B.) 6:23 7:00 8:01 9:00 10:01 11:00(1)
Arr. Luzern 70 minutes later

Sights in Luzern: See notes about city-sightseeing in Luzern at the start of this section.

Dep. Luzern 9:44 10:37 11:44 12:37 13:44 14:37(2)
Arr. Basle (S.B.B.) 70 minutes later

(1) Plus other departures from Basle on the hour from 12:00 to 21:00, plus 22:31. (2) Plus other departures from Luzern at frequent times from 15:44 to 22:40.

Basle - Rheinfelden - Basle 268

Dep. Basle (S.B.B.) 6:31 7:52 8:33 10:33 11:14 12:33(1)
Arr. Rheinfelden 15 minutes later

Sights in Rheinfelden: Tours of the Cardinal and Feldschlosschen breweries. The island park in the Rhine River.

Dep. Rheinfelden 8:06 9:06 10:23 11:06 12:23 13:06(2)
Arr. Basle (S.B.B.) 15 minutes later

(1) Plus other departures from Basle at 14:33, 15:14 and 16:33. (2) Plus other departures from Rheinfelden at frequent times from 15:06 to 0:06.

Basle - Strasbourg - Basle 176

Dep. Basle (SNCF)	5:10(1)	8:21(2)	11:12	12:44(2+3)
Arr. Strasbourg	6:40	9:44	12:40	14:28

Sights in Strasbourg: See very lengthy notes about sightseeing in Strasbourg in the "France" section, under "Paris-Strasbourg".

Dep. Strasbourg	12:11(2)	13:14	17:02(4)	20:37(2+5)
Arr. Basle (SNCF)	13:39	14:46	18:25	22:03

(1) Light refreshments. (2) Meal service. (3) Change trains in Mulhouse. (4) Supplement charged. Meal service. (5) Plus other departures from Strasbourg at 23:46(1) and 0:03.

Basle - Zurich - Basle 268

All of these trains have light refreshments.

Dep. Basle (S.B.B.) 6:09 6:58 7:52 8:58 9:54(1)
Arr. Zurich (Hbf.) 60 minutes later

Sights in Zurich: See notes about city-sightseeing in Zurich at the start of this section.

Dep. Zurich (Hbf.) Frequent times from 10:57 to 23:09
Arr. Basle (S.B.B.) 60 minutes later

(1) Plus other departures from Basle at frequent times from 10:12 to 22:25.

Bern - Basle - Bern 260

All of these trains have light refreshments.

Dep. Bern	6:45	7:45	8:45	9:45	10:45(1)
Arr. Basle (S.B.B.)	70 minutes later				

Sights in Basle: See notes about city-sightseeing in Basle at the start of this section.

Dep. Basle (S.B.B.)	10:56	11:46	12:56	13:46	14:56(2)
Arr. Bern	70 minutes later				

(1) Plus other departures from Bern at frequent times from 11:45 to 21:45. (2) Plus other departures from Basle at frequent times from 15:52 to 22:18.

Bern - Geneva - Bern 256

Dep. Bern	6:34(1)	7:16	7:34	8:16(2)	9:16(3)
Arr. Geneva (Corn.)	8:28	8:57	9:28	9:57	10:57

Sights in Geneva: See notes about city-sightseeing in Geneva at the start of this section.

Dep. Geneva (Corn.)	12:57(2)	13:26(1)	13:57(2)	14:57(2)	15:57(2+4)
Arr. Bern	14:38	15:20	15:38	16:38	17:38

(1) Light refreshments. (2) Meal service. (3) Plus other departures from Bern at frequent times from 9:34 to 13:16. (4) Plus other departures from Geneva at frequent times from 16:57 to 20:57 plus 22:26.

Bern - Interlaken - Bern 260

Dep. Bern	6:40	7:27	8:27	9:27(1)
Arr. Interlaken (West)	7:28	8:15	9:27	10:15
Arr. Interlaken (Ost)	5 minutes later			

Sights in Interlaken: See notes about city-sightseeing in Interlaken at the start of this section.

Dep. Interlaken (Ost)	7:34	8:24	9:34	10:24(2)
Dep. Interlaken (West)	5 minutes later			
Arr. Bern	8:27	9:27	10:27	11:27

(1) Plus other departures from Bern at frequent times from 10:27 to 22:21. (2) Plus other departures from Interlaken at frequent times from 11:34 to 22:30.

Bern - Lausanne - Bern 256

Dep. Bern	Frequent departures from 6:34 to 22:16
Arr. Lausanne	70 minutes later

Sights in Lausanne: The Cathedral. The Castle of St. Maire. City Hall. The Federal Palace of Justice.

Dep. Lausanne	Frequent departures from 5:29 to 23:09
Arr. Bern	70 minutes later

Bern - Fribourg - Lausanne - Bern

It is possible to stop and sightsee in both Fribourg and Lausanne on the same one-day excursion.

256

Dep. Bern	8:16	9:16	10:16	11:16	12:16
Arr. Fribourg	8:37	9:37	10:37	11:37	12:37

Sights in Fribourg: The world-famous organ in the 18th century Church and Convent of the Cordeliers was missing in 1982. See the 17th century altar in the Church of the Augustines. Farmers and their wives in traditional local dress, at the Wednesday and Saturday markets. The many stone fountains in the winding streets that lead to the 16th century Town Hall.

Dep. Fribourg	10:38	11:38	12:38	13:38	14:38
Arr. Lausanne	11:22	12:22	13:22	14:22	15:22

Sights in Lausanne: See notes in preceding listing.

Dep. Lausanne	13:32	14:32	15:32	16:32	17:32(1)
Arr. Bern	60 minutes later				

(1) Plus other departures from Lausanne at 18:32, 19:32, 20:09, 20:32, 21:32 and 23:09.

Bern - Fribourg - Bern

Here are the schedules for a one-day excursion involving only Fribourg.

256

Dep. Bern	Frequent times from 6:34 to 22:16
Arr. Fribourg	20 minutes later

Sights in Fribourg: See notes in preceding listing.

Dep. Fribourg	Frequent times from 6:16 to 23:58
Arr. Bern	20 minutes later

Bern - Luzern - Bern

Outstanding farm and forest scenery as you travel through Switzerland's beautiful Emmental (valley of the Emme River).

Most of these trains have light refreshments.

262

Dep. Bern	6:44	7:44	9:44	10:00	11:44	13:44
Arr. Luzern	8:01	9:01	11:01	11:49	13:01	15:01

Sights in Luzern: See notes about city-sightseeing in Luzern at the start of this section.

Dep. Luzern	11:51	13:51	15:51	16:51	17:51	18:51(1)
Arr. Bern	13:09	15:09	17:09	18:09	19:09	20:09

(1) Plus other departures from Luzern at 19:51, 20:51 and 22:03.

Bern - Langnau - Luzern - Bern 262

It is possible to stop and sightsee in both Langnau and Luzern on the same one-day excursion.

Most of these trains have light refreshments.

Dep. Bern	7:44	9:44	10:00	11:44	13:44
Arr. Langnau	30 minutes later				

Sights in Langnau: The antique household utensils and local industry products (linen-weaving, tanning, embroidery) in the museum housed in a 16th century wood building.

Dep. Langnau	10:45	12:15	14:15
Arr. Luzern	11:49	13:01	15:01

Sights in Luzern: See notes in preceding listing.

Dep. Luzern	11:51	13:51	15:51	16:51	17:51(1)
Arr. Bern	13:09	15:09	17:09	18:09	19:09

(1)Plus other departures from Luzern at 18:51, 19:51, 20:51 and 22:03.

Bern - Langnau - Bern 262

Here are the schedules for a one-day excursion involving only Langnau.

Dep. Bern	7:44	9:44	10:00	11:44	13:44
Arr. Langnau	30 minutes later				

Sights in Langnau: See notes in preceding listing.

Dep. Langnau	10:41	12:41	14:41	16:41	17:41(1)
Arr. Bern	30 minutes later				

(1)Plus other departures from Langnau at 18:41, 19:41, 20:41, 21:41 and 23:25.

Bern - Neuchatel - Bern
253

Dep. Bern	8:40	9:20	9:40	10:40	11:20	11:40(1)
Arr. Neuchatel	40-60 minutes later					

Sights in Neuchatel: After many years of recommending a visit to the Suchard chocolate factory, we received a letter from the Suchard people telling us it does not offer tours during July and August when its employees take vacations and it slows down production during those months. At any time of year, Suchard requires advance notice "of at least a couple of days" before it can provide a factory tour. For chocolate maniacs such as we are, if a tour of Suchard is imperative try phoning them at (038) 21-11-55. Failing the Suchard tour, see the city's museum of mechanical dolls and music boxes. Take a stroll up winding streets, past elegant Renaissance and 17th century houses, to the hilltop Castle. Visit the Fine Arts Museum. Take the funicular to the top (3,839 feet) of Chaumont for a view of the Alps.

Boat rides on the 3 lakes (Neuchatel, Biel and Morat) are covered by Eurailpass.

Try the great Fondue Neuchatelois, made from white wine and kirsch schnapps. On the first Sunday of October, the local grape harvest is celebrated with a colorful Parade and Battle of Flowers. On this day, wine flows from the city's outdoor fountains instead of water.

Dep. Neuchatel	10:56	11:28	13:08	13:28	14:56	15:28(2)
Arr. Bern	40-60 minutes later					

(1)Plus other departures from Bern at 12:40, 13:20, 13:47 and 14:40.
(2)Plus other departures from Neuchatel at frequent times from 16:20 to 23:20.

Bern - Zurich - Bern 256

All of these trains have meal service or light refreshments.

Arr. Zurich (Hbf.)	9:29	9:54	10:54	11:54	12:54	13:54
Dep. Bern	7:50	8:41	9:41	10:41	11:41	12:41

Sights in Zurich: See notes about city-sightseeing in Zurich at the start of this section.

Dep. Zurich (Hbf.)	Frequent times from 6:33 to 23:00
Arr. Bern	1-1½ hours later

Geneva - Annecy - Geneva 158

Dep. Geneva (Eaux-Vives)	6:33	10:26	12:27
Arr. Annemasse	6:41	10:34	12:35
Change trains.			
Dep. Annemasse	7:14	10:43(1)	12:41
Arr. La Roche-sur-Foron	7:35	11:04(1)	13:00
Change trains.			
167			
Dep. La Roche-sur-Foron	8:48(2)	11:09(1)	13:30
Arr. Annecy	9:35	11:43	14:08

Sights in Annecy: This is a beautiful lake resort. See the 12th century Island Palace. The shops in the old quarter.

Dep. Annecy	12:23	14:56	18:09
Arr. La Roche-sur-Foron	13:01	15:28	18:55
Change trains.			
158			
Dep. La Roche-sur-Foron	13:23	15:35	20:00(3)
Arr. Annemasse	13:41	15:52	20:18
Change trains.			
Dep. Annemasse	14:04	16:30	20:23
Arr. Geneva (Eaux-Vives)	8 minutes later		

(1)Direct train. No train change in La Roche-sur-Foron. (2)Bus. (3)Runs from late June to early September.

Geneva - Basle - Geneva 266

Dep. Geneva (Corn.)	6:26(1)	8:03(2)	9:26(1)	11:03(2)
Arr. Basle (S.B.B.)	9:33	10:54	12:33	13:54

Sights in Basle: See notes about city-sightseeing in Basle at the start of this section.

Dep. Basle (S.B.B.)	14:18	15:18(1)	16:18	17:18(1+3)
Arr. Geneva (Corn.)	17:28	18:28	19:28	20:28

(1) Light refreshments. (2) Meal service. (3) Plus other departures from Basle at 17:59(2), 19:15 and 20:18.

Geneva - Bern - Geneva 256

All of these trains have meal service or light refreshments.

Dep. Geneva (Corn.)	6:57	7:57	8:57	9:57	10:57	11:57	12:57
Arr. Bern	8:38	9:38	10:38	11:38	12:38	13:38	14:38

Sights in Bern: See notes about city-sightseeing in Bern at the start of this section.

Dep. Bern	12:16	13:16	14:16	15:16	16:16	17:16	18:16(1)
Arr. Geneva (Corn.)	13:57	14:57	15:57	16:57	17:57	18:57	19:57

(1) Plus other departures from Bern at 19:16, 20:16, 21:16 and 22:16.

Geneva - Dijon - Geneva 152

Both of these trains have meal service.

Dep. Geneva (Corn.)	7:27	Dep. Dijon	19:33
Arr. Dijon	10:52	Arr. Geneva (Corn.)	22:52

Sights in Dijon: Town Hall, formerly the palace of those swashbuckling dukes of Burgundy and now one of the richest museums in France. The Church of Notre Dame. The 13th century Cathedral of St. Benigne archaeological museum. The Palace of Justice. The Magnin Museum. The 14th century Chartreuse de Champmol, with its famous chapel portrait and Moses Fountain. Rude Museum. Don't fail to have lunch in Dijon, France's food and wine capital.

Geneva - Grenoble - Geneva 165

Dep. Geneva (Corn.)	8:12(1)	9:26	10:30(2)	11:27(3)
Arr. Grenoble	10:28	11:22	12:27	13:34

Sights in Grenoble: See very lengthy notes about sightseeing in Grenoble in the "France" section, under "Lyon-Grenoble".

Dep. Grenoble	15:13	17:39(3)	19:04(1)	20:59(4)
Arr. Geneva (Corn.)	17:12	19:44	21:27	23:27

(1) Runs from late June to mid-September. (2) Runs from late May to late September. Light refreshments. (3) Supplement charged. Meal service. (4) Change trains in Bellegarde.

Geneva - Lausanne - Geneva 256

Dep. Geneva (Corn.) Frequent times from 6:20 to 23:42
Arr. Lausanne 40 minutes later

Sights in Lausanne: See notes about sightseeing in Lausanne earlier in this section, under "Bern-Lausanne".

Dep. Lausanne Frequent times from 7:49 to 23:30
Arr. Geneva (Corn.) 40 minutes later

Geneva - Lyon - Geneva 155

Occasionally, 2 trains depart from the same track at Lyon's Perrache railstation, heading in opposite directions. Be sure to stand at the correct end (North or South) of the track in order to board the train you want to ride. Check the departure signs at the underground passageway. Do not rely merely on a track number when departing from Perrache railstation !

Next to the North passageway of Track "A" is a take-out restaurant, handy for provisioning your trip.

A metropolitan train connects Lyon's Brotteaux and Perrache railstations. The ride is 15 minutes.

Dep. Geneva (Corn.)	6:30	10:38	12:28
Arr. Lyon (Brot.)	8:40	12:49	14:31
Arr. Lyon (Per.)	10 minutes later		

Sights in Lyon: See very lengthy notes about sightseeing in Lyon at the start of the "France" section.

Dep. Lyon (Per.)	14:13	16:09	18:19
Dep. Lyon (Brot.)	10 minutes later		
Arr. Geneva (Corn.)	16:05	18:08	20:31

Geneva - Montreux - Geneva 251

Dep. Geneva (Corn.) 8:03(1) 8:46 9:46(1) 10:46(1) 11:46(2)
Arr. Montreux 70 minutes later
Arr. Montreux 70 minutes later

Sights in Montreux: Chillon Castle, about 1½ miles from Montreux, immortalized by Byron. Its dungeon, used as a model for many movies, is the attraction. Board the bus to Chillon across from the Montreux railstation.

Dep. Montreux 11:06 11:43(1) 13:06 13:43(1) 14:06(1+3)
Arr. Geneva (Corn.) 70 minutes later

(1)Light refreshments. (2)Plus other departures from Geneva at 11:57, 12:57, 13:46(1) and 14:46(1). (3)Plus other departures from Montreux at frequent times from 14:43 to 23:06.

Geneva - Neuchatel - Geneva 266

Dep. Geneva (Corn.)	7:26(1+2)	8:03(3)	8:26(1)	9:26(1+2+4)
Arr. Neuchatel	1½ hours later			

Sights in Neuchatel: See notes about city-sightseeing in Neuchatel earlier in this section, under "Bern-Neuchatel".

Dep. Neuchatel	10:54(1)	11:54(1+2)	12:24(3)	12:54(1+5)
Arr. Geneva (Corn.)	1½ hours later			

(1) Light refreshments. (2) Change trains in Lausanne. (3) Meal service. (4) Plus other departures from Geneva at 10:26(2), 11:03(2), 11:26-(1+2), 12:26(1) and 13:26(1+2). (5) Plus other departures from Neuchatel at frequent times from 13:54 to 21:54.

Geneva - Zurich - Geneva

All of these trains have meal service, unless otherwise designated.
256

Dep. Geneva (Corn.)	5:47	6:57	7:57	8:57(1)	9:57
Arr. Zurich (Hbf.)	8:54	9:54	10:54	11:54	12:54

Sights in Zurich: See notes about sightseeing in Zurich at the start of this section.

Dep. Zurich (Hbf.)	13:00	14:00(2)	15:00	15:50	17:00(3)
Arr. Geneva (Corn.)	15:57	16:57	17:57	18:57	19:57

(1) Light refreshments. (2) Neither meal service nor light refreshments. (3) Plus other departures from Zurich at 18:00, 19:00, 20:00 and 21:00.

Interlaken - Bern - Interlaken 260

All of these trains have light refreshments.

Dep. Interlaken (Ost)	7:34	8:24	9:34	10:24	11:34
Dep. Interlaken (West)	5 minutes later				
Arr. Bern	8:27	9:27	10:27	11:27	12:27

Sights in Bern: See notes about sightseeing in Bern at the start of this section.

Dep. Bern	12:27	13:27	14:27	15:27	16:27(1)
Arr. Interlaken (West)	13:27	14:27	15:15	16:27	17:15
Arr. Interlaken (Ost)	5 minutes later				

(1) Plus other departures from Bern at frequent times from 17:27 to 23:27.

Interlaken - Lausanne - Interlaken 260

Dep. Interlaken (Ost)	6:34	7:34	8:24	9:34	10:24
Dep. Interlaken (West)	5 minutes later				
Arr. Bern	7:34	8:27	9:27	10:27	11:27
Change trains. 256					
Dep. Bern	8:16(1)	9:16	10:16(1)	11:16(1)	12:16(1)
Arr. Lausanne	9:22	10:22	11:22	12:22	13:22
	*	*	*		
Dep. Lausanne	11:32(1)	12:32(1)	13:32(1)	14:32(1)	15:32(1+2)
Arr. Bern	12:38	13:38	14:38	15:38	16:38
Change trains. 260					
Dep. Bern	13:27	14:27	15:27	16:27	17:27(3)
Arr. Interlaken (West)	14:27	15:15	16:27	17:15	18:15
Arr. Interlaken (Ost)	5 minutes later				

(1) Meal service. (2) Plus other departures from Lausanne at 16:32(1), 17:32(1), 18:32(1), 19:32(1) and 20:32(1). (3) Plus other departures from Bern at 18:27, 19:27, 20:27, 21:21 and 22:21.

Interlaken - Murren - Jungfraujoch - Interlaken

This one-day trip covers the heart of the Bernese Oberland area. (It is not covered by Eurailpass or Eurail Youthpass.) There have been top ski resorts in this area since 1906. Jungfraujoch is the hightest (11,333 feet) railstation in Europe. From there, you can see the Jungfrau, Eiger and Monch peaks. It is great to see the fabulous views from the revolving restaurant, which rotates every 50 minutes. The highest waterfall in Europe (2,000-foot drop) is spectacular in late Spring and early Summer.

287

Dep. Interlaken (Ost)	9:40
Arr. Lauterbrunnen	10:50
Change to funicular.	
Dep. Lauterbrunnen	10:15
Arr. Murren	10:43
Change funiculars.	
Dep. Murren	11:13(1)
Arr. Lauterbrunnen	11:41
Change to train.	
Dep. Lauterbrunnen	12:10
Arr. Scheidegg	12:54
Change trains.	

288

Dep. Scheidegg	13:05
Arr. Jungfraujoch	13:56
Change trains.	
Dep. Jungfraujoch	14:05(1)
Arr. Scheidegg	14:50
Change trains. 287	
Dep. Scheidegg	14:57
Arr. Interlaken (Ost)	16:23

(1) There are other departures at frequent times.

Interlaken - Luzern - Interlaken 264

Dep. Interlaken (Ost)	6:37	7:38	8:37	9:39(1)	10:37
Arr. Luzern	8:56	9:37	10:56	11:37	12:56

Sights in Luzern: See notes about city-sightseeing in Luzern at the start of this section.

Dep. Luzern	11:17	11:57	13:17(1)	13:57	15:17(2)
Arr. Interlaken (Ost)	13:17	15:19	15:17	16:19	17:17

(1)Light refreshments. (2)Plus other departures from Luzern at 15:57, 17:17, 17:57, 18:57 and19:59.

Lausanne - Sion - Lausanne 251

Dep. Lausanne	7:50	8:22(1)	Dep. Sion	10:53	11:38(2)
Arr. Sion	8:59	9:14	Arr. Lausanne	12:04	12:32

(1)Plus other departures from Lausanne at frequent times from 8:50 to 14:28. (2)Plus other departures from Sion at frequent times from 12:16 to 22:21.

Sights in Sion: Ruins of a 13th century castle. The 11th century church-fortress. The astronomical clock and carved doors of the 12th century Town Hall. The Cantonal Museum of Fine Arts in The Majorie, once an ecclesiastical palace. Nearby, Roman relics from this area, in the Archaeological Museum. The ancient Tour de Sorciers (Tower of the Wizards). The 9th century Romanesque tower of the Cathedral.

Luzern - Andermatt - Luzern 277

The Goschenen-Andermatt-Goschenen portion of this one-day excursion is by rack railway and is not covered by Eurailpass.

Dep. Luzern	8:04(1)	9:04	10:04(2)	12:04(2)	14:04
Arr. Goschenen	9:42	10:37	11:47	13:47	15:47

Change trains.
295

Dep. Goschenen	9:55	11:08	11:53	13:55	15:55
Arr. Andermatt	10:10	11:23	12:08	14:10	16:10

Sights in Andermatt: A great ski resort.

Dep. Andermatt	12:40	13:30	14:40	16:18	16:37(3)
Arr. Goschenen	12:55	13:45	14:55	16:33	16:52

Change trains.
277

Dep. Goschenen	13:04(2)	14:44	15:05	16:40	17:01
Arr. Luzern	14:29	16:21	16:29	18:21	18:29

(1)Light refreshments. (2)Change trains in Arth Goldau. (3)Plus other departures from Andermatt at 18:40, 19:25, 19:47 and 21:12.

Luzern - Basle - Luzern 277

Dep. Luzern	6:37	7:37	8:37	9:44(1+3)
Arr. Basle (S.B.B.)	7:54	8:54	9:54	10:53

Sights in Basle: See notes about city-sightseeing in Basle at the start of this section.

Dep. Basle (S.B.B.)	11:00(2)	12:01(2)	13:00(1)	14:01(1+4)
Arr. Luzern	12:16	13:10	14:16	15:10

(1)Light refreshments. (2)Meal service. (3)Plus other departures from Luzern at 10:57(2), 12:37(1) and 13:44(2). (4)Plus other departures from Basle at frequent times from 15:00 to 22:31.

Luzern - Bern - Luzern 262

Dep. Luzern	6:51(1)	7:51(1)	9:51(1)	11:51(1)	13:51(1)
Arr. Bern	8:09	9:09	11:09	13:09	15:09

Sights in Bern: See notes about city-sightseeing in Bern at the start of this section.

Dep. Bern	9:44(1)	10:00	11:44(1)	13:44(1)	15:44(1+2)
Arr. Luzern	11:01	11:49	13:01	15:01	17:01

(1)Light refreshments. (2)Plus other departures from Bern at 16:44(1), 17:44(1), 19:44 and 21:44.

Luzern - Interlaken - Luzern 264

Dep. Luzern	6:06	7:17	8:00(1)	9:17(1)	9:57(2)
Arr. Interlaken (Ost)	8:19	9:17	10:00	11:17	12:19

Sights in Interlaken: See notes about city-sightseeing in Interlaken at the start of this section.

Dep. Interlaken (Ost)	8:37	9:39(1)	10:37	11:39(1)	12:37(3)
Arr. Luzern	10:56	11:37	12:56	13:37	14:56

(1)Light refreshments. (2)Plus other departures from Luzern at 11:17, 11:57, 13:17(1) and 13:57. (3)Plus other departures from Interlaken at frequent times from 13:39 to 20:37.

Luzern - Zurich - Luzern 254

Most of these trains have light refreshments.

Dep. Luzern	Frequent times from 7:09 to 22:19
Arr. Zurich	50 minutes later

Sights in Zurich: See notes about city-sightseeing in Zurich at the start of this section.

Dep. Zurich	Frequent times from 6:25 to 23:17
Arr. Luzern	50 minutes later

Luzern - Schwyz - Luzern

277

Dep. Luzern	8:31	9:31				
Arr. Schwyz	40 minutes later					

Sights in Schwyz: The Staatsarkivmuseum (National Archive Museum), to see the 13th century Oath of Eternal Alliance, the document which marks the founding of Switzerland. This village's name became the name of the country (Schweiz). The Museum is one mile (uphill) from the railstation. A bus meets every train.

Dep. Schwyz	10:40	11:40	13:37	15:40	16:40	17:36(1)
Arr. Luzern	40 minutes later					

(1)Plus other departures from Schwyz at 17:36, 18:40, 19:40, 20:40, 21:30 and 22:29.

Zurich - Andermatt - Zurich

The Goschenen-Andermatt-Goschenen portion of this one-day excursion is by rack railway and is not covered by Eurailpass.

277

Dep. Zurich (Hbf.)	6:27(1)	8:04(1)	9:04(2)	10:04(3)
Arr. Goschenen	8:05	9:41	10:36	11:46

Change trains.

295

Dep.Goschenen	8:24	9:55	10:48	11:53
Arr. Andermatt	15 minutes later			

Sights in Andermatt: A great ski resort.

Dep. Andermatt	10:48	12:45	13:55	16:42(4)
Arr. Goschenen	11:03	13:00	14:10	16:57

Change trains.

277

Dep. Goschenen	11:04(3)	13:04	15:05(1+3)	17:10(1)
Arr. Zurich (Hbf.)	12:50	14:50	16:50	18:50

(1)Light refreshments. (2)Meal service. (3)Change trains in Arth Goldau.

Zurich - Arosa - Zurich

268

Dep. Zurich (Hbf.)	6:24(1)	7:07(1)	8:07(2)	9:07(1)	10:07(1)
Arr. Chur	7:55	8:38	9:30	10:38	11:30

Change trains.

303

The Chur-Arosa-Chur trips are not covered by Eurailpass or Eurail Youthpass. The cogwheel train to Arosa leaves from the front of the Chur railstation. It is a very scenic ride.

Dep. Chur	8:02	8:50	9:38	10:50	11:40
Arr. Arosa	9:03	9:51	10:39	11:51	12:41

Sights in Arosa: Great Summer and Winter sports. Fantastic mountain scenery.

Dep. Arosa	10:00	11:00	12:03	13:00	16:03(3)
Arr. Chur	11:01	12:01	13:04	14:01	16:04

Change trains.

268

Dep. Chur	11:16(2)	12:24(1)	13:16(1)	14:24(2)	16:24(1)
Arr. Zurich (Hbf.)	12:47	13:47	14:47	15:47	17:47

(1) Light refreshments. (2) Meal service. (3) Plus other departures from Arosa at 17:15, 18:06 and 19:05 that connect with Chur-Zurich service.

Zurich - Basle - Zurich

268

Most of these trains have light refreshments or meal service.

Dep. Zurich (Hbf.) Frequent times from 6:43 to 23:09
Arr. Basle (S.B.B.) 60-70 minutes later

Sights in Basle: See notes about sightseeing in Basle at the start of this section.

Dep. Basle (S.B.B.) Frequent times from 6:09 to 22:25
Arr. Zurich (Hbf.) 60-70 minutes later

Zurich - Bern - Zurich 256

Most of these trains have meal service.

Dep. Zurich Frequent times from 7:00 to 23:00
Arr. Bern 1½ hours later

Sights in Bern: See notes about city-sightseeing in Bern at the start of this section.

Dep. Bern Frequent times from 4:50 to 22:41
Arr. Zurich 1½ hours later

Zurich - Chur - Zurich 268

Most of these trains have light refreshments or meal service.

Dep. Zurich (Hbf.)	Frequent times from 6:24 to 22:07
Arr. Chur	1½ hours later

Sights in Chur: This 2100-year old village is located at what has been a strategic pass in the Alps since Roman times. Walk from the station up through the small business area to a hilltop church and see the unusual cemetery there. The modern portion of it has rows of graves that are solidly decorated with living, blossoming plants. Also see the fine stained-glass and the 12th century altar in the 15th century St. Martin's Church. The Bishop's Palace. A one-hour walking tour of Chur is made easy by following red and green footprints painted on the sidewalks. The footprints are matched to a map available at the city's tourist office.

Dep. Chur	Frequent times from 6:08 to 20:58
Arr. Zurich (Hbf.)	1½ hours later

Zurich - Davos - Zurich 268

Dep. Zurich (Hbf.)	7:20(1)	8:07(2)	9:07(1)	10:07(1+3+4)
Arr. Landquart	8:33	9:19	10:27	11:19

Change trains.

301

The Landquart-Davos-Landquart trips are not covered by Eurailpass or Eurail Youthpass.

Dep. Landquart	8:40	9:30	10:35	11:30(3)
Arr. Davos (Platz)	9:48	10:42	11:45	12:41

Sights in Davos: One of the world's most popular ski resorts. Also popular for its skating rinks, hiking trails, a sled run, horse-drawn sleigh rides, indoor swimming, hang-gliding, horseback riding and ice hockey.

Take the 22-minute ride on the Parsenn cable railway, once described by Vogue Magazine as "the Rolls Royce of mountain railways", to the ridge of Weissfluh. A cable car ascends from there to the summit, the start of the different ski runs to Serneus, Sass and Klosters.

Davos has 35 mountain railways and ski lifts with a capacity for transporting 32,000 people every hour. A general-fare ticket, costing about $80 (U.S.) allows unlimited use of the entire network of funicular railways, ski lifts and cable cars for 6 days. There is also bus service every 15 minutes from one end of Davos to the other.

Dep. Davos (Platz)	12:11	12:56(3)	14:10	15:13(3+5)
Arr. Landquart	13:20	14:20	15:20	16:27

Change trains.

268

Dep. Landquart	13:27(1)	14:35(2)	15:27(1)	16:35(1)
Arr. Zurich (Hbf.)	14:47	15:47	16:47	17:47

(Timetable notes appear on next page.)

(1)Light refreshments. (2)Meal service. (3)Runs from mid-June to late September. (4)Plus other departures from Zurich at 11:07(1) and 13:07(1). (5)Plus other departures from Davos at 16:10(1), 17:05-(2+3), 18:13(1) and 19:14(1) that connect with Landquart-Zurich service.

Zurich - Frankfurt - Zurich

73

Both of these trains charge a supplement and have meal service.

Dep. Zurich (Hbf.)	6:57	Dep. Frankfurt (Hbf.)	17:37
Arr. Frankfurt (Hbf.)	11:17	Arr. Zurich (Hbf.)	21:57

Sights in Frankfurt: Goethe's House. The Goethe Museum. The Zoo. The emperor's coronation hall in the Romer complex at medieval Romerberg square. The wonderful doors in the 13th century Leonhardskirche. The 13th century chapel of Saalhof in the remains of the palace of Frederick Barbarossa. Cloth Hall. The Botanical Garden. The pews and murals in the Cathedral of St. Bartholomew. The Church of St. Nicholas. The Church of St. Paul. Senckenberg Natural History Society's Museum. Stadel Museum and Liebighaus (sculpture). The Museum of Plastic Art. Sachsenhausen, the old quarter of the city, across the Main River from the commercial district. The major shopping streets: Zeil and Kaiserstrasse.

Zurich - Geneva - Zurich

256

Most of these trains have meal service.

Dep. Zurich (Hbf.)	Frequent times from 7:00 to 21:00
Arr. Geneva (Corn.)	3 hours later

Sights in Geneva: See notes about sightseeing in Geneva at the start of this section.

Dep. Geneva (Corn.)	Frequent times from 5:47 to 20:57
Arr. Zurich (Hbf.)	3 hours later

Zurich - Lugano - Zurich 277

Dep. Zurich (Hbf.)	6:27(1)	7:04(2)	8:04(1)	8:39(3)	9:04(2+4)
Arr. Lugano	9:46	10:03	11:17	11:35	12:10

Sights in Lugano: See lengthy notes about sightseeing in Lugano in "Italy" section under "Milan-Lugano".

Dep. Lugano	10:43(2)	11:26	12:43(2)	14:43(1)	15:32(1+5)
Arr. Zurich (Hbf.)	13:50	14:50	15:50	17:50	18:50

(1) Light refreshments. (2) Meal service. (3) TEE. Reservation required. Meal service. (4) Plus another departure from Zurich at 11:04(2). (5) Plus other departures from Lugano at 16:43(2), 17:55(3), 18:36(2) and 20:05(2).

Zurich - Luzern - Zurich 254

Most of these trains have light refreshments.

Dep. Zurich (Hbf.)	Frequent times from 6:12 to 23:10
Arr. Luzern	50 minutes later

Sights in Luzern: See notes about city-sightseeing in Luzern at the start of this section.

Dep. Luzern	Frequent times from 6:23 to 22:07
Arr. Zurich (Hbf.)	50 minutes later

Zurich - Milan - Zurich 277

Dep. Zurich (Hbf.)	7:00(1)	8:47(2)
Arr. Milan (Cent.)	11:20	12:40

Sights in Milan: The Duomo Cathedral, holding more than 20,000 people, begun in 1386 and taking 5 centuries to complete. There are more than 3,000 statues on its exterior. Then, through the beautiful shopping arcade to La Scala, one of the world's greatest theaters, constructed in 1776-78. During the day, you can visit its opera museum and, if your timing is right, see a moment of a rehearsal. You will also want to see Da Vinci's "Last Supper" at Santa Maria della Grazie. Do not miss the enormous crypts at the Monumental Cemetery.

Dep. Milan (Cent.)	17:00(2)	18:40(1)
Arr. Zurich (Hbf.)	21:03	23:10

(1) Meal service. (2) TEE. Reservation required. Meal service.

Zurich - Munich - Zurich 256

Dep. Zurich (Hbf.)	7:04(1)	Dep. Munich (Hbf.)	16:03(2)	17:35
Arr. Munich (Hbf.)	12:06	Arr. Zurich (Hbf.)	20:37	22:50

(1) Light refreshments. (2) Meal service.

Sights in Munich: The works of Durer, El Greco, Raphael, Holbein, Rembrandt and many other great painters at Alte Pinakothek. Frauenkirche Cathedral, and the view from its north tower . . . and then later get a view of Frauenkirche from the top of the Neues Rathaus (City Hall). The paintings of Cezanne, Gauguin, Renoir and other impressionists at the Haus der Kunst. Wittelsbach Fountain. The fine exhibits and planetarium at Deutsches Museum, considered the best scientific museum in the world. The view of the Alps from the top of Peterskirche. The best collection of tapestries and wood carvings in Germany, at the Bavarian National Museum. Munich's most famous beer palace, Hofbrauhaus. The Schatzkammer in the Residenz palace, and the flower gardens in the park north of it. The decorations in Asamkirche. Schack Gallery. Theatinerkirche. At Schloss (Castle) Nymphenburg: the porcelain in the showrooms of Nymphenburger Porzellan Manufaktur and in the Residenzmuseum, the enormous Festsaal, and the park outside the castle.

Zurich - Rheinfelden - Zurich 268

Dep. Zurich (Hbf.)	6:43(1)	7:09	8:09(1)	10:09	12:09(3)
Arr. Rheinfelden	55 minutes later				

Sights in Rheinfelden: Tours of the Cardinal and Feldschlosschen breweries. The island park on the Rhine River.

Dep. Rheinfelden	10:45	12:45(1)	14:45	16:45	18:45(4)
Arr. Zurich (Hbf.)	55 minutes later				

(1) Light refreshments. (2) Daily, except Sundays and holidays. (3) Plus another departure from Zurich at 14:09. (4) Plus other departures from Rheinfelden at 20:45, 22:37 and 23:48(2).

Zurich - St. Moritz - Zurich

268			269		
Dep. Zurich (Hbf.)	7:20(1)	8:07(2)	Dep. Chur	8:50(1)	9:38(3)
Arr. Chur	8:44	9:30	Arr. St. Moritz	10:52	11:41
Change trains.					

Sights in St. Moritz: The lovely scenery of the Alps, reflected on the Lake of St. Moritz. The curative waters. Great Summer (swimming, sailing, fishing, golf, mountain climbing) as well as Winter sports. The creme de la creme of the international jet set December to April.

See the collection of porcelain stoves, furniture and carved woodwork in the Engadine Museum, open Monday-Saturday 9:30-12:00 and

14:00-17:00, also on Sunday 10:00-12:00. Many paintings of this beautiful area by Giovanni Segantini in the Segantini Museum, open Monday-Saturday 9:30-12:00 and 14:00-16:00, on Sunday 14:30-16:00. Also visit the marvelous Engadin Museum.

269

Dep. St. Moritz	10:55	12:08(2+3)	12:55(1)
Arr. Chur	13:02	14:13	15:02

Change trains.

268

Dep. Chur	13:16(1)	14:24	15:16
Arr. Zurich (Hbf.)	14:47	15:47	16:47

(1) Light refreshments. (2) Meal service. (3) Runs from mid-June to late September.

Zurich - Schwyz - Zurich 277

Change trains in Arth Goldau.

Dep. Zurich	8:04	9:04	Dep. Schwyz	11:40	13:37(1)
Arr. Schwyz	9:11	10:11	Arr. Zurich	12:50	14:50

(1) Plus other departures from Schwyz at frequent times from 15:40 to 21:30.

Sights in Schwyz: See notes about city-sightseeing in Schwyz earlier in this section, under "Luzern-Schwyz".

Zurich - Solothurn - Zurich 266

All of these trains have light refreshments.

Dep. Zurich	Frequent times from 6:04 to 21:04
Arr. Solothurn	60 minutes later

Sights in Solothurn: Switzerland's oldest town. (It and Trier, in Germany, are the 2 oldest towns north of the Alps.) See the outstanding ancient art here. Holbein's Madonna in the Museum. The marvelous Assumption over the high altar in the Jesuit church. The bulb domes on the twin towers of the Town Hall. The comprehensive collection of arms and armor in the old Arsenal. The Italian belltower of the Cathedral. The town's many fine statues and fountains.

Dep. Solothurn	Frequent times from 6:47 to 21:47
Arr. Zurich	60 minutes later

Zurich - Stuttgart - Zurich 668

Dep. Zurich	6:31	8:10(1)	10:10
Arr. Stuttgart	10:04	11:24	13:47

* * *

Dep. Stuttgart	12:31(1)	15:18(1)	17:13(1)	20:18(2)
Arr. Zurich	15:44	18:44	20:44	23:44

(1) Light refreshments. (2) Reservation required.

Sights in Stuttgart: Outstanding contemporary architecture, built since World War II. Liederhalle, with its 3 concert halls. The Schillerplatz flower and vegetable market (Tuesday, Thursday and Saturday).

Zurich - Winterthur - Zurich 266

Dep. Zurich	Frequent times from 7:07 to 21:07
Arr. Winterthur	22 minutes later

Sights in Winterthur: More art treasures than any other place in Switzerland, at the country's National Gallery in the Am Roemerholz mansion. Great Austrian, German and Swiss paintings.

Dep. Winterthur	Frequent times from 6:31 to 22:17
Arr. Zurich	22 minutes later

Zurich - Zug - Zurich

254 + 277

Dep. Zurich	Frequent times from 6:12 to 0:01
Arr. Zug	26 minutes later

Sights in Zug: This village is located on the northeast shore of the 14-mile long Lake Zug. See the spires and massive towers of the 15th century Church of St. Oswald. The stained-glass for which this area is noted and also gold and silver work, embroidery and wood carvings in the Museum at the 16th century Town Hall.

The view from the peak of the Zugerberg, 4000 feet above the town. From there, one can see the peaks of Rigi, Pilatus, Jungfrau, Eiger, Moench and Finsteraarhorn.

Try the local specialties: rotel, a tasty salmon-like fish from the lake, the local cherries that are used for producing the liqueur kirsch, and the local cake, kirsch-torte, laced with the cherry liqueur.

Dep. Zug	Frequent times from 5:51 to 22:35
Arr. Zurich	26 minutes later

SCENIC RAIL TRIPS

Basle - Schaffhausen - Basle

An easy one-day roundtrip, to see the marvelous Rhine Falls.

674

Dep. Basle (Bad Bf.)	7:06	8:36	12:10	14:01	17:10
Arr. Schaffhausen	8:28	9:52	13:29	15:27	18:25
	*	*	*		
Dep. Schaffhausen	10:13	12:57	14:56	16:46	19:02
Arr. Basle (Bad Bf.)	11:26	14:06	16:06	18:06	20:20

Bern - Brig - Bern

An easy one-day roundtrip that affords a view of Rhone Valley and Lonza Valley farms, gorges, lakes and mountains plus the Lake Thun scenery at Spiez about which we enthuse in the "Geneva-Spiez" trip described later in this section . . . and going through the 9-mile Lotschberg Tunnel and over the Bietschtal Bridge. This structure takes the train 255 feet above the ravine it crosses. We recommend a stop in Spiez and a stroll there on either the outbound or homebound leg of the trip.

260

Most of these trains have light refreshments.

Dep. Bern	6:21	7:21	8:13	8:21	9:21(1)
Arr. Spiez	6:52	7:52	8:43	8:52	9:52
Dep. Spiez	6:54	7:54	8:45	8:54	9:54
Arr. Brig	8:00	9:00	9:43	10:00	11:00

Sights in Brig: Switzerland's largest private residence, the 17th century Stockalper Castle, built by a very successful businessman.

Dep. Brig	8:54	9:54	10:54	11:12	11:54(2)
Arr. Spiez	10:01	11:01	12:01	12:10	13:01
Dep. Spiez	10:03	11:03	12:03	12:12	13:03
Arr. Bern	31 minutes later				

(1) Plus other departures from Bern at frequent times from 10:21 to 20:21. (2) Plus other departures from Brig at frequent times from 12:54 to 21:54.

Bern - Brig - Domodossola - Bern

To see all of the scenery and Lotschberg Tunnel noted above under "Bern-Brig" plus having the experience of going through the 12-mile Simplon, longest main line rail tunnel in the world, make the Bern-Domodossola portion of the Bern-Milan trip. The Simplon is actually 2 tunnels, one southbound and a 65-foot longer bore for the separate northbound tunnel.

260

Dep. Bern	6:21	7:21	8:13	9:21(1)	11:21(1)
Arr. Domodossola	8:49	9:49	10:27	11:49	13:49
	*	*	*		
Dep. Domodossola	9:05(1)	-0-	10:32(1)	12:05(1)	15:05(1)
Arr. Bern	11:34	-0-	12:43	14:34	17:34

(1) Light refreshments.

Bern - Interlaken - Brienz - Interlaken - Bern

Fine gorge, lake and mountain scenery on this easy one-day roundtrip.

260					
Dep. Bern	7:27	8:27	9:27	10:27	11:27(1)
Arr. Interlaken (Ost)	8:20	9:32	10:20	11:32	12:20
Change trains.					
264					
Dep. Interlaken (Ost)	8:37	9:39	10:37	11:39	12:37
Arr. Brienz	8:58	9:55	10:59	11:55	12:58
	*	*	*		
Dep. Brienz	8:59	9:56	10:59	11:56	12:59
Arr. Interlaken (Ost)	9:17	10:19	11:17	12:19	13:17
Change trains.					
260					
Dep. Interlaken (Ost)	9:34	10:24	11:34	12:24	13:24
Arr. Bern	10:27	11:27	12:27	13:27	14:27

(1)Plus other departures from Bern (that allow the same roundtrip) at 12:27, 13:27, 14:27, 15:27, 16:27 and 17:27.

Bern - Interlaken - Jungfraujoch - Wengen - Interlaken - Bern

Very good gorge, lake and mountain scenery on this easy one-day roundtrip. Jungfraujoch is the highest (11,333 feet) railstation in Europe. The Interlaken-Jungfraujoch-Interlaken portion of this trip is not covered by Eurailpass or Eurail Youthpass.

We suggest, for variety, you go from Interlaken to Jungfraujoch via Wengen and then return to Interlaken via Grindelwald.

260		
Dep. Bern	7:27	8:27
Arr. Interlaken (Ost)	8:20	9:32
Change trains. Go to Jungfraujoch via Wengen.		
287		
Dep. Interlaken (Ost)	8:40	9:40
Arr. Scheidegg	10:02	11:02
Change trains.		
288		
Dep. Scheidegg	10:07	11:07
Arr. Jungfraujoch	10:58	11:58

288		
Dep. Jungfraujoch	12:05	13:05
Arr. Scheidegg	12:52	13:50
Change trains. Go to Interlaken via Grindelwald.		
287		
Dep. Scheidegg	12:57	13:57
Arr. Interlaken (Ost)	14:23	15:36
Change trains.		
260		
Dep. Interlaken (Ost)	14:34	16:34
Arr. Bern	15:27	17:27

Bern - Lausanne - Brig - Spiez - Bern

Excellent gorge, lake and mountain scenery on this easy one-day circle trip. This is a portion of the "Geneva-Spiez-Geneva" trip listed later in this section. There is time for a stopover in Lausanne and/or Spiez. You go through the 9-mile Lotschberg Tunnel after leaving Brig.

256

Dep. Bern	6:34(1)	7:34	8:16(2)	9:16(3)
Arr. Lausanne	7:45	8:45	9:22	10:22

Change trains.

251

Dep. Lausanne	7:50	8:50(1)	9:28(2)	10:28(1)
Arr. Brig	9:40	10:47	11:08	12:17

Change trains.

260

Dep. Brig	9:54(1)	10:54(2)	11:12(1)	12:54(1)
Arr. Spiez	11:01	12:01	12:10	14:01
Dep. Spiez	11:03	12:03	12:12	14:03
Arr. Bern	11:34	12:34	12:43	14:34

(1) Light refreshments. (2) Meal service. (3) The same circle trip can be made leaving Bern at frequent times from 9:34 to 14:16.

Bern - Locarno - Bern

Complete notes on the Domodossola-Locarno portion of this easy one-day roundtrip appear later in this section, under "Brig-Domodossola-Locarno".

260

Dep. Bern	7:21	9:21
Arr. Domodossola	9:49	11.49

Change trains. Walk outside the Domodossola station and go to the underground Centovalli track.

252

Dep. Domodossola	10:05	12:05
Arr. Locarno	11:50	13:48

252

Dep. Locarno	15:00	17:20(1)
Arr. Domodossola	15:43	19:00

Change trains. Walk from the underground Centovalli track, up to the main Domodossola station.

260

Dep. Domodossola	17:05	19:15
Arr. Bern	19:34	21:34

(1) Plus another departure from Locarno at 18:40, arriving Bern at 23:34.

Sights in Locarno: Stroll the gardens along the shore of Lake Maggiore and take the funicular ride to the church high above the village for a fine view of Locarno and Lake Maggiore.

Bern - Mt. Pilatus - Bern

Very nice gorge, lake and mountain scenery on this easy one-day roundtrip that can include a stopover in Luzern.

The Pilatus Rack Railway trip (Alpnachstad-Pilatus-Alpnachstad) operates only April 1 to October 31. It is not covered by Eurailpass. Costs about 34 Swiss Francs for the roundtrip. There are good views and several restaurants at the peak of Pilatus.

262

Dep. Bern	6:44(1)	7:44(1)	10:00	11:44(1)
Arr. Luzern	8:01	9:01	11:49	13:01

Change trains.

264

Dep. Luzern	8:09	9:57	11:57	13:57
Arr. Alpnachstad	8:26	10:13	12:13	14:13

Change to rack railway for the ride to the top of Mt. Pilatus.

290

Dep. Alpnachstad	8:45	10:20	12:25	14:20
Arr. Pilatus Kulm	9:25	11:00	13:05	15:00

* * *

Dep. Pilatus Kulm	9:33	10:53	13:15	15:40
Arr. Alpnachstad	10:13	11:33	13:55	16:20

Change trains.

264

Dep. Alpnachstad	10:38	12:38	14:38	16:38
Arr. Luzern	10:56	12:56	14:56	16:56

Change trains.

262

Dep. Luzern	11:51(1)	13:51(1)	15:51(1)	17:51(2)
Arr. Bern	13:09	15:09	17:09	19:09

(1) Light refreshments. (2) Plus other departures from Luzern at 19:51(1), 20:51(1) and 22:03.

Bern - Spiez - Bern

Great gorge, lake and mountain scenery on this easy one-day roundtrip. This is a portion of the "Geneva-Spiez-Geneva" trip listed later in this section. Plenty of time to stroll in Spiez and enjoy the beauty of Lake Thun and the mountains above it.

260

Dep. Bern	Frequent times from 6:21 to 20:21
Arr. Spiez	30 minutes later

* * *

Dep. Spiez	Frequent times from 7:03 to 23:03
Arr. Bern	30 minutes later

Bern - Spiez - Brig - Lausanne - Bern

Marvelous gorge, lake, mountain and river scenery on this easy one-day circle trip. This is the reverse of the "Bern-Lausanne-Spiez-Bern" ride listed earlier in this section. A stroll in Spiez is a nice way to break the journey. You go through the 10-mile Lotschberg Tunnel after leaving Spiez.

260					
Dep. Bern	7:21	8:21(1)	9:21(1)	10:21(1)	11:21(1)
Arr. Spiez	7:52	8:52	9:52	10:52	11:52
Dep. Spiez	7:54	8:54	9:54	10:54	11:54
Arr. Brig	9:00	10:00	11:00	12:00	13:00
Change trains.					
251					
Dep. Brig	9:06(1)	10:06(1)	11:07(2)	12:06(1)	13:46
Arr. Lausanne	11:04	12:04	12:32	14:04	15:26
Change trains.					
256					
Dep. Lausanne	11:32(3)	12:09	13:32(3)	14:09(1)	15:32(3+4)
Arr. Bern	12:38	13:20	14:38	15:20	16:38

(1) Light refreshments. (2) Supplement charged. Light refreshments. A train without supplement departs Brig at 11:37. (3) Meal service. (4) Plus other departures from Lausanne at frequent times from 16:09 to 23:09.

Brig - Andermatt - Disentis - Brig

Fine gorge and mountain scenery on this easy one-day roundtrip. A stopover can be made (11:06-14:10) in Andermatt, a great ski resort. This trip is not covered by Eurailpass or Eurail Youthpass.

315					
Dep. Brig	8:15(1)	9:20(1)	10:44(1+2)	11:44(3)	11:58(2)
Arr. Andermatt	10:11(1)	11:08(1)	12:34(1)	13:27(3)	14:10(2)
Arr. Disentis	11:25	12:32	13:50	14:40	15:28
		*	*	*	
Dep. Disentis	12:17(3)	13:09(1)	15:09(1+2)	16:29(1+2)	
Dep. Andermatt	13:28(3)	14:30(1)	15:35(1+2)	18:23(1+2)	
Arr. Brig	15:12	16:35	17:39	20:37	

(1) Light refreshments. (2) Change trains in Andermatt. (3) "Glacier Express". Meal service.

Brig - Arona - Brig

Beautiful lake and mountain scenery on this easy one-day roundtrip, which can also be seen as a portion of the Lausanne-Milan route. This ride takes you through Europe's longest (19.8km - 11.9 miles) tunnel, the Simplon. It is the second longest tunnel in the world, after Japan's Daishimizu Tunnel (22.3km - 13.4 miles) between Tokyo and Niigata.

251

Dep. Brig	8:18	9:17	9:55	11:17	13:17	14:41
Arr. Arona	9:54	10:56	11:29	13:15	14:54	16:13
		*	*	*		
Dep. Arona	10:54	12:00	13:44	15:55	17:41	18:11(1)
Arr. Brig	12:37	13:37	15:37	17:37	19:27	19:45

(1) Plus other departues from Arona at 20:02 and 22:54.

Here is the schedule for the Lausanne-Milan route.

251

Dep. Lausanne	6:30	8:22	9:28	11:28	12:52(1)
Dep. Brig	8:18	9:55	11:17	13:17	14:41
Arr. Arona	9:54	11:29	13:15	14:54	16:13
Arr. Milan (Centrale)	11:00	12:25	14:30	16:00	17:00

(1) Light refreshments until Brig. Plus another departure from Brig at 15:22 that allows daylight viewing.

Brig - Bern - Brig

An easy one-day roundtrip that affords a view of Rhone Valley and Lonza Valley farms, gorges, lakes and mountains plus the Lake Thun scenery at Spiez about which we enthuse in the "Geneva-Spiez" trip described later in this section . . . and going through the 10-mile Lotschberg Tunnel and over the Bietschtal Bridge. This structure takes the train 255 feet above the ravine it crosses. We recommend a stop in Spiez and a stroll there on either the outbound or homebound leg of this trip.

260

All of these trains have light refreshments.

Dep. Brig	6:46	7:49	8:54	9:54	10:54	11:12(1)
Arr. Spiez	8:01	9:01	10:01	11:01	12:01	12:10
Dep. Spiez	8:03	9:03	10:03	11:03	12:03	12:12
Arr. Bern	30 minutes later					

		*	*	*		
Dep. Bern	9:21	10:21	11:21	12:21	12:54	13:21(2)
Arr. Spiez	9:52	10:52	11:52	12:52	13:25	13:52
Dep. Spiez	9:54	10:54	11:54	12:54	13:27	13:54
Arr. Brig	66 minutes later					

(1) Plus other departures from Bern that allow daylight viewing at frequent times from 11:54 to 17:54. (2) Plus other departures from Bern at frequent times from 14:21 to 20:21.

Brig - Domodossola - Locarno - Domodossola - Brig

We call the Domodossola-Locarno portion of this one-day roundtrip one of the 5 most scenic rail trips in Europe. It is a spectacular narrow-gauge local train ride offering great gorge, mountain and river scenery on the Centovalli (one hundred valleys) route. Be sure to have your passport with you. On this trip, you go from Switzerland to Italy, then Switzerland, back to Italy, and then again to Switzerland. In Locarno, take the chairlift to Cimetta for a magnificent view of Lake Maggiore and the Alps.

This ride takes you through Europe's longest (19.8km - 11.9 miles) tunnel, the Simplon (between Brig and Domodossola). It is the second longest tunnel in the world, after Japan's Daishimizu Tunnel (22.3km - 13.4 miles) between Tokyo and Niigata.

The 90-minute, 35-mile Locarno-Domodossola trip does not start from the Locarno railstation. You catch what looks like a trolley car at the central Locarno bus stop, across from the train station. Stops en route include Camedo, Intragna with its many churches, Verdasio which has a train connection to the mountain town of Rasa, Palagnedra which has a lake, and Druogno, highest point on this scenic route.

260		
Dep. Brig	8:18	11:17
Arr. Domodossola	8:49	11:49

Change trains. Walk outside the Domodossola station and go to the underground Centovalli track.

252		
Dep. Domodossola	9:05	12:05
Arr. Locarno	10:50	13:48

252		
Dep. Locarno	13:00	16:20
Arr. Domodossola	14:43	18:25

Change trains. Walk from the underground Centovalli track, up to the main Domodossola station.

260		
Dep. Domodossola	15:05	18:55
Arr. Brig	15:37	19:27

Brig - Spiez - Interlaken - Brienz - Interlaken - Brig

Very good gorge, lake and mountain scenery on this easy one-day roundtrip.

260			264		
Dep. Brig	9:54	10:54	Dep. Brienz	12:59	14:59
Arr. Spiez	11:01	11:59	Arr. Interlaken (Ost)	13:17	15:17
Change trains.			Change trains.		
260			260		
Dep. Spiez	11:07	12:00	Dep. Interlaken (Ost)	13:24	15:24
Arr. Interlaken (Ost)	11:32	12:20	Arr. Spiez	13:53	15:53
Change trains.			Change trains.		
264			260		
Dep. Interlaken (Ost)	11:39	12:37	Dep. Spiez	13:54	15:54
Arr. Brienz	11:56	13:01	Arr. Brig	15:05	17:00

Brig - Interlaken - Jungfraujoch - Interlaken - Brig

Excellent gorge, lake and mountain scenery on this easy one-day roundtrip. Jungfraujoch is the highest (11,333 feet) railstation in Europe. The Interlaken-Jungfraujoch-Interlaken portion of this trip is not covered by Eurailpass or Eurail Youthpass.

We suggest, for variety, you go from Interlaken to Jungfraujoch via Wengen and then return to Interlaken via Grindelwald.

260			288		
Dep. Brig	7:49	8:54	Dep. Jungfraujoch	14:05	15:07
Arr. Spiez	9:00	9:59	Arr. Scheidegg	14:50	15:50
Change trains.			Change trains. Go to Interlaken via Grindelwald.		
260			287		
Dep. Spiez	9:07	10:00	Dep. Scheidegg	14:57	15:57
Arr. Interlaken (Ost)	9:32	10:20	Arr. Interlaken (Ost)	16:23	17:23
Change trains. Go to Jungfraujoch via Wengen.			Change trains.		
287			260		
Dep. Interlaken (Ost)	9:40	10:40	Dep. Interlaken (Ost)	16:34	17:24
Arr. Scheidegg	10:54	11:54	Arr. Spiez	16:53	17:53
Change trains.			Change trains.		
288			260		
Dep. Scheidegg	11:33	12:07	Dep. Spiez	16:54	17:54
Arr. Jungfraujoch	12:27	12:58	Arr. Brig	18:00	19:00

Brig - Lausanne - Brig 251

Nice gorge, lake, mountain and river scenery on this easy one-day roundtrip.

Dep. Brig Frequent times from 5:29 to 21:46
Arr. Lausanne 1½-2 hours later

* * *

Dep. Lausanne Frequent times from 6:30 to 20:46
Arr. Brig 1½-2 hours later

Brig - Zermatt - Gornergrat - Zermatt - Brig

Great gorge and mountain scenery on this easy one-day roundtrip that includes an outstanding cogwheel train ride to Gornergrat (10,200 feet) for a close view of the Matterhorn (14,692 feet) and more than 50 other peaks. This trip is not covered by Eurailpass or Eurail Youthpass. The cost of the roundtrip is approximately 50 Swiss francs per person.

280
Dep. Brig Frequent times from 6:16 to 20:18
Arr. Zermatt 90 minutes later
Change trains.
281
Dep. Zermatt Frequent times from 7:35 to 17:35 (+18:00 from late June to late September)
Arr. Gornergrat 45 minutes later

* * *

Dep. Gornergrat Frequent times from 8:20 to 18:20 (+18:45 from late June to late September)
Arr. Zermatt 45 minutes later
Change trains.
280
Dep. Zermatt Frequent times from 6:04 to 21:05
Arr. Brig 90 minutes later

Chur - Brig - Zermatt - Gornergrat - Zermatt

There is fabulous Rhone Glacier scenery on this ride plus crossing Oberalp Pass (6,700 feet) and Furka Pass (7,100 feet) on the Chur-Brig portion. This trip crosses the highest bridges in Europe and includes the outstanding cogwheel train ride to Gornergrat (10,200 feet) for a close view of the Matterhorn (14,692 feet) and more than 50 other Alpine peaks. This trip is not covered by Eurailpass or Eurail Youthpass. The cost of the roundtrip is approximately 50 Swiss francs per person.

Table 315

Dep. Chur	8:53(1)
Arr. Zermatt	14:46

Change to narrow-gauge train.

281

Dep. Zermatt	15:05(2)	15:30	16:20	17:10(2)	17:35(3)
Arr. Gornergrat	16:40	16:15	17:05	17:55	18:15

* * *

Dep. Gornergrat	17:05	17:55(2)	18:20	18:45	-0-
Arr. Zermatt	45 minutes later				

(1)Light refreshments. (2)Runs from late June to late September. (3)Plus another departure from Zermatt at 18:00(2).

Chur - St. Moritz - Chur

Marvelous gorge, lake and mountain scenery on this easy one-day bus roundtrip. It is a very scenic ride involving going through double spiral tunnels and across the amazing Landwasser Viaduct.

346

Dep. Chur	7:15(1)	9:00	11:50	15:10
Arr. St. Moritz (Stn.)	9:51	11:33	14:26	17:44
Arr. St. Moritz (Post)	5 minutes later			

* * *

Dep. St. Moritz (Post)	8:30	13:30	16:05	17:25
Dep. St. Moritz (Stn.)	5 minutes later			
Arr. Chur	11:10	16:10	18:50	20:08

(1)Runs from late June to late September.

Geneva - Lausanne - Brig - Spiez - Bern - Geneva

One of the 5 most scenic rail trips in Europe. The succession of beautiful scenes defy verbal description: 15 miles of terraced vineyards and Lake Geneva shoreline between Geneva and Lausanne. Great river scenery en route from Martigny to Brig. After leaving Brig, you go through the 10-mile Lotschberg Tunnel. Take a seat on the side of the train that faces the Brig railstation.

After emerging from the tunnel, there is such beautiful farm and mountain scenery around tiny Kandersteg and Fruitigen that you want to get off the train and spend the rest of your life there.

We urge you to arrive Spiez near Noon and have the local specialty for lunch. Walk only 5 minutes from the Spiez railstation down a short hill to the dining-room of the little Hotel Krone, and order the delicious Geschnetzeltes und Rosti.

After lunch, it is only a 15-minute walk to the castle overlooking Lake Thun, the most beautiful lake scene on this planet. If the view of Lake Thun and the mountains reflected on its surface does not thrill you, pack up and go home because you will not find anything more beautiful to see in this world.

You can return to Geneva (via Bern) either by boarding a train in Spiez or by first taking the 45-minute boat ride (covered by Eurailpass) from Spiez to Thun village and then boarding the train in Thun. The lake steamer ties up 100 feet from Thun's railstation. If you resume the train ride in Spiez, look for the steamer when the train pulls into Thun. Look out the right side of the train.

It is possible to schedule a brief stop-over in Bern.

On the way back to Geneva from Bern, you pass through the same lake and vineyard scenery you saw between Lausanne and Geneva that morning, at the start of this fabulous one-day trip.

251					
Dep. Geneva (Corn.)	7:46	8:46	9:46(1)	10:46(1)	11:46(1)
Dep. Lausanne	8:22	9:28	10:28(1)	11:28(1)	12:28(1)
Arr. Brig	9:47	11:08	12:17	13:08	14:17
Change trains.					
260					
Dep. Brig	9:54(1)	11:12(1)	12:54(1)	13:54(1)	14:54(1)
Arr. Spiez	11:01	12:10	14:01	15:01	16:01
Dep. Spiez	11:03(1)	12:12(1)	14:03(1)	15:03(1)	16:03(1)
Dep. Thun	11:14(1)	12:23(1)	14:14(1)	15:14(1)	16:14(1)
Arr. Bern	11:34	12:43	14:34	15:34	16:34
Change trains.					
256					
Dep. Bern	12:16(2)	13:16(2)	15:16	16:16(2)	17:16(3)
Arr. Lausanne	13:22	14:22	16:22	17:22	18:22
Arr. Geneva (Corn.)	13:57	14:57	16:57	17:57	18:57

(1) Light refreshments. (2) Meal service. (3) Plus other departures from Bern at 17:34(1), 18:16(2), 19:16(2), 19:34, 20:16(2), 21:16(2) and 22:16(2).

Here are the Lake Thun (Spiez-Thun) boat schedules (covered by Eurailpass) to combine with departures from Thun village for Bern.

321					
Dep. Spiez	12:00	13:20	14:14	15:11	16:05(1)
Arr. Thun (Pier)	12:45	14:07	15:00	16:00	17:00

It is a 2-minute walk from the boat pier to the train.

260					
Dep. Thun (Stn.)	13:14	14:14	15:14	16:14	17:14
Arr. Bern	20 minutes later				

(1) Plus other boat departures from Spiez at 17:03, 18:01, 19:23 and 20:09, connecting in Thun with trains to Bern.

Geneva - Chamonix (Mt. Blanc) - Geneva

Be sure to have your passport with you on this trip filled with fantastic mountain scenery, as you will be going from Switzerland to France. From Chamonix, you should take the 2-mile-high cable-car ride that goes nearly to the top of the tallest mountain in Europe, the 15,771-foot Mt. Blanc, towering almost 10,000 feet above Chamonix, for a view of Alpine peaks extending 80 miles.

After descending, there is just time to also take the narrow-gauge train to see the "Sea of Ice" glacier bed. The tombstones in the small cemetery, a 5-minute walk from the railstation, are fascinating. Nearly one-fourth of the headstones read "died on the mountain". Climbers and their rescuers.

The train changes on this trip are easy cross-platform transfers taking only a minute.

158		167		
Dep. Geneva (Eaux-Vives)	9:35	Dep. Chamonix	15:29	18:20(1)
Arr. Annemasse	9:43	Arr. St. Gervais	16:05	18:56
Change trains.		Change trains.		
Dep. Annemasse	9:54	Dep. St. Gervais	16:15	19:06
Arr. La Roche-sur-Foron	10:11	Arr. La Roche	17:02	19:53
Change trains.		Change trains.		
167		158		
Dep. La Roche-sur-Foron	10:22	Dep. La Roche	17:15	20:00(1)
Arr. St. Gervais	11:18	Arr. Annemasse	17:33	20:18
Change trains.		Change trains.		
Dep. St. Gervais	11:28	Dep. Annemasse	17:40	20:23
Arr. Chamonix	12:05	Arr. Geneva (Eaux-Vives)	17:48	20:31

(1)Runs from late June to early September.

Geneva - Lausanne - Geneva

Here is a short trip packed with fine scenery of 15 miles of terraced vineyards, nearly the entire route following the lovely shoreline of Lake Geneva. Complete schedules are listed earlier in this section, under the "Geneva-Lausanne" one-day excursion.

Geneva - Lyon - Geneva

The Geneva-Amberieu portion of this easy one-day roundtrip is noted for scenic gorges.

Occasionally, 2 trains depart from the same track at Lyon's Perrache railstation, heading in opposite directions. Be sure to stand at the correct end (North or South) of the track in order to board the train you want to ride. Check the departure signs at the underground passageway. Do not rely merely on a track number when departing from Perrache railstation !

Next to the North passageway of Track "A" is a take-out restaurant, handy for provisioning your trip.

A metropolitan train connects Lyon's Brotteaux and Perrache railstations. The ride is 15 minutes.

155

Dep. Geneva (Corn.)	10:38		
Dep. Amberieu	12:24		
Arr. Lyon (Brotteaux)	12:49		
Arr. Lyon (Perrache)	12:58		
	*	*	*
Dep. Lyon (Perrache)	14:13	16:09	18:19
Dep. Lyon (Brotteaux)	14:21	16:17	18:28
Dep. Amberieu	-0- (1)	16:41	-0- (1)
Arr. Geneva (Corn.)	16:05	18:08	20:31

(1) Does not stop in Amberieu.

Geneva - Martigny - Geneva

This is a scenic trip of intermediate length, longer than the Geneva-Lausanne ride and shorter than the Geneva-Brig-Bern-Geneva circle trip. Very good gorge, lake, mountain and vineyard scenery.

251

Dep. Geneva (Corn.)	6:46	8:46	9:46(1)	10:46(1+3)
Arr. Martigny	8:16	10:16	11:19	12:16
	*	*	*	
Dep. Martigny	8:36(1)	10:36	12:31	13:08(1+2+4)
Arr. Geneva (Corn.)	10:08	12:08	14:08	14:57

(1) Light refreshments. (2) Change trains in Lausanne. (3) Plus other departures from Geneva at 11:46(1), 12:57(2), 13:46(1) and 14:57-(1+2). (4) Plus other departures from Martigny at frequent times from 13:36 to 22:36.

Geneva - Montreux - Zweisimmen - Spiez - Bern - Geneva

This variation on the scenic trip described earlier (Geneva-Brig-Bern-Geneva) runs parallel and north of the Martigny-Brig route. You miss going through the Lotschberg Tunnel, but you are able to see all of the Geneva-Lausanne vineyard and Lake Geneva scenery plus Lake Thun (Spiez) and a possible stopover in Bern, en route back to Geneva. See earlier notes about Spiez and taking a boat on Lake Thun from Spiez to Thun village.

The ascent from Montreux to Zweisimmen is very scenic as the train climbs from the shore of Lac Leman to Les Avants in a series of hairpin bends. The funicular ride from Les Avants to Sonloup is worthwhile.

251					
Dep. Geneva (Corn.)	9:46(1)	10:46(1)	11:46(1)	12:57(2)	13:46(1)
Arr. Montreux	10:47	11:47	12:47	14:10	14:47
Change trains.					
255					
Dep. Montreux	10:53	12:20	12:53	14:20(3)	14:53
Arr. Zweisimmen	12:55	14:06	14:55	16:06	16:55
Change trains.					
Dep. Zweisimmen	13:00	14:20	15:00	16:00	17:00
Arr. Spiez	13:51	14:57	15:51	16:51	17:51
Change trains.					
260					
Dep. Spiez	13:56	15:03	15:56	16:56	17:56(5)
Dep. Thun	14:07	15:14	16:07	17:07	18:07
Arr. Bern	14:27	15:34	16:27	17:27	18:27
Change trains.					
256					
Dep. Bern	15:16	16:16(4)	17:16(5)	17:34(1)	19:16(4+6)
Arr. Geneva (Corn.)	16:57	17:57	18:57	19:28	20:57

(1) Light refreshments. (2) Change trains in Lausanne. (3) "Panoramic Express". Has special observation cars. (4) Meal service. (5) Plus other departures from Spiez at frequent times from 18:56 to 23:03. (6) Plus other departures from Bern at 19:34, 20:16(4), 21:16(4) and 22:16(4).

Interlaken - Mt. Pilatus - Interlaken

Great gorge and mountain scenery on this easy one-day roundtrip. The Alpnachstad-Pilatus-Alpnachstad rack railway portion operates only from May to end of October and is not covered by Eurailpass. Costs about 34 Swiss francs for roundtrip. There are good views and several restaurants at the peak of Pilatus.

264

Dep. Interlaken (Ost)	6:37	8:37	10:37	12:37	
Arr. Alpnachstad	8:36	10:36	12:36	14:36	

Change to rack railway for the ride to the top of Mt. Pilatus.

290

Dep. Alpnachstad	8:45	11:00	13:20	14:58	
Arr. Pilatus Kulm	9:25	11:40	14:00	15:38	
	*	*	*		
Dep. Pilatus Kulm	9:33	11:00	13:20	14:58	17:15
Arr. Alpnachstad	10:13	11:40	14:00	15:38	17:55

Change to standard train.

264

Dep. Alpnachstad	10:15	12:15	14:15	16:15	18:15
Arr. Interlaken (Ost)	12:19	14:19	16:19	18:19	20:22

Interlaken - Spiez - Bern - Spiez - Interlaken

Excellent gorge, lake and mountain scenery on this easy one-day roundtrip that includes visiting Lake Thun and a possible stopover in Bern. See earlier notes about Spiez and taking a boat on Lake Thun from Spiez to Thun village, under the "Geneva-Brig-Bern-Geneva" scenic trip.

260

Dep. Interlaken (Ost)	7:34	8:24	9:34	10:24
Dep. Interlaken (West)	5 minutes later			
Dep. Spiez	7:56	8:56	9:56	10:56
Dep. Thun	8:07	9:07	10:07	11:07
Arr. Bern	20 minutes later			
	*	*	*	
Dep. Bern	Frequent times from 6:40 to 23:27			
Arr. Interlaken (West)	45-60 minutes later			
Arr. Interlaken (Ost)	5 minutes after arriving West station			

Interlaken - Spiez - Brig - Spiez - Interlaken 260

Nice gorge, lake and mountain scenery on this easy one-day round-trip which includes visiting Lake Thun and going through the 10-mile Lotschberg Tunnel. There is time to stopover in Spiez. See earlier notes about Spiez under the "Geneva-Brig-Bern-Geneva" scenic trip.

Dep. Interlaken (Ost)	7:34	8:24	9:34	10:24	11:34	12:24
Dep. Interlaken (West)	5 minutes later					
Arr. Spiez	7:53	8:53	9:53	10:53	11:53	12:53
Change trains.						
Dep. Spiez	7:54	8:54	9:54	10:54	11:54	12:54
Dep. Brig (1)	9:00	10:00	11:00	12:00	13:00	14:00
	*	*	*			

Dep. Brig	Frequent times from 4:30 to 21:54
Arr. Spiez	70 minutes later
Change trains.	
Dep. Spiez	Frequent times from 7:13 to 23:04
Arr. Interlaken (West)	15 minutes later
Arr. Interlaken (Ost)	5 minutes after arriving West station

(1) All of these trains have light refreshments.

Interlaken - Jungfraujoch - Interlaken

Great gorge and mountain scenery on this easy one-day roundtrip. This spectacular route ends at Europe's highest (11,333 feet) railstation. It includes 2 stops in the tunnel through Mount Eiger, for viewing through "windows" which the railroad's builders cut in the face of the cliff.

At Jungfraujoch, passengers alight to look down on the great Jungfrau glacier and stroll in the "Ice Palace" carved inside the glacier.

None of this trip is covered by Eurailpass or Eurail Youthpass.

For variety, we suggest you go from Interlaken to Jungfraujoch via Wengen, and then return to Interlaken via Grindelwald.

Grindelwald sits at 3400-feet altitude. The majestic peaks that rise around this village are: Jungfrau (13,642 feet), Eiger (13,026), Wetterhorn (12,142), Breithorn (12,409), Monch (13,449), Schreckhorn (13,380), Gspaltenhorn (11,277) and Tschingelhorn (11,736).

287							
Dep. Interlaken (Ost) (Via Wengen)	6:40	7:40	8:40	9:40	10:40	11:40	12:40
Arr. Scheidegg	7:55	8:54	9:54	10:54	11:54	12:54	13:54
Change trains.							
288							
Dep. Scheidegg	8:09	9:07	10:07	11:07	12:07	13:05	14:05
Arr. Jungfraujoch	9:00	9:59	10:58	11:58	12:58	13:56	15:02

	*	*	*				
Dep. Jungfraujoch	9:10	10:05	12:05	13:05	14:05	15:07	15:34(1)
Arr. Scheidegg	9:52	10:52	12:52	13:50	14:50	15:50	16:20
Change trains.							
287							
Dep. Scheidegg (Via Grindelwald)	10:14	11:14	12:57	13:57	14:57	15:57	16:36
Arr. Interlaken (Ost)	12:08	13:08	14:23	15:36	16:23	17:23	18:09

(1) Plus other departures from Jungfraujoch at 16:05, 16:58 and 17:57 for connections in Scheidegg with trains to Interlaken.

Lausanne - Brig - Lausanne 251

Fine gorge, lake, mountain and river scenery on this easy one-day roundtrip.

Dep. Lausanne	Frequent times from 6:30 to 21:28
Arr. Brig	1½-2 hours later
	* * *
Dep. Brig	Frequent times from 0:44 to 21:46
Arr. Lausanne	1½-2 hours later

Lausanne - Brig - Spiez - Bern - Lausanne

Marvelous gorge, lake, mountain and river scenery on this easy one-day roundtrip, a portion of the "Geneva-Lausanne-Spiez-Bern-Geneva" scenic trip listed earlier in this section and to which you should refer for complete schedules and sightseeing details.

Locarno - Camedo - Locarno

One of the 5 most scenic rail trips in Europe. Fantastic gorge, river and mountain scenery. You will see some hillside farms that are nearly vertical. The ride is called "Centovalli", and you will see a hundred valleys. This trip can be made either as an easy one-day roundtrip or as a portion of the Locarno-Milan or Locarno-Brig routes.

Please note that this trip does not start from the Locarno railstation. You catch what looks like a trolley car at the central bus stop, across from the train station.

At Camedo, there is only a tiny restaurant-bar and absolutely nothing to do while you wait for the return ride to Locarno.

Dep. Locarno	7:00	9:00	10:05(1)	12:00	13:00(1)	15:00	16:20
Arr. Camedo	7:50	9:47	10:45	12:47	13:41	15:41	17:08
		*	*	*			
Dep. Camedo	7:55	10:08(1)	11:08(1)	13:05(1)	15:05(1)	16:34	18:50

Arr. Locarno 45 minutes later

(1) Light refreshments.

Locarno - Domodossola - Brig - Domodossola - Locarno

Very good gorge, mountain and river scenery on this one-day roundtrip that includes the wonderful Centovalli ride described in the previous trip plus going through the 12-mile Simplon, longest main line rail tunnel in the world. Be sure to take your passport on this trip from Switzerland to Italy, Switzerland, back to Italy and then again to Switzerland.

The Domodossola-Brig (and v.v.) portion of this route takes you through Europe's longest (19.8km - 11.9 miles) tunnel, the Simplon. It is the world's second-longest tunnel, after Japan's Daishimizu Tunnel between Tokyo and Niigata (22.3km - 13.4 miles).

The 90-minute, 35-mile Locarno-Domodossola trip does not start from the Locarno railstation. You catch what looks like a trolley car at the central Locarno bus stop, across from the train station. Stops en route includes Camedo, Intragna with its many churches, Verdasio which has a train connection to the mountain town of Rasa, Palagnedra which has a lake, and Druogno, highest point on this scenic route.

252

Dep. Locarno	11:05(1)
Arr. Domodossola	12:44

Change trains. Walk from the underground Centovalli track, up to the main Domodossola station.

251

Dep. Domodossola	13:05
Arr. Brig	13:37

251

Dep. Brig	14:41
Arr. Domodossola	15:13

Change trains. Walk outside the Domodossola station and go to the underground Centovalli track.

262

Dep. Domodossola	15:30
Arr. Locarno	17:13

(1)Light refreshments.

Luzern - Brunnen - Luzern 319

Here is an excellent one-day roundtrip boat ride on Lake Luzern, covered by Eurailpass.

Dep. Luzern (Stn. Quay)	9:00	9:30	10:30	11:30	13:30(1)
Arr. Brunnen	10:54	11:54	12:50	14:02	15:33
	*	*	*		
Dep. Brunnen	12:32	13:52	14:40	15:45	17:26(2)
Arr. Luzern (Stn. Quay)	14:50	16:15	16:52	18:20	19:29

(1)Plus other departures from Luzern at 14:30 and 15:30. (2)Plus another departure from Brunnen at 18:19.

Luzern - Interlaken - Luzern

Great gorge and mountain scenery on this easy one-day roundtrip. Complete schedules are listed earlier in this section, under the "Luzern-Interlaken-Luzern" one-day excursion.

Luzern - Interlaken - Brig - Domodossola - Locarno - Luzern

This route includes going through the 9-mile Lotschberg Tunnel, the 12-mile Simplon and the 9-mile St. Gotthard, as well as seeing the beautiful Centovalli scenery between Domodossola and Locarno.

264	
Dep. Luzern	8:00(1)
Arr. Interlaken(Ost)	10:00
Change trains.	
260	
Dep. Interlaken (Ost)	10:24(1)
Arr. Spiez	10:53
Change trains.	
Dep. Spiez	10:54
Arr. Brig	12:00
Change trains.	
251	
Dep. Brig	13:17
Arr. Domodossola	13:49

252		
Dep. Domodossola	14:05(1)	
Arr. Locarno	15:47	
Change trains.		
261		
Dep. Locarno	15:53	18:31
Arr. Bellinzona	16:22	18:57
Change trains.		
277		
Dep. Bellinzona	17:20	19:05(2)
Arr. Luzern	19:37	21:37

(1) Light refreshments. (2) Meal service.

Luzern - Interlaken - Jungfraujoch - Interlaken - Luzern

Marvelous gorge, lake and mountain scenery on this easy one-day roundtrip. See details about Jungfraujoch earlier in this section, under "Interlaken-Jungfraujoch".

For variety, we suggest you go from Interlaken to Jungfraujoch via Wengen, and then return to Interlaken via Grindelwald. This portion is not covered by Eurailpass.

264		
Dep. Luzern	7:17	8:00(1)
Arr. Interlaken (Ost)	9:17	10:00
Change trains.		
287		
Dep. Interlaken (Ost) (via Wengen)	9:40	10:18
Arr. Scheidegg	10:54	11:36
Change trains.		
288		
Dep. Scheidegg	11:07	12:07
Arr. Jungfraujoch	11:58	12:58

288		
Dep. Jungfraujoch	12:05	13:05(2)
Arr. Scheidegg	12:52	13:50
Change trains.		
287		
Dep. Scheidegg (via Grindelwald)	12:57	13:57
Arr. Interlaken (Ost)	14:23	15:36
Change trains.		
264		
Dep. Interlaken (Ost)	14:37	15:39
Arr. Luzern	16:56	17:37

(1) Light refreshments. (2) Plus other departures from Jungfraujoch that allow connections for returning to Luzern, at frequent times from 14:05 to 17:57.

Luzern - Interlaken - Spiez - Brig - Andermatt - Goschenen - Luzern

Here is a marvelous one-day circle trip, crammed with outstanding scenery. Although this schedule allows only 50 minutes in Spiez, if you take a packed lunch from Luzern there are benches outside the Spiez railstation where you can sit while eating and have a fabulous view of the village, Lake Thun and the mountains reflected on its surface. From Spiez to Brig, there is a good view of the Matterhorn from the right side of the train. Walk to the front of the Brig railstation to board the train to Andermatt. En route from Brig to Andermatt, you see the beautiful Rhone Valley, pass the face of the Rhone Glacier, and cross Furka pass (7,100 feet).

The Brig-Andermatt-Goschenen portion of this trip is not covered by Eurailpass or Eurail Youthpass.

264	
Dep. Luzern	9:17
Arr. Interlaken (Ost)	11:17
Change trains.	
260	
Dep. Interlaken (Ost)	11:34
Arr. Spiez	11:52
Change trains.	
260	
Dep. Spiez	12:54
Arr. Brig	14:00
Change trains.	
315	
Dep. Brig	14:30
Arr. Andermatt	16:31
Change trains.	
295	
Dep. Andermatt	16:37
Arr. Goschenen	16:52
Change trains.	
277	
Dep. Goschenen	17:01
Arr. Luzern	18:29

Luzern - Mt. Pilatus - Luzern 264 + 290

Fine gorge and mountain scenery on this easy one-day roundtrip. The Alpnachstad-Pilatus-Alpnachstad rack railway portion operates only from May to end of October and is not covered by Eurailpass. Costs about 34 Swiss francs for the roundtrip. There are good views and several restaurants at the peak of Pilatus.

Dep. Luzern	8:09	9:57	11:57	13:57	14:57	15:57
Arr. Alpnachstad	8:26	10:13	12:13	14:13	15:13	16:13
Change to rack railway for the ride to the top of Mt. Pilatus.						
Dep. Alpnachstad	8:45	10:20	12:25	14:20	15:45	16:25
Arr. Pilatus Kulm	9:25	11:00	13:05	15:00	16:25	17:05
	*	*	*			
Dep. Pilatus Kulm	9:33	11:35	13:15	15:40	16:20	17:15
Arr. Alpnachstad	10:13	12:15	13:55	16:20	17:00	17:55
Change trains.						
Dep. Alpnachstad	10:38	12:38	14:38	16:38	17:38	18:38
Arr. Luzern	18 minutes later					

Luzern - Mt. Titlis - Luzern

Very good gorge and mountain scenery on this easy one-day roundtrip. The Engelberg-Titlis-Engelberg rack railway is not covered by Eurailpass or Eurail Youthpass and does not operate the month of November. The cost for that roundtrip is 41 Swiss francs. Engelberg is a popular ski resort. It also has more than 20 miles of level walking and hiking paths, toboggan runs, a gambling casino and indoor swimming pools. There are great views from the restaurant on the top of Mount Titlis.

291

Dep. Luzern	7:17(1)	7:55	9:26	9:53	11:17(2)
Arr. Engelberg	8:12	8:46	10:20	10:49	12:12

Change to the funicular.

Dep. Engelberg — Frequent times
Arr. Mt. Titlis — 60 minutes later

* * *

Dep. Mt. Titlis — Frequent times
Arr. Engelberg — 60 minutes later

Change to the train.

Dep. Engelberg — Frequent times from 6:24 to 20:50
Arr. Luzern — 60-65 minutes later

(1)Change trains in Hergiswil. (2)Plus other departures from Luzern at frequent times from 12:09 to 21:17.

Luzern - Mt. Titlis - Luzern - Mt. Pilatus - Luzern

May through October, both mountains can be ascended in one day by following this schedule.

291

Dep. Luzern	7:55(1)
Arr. Engelberg	8:46

Change to the funicular.

000

Dep. Engelberg	9:30(1+2)
Arr. Mt. Titlis	10:30(2)

* * *

Dep. Mt. Titlis	11:00(1+2)
Arr. Engelberg	12:00(2)

Change to the train.

291

Dep. Engelberg	12:30(1)
Arr. Luzern	13:37

264

Dep. Luzern	13:57
Arr. Alpnachstad	14:13

Change to the rack railway.

303

Dep. Alpnachstad	14:20(1)
Arr. Pilatus Kulm	15:00

* * *

Dep. Pilatus Kulm	15:40(1+3)
Arr. Alpnachstad	16:20

Change to the train.

264

Dep. Alpnachstad	16:38
Arr. Luzern	16:56

(1)Not covered by Eurailpass or Eurail Youthpass. (2)Estimated. (3)Plus another departure from Alpnachstad at 17:15, arriving Luzern at 18:56.

Luzern - Mt. Rigi (via Arth-Goldau) - Luzern

The excellent gorge and mountain scenery on this route is, unlike the route that follows, entirely by train. This is an easy one-day roundtrip. The rides between Arth-Goldau and Rigi are not covered by Eurailpass or Eurail Youthpass.

272 + 277						
Dep. Luzern	9:02	10:24	11:02	12:24	13:02	14:24(1)
Arr. Arth-Goldau	9:26	10:48	11:26	12:48	13:26	14:48
Change to rack railway.						
294						
Dep. Arth-Goldau	10:05	11:05	12:05	13:05	14:05	15:05
Arr. Rigi Kulm	10:40	11:40	12:40	13:40	14:46	15:40

* * *

Dep. Rigi Kulm	11:00	12:00	13:00	14:00	14:54	16:00(2)
Arr. Arth-Goldau	11:45	12:45	13:45	14:45	15:48	16:45
Change to standard train.						
272 + 277						
Dep. Arth-Goldau	11:47	13:11	14:26	15:11	15:52	16:52
Arr. Luzern	30-40 minutes later					

(1) Plus other departures from Luzern at 15:17, 15:31 and 16:24.
(2) Plus other departures from Rigi Kulm at 17:00, 18:00 and 19:00.

Luzern - Mt. Rigi (via Vitznau) - Luzern

The very nice gorge, lake and mountain scenery on this easy one-day roundtrip includes a boat ride, covered by Eurailpass, on Lake Luzern. All boats serve food. From Vitznau to Mt. Rigi, the train climbs 4,000 feet in 4¼ miles. Over 450,000 passengers take this ride every year. There is good skiing at Rigi in the Winter. This line was constructed in 1871. Vitznau-Rigi ride not covered by Eurailpass or Eurail Youthpass.

319 (Boat)					
Dep. Luzern (Stn. Quay)	9:00	9:30	10:30	12:00	13:00
Arr. Vitznau (Pier)	9:53	10:24	11:47	12:51	14:30
Change to rack railway. Not covered by Eurailpass.					
293					
Dep. Vitznau	10:00	10:40	11:55	13:00	14:40
Arr. Rigi Kulm	10:35	11:15	12:30	13:35	15:15

	*	*	*		
Dep. Rigi Kulm	10:40	11:40	12:45	14:30	15:20(1)
Arr. Vitznau	11:20	12:20	13:25	15:10	16:00
Change to boat.					
319					
Dep. Vitznau (Pier)	11:40	12:53	13:34	15:15	16:05
Arr. Luzern (Stn. Quay)	55-70 minutes later				

(1) Plus other departures from Rigi Kulm at 16:20, 17:35 and 19:30 to connect in Vitznau with boat departures to Luzern.

St. Moritz - Tirano - St. Moritz

Great mountain scenery on this easy one-day roundtrip. Take your passport ! The track reaches the height of 7,405 feet, making this Europe's highest main rail line.

304					
Dep. St. Moritz	7:40	8:40	11:35	13:30	
Arr. Tirano	10:12	11:26	14:13	16:15	
		*	*	*	
Dep. Tirano	10:30	12:30	14:47(1)	15:42	16:57
Arr. St. Moritz	13:08	15:02	17:00	18:14	19:20

(1) Light refreshments.

St. Moritz - Chur - Brig - Zermatt

Marvelous gorge, mountain and Rhone Glacier scenery on this ride, which goes on the highest bridges in Europe and crosses Oberalp Pass (6,700 feet) and Furka Pass (7,100 feet). The Chur-Brig and Brig-Zermatt trips are not covered by Eurailpass or Eurail Youthpass. Sit on the right-hand side for the best views.

269		
Dep. St. Moritz	6:00	8:55(1)
Arr. Chur	7:56	11:01
Change trains.		
315		
Dep. Chur	8:00(2)	-0-
Arr. Brig	12:26	-0-
Change trains.		
280		
Dep. Brig	13:22	15:18(1)
Arr. Zermatt	14:46	16:45

(1) Direct train to Zermatt. No train changes en route. Meal service.
(2) Change trains in Disentis.

Zermatt - Brig - Disentis - Chur - St. Moritz

280				
Dep. Zermatt	6:04	7:23	10:05(1)	12:05
Arr. Brig	7:30	8:46	11:34	13:33
Change trains.				
315				
Dep. Brig	8:15	9:20	-0-	13:44(2)
Arr. Disentis	11:25	12:32	-0-	-0-
Change trains.				
Dep. Disentis	11:32	12:45	-0-	-0-
Arr. Chur	12:56	14:07	-0-	18:04
Change trains.				
269				
Dep. Chur	13:50(3)	14:50	15:45(1)	18:50(4)
Arr. St. Moritz	15:49	16:54	17:52	20:49

(1) Direct train to St. Moritz. No train change en route. Meal service. (2) Direct train to Chur. Light refreshments. (3) Runs from mid-June to late September. (4) Meal service offered only from mid-June to late September.

Zermatt - Gornergrat - Zermatt

This is a great cogwheel train ride to 10,200-foot high Gornergrat for a close view of the Matterhorn (14,692 feet) and more than 50 other Alpine peaks. This ride is not covered by Eurailpass. Cost is approximately $43 (U.S.) per person for the roundtrip.

281	
Dep. Zermatt	Frequent times from 7:10 to 17:35(1)
Arr. Gornergrat	45 minutes later

(1) Also at 18:00 from late June to mid-September.

* * *

Dep. Gornergrat	Frequent times from 7:55 to 18:20(1)
Arr. Zermatt	45 minutes later

(1) Also at 18:45 from late June to mid-September.

Zurich - Buchs - Zurich

Fine lake scenery on this easy one-day roundtrip.

268				
Dep. Zurich	6:24(1)	7:20(1+2)	8:07(3)	9:20(2+4+5)
Arr. Sargans	7:31	8:18(2)	9:08	10:18
Change trains.				
Dep. Sargans	7:46	8:24	9:20	10:24
Arr. Buchs	10-15 minutes later			
	*	*	*	
Dep. Buchs	10:11(2)	11:14	12:20	13:14(6)
Arr. Sargans	10:23(2)	11:31	12:35	13:31
Change trains.				
Dep. Sargans	10:34	11:40(3)	12:46(1)	13:40(1)
Arr. Zurich	11:33	12:47	13:47	14:47

(1)Light refreshments. (2)Direct train. No train change in Sargans. (3)Meal service. (4)Reservation required. Meal service. (5)Plus other departures from Zurich at 10:07(1), 11:20(3), 12:16(1) and 13:20(3). (6)Plus other departures from Buchs at 12:20, 13:14, 14:17 and 15:15-(2+3) to connect in Sargans with trains to Zurich.

Zurich - Chur - Arosa - Chur - Zurich

Very good gorge, lake and mountain scenery on this easy one-day roundtrip. There is time for a stopover in Chur.

All of the Zurich-Chur and Chur-Zurich trains have light refreshments or meal service.

268					
Dep. Zurich	6:24	7:07	9:07	10:07	11:07(1)
Arr. Chur	7:55	8:38	10:38	11:30	12:38
Change trains.					
303					
Dep. Chur	8:02	8:50	10:50	11:40	12:50
Arr. Arosa	61 minutes later				
		*	*	*	
Dep. Arosa	9:03	10:00	11:00	12:03	13:00(2)
Arr. Chur	10:04	11:01	12:01	12:04	14:01
Change trains.					
268					
Dep. Chur	10:24	11:16	12:24	13:16	14:24
Arr. Zurich	11:47	12:47	13:47	14:47	15:47

(1)Plus other departures from Zurich at frequent times from 13:07 to 19:07. (2)Plus other departures from Arosa at 16:03, 17:15, 18:06 and 19:05 to connect in Chur with trains to Zurich.

Zurich - Chur - Disentis - Andermatt - Brig - Zermatt - Gornergrat - Zermatt

There is fabulous Rhone Glacier scenery on this ride plus crossing Oberalp Pass (6,700 feet) and Furka Pass (7,100 feet) on the Chur-Brig portion. This trip includes going over the highest bridges in Europe and, by departing Zurich at 7:07 or 9:07, you can include the outstanding cogwheel train ride to Gornergrat (10,200 feet) for a close view of the Matterhorn (14,692 feet) and more than 50 other Alpine peaks. Only the Zurich-Chur portion of this trip is covered by Eurailpass and Eurail Youthpass. The rest of this itinerary costs about $100(U.S.).

Do not let this timetable discourage you. This trip is easier to make than it was for us to prepare the table !

268			
Dep. Zurich	7:07(1)	9:07(1)	10:07(1)
Arr. Chur	8:38	10:38	11:30
Change trains.			
315			
Dep. Chur	8:53(2)	10:53(3)	11:41
Arr. Disentis	10:05(2)	12:08(3)	13:01
Change trains.			
Dep. Disentis	10:15(2)	12:17(3)	13:09
Arr. Brig	13:13	15:12	16:35
Change trains.			
280			
Dep. Brig	13:22	15:18	17:18
Arr. Zermatt	14:46	16:45	18:45
Change trains.			
281			
Dep. Zermatt	15:30	17:35	-0-
Arr. Gornergrat	16:15	18:15	-0-
	*	*	*
Dep. Gornergrat	17:05	18:20	-0-
Arr. Zermatt	17:50	19:05	-0-

(1) Light refreshments. (2) Direct train. No train change en route to Brig. Light refreshments. (3) "Glacier Express". Direct train to Brig. Meal service.

Zurich - Landquart - Davos - Landquart - Zurich

Excellent gorge, lake and mountain scenery on this easy one-day roundtrip. The Landquart-Davos-Landquart portion of this trip is not covered by Eurailpass or Eurail Youthpass.

268					
Dep. Zurich	7:07(1)	8:07(2)	9:07(1)	10:07(1+4)	
Arr. Landquart	8:27	9:19	10:27	11:19	
Change trains.					
301					
Dep. Landquart	8:45	9:30	10:35	11:35	
Arr. Davos Platz	10:00	10:42	11:45	13:37	
	*	*	*		
Dep. Davos Platz	10:00	10:57	12:11	13:47	14:10(5)
Arr. Landquart	11:12	12:28	13:20	15:15	15:20
Change trains.					
268					
Dep. Landquart	11:27(2)	12:35(1)	13:27(1)	14:35(2)	15:27(1)
Arr. Zurich	12:47	13:47	14:47	15:47	16:47

(1)Light refreshments. (2)Meal service. (3)Runs from late June to late September. (4)Plus other departures from Zurich at frequent times from 11:07 to 16:07. (5)Plus other departures from Davos at 15:37, 17:05(3) and 19:14, connecting in Landquart with trains to Zurich.

Zurich - Lugano - Milan

The Zurich-Lugano portion of the Zurich-Milan route can be seen on a one-day roundtrip from Zurich. That portion is a major part of one of the 5 most scenic rail trips in Europe (Zurich-Milan). A feast of beautiful farms, lakes, mountains, rivers and vineyards. You go through the 9.3-mile long Gotthard Tunnel.

Before the Gotthard was opened to traffic in 1882, there was no direct rail route from eastern Switzerland through the Alps to Italy. For 7 years and 5 months, 2500 men worked in 3 shifts day and night to build this engineering marvel.

Immediately after exiting the third of a series of 9 tunnels, the train passes the small, white Wassen Church to your right, and about 230 feet above the track. The next time the church comes into view, after leaving Wassen Station, it is also to your right, and nearly level with the track. Later, after exiting tunnel #7, you have a third view of the church. this time to your left and 170 feet above the track.

The turns inside 3 semi-circular tunnels in this area (Pfaffensprung, Wattinger and Leggistein) are engineered so well that there is no sensation of the curves that the train is making inside those tunnels.

Try this interesting experiment: make a pendulum of any object, holding the top of a weighted string, chain or handkerchief against the inner face of a train window (a left-hand window when inside Pfaffensprung and Wattinger, a right-hand window when inside Leggistein). As the train goes around a curve, the weighted bottom will move away from the window.

Climate on the Swiss side of the tunnel is usually much cooler than the Mediterranean temperature on the Italian end. There is a beautiful descent from the Italian end of the tunnel down the Ticino Valley. The train makes 3% gradients at 45-50 miles per hour.

At Bellinzona, the line forks. One branch goes to Locarno, the other to Lugano and Milan.

277

Dep. Zurich	7:04(1)	8:04(2)	8:39(3)	9:04(1)	11:04(1)
Arr. Lugano	10:03	11:17	11:35	12:10	14:10
		*	*	*	
Dep. Lugano	11:26	12:43(1)	14:43(2)	15:32(2)	16:43(1+4)
Arr. Zurich	14:50	15:50	17:50	18:50	19:50

(1) Meal service. (2) Light refreshments. (3) TEE. Reservation required. Meal service. (4) Plus other departures from Lugano at 18:36(1) and 20:05(1).

Zurich - Milan

Schedules for the complete Zurich-Milan trip appear later in this section, under "International Routes From Switzerland".

Zurich - Luzern - Mt. Pilatus - Luzern - Zurich

Fine gorge and mountain scenery on this easy one-day roundtrip. The Alpnachstad-Pilatus-Alpnachstad rack railway portion operates only from May to the end of October and is not covered by Eurailpass. Costs about 34 Swiss francs for the roundtrip. There are good views and several restaurants at the top of Pilatus.

254					
Dep. Zurich	6:58	8:58	10:58(1)	12:58(1)	13:58(1)
Arr. Luzern	7:46	9:46	11:46	13:46	14:46
Change trains.					
264					
Dep. Luzern	8:09	9:57	11:57	13:57	14:57
Arr. Alpnachstad	8:28	10:15	12:15	14:15	15:15
Change to rack railway.					
290					
Dep. Alpnachstad	8:45	10:20	12:25	14:20	15:45
Arr. Pilatus Kulm	9:25	11:00	13:05	15:00	16:25
	*	*	*		
Dep. Pilatus Kulm	9:33	11:35	13:15	15:40	16:20(2)
Arr. Alpnachstad	10:13	12:15	13:55	16:00	17:00
Change to standard train.					
264					
Dep. Alpnachstad	10:38	12:38	14:38	16:38	17:38
Arr. Luzern	10:56	12:56	14:56	16:56	17:56
Change trains.					
254					
Dep. Luzern	Frequent times from 6:23 to 22:42				
Arr. Zurich	50 minutes later				

(1) Light refreshments. (2) Plus another departure from Pilatus Kulm at 17:15 that connects with a train arriving Luzern at 18:56.

Zurich - Romanshorn - St. Gallen - Zurich

Very good lake and mountain scenery on this easy one-day roundtrip that visits Lake Konstanz.

Sights in St. Gallen: The history of lacemaking and embroidery from the 16th century to the present, and lacework worn by European nobility, at the Gewerbemuseum (Embroidery Museum). The 100,000 volumes (including illuminated manuscripts), more than 1,000 years old, in the rebuilt rococo library of the ancient abbey. The twin-towered baroque 18th century Cathedral. Near it, many old houses decorated with frescoes and oriel windows, in the city's old quarter.

266

Dep. Zurich (Hbf.)	7:07	8:07	9:07	10:07	11:07(2)
Arr. Romanshorn	8:16	9:16	10:16	11:16	12:16

Take time for a boat on Lake Konstanz.

272

Dep. Romanshorn	9:02	10:02	-0-	12:02	13:02(3)
Arr. St. Gallen	9:30	10:30	-0-	12:30	13:30

Change trains.

256

Dep. St. Callen (1)	9:40	10:40	-0-	12:40	13:40
Arr. Zurich (Hbf.)	11:00	12:00	-0-	14:00	15:00

(1)All of these departures have meal service. (2)Plus other departures from Zurich at frequent times from 12:07 to 16:07. (3)Plus other departures from Romanshorn (connecting in St. Gallens with trains to Zurich) at 14:02, 16:02, 17:02, 18:02 and 20:02.

Romanshorn - Friedrichshafen 323

There is ferry service between Romanshorn and Friedrichshafen (50% discount with Eurailpass).

Dep. Romanshorn	9:32	11:31	13:31	15:55	17:31
Arr. Friedrichshafen	40-45 minutes later				

* * *

Dep. Friedrichshafen	10:48	12:48	15:00	16:48	18:49
Arr. Romanshorn	40-45 minutes later				

Zurich - Schaffhausen - Zurich 668

To see the marvelous Rhine Falls.

Dep. Zurich	8:10	9:10	10:10	11:10	14:10(1)
Arr. Schaffhausen	42 minutes later				

* * *

Dep. Schaffhausen	10:03	12:03	14:03	15:03	17:03(2)
Arr. Zurich	42 minutes later				

(1) Plus other departures from Zurich at 15:10, 16:10 and 18:10. (2) Plus other departures from Schaffhausen at frequent times from 18:03 to 23:03.

Here is a great 7-day circle itinerary of Switzerland that gives you in the span of one week a visit to most of the country's major cities plus a view of much of Switzerland's great scenery:

Day 1 Geneva, Montreux, Zweisimmen, Spiez (Lunch), Lake Thun boat to Interlaken.
Day 2 Interlaken, Jungfraujoch, Grindelwald (lunch), Interlaken.
Day 3 Interlaken, Luzern.
Day 4 Luzern, Vitznau, Mt. Rigi (lunch), Arth-Goldau, Lugano.
Day 5 Lugano, Bellinzona, Locarno.
Day 6 Locarno, Domodossola, Bern.
Day 7 Bern to Geneva or Zurich.

INTERNATIONAL ROUTES FROM SWITZERLAND

The Swiss gateways for travel to West Germany are Basle (to Cologne) and Zurich (to Munich). Zurich is also the starting point for the train trip to Austria (Innsbruck, and on to Vienna and East Europe) and for train travel to Italy (Milan and beyond).

Basle is also a starting point for trips to Belgium, Holland and France (Paris, and on to London or Madrid).

Geneva (via Aosta, and on to Torino) as well as Bern and Brig (via Domodossola) are also departure cities for rail rides to Italy (Milan, and beyond).

There is also rail service from Geneva to Paris, and from Geneva to southern France (Avignon) and on to Spain (Barcelona).

Basle - Cologne 662

All of these trains charge a supplement and have meal service.

Dep. Basle (S.B.B.)	-0-	7:08(2)	8:08(1)	9:08(3+7)
Dep. Basle (Bad Bf.)	6:14(1)	7:14(2)	8:14(1)	9:14(3)
Arr. Cologne	10:57	11:57	12:57	13:57

(1) Daily, except Sundays and holidays. (2) Monday-Friday, except holidays. (3) Daily. (4) Daily, except Saturday. (5) TEE. Reservation required. Meal service. (6) Carries sleeping car. Also has couchettes. (7) Plus other departures from Basle at 10:08(3), 11:08(3), 12:08(4), 13:08(3), 14:08(3), 15:08(3), 16:08(4), 17:08(3), 18:08(4), 19:08(4), 22:40(6) and 0:15(6).

Zurich - Munich

685

Dep. Zurich	7:04(1)	9:19(2)	12:04(1)	14:19(1)	16:19(1)
Arr. Munich	12:06	13:46	17:06	19:09	21:13

(1) Light refreshments. (2) Meal service.

Zurich - Innsbruck - Vienna

About 2½ hours out of Zurich, the train passes through one of Europe's largest tunnels, the 6:3-mile long Arlberg. There is a very beautiful view of Alpine scenery as the train comes out of the tunnel.

268

Dep. Zurich	7:20(1)	9:20(2)	11:20(3)	13:20(3)	16:07(3+5)
Arr. Innsbruck	11:56(1)	13:24(2)	15:27(3)	17:30(3)	20:55
Arr. Vienna (Westbf.)	19:45	18:55	20:55	22:55	6:10

(1) Light refreshments. (2) Reservation required. Meal service. (3) Meal service. (4) Carries sleeping car. Also has couchettes. (5) Plus another departure from Zurich at 21:20(4).

Bern - Brig - Milan

This trip takes you on the marvelous scenic route via Spiez, noted earlier in this section under "Scenic Trips", and through both the 10-mile long Lotschberg Tunnel and the 11.9-mile long Simplon, longest tunnel in Europe and world's second longest, after Japan's 13.4-mile long Daishimizu Tunnel, between Tokyo and Niigata.

260

Dep. Bern	6:21(1)	8:13(1)	9:21(2)	11:21(1+2)	12:54(1+2+4)
Arr. Brig	8:00(1)	9:43(1)	11:00	13:00(1)	14:30(1+2)

Change trains.

251

Dep. Brig	8:18	9:55	11:17	13:17	14:41
Arr. Milan (Cent.)	11:00	12:55	14:30	16:00	17:00

(1) Direct train to Milan. No train change in Brig. (2) Light refreshments. (3) Has couchettes. (4) Plus other departures from Bern at 14:21(2), 16:21(2), 17:21(1+2) and19:21(2+3).

Zurich - Milan

277

Dep. Zurich	7:04(1)	8:39(2)	9:04(1)	10:04(1+3+7)
Arr. Milan (Cent.)	11:35	12:40	13:40	15:00

(1)Meal service (2)TEE. Reservation required. Meal service. (3)Change trains in Arth Goldau. (4)Light refreshments. (5)Change trains in Chiasso. (6)Has couchettes. (7)Plus other departures from Zurich at 11:04(1), 13:04, 14:04(4), 15:04(4), 16:04(4+5), 17:04(1) and 18:04(3+6).

Basle - Amsterdam

You see many castles in the Mainz-Koblenz area as you travel alongside the Rhine River.

	68	63	68	68	68
Dep. Basle (S.B.B.)	-0-	8:21(1)	12:22(2)	13:16(3)	22:40(4)
Dep. Basle (Bad Bf.)	5:18	-0-	12:27(2)	13:22(3)	22:46(4)
Arr. Amsterdam	14:26	18:03	19:57	22:34	9:36

(1)Departs from Basle's SNCF railstation. Runs from late September to late May. Change trains in Maastricht. Light refreshments. (2)TEE. Reservation required. Meal service. (3)Meal service. (4)Carries sleeping car. Also has couchettes.

Basle - Brussels

63 + 216

Dep. Basle (S.N.C.F.)	5:03(1)	8:21(1)	13:20(1)	16:45(1)	0:27(2)
Arr. Brussels (Q.L.)	11:42	14:15	19:15	22:44	7:18
Arr. Brussels (Nord)	11:54	14:25	19:25	22:54	7:28
Arr. Brussels (Cent.)	-0-	-0-	-0-	22:59	-0-
Arr. Brussels (Midi)	12:02	14:34	19:33	23:03	7:37

(1)Meal service. (2)Carries sleeping car. Also has couchettes.

Basle - Paris

171

Dep. Basle (S.N.C.F.)	8:13(1)	11:25(2)	12:44(2)	16:32(2+3+6)
Arr. Paris (Est)	13:04	16:16	18:09	21:19

(1)Supplement charged. Meal service. (2)Meal service. (3)Daily, except Saturday. (4)State meals required when reserving first-class seat. (5)Has couchettes. (6)Plus other departures from Basle at 18:30(4) and 0:10(5).

Geneva - Paris

152

Dep. Geneva (Cornavin)	7:09(1)	7:23(2)	18:09(1)
Arr. Paris (Lyon)	11:36	13:23	22:37

(1)TGV. Reservation required. Supplement charged. Meal service. (2)Meal service.

Geneva - Avignon - Barcelona

77

Dep. Geneva (Corn.)	8:12(1)	11:27(2)	21:28(3)
Arr. Avignon	12:49(1)	15:47(2)	1:53(3)
Dep. Avignon	12:52(1)	15:50(2)	1:56(3)
Arr. Narbonne	15:07(1)	17:39(2)	4:05(3)
Change trains.			
162			
Dep. Narbonne	15:11(1)	17:41(2)	4:18(3)
Arr. Port Bou	16:46	19:03	5:56
424			
Dep. Port Bou	17:25	19:18(2)	7:10(4)
Arr. Barcelona (Ter.)	20:15	21:16	9:39

(1)Runs from late June to mid-September. Direct train to Port Bou. No train change in Narbonne. (2)Direct train to Barcelona. No train changes en route. Supplement charged. Meal service. (3)Has couchettes. (4)Light refreshmnts.

Aosta - Torino Gateways to Italy

(1) Via San Bernardo Tunnel

Lausanne or Brig - Martigny - Aosta - Torino

251			251		
Dep. Lausanne	6:50	14:50	Dep. Brig	6:37	15:14
Arr. Martigny	7:43	15:43	Arr. Martigny	7:29	16:06

Change to bus.
337

Dep. Martigny (Stn.)	8:00	16:15
Arr. Aosta (P. Narbonne)	10:00	18:25

Change to train.
362

Dep. Aosta	12:19	19:38
Arr. Torino (P.N.)	16:20	21:35

(2) Via Mt. Blanc Tunnel

Geneva - Chamonix - Aosta - Torino 158

Dep. Geneva (Eaux-Vives)	9:35	12:20
Arr. Annemasse	9:43	12:28

Change trains. (All of the train changes Geneva-Chamonix are cross-platform, taking only one minute.)

Dep. Annemasse	9:54	12:46
Arr. Roche-sur-Foron	10:11	13:09

Change trains. 167

Dep. Roche-sur-Foron	10:22	13:14
Arr. St. Gervais	11:18	13:58

Change trains.

Dep. St. Gervais	11:28	14:12
Arr. Chamonix	12:05	14:49

Change to bus. 191

Dep. Chamonix N/A(1) N/A(1) N/A(1) N/A(1) N/A(1) N/A(1)
Arr. Aosta 2½ hours later

(1)Two departures per day in Winter. Six departures per day during July, August and early September.

Change to train 362

Dep. Aosta (P. Narbonne)	14:15	16:00	18:20	19:38
Arr. Torino (P.N.)	16:20	19:42	21:21	21:35

A good break in this journey is to spend the night in Aosta and continue on to Torino the next day. Here are the schedules for the early departures from Aosta:

Dep. Aosta (P. Narbonne)	5:15	6:13	9:10	12:19
Arr. Torino (P.N.)	7:32	9:00	11:16	15:55

WEST GERMANY

The German Federal Railroad operates over 20,000 passenger trains every day, linking 6,500 destinatioas. **Where no station is designated for cities in West Germany, the station is "Hauptbahnhof".**

West Germany's fast Intercity trains, connecting 50 important cities along 4 major rail routes, are identified by the abreviation "IC". These trains have easy cross-platform connections in such cities as Cologne, Wurzburg, Mannheim, Dortmund, etc.

A small supplement is charged for both first-class and second-class IC tickets. However, there is no additional charge for making a seat reservation on them. The supplement is not charged to passengers using a Eurailpass, Eurail Youthpass or GermanRail Tourist Card. (All of those passes are also valid on all commuter rail services in major German cities.) The IC supplement must be paid when using the Inter Rail Card.

Some of the Intercity trains have top speeds of 125 mph. A "conference compartment" in them can be rented for the cost of 4 first-class tickets. Worldwide telephone calls can be made from all IC trains.

When entering or leaving West Germany on an international train, the customs, passport and currency control are usually performed in the train. Because of this, passengers traveling across West Germany (such as from Amsterdam to Copenhagen) are required to travel in a special car or compartment.

Porter service may be reserved in advance.

The signs you will see at railstations in West Germany are the same as those listed earlier in this chapter, under "Austria".

SUMMER TIME

West Germany changes to Summer Time on the last Sunday of March and converts back to Standard Time on the last Sunday of September.

WEST GERMAN HOLIDAYS

A list of holidays is helpful because some trains will be noted later in this section as not running on holidays. Also, those trains which operate on holidays are filled, and it is necessary to make reservations for them long in advance.

January 1	New Year's Day	June 17	Commemorating East Berlin Uprisings
	Good Friday		
	Easter		
	Easter Monday	August 15	Assumption Day
May 1	Labour Day	November 1	All Saints Day
	Ascension Day	December 25	Christmas
	Whit Monday	December 26	Holiday

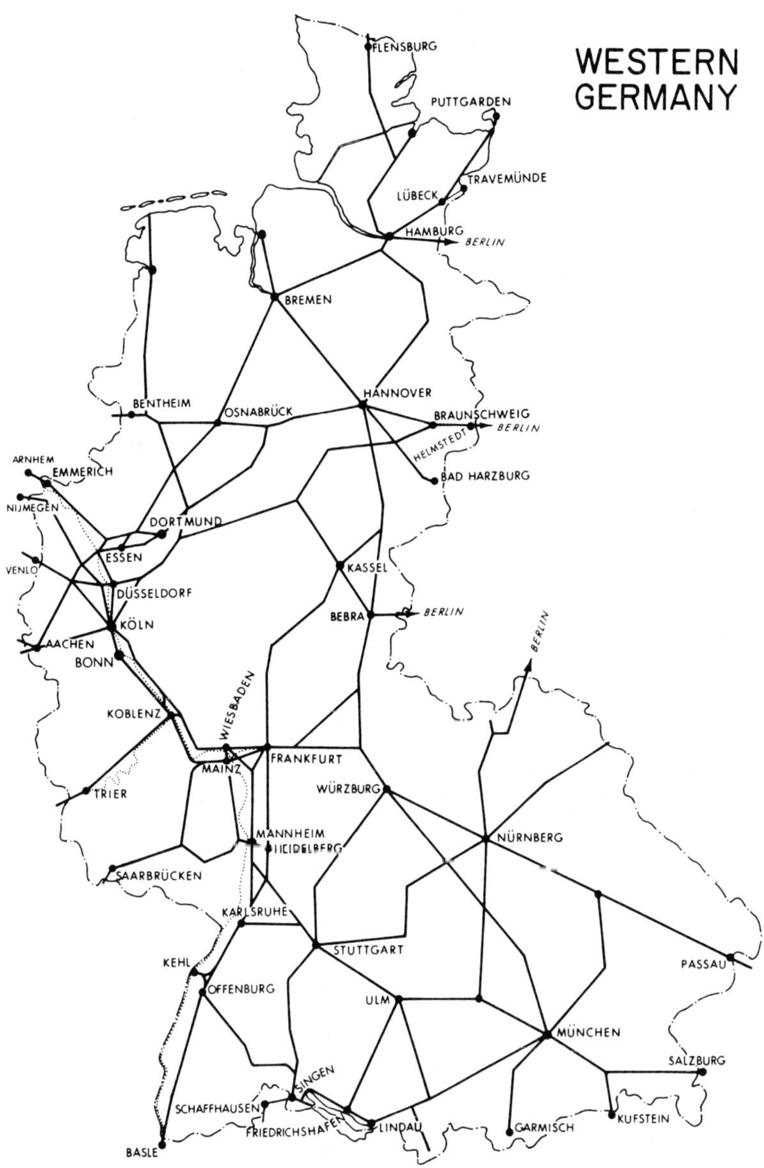
WESTERN
GERMANY
FLENSBURG
PUTTGARDEN
TRAVEMÜNDE
LÜBECK
HAMBURG
BERLIN
BREMEN
HANNOVER
BENTHEIM
OSNABRÜCK
BRAUNSCHWEIG
BERLIN
HELMSTEDT
BAD HARZBURG
ARNHEM
EMMERICH
NIJMEGEN
DORTMUND
VENLO
ESSEN
KASSEL
DÜSSELDORF
BEBRA
BERLIN
KÖLN
AACHEN
BONN
BERLIN
WIESBADEN
KOBLENZ
FRANKFURT
MAINZ
WÜRZBURG
TRIER
NÜRNBERG
MANNHEIM
SAARBRÜCKEN
KARLSRUHE
STUTTGART
PASSAU
KEHL
OFFENBURG
ULM
MÜNCHEN
SALZBURG
SINGEN
SCHAFFHAUSEN
KUFSTEIN
FRIEDRICHSHAFEN
LINDAU
GARMISCH
BASLE

EURAIL BONUSES IN WEST GERMANY

Two cruises: (1) Rhine (between Dusseldorf and Frankfurt), and (2) Mosel (between Trier and Koblenz). Eurail Youthpass holders must pay an extra charge on Express-steamers. One ferry crossing: Puttgarden to Rodby. Most of the Post/Railroad bus lines, including "Romantic Road" (Wiesbaden-Munich and vice versa) and "Castle Road" (Mannheim-Nurnberg and vice versa). Reduction of 50% on (1) Lubeck-Travemunde-Malmo ferry crossing, (2) cruises on Lake Constance, and (3) the Freiburg (Breisgau)-Schauinsland private railroad. A small reduction (only for Eurailpass, not for Eurail Youthpass) is allowed on the Garmisch-Partenkirchen-Grainau-Zugspitze private railroad.

GERMANY'S TRAIN PASSES

GermanRail Tourist Card Sold all over the world and also at many railstations and airports in West Germany. Unlimited train travel, valid for the Romantic Road and Frankfurt-Moselle bus rides, and also allows reduced fares on Rhine and Moselle Rivers excursion steamboats. First-class prices in 1983: 9 days $165(U.S.), 16 days $215. Second-class: 9 days $120, 16 days $155. Half-fare for children 4 to under 12.

Travelers arriving in West Germany by airplane can validate the GermanRail Tourist Card, Eurailpass or Eurail Youthpass at the airport ticket office, after exiting the customs area, and use any of those passes for the rail trip from the airport to the city.

Another benefit of the GermanRail Tourist Card is that it entitles the holder to a greatly reduced roundtrip rail ticket across part of East Germany to West Berlin plus a free sightseeing tour in West Berlin.

NOTE: The reduced-price ticket to Berlin can be purchased in West Germany either at GermanRail ticket offices or at an authorized DER travel agency.

National Netzkarte Sold only in West Germany. Unlimited train travel through *all* of West Germany for one month. The 1983 prices are: first-class DM-1,090, second-class DM-730.

Area Netzkarte Sold only in West Germany. Unlimited train travel in *one specified area* of the country. The 1983 prices are: first-class DM-660, second-class DM-440.

Tourenkarte Sold only in West Germany, after presentation of a roundtrip ticket that covers a distance of at least 201 km. Allows unlimited second-class train travel within 10 consecutive days over a network of approximately 1,000 km of rail lines. The 1983 prices are: 1 person DM-45, 2 persons DM-60, one family DM-75.

TRAIN TOUR PACKAGES

These are the train-hotel packages GermanRail offers in 1983:

Romantik Hotel Rail Tours

Includes a room for 6 nights in small inns and guest houses in any of 39 locations, continental breakfast every day, one gourmet dinner and a 9-day second-class GermanRail Tourist Card. The 1983 prices are: $325(U.S.) per person for double occupancy, DM-15 additional per night for single occupancy, payable in marks on arrival. Children up to 12 years of age (third bed in same room) pay DM-30 per night, also payable in marks on arrival. For a first-class GermanRail Tourist Card, the price is $370.

Travelers need not plan their itinerary in advance. Only the first night's accommodation must be reserved before arriving in West Germany.

The 39 locations include such places as Garmisch-Partenkirchen, Luneburg, Rothenburg ob der Tauber and Zweibrucken.

THE ISLAND OF WEST BERLIN

The city of West Berlin is a virtual island within the sometimes stormy sea of East Germany. Travel to West Berlin must cross through East Germany. The portion of the train trip through East Germany is not covered by Eurailpass, Eurail Youthpass or GermanRail Tourist Card.

In order to avoid being in East Berlin by mistake, be certain to leave the train only at Berlin's Zoo railstation.

Tickets from Berlin to West Germany must be paid in West German marks. The East Germany rail authorities will not accept East German currency.

Sightseeing tours can be arranged from West Berlin to such East German cities as Potsdam, Dresden and Karl Marx Stadt. For reservations, write to: Deutsches Reiseburo, Kurfurstendamm 17, Berlin W. 30, West Germany.

The key cities in West Germany for rail connections to and from West Berlin are Frankfurt, Hamburg, Hannover and Munich.

Two-hour and 4-hour tours of West Berlin begin at 10:00 and occur at frequent intervals during the day, from 220 Kurfurstendamm, 216 Kurfurstendamm, and opposite from the bombed-out Gedachtniskirche (Memorial Church).

Sights in West Berlin: The stroll down tree-lined Kurfurstendamm is almost mandatory, to observe the city's fine stores, theaters, cafes, movie houses and bars. See the Zoo and Aquarium, one of Europe's oldest and best animal exhibits. The New National Gallery. The bust of Nefertiti and other important items in the Egyptian Museum at 70 Schloss Strasse. The rooms and gardens of Charlottenburg Castle, opposite the Egyptian Museum. The 1936 Olympic Stadium. The reconstructed Reichstag Building. The tent-shaped Philharmonic Hall. Take a boat ride on the Havel River.

Visit the sixth floor (called Feinschmecker Etage — "the gourmet's floor") of Kaufhaus des Westens, a large department store on Tauentzienstrasse. It is the largest food store in Europe: 500 sales clerks dispensing 25,000 different products. Fruits and vegetables sold there include limes from Brazil, rare wild mushrooms from France and Poland, avocados from Israel, tiny beans from Kenya, tomatoes from Spain, apples from Hungary. The meats available there go far beyond the 1,000 kinds of wurst and 250 varieties of salami. Then there are eels, crawfish, catfish and carp. Live lobsters are delivered to the store in tank trucks. You will also find hundreds of pastries and breads. Three separate cheese counters for items from France, Italy and from all other countries. Eighteen kinds of herring salad. And much more.

The Weissbierstube Restaurant in the Berlin Museum is acclaimed for its bounteous buffet tables. Both the Restaurant and the Museum are open daily except Mondays 11:00-18:00.

To see East Berlin, take the elevated railway from West Berlin's Zoo station to the Friedrichstrasse station, where entry visas can be obtained.

On leaving Friedrichstrasse station, turn right and walk 3 blocks to reach Berlin's famous boulevard, Unter den Linden. A few blocks further, at the end of the boulevard, is the classical Brandenburg Gate and the Berlin Wall. Also see the Museum of German History. The State Opera. The tiny 14th century church, Marienkirche. The archaeological exhibits in the Pergamon Museum.

GATEWAYS TO BERLIN

Here are the schedules for the major routes to and from Berlin.

Frankfurt - West Berlin

776			
Dep. Frankfurt	8:51(1)	15:26(1)	22:35(2)
Arr. Berlin (Zoo)	16:10	22:31	6:19
	*	*	*
Dep. Berlin (Zoo)	6:37(1)	13:01(1)	22:54(2)
Arr. Frankfurt	13:56	20:26	7:13

(1) Meal service. (2) Carries sleeping car. Also has couchettes.

Hamburg - West Berlin 775

Dep. Hamburg (Hbf.)	8:07(1)	13:36(2)	17:27(2)	20:07(2+3)
Arr. Berlin (Zoo)	11:43	17:20	21:19	23:42

* * *

Dep. Berlin (Zoo)	8:00(2)	13:31(2)	17:24(1)
Arr. Hamburg (Hbf.)	11:38	17:08	20:58

(1) Light refreshments. (2) Meal service. (3) Operates Sundays and holidays all year. Also on Friday from late June to early August.

Hannover - West Berlin 764

Dep. Hannover	1:35(1)	2:39(2)	8:10(3)	10:11(3)	13:13(3+4)
Arr. Berlin (Zoo)	5:17	6:33	11:38	13:51	17:14

* * *

Dep. Berlin (Zoo)	0:35(1)	6:49(3)	8:17(3)	10:50(3)	12:54(3+5)
Arr. Hannover	4:06	10:27	12:02	14:37	16:45

(1) Runs from late May to late September. Carries sleeping car. (2) Carries sleeping car. Also has couchettes. (3) Meal service. (4) Plus other departures from Hannover at 14:15(3), 17:06(3) and 19:10(3). (5) Plus other departures from Berlin at 15:44(3), 16:49(3) and 23:30(2).

Munich - West Berlin
771

Dep. Munich	7:44(1)	12:29(1)	19:25(2)	22:27(3)
Arr. Berlin (Zoo)	16:49	21:53	5:33	7:31

* * *

Dep. Berlin (Zoo)	7:02(1)	9:05(1)	21:50(3)	23:41(2)
Arr. Munich	16:05	18:25	7:29	9:24

(1) Meal service. (2) Runs from late June to mid-August. (3) Carries sleeping car. Also has couchettes.

ONE-DAY EXCURSIONS AND CITY-SIGHTSEEING

Here are 60 one-day rail trips that can be made comfortably from 4 major cities in West Germany, returning to them in most case before dinnertime. Notes are provided on what to see at each destination. The number below the name of each route is the Cook's timetable.

Details on 11 other rail trips recommended for exceptional scenery and schedules for international connections conclude this section.

The 4 base cities are Cologne (Koln), Frankfurt/Main, Hannover and Munich (Munchen).

Cologne (Koln)

It is a 10-minute bus ride from the Cologne/Bonn Airport to the center of Cologne.

Your city-sightseeing in Cologne should include, above all, the Cathedral. Started in 1248 and not completed until 1880, it houses the world's largest reliquary, containing relics of the 3 kings, the Magi. See the view of Cologne and the Rhine Valley from the top of the Cathedral, very close to the railstation.

Near the Cathedral, explore ancient Cologne. The Praetorium, a palace for Roman governors several centuries before Christ. The 3rd century Dionysus mosaic (once the dining hall floor of a Roman house) in the Roman Museum, open Tuesday-Sunday 10:00-20:00. Also on view there is an outstanding collection of Roman glass and 4th century jewelry. See the 3rd century Roman Tower.

All museums in Cologne are closed on Monday. See the collection of paintings by Cologne masters of the Middle Ages, also Impressionists, Expressionists and post World War II art at the Wallraf Richartz Museum, open 10:00-17:00 (until 20:00 on Tuesday and Thursday).

See the Zoo. The 15th century Gurzenich. The Metropolitan Historical Museum. The Town Hall. St. Pantaleon Church. St. Andreas Church. Relics and treasures in the Golden Room at the Church of St. Ursula. The luxury shops on Hohestrasse and Schildergasse.

Frankfurt

There is frequent rail service from Frankfurt's Hauptbahnhof railstation to the city's airport and vice versa (16-minute travel time) every 25-30 minutes from 5:00 to 23:30. One train per hour continues beyond the airport station to Mainz and Wiesbaden. Trains also depart the Airport at 9:19, 13:09 and 20:58 for Darmstadt (20 minutes), Mannheim (60 minutes) and Ludwigshafen (66 minutes).

Goethe's house. The Goethe Museum. The Zoo. The emperor's coronation hall in the Romer complex at medieval Romerberg square. The wonderful doors in the 13th century Leonhardskirche. The 13th century chapel of Saalhof in the remains of the palace of Frederick Barbarossa. Cloth Hall. The Botanical Garden. The pews and murals in the Cathedral of Bartholomew. The Church of St. Nicholas. The Church of St. Paul. Senckenberg Natural History Society's Museum. Stadel Museum and Liebighaus (sculpture). The Museum of Plastic Art. Sachsenhausen, the old quarter of the city, across the Main River from the commercial district. The major shopping streets: Zeil and Kaiserstrasse.

Hannover

The bus ride between Langenhagen Airport and Hannover's railstation takes 30 minutes. The bus terminal is located next to Track #14.

For an interesting 2-hour walking tour of Hannover, obtain the detailed brochure available at either of the railstation's 2 tourist information offices. Walk out of the station to the statue in front of the station, and start to follow the painted red line which leads to Passerelle (a pedestrian mall), the 19th century Opera House, the old city wall, Town Hall, and Hannover's oldest (16th century) half-timbered structure.

See the bronze doors by Marcks at Market Church. The outstanding collection of Egyptian antiquities in the Kestner Museum. The prehistorical objects in the Museum of Lower Saxony. Take streetcars #5 or #16 from the Central railstation to the absolutely fantastic baroque Royal Gardens of Herrenhausen. Its ornamental fountains perform in Summer Monday-Friday 11:00-12:00 and 15:30-16:30. On Saturdays and Sundays, they can be seen 10:00-12:00 and 15:30-17:30. Next to Herrenhausen is the natural park, Georgengarten. Nearby, see the exotic plants in the greenhouses at Berggarten.

Take streetcar #6 from the Central railstation to Hannover's outstanding Zoo.

Munich (Munchen)

A metropolitan train connects Munich's Hauptbahnhof and Ostbanhof railstations. It is a 10-minute bus ride between Munich's Reim Airport and the Hauptbahnhof railstation, where the city's monthly program of events (theaters, museums, exhibits, concerts, plays, etc.) can be obtained. The program is also sold at newsstands.

The works of Durer, El Greco, Raphael, Holbein, Rembrandt and many other great painters at Alte Pinakothek. Frauenkirche Cathedral, and the view from its north tower . . . and then later see the view of Frauenkirche from the top of Neues Rathaus (City Hall). The paintings of Cezanne. Gauguin, Renoir and other impressionists at the Haus der Kunst. Wittelsbach Fountain. The fine exhibits and plantarium at Deutsches Museum, considered the best scientific museum in the world. The view of the Alps from the top of Peterskirche. The best collection of tapestries and wood carvings in Germany, at the Bavarian National Museum. Munich's most famous beer palace, Hofbrauhaus. The Schatzkammer in the Residenz palace, and the flower gardens in the park north of it. The decorations in Asamkirche. Schack Gallery. Theatinerkirche. At Schloss (Castle) Nymphenburg: the porcelain in the showrooms of Nymphenburger Porzellan Manufaktur and in the Residenzmuseum, the enormous Festsaal, and the park outside the castle. Closed on Mondays. A short ride from the center of Munich by streetcars #17 or #21, or by buses #41 or #42.

On the island in the river, visit the Deutsches Museum (science and engineering). See the history of Munich in the Isartorplatz Museum. The 19th and 20th century art in the Neue Pinakothek. The collection of Klee, Kandinsky and Marc paintings in the Stadtische Galerie on Lenbachplatz.

Infamous Dachau is a 40-minute ride by Subway train #3 or bus

#11. Although there are no guides at Dachau, an exhibit there details the operation of the concentration camp, and an English-language film is shown at 11:30 and 15:30.

Since 1870, an Alois Dallmayr food store has offered gourmet delicacies in Munich. It added a restaurant in 1978. As Fauchon's in Paris does, Dallmayr has a vast section of imported foods. Its most notable feature, however, is the enormous array it offers of West Germany's finest lunch meats, 22 varieties of smoked fish and 27 types of bread. If you eat none of the splendid food there, at least see the statues, marble pillars and mounted deer heads inside the store.

Nearly everything edible can be found at Dallmayr's: local and imported fruits, cooked meats and poultry, fresh fish, wines, more than 50 different salads, chocolates, 18 types of ham, and they also sell special cigars.

In the following timetables, where a city has more than one railstation we have designated the particular station after the name of the city (in parentheses). Where no station is designated for cities in Austria, Switzerland and West Germany, the station is "Hauptbahnhof".

It is not necessary to be staying in East Germany in order to tour that area. Sightseeing tours to Potsdam, Dresden and Karl Marx Stadt start in West Berlin at Parkplatz Rankestrasse, near the Kurfurstendamm. For reservations, contact Deutsches Reiseburo, Berlin W.30, Kurfurstendamm 17.

Cologne - Amsterdam - Cologne 221

Dep. Cologne	6:17	7:27	8:54(1)	9:15	10:29(2)
Arr. Amsterdam	9:36	10:42	11:45	12:42	13:26

Sights in Amsterdam: The Rijksmuseum collection of Rembrandt paintings. Rembrandt's house and, near it, the Flea Market. Anne Frank's house at Prisengracht 263. The Tropical Museum, with its display of Indonesian and Far Eastern art and anthropology. The Amsterdam Historical and Jewish Historical Museum. A 75-minute ride in a glass-roofed canal boat, starting at the piers in front of Central Railstation or at Stadhouderskade, near the Rijksmuseum. Royal Palace. The Tower of Tears. The attic church of the Amstelkring Museum. Mint Tower. The Maritime Museum.

Dep. Amsterdam	13:55(2)	14:49(3)	16:55(1)	17:19(4)	18:17(5)
Arr. Cologne	16:45	18:38	19:59	20:42	21:36

(1)Supplement charged. Meal service. (2)TEE. Reservation required. Meal service. (3)Light refreshments. (4)Runs from late May to late September. (5)Plus other departures from Amsterdam at 19:19 and 19:49.

Cologne - Bonn - Cologne

637 + 662

Dep. Cologne	Frequent times from 7:21 to 0:22
Arr. Bonn	22 minutes later

Sights in Bonn: The government buildings in the capital of West Germany, including Bundeshaus where its legislature meets. Beethoven-Halle and the museum at Bonngasse 20, where Beethoven was born in 1770. Drachenfels Mountain and the castle ruins that Byron immortalized. The 13th century Remigius Church. Jesu Church. The view of the Rhine and Siebengebirge from Alte Zoll. The university in the Electors' Castle. The Rhineland Museum.

Dep. Bonn	Frequent times from 6:23 to 0:06
Arr. Cologne	22 minutes later

Cologne - Brussels - Cologne

206

Dep. Cologne	4:47(1)	5:12(2)	7:05(3)	9:06(4+7)
Arr. Brussels (Nord)	7:55	8:08	9:48	11:19
Arr. Brussels (Cent.)	-0-	-0-	9:53	11:25
Arr. Brussels (Midi)	8:04	8:19	9:57	11:29

Sights in Brussels: The gilded buildings in Grand Place. Town Hall. The Law Courts. The Royal Palace. The tapestries in the 13th century Cathedral of St. Michael. Flemish paintings in the Museum of Ancient Art. The Museum of Modern Art. The Central Africa Museum. The Brussels City Museum. The Museum of Arms and Armor. The Postal Museum. The Brewery Museum. The Royal Greenhouses. The Bruegel Museum, in the house where the painter lived his last 6 years. The view from the Palais de Justice. A bus takes you 10 miles to Waterloo.

Dep. Brussels (Midi)	12:10(3)	15:10(1)	16:00(4)	18:10(4+8)
Dep. Brussels (Cent.)	12:14(3)	15:15(1)	-0-	18:15(4)
Dep. Brussels (Nord)	12:20(3)	15:20(1)	16:07(4)	18:20(4)
Arr. Cologne	14:48	17:49	18:48	20:44

(1) Light refreshments. (2) Runs from mid-June to late August. (3) Meal service. (4) Supplement charged. Meal service or light refreshments. (5) Reservation required. (6) Daily, except Sundays and holidays. Runs from late May to late September. (7) Plus other departures from Cologne at 9:43(3) and 11:12(1). (8) Plus other departures from Brussels Midi at 18:27(3+5) and 18:52(3+6).

Cologne - Dortmund - Cologne

633 + 634

Dep. Cologne Frequent times from 5:50 to 23:45
Arr. Dortmund 70 minutes later

Sights in Dortmund: The view of the city from the top of the Television Tower. Westphalia Park. The Ostwall Museum.

Dep. Dortmund Frequent times from 5:40 to 22:24
Arr. Cologne 70 minutes later

Cologne - Dusseldorf - Cologne

There is frequent rail service between Dusseldorf's railstation and the Lohhausen Airport. Travel time is 15 minutes.

634

Dep. Cologne Frequent times from 5:36 to 0:38.
Arr. Dusseldorf 24-28 minutes later.

Sights in Dusseldorf: Many sensational modern buildings. The Paul Klee collection at Kunsttammlung Nordhein-Westfallen. The Goethe Museum, with its first editions, paintings and over 30,000 manuscripts. The Aquarium at the Museumbunker am Zoo. Hofgarten. The Fine Arts Museum. Jagerhof Castle.

Dep. Dusseldorf Frequent times from 6:30 to 23:44.
Arr. Cologne 24-28 minutes later.

Cologne - Essen - Cologne

634

Dep. Cologne Frequent times from 5:36 to 0:38.
Arr. Essen 48-52 minutes later.

Sights in Essen: The Folkwang Museum. The 10th century Cathedral and its collection of priceless 10th and 11th century processional crosses, the crown of the Gold Madonna, and the sword of Cosmas and Damian, the martyr saints. The museum and park at Villa Hugel.

Dep. Essen Frequent times from 6:02 to 23:06.
Arr. Cologne 48-52 minutes later.

Cologne - Frankfurt - Cologne
662

Dep. Cologne	7:03(1)	7:27(2)	8:03(1+3)	8:17(2+7)
Arr. Frankfurt	9:26	9:55	10:26	10:43

Sights in Frankfurt: See notes about city-sightseeing in Frankfurt at the start of this section.

Dep. Frankfurt	12:29(1)	13:29(1+3)	14:29(1+5)	15:19(4+8)
Arr. Cologne	14:51	15:51	16:51	17:56

(1) Supplement charged. Meal service. (2) Meal service. (3) Daily, except Sundays and holidays. (4) Light refreshments. (5) Daily, except Saturday. (6) TEE. Reservation required. Meal service. (2) Plus other departures from Cologne at 9:03(1), 9:32(4), 10:03(1) and 11:03(1). (8) Plus other departures from Frankfurt at 15:29(1), 15:42(2), 16:24(4), 16:29(1), 16:37(6), 17:08(4), 17:29(1), 18:11(2), 18:29(1), 19:29(1), 20:29(1+5) and 21:49(1).

Cologne - Hamburg - Cologne 638

Dep. Cologne	5:32(1+2)	7:00(1)	7:15(3)	9:00(1)
Arr. Hamburg	9:49	11:17	12:04	13:17

Sights in Hamburg: The port, one of the busiest in the world. Hagenbeck Zoo. St. James Church, with its famous organ, built in 1693. Rathausmarkt Square. The models of Old Hamburg, the port and the city's railway system, in the Historical Museum. The Counting Houses in the business quarter, around Burchardplatz. The notorious Reperbahn.

Dep. Hamburg	13:40(1)	14:40(1+4)	15:40(1)	16:40(1+4+5)
Arr. Cologne	17:53	18:53	19:53	20:53

(1) Supplement charged. Meal service. (2) Daily, except Sundays and holidays. (3) Light refreshments. (4) Daily, except Saturday. (5) Plus other departures from Hamburg at 18:40(1+4) and 19:40(1).

Cologne - Heidelberg - Cologne
662

Dep. Cologne	7:21(1)	7:49(2)	7:57(3)	8:57(3+4)	10:57(3+7)
Arr. Heidelberg	10:16	10:20	10:38	11:38	13:38

Sights in Heidelberg: The gardens, Library, Great Terrace, Fat Tower, Elizabeth Gate, Freidrich's Wing, the Otto-Heinrich Wing and the Mirror Room Wing at Heidelberg Castle. Germany's oldest (13th century) university, immortalized in "The Student Prince" opera. The astounding 16th century carved wood Altar of the Twelve Apostles in the

Kurpfalzisches Museum. The Jesuit Church. The Church of the Holy Ghost. The German Pharmaceutical Museum. The Electors of The Palatinate Museum. Knight's Mansion. Student's Gaol.

Dep. Heidelberg	13:14(3)	14:14(3)	15:14(3)	15:51(5)	17:14(3+8)
Arr. Cologne	15:57	16:57	17:57	19:12	19:57

(1) Meal service. (2) TEE. Reservation required. Meal service. (3) Supplement charged. Meal service. (4) Daily, except Sundays and holidays. (5) Runs from early July to early September. Meal service. (6) Daily, except Saturday. (7) Plus another departure from Cologne at 11:57(3). (8) Plus other departures from Heidelberg at 18:14(3), 20:14(3+6) and 21:14(3+6).

Cologne - Koblenz - Cologne 662

(There is a description later in this section of a marvelous scenic trip from Cologne to Koblenz and Bullay and back to Koblenz which does not permit much time for sightseeing in Koblenz.)

Dep. Cologne (Hbf.)	Frequent times from 6:10 to 0:21.
Arr. Koblenz	One hour later.

Sights in Koblenz: Old Town. St. Castor's Church. The Middle Rhine Museum.

Dep. Koblenz	Frequent times from 5:21 to 23:24.
Arr. Cologne (Hbf.)	One hour later.

Cologne - Luxembourg - Cologne

662		
Dep. Cologne	7:57(1)	11:03(1)
Arr. Koblenz	8:49	11:55
Change trains.		
625		
Dep. Koblenz	9:10	12:10
Arr. Luxembourg	11:15	14:15

625		
Dep. Luxembourg	17:40	19:20(2)
Arr. Koblenz	19:43	21:43
Change trains.		
662		
Dep. Koblenz	19:58	21:58(1+3)
Arr. Cologne	20:51	22:51

(1) Supplement charged. Meal service. (2) Change trains in Trier. (3) Daily, except Saturday.

Sights in Luxembourg: The Citadel, with its 53 forts connected by 16 miles of tunnels. Fish Market, site of the city's oldest buildings. The National Museum. The Palace. City Hall. The old quarter of Pfaffenthal, with its medieval buildings. The Fort of Three Acorns. Malakoff Tower. The Church of St. Michael. The Three Towers, marking the outer limits of the town in 1050. Notre Dame Cathedral. The 4th century Chapel of St. Quirinus, one of the oldest shrines in Christendom. The Museum of History and Art. General Patton's grave in the U.S. Military Cemetery, 3 miles away, at Hamm.

Cologne - Mainz - Cologne 700

Here is a way to combine a cruise on the Rhine with a scenic rail trip.

Dep. Cologne (Frankenwerk) by boat	7:00(1)	9:00(2)
Dep. Bonn	9:15	9:40
Dep. Koblenz	14:00	11:05
Arr. Mainz	21:00	13:10

(1) Covered by Eurailpass. Runs daily from mid-April to mid-September. Ticket buyers must pay a supplement for the Koblenz-Mainz portion. (2) Hydrofoil boat express service. Not covered by Eurailpass. Runs daily, except Monday. Runs from early May to early October.

During the Koblenz-Bingen portion of this cruise, you will see the best scenery on the Rhine, many hilltop castles, and the Lorelei. Have lunch and Rhine wine on board just before arriving Mainz. Early in the trip, you can see Drachenfels Castle, near Bonn.

Sights in Mainz: The art collection in the Cathedral. The Museum of the Central Rhineland. The rare books in the World Museum of Printing in the Romischer Kaiser. The restored Baroque mansion on the Schillerplatz and Schillerstrasse, in the Kirschgarten. Old Town. The sculptures in the Diocesan Museum.

Then for the train ride back to Cologne:

662

Dep. Mainz	Frequent times from 7:06 to 22:24
Arr. Koblenz	50 minutes after departing Mainz
Arr. Bonn	1½ hours after departing Mainz
Arr. Cologne	2 hours after departing Mainz

Here is the schedule for visiting Mainz by taking the train both ways:

662

Dep. Cologne (Hbf.)	Frequent times from 7:06 to 22:36.
Arr. Mainz (Kastel)	2 hours later.

* * *

Arr. Cologne (Hbf.)	Frequent times from 7:06 to 22:24.
Dep. Mainz (Kastel)	2 hours later.

Cologne - Siegen - Cologne 636

Dep. Cologne	8:06	9:15	10:12	11:06(1)	12:08
Arr. Siegen	9:56	11:15	11:52	12:31	13:58

Sights in Siegen: The Upper Castle, with its Reubens paintings. (He was born here.) The crypts of the Princes of Nassau-Orange in the Castle.

Dep. Siegen	11:07(1)	12:01	13:04	14:07	14:56(2)
Arr. Cologne	12:48	13:48	14:48	15:45	16:30

(1) Daily, except Sundays and holidays. (2) Plus other departures from Siegen at frequent times from 15:28 to 20:31.

Cologne - Mannheim - Cologne

662

Dep. Cologne	6:57(1)	7:57(1)	8:17(2)	8:57(1+3+7)
Arr. Mannheim	9:24	10:24	11:00	11:24

Sights in Mannheim: The first thing that strikes you about Mannheim is its "Squareness". Built to be a fortified town, it was designed as a chessboard of 144 residential blocks, each known by a letter and number that identifies its position on the grid. The Squared Town. See the Fine Arts Museum. The Reiss Municipal Museum. The Cathedral, Europe's largest Romanesque church. The Water Tower. The old Town Hall and parish church in the Marketplatz. The Castle.

Dep. Mannheim	12:30(1)	13:30(1)	13:46(5)	14:30(1)	15:30(1+8)
Arr. Cologne	14:57	15:57	16:32	16:57	17:57

(1) Supplement charged. Meal service. (2) Light refreshments. (3) Daily, except Sundays and holidays. (4) TEE. Reservation required. Meal service. (5) Meal service. (6) Daily except Saturday. (7) Plus other departures from Cologne at 9:25(2), 9:39(2), 9:57(1), 10:49(4), 10:57(1) and 11:38(5). (8) Plus other departures from Mannheim at 16:30(1), 17:30(1), 18:30(1), 19:30(1), 20:30(1+6) and 21:30(1+6).

Frankfurt - Baden Baden - Frankfurt

664

Dep. Frankfurt	7:25(1)	7:37(2)	8:57	9:37(2)
Arr. Baden Baden	9:31	9:15	11:19	11:15

Sights in Baden Baden: See very lengthy notes about sightseeing in Baden Baden earlier in this chapter ("Basle-Baden Baden", under "Switzerland").

Dep. Baden Baden	13:37(1+3)	15:37(4)	17:57	19:47(1)	21:30
Arr. Frankfurt	15:17	17:48	20:26	22:14	23:39

(1) Light refreshments. (2) Supplement charged. Meal service. (3) Daily, except Saturday. (4) Change trains in Mannheim.

Frankfurt - Basle - Frankfurt

664

Dep. Frankfurt	6:32(1+2)	7:37(1)	9:37(1)	10:37(1+2)
Arr. Basle (Bad Bf.)	9:39	10:40	12:39	13:39
Arr. Basle (S.B.B.)	7 minutes later			

Sights in Basle: The Cathedral, with the tombs of Queen Anne and Erasmus of Rotterdam. The superb Holbein, Delacroix, Gauguin, Matisse, Ingres, Courbet and Van Gogh paintings in the Kunstmuseum. The Historical Museum in the Franciscan church in Barfusserplatz. The

Municipal Casino. The collection of 18th century clothing, ceramics and watches in the Kirschgarten mansion. Shop on Freiestrasse. The 16th century Town Hall. The fishmarket. The 15th century New University. Take a boat excursion from the pier in the back of Hotel Three Kings. The beautiful Munsterplatz. See the view of the city from the Wettstein Bridge.

Dep. Basle (S.B.B.)	14:08(1+3)	15:08(1)	16:08(1+4)	17:29(5)
Dep. Basle (Bad Bf.)	6 minutes later			
Arr. Frankfurt	17:17	18:17	19:17	22:14

(1) Supplement charged. Meal service. (2) Daily, except Sundays and holidays. (3) Change trains in Mannheim. (4) Daily, except Saturday. (5) Light refreshments. (6) Plus other departures from Basle at 18:08(1), 19:08(1+4), 19:23 and 20:08(1).

Frankfurt - Bremen - Frankfurt 664

Dep. Frankfurt	7:23(1+2)	8:23(2)	9:23(1+2)
Arr. Hannover	10:43	11:43	12:43
Change trains.			
Dep. Hannover	11:04	11:48(1)	13:02
Arr. Bremen	12:32	12:50	14:36

Sights in Bremen: It is an easy walk, down Bahnhofstrasse, from the railstation to the fine buildings in Market Square and to the 17th century Rathaus (Town Hall), Liebfrauenkirche, and the 11th century Cathedral, with its ancient crypt. From Market Square, walk down Bottcherstrasse to see the Porcelain Carillon and the Atlantis House, decorated with Zodiac signs.

Visit the Overseas Museum. Rampart Walk. The Focke Museum of Folklore. The Municipal Weights and Measures Office. Martini Church, from which 75-minute harbor cruises depart frequently every day in Summer. See the old workshops, inns and houses in the Schnoor residential area.

Dep. Bremen	16:08(2+3)	17:29
Arr. Hannover	17:05	18:45
Change trains.		
Dep. Hannover	17:10(2+3)	19:10(2+3)
Arr. Frankfurt	20:31	22:31

(1) Daily, except Sundays and holidays. (2) Supplement charged. Meal service. (3) Daily, except Saturday.

Frankfurt - Brussels - Frankfurt 64

Dep. Frankfurt	6:41(1)	6:55(2)	8:29(1+3)	
Arr. Cologne	8:51	9:23(2)	10:51	
Change trains.				
Dep. Cologne	9:06(1)	9:43(2)	11:12(4)	
Arr. Brussels (Nord)	11:19	12:23	13:45	
Arr. Brussels (Midi)	10 minutes later			

Sights in Brussels: See notes about sightseeing in Brussels earlier in this section, under "Cologne-Brussels".

Dep. Brussels (Midi)	15:10(4)	16:00(1)	18:10(1)	18:27(2+6)
Dep. Brussels (Nord)	15:20(4)	16:07(1)	18:20(1)	18:35(2+6)
Arr. Cologne	17:49	18:48	20:44	21:23(2)
Change trains.				
Dep. Cologne	18:03(1)	19:03(1+5)	21:03(1+5)	21:35(2)
Arr. Frankfurt	20:26	21:26	23:14	24:00

(1) Supplement charged. Meal service or light refreshments. (2) Direct train. No train change in Cologne. Light refreshments. (3) Daily, except Sundays and holidays. (4) Daily. Light refreshments. (5) Daily, except Saturday. (6) Reservation required.

Frankfurt - Cologne - Frankfurt 662

Dep. Frankfurt	6:41(1)	7:05(2+3)	7:28(1+4)	8:23(9)
Arr. Cologne	8:51	9:10	9:51	10:43

Sights in Cologne: See notes about city-sightseeing in Cologne at the start of this section.

Dep. Cologne	12:03(1)	13:03(1+6)	14:03(1)	14:11(8+10)
Arr. Frankfurt	14:27	15:27	16:27	16:55

(1) Supplement charged. Meal service. (2) TEE. Reservation required. Meal service. (3) Runs Monday-Friday. Does not run from early June to late August. (4) Daily, except Sundays and holidays. (5) Meal service. (6) Monday-Friday, except holidays. (7) Daily, except Saturday. (8) Light refreshments. (9) Plus other departures from Frankfurt at 8:29(1+4), 8:49, 9:29(1), 9:40, 10:29(1+4) and 11:29(1+4). (10) Plus other departures frm Cologne at 15:03(1+7), 15:06, 16:03(1+7), 17:03(1) 17:44(2+3), 18:03(1), 18:27(8), 19:03(1+7), 19:21, 20:03(1) 21:03(1+7) and 21:35(5).

Frankfurt - Dusseldorf - Frankfurt

662

Dep. Frankfurt	6:41(1)	7:05(2)	8:23	9:28(3)
Arr. Dusseldorf	9:17	9:35	11:15	12:25

Sights in Dusseldorf: See notes about city-sightseeing in Dusseldorf earlier in this section, under "Cologne-Dusseldorf".

Dep. Dusseldorf	12:30(3+4)	13:44(5)	14:31	17:20(6+7)
Arr. Frankfurt	15:26	16:56	18:05	19:51

(1) Supplement charged. Meal service. (2) TEE. Reservation required. Meal service. (3) Supplement charged. (4) Monday-Friday, except holidays. (5) Light refreshments. (6) TEE. Reservation required. Meal service. Monday-Friday. Runs from late August to late May. (7) Plus other departures from Dusseldorf at 17:30(1), 17:52(5), 18:45, 19:35(1) and 21:57(5).

Frankfurt - Essen - Frankfurt

662

Dep. Frankfurt	7:05(1)	7:02(2)	9:28(3)
Arr. Essen	9:59	10:46	12:52

Sights in Essen: See notes about city-sightseeing in Essen earlier in this section, under "Cologne-Essen".

Dep. Essen	13:08(4)	16:55(1)	17:02(5)	18:10	19:30(2+6)
Arr. Frankfurt	16:55	19:51	20:27	22:09	23:20

(1) TEE. Reservation required. Meal service. Runs Monday-Friday. Does not run June, July and August. (2) Runs from late May to late September. (3) Supplement charged. (4) Light refreshments. (5) Supplement charged. Meal service. (6) Plus another departure from Essen. at 21:14(4).

Frankfurt - Hamburg - Frankfurt

664

Dep. Frankfurt	7:02(1)	7:23(2+3)	8:23(2)	9:23(2)
Arr. Hamburg	13:44	12:09	13:09	14:09

Sights in Hamburg: See notes about city-sightseeing in Hamburg earlier in this section under "Cologne-Hamburg".

Dep. Hamburg	15:45(2)	16:45(2)	17:45(2+4)
Arr. Frankfurt	20:31	21:31	22:31

(1) Light refreshments. (2) Supplement charged. Meal service. (3) Daily, except Sundays and holidays. (4) Daily, except Saturday.

Frankfurt - Hannover - Frankfurt

664

Dep. Frankfurt	7:02(1)	7:23(2+3)	8:23(2)	9:23(2+5)
Arr. Hannover	11:33	10:43	11:43	12:43

Sights in Hannover: See notes about sightseeing in Hannover earlier in this section at the start of "One-Day Excursions".

Dep. Hannover	14:07(2)	15:07(2)	16:07(2)	17:07(2+6)
Arr. Frankfurt	17:31	18:31	19:31	20:31

(1) Light refreshments. (2) Supplement charged. Meal service. (3) Daily, except Sundays and holidays. (4) Daily, except Saturday. (5) Plus another departure from Frankfurt at 10:25(2). (6) Plus other departures from Hannover at 18:00(2), 18:07(2) and 19:07(2+4).

Frankfurt - Heidelberg - Frankfurt

662 + 664

Dep. Frankfurt	Frequent times from 7:25 to 21:38
Arr. Heidelberg	One hour later

Sights in Heidelberg: See notes about city-sightseeing in Heidelberg earlier in this section, under "Cologne-Heidelberg".

Dep. Heidelberg	Frequent times from 7:41 to 23:03
Arr. Frankfurt	One hour later

Frankfurt - Luxembourg - Frankfurt

657

Dep. Frankfurt	7:08
Arr. Koblenz	8:52

625

Dep. Koblenz	9:10
Arr. Luxembourg	11:15

625

Dep. Luxembourg	17:40
Arr. Koblenz	19:43

657

Dep. Koblenz	20:03
Arr. Frankfurt	21:58

Sights in Luxembourg: See notes about city-sightseeing in Luxembourg earlier in this section, under "Cologne-Luxembourg".

Frankfurt - Mainz - Frankfurt

	662	662	622	622	662
Dep. Frankfurt	8:25	8:49	10:37	12:38	15:19
Arr. Mainz	30 minutes later				

Sights in Mainz: See notes about city-sightseeing in Mainz earlier in this section, under "Cologne-Mainz".

Dep. Mainz	Frequent times from 11:12 to 23:32
Arr. Frankfurt	30 minutes later

Frankfurt - Mannheim - Frankfurt

664

Dep. Frankfurt	7:37(1)	8:37(1)	9:37(1+2)	10:37(1+2+4)
Arr. Mannheim	50 minutes later			

Sights in Mannheim: See notes about sightseeing in Mannheim earlier in this section, under "Cologne-Mannheim".

Dep. Mannheim	11:33(1)	12:33(1)	13:33(1)	14:33(1+3+5)
Arr. Frankfurt	50 minutes later			

(1) Supplement charged. Meal service. (2) Daily, except Sundays and holidays. (3) Daily, except Saturday. (4) Plus other departures from Frankfurt at 11:37(1+2), 12:37(1) and 13:37(1). (5) Plus other departures from Mannheim at 15:33(1), 16:33(1+3), 17:33(1), 18:33(1+3), 19:33(1), 20'33(1), 21:33(1+3), 22:33(1) and 22:44.

Frankfurt - Munich - Frankfurt

663

Dep. Frankfurt	6:32(1+2)	8:32(1)	9:32(1)
Arr. Munich	10:28	12:23	13:42

Sights in Munich: See notes about city-sightseeing in Munich at the start of this section.

Dep. Munich	12:30(1)	13:14(1)	14:14(1)	15:30(1+4)
Arr. Frankfurt	16:23	17:23	18:23	19:23

(1) Supplement charged. Meal service. (2) Daily, except Sundays and holidays. (3) Daily, except Saturday. (4) Plus other departures from Munich at 16:30(1+3), 17:14(1) and 19:30(1+3).

Frankfurt - Nurnberg (and Bayreuth) - Frankfurt

663

Dep. Frankfurt	7:32(1)	7:54(2)	9:32(1)	10:06(3)
Arr. Nurnberg	9:57	10:51	11:56	12:49

Sights in Nurnberg: The bronze and silver Sebaldusgrab in the 13th century St. Sebaldus Church. The Kaiserburg (Imperial Castle), Burggrafenburg and Imperial Stables in the fort. Albrecht Durer Haus, with copies of his paintings. The Rosette window, wood carving and statues in St. Lorenz Church. The 14th century Frauenkirche. The Alstadt Museum. The collection of toys, doll houses and other works in the Germanic National Museum. The 40 gold figures of artists, emperors, philosophers, prophets and popes around the Schoner Brunnen (Beautiful Fountain).

On the little island in the Pegnitz River, the Holy Ghost Hospital, locale of the legendary Till Eulenspiegel. Disguised as a doctor, this is where the 14th century peasant clown told the man in charge of the hospital that he could cure all the patients in one day.

The hospital authorities believed Till was a miracle worker when the patients rose from their beds and left the hospital after he whispered in each one's ear. "Those of you who are the most sick are going to be burned into a powder the hospital will use to heal the others," he told the patients.

See, every Noon, the moving figures in the clock on the front of the Church of Our Lady in the marketplace, and then lunch at a bratwurst restaurant. One is next to St. Sebaldus Church; another is behind the rebuilt 17th century Rathaus (City Hall). In the Rathaus, there are guided tours of the 14th century catacombs.

In St. Sebaldus, see the carved tomb of the Saint for whom the church is named. Visit the collection of Porcelains at Fembo House (The City Museum), 15 Burgstrasse.

From Nurnberg, it's a short trip to Bayreuth, site of a 5-week annual (over 100 years) Wagner opera festival at Festspielhaus, every year from late July to late August at 16:00. See Haus Wahnfried, Wagner's home. Marvelous sights in Bayreuth: The breathtaking opera house. The Orangerie castle, open daily 10:00-11:30 and 13:30-15:00. Eremitage Park.

Dep. Nurnberg	13:01(1)	14:05(4)	15:01(1)	15:25(3)	16:01(1+5)
Arr. Frankfurt	15:23	16:59	17:23	18:02	18:23

(1)Supplement charged. Meal service. (2)Does not run from mid-July to late August. Meal service. (3)Meal service. (4)Light refreshments. (5)Plus other departures from Nurnberg at 19:01(1), 19:09 and 20:03(1).

Here are the connections between Nurnberg and Bayreuth:

678

Dep. Nurnberg	13:04	15:04	Dep. Bayreuth	16:30	20:37
Arr. Bayreuth	14:19	16:17	Arr. Nurnberg	17:53	21:53

Frankfurt - Siegen - Frankfurt

635

Dep. Frankfurt	6:03	Dep. Siegen	12:00
Arr. Siegen	7:55	Arr. Frankfurt	13:55

Sights in Siegen: The Upper Castle, with its Reubens paintings. (He was born here.) The crypts of the Princes of Nassau-Orange in the Castle.

Frankfurt - Strasbourg - Frankfurt

670

Dep. Frankfurt	7:25	9:37	Dep. Strasbourg	16:20(1)	19:33(2)
Arr. Strasbourg	10:05	12:28	Arr. Frankfurt	20:26	22:26

(1)Change trains in Offenburg. (2)Daily, except Sundays and holidays. Supplement charged. Change trains in Offenburg.

Sights in Strasbourg: The famous astronomical clock in the Cathedral. The Alsatian Museum at 23 Quai St. Nicolas. Place Kleber. The Chateau des Rohan museums of archaeology, fine arts and decorative arts.

Frankfurt - Stuttgart - Frankfurt

662

Dep. Frankfurt	6:07	7:56(1)	8:37(2)	9:15(1)	9:40
Arr. Stuttgart	8:38	10:17	10:51	11:29	12:06

Sights in Stuttgart: Outstanding contemporary architecture, built since World War II. Liederhalle, with its 3 concert halls. The Schillerplatz flower and vegetable market (Tuesday, Thursday and Saturday).

Dep. Stuttgart	11:26	15:13(1)	16:49(1)	19:44(1)	21:07
Arr. Frankfurt	14:12	17:20	19:20	22:01	23:59

(1)Light refreshments. (2)Supplement charged. Meal service.

Frankfurt - Wiesbaden - Frankfurt

657 + 662

Dep. Frankfurt	Frequent times from 7:07 to 20:08
Arr. Wiesbaden	30-40 minutes later

Sights in Wiesbaden: One of Europe's top mineral bath resorts. See the longest colonnade in Europe: Brunnenkolonnade.

Dep. Wiesbaden	Frequent times from 6:21 to 22:53
Arr. Frankfurt	30-40 minutes later

Hannover - Berlin - Hannover

764

Dep. Hannover	8:10(1)	10:11(1)
Arr. Berlin (Zoo)	11:35	13:52

Sights in Berlin: See lengthy notes about sightseeing in Berlin earlier in this section, under "The Island of West Berlin".

Dep. Berlin (Zoo)	15:44(1)	16:49	23:31(2)	23:55(2)	0:35(3)
Arr. Hannover	19:27	20:15	3:11	3:46	4:06

(1) Meal service. (2) Carries sleeping car. Also has couchettes. (3) Carries sleeping car. Runs from late May to late September.

Hannover - Bremen - Hannover

645

Dep. Hannover	7:48(1)	9:21	11:01	11:48(2)	12:58
Arr. Bremen	9:05	10:46	12:28	12:49	14:29

Sights in Bremen: See notes about sightseeing in Bremen earlier in this section, under "Frankfurt-Bremen".

Dep. Bremen	13:08(3)	13:14	14:11	15:04	16:08(4+5)
Arr. Hannover	14:05	14:49	15:34	16:35	17:05

(1) Light refreshments. (2) Daily, except Sundays and holidays. (3) Supplement charged. Meal service. (4) Daily, except Saturday. (5) Plus other departures from Bremen at 16:15, 17:04(4), 17:25, 19:04, 20:53, 22:28 and 23:53.

Hannover - Celle - Hannover 658

Dep. Hannover	9:21	10:10	11:51	12:50
Arr. Celle	25 minutes later			

Sights in Celle: The 13th century Duke's Castle. The marvelous 16th-19th century homes in the old section. The 14th century Church and Town Hall. The Museum, with its Lower Saxon exhibits.

Dep. Celle	12:08	13:19	14:30	15:41	16:33	19:48(1)
Arr. Hannover	25 minutes later					

(1) Plus other departures from Celle at frequent times from 20:13 to 0:10.

Hannover - Frankfurt - Hannover 664

Dep. Hannover	6:10(1+2)	7:10(1+2)	7:51(3)	8:10(1+2+6)
Arr. Frankfurt	9:30	10:31	12:06	11:31

Sights in Frankfurt: See notes about sightseeing in Frankfurt at the start of this section on West German "One-Day Excursions".

Dep. Frankfurt	15:04(3)	15:23(1+4)	16:23(1)	17:02(3+7)
Arr. Hannover	18:30	18:43	19:43	21:20

(1) Supplement charged. Meal service. (2) Daily, except Sundays and holidays. (3) Light refreshments. (4) Daily, except Saturday. (5) Adjustment footnote. (6) Plus other departures from Hannover at 8:35(3), 9:10(1) and 10:10(1). (7) Plus other departures from Frankfurt at 17:23(1+4), 18:23(1), 19:23(1+4) and 20:33(1+4).

Hannover - Goslar 653

Dep. Hannover	7:24(1)	7:55(2)	10:36
Arr. Goslar	8:36	9:19	11:48

Sights in Goslar: The many 13th-16th century half-timbered buildings and 19th century houses. The Eagle Fountain. The five 13th century churches. The chandeliers of reindeer horns in the 15th century Town Hall. The 16th century towers and old city walls. The 11th century Imperial Palace. The museums of natural science and antiquities. Goslar is a popular base for touring the Harz Mountains.

Dep. Goslar	12:27	13:19	15:15	16:32(3)	17:23(4)
Arr. Hannover	13:47	14:33	16:33	18:02	18:51

(1) Sundays and holidays only. (2) Daily, except Sundays and holidays. (3) Change trains in Lehrte. (4) Plus other departures from Goslar at 18:47 and 21:27.

Hannover - Hamburg - Hannover 658

Dep. Hannover (Hbf.)	6:21	7:43	9:21(1)	10:45(2+3+5)
Arr. Hamburg (Hbf.)	8:19	9:39	11:10	12:09

Sights in Hamburg: See notes about sightseeing in Hamburg earlier in this section, under "Cologne-Hamburg".

Dep. Hamburg (Hbf.)	12:45(2)	12:55(1)	13:45(2)	14:30(2+6)
Arr. Hannover (Hbf.)	14:08	14:57	15:08	16:03

(1) Light refreshments. (2) Supplement charged. Meal service. (3) Daily, except Sundays and holidays. (4) Daily, except Saturday. (5) Plus other departures from Hannover at 11:45(2) and 12:45(2). (6) Plus other departures from Hamburg at 14:45(2), 14:55, 15:45(2), 16:45(2), 17:45(2+4), 18:00, 18:50(1), 19:55 and 20:55.

Hannover - Hameln - Hannover

654

Dep. Hannover	7:38	10:23	12:54	13:20	
Arr. Hameln	35-50 minutes later				

Sights in Hameln: Every Sunday at Noon (mid-May through mid-September), see the reenactment of the Pied Piper leading children through the Town Square. Take the 90-minute guided walking tour (10:00-11:30) from the tourist information office. A stroll through the surrounding woods is pleasant. Or, try a steamboat trip on the Weser River.

Dep. Hameln	13:37	14:49	15:52	19:16	20:29(1)
Arr. Hannover	35-50 minutes later				

(1) Plus another departure from Hameln at 21:49.

Hannover - Hildesheim - Hannover

653

Dep. Hannover	7:24(1)	7:55(2)	10:35	13:25	14:19
Arr. Hildesheim	25-30 minutes later				

Sights in Hildesheim: The supposedly 1,100-year old rose tree (probably 300-500 years old) which survived World War II bombings that literally destroyed the city, on the grounds of the Cathedral, which houses marvelous 11th century art. Also see the Egyptian and Greco-Roman objects in the Roemer und Pelizaeus Museum. The 12th century painted ceiling in St. Michael's Church. The 15th century Tempelhaus. The Gothic Town Hall.

Take a local train for the short ride to Nordstemmen and then it is a 20-minute walk from that railstation to see the medieval castle, Schloss Marianburg.

Dep. Hildesheim	11:42	13:10	14:06	16:03	18:20(3)
Arr. Hannover	25-30 minutes later				

(1) Sundays and holidays only. (2) Daily, except Sundays and holidays. (3) Plus other departures from Hildesheim at 19:36 and 22:27.

Hannover - Kassel - Hannover

There is beautiful Fulda River Valley scenery 20 minutes before arriving in Kassel.

664

All of these trains have light refreshments, unless designated otherwise.

Dep. Hannover	7:51	8:35	10:40
Arr. Kassel	9:49	10:35	12:38

Sights in Kassel: Take the bus #13 to see the enormous 233-foot high statue of Hercules, the 19th century Wilhelmshohe Castle, and the art museums inside the Castle. Open daily except Monday, March-October, 10:00-17:00. Also see the collection of Brothers Grimm memorabilia in the City Museum. They wrote their fairy tales here. Other interesting sights are the 18th century Orangery Palace in Karlsaue Park. The paintings in the Landesmuseum. The Tapestry Museum. The Fredericianum Museum.

Dep. Kassel	13:07	15:01	16:57	19:21
Arr. Hannover	15:25	17:04	19:02	21:20

Hannover - Luneburg - Hannover

658

Dep. Hannover	7:43	9:21(1)	10:10	11:51(1)	12:50(2)
Arr. Luneburg	9:00	10:32	11:40	13:08	13:48

Sights in Luneburg: The twisted-brick cornices on many old buildings. Fine art pieces in the churches: St. Nicholas, St. John and St. Michael. The 18th century crane at the waterfront. Guided tours of Town Hall, constructed over 5 centuries (1300-1800). The 17th century Ducal Palace.

Dep. Luneburg	11:06	12:21	13:35(1)	15:03(2)	15:33(4)
Arr. Hannover	12:34	13:45	14:56	16:03	16:59

(1) Light refreshments. (2) Supplement charged. Meal service. (3) Daily, except Saturday. (4) Plus other departures from Luneburg at 18:40, 19:27(1), 20:32, 21:32 and 22:47.

Munich - Augsburg - Munich

662

Dep. Munich	Frequent times from 6:43 to 23:31
Arr. Augsburg	30-40 minutes later

Sights in Augsburg: The 11th century bronze doors, Romanesque stained-glass and Holbein altarpiece at the Cathedral. The three 16th century fountains. The Mozart Museum in the house of the composer's father. The collection of manuscripts and drawings in the Municipal Library.

Dep. Augsburg	Frequent times from 8:23 to 0:32
Arr. Munich	30-40 minutes later

Munich - Bayreuth - Munich

658

Dep. Munich	10:05	12:18	
Arr. Nurnberg	12:42	14:50	

Change trains.

678

Dep. Nurnberg	13:04	15:04	
Arr. Bayreuth	14:19	16:17	

Sights in Bayreuth: See notes about sightseeing in Bayreuth earlier in this section, under "Frankfurt-Bayreuth".

Dep. Bayreuth	14:40	16:30	20:37
Arr. Nurnberg	15:52	17:53	21:53

Change trains.

658

Dep. Nurnberg	16:02	18:11	22:02(1)
Arr. Munich	17:45	20:36	23:46

(1) Supplement charged. Meal service.

Munich - Frankfurt - Munich

662

Dep. Munich	6:30(1+2)	7:15(1+2)	8:30(1)	9:14(1+2)
Arr. Frankfurt	10:23	11:23	12:23	13:23

Sights in Frankfurt: See notes about city-sightseeing in Frankfurt at the start of this section.

Dep. Frankfurt	14:32(1)	15:32(1+3)	16:32(1)	17:32(1+4+5)
Arr. Munich	18:26	19:44	20:23	21:45

(1) Supplement charged. Meal service. (2) Daily, except Sundays and holidays. (3) Monday-Friday, except holidays. (4) Daily, except Saturday. (5) Plus other departures from Frankfurt at 18:32(1+4) and 19:32(1).

Munich - Heidelberg - Munich

662

Dep. Munich	6:43(1+2)	6:55(3)	7:43(1)	8:43(1+5)
Arr. Heidelberg	10:12	11:06	11:12	12:12

Sights in Heidelberg: See notes about city-sightseeing in Heidelberg earlier in this section, under "Cologne-Heidelberg".

Dep. Heidelberg	13:40(1)	14:40(1)	15:40(1)	16:40(1+6)
Arr. Munich	17:10	18:10	19:10	20:10

(1) Supplement charged. Meal service. (2) Daily, except Sundays and holidays. (3) Light refreshments. (4) Daily, except Saturday. (5) Plus another departure from Munich at 9:43(1). (6) Plus other departures from Heidelberg at 17:40(1+4), 17:43(3), 18:40(1), 19:41(1) and 20:48.

Munich - Innsbruck - Munich

758

Dep. Munich	7:40(1)	8:05(2+3)	8:24(3+4)
Arr. Innsbruck	9:50	10:21	10:31

Sights in Innsbruck: Marvelous Winter resort. Gateway to many cable railway trips (Hungerburg, Hafelekar, Igls, Patscherkofel). See the gilded copper shingles on Goldenes Dachl (Golden Roof). The 18th century Roman style Triumphal Arch. The paintings and furniture in the 18th century Hofburg Palace. The enormous and magnificent tomb of Maximilian I and the effigy of King Arthur in the 16th century Imperial Church. The silver altar at the Silver Chapel. Costumes and rustic furniture in the Tyrolean Folk Art Museum.

Dep. Innsbruck	12:08(5)	12:26(1+3)	14:12(2)	15:10(6)
Arr. Munich	13:54	14:33	16:25	18:24

(1) Meal service. (2) Light refreshments. (3) Runs from late May to late September. (4) Departs/Arrives Munich's Ost station. (5) TEE. Reservation required. Meal service. (6) Plus other departures from Innsbruck at 18:38(2+3), 19:12(2+3), 20:00(1) and 23:35(3+4).

Munich - Mainz - Munich

662

Dep. Munich	6:43(1+2)	8:43(1)	9:43(1)	
Arr. Mainz	11:11	13:11	14:11	

Sights in Mainz: See notes about city-sightseeing in Mainz earlier in this section, under "Cologne-Mainz".

Dep. Mainz	13:43(1)	14:43(1)	15:43(1)	16:43(1+3+5)
Arr. Munich	18:10	19:10	20:10	21:13

(1)Supplement charged. Meal service. (2)Daily, except Sundays and holidays. (3)Daily, except Saturday. (4)Light refresments. (5)Plus other departures from Mainz at 17:43(1) and 19:30(4).

Munich - Mannheim - Munich

662

Dep. Munich	5:43(1+2)	6:43(1+3)	7:43(1)	8:43(1+6)
Arr. Mannheim	9:27	10:27	11:26	12:27

Sights in Mannheim: See notes about city-sightseeing in Mannheim earlier in this section, under "Cologne-Mannheim".

Dep. Mannheim	13:27(1)	14:27(1)	15:27(1)	16:27(1+7)
Arr. Munich	17:10	18:10	19:10	20:10

(1)Supplements charged. Meal service. (2)Monday-Friday, except holidays. (3)Daily, except Sundays and holidays. (4)Daily, except Saturday. (5)Light refreshments. (6)Plus other departures from Munich at 9:43(1) and 10:43(1). (7)Plus other departures from Mannheim at 17:27(1+4), 18:27(1), 19:28(1) and 20:32(5).

Munich - Nurnberg - Munich

663

Dep. Munich	7:15(1+2)	8:15(1)	9:15(1+2)	10:15(1+3+6)
Arr. Nurnberg	8:55	9:55	10:55	11:55

Sights in Nurnberg: See notes about city-sightseeing in Nurnberg earlier in this section, under "Frankfurt-Nurnberg".

Dep. Nurnberg	13:02(1)	14:02(1)	14:07	15:02(1+7)
Arr. Munich	14:42	15:42	16:05	16:42

(1) Supplement charged. Meal service. (2) Daily, except Sundays and holidays. (3)Daily, except Saturday. (4)Meal service. (5)Monday-Friday, except holidays. (6)Plus other departures from Munich at 11:13(1) and 12:13(1+3). (7)Plus other departures from Nurnberg at 15:17, 16:02(1), 16:14, 17:02(1), 18:02(1+5), 18:11, 19:02(1), 20:02(1+3), 20:06, 21:02(1+3) and 22:02(1).

Munich - Oberammergau - Munich

683

Dep. Munich	7:30(1)	8:50	10:00	11:00	12:00
Arr. Murnau	8:27	9:51	10:55	11:55	12:55

Change trains.

682

Dep. Murnau	8:33	10:03	11:03	12:15	13:12
Arr. Oberammergau	9:10	10:45	11:45	12:55	13:54

Sights in Oberammergau: Every year ending in zero (1980, 1990, etc.), the famous Passion Play. Three hundred years ago the villagers here promised to produce this play every 10 years if the Black Plague ended. In the interval between decades, you can still see the unique theater and enjoy this interesting woodcarving capital of Bavaria. There is time to take a bus trip and see the lapis lazuli, gilt and crystal in King Ludwig II's glorious palace, Schloss Linderhof.

682

Dep. Oberammergau	10:05	11:05	12:11	13:10	15:13(3)
Arr. Murnau	10:45	11:45	12:52	13:52	15:53

Change trains.

683

Dep. Murnau	10:59	11:59(2)	12:58	13:58	16:04
Arr. Munich	11:56	12:56	13:58	14:55	17:13

(1)Light refreshments. (2)Supplement charged. Meal service. (3)Plus other departures from Oberammergau at 16:13, 17:10, 18:19, and 19:57.

Munich - Salzburg - Munich

684

Dep. Munich	7:19(1)	7:55(2)	9:02(1)	9:22(2)	9:46(2+5)
Arr. Salzburg	9:27	9:38	10:42	11:05	11:27

Sights in Salzburg: The most amusing place in Europe, the 17th century Hellbrun Palace. The 16th century 200-pipe barrel organ in the 12th century fortress, 500 feet above the town, Festung Hohensalzburg. The traditional Music Festival (last week of July until the end of August). The State Rooms in The Residenz, the 17th century city palace of Salzburg's archbishops. The painted ceilings in the 17th century Festspeilhaus. The collection of Mozart musical instruments and family memorabilia in the Mozart Museum, his birthplace. The vast musical library at Bibliotheca Mozartiana. St. Sebastian's Cemetery at Linzergasse 41. The 17th century Cathedral. The Universitatkirche. The Gothic cloister in the 9th century Benedictine Abbey of St. Peter. The Glockenspiel Tower, particularly at 7:00, 11:00 and 18:00 for the Carillon concerts. The ancient marketplace, Alter Markt. The marble Angel Staircase in the 17th century Schloss Mirabell, and the garden there. Take the cable car to the top (5,800 feet) of Untersberg for a breathtaking view of Salzburg and the Alps.

Dep. Salzburg	13:45(1)	14:47	15:31(3)	16:13	17:41(1+6)
Arr. Munich	15:33	16:58	17:31	18:24	19:59

(1)Light refreshments. (2)Meal service. (3)Supplement charged. Meal service. (4)Runs from late June to late August. (5)Plus other departures from Munich at 10:20 and 11:31. (6)Plus other departures from Salzburg at 18:52(2), 19:05(1), 19:54(4) and 20:47(2).

Munich - Stuttgart - Munich

662

Dep. Munich	Frequent times from 6:55 to 23:30
Arr. Stuttgart	2-3 hours later

Sights in Stuttgart: See notes about city-sightseeing in Stuttgart earlier in this section, under "Frankfurt-Stuttgart".

Dep. Stuttgart	Frequent times from 5:53 to 22:26
Arr. Munich	2-3 hours later

Munich - Tegernsee and Schliersee - Munich

1000

Take a local train from Holzkirchner Bahnhof, a wing of Munich's Hauptbahnhof, for this 36-mile ride.

At the northern end of Tegernsee (an exceptionally beautiful lake) is Gmund, not to be confused with the 2 Austrian villages also named Gmund. A mile away from this Gmund is a smaller lake, Schliersee. It is only a 4-mile walk around Schliersee. There is a lovely view of the lake from the ruins of Hohenwaldeck Castle and also from one of the many benches along the lake's shore. Also much sports (tennis, sailing, swimming) in this area. The Taubenstein mountain railway goes to an area that provides extensive mountain hiking. Wandering through the Weissachau Wildlife preserve, with its rare flowers, is worthwhile. Local food specialties in this region are white sausage, liver loaf, big white radishes and spicy Miesbacher cheese.

Sights in Tegernsee: The concerts (May-September) in the enormous Baroque dining hall of the Castle. The large collection of rustic furniture, weapons, craft utensils, traditional costumes and ancient books in the Tegernsee Museum. The drawings, illustrations, sketches and caricatures by Olaf Gulbransson at the Kurpark Museum. The lakeside gambling casino. The 10-minute boat trip (every half hour) across the lake to Wiessee. Both Tegernsee and Wiessee have been popular for centuries for their curative mineral waters, laden with iodine and sulphur. Swimming in the pure lake is marvelous.

Take the cable car from nearby Rottach-Egern to the top of Wallberg for a view of the Tegernsee Valley and Austria's highest peak, the Grossglockner.

Munich - Wurzburg - Munich 658

Dep. Munich	6:30(1+2)	7:30(1+2)	9:30(1)	10:30(1+3)
Arr. Wurzburg	8:57	9:57	11:57	12:57

Sights in Wurzburg: Vineyards and wineries galore. The tourist information center is located in Falcon House, on the square where bratwurst, vegetables, fruits and flowers are sold. See the Main-Franconia Museum (sculptures, wine presses, etc.) in the 13th century Marienberg Fortress. The view of the city from the restaurant at the Fortress. The roccoco garden in the nearby Schloss Veitshochheim. The 12 statues of saints on the Old Main Bridge. Pilgrimage Church. The Tiepolo ceiling and the Emperor's Hall, in the Residenz. Neumunster Church. The Cathedral. The fine sculptures in the Mainfrankisches Museum at the Festung. Take a boat trip on the River Main to see Randersacker and Sommerhausen.

Dep. Wurzburg	12:58(1+2)	13:58(1)	16:58(1)	18:58(1+3+5)
Arr. Munich	15:25	16:25	19:25	21:28

(1) Supplement charged. Meal service. (2) Daily, except Sundays and holidays. (3) Daily, except Saturday. (4) Light refreshments. (5) Plus other departures from Wurzburg at 19:21, 20:58(1+3) and 21:58(3+4).

Munich - Ulm - Munich 662

Dep. Munich	Frequent times from 6:55 to 23:30
Arr. Ulm	70-80 minutes later

Sights in Ulm: The Bakery Museum (tools, library, artwork pertaining to bread) on Fuerstenecker Strasse. The display there includes breads made in ancient Egypt and in the Middle Ages. Open Monday-Friday 10:00-12:00 and 15:00-17:30.

The 14th century Gothic Cathedral, which has one of the highest towers (528 feet) in the world. The 17th century Schworhaus, where Town Council members once took their oaths to perform their duties (where they were "sworn in").

Dep. Ulm	Frequent times from 7:13 to 23:39
Arr. Munich	70-80 minutes later

Munich - Zurich - Munich 685

Dep. Munich	9:05(1)	Dep. Zurich	16:19(1)
Arr. Zurich	13:50	Arr. Munich	21:13

(1) Light refreshments.

Sights in Zurich: Here is a great 2-hour walk. Upon arriving at the Zurich railstation, take the escalator down one level and enjoy a snack or meal in Shopville, the enormous underground shopping center under Bahnhof Platz, just alongside the station. Come up from Shopville on the other side of Bahnhof Platz, and then walk one mile down one side of Bahnhofstrasse, lined with smart stores, until this city's Fifth Avenue ends at the shore of Lake Zurich. After viewing the lakeside promenade, return to the railstation down the opposite side of Bahnhofstrasse that you walked earlier. Upon returning to the station, go all the way through it, cross Museumstrasse, and visit the National Museum. Other sights to see: the Bellevue Platz amusement center. The paintings and sculptures at the Kunsthaus. African and Asian art at the Rietberg Museum. Kunstgewerbemuseum (The Museum of Applied Arts: handicrafts, architecture and industrial design).

SCENIC RAIL TRIPS

Cologne - Koblenz - Bullay - Cologne

There is beautiful farm, mountain and vineyard scenery on this easy one-day trip through the Moselle Valley.

662					
Dep. Cologne	7:57(1)	9:03(1)	10:47(1)	12:57(1)	
Arr. Koblenz	8:49	9:55	11:46	13:49	
Change trains.					
625					
Dep. Koblenz	9:10	10:10	12:10	14:10(2)	
Arr. Bullay	9:53	10:50	12:51	14:50	
	*	*	*		
Dep. Bullay	12:59	14:59	17:02	19:02	20:59
Arr. Koblenz	13:43	15:43	17:43	19:43	21:43
Change trains.					
662					
Dep. Koblenz	13:58(1)	16:04(1)	17:58(1)	20:04(1)	21:58(1+3)
Arr. Cologne	14:51	16:57	18:51	20:57	22:51

(1) Supplement charged. Meal service or light refreshments. (2) Monday-Friday, except holidays. (3) Daily, except Saturday.

Cologne - Mainz

Fine mountain, vineyard and Rhine river scenery. Complete schedules appear under the "Cologne-Mainz-Cologne" one-day excursion.

Cologne - Siegen - Frankfurt - Cologne

Excellent mountain scenery on this ride, which can be made as a circle trip from either Cologne or Frankfurt.

636

Dep. Cologne	10:12
Arr. Siegen	11:52

Change trains.

635

Dep. Siegen	12:00
Arr. Frankfurt	13:55

662

Dep. Frankfurt	14:29(1+2)	15:29(1)	15:42(3)	16:29(1)	16:37(4+6)
Arr. Cologne	16:51	17:51	18:29	18:51	18:43

(1) Supplement charged. Meal service. (2) Daily, except Saturday. (3) Meal service. (4) TEE. Monday-Friday, except holidays. Reservation required. Meal service. (5) Light refreshments. (6) Plus other departures from Frankfurt at 17:08(5), 17:29(1), 18:11(3), 18:29(1), 19:29(1), 20:29(1+2) and 21:49(1).

Here is the Frankfurt version of this circle trip:

635

Dep. Frankfurt	6:01	10:02
Arr. Siegen	7:54	11:56

Change trains.

636

Dep. Siegen	8:17	12:01
Arr. Cologne	9:47	13:56

657

Dep. Cologne	10:26(1)	16:40
Arr. Frankfurt	13:12	20:23

(1) Light refreshments.

Freiburg - Donaueschingen

The train runs through the heart of the Black Forest. Very good mountain scenery on this spur of the Frankfurt-Basle route.

664

Dep. Frankfurt	6:30(1+2)	13:37(1)
Arr. Freiburg	9:01	16:01

Change trains.

690

Dep. Freiburg	9:51(2)	16:09
Arr. Donaueschingen	11:28	17:44

* * *

Dep. Donaueschingen	12:56	17:50
Arr. Freiburg	14:30	19:30

Change trains.

664

Dep. Freiburg	15:04(1)	20:02(1)
Arr. Basle (S.B.B.)	15:46	20:46

(1) Supplement charged. Meal service. (2) Daily, except Sundays and holidays. (3) Meal service.

Koblenz - Giessen

There is fine river scenery on this easy one-day roundtrip. This area can also be seen by taking an indirect route from Koblenz to Frankfurt. For the first way:

650

Dep. Koblenz	9:12(1)	11:12(1)	14:19		
Arr. Giessen	11:23	13:06	16:18		
		*	*	*	
Dep. Giessen	11:38	13:28	16:19	17:52	18:41
Arr. Koblenz	14:18	15:42	18:30	20:00	21:26

Here is the long route to Frankfurt that offers the same scenery:

650

Dep. Koblenz	7:01(1)	9:12(1)	11:12(1)	14:19
Arr. Giessen	9:09	11:22	13:06	16:18

Change trains.

664

Dep. Giessen	9:39	11:23	14:05	17:16
Arr. Frankfurt	10:24	12:08	14:44	18:04

(1) Daily, except Sundays and holidays. (2) Monday-Friday, except holidays

The schedule for the reverse trip:

664

Dep. Frankfurt	10:02	10:41	12:31	14:31	17:02
Arr. Giessen	10:53	11:26	13:16	15:15	17:45

Change trains.

650

Dep. Giessen	10:58(1)	11:38	13:28	16:19	17:52
Arr. Koblenz	12:44	14:18	15:42	18:30	20:00

(1) Daily, except Sundays and holidays.

Munich - Innsbruck - Garmisch - Zugspitz - Munich

Fine mountain scenery on this easy one-day circle trip.

758

Dep. Munich	7:40(1)	8:05(2)	8:24(2)	10:06(3)	13:38(4)
Arr. Innsbruck	9:50	10:21	10:31	12:25	15:51

Change trains.

756

Dep. Innsbruck	10:45	11:45(5)	13:53	14:56(5)	16:45(7)
Arr. Garmisch	12:22	13:24	15:26	16:23	18:24

(1) Meal service. (2) Runs from late May to late September. Light refreshments. (3) Runs from mid-July to late September. (4) Light refreshments. (5) Privilege train (no border formalities). Special ticket required.

(6) Change trains in Mittenwald. (7) Plus other departures from Innsbruck at 17:42(6) and 18:25(5).

The following schedule allows one to ride one cable railway to the summit of Zugspitz and ride a different cable railway en route back to Garmisch.

693				
Dep. Garmisch	13:00	14:00	15:00	16:00(1)
Arr. Eibsee	13:38	14:38	15:38	16:38
Change trains.				
Dep. Eibsee	13:45	14:45	15:45	16:45
Arr. Zugspitz	13:55	14:55	15:55	16:55
Change trains.				
Dep. Zugspitz	14:00	15:00	16:00	17:00
Arr. Schneefernerhaus	14:04	15:04	16:04	17:04
Change trains.				
Dep. Schneefernerhaus	14:25	15:25	16:25	17:25
Arr. Garmisch	15:45	16:45	17:45	18:45
Change trains.				
683				
Dep. Garmisch	16:34	17:32	18:41	20:06
Arr. Munich	17:56	18:56	20:19	21:34

(1) Runs July and August.

Munich - Nurnberg - Heilbronn - Heidelberg

This schedule follows the route of the "Castle Road" and "Romantic Road" bus trips.

663				
Dep. Munich	10:14(1+2)	11:14(1)	12:14(1)	13:14(1)
Arr. Nurnberg	11:55	12:55	13:55	14:55
Change trains.				
679				
Dep. Nurnberg	-0-	-0-	-0-	15:22(3)
Arr. Heilbronn	-0-	-0-	-0-	17:24
Change trains.				
Dep. Heilbronn	-0-	-0-	-0-	17:30
Arr. Heidelberg	-0-	-0-	-0-	18:55

(1) Supplement charged. Meal service. (2) Daily, except Saturday. (3) Light refreshments.

Munich - Salzburg

This route offers good mountain scenery and is an easy one-day roundtrip. See schedules earlier in this section, under "One-Day Excursions".

Offenburg - Konstanz - Offenburg 675

This trip is recommended for exceptional mountain scenery.

Dep. Offenburg	8:07	8:42(1)	10:37	12:43(1)	13:32	14:45
Arr. Konstanz	10:37	11:16	13:02	15:34	16:06	17:23
		*	*	*		
Dep. Konstanz	11:50	13:40	14:42	16:34	18:18	21:00(2)
Arr. Offenburg	14:12	16:08	17:08	19:06	20:50	23:23

(1) Daily, except Sundays and holidays. (2) Daily, except Saturday.

Offenburg - Singen - Schaffhausen

Excellent Black Forest scenery on this route. This trip can also be made as a detour en route from Frankfurt to Basle.

675					
Dep. Offenburg	8:07	10:37	12:43	13:32(1)	15:53
Arr. Singen	10:10	12:36	14:58	15:38	17:58
Change trains.					
668					
Dep. Singen	11:38	14:39	-0-	17:38	19:38
Arr. Schaffhausen	11:54	14:54	-0-	17:54	19:54

(1) Meal service.

Here is the detour from the Frankfurt-Basle ride:

664	
Dep. Frankfurt	7:35(1)
Arr. Offenburg	10:02
Change trains.	
675	
Dep. Offenburg	10:38
Arr. Singen	12:38
Change trains.	
674	
Dep. Singen	12:41
Arr. Schaffhausen	12:55
Dep. Schaffhausen	12:57
Arr. Basle (Bad Bf.)	14:06

(1) Light refreshments.

Wurzburg - Zurich

Exceptional Black Forest scenery on this ride.

672				
Dep. Wurzburg	9:59	12:22	15:08	17:06(1)
Arr. Stuttgart	12:16	14:45	17:30	19:19
Change trains.				
668				
Dep. Stuttgart	12:31(1)	15:18(1)	17:13(1)	20:18(2)
Arr. Zurich	15:44	18:44	20:44	23:44

(1) Light refreshments. (2) Reservation required.

RHINE RIVER CRUISES

A variety of cruising on the Rhine is offered. The complete 5-day downstream route (from Basle to Amsterdam or Rotterdam) and the complete 6-day upstream route (Amsterdam or Rotterdam to Basle) are offered April to October.

A shorter portion (Rotterdam-Strasbourg and vice versa) is also available April to October. It is 4 days downstream and 5 upstream.

Still another service (3 days downstream and 4 upstream), between Amsterdam or Rotterdam and Mainz, is offered April to September.

On any of these, passengers may stop-over at points en route and resume the journey later (Dusseldorf, Cologne, etc.).

The most popular stretch of the Rhine, Dusseldorf to Frankfurt, is covered by the Eurailpass. This is the portion famed for scenic vineyards and hilltop castles. The entire Rhine trip is not covered by Eurailpass. With a Eurailpass, there is no charge for either the Mainz-Cologne boat trip or for the Cologne-Mainz train ride.

The scenery between Mainz and Koblenz can be seen as well from a train as from a boat because the track on this run goes along the river bank.

Here are the schedules for taking the boat Mainz-Cologne and returning to Mainz by train the same day:

700 (Boat)		662 (Train)		
Dep. Mainz	8:45(1)	Dep. Cologne (Hbf.)	18:46(2)	19:21(5)
Arr. Koblenz	13:20	Dep. Koblenz	19:48(2)	20:36
Arr. Cologne (Frankenwrft.)	18:00	Arr. Mainz	20:59	21:36

(1) Runs from mid-April to late October. (2) Light refreshments. (3) Supplement charged. Meal service or light refreshments. (4) Daily, except Saturday. (5) Plus other departures from Cologne at 21:03(3+4), 21:35(3) and 22:36(3).

SCENIC BUS TRIPS COVERED BY EURAILPASS

Both of these extremely popular bus trips are covered by Eurailpass: "Romantische Strasse" (Romantic Road) and "Burgenstrasse" (Castle Road). Advance seat reservations should be made. They can be obtained at no cost by writing to: Bahnbusverkehrstelle, Hauptbahnhof, Augsburg, West Germany. Be sure to indicate the dates you want to journey, which of the 2 different lines you want to travel, where you will start and end your trip, and the number of seats you want.

Passengers are allowed to break the journey at as many stops as they desire on both bus lines, and we recommend some specific places to do so in the text that follows. If that is your plan, be sure to provide all the specific dates this will involve when requesting a reservation.

The 2 lines connect in Rothenburg, making it easy to ride on all or part of both trips. Lodging in Rothenburg is good quality, but the supply is small and the demand very great. The Encyclopedia Britannica calls Rothenburg "probably the finest surviving example of a medieval town". It has been there for 1,000 years. Its 30 watchtowers and many dungeons, churches, patrician homes, ornamental fountains and market squares are perfectly preserved.

The town's most important buildings are on the old Market Square: Town Hall, Virgin's Pharmacy (Marienapotheque), the lovely stone fountain (Herterichbrunnen), the ancient city council drinking hall, and the mechanical clock that performs at 11:00, 13:00 and 14:00 the Meistertrunk legend.

When the town was under siege in the 17th century, the commander of the victorious Imperial Army was given his first taste of wine by the inhabitants. He offered to spare the lives of the city officials if any of them could empty in one drink the content of a tankard holding almost one gallon. One burgermeister rose to the challenge, accomplished the feat, and even quaffed more.

That 3.24 liter Meistertrunk tankard is on display in the town's Reichstadt Museum. The legend is recreated every year in a pageant held on Whitsunday, 7 weeks after Easter.

Statues of the 7 deadly sins and 7 virtues adorn the Baumeisterhaus, on Schmiedgasse, near Market Square. This chiseled house is well worth seeing. The torture museum at the Dominican Nunnery is another attraction in the town.

Rothenburg has 15 hotels with 11 to 145 rooms each. It is an ideal stopover either for breaking the Romantische Strasse ride into 2 days or for transferring from or to the Burgenstrasse ride.

Another recommended stopover on the Romantische Strasse ride is Dinkelsbuhl, another finely preserved medieval town with a surfeit of gates, bastions, towers, a moat equipped with floating swans and a sharp sense of ancient history. Its major pageant is every July, complete with sword dances and historic tableaux.

Augsburg is an ancient castled city, complete with splendid Gothic gate, moat, bridge, tower and ramparts. The oldest (12th century) stained-glass in the world, an 11th century bronze door and an altar painting by Holbein are features worth seeing in the 10th century Cathedral. The best Renaissance street in Germany is Augsburg's Maximilianstrasse.

Romantic Road

The portion of this trip that has the principal sights is Wurzburg-Augsburg (and v.v.). A stewardess-guide is provided for this part of the 4 schedules shown below.

	1635	1636
Dep. Wiesbaden	7:05(1)	-0-
Dep. Frankfurt	8:15	-0-
Dep. Wurzburg	10:15(2)	9:00(4)
Arr. Rothenburg	11:35(3)	12:00(3)
Dep. Rothenburg	13:45	13:10
Arr. Dinkelsbuhl	14:40(3)	14:10(3)
Dep. Dinkelsbuhl	15:30	14:45
Arr. Augsburg	17:35	16:45
Arr. Munich	18:55	0-
Arr. Fussen	-0-	19:55

	1635	1636
Dep. Fussen	-0-	8:45(4)
Dep. Munich	9:00(1)	-0-
Arr. Augsburg	10:10	12:15(3)
Arr. Dinkelsbuhl	12:35(3)	14:50
Dep. Dinkelsbuhl	14:15	15:10
Arr. Rothenburg	15:15(3)	16:15(3)
Dep. Rothenburg	17:00	17:00
Arr. Wurzburg	18:09	19:20
Arr. Frankfurt	20:00	-0-
Arr. Wiesbaden	20:45	-0-

(1) Runs from late March to early November. (2) No boarding or leaving this bus in Wurzburg from mid-June to late September. (3) Meal stop. Time to stroll. (4) Runs from mid-June to late September.

Castle Road 1636

	1636
Dep. Mannheim	7:15(1)
Dep. Heidelberg	7:45(1)
Arr. Rothenburg	12:00

	1636
Dep. Rothenburg	16:50(1)
Arr. Heidelberg	20:25
Arr. Mannheim	20:45

(1) Runs from early June to late September.

INTERNATIONAL ROUTES FROM WEST GERMANY

The West German gateway for travel to Amsterdam and Brussels (and on to London) and Paris (and on to Barcelona and Madrid) is Cologne. Notes on the route to London appear in Chapter 10. Frankfurt is the access point for travel to Basle and Zurich (and on to Milan and Genoa). Munich is the nearest starting point for trips to Vienna (and on to Belgrade and Budapest), Venice and Rome. Hamburg is the gateway to Copenhagen (and on to Oslo and Stockholm).

Cologne - Amsterdam 68

Dep. Cologne	6:17	10:46	17:06(1)	19:17(2)
Arr. Amsterdam	9:36	14:26	19:57	22:34

(1)TEE. Reservation required. Meal service. (2)Meal service.

Cologne - Brussels 62 + 64 + 206

Dep. Cologne	4:47(1)	5:12(1+2)	7:05(1)	9:06(1)	9:43(1+4)
Arr. Brussels (Nord)	7:55	8:08	9:48	11:19	12:23
Arr. Brussels (Cent.)	-0-	-0-	9:51	-0-	-0-
Arr. Brussels (Midi)	8:04	8:19	9:57	11:29	12:30

(1)Supplement charged. Meal service or light refreshments. (2)Runs from mid-June to late August. (3)Runs from late May to late September. (4)Plus other departures from Cologne at 11:12(1), 13:21(1), 15:08(1), 17:06(1), 18:18(1), 20:20(1) and 20:50(1+3).

Cologne - Paris 62

Dep. Cologne	3:18(1+2)	7:15(3)	8:13(4+7)
Arr. Paris (Nord)	8:40	12:30	14:42

(1)Reservation required. Supplement charged. (2)Carries sleeping car. Also has couchettes. (3)From late June to early September: daily. From late September to early June: Monday-Friday, except holidays. Supplement charged. Meal service. (4)Supplement charged. (5)Light refreshments. (6)Meal service. (7)Plus other departures from Cologne at 13:21(4+5), 16:35(3+5) and 23:37(2).

Frankfurt - Basle and Zurich 73

All of these trains charge a supplement and have meal service.

Dep. Frankfurt	9:37	12:37	14:37
Arr. Basle (S.B.B.)	13:46	15:46	17:46
Arr. Zurich	70 minutes later		

Hamburg - Copenhagen 648

All of these trains charge a supplement.

Dep. Hamburg	2:21(1)	3:20(2)	7:00	8:39	11:32(6)
Arr. Copenhagen (Cent.)	8:09	9:09	12:09	14:09	16:29

(1) Has couchettes. (2) Carries sleeping car. Also has couchettes. (3) Runs from mid-June to early September. (4) Adjustment footnote. (5) Adjustment footnote. (6) Plus other departures at 14:46, 17:40(2), 19:37(2+3) and 23:35(2).

Munich - Rome 74

Dep. Munich (Hbf.)	7:40(1)	13:38	16:16(3+4)	19:20(4+5+7)
Arr. Rome (Ter.)	21:12	6:18(2)	7:58	10:15

(1) Meal service. (2) Arrives at Rome's Tiburtina station. (3) Light refreshments to 19:35. (4) Carries sleeping car. Also has couchettes. (5) Runs from late May to late September. (6) Light refreshments. on Day 2. (7) Plus another departure from Munich at 23:20(4+6).

Munich - Vienna 61

Dep. Munich	6:46(1+2)	9:49(2)	17:20(2)	23:35(3)
Arr. Vienna (Westbf.)	11:55	15:28	22:45	6:10

(1) From late May to late September: daily. From late September to late May: daily, except Sundays and holidays. (2) Meal service. (3) Has couchettes.

Munich - Venice 381

Dep. Munich	7:40(1)	13:38	16:26
Arr. Verona (P.N.)	14:25(1)	20:59	0:14
Change trains.			
Dep. Verona (P.N.)	15:12	22:08	2:44
Arr. Venice (S.L.)	16:48	23:48	4:32

(1) Direct train. No train change in Verona.

Munich - Zurich 685

All of these trains charge a supplement and have light refreshments.

Dep. Munich	7:00	9:05	11:19	16:03	17:35
Arr. Zurich	11:37	13:50	16:18	20:37	22:50

Chapter 7

EUROPE'S GREATEST TRAINS

For train travel that is the ultimate in speed, comfort and service, nothing in the world equals the 28 Trans Europ Express trains, the 26 International Inter-City trains and the Trains à Grande Vitesse (trains of great speed). Those which have an international route provide on-board customs inspection during trainsit.

The complete itineraries for all of these trains appear in this chapter. The name in parenthesis after a city-name refers to the correct station where a city has 2 or more railstations. Unless designated otherwise, all stations in Austria, Switzerland and West Germany are "Hauptbahnhof".

Trans Europ Express Trains

All TEE trains charge first-class fare plus a supplement. Holders of Eurailpass need not pay the supplemental charge but must pay the same $2(U.S.) reservation fee required of any passenger traveling by a regular ticket.

If you board a TEE train without a seat reservation and there is vacant space, the conductor can allocate space after collecting the reservation fee. If all the seats are taken, you can be required to leave the train at the next stop.

A special telex network exists between the principal cities served by TEE trains. Except where a return ride begins in Spain, both outward and return reservations can be made quickly at the same time.

Holders of Eurail Youthpass can ride TEE trains by paying the difference between the second-class fare for a particular route and the TEE fare (first-class price plus supplemental charge).

Space on TEE trains can be reserved 2 months in advance of travel date. It is advisable to reserve TEE space before arriving in Europe. All of these special trains have a fixed maximum capacity. They do not add cars beyond that limit in peak travel periods, as many ordinary trains do. Often, demand for seats is greater than capacity.

For example, the outstanding "Settebello" consists of only 4-8 cars, with 144-384 seats. It was sold-out on many rides we made on it. (Don't fail to seek the conductor as early as possible so as to reserve some time in the limited area of the locomotive's unique glass nosecone).

As noted in Chapter 3, you can make reservations on TEE trains either through travel agents or directly with those offices of European railroads that sell Eurailpass which we listed in Chapter 2.

The numeral following the name of each TEE train refers to the following index:

(1) 6-12 cars, 230-460 seats in compartments and open saloons. Meals are served at passengers' own seats in the open saloons. Passengers desiring meals should specify so when ordering seats.

(2) 3-9 cars, 150-461 seats in compartments and open saloons. Meals are served in a 42-seat restaurant car.

(3) 5 cars, 168 seats in open saloons. Meals are served in a 48-seat restaurant car.

(4) 7-9 cars, 230-320 seats in compartments. Meals are served in a 48-seat restaurant car.

(5) 4-8 cars, 144-384 seats in compartments and open saloons. Meals are served in a restaurant car.

International Inter-City Trains

These comprise the second stage of quality train service that began with the introduction of the marvelous TEE trains in the 1960's. Many former TEE trains ("Catalan", "Ligure", "Prinz Eugen", etc.) have been converted to IIC status.

Unlike the first-class-only TEE trains, the IIC trains have offered since their introduction in 1980 both first and second-class coaches.

A supplement is charged by some IIC trains and some IIC trains are air-conditioned. Most IIC trains do not require reservation.

Trains a Grande Vitesse

The third, and most revolutionary, stage in the modern development of European train transportation was the 1982 introduction of France's air-conditioned TGV service—the fastest trains on earth, capable of 236 miles-per-hour and often operated at 162 mph.

The previous 3 hours 30 minutes time to travel the 265 miles between Paris and Lyon has been reduced to 2 hours 30 minutes. The ordinary train ride of 7 hours from Paris to Marseille now takes only 4 hours 50 minutes on a TGV. The usual 6 hours to go from Paris to Geneva requires only 4 hours 15 minutes aboard a TGV.

Each TGV train is a single 660-foot-long unit with an engine at both ends, consisting of 8 passenger cars that accommodate 111 persons in first-class and 275 in second-class.

Advance reservation on TGV's are essential since French National Railways often cannot handle all the people who have switched from either airplane or auto travel to the TGV. Where a TGV has not been sold-out, a reservation can be made at an automatic machine in the rail-station.

On a TGV, no one sits over the wheels. These trains ride smoothly due to running on continuous-welded rails that were specially built for the TGV. Seating in first-class consists of a single place on one side of the aisle and 2 seats on the other side. Second-class is 2 by 2 seating.

Each car has its own galley. The meals a passenger desires must be stated when reserving a first-class seat and are served to the passenger's seat airline style in 2 of the first-class cars, an attendant wheeling a cart down the aisle. Some TGV's offer light refreshments. Every TGV has a bar mid-train.

Normal fares are charged at off-peak times. A supplement is charged on peak travel days and at peak travel times.

Departure and arrival times shown in this chapter are for the Summer period (late May to late September).

All times given in this chapter and throughout our book should be verified, as they are subject to change.

INDEX OF EUROPE'S GREATEST TRAINS

FRANKFURT

GENEVA

HAMBURG

MILAN

Bari 1
Basel 33, 56
Bolgona 1, 3, 54, 58
Bonn 33
Brig 10, 27
Cannes 28
Cologne 33
Como 18
Dijon 10
Dortmund 33
Dusseldort 33
Florence 3, 54, 58
Frankfurt 36
Geneva 27
Genoa 28
Hamburg 56
Hannover 56
Innsbruck 30
Koblenz 33
Lausanne 10, 27
Lugano 18, 33, 56
Luzern 33, 56
Lyon 36
Mainz 33
Mannheim 33
Marseille 28
Modane 36
Monaco 28
Munich 30
Naples 3, 54, 58
Nice 28
Paris 10
Pescara 1
Rimini 1
Rome 3, 54, 58
Stresa 27
Torino 36
Verona 30
Zurich 18

MUNICH

Amsterdam 11
Bonn 6, 11, 37
Bremen 35
Cologne 6, 11, 37
Dortmund 6, 37
Dusseldorf 11, 37
Frankfurt 6, 11
Hannover 35
Heidelberg 37
Innsbruck 11, 30, 35, 37
Koblenz 6, 11, 37
Mainz 37
Mannheim 37
Milan 30
Nurnberg 6, 11, 35
Salzburg 6
Stuttgart 37
Verona 30
Wiesbaden 6
Wurzburg 6, 35

PARIS

Amsterdam 13, 21, 40
Annecy 39
Antwerp 13, 21, 40
Avignon 45-B
Basel 5
Bordeaux 4, 12
Brig 10, 44
Brussels 7, 13, 21, 31, 38, 40, 52
Cologne 34
Den Haag 13, 21, 40
Dijon 10, 41
Dortmund 34
Frankfurt 42
Geneva 43
Grenoble 39
Lausanne 10
Lille 14, 16, 59
Limoges 8
Lyon 45-A
Marseille 45-B

Milan 10
Nancy 26, 55
Nantes 24
Rotterdam 13, 21, 40
Strasbourg 26, 55
Toulouse 8
Tourcoing 14, 16, 59
Zurich 5

ROME

Bologna 3, 54, 58
Florence 3, 54, 58
Milan 3, 54, 58
Naples 58

VIENNA

Frankfurt 23
Hamburg 46
Hannover 46
Linz 23, 46
Nurnberg 23, 46

ZURICH

Basel 5, 20, 22, 47, 50
Bonn 50
Bremen 50
Brussels 22
Chur 22, 47
Cologne 50
Como 18
Dusseldorf 50
Frankfurt 20, 47
Hamburg 20, 47, 50
Hannover 20, 47
Koblenz 50
Lugano 18
Luxembourg 22
Mainz 50
Mannheim 50
Milan 18
Paris 5
St. Moritz 47
Strasbourg 22

1 **ADRIATICO** TEE Type #5

Arr.	Dep.	↓	↑	Arr.	Dep.
	9:30	Milan (Centrale)		19:05	
11:22	11:27	Bologna		17:04	17:12
12:35	12:37	Rimini		15:49	15:52
13:36	13:41	Ancona		14:43	14:47
15:16	15:19	Pescara (Centrale)		13:02	13:05
17:37	17:40	Foggia		10:50	10:54
18:55		Bari			9:40

2 ALBERT SCHWEITZER TEE Type #2

Runs Monday-Friday. Light refreshments only.

Arr.	Dep.		Station		Arr.	Dep.
	6:35	↓	Dortmund	↑	20:55	
6:54	6:55		Essen		20:33	20:34
7:07	7:09		Duisburg		20:22	20:23
7:22	7:23		Dusseldorf		20:09	20:10
7:46	7:49		Cologne		19:44	19:46
8:07	8:08		Bonn		19:22	19:23
8:40	8:41		Koblenz		18:50	18:51
9:31	9:33		Mainz		17:59	18:01
9:52	9:53		Darmstadt		17:37	17:39
10:21	10:22		Heidelberg		17:08	17:09
10:48	10:49		Karlsruhe		16:38	16:39
11:04	11:05		Baden-Baden		16:19	16:20
11:30	11:40		Kehl		15:44	15:54
11:50			Strasbourg			15:35

3 AMBROSIANO TEE Type #5

Arr.	Dep.		Station		Arr.	Dep.
	16:50	↓	Milan (Centrale)	↑	17:40	
18:48	18:53		Bologna		15:38	15:46
20:08	20:18		Florence		14:13	14:23
23:05			Rome (Termini)			11:30

4 AQUITANE TEE Type #4

This is one of Europe's fastest trains (125 mph in open country, averaging 87 mph on its 360-mile run). Gourmet food is served on this beautiful train. Meals desired must be specified when reserving seat. Runs Monday-Friday, from early September to late June.

Arr.	Dep.		Station		Arr.	Dep.
	17:47	↓	Paris (Austerlitz)	↑	12:02	
19:23	19:24		St. Pierre des Corps		10:23	10:24
20:04	20:05		Poitiers		9:43	9:44
20:51	20:52		Angouleme		8:58	8:58
21:50			Bordeaux			8:00

5 ARBALETE IIC (Meal service)

Arr.	Dep.		Station		Arr.	Dep.
	17:03	↓	Paris (Est)	↑	13:04	
	20:57		Belfort			9:10
	21:25		Mulhouse			8:35
21:46	22:00		Basel (S.B.B.)		7:56	8:13
23:02			Zurich			6:57

6 **BLAUER ENZIAN** IIC (Meal service)

Arr.	Dep.		Station		Arr.	Dep.
	5:40	↓	Dortmund	↑	22:14	
	6:04		Hagen		21:58	
	6:22		Wt. Elberfeld		21:34	
6:51	7:03		Cologne		20:51	21:03
	7:23		Bonn			20:31
	7:57		Koblenz			19:58
	9:00		Wiesbaden			19:01
	9:32		Frankfurt			18:29
	10:59		Wurzburg			17:02
	12:02		Nurnberg			16:01
13:42	13:52		Munich		14:02	14:14
	15:26		Salzburg			12:26
	18:52		Villach			9:08
19:30		↓	Klagenfurt	↑		8:25

7 **BRABANT** TEE Type #1

One of Europe's fastest trains. Averages 78 miles per hour.

Arr.	Dep.		Station		Arr.	Dep.
	17:17	↓	Brussels (Midi)	↑	14:03	
19:44		↓	Paris (Nord)	↑		11:37

8 **CAPITOLE** TEE Type #4

From Paris to Toulouse: daily, except Saturday. From Toulouse to Paris: daily, except Sundays and holidays.

Arr.	Dep.		Station		Arr.	Dep.
	18:00	↓	Paris (Austerlitz)	↑	13:47	
20:50	20:52		Limoges		10:47	10:49
21:51	21:52		Brive-la-Gaillarde		9:47	9:48
22:53	22:54		Cahors		8:46	8:47
23:30	23:31		Montauban		8:08	8:09
23:59		↓	Toulouse (Matabiau)	↑		7:43

9 **CATALAN** IIC

Supplement charged. Meals are served in a 48-seat restaurant car. Also has bar. All cars are air-conditioned.

Arr.	Dep.		Arr.	Dep.
	11:27	Geneva (Cornavin)	19:44	
11:57	11:58	Bellegarde	19:11	19:12
12:45	12:55	Chambery	18:16	18:25
13:34	13:35	Grenoble	17:38	17:39
14:33	14:47	Valence	16:28	16:37
15:47	15:50	Avignon	15:27	15:29
16:16	16:18	Nimes	14:58	15:00
16:44	16:46	Montpellier	14:31	14:33
17:23	17:25	Beziers	13:52	13:54
17:39	17:41	Narbonne	13:36	13:38
18:14	18:16	Perpignan	13:01	13:03
18:43	18:48	Cerbere	12:30	12:35
19:03	19:18	Port Bou	12:00	12:15
20:09	20:11	Gerona	11:06	11:08
21:16		Barcelona (Termino)		10:02

10 **CISALPIN** TEE Type #4

Meal service from Paris to Lausanne and v.v. Light refreshments from Paris to Milan and v.v.

Arr.	Dep.		Arr.	Dep.
	12:30	Paris (Lyon)	23:25	
14:52	14:53	Dijon	21:00	21:01
15:22	15:23	Dole	20:33	20:34
16:39	16:47	Vallorbe	19:16	19:26
17:19	17:22	Lausanne	18:32	18:42
18:15	18:16	Sion	17:37	17:38
18:47	18:50	Brig	17:04	17:07
19:22	19:32	Domodossola	16:22	16:32
21:00		Milan (Centrale)		14:55

11 **ERASMUS** IIC

Supplement charged. Meal service. The Munich-Innsbruck portion and v.v. runs from late May to late September.

Arr.	Dep.		Arr.	Dep.
	6:57	Amsterdam	20:52	
9:32	9:35	Dusseldorf	18:18	18:20
9:59	10:03	Cologne	17:51	17:54
10:21	10:23	Bonn	17:29	17:31
10:55	10:57	Koblenz	16:56	16:58
12:26	12:32	Frankfurt	15:23	15:29
14:56	16:01	Nurnberg	12:55	13:01
16:44	16:55	Munich	11:03	11:14
19:00		Innsbruck		8:55

12 **ETENDARD** TEE Type #4

From Paris to Bordeaux: Monday-Friday, except holidays. From Bordeaux to Paris: daily, except Saturday. Specify meals desired when reserving seat.

Arr.	Dep.		Station		Arr.	Dep.
	7:51	↓	Paris (Austerlitz)	↑	21:46	
9:23	9:24		St. Pierre des Corps		20:08	20:09
10:01	10:02		Poitiers		19:29	19:30
10:50	10:51		Angouleme		18:40	18:41
11:56			Bordeaux (St. Jean)			17:44

13 **ETOILE DU NORD** TEE Type #1

Arr.	Dep.		Station		Arr.	Dep.
	8:56	↓	Amsterdam	↑	22:45	
9:37	9:38		Den Haag		22:07	22:08
9:53	9:54		Rotterdam		21:50	21:52
10:29	10:31		Roosendaal		21:14	21:15
10:56	10:57		Antwerp (Berch.)		20:48	20:49
11:26	11:28		Brussels (Nord)		20:18	20:20
11:33	11:43		Brussels (Midi)		20:05	20:13
14:08			Paris (Nord)			17:42

14 **FAIDHERBE** TEE Type #4

Runs Monday-Friday, except holidays. Does not operate from mid-July to late August.

Arr.	Dep.		Station		Arr.	Dep.
	7:30	↓	Paris (Nord)	↑	9:03	
-0-	-0-		Arras		7:34	7:35
9:06	9:07		Douai		7:20	7:21
9:26	9:32		Lille		6:56	7:02
9:42	9:43		Roubaix		6:45	6:46
9:49			Tourcoing			6:39

15 **GAMBRINUS** TEE Type #2

Runs Monday-Friday.

Arr.	Dep.		Station		Arr.	Dep.
	14:33	↓	Dortmund	↑	16:50	
14:43	14:44		Bochum		16:35	16:36
14:54	14:55		Essen		16:26	16:27
15:06	15:07		Duisburg		16:15	16:16
15:18	15:19		Dusseldorf		16:02	16:03
15:42	15:44		Cologne		15:36	15:38
16:02	16:03		Bonn		15:16	15:17
16:34	16:35		Koblenz		14:45	14:46
17:25	17:27		Mainz		13:53	13:55
17:45	17:46		Darmstadt		13:32	13:33
18:16	18:17		Heidelberg		13:03	13:04
19:28			Stuttgart			11:57

16 **GAYANT** TEE Type #4

Runs Monday-Friday, except holidays.

Arr.	Dep.		Station		Arr.	Dep.
	11:56	↓	Paris (Nord)	↑	14:02	
13:21	13:22		Arras		12:30	12:31
13:37	13:38		Douai		12:16	12:17
13:58	14:04		Lille		11:51	11:57
14:14	14:15		Roubaix		11:40	11:41
14:21			Tourcoing			11:34

17 **GOETHE** TEE Type #2

Runs Monday-Friday.

Arr.	Dep.		Station		Arr.	Dep.
	5:33	↓	Dortmund	↑	19:57	
5:43	5:44		Bochum		19:43	19:44
5:54	5:55		Essen		19:33	19:34
6:06	6:08		Duisburg		19:22	19:23
6:22	6:23		Dusseldorf		19:09	19:10
6:46	6:49		Cologne		18:43	18:45
7:07	7:08		Bonn		18:22	18:23
7:40	7:41		Koblenz		17:50	17:51
8:33	8:34		Mainz		17:00	17:01
8:58			Frankfurt			16:37

18 **GOTTARDO** TEE Type #3

Arr.	Dep.		Station		Arr.	Dep.
	8:39	↓	Zurich	↑	20:53	
11:08	11:10		Bellinzona		18:23	18:25
11:35	11:38		Lugano		17:52	17:55
12:04	12:06		Como		17:23	17:25
12:40			Milan (Centrale)			16:50

19 **HEINRICH HEINE** TEE Type #2

Runs Monday-Friday from late August to late May.

Arr.	Dep.		Station		Arr.	Dep.
	16:33	↓	Dortmund	↑	10:22	
16:43	16:44		Bochum		10:08	10:09
16:53	16:55		Essen		9:59	10:00
17:06	17:07		Duisburg		9:48	9:49
17:18	17:20		Dusseldorf		9:35	9:36
17:42	17:44		Cologne		9:10	9:12
18:02	18:03		Bonn		8:49	8:50
18:34	18:35		Koblenz		8:18	8:19
19:26	19:27		Mainz		7:28	7:29
19:51			Frankfurt			7:05

20 **HELVETIA** IIC

Supplement charged. Meal service.

Arr.	Dep.		Arr.	Dep.
	12:45	Hamburg (Hbf.)	16:09	
14:07	14:10	Hannover	14:43	14:45
17:31	17:37	Frankfurt	11:17	11:23
20:39	20:41	Basel (Bad. Bf.)	8:13	8:14
10:46	20:58	Basel (S.B.B.)	7:56	8:08
21:57		Zurich		6:57

21 **ILE DE FRANCE** TEE Type #1

From Amsterdam to Paris: Runs daily except Saturday. From Paris to Amsterdam: Runs daily except Sunday.

Arr.	Dep.		Arr.	Dep.
	17:55	Amsterdam	12:30	
18:39	18:40	Den Haag	11:49	11:50
18:56	18:57	Rotterdam	11:31	11:33
19:34	19:35	Roosendaal	10:50	10:53
19:59	20:00	Antwerp (Berchem)	10:24	10:25
20:29	20:30	Brussels (Nord)	9:55	9:56
20:35	20:45	Brussels (Midi)	9:43	9:50
23:10		Paris (Nord)		7:19

22 **IRIS** IIC

Meal service or light refreshments.

Arr.	Dep.		Arr.	Dep.
	12:12	Brussels (Midi)	19:33	
12:15	12:20	Brussels (Nord)	19:25	19:30
14:44	14:54	Luxembourg	16:49	16:59
16:59	17:02	Strasbourg	14:37	14:39
18:25	18:58	Basel (S.B.B.)	12:56	13:20
19:57	20:07	Zurich	11:47	11:57
21:30	-0-	Chur	10:20	10:24
-0-	-0-	St. Moritz		7:35

23 **JOHANN STRAUSS** IIC

Supplement charged in Germany. Meal service.

Arr.	Dep.		Arr.	Dep.
	7:32	Frankfurt	22:26	
	8:59	Wurzburg		21:02
	9:59	Nurnberg		20:03
	11:01	Regensburg		18:59
12:08	12:12	Passau	17:37	17:51
13:21		Linz		16:20
15:24		Vienna (Westbf.)		14:20

24 **JULES VERNE** TEE Type #4

Runs Monday-Friday from late August to mid-July.

Arr.	Dep.		Station		Arr.	Dep.
	19:03	↓	Paris (Montparnasse)	↑	9:32	
21:31	21:32	↓	Angers-St. Laud	↑	7:04	7:05
22:20		↓	Nantes	↑		6:15

25 **KARWENDEL** IIC

Runs the Garmisch-Innsbruck and v.v. portion only from late May to late September. Meal service.

Arr.	Dep.		Station		Arr.	Dep.
	7:08	↓	Bremen	↑	19:46	
	8:15	↓	Hannover	↑	18:38	
	9:13	↓	Gottingen	↑		17:40
	10:07	↓	Bebra	↑		16:48
	11:59	↓	Wurzburg	↑		15:07
	13:02	↓	Nurnberg	↑		14:01
14:45	14:55	↓	Munich	↑	11:56	12:14
16:11	16:24	↓	Garmisch	↑	10:24	10:36
16:44		↓	Mittenwald	↑		10:03
17:46		↓	Innsbruck	↑		9:00

26 **KLEBER** TEE Type #4

Kleber was reduced to a Rapide train in 1982.

27 **LEMANO** IIC

Supplement charged in Italy. Light refreshments.

Arr.	Dep.		Station		Arr.	Dep.
	14:46	↓	Geneva (Cornavin)	↑	13:08	
15:19	15:22	↓	Lausanne	↑	12:32	12:35
16:15	16:16	↓	Sion	↑	11:37	11:38
16:47	16:50	↓	Brig	↑	11:04	11:07
17:22	17:37	↓	Domodossola	↑	10:22	10:32
18:01	18:02	↓	Stresa	↑	9:54	9:55
19:05		↓	Milan (Centrale)	↑		9:00

28 **LIGURE** IIC

Supplement charged in Italy. Same description as TEE Type #5.

Arr.	Dep.			Arr.	Dep.
	6:40	↓	Milan (Centrale)	23:30	
8:15	8:23		Genoa (P.P.)	21:47	21:55
8:51	8:53		Savona	21:16	21:18
9:45	9:47		Imperia P. Maurizio	20:28	20:29
10:09	10:11		San Remo	20:06	20:08
10:28	10:44		Ventimiglia	19:40	19:53
10:54	10:55		Menton	19:28	19:29
11:03	11:04		Monaco-Monte Carlo	19:19	19:20
11:16	11:20		Nice	19:04	19:06
11:33	11:34		Antibes	18:49	18:50
11:43	11:45		Cannes	18:39	18:41
12:07	12:09		St. Raphael	18:15	18:17
12:54	12:56		Toulon	17:28	17:30
13:38			Marseille (St. Ch.) ↑		16:49

29 **LOTSCHBERG** IIC

Meal service. From Hamburg to Munster: daily, except Sundays and holidays. From Munster to Hamburg: daily, except Saturday. From Dortmund to Brig and v.v.: daily.

Arr.	Dep.			Arr.	Dep.
	5:26	↓	Hamburg (Altona)	23:35	
	5:40		Hamburg (Hbf.)	23:19	
	6:40		Bremen	22:17	
	8:03		Munster	20:53	
	8:37		Dortmund	20:18	
	9:02		Essen		19:54
	9:30		Dusseldorf		19:27
9:53	9:57		Cologne	18:57	19:00
	10:17		Bonn		18:37
	10:51		Koblenz		18:04
	11:43		Mainz		17:13
	12:29		Mannheim		16:30
	13:00		Karlsruhe		15:56
	14:03		Freiburg (Breisgau)		14:50
14:39			Basel (Bad. Bf.)		14:14
14:46	14:56		Basel (S.B.B.)	13:58	14:08
16:09			Bern		12:45
17:20			Interlaken (Ost)		11:34
18:00			Brig ↑		10:54

30 **MEDIOLANUM** TEE Type #5

Arr.	Dep.		Station		Arr.	Dep.
	15:38	↓	Munich	↑	13:54	
16:38	16:43		Kufstein		12:51	12:53
17:26	17:29		Innsbruck		12:05	12:08
18:04	18:17		Brennero		11:19	11:32
19:34	19:36		Bolzano		9:57	10:00
20:08	20:09		Trento		9:24	9:26
21:13	21:24		Verona (P.N.)		8:11	8:23
21:58	21:59		Brescia		7:34	7:35
22:50			Milan (Centrale)			6:50

31 **MEMLING** TEE Type #1

Runs Monday-Friday, except holidays, from early September to late June.

Arr.	Dep.		Station		Arr.	Dep.
	18:38	↓	Brussels (Midi)	↑	**9:11**	
21:06			Paris (Nord)			**6:41**

32 **MERKUR** IIC

Departs Freiburg Monday-Friday, except holidays. Runs from all other cities daily. Meal service. Hamburg-Karlsruhe and v.v.

Arr.	Dep.		Station		Arr.	Dep.
	10:15	↓	Copenhagen (H.)	↑	19:40	
	12:10		Rodby Ferry		17:30	
	13:34		Puttgarden		16:25	
	14:30		Lubeck		15:24	
15:07	15:40		Hamburg		14:17	14:46
	16:40		Bremen			13:19
	18:03		Munster			11:55
	18:37		Dortmund			11.23
	19:02		Essen			10:54
	19:30		Dusseldorf			10:27
19:53	19:57		Cologne		9:57	10:00
	20:17		Bonn			9:37
	20:51		Koblenz			9:04
	21:43		Mainz			8:13
22:25			Mannheim			6:56
22:58			Karlsruhe			6:02
	-0-		Freiburg (Breisgau)			

33 **METROPOLITANO** IIC

Meal service.

Arr.	Dep.		Station		Arr.	Dep.
	5:37	↓	Dortmund	↑	23:18	
	6:02		Essen		22:52	
	6:30		Dusseldorf		22:25	
6:53	6:57		Cologne		21:57	22:00
	7:17		Bonn			21:37
	7:51		Koblenz			21:04
	8:43		Mainz			20:13
	9:29		Mannheim			19:30
	10:00		Karlsruhe			18:56
	11:03		Freiburg (Breisgau)			17:50
11:39			Basel (Bad. Bf.)			17:14
11:46	12:01		Basel (S.B.B.)		16:53	17:08
13:10			Luzern			15:44
15:34			Bellinzona			13:20
16:03			Lugano			12:50
16:29			Chiasso			12:25
17:35			Milan (Centrale)			11:20

34 **MOLIERE** IIC

From late June to early September: daily. From early September to late June: Monday-Friday.

Arr.	Dep.		Station		Arr.	Dep.
	17:45	↓	Paris (Nord)	↑	12:30	
22:51	22:53		Cologne		7:11	7:15
	0:08		Dortmund			5:44

35 **MONT-BLANC** IIC

Meal service. Connects in Geneva with trains to and from Barcelona.

Arr.	Dep.		Station		Arr.	Dep.
	9:31	↓	Hamburg (Altona)	↑	19:25	
9:41	9:45		Hamburg (Hbf.)		19:09	19:14
11:07	11:10		Hannover		17:43	17:45
12:05	12:07		Gottingen		16:43	16:45
14:31	14:37		Frankfurt		14:17	14:23
15:21	15:29		Mannheim		13:25	13:33
15:58	16:00		Karlsruhe		12:54	12:56
17:01	17:03		Freiburg (Breisgau)		11:48	11:50
17:39	17:41		Basel (Bad. Bf.)		11:13	11:14
17:46	17:59		Basel (S.B.B.)		10:54	11:08
19:02	19:04		Biel		9:49	9:51
19:23	19:24		Neuchatel		9:28	9:29
20:12	20:17		Lausanne		8:36	8:41
20:50	21:28		Geneva (Cornavin)		7:25	8:03

CONNECTION TO BARCELONA/GENEVA

Arr.	Dep.		Station		Arr.	Dep.
23:25	23:29	↓	Lyon (Brotteaux)	↑	5:15	5:19
9:41		↓	Barcelona	↑		19:00

36 **MONT-CENIS** IIC

Supplement charged in Italy. Light refreshments.

Arr.	Dep.				Arr.	Dep.
	17:07	↓	Lyon (Perrache)	↑	13:01	
	17:15	↓	Lyon (Brotteaux)	↑	12:52	
	18:33	↓	Chambery	↑		11:30
19:40	19:52	↓	Modane	↑	10:15	10:25
21:26	21:40	↓	Torino (P.N.)	↑	8:30	8:40
	23:10	↓	Milan (Centrale)	↑		7:00

37 **NYMPHENBURG** IIC

Meal service. The Munich-Innsbruck portion and v.v. runs only from late May to late September.

Arr.	Dep.				Arr.	Dep.
	6:37	↓	Dortmund	↑	22:18	
	7:02	↓	Essen	↑	21:52	
	7:30	↓	Dusseldorf	↑	21:25	
7:54	7:57	↓	Cologne	↑	20:57	21:00
	8:17	↓	Bonn	↑		20:37
	8:51	↓	Koblenz	↑		20:04
	9:43	↓	Mainz	↑		19:13
	10:27	↓	Mannheim	↑		18:30
	10:40	↓	Heidelberg	↑		18:14
	11:57	↓	Stuttgart	↑		17:03
	12:55	↓	Ulm	↑		15:59
14:10	14:21	↓	Munich	↑	14:33	14:43
	15:40	↓	Kufstein	↑		13:31
16:38		↓	Innsbruck	↑		12:26

38 **OISEAU BLEU** TEE Type #1

From Brussels to Paris: Runs daily except Sunday. From Paris to Brussels: Runs daily except Saturday.

Arr.	Dep.				Arr.	Dep.
	7:13	↓	Brussels (Nord)	↑	23:08	
7:20	7:30	↓	Brussels (Midi)	↑	22:59	23:02
10:01		↓	Paris (Nord)	↑		20:29

39 **PARIS-ANNECY-GRENOBLE** TGV

Service is expected to start in 1983.

Arr.	Dep.				Arr	Dep.
		↓	Paris	↑		
		↓	Annecy	↑		
		↓	Grenoble	↑		

40 PARIS-BRUSSELS-AMSTERDAM IIC

Supplement charged. From Paris to Brussels: runs from late June to early September. Light refreshments. From Brussels to Paris: daily from late June to late September. . . . daily except Saturday from late September to late June. Meal service.

Arr.	Dep.			Arr.	Dep.
	16:46	↓	Paris (Nord)	↑ 20:35	
19:31	19:44		Brussels (Midi)		17:53
19:49	19:51		Brussels (Nord)	-0-	
10:15	20:22		Antwerp (Berchem)	-0-	
21:33	21:38		Rotterdam	-0-	
21:53	21:58		Den Haag	-0-	
22:38			Amsterdam	-0-	

41 PARIS-DIJON TGV

Dep. Paris (Lyon)	6:36(1)	12:08(2)	19:35(3)
Arr. Dijon	8:57	14:18	21:45
	*	*	*
Dep. Dijon	7:48(4)	9:51	14:48(2)
Arr. Paris (Lyon)	10:00	12:06	17:00

(1) Daily, except Sundays and holidays. Supplement charged, except on Saturday. (2) Monday-Friday. Does not run from early July to late August. (3) Daily. Supplement charged on Friday and Sunday. (4) Daily. Supplement charged on Monday.

42 PARIS-FRANKFURT IIC

Meal service.

Arr.	Dep.			Arr.	Dep.
	17:15	↓	Paris (Est)	↑ 14:05	
	20:04		Metz		11:17
	20:49		Forbach		10:27
20:56			Saarbrucken		10:11
22:21			Mannheim		8:44
23:09			Frankfurt		7:55

43 PARIS-GENEVA TGV

All of these trains run daily.

Dep. Paris (Lyon)	7:45(1)	19:12(2)	
Arr. Geneva (Corn.)	12:00	23:27	
	*	*	*
Dep. Geneva (Corn.)	7:09(3)	18:09(4)	
Arr. Paris (Lyon)	11:34	22:37	

(1) Supplement charged on Saturday. (2) Supplement charged daily, except Saturday. (3) Supplement charged on Monday. (4) Supplement charged every day.

44 **PARIS-LAUSANNE** TGV

Service is expected to start in 1984.

Dep. Paris (Lyon)
Arr. Lausanne

* * *

Dep. Lausanne
Arr. Paris (Lyon)

45-A **PARIS-LYON** TGV

Supplement for these trains are charged on various days.

Dep. Paris (Lyon)	6:15(1)	7:15	8:15(2)	9:15(6)
Arr. Lyon (Brot.)	8:54	10:07	10:53	11:54
Arr. Lyon (Per.)	10 minutes later			
	*	*	*	
Dep. Lyon (Per.)	5:50(1)	6:50(2)	7:50(3)	8:50(7)
Dep. Lyon (Brot.)	6:00(1)	7:00(2)	8:00(3)	9:00
Arr. Paris (Lyon)	8:52	9:42	10:42	11:40

(1)Monday-Friday. (2)Daily, except Sundays and holidays. (3)Saturday and Sunday only. (4)Daily, except Saturday. (5)Sunday only. (6)Plus other departures from Paris at 11:15(4), 13:15, 14:15, 16:15. 17:15, 18:15(4), 19:20 and 20:15(4). (7)Plus other departures from Lyon at 10:50, 11:50, 13:50(2), 14:50, 15:50(4), 16:50, 17:50, 18:50, 19:50 and 20:50(5).

45-B **PARIS-AVIGNON-MARSEILLE** TGV

All of these trains run daily.

Dep. Paris (Lyon)	7:10(1)	9:07(2)	10:55	12:45(3)
Arr. Avignon	11:49(1)	13:45(2)	15:37	-0-
Arr. Marseille	12:55	14:47	16:39	18:18
	*	*	*	
Dep. Marseille	13:58	15:09(4)	16:37(4)	17:41(5)
Dep. Avignon	14:59	16:09(4)	17:38(4)	18:47(5)
Arr. Paris (Lyon)	19:37	20:47	22:20	23:30

(1)Supplement charged Monday-Friday. (2)Supplement charged on Saturday. (3)Supplement charged daily, except Sundays and holidays. (4)Supplement charged daily, except Saturday. (5)Supplement charged daily, except Friday and Sunday.

46 **PRINZ EUGEN** IIC

Supplement charged in Germany. Meal service.

Arr.	Dep.	↓		↑	Arr.	Dep.
	9:16		Hamburg (Altona)		19:38	
	9:30		Hamburg (Hbf.)		19:24	
	11:15		Hannover			17:50
	12:13		Gottingen			16:40
	13:07		Bebra			15:48
	15:03		Wurzburg			14:07
	16:04		Nurnberg			12:56
	17:05		Regensburg			11:52
18:11	18:20		Passau		10:39	10:46
19:25			Linz			9:34
21:25			Vienna (Westbf.)			7:35

47 **RATIA** IIC

Runs only in one direction. Supplement charged. Meal service.

Arr.	Dep.	↓		↑	Arr.	Dep.
	7:35		St. Moritz			
10:22	10:24		Chur			
11:52	11:57		Zurich			
12:56	13:08		Basel (S.B.B.)			
13:13	13:14		Basel (Bad. Bf.)			
16:17	16:23		Frankfurt			
19:43	19:45		Hannover			
21:09			Hamburg			

48 **REMBRANDT** TEE Type #2

Arr.	Dep.	↓		↑	Arr.	Dep.
	13:53		Amsterdam		13:26	
14:25	14:28		Utrecht		12:55	12:58
15:00	15:03		Arnhem		12:17	12:19
15:21	15:34		Emmerich		11:40	11:51
16:09	16:10		Duisburg		11:05	11:06
16:22	16:23		Dusseldorf		10:52	10:53
16:45	16:49		Cologne		10:27	10:29
17:07	17:08		Bonn		10:05	10:06
17:41	17:42		Koblenz		9:34	9:35
18:32	18:34		Mainz		8:42	8:44
18:53	18:54		Darmstadt		8:22	8:23
19:24	19:25		Heidelberg		7:53	7:54
20:37			Stuttgart			6:46

49 **RHEINGOLD** TEE Type #2

Arr.	Dep.		Arr.	Dep.
	7:49	Amsterdam	19:57	
8:17	8:21	Utrecht	19:25	19:28
8:58	9:01	Arnhem	18:50	18:52
9:21	9:34	Emmerich	18:18	18:29
10:09	10:10	Duisburg	17:43	17:44
10:22	10:23	Dusseldorf	17:29	17:31
10:46	10:49	Cologne	17:03	17:06
11:07	11:08	Bonn	16:41	16:42
11:40	11:41	Koblenz	16:09	16:10
12:32	12:34	Mainz	15:17	15:19
13:15	13:17	Mannheim	14:35	14:37
13:46	13:47	Karlsruhe	14:05	14:06
14:01	14:02	Baden-Baden	13:49	13:50
14:48	14:49	Freiburg	13:03	13:04
15:25	15:27	Basle (Bad. Bf.)	12:27	12:29
15:32		Basle (S.B.B.)		12:22

50 **RHEINPFEIL** IIC

Change trains in Basel, en route to and from Zurich. Meal service.

Arr.	Dep.		Arr.	Dep.
	12:26	Hamburg (Altona)	18:31	
	12:40	Hamburg (Hbf.)	18:17	
	13:40	Bremen	17:17	
	15:03	Munster	15:53	
	15:37	Dortmund	15:18	
	16:02	Essen		14:54
	16:30	Dusseldorf		14:27
16:54	16:57	Cologne	13:57	14:00
	17:12	Bonn		13:37
	17:51	Koblenz		13:04
	18:43	Mainz		12:13
	19:29	Mannheim		11:30
	20:00	Karlsruhe		10:56
	21:03	Freiburg (Breisgau)		9:50
21:39		Basel (Bad. Bf.)		9:14
21:46	22:02	Basel (S.B.B.)	8:56	9:08
	23:02	Zurich		7:57

51 **RHODANIEN** IIC

Meal service.

Arr.	Dep.		Arr.	Dep.
	16:08	Geneva	12:09	
18:14	18:15	Grenoble	10:33	10:34
20:27		Avignon		8:15
21:31		Marseille		7:11

52 **RUBENS** TEE Type #1

Runs Monday-Friday, except holidays, from early September to late June.

Arr.	Dep.				Arr.	Dep.
	6:42	↓	Brussels (Midi)	↑	21:05	
9:05		↓	Paris (Nord)	↑		18:44

53 **SAPHIR** IIC

Supplement charged. Meal service.

Arr.	Dep.				Arr.	Dep.
	16:49	↓	Dostende	↓	12:43	
18:02	18:10	↓	Brussels (Midi)	↓	11:29	11:33
18:15	18:20	↓	Brussels (Nord)	↓	11:19	11:24
	20:44	↓	Cologne	↓		9:06

54 **SETTEBELLO** TEE Type #5

Sitting in the nosecone of Settebello's locomotive is one of the world's greatest train travel experiences.

Arr.	Dep.				Arr.	Dep.
	8:10	↓	Milan (Centrale)	↑	13:55	
10:03	10:06	↓	Bologna	↑	11:56	12:00
11:17	11:22	↓	Florence	↑	10:37	10:42
14:05		↓	Rome (Termini)	↑		7:55

55 **STANISLAS** TEE Type #4

From Paris to Strasbourg: daily, except Sundays and holidays, running from early September to late June. From Strasbourg to Paris: daily, except Saturday, running all year.

Arr.	Dep.				Arr.	Dep.
	11:00	↓	Paris (Est)	↑	21:08	
13:36	13:37	↓	Nancy	↑	18:29	18:31
14:52		↓	Strasbourg	↑		17:13

56 **TIZIANO** IIC

Supplement charged. Meal service from Hamburg to Chiasso and v.v.

Arr.	Dep.				Arr.	Dep.
	7:45	↓	Hamburg (Hbf.)	↓	23:09	
9:07	9:10	↓	Hannover	↓	21:43	21:45
12:31	12:37	↓	Frankfurt	↓	18:17	18:23
15:39	15:41	↓	Basel (Bad. Bf.)	↓	15:13	15:14
15:46	16:01	↓	Basel (S.B.B.)	↓	14:53	15:08
17:10	17:12	↓	Luzern	↓	13:42	13:44
20:03	20:05	↓	Lugano	↓	10:48	10:50
20:29	20:31	↓	Chiasso	↓	10:20	10:25
21:40		↓	Milan (Centrale)	↓		9:20

57 **VAN BEETHOVEN** IIC

Supplement charged. Meal service.

Arr.	Dep.		Arr.	Dep.
	16:55	Amsterdam	11:45	
19:32	19:35	Dusseldorf	9:17	9:19
19:59	20:03	Cologne	8:51	8:54
20:21	20:23	Bonn	8:29	8:31
20:55	20:57	Koblenz	7:56	7:58
21:58	22:00	Wiesbaden	-0-	-0-
-0-	-0-	Mainz	7:04	7:06
	22:26	Frankfurt		6:41

58 **VESUVIO** TEE Type #5

Arr.	Dep.		Arr.	Dep.
	11:50	Milan (Centrale)	23:42	
13:45	13:50	Bologna	21:43	21:48
15:01	15:11	Florence	20:24	20:34
17:46	18:00	Rome (Termini)	17:25	17:40
20:10		Naples (Mergellina)		15:30

59 **WATTEAU** TEE Type #4

Runs Monday-Friday, except holidays. Does not operate from mid-July to late August.

Arr.	Dep.		Arr.	Dep.
	18:07	Paris (Nord)	20:07	
19:32	19:33	Arras	-0-	-0-
19:46	19:47	Douai	18:27	18:28
20:06	20:12	Lille	18:03	18:09
20:22	20:23	Roubaix	17:52	17:53
20:29		Tourcoing		17:46

Chapter 8

ENGLAND, WALES, SCOTLAND, NORTHERN IRELAND

On British trains, first-class sleeping cars have single compartments; second-class cars have 2-berth compartments. Passengers are served morning tea and biscuits free of charge. Generally, passengers may remain in sleeping cars at destinations until 7:30.

British trains continually increase speed as a result of the country's rail modernization program. Its 1,800 "Inter-City" trains, linking more than 200 towns each weekday, average 98 to 100 miles per hour on some routes. The 17:45 departure from London for Glasgow, a train that averages almost 100 mph, makes that 401-mile trip in 4 hours and 16 minutes versus 5 hours or more by other trains. The 393-mile run between London and Edinburgh is covered by the "Flying Scotsman" (10:00 departure) in 4 hours and 43 minutes, while other trains take 6 hours or more.

Reservations are required on fast day trains. If there are vacant spaces, the conductor at the departure platform can allocate available places.

BritRail Pass

The BritRail Pass, similar to Eurailpass (which does not cover Britain), provides unlimited rail travel in England, Scotland and Wales. Youth-Pass, limited to ages 16 to under 26, is for Economy-class space. Prices in U.S. dollars April 1, 1983 to March 31, 1984 are:

	First-class	Economy	Youth
7 days	$ 147	$ 107	$ 93
14 days	219	162	144
21 days	272	205	183
1 month	317	243	215

Children from 5 to under 16 are charged half of either the First-class or Economy fare.

These passes do not cover travel in the Irish Republic or in Northern Ireland. They cannot be purchased in Britain. They can be purchased through the offices of BritRail Travel International, its representatives, and travel agencies outside Britain.

Validate these passes at the railstation's "Travel Centre" before starting your first trip with them. The rail official will mark your pass with that day's date and also the appropriate expiration date.

It is a good idea to protect yourself from having your pass rendered partly or wholly invalid because the validity dates were entered incorrectly.

Before the rail official writes on the pass the first and last day it can be used, you should write a note with what you believe are the correct validity dates, show it to him, and ask if he agrees with those dates.

(Be sure to follow the European custom of showing the day of the month first, followed by the number of the month. In Europe, July 8 is 8/7. If you wanted to take a train to Edinburgh, leaving at 1:50 PM on July 8, your note for a reservation would read: "Edinburgh—13:50—8/7".)

Only when the official says your dates are correct, or explains why they are not, should you hand your pass to him for the dates to be

BritRail Seapass

Can be purchased only as an addition to a Britrail Pass.

The Britrail Seapass covers travel by train from London and then by economy class on either ordinary ships or on hovercraft from several British ports (Dover, Folkestone, Harwich, Newhaven or Weymouth) to various European ports (Boulogne, Calais, Cherbourg, Dieppe, Dunkerque, Hoek van Holland, Oestende).

The 1983 price for BritRail Seapass is $25(U.S.) for each crossing of the Channel, a savings of up to 50% compared to buying ordinary tickets. Valid for 6 months after issue date.

Irish Seapass

Can be purchased only as an addition to a BritRail Pass. Good for rail service from London to Fishguard and Holyhead, plus the boat passage (economy class) from those English ports to Rosslare and Dun Laoghaire on the Irish coast.

The 1983 price for Irish Seapass is $37(U.S.) for each one-way trip. Valid for 6 months after issue date.

Young Person's Railcard

Can be purchased only in Britain and available only to a bona-fide student aged 18-30 registered for the scholastic year at a British establishment of higher education. The current Young Person's Railcard is valid from September 15, 1982 to September 30, 1983. Its price is 10 Pounds. Entitles the bearer to 50% discount on second-class space.

Senior Citizens BritRail Pass

Can be purchased only outside Britain. For people over 65. Allows first-class space at the economy price. The 1983 prices are: $107(U.S.) for 7 days, $162 for 14 days, $205 for 21 days, and $243 for one month.

Scottish Highland and Islands Travel Pass

Allows unlimited travel on most train, bus and ship routes in Scotland. Both the pass for 5 consecutive days at $68(U.S.) and another for 10 consecutive days at $113 can be purchased either outside Britain or after arriving in Britain. Two other versions (for 7 days and for 12 days) are sold only in Scotland.

Family Railcard

With this card, one adult pays full fare, and a second adult plus up to 4 children pay $1.25(U.S.) for any rail trip, except at peak travel hours. Price is 10 Pounds. The card is valid from March 1 to the end of the following February. Only families resident in the U.K. can buy Family Railcard.

North Wales Rideabout Ticket

Can be purchased only in Britain. Covers 7 days of rail and bus travel. Provides a substantial savings. Costs 6 Pounds.

Southwest Wales Runabout Ticket

Can be purchased only in Britain. Covers 7 days of rail and bus travel. Provides a substantial savings. Costs 10.70 Pounds.

Day Return

When buying rail tickets for a one-day roundtrip rail excursion, be sure to use this economy. The price of the return ride will be about only 12% of the cost of the outgoing ride.

Weekend Return

Another good discount, if your outbound train ride is on a Friday, Saturday or Sunday—and your return trip is Saturday, Sunday or Monday of the same weekend.

Makes the cost of the return ride a fraction of the outgoing ride.

Monthly Return

Makes the cost of the return ride a fraction of the outgoing ride, if both rides are within one month of each other.

BRITAINSHRINKERS

Available March 1 to October 31. Guided one-day excursions from London by train and bus to Bath and Stonehenge, Canterbury and Dover, Stratford-upon-Avon, York, Brighton, Oxford and the Cotswolds. Cambridge and Ely, Leeds Castle and Canterbury, Devon, and Stratford and Oxford.

From the time you board a specially marked car on the designated train, a red-uniformed escort accompanies you to the day's destination: onto a waiting deluxe motorcoach, that day's sightseeing (including admission fees), and on the ride back to London. Lunch at a pub is included. Purchased in conjunction with a BritRail Pass and taken during the BRP's validity period, these tours are priced at a great discount. The 1983 prices range from U.S.$41 ($29 with a BRP) to $65 ($35 with a BRP) per adult, and 30%-40% less for a child. A $201 Scotland overnight tour is only $149 with a BRP, and a 2-night $289 York-and-Scotland tour is $237 with a BRP.

Three overnight (2-day) tours are also offered: Scotland, a combination of York and Scotland, and Shakespeare Country.

When planning to travel both in Britain and on the Continent, keep in mind that the maximum value of combining a British pass with Eurailpass is achieved by scheduling Britain for either the start or end of a tour.

For example, to start a tour in Amsterdam and have one's itinerary then go to Paris, London and then return to the Continent for additional Eurailpass traveling would require a longer and therefore more expensive Eurailpass since the time spent in Britain consumes Eurailpass days.

Conversely, to start a tour in London, followed by travel on the Continent, and then concluding with more travel in Britain will require a longer and therefore more expensive BritRail Pass since the time spent on the Continent will consume BritRail Pass days.

In either direction, the "bridge" for using both the BritRail Pass and a Eurailpass is to also have a BritRail Seapass.

We present in this chapter descriptions of 4 categories of rail service. First, the train connection services between London and the Continent (Paris, Brussels and Amsterdam). Next, 43 one-day rail trips that can be made comfortably out of London, with details as to departure and arrival times plus what to see in each destination before returning to London, in most cases, at dinnertime.

Third, you will find itineraries for 3 long trips from and to London: Shannon Airport, Dublin and Edinburgh. This chapter concludes with details on many rail trips in Scotland.

Several of the routes are noted for outstanding scenery.

Always—without exception—before commencing each journey doublecheck the times given here or in any published timetable, as they are subject to change without prior notice. Eurail® Guide has made every effort to publish correct departure and arrival times, but schedules are constantly changed.

Changes will usually be minor and have no effect on the trips recommended in this book. However, in being one-minute late for a connection, the proverbial "a miss is as good as a mile" applies. WE DO NOT WANT YOU TO BE STRANDED!

The extensive notes on train connections in this book are intended to help you plan your itinerary before you start your trip. These notes are also useful after your trip begins (if you bring Eurail® Guide along!) for making impromptu, last-minute travel plans.

WARNING: Many cities have 2 or more railstations. London has 8 railstations. We take pains to tell you for every trip in this book the name of the railstation from which your train departs, by noting the station in parenthesis immediately after the name of the city. PAY HEED!

BRITAIN
THURSO
WICK
INVERNESS
KYLE OF LOCHALSH
ABERDEEN
MALLAIG
AVIEMORE
FORT WILLIAM
DUNDEE
PERTH
ST. ANDREWS
GLENEAGLES
OBAN
STIRLING
GLASGOW
EDINBURGH
BERWICK
TURNBERRY
DUMFRIES
NEWCASTLE
SUNDERLAND
CARLISLE
STRANREAR
HARTLEPOOL
SALTBURN
DARLINGTON
MIDDLESBROUGH
WINDERMERE
SCARBOROUGH
HARROGATE
BARROW
YORK
HEYSHAM
HULL
PRESTON
LEEDS
SELBY
BLACKPOOL
BRADFORD
DONCASTER
MANCHESTER
GRIMSBY
SHEFFIELD
LIVERPOOL
LINCOLN
HOLYHEAD
LLANDUDNO
RETFORD
SKEGNESS
CREWE
NEWARK
STOKE
CHESTER
GRANTHAM
YARMOUTH
DERBY
PWLLHELI
KING'S LYNN
STAFFORD
NOTTINGHAM
NORWICH
SHREWSBURY
PETERSBOROUGH
LEICESTER
ELY
WOLVERHAMPTON
ABERYSTWYTH
COVENTRY
BURMINGHAM
CAMBRIDGE
HARWICH
RUGBY
IPSWICH
WORCESTER
NORTHAMPTON
FISHGUARD
HEREFORD
STRATFORD UPPON AVON
COLCHESTER
CHELTENHAM
CLACTON
CLOUCESTER
OXFORD
SWANSEA
READING
SWINDON
LONDON
NEWPORT
SOUTHEND
WINDSOR
CANTERBURY
CARDIFF
BRISTOL
BATH
ASHFORD
DOVER
SALISBURY
BARNSTAPLE
TAUNTON
FOLKSTONE
SOUTHAMPTON
HASTINGS
EASTBOURNE
NEWHAVEN
BRIGHTON
WORTHING
PORTSMOUTH
EXETER
BOURNEMOUTH
WEYMOUTH
NEWTON ABBOT
TORQUAY
PLYMOUTH
ST. IVES
PENZANCE

All of London's railstations are interconnected by subway service, providing far easier and quicker transfers than by surface streets. For example, when entering England by rail from France, at Dover, you will come into Victoria station. To continue directly to Edinburgh, it is necessary to take a train from King's Cross station, on the opposite side of London from Victoria station.

A brief description of the areas served by London's 8 major railstations:

CHARING CROSS STATION

This station services suburban commuters between London and Folkestone, and between London and Hastings. It connects at Dover (Priory station) with Hovercraft service to and from France.

EUSTON STATION

A part of Central England and the Northwestern area of Britain are reached from Euston station, starting with Coventry and Birmingham, and then running through Stafford, Chester, Liverpool, Manchester and Blackpool, on into Glasgow. Also, Holyhead, gateway to Dublin.

KING'S CROSS STATION

Northeastern England (Leeds, York, Hull, Newcastle) and Edinburgh are reached by trains from King's Cross station. Newcastle is the gateway to Norway. Hull is a gateway to Denmark, Germany and Holland.

LIVERPOOL STREET STATION

This station services the area immediately Northeast of London: Colchester, Cambridge, Ipswich, Harwich (gateway to Holland, Germany, Austria, Yugoslavia and Norway), Norwich and King's Lynn.

PADDINGTON STATION

The area in Southern England, West from Weymouth (Exeter, Plymouth and Penzance), is reached out of Paddington station—as is also that portion of Southwestern England running North to Bristol, Swansea, Fishguard (gateway to Rosslare, at the Southeastern tip of the Republic of Ireland), Gloucester, Worcester, Hereford and Oxford.

ST. PANCRAS STATION

Trains going due North from London to Leicester, Derby, Nottingham and Sheffield leave from St. Pancras station.

VICTORIA STATION

The London airport for charter flights is Gatwick, which is serviced from 6:00 to 24:00 by a train every 15 minutes (and hourly from 1:00 to 5:00) for the 40-minute ride to London's Victoria station.

The transfer from airplane to train, or vice versa, is entirely indoor as the railstation at Gatwick is a part of the airport.

Victoria station services the small area of Southern England just

East of but not including Portsmouth: Worthing, Brighton, Newhaven, Eastbourne, Hastings and Dover (gateway to France, Spain, Belgium. Switzerland, Italy, Austria and Yugoslavia).

WATERLOO STATION

Services South Central England: Portsmouth, Southampton, Bournemouth and Weymouth.

London Underground Connection with Heathrow

Opened in mid-1977, the direct subway service between Heathrow Airport and central London allows one to take a direct train from and to any station on Piccadilly Line and London's airport for scheduled airlines.

SUMMER TIME

Britain changes to Summer Time on the last Sunday of March and converts back to Standard Time on the last Sunday of October.

Days of the Week Variances

For the time schedules given in this book, "daily" means Monday through Sunday. Where Sunday departure and arrival times are specified in conjunction with a list of daily schedules, this refers to additional service on Sunday, not to substitute service.

In other words, if a daily schedule lists departures at 10:00 and 11:12, and the Sunday schedule indicates a departure at 13:05, there are 3 departures on Sunday: at 10:00, 11:12 and 13:05.

Conversely, if Monday-Friday or Monday-Saturday schedules show departures at 10:00 and 11:12, and there is a listing of a Sunday departure at 13:05, then the only departure on Sunday for that trip is 13:05.

The same treatment applies to "Saturday only" schedules in connection with times given as "Monday-Friday" or as "daily".

Summer and Winter Schedules

In most European countries, a Winter timetable goes into effect on the last Saturday in September. Outside Britain, Winter schedules usually start on the Sunday following the last Saturday of September and run until and including the Saturday preceding the last Sunday in May of the following year.

British timetables differ from the Continental pattern.

Summer timetables for British rail service begin on the third Monday in May. The change to a Winter schedule occurs on the first Monday in October and on the first Monday in January.

Unless designated otherwise, the departure and arrival times given in this chapter are for the Summer season and apply to trips that are made from early May to October.

LONDON

The capital of England. See the changing of the guard at Buckingham Palace. Downing Street, official residence of the Prime Minister. The Tower of London. London Bridge. The Houses of Parliament. The Wellington Museum. Hyde Park.

The Kensington Gardens complex of Royal Albert Hall, the Science Museum and the Natural History Museum. Globe Theater. Piccadilly Circus. The National Gallery. The British Museum. Dickens' House. St. Paul's Cathedral. Gray's Inn. The Imperial War Museum. Kew Gardens. Regent's Park.

Westminster Abbey. The Geological Museum. The National Portrait Gallery. Nelson's Monument in Trafalgar Square. The Victoria and Albert Museum. St. James Palace. The 53-acre Green Park. The Wellington Arch. Admiralty Arch. The Sunday orators at Speaker's Corner. Marble Arch. Lambeth Palace, the residence of the Archbishop of Canterbury. The newspaper offices along Fleet Street.

The dragon at Temple Bar Memorial. Mansion House, the residence of the Lord Mayor of London. Tower Bridge. The South Bank Arts Centre complex of National Theatre, Queen Elizabeth Hall, Royal Festival Hall, and Hayward Gallery. The Victoria Tower. Whitehall, the compound of government offices. The beautifully uniformed sentries outside The Horse Guards. Piccadilly Circus.

One of the world's greatest food stores, in Harrods Department Store, presents a spectacle of more than 500 cheeses, 120 different breads, 21 kinds of butter, produce from California, and a meat hall 90 feet long by 60 feet wide containing hams, pork, sausages, beef and lamb. There is also venison, shellfish, poultry, salmon (smoked and fresh), tinned foods from all over the world, eggs, teas from everywhere, caviars, wine, and the list goes on forever.

CONNECTIONS WITH THE CONTINENT

The shortest route from England to the Continent is Dover (Marine) to Calais, or Dover (Priory) to Boulogne.

The validity of one's BritRail Pass stops or starts, as the case may be, at the British shore. Similarly, the validity of one's Eurailpass stops or starts at the Continental port where your boat ride begins or ends.

In all cases, the channel boat fare is not covered by either pass.

Regular ferries run the following routes: Dover-Boulogne, Dover-Calais, Dover-Dunkerque, Dover-Oostende, Folkestone-Boulogne, Folkestone-Calais, Harwich-Hoek van Holland and Newhaven-Dieppe.

Hovercraft service, faster and more expensive, is provided Dover-Boulogne, Dover-Calais, Dover-Zeebrugge, Newhaven-Dieppe, Portsmouth-Cherbourg, Portsmouth-Le Havre, Ramsgate-Calais, Ramsgate-

Dunkerque, Southampton-Cherbourg and Southampton-Le Havre.
Both regular ferries and hovercraft carry autos.

London - Paris via Dieppe (regular ferry) 51

Dep. London (Vict.)	7:50(1)	8:36(3)	11:10(4)	20:10(5)
Dep. Gatwick Airport	8:28	9:11	11:46	20:46
Arr. Newhaven Harbour	9:12	10:01	12:27	21:29
Change to ferry.				
Dep. Newhaven Harbour	10:00	11:00	13:00	22:00
Set your watch forward one hour, except from late Sept. to late Oct.				
Arr. Dieppe	15:00	15:00	18:00	3:00
Change to train.				
Dep. Dieppe	15:50(2)	15:50(2)	18:40	4:00
Arr. Rouen (Rive Dr.)	16:43	16:43	-0- (4)	4:56
Arr. Paris (St. Laz.)	18:11	18:11	21:05	6:25

* * *

Dep. Paris (St. Laz.)	10:45(1+2)	10:45(3)	22:36(5)
Dep. Rouen (Rive Dr.)	12:12	12:12	0:03
Arr. Dieppe	13:10	13:10	0:56
Change to ferry.			
Dep. Dieppe	13:45	13:45(3)	2:00
Set your watch back one hour, except from late Sept. to late Oct.			
Arr. Newhaven Harbour	16:45	17:45	5:00
Change to train.			
Dep. Newhaven Harbour	17:26	18:26	5:40
Arr. Gatwick Airport	18:04	19:05	6:18
Arr. London (Vict.)	18:46	19:46	6:57

(1) Daily. Runs from late May to late September. (2) Light refreshments. (3) Daily. Runs from late September to late October. No time change during this period. (4) Daily. Runs from late May to late September. Departs London at 10:55 on Saturday. Only the Sunday departure stops in Rouen. (5) Daily. Runs from mid-June to mid-September. Departs London at 19:55 on Saturday.

The other Channel-crossing schedules are:

London - Paris (regular ferry)

50

Dep. London (Vict.)	8:00(1)	9:58(2)	11:58(3)	13:58(7)
Set your watch forward one hour, except from late Sept. to late Oct.				
Arr. Paris (Nord)	16:18	18:25	20:20	22:30
Arr. Paris (Lyon)	-0-	20:06	-0-	23:20(4)
	*	*	*	
Dep. Paris (Lyon)	-0-	9:30(3)	-0-	-0-
Dep. Paris (Nord)	8:10(3)	10:37(3)	12:20(5)	14:25(3+8)
Set your watch back one hour, except from late Sept. to late Oct.				
Arr. London (Vict.)	14:17	16:55	19:02	21:17

(1)Runs from late July to late August. (2)Light refreshments. (3)Runs from late May to late September. Light refreshments from Boulogne to Paris and v.v. (4)Terminates at Lyon station only from late May to late September. (5)Meal service Paris to Calais. (6)Light refreshments Dunkerque to Paris. (7)Plus another departure from London at 20:58(6). (8)Plus another departure from Paris(Nord) at 22:35.

London - Paris (hovercraft)

49

Dep. London (Charing X)	7:20(1)	9:00(2)	11:30(2)	14:00(2)	16:00(1)
Set your watch forward one hour, except from late Sept. to late Oct.					
Arr. Paris (Nord)	14:15	16:12	18:15	20:40	23:02
		*	*	*	
Dep. Paris (Nord)	6:52(3)	9:05(1)	11:00(2)	13:00(2)	14:20(2+4)
Set your watch back one hour, except from late Sept. to late Oct.					
Arr. London (Charing X)	12:40	13:40	15:40	17:43	18:40

(1)Runs from late May to late September. (2)Light refreshments from Boulogne to Paris and v.v. (3)Monday-Friday. (4)Plus another departure from Paris at 16:37(1).

London - Brussels via Oostende (Jetfoil) 52a

Reservations are advisable on all of these trains.

Dep. London (Vict.)	8:44	11:28(1)	13:44	15:58
Dep. Dover Docks	10:35	13:20	15:40	17:50
Set your watch forward one hour, except from late Sept. to late Oct.				
Arr. Oostende	13:15	16:00	18:20	20:30
Change to train.				
Dep. Oostende	13:53	16:53	18:53	21:15
Arr. Brussels (Midi)	15:06	18:06	20:06	22:31
Arr. Brussels (Nord)	12 minutes later			

(1)Daily from late May to late September. Monday-Friday from late September to mid-November, mid-December to early January, and mid-March to late May.

London - Brussels via Oostende (regular ferry) 52

Dep. London (Vict.)	8:44	11:28(1)	13:44	15:58
Set your watch forward one hour, except from late Sept. to late Oct.				
Arr. Brussels (Midi)	15:06	18:06	20:06	22:31
Arr. Brussels (Nord)	12 minutes later			

(1)Daily from late May to late September. (2)Monday-Friday from late September to mid-November, mid-December to early January, and mid-March to late May.

London - Amsterdam via Hoek van Holland (regular ferry) 66

All of these trains have light refreshments.

Dep. London (L'pool)	9:40	19:40
Set your watch forward one hour, except from late Sept. to late Oct.		
Arr. Amsterdam (C.S.)	20:55	9:01

* * *

Dep. Amsterdam (C.S.)	9:30	21:16
Set your watch back one hour, except from late Sept. to late Oct.		
Arr. London (L'pool)	19:23	9:14

One-Day Excursions from London

The notation "frequent times" in these schedules means at least one (and usually more) departures every hour.

London - Arundel - London

520

Dep. London (Victoria) Frequent times from 8:28 to 13:28
Arr. Arundel 80 minutes later

Sights in Arundel: A lovely town, dominated by the magnificent Castle of the Dukes of Norfolk, open late March to late October, Monday-Friday plus Sundays in August, 12:00-17:00.

Dep. Arundel Frequent times from 12:38 to 20:38
Arr. London (Victoria) 80 minutes later

London - Bath - London

535

Dep. London (Pad.)	Mon.-Sat. Frequent times from 7:20				
	Sun.	**7:45**	**8:45**	**9:45**	**11:45**
Arr. Bath	90 minutes later.				

Sights: The Roman baths. Antique shops around Abbey Green. The Costume Museum in the Assembly Rooms. The Pump Room. The Royal Crescent row of town houses. Queen Square. The shops on Pulteney Bridge. The Circus. The American Museum at Claverton Manor, open daily except Monday 14:00-17:00. The collection of Eltonware and Nailsea glass in the 14th century Clevedon Court manor house, open Wednesday, Thurday and Sunday 14:30-17:30.

Bath is a great base for seeing much of the best sights in England. Several good, inexpensive motorcoach tours go to Gloucester, Salisbury, Stonehenge and Cheddar Gorge. These buses stop for photo-taking along the way.

Dep. Bath Spa	Mon-Sat	Frequent times to 21:30
	Sun.	Frequent times to 21:27
Arr. London (Pad.)	90 minutes later.	

London - Bournemouth - London 522

Dep. London (Waterloo) Mon-Sat Frequent times from 5:46
Sun Frequent times from 8:30
Arr. Bournemouth 2 hours later.

Sights: A large seaside resort. Stroll through Pavillion Rock Garden. Three gambling casinos. Many lovely parks and gardens.

Dep. Bournemouth Mon-Sat Frequent times to 23:57
Sun Frequent times to 22:00
Arr. London (Waterloo) 2 hours later.

London - Brighton - London 518

Dep. London (Victoria) Frequent times from 6:20
Arr. Brighton 55-70 minutes later.

Sights: The Aquarium at Palace Pier. Antique shops in the many alleys, called "The Lanes". Plenty of Regency architecture. The Royal Pavillion. The ornate chandelier in Banquet Hall.

Dep. Brighton Frequent times to 23:10
Arr. London (Victoria) 55-70 minutes later.

London - Bristol - London 535

Dep. London (Paddington) Frequent times from 7:20
(from 7:45 on Sundays)
Arr. Bristol (Temple Meads) 2 hours later

* * *

Dep. Bristol (Temple Meads) Frequent times to 21:30 (21:15 on Sun.)
Arr. London (Paddington) 2 hours later

Sights: A famous seaport. Everything here is either a short walk or can be reached by bus. The city operates 1½-hour guided walking tours June, July and August from the Exchange on Corn Street at 11:00 on Monday and Tuesday, at 14:30 on other days. Some of Bristol can be seen from a tour boat at the harbor. That tour operates daily at 12:00, 14:00, 15:00 and 16:00.

See the many excellent Georgian buildings on Royal York Crescent, Cornwallis Crescent, Windsor Terrace, West Mall, Caledonia Place, Queen Square and Berkeley Square. The Christmas Steps, built in 1669. The 12th century St. James' Church.

The John Wesley Chapel, world's first Methodist preaching house, with a bronze statue of Wesley in the courtyard. The 11th century St. Mary-le-Port Church. St. John's Church. The 13th century St. Mary Redcliffe, one of England's largest churches. The 12th century Cathedral.

The exhibit of period furniture in the 18th century Georgian House. The view from the top of Cabot Tower, on Brandon Hill. The collection of porcelain, models of early sailing ships and paintings of the waterfront in the Bristol Museum and Art Gallery, open every day 10:00-17:00. See the rare animals (including white tigers) at the Zoo. Brunel's Clifton Suspension Bridge, built in 1864, striding Avon Gorge, 245 feet above the water. Tour Brunel's iron steamship, The Great Britain (the first ocean screw steamship, launched in 1843), returned to Bristol in 1970 from the Falkland Islands. It is open to visitors 10:00-18:00.

London - Cardiff - London 540

Dep. London (Pad.) Frequent times from 7:00 (8:15 on Sun.)
Arr. Cardiff (Cent.) 2 hours later

Sights: Llandaff Cathedral. Cardiff Castle. The National Museum of Wales, featuring Welsh handicraft and art.

Dep. Cardiff (Cent.) Frequent times to 21:30 (21:20 on Sun.)
Arr. London (Pad.) 2 hours later

London - Bristol - Cardiff - London

As these schedules indicate, it is easy to visit both Cardiff and Bristol in one day. These schedules are only for Monday-Friday travel.

535

Dep. London (Pad.) 8:20
Arr. Bristol (T.M.) 9:52

Sightsee in Bristol.
Change trains.

539

Dep. Bristol (T.M.) 13:01
Arr. Cardiff (Cent.) 14:10

540

Dep. Cardiff (Central) 16:38(1)
Arr. London (Pad.) 18:31

Plus other departures from Cardiff at 17:31, 18:38, 19:31 and 21:26.

London - Cambridge - London 589

Dep. London (L'pool) 7:28(1) 8:35(2+3) 9:35(2) 10:35(4+6)
Arr. Cambridge 70-80 minutes later

Sights: To see buildings that have housed great colleges for more than 700 years, take bus #101 to Market Street. See King's College Chapel and Queen's College. Visit the Wren Library at Trinity College, the tapestries and manuscripts in the Fitzwilliam Museum, and the Botanical Gardens. Hire a boat at Mill Bridge or Anchor Inn, and paddle along the idyllic Cam River. Four miles away is the American Cemetery.

Dep. Cambridge 12:20(2) 13:44(3) 14:20(4) 15:34(1+7)
Arr. London (L'pool) 70-80 minutes later

(1) Monday-Friday, except holidays. (2) Light refreshments. (3) Daily, except Sundays and holidays. (4) Meal service. (5) Sunday only. (6) Plus other departures from London at 11:05(3), 12:05(1+2) and 12:35(4). (7) Plus other departures from Cambridge at 16:20(2+5), 17:00(3+4), 17:20(2), 18:20(4), 19:20(5), 20:00(3) and 20:24(5).

London - Canterbury - London

The easiest way to make a one-day excursion to Canterbury is to start by departing from either London's Waterloo or Charing Cross railstations. Trains running frequently arrive 70 minutes later at Canterbury's West railstation. The walk from it to the famous Cathedral allows you to view interesting buildings.

For the ride back to London, depart from Canterbury's East railstation, nearer to the Cathedral than the West station. A departure from Canterbury's East station will take you to London's Victoria station. Or, you can depart from Canterbury's West station, arriving London's Waterloo or Charing Cross stations.

Sights: The great Cathedral, housing the tomb of Thomas á Becket. Medieval inns (Falstaff, Beverlie, Olive Branch). The cemetery, where Christopher Marlowe and Joseph Conrad are buried. Shops, plays, ballet, cricket.

London - Chester - London 557

Dep. London (Euston)	9:00(1)	10:00(1)	10:55(2)	
Arr. Chester	11:47	12:50	13:54	
	*	*	*	
Dep. Chester	14:13(3)	16:05(3+4)	17:59(5)	19:46(5+6)
Arr. London (Euston)	16:56	18:48	20:40	22:27

(1) Light refreshments. (2) Monday-Friday. (3) Meal service. (4) Daily. (5) Sunday only. (6) Runs from late July to mid-September.

Sights: The excellent collection of Roman artifacts (glass, tools, coins, weapons, tombstones) at Grosvenor Museum. The "Rows", long covered balconies (to protect shoppers from rain) that are full-length streets above the streets of Chester. These are lined with shops. Also see the Cathedral. The castle overlooking the River Dee. The ancient city walls. The marvelous carving of animals and historic scenes on the front of the 17th century Bishop Lloyd's House. The 16th century mansion, Stanley Palace. The 30-minute slide show of Chester's history, in the British Heritage Centre. The Tourist Office at City Hall offers a free guided 2½-hour walking tour.

London - Chartwell - London

There are many departures daily from London's Charing Cross railstation for the 45-minute ride to Sevenoaks. Take a taxi for the 7-mile trip from Sevenoaks to Chartwell.

Sights in Chartwell: The country house that Winston Churchill bought in 1922, where he painted and wrote his books during the years he was out of power. You will see here the best collection of Churchilliana in the world: his collection of eccentric hats, his World War II "jump suit", Knight of the Garter uniform, many of his paintings, and a model of the Invasion Day harbor at Arromanches. Also the brick wall and cottage he built with his own hands on a small part of the 79 acres there. The main house is open Wednesday, Thurday, Saturday and Sunday from April to mid-October.

London - Chichester - London

520

Dep. London (Victoria) 6:48(1) 8:28(2) 9:28 10:28(3+4)
Arr. Chichester 2 hours later

Sights in Chichester: The museum and mosaic floors in the Palace at Fishbourne, one mile away, the largest Roman residence in Britain, built in the 3rd century.

Dep. Chichester Mon-Sat Frequent times from 13:19 to 21:39
Sun Frequent times from 9:27 to 21:27
Arr. London (Victoria) 2 hours later

(1) Daily, except Saturday. (2) Light refreshments. (3) Daily, except Sundays and holidays. (4) Plus other departures from London at 10:28(2+3), 11:28(3), 12:28(3) and 13:28(3).

London - Coventry - London

552

Dep. London (Euston) Mon-Sat Frequent times from 7:02
Sun Frequent times from 9:40
Arr. Coventry 1-1½ hours later

Sights: Completely rebuilt since the Nazi air attacks, Coventry was the site of Lady Godiva's notorious horseback ride. See the Graham Sutherland tapestry, the abstract stained-glass windows and the enormous engraved glass wall at the new (1962) Cathedral.

Dep. Coventry Frequent times to 21:58 (22:09 on Sundays)
Arr. London (Euston) 1-1½ hours later

London - Dover - London

512

Dep. London (Victoria) Frequent times from 6:55 to 21:55
Arr. Dover (Priory) 2 hours later

Sights: The legendary white cliffs. The mighty castle. The busy harbor.

Dep. Dover (Priory) Frequent times from 6:32 to 22:18
Arr. London (Victoria) 2 hours later

London - Exeter - London #1

530

Dep. London (Pad.)

	Mon-Fri	Frequent times from 7:15 to 20:25
	Sat	Frequent times from 7:25 to 23:25
	Sun	Frequent times from 8:25 to 23:00
Arr. Exeter (St. David's)		2½ hours later

Sights: The 11th century Cathedral, with its 300-foot nave and row of statues. Rougemont Castle. The Mint. The underground water channel at Princesshay. The paintings and oak paneling in Exeter Guildhall.

The exhibit of boats from all parts of the world at the very interesting Maritime Museum.

Dep. Exeter (St. David's)

	Mon-Fri	Frequent times from 6:59 to 20:09
	Sat	Frequent times from 6:59 to 20:09
	Sun	Frequent times from 8:30 to 22:23
Arr. London (Pad.)		2½ hours later

OR

London - Exeter - London #2

523

Dep. London (Waterloo)	6:50(1)	8:37(2)	9:10(3)	
Arr. Exeter (Central)	10:33	11:47	12:31	
Arr. Exeter (St. David's)	5 minutes later			

* * *

(Monday-Saturday)

Dep. Exeter (St. David's)	14:20(4)	16:20(4)	18:20	20:20(5)
Dep. Exeter (Central)	5 minutes later			
Arr. London (Waterloo)	17:53	19:47	21:48	0:33

(Sundays)

Dep. Exeter (St. David's)	15:24(4)	16:05	17:39	18:25
Dep. Exeter (Central)	5 minutes later			
Arr. London (Waterloo)	18:43	19:30	20:56	21:43

(1) Monday-Saturday. (2) Saturdays only. (3) Light refreshments, except Sundays. (4) Light refreshments. (5) Change trains at Basingstoke.

London - Greenwich - London

There is commuter train service from London to Blackheath, from where it is a short walk through Greenwich Park to the Observatory, the Cutty Sark and the Royal Navy College. Allow 3 hours for the walk and sightseeing.

0000

Dep. London (Charing X)	On the half-hour
Arr. Blackheath	20 minutes later

Sights: Greenwich is the location of the world's prime meridian, from which all distances and hours worldwide are measured. See the 1870 clipper ship, Cutty Sark, at Greenwich Pier. Nearby, the 53-foot Gypsy Moth sailboat which Chichester sailed around the world in 1966-67. The Royal Navy College, and its magnificent Painted Hall. The Royal Observatory. The marvelous exhibits in the National Maritime Museum. The Meridian Building.

Dep. Blackheath	Frequent times
Arr. London (Charing X)	20 minutes later

London - Hampton Court - London

0000

Dep. London (Waterloo)	Frequent times
Arr. Hampton Court	35 minutes later

Sights in Hampton Court: The riverside Palace built by Cardinal Wolsey and then given to Henry VIII.

Dep. Hampton Court	Frequent times
Arr. London (Waterloo)	35 minutes later

London - Hastings - London

516

These trains have light refreshments daily, except Sun. and holidays.

Dep. London (Vict.)	8:52	9:52	10:52	11:52
Arr. Hastings	2 hours later			

Sights: This is where William became the Conqueror, of the Saxons. Visit the old fishing harbor.

Dep. Hastings	28 minutes after each hour to 21:28
Arr. London (Vict.)	2 hours later

London - Hatfield - London

0000

Dep. London (King's X)	Frequent times
Arr. Hatfield	35 minutes later

Sights in Hatfield: The fine state rooms in the 17th century Hatfield House, open from late March to early October, Tuesday-Saturday 12:00-17:00 and Sundays 14:00-17:30.

Dep. Hatfield	Frequent times
Arr. London (King's X)	35 minutes later

London - Isle of Wight - London (via Portsmouth) #1

521

Dep. London (Waterloo)	7:50	8:40	9:40
Arr. Portsmouth (Harbor)	9:27	10:16	11:17
Change to boat.			
Dep. Portsmouth (Harbor)	9:35	10:25	11:25
Arr. Ryde Pier Head	10:00	10:50	11:50
Change to train.			
Dep. Ryde Pier Head	10:07	11:05	12:05
Arr. Shanklin	10:29	11:29	12:29

* * *

Three different bus tours on the Isle of Wight operate on different Sundays from June through early September. These are offered as a package that includes the roundtrip train fare from London (the 9:50 departure). The bus tours end in Ryde, connecting with the hovercraft departure from there for Portsmouth that is timed for the train that arrives back in London at 20:17.

Dep. Shankin	Frequent times from 12:41 to 21:11
Arr. London (Waterloo)	3 hours later

OR

London - Isle of Wight - London (via Lymington) #2

522

Dep. London (Waterloo)	8:46
Arr. Brockenhurst	10:28
Change trains.	
522a	
Dep. Brockenhurst	10:41
Arr. Lymington Pier	10:54
Change to ferry.	
Dep. Lymington Pier	11:00
Arr. Yarmouth	11:30

522a

Dep. Yarmouth	14:00
Arr. Lymington Pier	14:30
Change to train.	
Dep. Lymington Pier	15:00
Arr. Brockenhurst	15:13
Change trains.	
522	
Dep. Brockenhurst	16:02
Arr. London (Waterloo)	18:04

London - Leicester - London

Dep. London (St. Pancras) Frequent times from 7:45 to 23:05
Arr. Leicester 1½-2 hours later

Sights: The Jewry Wall, to see outstanding Roman ruins. The Church of St. Mary de Castro.

Dep. Leicester Frequent times from 8:26 to 20:51
Arr. London (St. Pancras) 1½-2 hours later

London - Lincoln - London 576

Change trains in Newark.

Dep. London (King's X)	8:04(1+2)	9:50(1+2)	11:05(3+6)
Arr. Lincoln (St. Marks)	10:06	11:30	13:35

Sights: The wonderful Cathedral. Newport Arch. Roman relics in the City and County Museums. The houses on High Bridge.

Dep. Lincoln (St. Marks)	14:17(4)	16:38(2+5)	17:10(3+7)
Arr. London (King's X)	16:42	18:49	19:11

(1) Monday-Saturday. (2) Meal service. (3) Sunday only. Meal service. (4) Daily. Meal service Monday-Saturday. Only light refreshments on Sunday. (5) Monday-Friday, except holidays. (6) Plus another departure from London at 12:04(1+2). (7) Plus other departures from Lincoln at 18:26(1), 19:10(3) and 20:24(1+2).

London - Norwich - London 590

Dep. London (Liverpool)	8:30(1)	9:30(1)	10:30(1)	11:30(2)	12:30(1)
Arr. Norwich	10:44	11:27	12:40	13:27	14:40

Sights: Norwich Grammar School. (Its alumni include Lord Nelson.) The Cathedral. The collection of lace, pottery, teapots, paintings and coins at the Museum in the Castle, and the view of Norwich from the Castle. Assembly House. The Strangers Hall. Walk down the Elm Hill alley.

Dep. Norwich	14:31(1)	15:46(3)	16:31(1)	17:46(1)	18:46(4+7)
Arr. London (Liverpool)	16:45	17:45	18:45	19:44	21:01

(1) Daily. Meal service, except on Saturday and Sunday. Light refreshments on Saturday. (2) Monday-Saturday. Meal service. (3) From late May to early September: daily. From early September to late May: Monday-Saturday. (4) Daily. Departs 18:20 on Sunday. (5) Sunday only. (6) Daily. (7) Plus other departures from Norwich at 19:00(5) and 19:54(6).

London - Nottingham - London

570

Dep. London (St. Pan.) 8:10(1+2) 8:45(3) 10:00(4+12)
Arr. Nottingham 2 hours later

Sights: The Duke of Newcastle's castle, which was a new Newcastle castle in 1679, with its art collection. The great council house. The Natural History Museum in Wollaton Hall.

Dep. Nottingham 13:00(1) 13:17(5) 14:10(4+13)
Arr. London (St. Pan.) 2 hours later

(1) Monday-Friday, except holidays. (2) Meal service. (3) Saturday and Sunday only. (4) Monday-Saturday. Meal service, except only light refreshments on Saturday. (5) Sunday only. Light refreshments. (6) Daily. Meal service Monday-Friday. Only light refreshments on Saturday and Sunday. (7) Monday-Saturday. (8) Sunday only. (9) Monday-Saturday. Light refreshments except on Saturday. (10) Daily, except Saturday. (11) Saturday only. (12) Plus another departure from London at 11:00(4). (13) Plus other departures from Nottingham at 15:06(6). 16:05(7), 16:30(8), 17:05(1), 17:30(3), 18:30(8), 19:06(9), 19:30(8), 20:10(10), 20:30(11) and 21:06(8).

London - Leicester - Nottingham - London

As these schedules indicate, it is easy to visit both Leicester and Nottingham in one day. Monday-Saturday service.

570

Dep. London (St. Pancras) 7:50
Arr. Leicester 9:22
Sightsee in Leicester.
Dep. Leicester 13:05
Arr. Nottingham 13:39

Dep. Nottingham 17:00(1)
Arr. London (St. Pancras) 19:09
(1) Plus frequent other departures to 20:03.

London - Oxford - London 527 + 538

Dep. London (Pad.)	Frequent times from 6:50 to 19:50
Arr. Oxford	60-75 minutes later

* * *

Dep. Oxford	Frequent times from 8:30 to 22:25
Arr. London (Pad.)	60-75 minutes later

Sights: This is the home of one of the greatest universities in the world, comprising 28 different colleges. Start your stroll at the center of Oxford, Carfax Tower, where the Information Center is located and from which a 2-hour guided tour can be taken at 10:45 and 14:15 Monday-Saturday. There is bus service from the railstation to Carfax Tower.

Begin by walking south from Carfax Tower, down St. Aldates Street, to Folly Bridge, Christ Church and Pembroke College.

Later, see Merton College and Corpus Christi before continuing on to Oriel and then into High Street. See Bodleian Library, which has a copy of every book published in England. Most popular among visitors is Magdalen College, with its beautiful main quadrangle.

Nearby Blenheim Palace Churchill's Birthplace

To see lovely Blenheim Palace, take a bus in Oxford from Gloucester Green bus station for the 8-mile trip to Woodstock. This magnificent 18th century structure was the birthplace of Winston Churchill in 1874.

A gift from Britain to the Duke of Marlborough after this ancestor of Churchill defeated the French in 1704 at Blenheim in Bavaria, the beautiful 300-room mansion is open daily March-October, with guided tours 11:30-17:00.

Letters, documents, photos, even a lock of Churchill's hair (at the age of 5) are exhibited in the tiny room where he was born prematurely and unexpectedly on November 30, 1874, in his mother's seventh month of pregnancy. Other rooms throughout the palace have more memorabilia: some of Churchill's paintings (see "London-Chartwell", earlier in this chapter), recordings of his speeches, his letters, etc. A visit here is worthwhile if only to see the 180-foot-long library, with its marvelous Willis pipe organ.

There is time in the same day to visit nearby Bladon Churchyard. A simple tombstone there that reads merely "Winston Leonard Spencer Churchill 1874/1965" marks the burial place, alongside his American mother Jenny Spencer, of the greatest Englishman of the last 1,000 years.

London - Penzance - London 530

These trains have meal service.

Dep. London (Pad.)	8:25	Dep. Penzance	16:25(1)
Arr. Penzance	13:33	Arr. London (Pad.)	22:00

(1) Departs at 15:40 on Sunday.

Sights: The primitive beauty of the barren westernmost tip of England. Subtropical plants and palm trees grow here! It is only a 3-mile bus trip to St. Michel's Mount, and a 9-mile bus ride to Land's End.

London - Portsmouth - London **#1**

520

Dep. London (Victoria) 28 minutes after each hour, from 8:28 to 20:28
Arr. Portsmouth (Hbr.) 2 hours later

Sights: England's great naval base. See Lord Nelson's flagship, H.M.S. Victory, which won the battle of Trafalgar over the combined Spanish and French fleets. The nearby Victory Museum. The Dickens Museum at the house where the author was born, 393 Commercial Road.

Dep. Portsmouth (Hbr.) 49 minutes after each hour, from 8:49 to 19:49(1)
Arr. London (Victoria) 2 hours later

(1) On Sundays, depart Portsmouth at 2 minutes after each hour, from 9:02 to 21:02.

OR

London - Portsmouth - London **#2**

521

Dep. London (Waterloo) Frequent times from 6:48 to 20:28
Arr. Portsmouth (Hbr.) 1½-2 hours later

* * *

Dep. Portsmouth (Hbr.) Frequent times from 5:27 to 21:12
Arr. London (Waterloo) 1½-2 hours later

London - Portsmouth - Isle of Wight - London

As these schedules indicate, it is easy to visit both Portsmouth and the Isle of Wight in one day by stopping-over in Portsmouth from 9:25 to 11:20 or 12:33.

521

Dep. London (Wat.)	7:50(1)	8:50(1)
Arr. Portsmouth (Hbr.)	9:25	10:24
Sightsee in Portsmouth. Then take hovercraft to Isle of Wight.		
Dep. Portsmouth (Hbr.)	11:20(2)	12:33
Arr. Ryde Pier Head	11:50	12:58
Change to train.		
Dep. Ryde Pier Head	11:55	13:05
Arr. Shanklin	12:16	13:31

Dep. Shanklin	15:35(3)
Arr. Ryde Pier Head	16:03
Change to hovercraft.	
Dep. Ryde Pier Head	16:10
Arr. Portsmouth (Hbr.)	16:42
Change to train.	
Dep. Portsmouth (Hbr.)	16:53(1)
Arr. London (Wat.)	18:25

(1) Meal service Monday-Friday. Only light refreshments on Saturdays. (2) Departs 11:10 on Saturdays. (3) Plus frequent other departures from Shanklin to 21:11.

London - Rochester - London 514

Dep. London (Vict.)	MON-FRI	Frequent times from 6:25 to 23:23
	SAT & SUN	Frequent times from 5:23 to 22:23
Arr. Chatham	60 minutes later	

Change to suburban train for the 1-mile ride from Chatham to Rochester.

Sights in Rochester: The 17th century Bull Hotel, where Dickens' characters, Pickwick and his friends, spent the first night of their long and memorable trip. The house where Dickens lived his last 10 years and where he died is here, a red brick mansion. The cemetery has many markers from which Dickens took the names for the people he cast in his stories. Alongside the cemetery is the 15th century Gatehouse Teashoppe.

Visit the City Museum in Eastgate House, open daily except Friday 14:00-17:30. See the little house at 11 Ordinance Terrace, where Dickens lived from the time he was 4 until he was 9 years old.

Dep. Chatham	MON-FRI	Frequent times from 5:57 to 23:21
	SAT & SUN	Frequent times from 8:51 to 22:21
Arr. London (Vict.)	60 minutes later	

London - Rye - London 0000

Dep. London (Charing X)	Frequent times
Dep. London (Waterloo)	Frequent times
Arr. Rye	1½ hours later

Sights in Rye: The old houses and inns along the cobbled streets in this delightful little hilltop town, once an important seaport but now 2 miles from the sea.

Dep. Rye	Frequent times
Arr. London (Waterloo)	1½ hours later
Arr. London (Charing X)	1½ hours later

London - Salisbury - Stonehenge - London
523

Dep. London (Wat.)	7:45(1+2)	8:37(3)	9:10(4)	10:10(1+7)
Arr. Salisbury	9:21	9:54	10:34	11:53

Sights: The Cathedral, with its tombs of Crusaders and one of the 4 existing copies of the Magna Carta. Take a bus from Salisbury to Stonehenge to view the mysterious oval of huge stones there, about 4,000 years old. This is the most important prehistoric relic in Britain. How were these stupendous weights moved many miles from their quarry, and why ?

Dep. Salisbury	12:10(3)	13:10(5)	14:15(4)	15:10(5+8)
Arr. London (Wat.)	13:48	14:48	15:48	16:48

(1)Monday-Saturday. (2)Change trains in Basingstoke. (3)Saturdays only. (4)Light refreshments. (5)Monday-Friday, except holidays. (6)Saturday and Sunday. (7)Plus another departure from London at 11:10(4). (8)Plus other departures from Salisbury at 16:20(4), 17:10(6), 17:30(5), 18:20(1), 20:20, 21:20(2) and 22:24(1+2).

London - Salisbury - Exeter - London 523

As these schedules indicate, it is easy to visit both Salisbury and Exeter in one day.

Dep. London (Waterloo)	9:10
Arr. Salisbury	10:36
Sightsee in Salisbury.	
Dep. Salisbury	12:40
Arr. Exeter (Central)	14:41
Arr. Exeter (St. Davids)	14:45

Dep. Exeter (St. Davids)	18:20
Dep. Exeter (Central)	18:24
Arr. London (Waterloo)	21:48

London - St. Albans - London 570

Dep. London (St. Pancras)	6:41(1) 10:06(1)
Arr. St. Albans	20 minutes later

Sights in St. Albans: The beautiful Cathedral. The Roman ruins.

Dep. St. Albans	19:30(2)
Arr. London (St. Pancras)	20 minutes later

(1) Monday-Saturday, except holidays. (2) Monday-Friday, except holidays.

London - Stratford on Avon - London 527

Dep. London (Pad.)	6:50(1)	9:00	10:40(1+2+3)
Arr. Leamington Spa	8:49	10:46	12:54
Change trains.			
Dep. Leamington Spa	9:15(1)	10:50	13:14(1)
Arr. Stratford	9:46	11:21	13:45

Many people prefer fully-escorted day tours to Stratford that start and end in London. Details are available from British Tourist Authority, 64 St. James Street, near Piccadilly Circus.

A special "Shakespeare Connection" train departs from London's *Euston* station at 8:40 Monday-Saturday (9:40 on Sundays), arriving Coventry about one hour later. A special bus transfers passengers from Coventry to Stratford-on-Avon, a one-hour ride. This bus stops near the Stratford office that books various local tours. After 7 hours of leisurely sightseeing, passengers leave Stratford at 17:30 for the train departing Coventry at 18:30 for London. Those wishing to attend a performance at the Royal Shakespeare Theater are provided a bus at 11:38 for the 0:38 train from Coventry, arriving back in London, reaching there at 1:25.

There are many restaurants and pubs in Stratford, and visitors may picnic either by the theater or in the garden along the river.

It is a 10-minute walk from the railstation to Shakespeare's birthplace. See the house of Mary Arden, his mother. The cottage of Anne Hathaway, his wife. Shakespeare's tomb in Trinity Church. The home of John Harvard, founder of America's great university. There are afternoon performances at the Royal Shakespeare Theater on some Thursdays and Saturdays.

Dep. Stratford	12:31(1)	13:05(4)	15:32(1)	18:42(1+5)
Arr. Leamington Spa	13:03	14:00	16:04	19:05
Change trains.				
Dep. Leamington Spa	13:09(1)	14:12(4)	16:19(1)	19:10(1)
Arr. London (Pad.)	15:07	16:24	18:18	21:13

(1) Monday-Saturday, except holidays. (2) Light refreshments. (3) Change trains in Reading. (4) Sundays only. (5) Plus other departures from Stratford at 19:05(4), 20:05(4) and 20:40(1).

London - Torquay - London 530

Most of these trains have meal service or light refreshments.

Dep. London (Pad.)	7:15(1)	7:25(2+3)	8:25(3+4+6)
Arr. Torquay	10:41	11:03	12:17

Sights in Torquay: An 11-mile coastline that resembles a Mediteranean resort, palm trees and all.

Dep. Torquay	12:05(2)	13:16(1)	13:36(4+7)
Arr. London (Pad.)	15:29	16:36	17:38

(1) Monday-Friday, except holidays. (2) Saturday only. (3) Change trains in Newton Abbott. (4) Sundays only. (5) Runs from early July to late September. (6) Plus other departures from London at 8:27(2), 9:15(1), 9:25(3+4), 9:30(2), 10:27(2) and 10:45(4). (7) Plus other departures from Torquay at 14:02(2+5), 14:09(1+3), 15:01(2), 15:06(4), 15:15(1), 16:05(2), 16:44(1+3), 16:56(3+4), 17:08(2+3), 17:46(4), 18:35(1+3), 18:46(2+3), 18:53(3+4) and 21:05(3+4).

London - Winchester - London 522

Dep. London (Wat.)	MON-SAT	Frequent times from 5:45 to 23:46
	SUN	Frequent times from 8:45 to 22:46
Arr. Winchester	65 minutes later	

Sights: King Arthur's roundtable in the Great Hall at the Castle. The 11th century Cathedral, with the tombs of King Alfred, Jane Austen and Izaak Walton.

Dep. Winchester	MON-SAT	Frequent times from 10:01 to 22:55
	SUN	Frequent times from 9:04 to 23:04
Arr. London (Wat.)	65 minutes later	

London - Windsor - London 525

Dep. London (Waterloo)	Frequent times from 7:11 to 22:12
Arr. Windsor (Riverside)	50-60 minutes later

Sights in Windsor: Windsor Castle with its collection of Da Vinci drawings and, occasionally, members of the Royal Family. See the Changing of the Guard there, at 10:25. Queen Mary's Doll House. St. George's Chapel.

In the town, stroll down the 3-mile "Long Walk". See Eton College, where once it did not matter if you won or lost, in the days when observing amenities was more important than the final score.

Dep. Windsor (Riverside) Frequent times from 8:10 to 22:44
Arr. London (Waterloo) 50-60 minutes later

London - York - London

575

Most of these trains have meal service.

MONDAY-SATURDAY

Dep. London (King's X)	7:25	8:00	8:50	9:30(1)
Arr. York	9:40	10:14	11:22	11:41
	*	*	*	
Dep. York	14:56	15:17	16:48	17:49(2)
Arr. London (King's X)	16:49	17:26	18:55	19:55

SUNDAYS

Dep. London (King's X)	8:45	9:30	10:00	11:00(3)
Arr. York	11:49	11:57	12:33	13:21
	*	*	*	
Dep. York	14:29	15:12	15:20	16:27(4)
Arr. London (King's X)	16:59	17:25	18:00	18:43

(1)Plus other departures from London (Mon-Sat) at 10:00, 11:00, 11:30 and 12:00. (2)Plus other departures from York (Mon-Sat) at 18:48 and 20:53. (3)Plus other departures from London (Sun) at 12:00 and 12:30. (4)Plus other departures from York (Sun) at 17:12, 17:27, 18:09, 18:48, 19:45 and 20:48.

Sights: York Minister, the Cathedral with fantastic 15th century stained-glass. The collection of antiques at York Castle Museum. Walk down "The Shambles".

National Railway Museum, to which there are special excursion trains a few days in August, September, October and November. The all-day event includes roundtrip train service from London and 4 hours at the Museum.

SCENIC TRAIN TRIPS

There is much fine scenery on nearly every rail route in England. The next 3 train rides offer exceptional scenic views.

London - Pwllheli - London

There is fine coastal scenery plus a splendid view of Harlech Castle on this ride. It is not possible to make this trip without staying overnight in Pwllheli.

552			
Dep. London (Euston)	9:35(1+2)		
Arr. Wolverhampton	11:34		
Change trains.			
547			
Dep. Wolverhampton	11:50		
Arr. Shrewsbury	12:34		
Change trains.			
554			
Dep. Shrewsbury	12:40(3)		
Arr. Pwllheli	16:50		
	*	*	*
Dep. Pwllheli	8:00(4)	10:25(4)	12:00(1+5)
Arr. Shrewsbury	12:17	14:19	16:11
Change trains.			
547			
Dep. Shrewsbury	12:34(1)	14:34(1)	16:31(1)
Arr. Wolverhampton	13:20	15:20	17:19
Change trains.			
552			
Dep. Wolverhampton	13:30(1+2)	15:30(1+2)	17:30(1+6)
Arr. London (Euston)	15:33	17:36	19:31

(1) Monday-Saturday, except holidays. (2) Meal service. (3) Monday-Friday. Runs from late May to mid-September. (4) Saturdays only. Runs from late May to mid-September. (5) Change trains in Dovey Junction. (6) Light refreshments.

London - Windermere - London 565

These trains run Monday-Saturday, except holidays

Dep. London (Euston)	8:45(1)		
Arr. Preston	11:24		
Change trains.			
Dep. Preston	11:49		
Arr. Oxenholme	12:19		
Change trains. 563			
Dep. Oxenholme	12:26		
Arr. Windermere	12:51		

Sights in Windermere: Breathtaking lake scenery.

Dep. Windermere	14:45	16:55	
Arr. Oxenholme	15:08	17:18	
Change trains. 565			
Dep. Oxenholme	15:17(2)	17:40	-0-
Arr. Preston	-0- (2)	18:20	-0-
Change trains.			
Dep. Preston	-0- (2)	18:45(3)	19:51(1)
Arr. London (Euston)	19:03	21:34	22:37

(1) Meal service. (2) Direct train. No train change in Preston. (3) Runs from late May to early October.

A DAY THROUGH WALES

There is a marvelous one-day circle train trip from London that takes you through the incredibly beautiful rural scenery in the heart of Wales, between Swansea and Shrewsbury. As shown below, this trip can be made either clockwise or counter-clockwise.

London - Swansea - Shrewsbury - London

The following schedules are daily, except Sundays and holidays.

540		552	
Dep. London (Pad.)	9:15	Dep. London (Euston)	7:40
Arr. Swansea	11:54	Arr. Wolverhampton	9:39
Change trains. (548)		Change trains. (547)	
Dep. Swansea	12:25	Dep. Wolverhampton	9:50
Arr. Shrewsbury	16:05	Arr. Shrewsbury	10:26
Change trains. (547)		Change trains. (548)	
Dep. Shrewsbury	16:31	Dep. Shrewsbury	10:46
Arr. Wolverhampton	17:19	Arr. Swansea	14:35
Change trains. (552)		Change trains. (540)	
Dep. Wolverhampton	17:30	Dep. Swansea	14:42
Arr. London (Euston)	19:31	Arr. London (Pad.)	17:24

RAIL CONNECTIONS WITH IRELAND

London - Limerick (Shannon Airport) or Dublin via Fishguard 504

Dep. London (Pad.)	9:10(1)	20:55(3)	21:25(5)
Arr. Fishguard (Har.)	13:39	2:25(4)	2:25
Change to boat.			
Dep. Fishguard (Har.)	14:45	3:10(4)	3:10
Arr. Rosslare (Har.)	18:15	6:40(4)	6:40
Change to train.			
Dep. Rosslare (Har.)	19:15(2)	9:15(4)	7:35(2)
Arr. Dublin (Con.)	-0-	10:27(4)	10:40
Arr. Limerick (Colb.)	23:40(6)	-0-	-0-
	*	*	*
Dep. Limerick (Colb.)	16:05(2)	-0-	-0-
Dep. Dublin (Con.)	-0-	18:00(4)	18:20(2)
Arr. Rosslare (Har.)	20:10	21:05	21:30
Change to boat.			
Dep. Rosslare (Har.)	21:40(2)	21:40(4)	21:40(2)
Arr. Fishguard (Har.)	1:10	1:10	1:10
Change to train.			
Dep. Fishguard (Har.)	2:00(7)	2:00(8)	2:00(7)
Arr. London (Pad.)	6:57(7)	6:57(8)	6:57(7)

(1) Monday-Friday. Also operates Saturdays from late June to mid-September. Change trains in both Cardiff and Swansea from late August to early July. Direct train from early July to late August. (2) Monday-Saturday. (3) Saturdays only. Runs from early July to mid-August. (4) Sundays only. (5) From late July to early September: runs Monday-Thursday. From early July to mid-September: runs Fridays also. (6) Change to bus for the short ride to Shannon Airport. (7) Tuesday-Sunday. (8) Mondays only.

London - Dublin via Holyhead	501		
Dep. London (Euston)	8:55(1+3)	10:00(2+3+4)	13:00(5+13)
Arr. Holyhead	14:17	14:27	17:53
Change to boat.			
Dep. Holyhead	15:00	15:00	19:00
Arr. Dun Laoghaire	18:30	18:30	22:30
Change to bus.			
Arr. Dublin (Con.)	19:35	19:35	23:30
	* * *		
Dep. Dublin (Con.)	8:00(4+8)	12:40(10)	13:05(11+14)
Change to boat.			
Dep. Dun Laoghaire	8:45	14:00	14:00
Arr. Holyhead	12:15	17:30	17:30
Change to train.			
Dep. Holyhead	12:48	18:07(10)	18:05(11)
Arr. London (Euston)	16:56(9)	22:27	22:16

(1)Sun. only. (2)Mon-Sat, except holidays. (3)Change trains in both Crewe and Chester. (4)Light refreshments. (5)Mon-Fri. Meal service. Runs from late July to early September. (6)Sat. only. Change trains in Crewe. Carries sleeping car. Light refreshments. (7)From early September to late July: runs daily except Sat. From late July to early September: runs Tues-Sat. (8)Daily. Carries sleeping car. Light refreshments. (9)Arrives 18:15 on Sun. (10)Sun. only. Change trains in Crewe. (11)Mon-Sat. (12)On Sun., depart Dublin at 19:40. (13)Plus other departures from London at 21:25(6) and 21:45(7). (14)Plus another departure from Dublin at 19:05(3+8+12).

RAIL CONNECTIONS WITH SCOTLAND

These are the schedules for rail travel between London and the capital of Scotland.

London - Edinburgh 575

MONDAY-SATURDAY

Dep. London (King's X)	0:05	1:55(1)	7:25(2)	8:00(3)	9:00(3)	10:00(3+9)
Arr. Edinburgh	8:21	9:17	12:34	12:55	13:55	14:51

* * *

Dep. Edinburgh	0:15(1+6)	7:00(3)	8:00(3)	9:00(3)	10:15(4)	11:00(3+10)
Arr. London (King's X)	7:18	12:00	12:55	13:55	14:53	15:52

(1) Carries sleeping car. (2) Sat. only. Meal service. (3) Meal service. (4) "Flying Scotsman". Limited accommodations. Reservation advisable. (5) Mon-Fri. Carries sleeping car. (6) Mon-Fri. (7) Reservation required. Light refreshments. (8) Sat. only. Carries sleeping car. (9) Plus other departures from London at 10:35(3+4), on the hour from 11:00(3) to 18:00(3), 20:00(5), 20:15(6), 21:00(5), 22:05(7), 22:30 and 23:35(1). (10) Plus other departures from Edinburgh on the hour from 12:00(3) to 18:00(3), 13:25(2), 20:25(5), 21:05(5), 21:40(8), 22:15(8), 22:30, 22:45(5), 23:00(8), 23:20(5), 23:30(8) and 23:40(7).

SUNDAYS

Most of these trains have meal service.

Dep. London (King's X)	9:30	10:00	11:00	12:00	13:00	14:00	15:00(4)
Arr. Edinburgh	15:11	15:43	16:34	17:22	18:24	19:25	20:16

* * *

Dep. Edinburgh	10:00	10:15	11:00	12:00	13:00	13:10	14:00(5)
Arr. London (King's X)	15:54	16:23	16:59	17:25	18:11	18:43	19:26

(1) Train has only sleeping cars. (2) Second-class only. (3) Carries sleeping car. (4) Plus other departures from London on the hour from 15:00 to 20:00, 22:40 and 23:55(1). (5) Plus other departures from Edinburgh at 14:00, 15:00, 16:00, 17:00(2), 18:00, 20:25, 21:00(1), 22:30(3), 22:45 and 23:20(1).

SCOTLAND

The 2 rail trips north from Edinburgh (to Dundee-Aberdeen and to Perth-Inverness) are very scenic. There is also train service between Aberdeen and Inverness.

From Inverness, there is a rail route to Wick in northernmost Scotland, and to Kyle of Lochalsh on the west coast of Scotland. Other train routes to the same coastal area are from Glasgow to both Oban and to Mallaig. The other principal rail service in Scotland is between Edinburgh and Glasgow.

Edinburgh

The capital of Scotland. Most of the 25-acre railstation is under glass. Visit Edinburgh Castle, sitting on a cliff 270 feet above the city, on a site where there have been forts since the 6th century. A cannon has been fired from there every day since 1858. The Castle is open every day in the Summer: 9:30-18:00 Monday-Saturday, 11:00-18:00 on Sundays. The panoramic view of Edinburgh from the Castle is breathtaking. At the Castle, see the hammer-beamed timbered ceiling in the Great Hall of James IV, the Scottish Crown Jewels, the small St. Margaret's Chapel, and the State Apartments, including the rooms once occupied by Mary Queen of Scots.

Below the Castle is the 37-acre Princess Street Gardens, with the city's main rail tracks running through it, at a lower level than the surface of the park.

Also visit the 17th century Palace of Holyrood House to see the Throne Room and also the portraits of 110 Scottish kings (painted by the same artist) in the gallery. You will notice that all 110 noses are the same ! Stroll through 648-acre Holyrood Park, which has 3 lakes.

Other interesting sights in Edinburgh: the paintings at both the National Gallery of Scotland and in the National Portrait Gallery. The National Museum of Antiquities. The collection of technology, art, archaeology, geology and natural history in the Royal Scottish Museum. The Museum of Childhood (historic books, toys and materials about child rearing), closed on Sundays. The adaptation of Athens' Temple of Thesus. The month-long International Festival of Music and Drama.

Edinburgh - Dundee - Aberdeen 606

This is a very scenic rail trip.

Dep. Edinburgh	7:00(1+2)	9:05(3+4)	10:30
Arr. Dundee	8:11	10:41	11:54
Arr. Aberdeen	9:24	12:33	13:34

* * *

Dep. Aberdeen	6:05(1+2)	7:30(1+5)	8:40(1+5)	10:25(3+5+8)
Arr. Dundee	7:27	8:44	9:50	11:41
Arr. Edinburgh	8:50	9:54	10:55	13:03

(1) Monday-Saturday, except holidays. (2) Light refreshments. (3) Daily. (4) Change trains in Dundee. (5) Meal service. (6) Sun. only. (7) Plus other departures from Edinburgh at 11:17(1+4), 12:35(1), 13:17(1+4), 15:00(5), 17:00(1), 17:30(5+6), 18:00(1+2), 18:05(4+6) and 20:30(5+6). (8) Plus other departures from Aberdeen at 11:50(1+2), 12:05(5+6), 13:25(4+6), 13:50(1+2), 14:55(1+4), 16:25(2+3), 17:25(4+6), 18:25(4+6), 18:30(1+2), 18:55(1+4) and 19:25(6).

Sights in Dundee: A very ancient city, predating Roman occupation. Mountains of jam and preserves are processed here.

Sights in Aberdeen: A very popular tourist center and busy seaport. The center of Scotland's fishing industry. Straddles 2 rivers. See the 15th century Cathedral of St. Machar. Streets that were laid out in the 13th and 14th centuries. The local history museum in the 17th century Provost Skene's House.

The 16th century Provost Ross's House. The 18th century St. Nicholas Church. Two very old bridges: the 14th century Brig o'Balgownie and the 16th century Old Bridge of Dee. The 19th century Music Hall. The 19th century Marischal College, considered the world's largest and finest granite building.

Edinburgh - Perth - Inverness 611

A very scenic train ride.

Dep. Edinburgh	9:22(1)	13:22(1)	17:10(2)	23:05(3)
Arr. Perth	10:46	14:44	18:31	0:34
Arr. Inverness	13:26	17:26	21:48	4:49

* * *

Dep. Inverness	8:30(1)	16:30(1)	17:10(2+4)	17:30(2+5+6)
Dep. Perth	11:15(1)	19:25(1)	20:21(2+4)	20:18(2+5)
Arr. Edinburgh	12:36	20:48	21:58	21:43

(1) Mon-Sat, except holidays. Light refreshments. (2) Sun. only. Light refreshments. (3) Daily, except Sat. Carries sleeping car. (4) Runs from mid-September. to mid-June. (5) Runs from late June to early September. (6) Plus another departure from Inverness at 23:50(3).

Sights in Perth: A popular tourist center. There is much whiskey distilling and weaving of tartans here. Good Winter sports. Sailing and water skiing in the Summer.

Sights in Inverness: Located in the mountainous Highlands. Very cold Winters and cool Summers here. A popular tourist resort for hunting of grouse and deer, hiking, fishing, sailing, camping and Winter sports. Many whiskey distillers in this area. Nearby is Great Britain's highest mountain, Ben Nevis (4,406 feet).

Aberdeen - Inverness 605

Dep. Aberdeen	7:36(1+2)	9:50(1)	11:50(1+2)	12:43(3+5)
Arr. Inverness	10:19	12:18	14:20	15:10

* * *

Dep. Inverness	5:40(1)	8:40(4)	10:40(1+2)	12:40(1+2+6)
Arr. Aberdeen	8:25	11:09	13:06	15:06

(1) Mon-Sat, except holidays. (2) Light refreshments. (3) Sun. and holidays only. (4) Daily. (5) Plus other departures from Aberdeen at 13:50(1+2), 15:50(1+2), 16:43(2+3), 17:50(1+2) and 20:50(1). (6) Plus other departures from Inverness at 14:40(1+2), 15:40(2+3), 17:40(1+2) and 20:40(1).

Inverness - Wick 610

Dep. Inverness	6:15(1)	8:00(2)	11:10(1)	17:20(1)
Arr. Wick	11:12	13:17	15:47	21:49

* * *

Dep. Wick	5:30(1)	11:15(2)	11:45(1)	17:46(1)
Arr. Inverness	10:13	15:48	16:14	22:30

(1) Monday-Saturday, except holidays. Light refreshments. (2) Sundays only. Runs from mid-June to mid-September.

Inverness - Kyle of Lochalsh - Inverness 610

This is one of the most scenic train trips in Britain. The track climbs and descends, turns and twists through the Wester Ross mountains as it often goes along the shoreline of lovely lakes through the heart of the Highlands. In the Spring, there are fields of red and orange rhododendrons. The fields of purple heather can be seen all year.

In the high Luib Summit area there are forests and snowcapped mountains. It is only an 8-minute ferry-boat ride from Kyle to the Isle of Skye.

All of these trains run Monday-Saturday, except holidays.

Dep. Inverness	6:34	10:35(1)	18:05
Arr. Kyle	9:35	13:40	20:43

* * *

Dep. Kyle	7:00	11:08	17:14(1)
Arr. Inverness	9:31	13:51	20:11

(1)Light refreshments from early June to mid-September. Carries an observation car Monday-Friday from early June to mid-September, for which a supplement is charged.

Edinburgh - Dunbar - Edinburgh 575

Dep. Edinburgh	7:05(1)	9:00(1)	10:15(2)	12:00(3)
Arr. Dunbar	25-40 minutes later			

Sights in Dunbar: A small fishing port, the birthplace of naturalist John Muir (128 High Street). See the Castle ruins at the harbor. Take the 45-minute walk and visit the Old Harbor with its lifeboat museum, the roost for domesticated pigeons in Friar's Croft, and the Georgian houses (Castellau and Lauderdale). This walk is detailed in a guidebook available at the town's tourist information center in the 17th century Town House on High Street.

Also visit the 1,667-acre John Muir Country Park, containing a wide variety of birds and plants. Near it are the restored 17th century Preston watermill and many old towns and villages: Gifford, Haddington, Dirleton and North Berwick.

A list of hotels, guest houses and bed-and-breakfast places can be obtained by writing to the Dunbar Tourist Information Centre, if sufficient international reply coupons are enclosed.

Dep. Dunbar	8:39(1)	9:51(1)	11:51(1)	12:17(2)	13:29(1+4)
Arr. Edinburgh	25-40 minutes later				

(1)Monday-Saturday, except holidays. (2)Sundays only. (3)Daily. (4)Plus other departures from Dunbar at 17:40(1), 18:59(2), 20:42(2), 21:00(2) and 21:27(1).

Edinburgh - Glasgow - Edinburgh 600

Dep. Edinburgh	Frequent times from 7:00 to 23:00
Arr. Glasgow	45 minutes later

Sights in Glasgow: A major seaport. Largest city in Scotland. See the 12th century Cathedral. The fine collections in Kelvingrove Art Galleries and Museum. The Hunterian Museum.

Dep. Glasgow	Frequent times from 6:20 to 23:00
Arr. Edinburgh	45 minutes later

Glasgow - Oban - Glasgow 604

Marvelous Highland scenery on this route. The train service is Monday-Saturday except holidays. As indicated below, a one-day excursion (Glasgow-Oban-Glasgow) is possible.

Dep. Glasgow (Queen St.)	8:06(1)	12:55	18:18
Arr. Oban	11:16	16:00	21:30

Sights in Oban: This has been a holiday resort for nearly a century, and a fishing port for even longer.

Dep. Oban	7:40	12:26	17:55
Arr. Glasgow (Queen St.)	10:51	15:37	21:02

(1) Light refreshments.

Glasgow - Mallaig - Glasgow 604

A very scenic rail trip. The train service is Monday-Saturday except holidays. As indicated below, a one-day excursion (Glasgow-Mallaig-Glasgow) is possible.

Dep. Glasgow (Queen St.)	6:00(1)	8:37(1+2)	16:35(1)
Arr. Mallaig	11:38	14:49	22:33

* * *

Dep. Mallaig	7:00(1)	12:45(1+2)	16:10
Arr. Glasgow (Queen St.)	13:14	19:02	22:28

(1) Light refreshments. (2) Runs from early June to mid-September.

Glasgow - Stranraer - Glasgow 603

A trip through the beautiful moor of southwest Scotland.

Dep. Glasgow (Cent.)	8:35(1)	9:00(2)	11:35(1)	22:00(1)
Arr. Stranrear	11:29	11:48	14:09	0:42

* * *

Dep. Stranrear	7:32(1)	13:06(3)	15:30(4)	18:07(5)	21:25(6)
Arr. Glasgow (Cent.)	10:23	15:57	18:30	20:52	0:01

(1) Mon-Sat. (2) Sun. only. Runs from late May to mid-September. (3) Sun. only. Runs from late June to late August. (4) Mon-Fri. Runs from late May to early September. (5) Daily. (6) Fri. and Sat.

Stranrear - Belfast Boat 505

The boat connection with Northern Ireland.

Dep. Stranrear (Har.)	7:00(1)	7:30(2)	12:00(3)	14:30(4)	19:00(3)
Arr. Belfast (York Rd.)	10:46	11:00	15:28	18:17	22:25

(1) Sat. only. Runs from mid-June to early September. (2) Daily. except Sat. (3) Daily. (4) Daily, except Sun.

Chapter 9

EASTERN EUROPE

ALBANIA

There are no rail connections between Albania and other countries. The really long train ride in little Albania is 43 miles, from Durres to Elbasan, taking nearly 2 hours.

Durres - Elbasan **Elbasan - Durres**

838

Dep. Durres	7:55	16:15	Dep. Elbasan	4:30	16:01
Arr. Elbasan	10:10	19:05	Arr. Durres	6:45	18:20

Sights in Durres: Albania's Adriatic port. Excellent sand beaches. Bus tours to such interesting villages as Apollonia, Kruja (ruins of the 15th century Skanderbeg fortress), Shkodra (great Moslem mosques and bazaara), and Gjirokastra.

Sights in Elbasan: Many interesting ruins.

Durres - Tirana

This 23-mile ride takes about 62 minutes.

837

Dep. Durres 5:30 6:45 8:00 14:35 17:05 18:20

Sights in Tirana: This is Albania's capital. The prehistoric and Illyrian objects and folk art in the Museum. Tours of the textile factory and film studio. Moslem mosques and bazaars.

Dep. Tirana 5:40 6:55 10:20 15:10 18:30 21:35

BULGARIA

Bulgaria's express trains are called Ekspresen. The name for its fast trains is Brzi, and the slow trains are Putnichki.

BULGARIAN HOLIDAYS

January 1	New Year's Day	June 2	Memorial Day
May 1 and 2	Labor Day	Sept. 9 and 10	Liberation Day
May 24	Education Day	November 7	Revolution Day

SUMMER TIME

Bulgaria changes to Summer Time on the last Sunday of March and converts back to Standard Time on the last Sunday of September.

ONE-DAY EXCURSIONS AND CITY-SIGHTSEEING

Here are 2 one-day rail trips that can be made comfortably from Sofia and one longer ride. Notes are provided on what to see at each destination. The number below the name of each route is the Cook's timetable.

Schedules for one other train route and international connections conclude this section.

Sofia

The capital of Bulgaria. See the beautiful icons at Alexander Nevsky Memorial Church. The Archaeological Museum in the city's largest mosque, Bouyouk. The Byzantine Sancta Sophia Church. The city's many monuments. The 14th century frescos at the Church of St. Georgi.

Sofia - Burgas - Sofia 823

Dep. Sofia	6:10(1)	7:28	10:00(2)	16:00(1)	21:30(3)
Arr. Burgas	12:43	14:12	17:42	21:52	5:30

* * *

Dep. Burgas	5:00(1)	9:35(2)	16:04(4)	16:20(1)	23:36(3)
Arr. Sofia	10:47	17:28	23:00	22:50	7:27

(1) Reservation required. Light refreshments. (2) Meal service. (3) Carries sleeping car. (4) Light refreshments.

Sights in Burgas: A good beach resort.

Sofia - Plovdiv - Sofia 823

Dep. Sofia	6:10(1)	10:00(2)	15:50(1)	21:30
Arr. Plovdiv	8:35	12:49	18:09	0:25

Sights in Plovdiv: This city has been a commercial center for more than 2,000 years, serving the early caravans that moved between Europe, Asia and Africa. There are excellent exhibits of Thracian gold utensils in the Archaeological Museum. See the Bachkovo Monastery and, near it, the ruins of Tsar Ivan Asen II's fort.

Dep. Plovdiv	4:18	6:50(1)	14:30(2)	20:25(1)
Arr. Sofia	7:27	9:12	17:28	22:50

(1) Reservation required. Light refreshments. (2) Meal service.

Sofia - Varna 823

Dep. Sofia	6:15(1+2)	9:10(2)	14:10	20:15(3)	22:55
Arr. Varna	15:40	18:55	22:30	6:20	7:42

Sights in Varna: An important seaport and a very popular beach resort. Many museums and art galleries.

Dep. Varna	7:26	9:25(2)	13:25(1+2)	21:15(3)	21:45(3)
Arr. Sofia	16:29	20:00	22:52	5:51	8:26

(1) Reservation required. (2) Meal service. (3) Carries sleeping car. Also has couchettes.

INTERNATIONAL ROUTES FROM BULGARIA

Sofia is the gateway for train travel to Yugoslavia (and on to Western Europe), Romania and Greece (and on to Turkey).

Sofia - Belgrade

There is great mountain scenery on the Dragomagoman-Crveni Krst portion of this route.

821

Dep. Sofia 7:26(1) 8:40(2) 11:24(3)

During Bulgarian Summer Time, set your watch back 2 hours.

Arr. Belgrade 13:50 16:20 19:08

(1)Reservation required. (2)Runs from late September to late May. (3)Runs from late May to late September.

Sofia - Bucharest

822

Dep. Sofia	8:20	11:30(1)	21:26(2)
Arr. Bucharest	19:20	22:34	8:15

(1)Meal service. (2)Carries sleeping car. Also has couchettes.

Sofia - Athens

88

Dep. Sofia	11:45(1)
Arr. Athens	7:10

(1)Carries sleeping car. Also has couchettes.

CZECHOSLOVAKIA

A supplement is charged when traveling on Czechoslovakia's express trains, except for passengers holding tickets purchased outside the country.

Prague is the rail center for Czechoslovakia. International trains depart from both its Hlavni(Main) and Stredni(Central) railstations. The city's 2 other stations are Liben and Smichov (for suburban trains).

Reservations can be made at the office of CEDOK, the State Tourist Organization, a short walk from Hlavni station.

The volume of rail service in Czechoslovakia is evidenced by the fact that its timetable book has 683 pages of tables.

CZECHOSLOVAKIAN HOLIDAYS

January 1	New Year's Day	May 9	Liberation Day
	Easter	October 28	Nationalization Day
	Easter Monday	December 25	Christmas Day
May 1	Labor Day	December 26	Additional Holiday

SUMMER TIME

Czechoslovakia changes to Summer Time on the last Sunday of March and converts back to Standard Time on the last Sunday of September.

ONE-DAY EXCURSIONS AND CITY-SIGHTSEEING

Here are 7 one-day rail trips that can be made comfortably from Prague, returning there in most cases before dinnertime. Notes are provided on what to see at each destination. The number below the name of each route is the Cook's timetable.

Details on 3 other rail trips recommended for exceptional scenery and schedules for international connections conclude this section.

Prague

See the beautiful frescos in the 18th century St. Nicolas Church. The 13th century Synagogue. The statue of John Huss at Staromestke Namesti (Old Town Square). The ceremony performed by the 15th century Town Hall Clock. Dalibor Tower, a medieval prison.

The complex of interesting buildings on Castle Hill: The thousand-year old Hradcany Castle. The illuminated manuscripts and ancient globes in the library of Strahov Monastery, near Loretanski Square. The burial place of many Czech kings and the exhibit of crown jewels at St. Vitus Cathedral, in the Castle's third courtyard. The changing of the guard, outside the Cathedral.

Also visit the 14th century Charles Bridge with its 30 statues of saints, straddling the Vltava River. The 14th century Tyn Cathedral. The 17th century Wallenstein Palace.

The Prague House of Artists. The memorial to Mozart at Bertramka. The Laterna Magica. The hall at Vladislav Palace, so large that knights on horseback once jousted in it. The tiny houses on Zlata Ulicka (Golden Lane). The 7 centuries of art exhibited in the 5 wings of the National Gallery, in Sternbeck Palace. Near Sternbeck is Lookout Point, a paved terrace that offers a good view of the city below. Then, see Belvedere, the royal Summer Palace, and visit the tiny museum across from it. See the Old Jewish Cemetery and Museum.

Prague - Bratislava - Prague

812

Dep. Prague (Hlavni)	4:12(1+2)	6:15(3)	8:15(3+4)
Arr. Bratislava	10:07	11:48	13:46

Sights in Bratislava: An important Danube port in ancient Roman times. See the 14th-15th century castle. The Hussite House. The Old City Hall. The Cathedral. The palaces on Mirove Square, Michalska Street and Gottwald Square.

Dep. Bratislava	14:38(3)	16:35(3+4)	18:22(3+4)
Arr. Prague (Hlavni)	21:03(2)	22:21	0:11

(1) Runs from late June to early September. (2) Depart/Arrive Prague's Stredni station. (3) Meal service. (4) Reservation required.

Prague - Brno - Prague

812

Dep. Prague (Hlavni)	6:15(1)	8:15(1+2)	8:50(1+3)
Arr. Brno	9:45	11:42	12:53

Sights in Brno: The folk-art exhibit of woodcarvings, laces, pottery and costumes in the Moravian Museum. Brno Castle. Take a cruise on one of the underground rivers to see the Macocha and Sloup grottos. The outstanding 13th century Pernstejn Castle, near Brno.

Dep. Brno	14:05	16:56(1)	18:41(1+2)	20:32(1+2)
Arr. Prague (Hlavni)	18:25	21:03(3)	22:21	0:11

(1) Meal service. (2) Reservation required. (3) Depart/Arrive Prague's Stredni station.

Prague - Ceske Budejovice - Prague

810a

Dep. Prague (Main)	7:57	Dep.		
Arr. Ceske Budejovice	11:00	Ceske Budejovice	12:55	18:22
		Arr. Prague (Main)	15:56	21:28

Sights in Ceske Budejovice: A city that appears as it did in the Middle Ages. Visit the Budvar brewery.

Prague - Karlovy Vary - Prague

810

Dep. Prague (Stredni)	5:57(1)	9:16(2)
Arr. Karlovy Vary	10:40	14:14

Sights in Karlovy Vary: Once called Carlsbad, still famous for its curative waters. An international film festival, held here every July. The Moser crystal glass factory. An interesting porcelain factory in nearby Slakov.

Dep. Karlovy Vary	13:13(2)	16:57
Arr. Prague (Stredni)	18:12	21:43

(1) Departs from Prague's Hlavni station. (2) Meal service.

Prague - Marianske Lazne - Prague

809

Dep. Prague (Hlavni)	8:30	11:00(1)
Arr. Marianske Lazne	12:04	14:33

Sights in Marianske Lazne: Once called Marienbad, still a famous health spa.

Dep. Marianske Lazne	15:13	17:15
Arr. Prague (Hlavni)	18:35	20:55

(1) Reservation required.

Prague - Plzen - Prague

809

Dep. Prague (Hlavni)	8:30	11:00(1)
Arr. Plzen	10:35	13:05

Sights in Plzen: Visit the enormous Urquell brewery, where more than 200 million pints of beer are bottled annually. They have been producing beer here for over 800 years.

Dep. Plzen	14:00	16:37	18:43
Arr. Prague (Hlavni)	16:13	18:35	20:55

(1) Reservation required.

Prague - Tabor - Prague

810-a

Dep. Prague (Main)	7:50	13:05	Dep. Tabor	13:54	19:44
Arr. Tabor	10:02	15:28	Arr. Prague (Main)	15:51	21:41

Sights in Tabor: A museum town, preserved to immortalize the unusual Hussite 14th century reform movement which held that all people are brothers and equal.

SCENIC RAIL TRIPS

Bratislava - Kosice **Kosice - Bratislava** 811

Very good mountain scenery, through the Low and High Tatras Mountains.

Dep. Bratislava	9:18(1)	13:40(1)	15:40(1+2)	22:25(3)	23:25(3+5)
Arr. Kosice	17:31	22:09	23:03	6:47	7:06

* * *

Dep. Kosice	0:45(3)	6:20(1)	13:05(1)	15:20(1+2)	21:15(3+6)
Arr. Bratislava	8:44	14:23	21:17	22:30	5:55

(1) Meal service. (2) From late May to late September: daily. From late September to late May: daily, except Saturday. (3) Carries sleeping car. (4) Also has couchettes. (5) Plus another departure from Bratislava at 23:50(3+4). (6) Plus another departure from Kosice at 23:25(3+4).

Poprad - Tatry to Stary Smokovec 815

This spur off the Prague-Kosice route is the most scenic rail trip in Czechoslovakia. Forty minutes of the spectacular Tatras Mountains. Then, you can continue on to the Tatranska Lomnica ski resort and take a funicular to the top of 8,645-foot Lomnicky Stit.

Dep. Prague (Hlavni)	0:15	12:34(1)	15:46(2)	16:32(3+7)
Arr. Poprad-Tatry	11:22	21:34	1:18	2:01

* * *

Dep. Poprad-Tatry	0:56(2+4)	3:12(3)	7:51(2)	10:33(1+8)
Arr. Prague (Hlavni)	11:55	12:28	17:38	19:42

(1) Reservation required. Meal service. (2) Meal service. (3) Train of only sleeping cars. (4) Carries sleeping car. Also has couchettes. (5) Arrive/Depart Prague's Stredni station. (6) Has couchettes. (7) Plus other departures from Prague at 18:00(4), 18:57(2+4), 20:00(3) and 21:12(5+6). (8) Plus other departures from Poprad-Tatry at 17:55, 19:23(5+6), 21:42(3) and 22:21(4).

Change trains.

814

Dep. Poprad-Tatry	26 times daily
Arr. Stary Smokovec	40 minutes later

Change trains.

Dep. Stary Smokovec	Frequent times
Arr. Tatranska Lomnica	15 minutes later

Dep. Poprad-Tatry	1:22	4:59	6:35	7:24	11:26	15:44(3)
Arr. Kosice	3:04	6:47	8:23	9:11	13:13	17:31

(1) Meal service. (2) Reservation required. (3) Plus other departures from Poprad-Tatry at 20:21(1), 21:26(1) and 21:36(1+2).

Strbа - Strbske Pleso

This is another great Tatras Mountain scenic rail trip. Much winter sports in this area.

815

Dep. Prague (Hlavni)	0:15	12:34(1)	18:57(2+3+7)
Arr. Strba	11:07	21:19	6:26

Change trains.

814

Dep. Strba	24 times daily in Summer
Arr. Strbske Pleso	18 times daily in Winter

(1)Reservation required. Meal service. (2)Carries sleeping car. Meal service. (3)Has couchettes. (4)Meal service. (5)Train of only sleeping cars. (6)Departs from Prague's Stredni station. (7)Plus other departures from Prague at 20:00(5) and 21:12(3+6).

INTERNATIONAL ROUTES FROM CZECHOSLOVAKIA

Prague is Czechoslovakia's gateway to Vienna (and on to Budapest, Bucharest and Athens), Berlin (and on to Copenhagen and all of Scandinavia), Warsaw (and on to Moscow), and Nurnberg (and on to the rest of Western Europe).

Prague - Budapest 812

Dep. Prague (Hlavni)	-0-	-0-	6:15(3+4+5)
Dep. Prague (Liben)	0:32(1+2+3)	4:12(1+3)	-0-
Arr. Budapest (Nyugati)	10:33	-0-	16:23
Arr. Budapest (Kelcti)	-0-	14:20	-0-

(1)Runs from late June to early September. (2)Carries sleeping car. Also has couchettes. (3)Meal service. (4)Reservation required. (5)Plus other departures from Prague(Hlavni) at 8:15(3+4), 13:55(3), 19:05(2) and 22:00(2).

Prague - Vienna 746

Dep. Prague (Main)	7:47	15:30(1)
Arr. Vienna (Franz Josefs Bf.)	16:05	21:27

(1)Meal service.

Prague - Berlin 87 + 780

Dep. Prague (Hlavni)	0:50(1)	5:30(2+3)	10:26(3+5)
Arr. Berlin (Ost)	8:24	12:26	18:01(4)

(1) Carries sleeping car. Also has couchettes. Meal service. (2) Reservation required. (3) Meal service. (4) Arrives at Berlin's Lichtenberg station. (5) Plus other departures at 11:35(3), 15:35(2+3), 16:45(2+3) and 23:08(1+2+4).

Prague - Warsaw
819

Dep. Prague (Hlavni)	18:48(1)	22:35(2)
Arr. Warsaw	8:57	11:40

(1) Carries sleeping car. Also has couchettes. (2) Train of only sleeping cars.

Prague - Nurnberg
809

Dep. Prague (Hlavni)	11:00(1)	23:30
Arr. Nurnberg	18:53	6:52

(1) Reservation required. Meal service.

EAST GERMANY

The signs you will see at railstations in East Germany are the same as those listed in Chapter 6, under the section on "Austria".

Supplements are charged for East Germany's 3 categories of fast trains: Ex (Express diesel trains), D (ordinary express trains) and E (semi-fast trains). Local trains, stopping at all stations, are called Personnenzug. Reservations are essential on the routes from East Berlin to Poland. Most Hauptbahnhof (main) railstations have food facilities.

Train trips from Berlin to West Germany are not covered by Eurailpass. Tickets for trips from Berlin to West Germany must be paid in West German marks. The East Germany rail authorities will not accept East German currency for tickets from Berlin to West Germany.

There is suburban train service between Schonefeld Airport and East Berlin every 20 minutes from 4:00 to 1:00. Bus service to West Berlin is hourly from 4:00 to 23:00 and takes 90 minutes.

Where no station is designated for cities in East Germany, the station is Hauptbahnhof.

EAST GERMAN HOLIDAYS

January 1	New Year's Days	October 7	Republic Day
	Easter	December 25	Christmas Day
	Easter Monday	December 26	Additional Holiday
May 1	Labor Day		

ONE-DAY EXCURSIONS AND CITY-SIGHTSEEING

Here are 19 one-day rail trips that can be made comfortably from 3 major cities in East Germany, returning to them in most cases before dinnertime. Notes are provided on what to see at each destination. The number below the name of each route is the Cook's timetable.

It is not necessary to be staying in East Germany in order to tour that area. Sightseeing tours to Potsdam, Dresden and Karl Marx Stadt start in West Berlin at Parkplatz Rankestrasse, near the Kurfurstendamm. For reservation, contact Deutsches Reiseburo, Berlin W. 30, Kurfurstendamm 17.

Schedules for international connections conclude this section.

The 3 base cities are: Dresden, East Berlin and Leipzig.

Dresden

Major works of Raphael, Rembrandt, Rubens, Tintoretto, Van Eyck, Vermeer and other great 16th and 17th century painters at the Picture Gallery in the Semper Building of Zwinger Palace. Another excellent collection of paintings in the National Gallery.

Hear the Silberman organ (228 years old in 1983) at the cathedral, Hofkirche, Visit the baroque Opera House. The Zoo in Stadtpark (also called Volkspark). The Block House. Dresden Palace. The Japanese Castle. The treasures at the Albertinium Museum. The Palace of Culture. Take the cable car to Weisser Hirsch for the view of Dresden from the top of that hill.

It is a 17-mile ride by suburban railway from Dresden to Meissen. See the 15th century castle (Albrechtsburg) and the Cathedral there. Shop in Meissen for Dresden china and Albrecht porcelain.

East Berlin

The reconstructed St. Hedwig's Cathedral, National Gallery and 18th century State Opera. The tremendous collection of Near East monuments, the Market Gate of Milet and the impressive Pergamon Altar, all at the Pergamon Museum. The enormous Soviet Embassy on Unter den Linden. Palace of the Republic. Bode Museum. The Altes Museum.

Leipzig

Concentrate on the area around Market Place. Visit the Museum of the History of Leipzig in the Renaissance Old Town Hall. The 17th century stock exchange (Alte Bourse), rebuilt in 1963. The weighing-house (Alte Waage), where taxes were levied on imported goods. Auerbachs Keller, the old tavern on which Goethe based the locale of his Faust drama. Bach's tomb, at St. Thomas Church. The Museum of Fine Arts.

West of Market Place is the church where Johann Sebastian Bach is buried. Bach composed in that church the last 27 years of his life. Also see Gohliser Schlosschen, a rococco palace. Gohlis, the home of the poet Schiller. The Opera House in Karl Marx Platz. It is impossible to find a room in Leipzig during the semi-annual (March and September) trade fairs that attract visitors from all over the world.

Dresden - East Berlin - Dresden 780

Dep. Dresden	6:00(1)	9:54(1)
Arr. Berlin (Ost)	8:49	12:26

Sights in East Berlin: See notes on city-sightseeing in East Berlin at the start of this section.

Dep. Berlin (Ost)	12:36(1+2)	14:20(1+3)	16:36(1)	19:12(1+4)
Arr. Dresden	15:09	17:01	19:09	21:50

(1) Meal service. (2) Reservation required. (3) Departs from Berlin's Lichtenberg station. (4) Plus another departure at 21:36(1).

Dresden - Karl Marx Stadt - Dresden

	774	777	777
Dep. Dresden (Hbf.)	8:00	8:24	13:20
Arr. Karl Marx Stadt	9:15	9:37	14:37

Sights in Karl Marx Stadt: An East German post-World War II showplace new city.

	774	777	774	774	777	777
Dep. Karl Marx Stadt	11:32	12:54	14:40	17:00	17:22	20:00
Arr. Dresden (Hbf.)	12:47	14:07	15:55	18:14	18:36	21:16

Dresden - Leipzig - Dresden 768

Dep. Dresden	7:25(1)	7:48	8:35	8:52	9:57(1+4)
Arr. Leipzig	8:44	9:28	10:11	10:39	11:16

Sights in Leipzig: See notes about city-sightseeing in Leipzig at the start of this section.

Dep. Leipzig	12:54	14:06	15:02	16:06	17:08(5)
Arr. Dresden	14:22	15:37	16:24(1)	17:30(1)	18:33

(1) Depart/Arrive Dresden's Neustadt station. (2) Runs from mid-June to early September. (3) Sundays and holidays only. (4) Plus other departures from Dresden at 10:58, 11:30(2), 11:33(1), 11:50(2) and 13:06. (5) Plus other departures from Leipzig at 17:50, 19:02(2), 20:14, 21:29(2), 22:02 and 22:31(3).

East Berlin - Dresden - East Berlin

780

Dep. Berlin (Ost)	6:36(1)	8:34(1)	10:56(2+3)		
Arr. Dresden	9:18	11:03	13:22		

Sights in Dresden: See notes about city-sightseeing in Dresden at the start of this section.

Dep. Dresden	11:55(3)	15:21(3)	15:49(3)	19:53(1)	20:54(1)
Arr. Berlin (Ost)	14:47(2)	18:01(2)	18:26	22:29	23:39

(1) Reservation required. Meal service. (2) Departs/Arrives Berlin's Lichtenberg station. (3) Meal service.

East Berlin - Erfurt - East Berlin 776

Dep. Berlin (Lichtenberg)	6:02(1)	6:56	-0-
Dep. Berlin (Schoneweide)	-0-	-0-	9:37(1)
Dep. Berlin (Schonefeld)	6:28(1)	7:22	9:52(1)
Arr. Erfurt	9:51	11:07	13:33

Sights in Erfurt: The exquisite Gothic and German Renaissance houses. The Cathedral, where Martin Luther was ordained in 1507. The bridge, on which 33 houses stand. St. Severin Church.

Dep. Erfurt	13:27(2)	17:19(1)
Arr. Berlin (Schonefeld)	16:58	20:34
Arr. Berlin (Schoneweide)	17:13	-0-
Arr. Berlin (Lichtenberg)	-0-	21:01

(1) Meal service. (2) Light refreshments.

East Berlin - Karl Marx Stadt - East Berlin

All of these trains have light refreshments.

772a

Dep. Berlin (Schoneweide)	6:07	-0-
Dep. Berlin (Lichtenberg)	-0-	9:30
Dep. Berlin (Schonefeld)	6:22	9:58
Arr. Karl Marx Stadt	9:59	13:39

Sights in Karl Marx Stadt: This is an East German post-World War II showplace new city.

Dep. Karl Marx Stadt	13:53	17:49	20:57
Arr. Berlin (Schonefeld)	17:22	21:16	0:28
Arr. Berlin (Lichtenberg)	-0-	-0-	-0-
Arr. Berlin (Schoneweide)	17:37	21:31	-0-

Sights in Karl Marx Stadt: An East German post-World War II showplace new city.

East Berlin - Leipzig - East Berlin 776

Dep. Berlin (Lichtenberg)	6:14(1+2)	6:44(3)	6:58(2)	8:55(2+4)
Dep. Berlin (Schonefeld)	6:40(1+2)	7:10(3)	7:28(2)	9:10(2)
Arr. Leipzig	8:53	9:34	9:47	11:43

Sights in Leipzig: See notes about sightseeing in Leipzig at the start of this section.

Dep. Leipzig	13:23(2)	13:35(3)	15:36(1+2)	16:11(2+6)
Arr. Berlin (Schonefeld)	15:28	15:46	17:40	18:28
Arr. Berlin (Schoneweide)	15:43	-0-	-0-	18:43
Arr. Berlin (Lichtenberg)	16:02	16:13	18:07	-0-

(1) Monday-Friday, except holidays. (2) Meal service. (3) Light refreshments. (4) Departs from Berlin's Schoneweide station. (5) Arrives at Berlin's Schonefeld and Ost station. (6) Plus other departures from Leipzig at 18:19(3), 19:41(3) and 21:05(3+5).

East Berlin - Potsdam -East Berlin

There is inexpensive local suburban train service (50 minutes) from the center of East Berlin to Potsdam, and v.v.

Sights in Potsdam: The Concert Room and the great paintings in the Picture Gallery at the 18th century Sanssouci Palace. The 17th century Palace, Cecillienhof, where Truman, Attlee and Stalin signed the Potsdam Agreement in 1945.

East Berlin- Rostock - East Berlin 769

Dep. Berlin (Zoo)	7:58(1+2)	Dep. Rostock	18:19(3)	22:48(5)
Dep. Berlin (Fr'str.)	8:25	Arr. Berlin (Ost)	21:39(4)	1:46(4)
Dep. Berlin (Ost)	8:50	Arr. Berlin (Fr'str.)	-0-	-0-
Arr. Rostock	12:06	Arr. Berlin (Zoo)	-0-	-0-

(1) Light refreshments. (2) Reservation required. (3) Meal service. (4) Arrives at Berlin's Lichtenberg station. (5) Runs from late May to late September.

Sights in Rostock: East Germany's largest seaport. St. Mary's Church. The ancient Town Hall.

East Berlin - Stralsund - East Berlin 765a

Dep. Berlin (Ost)	6:21(1+2)	12:28(3)
Arr. Stralsund	9:42	15:58

Sights in Stralsund: Many old red-brick buildings and churches along the city's quaint Hanseatic streets.

Dep. Stralsund (Rotterdam)	14:57(2)	18:54(2)
Arr. Berlin (Ost)	18:35	22:15

(1) Departs from Berlin's Lichtenberg station. (2) Meal service. (3) Light refreshments.

East Berlin - Warnemunde - East Berlin

769

Dep. Berlin (Zoo)	7:58(1)	Dep. Warnemunde	16:27(2)	22:19(3)
Dep. Berlin (Fr'str.)	8:25(1)	Arr. Berlin (Ost)	21:39	1:46
Dep. Berlin (Ost)	8:50(1)	Arr. Berlin (Fr'str.)	-0-	-0-
Arr. Warnemunde	12:22	Arr. Berlin (Zoo)	-0-	-0-

(1) Reservation required. Light refreshments. (2) Meal service. (3) Runs from late May to late September.

Sights in Warnemunde: A famous beach resort. A ferry connection to Denmark.

East Berlin - Weimar - East Berlin

776

Dep. Berlin (Lichtenberg)	6:02(1)	6:56	9:37(1+2)
Dep. Berlin (Schonefeld)	6:28	7:22	9:52
Arr. Weimar	9:44	10:51	13:19

Sights in Weimar: The marvelous atmosphere of the era when German princes lived here.

Dep. Weimar	13:42(3)	17:34(1)
Arr. Berlin (Schonefeld)	16:58	20:34
Arr. Berlin (Lichtenberg)	17:13(2)	21:01

(1) Meal service. (2) Depart/Arrive Berlin's Schoneweide station. (3) Light refreshments.

Leipzig - Dresden - Leipzig

768

Dep. Leipzig	8:02	8:45	9:30	11:06	11:16(1+3)
Arr. Dresden (Neustadt)	9:25	10:05	10:46	12:25	12:39
Arr. Dresden (Hbf.)	9:33	-0-	10:56	12:33	12:47

Sights in Dresden: See notes about city-sightseeing in Dresden at the start of this section.

Dep. Dresden (Hbf.)	13:06	15:00	16:00	16:53	18:23
Dep. Dresden (Neustadt)	8 minutes later				
Arr. Leipzig	14:36	16:32	17:27	18:13	19:53

(1) Light refreshments. (2) Meal service. (3) Plus another departure from Leipzig at 12:54. (4) Plus other departures from Dresden Hauptbahnhof at 20:22(2) and 22:00.

Leipzig - East Berlin - Leipzig 776

Dep. Leipzig	6:57(1+2)	7:39(2)	8:19(3)	8:54(3)
Arr. Berlin (Schonef.)	8:58	9:46	10:40	10:58
Arr. Berlin (Licht.)	9:25	10:01(4)	-0-	11:13
Arr. Berlin (Ost)	-0-	-0-	11:08	-0-

Sights in East Berlin: See notes about sightseeing in East Berlin at the start of this section.

Dep. Berlin (Licht.)	13:32(3)	14:07(3+4)	15:26(1+2)	15:38(3+5)
Dep. Berlin (Schonef.)	-0-	14:22(3)	15:52(1+2)	16:04(3+6+7)
Arr. Leipzig	16:30	16:41	18:07	18:30

(1) Monday-Friday, except holidays. (2) Meal service. (3) Light refreshments. (4) Arrive/Depart Berlin's Schoneweide station. (5) Plus another departure from Berlin Lichtenberg at 21:29(3). (6) Plus another departure from Berlin Schoneweide at 16:55(2). (7) Plus other departures from Berlin Schonefeld at 17:10(2) and 21:58(3).

Leipzig - Erfurt - Leipzig 776

Dep. Leipzig	7:39	8:39	10:30	12:09(1)
Arr. Erfurt	8:56	10:08	11:58	13:38

Sights in Erfurt: The exquisite Gothic and German Renaissance houses. The Cathedral. The bridge, on which 33 houses stand. St. Severin Church.

Dep. Erfurt	13:15	13:59	16:33	18:14	19:57	20:22
Arr. Leipzig	14:48	15:27	18:10	19:40	21:30	21:47

(1) Daily, except Sundays and holidays.

Leipzig - Karl Marx Stadt - Leipzig 768a

Dep. Leipzig (Hbf.)	7:53	9:57	Dep. Karl Marx Stadt	14:24	17:25
Arr. Karl Marx Stadt	9:18	11:24	Arr. Leipzig	15:46	18:55

Sights in Karl Marx Stadt: An East German post-World War II showplace new city.

Leipzig - Naumberg - Leipzig 776

Dep. Leipzig 7:26 8:34 12:05(1) 13:36
Arr. Naumberg 40 minutes later

Sights in Naumberg: A gem of a Medieval village.

Dep. Naumberg 11:35 13:47 14:46 17:28 19:02(2)
Arr. Leipzig 40 minutes later

(1) Daily, except Sundays and holidays. (2) Plus other departures from Naumberg at 20:43 and 21:06.

Leipzig - Rostock - Leipzig 767

Dep. Leipzig	7:14(1)	Dep. Rostock	15:43(1)	17:58(1)
Arr. Rostock	12:45	Arr. Leipzig	21:29	23:47

(1) Light refreshments.

Sights in Rostock: East Germany's largest seaport. St. Mary's Church. The ancient Town Hall.

Leipzig - Schwerin - Leipzig 767

Dep. Leipzig	7:14(1)	8:11(2)	Dep. Schwerin	17:02(1)	19:19(1)
Arr. Schwerin	11:36	12:40	Arr. Leipzig	21:29	23:47

(1) Light refreshments. (2) Meal service.

Sights in Schwerin: The Opera House. The fine castle.

INTERNATIONAL ROUTES FROM EAST GERMANY

Berlin is East Germany's principal gateway to Copenhagen (and on to the rest of Scandinavia), Frankfurt/Main (and on to the rest of Western Europe), Munich (and on to Western Austria, Switzerland and Italy), Prague (and on to Eastern Austria, Italy, Romania, Yugoslavia, Greece and Turkey), and Warsaw (and on to Russia).

Berlin - Copenhagen 769

Dep. Berlin (Zoo)	7:57(1)	22:10(2)
Dep. Berlin (Fr'str.)	8:25(1)	22:34(2)
Dep. Berlin (Ost)	8:50(1)	23:51(2)
Arr. Copenhagen	17:25	9:41

(1) Reservation required. Light refreshments on train. Meal service on ship 12:50-14:50. (2) Carries sleeping car. Also has couchettes.

Berlin - Frankfurt/Main 776

Dep. Berlin (Fr'str.)	5:48(1)	12:35(1)	22:20(2)
Dep. Berlin (Zoo)	6:40(1)	13:06(1)	23:06(2)
Arr. Frankfurt/Main	13:56	20:27	7:13

(1) Meal service. (2) Carries sleeping car. Also has couchettes.

Berlin - Munich 771

Dep. Berlin (Ost)	-0-	8:18(1)	-0-	-0-
Dep. Berlin (Fr'str.)	6:36(1)	8:46(1)	21:21(2)	22:38(3)
Dep. Berlin (Zoo)	7:03(1)	9:06(1)	21:51(2)	22:44(3)
Arr. Munich	16:08	18:23	7:30	9:24

(1) Meal service. (2) Carries sleeping car. Also has couchettes. (3) Runs from late June to mid-August. Carries sleeping car on Fridays.

Berlin - Prague 780

Dep. Berlin (Ost)	-0-	-0-	6:36(1+4+6)
Dep. Berlin (Licht.)	0:02(1+2)	2:08(3+5)	-0-
Dep. Berlin (Schonef.)	0:28(1+2)	2:34(3)	7:04(1+4+7)
Arr. Prague (Hlavni)	7:43	10:00	13:40

(1)Reservation required. (2)Carries sleeping car. Also has couchettes. (3)Has couchettes. (4)Meal service. (5)Plus another departure from Berlin Lichtenberg at 10:56(4). (6)Plus other departures from Berlin Ost at 8:34(1+4), 12:36(1+4), 16:36(1) and 21:36(1). (7)Plus other departures from Berlin Schonefeld at 9:04(1+4), 11:22(4), 13:04(1+4). 17:04(1) and 22:04(1).

Berlin - Vienna 746 + 747

Dep. Berlin (Ost)	8:34(1)	16:36(2)
Arr. Vienna (F. Josef Bf.)	21:27	8:25(3)

(1)Meal service. (2)Carries sleeping car. (3)Arrives at Vienna's Sudbahnhof station.

Berlin - Warsaw 847

Dep. Berlin (Ost)	0:30(1+2)	6:15(1)	7:34(1)	8:28(1)	10:10(3+4)
Arr. Warsaw (Centralna)	9:30	-0-	-0-	-0-	-0-
Arr. Warsaw (Gdanska)	-0-	14:57	16:14	17:11	19:40

(1)Meal service. (2)Carries sleeping car. (3)Runs from late May to late September. (4)Plus other departures from Berlin at 15:02(1), 20:14(1+2) and 22:03(2).

HUNGARY

Timetables (Hivatalos Menetrend) can be purchased at Hungary's main railstations. The larger stations in Hungary have food service.

Budapest's railstations are: Keleti (Eastern, for arrivals from and departures to Berlin, Prague and Vienna), Nyugati (Western, for arrivals from and departures to Berlin, Prague and Stockholm), and Deli (Southern, for arrivals from and departures to eastern Yugoslavia).

HUNGARIAN HOLIDAYS

January 1	New Year's Day	August 20	Constitution Day
	Easter	November 7	Revolution Remembrance Day
	Easter Monday		
April 4	Liberation Day	December 25	Christmas Day
May 1	Labor Day	December 26	Additional Holiday

SUMMER TIME

Hungary changes to Summer Time on the last Sunday of March and converts back to Standard Time on the last Sunday in September.

ONE-DAY EXCURSIONS AND CITY-SIGHTSEEING

Here are 3 one-day rail trips that can be made comfortably from Budapest, returning there in most cases before dinnertime. Notes are provided on what to see at each destination. The number below the name of each route is the Cook's timetable.

Schedules for international connections conclude this section.

Budapest

The capital of Hungary. Actually 2 cities, there is the dominant Buda on the west side of the Danube and the youthful Pest, extending east of the river.

In Buda, be sure to see the 112-acre garden island, Margitziget (Margaret Island). The Celtic and Roman ruins. The 250-foot Gothic tower at the 14th century Mathias Church. The view of the Danube and Pest from the tower of the nearby Fisherman's Bastion. The State Opera House. Heroes' Spuare. The National Gallery and Art Museum. The Railway Museum. The old stone fort.

The display of pottery, weaving, wood-carving, embroidery and costumes in the Ethnographical Museum. The 13th century Coronation Church. The exhibits of pre-history, Roman, medieval and Turkish objects in the National Museum. The Aquincum Museum. The tomb of the 16th century Turkish poet, Gul-Baba. The collection of medieval art in the museum at the Royal Palace.

The view of mountains, Buda Castle, Parliament, Pest and all of the Danube bridges from the top of the 770-foot hill called Gellerthegy. Take the cogwheel railway to the tops of Varhegy (Castle Hill) and Rozsadomb (Hill of Roses).

In Pest: The 12th century church, Belvarosi Templom. Window-shop on Vaci Ucta. The great Zoo and Central Europe's largest amusement park, both in Varosliget Park. The city's best restaurants and shops are in Pest.

Budapest - Kecskemet - Budapest 803

All these trains have meal service.

Dep. Budapest (West)	7:15	13:50	Dep. Kecskemet	14:51	19:05
Arr. Kecskemet	8:40	15:23	Arr. Budapest (West)	16:25	20:30

Sights in Kecskemet: Home of the ancient art of distilling barack, apricot brandy.

Budapest - Lake Balaton (Siofok and Balantonszentgyorgy) - Budapest

It is a short train and bus ride to reach Hungary's most popular resort area, the 46-mile long Lake Balaton, circled with spas, motels and campgrounds along its 118 miles of shoreline. Great sailboating and fishing here. Frequent ferries link the many towns on both sides of the lake.

Sights in Siofok: Many resort hotels and sidewalk cafes.

Sights in Balatonszentgyorgy: The attraction here is the curative carbonated water from the town's 11 mineral springs.

In Keszthely: The Balaton Museum of the lake's natural history and the large collection of paintings and rare books in the Helicon Library at the 18th century Festetics mansion.

In Heviz: The thermal waters. This has been famous as a health spa for more than 600 years.

799

Dep. Budapest (South)	6:45(1)	7:45	11:38(2)		
Arr. Siofok	8:40	9:21	13:51		
Arr. Balatonszentgyorgy	9:43	-0-	15:33		
	*	*	*		
Dep. Balatonszentgyorgy	14:37(1)	15:34	16:51	17:42(1)	18:43(1)
Dep. Siofok	15:58	17:05	18:10	18:49	20:46
Arr. Budapest (South)	17:35	18:50	19:56	20:35	22:55

(1) Meal service. (2) Light refreshments.

Budapest - Szeged - Budapest 803

All of these trains have meal service.

Dep. Budapest (W)	7:05(1)	Dep. Szeged	13:50	18:00(1)
Arr. Szeged	9:20	Arr. Budapest (W)	16:30	20:15

(1) Reservation required.

Sights in Szeged: Many Summer festivals.

INTERNATIONAL CONNECTIONS FROM HUNGARY

Budapest is Hungary's gateway for rail travel to Belgrade (and on to Athens and Istanbul), Moscow, Prague (and on to Berlin and Scandinavia), Vienna (and on to the rest of Western Europe), and Zagreb (and on to Italy).

Budapest - Belgrade 791

Dep. Budapest (Keleti)	6:50(1)	17:05	23:25(1+2)
Arr. Belgrade	11:50	22:38	7:09

(1)Reservation required. (2)Departs from Budapest's Nyugati station. Carries sleeping car. Also has couchettes.

Budapest - Moscow 806

Dep. Budapest (Keleti)	20:05(1)	23:10(1+2)
Arr. Moscow	7:15(3)	13:05(3)

(1)Carries sleeping car. (2)From late May to late September: daily. From late September to mid-November: runs Tues., Fri. and Sun. (3)Day 3.

Budapest - Prague 812

Dep. Budapest (Nyugati)	8:00(1)	13:00(1)	14:30(1+2+7)
Arr. Prague (Hlavni)	16:29	22:21	0:11

(1)Meal service. (2)Reservation required. (3)Runs from late June to early September. (4)Carries sleeping car. Also has couchettes. (5)Arrives at Prague's Liben station. (6)Runs from late May to late September. (7)Plus other departures from Budapest Nyugati station at 18:05(1+3+4+5) and 22:25(1+4+6) ...and from Budapest Keleti station at 21:15(1+3+4+5) and 23:30(4).

Budapest - Vienna 798

Dep. Budapest (Keleti)	9:20(1)	16:10(1)	18:30(1+2)
Arr. Vienna (Westbf.)	13:25	20:15	22.00(3)

(1)Meal service. (2)From late May to late September: daily. From late September to late May: runs Sat. and Sun. (3)Arrives at Vienna's Sudbahnhof station.

Budapest - Zagreb 805

Dep. Budapest (Keleti)	12:35(1)	-0-
Dep. Budapest (Deli)	-0-	22:25(1+2)
Arr. Zagreb	18:35	5:05

(1)Reservation required. (2)Runs from late May to late September.

POLAND

POLISH HOLIDAYS

January 1	New Year's Day	July 22	National Day
	Easter	November 1	All Saints' Day
	Easter Monday	December 25	Christmas Day
May 1	Labor Day	December 26	Additional Holiday
	Corpus Christi		

SUMMER TIME

Poland changes to Summer Time on the last Sunday of March and converts back to Standard Time on the last Sunday in September.

POLRAILPASS

Unlimited train travel. Non-transferable. Can be purchased in Poland at any office of Polish Travel Bureau (Orbis). Also sold at Orbis offices in London, Cologne, Stockholm and New York (500 Fifth Ave., New York, N.Y. 10036). The 1983 prices for first-class are: 8 days $45(U.S.), 15 days $60, 21 days $75, one month $90. Second-class: $30, $40, $50 and $60. Children under 10 pay half-fare.

ONE-DAY EXCURSIONS AND CITY-SIGHTSEEING

Here are 9 one-day rail trips that can be made comfortably from Warsaw, returning there in most cases before dinnertime. Notes are provided on what to see at each destination. The number below the name of each route is the Cook's timetable.

Warsaw

See the priceless collection of coins, jewelry, paintings and Polish crown jewels in 15 large rooms on the second floor of the rebuilt (1974) 16th century Royal Castle, destroyed during World War II. Also, see the Sigismund Column at the Castle.

Visit the churches, houses, Barbicon Wall, Blacha Palace and the ancient market in the reconstructed Old Quarter. The University in Casimir Palace. The reconstructed "Chopin Family Drawing Room" in the side wing of the former Raczynski Palace. The very colorful changing of the guard (Sundays) in Victory Square. Lazienki, the wonderful park with its enormous Chopin monument and Island Palace. Belvedere Palace. Wilanow Park and its 18th century Palace. Contemporary art in Zacheta Museum, located in Malachowskiego Palace. The Monument to the Heroes of the Ghetto.

In the city center: The 37-story Palace of Culture and Science, highest building in Warsaw, and the view of the city and the Vistula River from the top of it. Amfora, a strolling street. The National Philharmonic Hall. Warka, the museum devoted to General Pulaski and to the Polish emigration to America. The collection of picturesque folk costumes and hand-painted furniture and dishes in the Lowicz Museum.

The Zoological Gardens. The ancient Polish weapons at the Army Museum. The Jewish Historical Museum. The Curie Museum. The City Historical Museum.

Warsaw - Czestochowa - Warsaw 845

Dep. Warsaw (Cent.)	6:29(1+2+3)	12:16(1+2)
Arr. Czestochowa	9:40	15:28

Sights in Czestochowa: The Black Madonna in the 14th century Jasna Gora Monastery. The 2,600-year old cemetery.

Dep. Czestochowa	12:08(2)	16:40(2)	18:05(1+2+4)
Arr. Warsaw (Cent.)	15:52	20:21	21:19

(1) Reservation required. (2) Meal service. (3) Runs from late May to late September. (4) Plus another departure from Czestochowa at 19:23(2+3).

Warsaw - Gdansk - Warsaw 846

846

Dep. Warsaw (Cent.)	5:45(1)	Dep. Gdansk	14:55(2)	17:28(1)
Dep. Warsaw (Wsch.)	6:00(1)	Arr. Warsaw (Wsch.)	19:54	22:03
Arr. Gdansk	10:20	Arr. Warsaw (Cent.)	20:28	22:20

(1) Reservation required. Meal service. (2) Meal service.

Sights in Gdansk: A major Polish seaport. See the reconstructed Old Town. The immense Church of St. Mary. Town Hall. The Armory. Artus Mansion. The 600-pipe organ in nearby Oliwa.

Warsaw - Gdynia - Warsaw 846

Dep. Warsaw (Cent.)	5:45(1)	Dep. Gdynia	14:20(2)	17:00(1)
Dep. Warsaw (Wsch.)	6:00(1)	Arr. Warsaw (Wsch.)	19:54	22:03
Arr. Gdynia	10:51	Arr. Warsaw (Cent.)	20:28	22:20

(1) Reservation required. Meal service. (2) Meal service.

Sights in Gdynia: A leading Polish seaport.

Warsaw - Krakow - Warsaw 842

Dep. Warsaw (Cent.)	6:00(1)	Dep. Krakow	16:25(2)	18:22(1)
Arr. Krakow	10:31	Arr. Warsaw (Cent.)	21:29	22:50

(1) Reservation required. Meal service. (2) Meal service.

Sights in Krakow: Undamaged in World War II, it is one of Europe's most beautiful Medieval towns. See such historical monuments at Wawel Castle, with its priceless collection of tapestries. The unique 15th century Carved wood altar in St. Mary's Church. The very interesting library in the 14th century Jagiellonian University. The interior of the old Remuh Synagogue. The tombs of all of Poland's kings and queens, plus many national heroes and poets, in the 14th century Cathedral. The gold dome of Sigismund Chapel.

There are 3 guided half-day bus tours: The Museum of Martyrdom at the death camp in Oswiecim (Auschwitz). The underground sculptures, great hall, chapels, lakes and even tennis courts and a sanatarium in the 10th century salt mines at Wieliczka. The Ethnological Museum at Zubrzyca Gorna, a collection of houses typifying the lifestyles of several centuries of both peasants and wealthy people (primitive cooking utensils, elegant inlaid wood chests, furniture, etc.).

Warsaw - Lublin - Warsaw 844

All of these trains have meal service.

Dep. Warsaw (Centralna)	6:18	7:43
Dep. Warsaw (Wschodnia)	6:40	8:20
Arr. Lublin	9:17	11:47

Sights in Lublin: One of Poland's oldest cities. Many outstanding churches. The Castle, above Lublin. The Gothic Krakowski Gate.

Dep. Lublin	11:15	18:00	20:05
Arr. Warsaw (Wschodnia)	14:55	21:58	22:50
Arr. Warsaw (Centralna)	15:27	22:19	23:10

Warsaw - Poznan - Warsaw 847

Dep. Warsaw (Gdanska)	-0-
Dep. Warsaw (Centralna)	6:48(1)
Arr. Poznan	10:27

Sights in Poznan: Przemyslaw Castle. The sculptures at Dzialynski Castle. Gorki Palace. Parish Church. Franciscan Church. The State Ballet School. The stained-glass at the Church of the Holy Virgin. The Cathedral. The 12th century Church of St. John of Jerusalem.

Dep. Poznan	15:20(2)	18:50(1)
Arr. Warsaw (Centralna)	-0-	22:49
Arr. Warsaw (Gdanska)	19:50	-0-

(1) Meal service. (2) Runs from early June to late September.

Warsaw - Sopot - Warsaw 846

Dep. Warsaw (Cent.)	5:45(1)
Dep. Warsaw (Wsch.)	6:00
Arr. Sopot	10:38

Dep. Sopot	14:32(2)	17:14(1)
Arr. Warsaw (Wsch.)	19:54	22:03
Arr. Warsaw (Cent.)	20:28	22:20

(1) Reservation required. Meal service. (2) Meal service.

Sights in Sopot: The International Music (Jazz) Festival, every August. This is a popular beach resort on the Baltic, with concerts on the half-mile pier.

Warsaw - Torun - Warsaw 852a

These trains have meal service.

Dep. Warsaw (Cent.)	6:25
Arr. Torun	9:47

Dep. Torun	17:10
Arr. Warsaw (Cent.)	22:11

Sights in Torun: A 13th century town on the banks of the Vistula River. The birthplace of Nicholas Copernicus in 1473. See the house where he was born. The instruments he used to determine that the earth revolves around the sun are exhibited there. Visit the ancient 3-story Town Hall. The Church of St. John contains one of the largest bells in Poland.

Warsaw - Krakow - Zakopane 842

Dep. Warsaw (Cent.)	6:00(1)	8:38(2)	17:18(1)	20:45(3+4+7)
Arr. Krakow (Gl.)	10:32	15:40	21:47	2:17(3+4)
Change trains.				
Dep. Krakow (Gl.)	10:50	16:05	23:17	2:24(3+4+8)
Arr. Zakopane	15:53	21:52	4:22	6:53

Sights in Zakopane: Good mountain scenery. Great Winter and Summer sports. Poland's most popular health resort. Take a ride on a horsedrawn sleigh. Ride the chairlift to the top of Mt. Kasprowy.

(Timetable continues on next page.)

Dep. Zakopane	0:03	9:00	12:40	18:50(3+5+9)
Arr. Krakow (Gl.)	5:30	14:25(6)	17:31	23:36(3+5)
Change trains.				
Dep. Krakow (Gl.)	8:55(2)	16:25(2+6)	18:22(1)	23:50(3+5+10)
Arr. Warsaw (Cent.)	15:36	21:27	22:53	5:44

(1) Reservation required. Meal service. (2) Meal service. (3) Direct train. No train change in Krakow. (4) Carries sleeping car. Also has couchettes. (5) Has couchettes Warsaw-Zakopane and v.v. Carries sleeping car only Warsaw-Krakow and v.v. (6) Change trains in Krakow Plasow. (7) Plus another departure from Warsaw at 22:11(3+5). (8) Plus another departure from Krakow at 4:25(3+5). (9) Plus another departure from Zakopane at 20:50(3+4). (10) Plus another departure from Krakow at 1:00(3+4).

INTERNATIONAL CONNECTIONS FROM POLAND

Warsaw is Poland's gateway for rail travel to Berlin (and on to both Scandinavia and northwestern Europe), Moscow, and Vienna (and on to Italy, southeastern Europe and southwestern Europe).

Warsaw - Berlin 847

Dep. Warsaw (Wsch.)	6:33(1)	10:48(1)	-0-	-0-
Dep. Warsaw (Gdan.)	-0-	-0-	14:18	-0-
Dep. Warsaw (Cent.)	6:48	10:56	-0-	22:20(1+3)
Arr. Berlin (Ost)	14:26	20:06	23:35	8:46

(1) Meal service. (2) Runs from late May to late September. (3) Carries sleeping car.

Warsaw - Moscow 847

Dep. Warsaw (Cent.)	9:30(1)	14:10(2)	-0-	-0-
Dep. Warsaw (Gdan.)	-0-	-0-	16:50(1)	17:50(2+3+4)
Dep. Warsaw (Wsch.)	9:50(1)	14:20(2)	-0-	-0-
Set your watch forward 2 hours.				
Arr. Moscow (Byel.)	8:16	10:57	15:03	15:03

(1) Carries sleeping car. Meal service. (2) Carries sleeping car. (3) Runs from late May to late September. (4) Plus another departure from Warsaw (Gdan.) at 20:03(3).

Warsaw - Vienna 845

Dep. Warsaw (Wschadnia)	6:17(1+2)	-0-
Dep. Warsaw (Centralna)	6:29(1+2)	17:56(1+3)
Arr. Vienna (Sudbf.)	20:20	8:25

(1) Reservation required. Meal service. (2) Runs from late May to late September. (3) Departs from Warsaw's Gdanska station. Carries sleeping car. Also has couchettes.

ROMANIA

Romania has 3 classes of trains: Rapide (the fastest), Accelerate and Personal. Avoid travel on the very slow, very crowded, very filthy "Personal" trains. Supplements are charged for travel on "Rapide" and "Accelerate" trains, except for passengers holding tickets purchased outside Romania. Reservations are required for the fast trains. To buy a Romanian timetable, ask for "Mersul Trenurillor".

ROMANIAN HOLIDAYS

January 1	New Year's Day	August 23	Liberation Day
January 2	Additional Holiday	August 24	Additional Holiday
May 1	Labor Day	December 30	Republic Day
May 2	Additional Holiday		

SUMMER TIME

Romania changes to Summer Time on the last Sunday of March and converts back to Standard Time on the last Sunday in September.

ONE-DAY EXCURSIONS AND CITY-SIGHTSEEING

Here are 5 one-day rail trips that can be made comfortably from Bucharest, returning there in most cases before dinnertime. Notes are provided on what to see at each destination. The number below the name of each route is the Cook's timetable.

Schedules for international connections conclude this section.

Bucharest

See the lakes and fountains at Cismigiu Gardens on Gheorghiu-Dej Blvd. Great paintings at the Arth Museum in the Royal Palace, the lovely Athenaeum Concert Hall, and the Folk Art Museum, all on Calea Victoriei. Near that museum, in Herastrau Park, is the city's major attraction, Village Museum (on Kisselef Ave.), featuring perfect replicas of 17th-20th century peasant homes, workplaces, shops, barns and churches, which have been moved from all over Romania to this site.

On Piata Victoriei, you will find the Statue of Soviet Heroes, the Geological Institute, the Natural Science Museum, the Council of Ministers. Other interesting places: The Zoo. Fine paintings at the National Gallery of Art, in the former Royal Palace. A great collection of gold treasures and crown jewels in the Museum of Romanian History. The

Technical Museum. The Art Collection Museum. The vast Northern Train Station, built in 1870 and restored in 1945.

Guides at the Jewish Federation office, Strada Dmitri Rakovita 8, escort visitors to the well-preserved 200-year-old synagogue at Strada Sfintul Veneri 9, to the kosher "soup kitchen" that is subsidized by American Jewish charities, and to the Jewish Museum.

Bucharest - Brasov - Bucharest 831

Dep. Bucharest (Nord)	6:40(1)	9:20(1)
Arr. Brasov	9:18	11:58

Sights in Brasov: Excellent Transylvania Mountain scenery in this area. See the 14th century Black Church. The Museum of History. The Art Museum. The Museum of the Romanian School. A popular Winter resort, Poiana Brasov, is 9 miles from here.

Dep. Brasov	16:16(1)	18:26(1)
Arr. Bucharest (Nord)	18:40	20:55

Bucharest - Constantza (Eforie, Mangalia) - Bucharest 827

Dep. Bucharest (Nord)	5:25(1+2)	5:45(3)	7:25(4)
Arr. Constantza	8:11	9:20	10:37
Dep. Constantza	8:29(1+2)	-0-	10:51(4)
Arr. Eforie Nord	9:04	-0-	11:15
Arr. Mangalia	9:50	-0-	12:00

* * *

Dep. Mangalia	12:05(3)	15:10	-0-	18:30(2)
Dep. Eforie Nord	12:49(3)	15:56	-0-	19:14(2)
Dep. Constantza	13:27(3)	16:35	18:45(3)	19:48(2)
Arr. Bucharest (Nord)	17:20	20:10	22:25	22:55(1)

(1)Depart/Arrive Bucharest's Baneasa station. (2)Runs from mid-June to mid-September. (3)Light refreshments. (4)Meal service.

Sights: Constantza is a very large resort. Eforie and Mangalia are popular Black Sea beach resorts. In Constantza, see the Museum of Archaeology Parvan. The Open Air Museum of Archaeology. The Roman Mosaic. The Museum of the Black Sea.

Bucharest - Galati - Bucharest
836

Dep. Bucharest (Nord)	5:50(1)	13:35(1)
Arr. Galati	8:59	16:47

Sights in Galati: The most splendid array of birdlife in all of Europe.

Dep. Galati	15:32(1)	19:35(1)
Arr. Bucharest (Nord)	18:47	22:37

(1)Light refreshments.

Bucharest - Sighisoara - Bucharest

826

Dep. Bucharest (Nord)	6:40(1)	Dep. Sighisoara	14:24(1)	18:28(1)
Arr. Sighisoara	11:17	Arr. Bucharest (Nord)	18:35	22:40

(1) Meal service.

Sights in Sighisoara: This is an interesting medieval fortress city. See the Museum of the Walled Town. Stroll through the old section.

Bucharest - Sinaia - Bucharest

831

All of these trains have meal service.

Dep. Bucharest (Nord)	6:40	9:25	10:25
Arr. Sinaia	8:21	11:07	12:21

Sights in Sinaia: This is a major Winter resort.

Dep. Sinaia	11:50	18:39	19:17
Arr. Bucharest (Nord)	13:30	20:20	10:55

INTERNATIONAL ROUTES FROM ROMANIA

Bucharest is Romania's gateway for rail travel to Belgrade (and on to Yugoslavia's Adriatic cities), Budapest (and on to Western Europe), Kiev (and on to Moscow and Leningrad), and Sofia (and on to Athens and Istanbul).

Bucharest - Belgrade

795

Dep. Bucharest (Nord)	22:37(1)
Arr. Belgrade (Dunav)	9:20

(1)Carries sleeping car.

Bucharest - Budapest

826 + 831

Dep. Bucharest (Nord)	7:00(1+2)	-0-	9:25(2+9)
Dep. Bucharest (Chitila)	-0-	8:20(3+4+8)	-0-
Arr. Budapest (Nyugati)	21:40(1+2)	-0-	-0-
Arr. Budapest (Keleti)	-0-	-0-	22:33
Arr. Budapest (Zuglo)	-0-	23:10	-0-

(1)Runs from late May to late September. (2)Meal service. (3)Runs from early June to late September. (4)Reservation required. (5)Carries sleeping car. Also has couchettes. (6)Light refreshments. (7)Runs from early June to early September. (8)Plus another departure from Bucharest Chitila at 23:45(7), arriving Budapest Zuglo at 15:05. (9)Plus other departures from Bucharest Nord at 18:30(2+4+5), arriving Budapest Keleti at 7:38 . . . at 22:05(4+5+6), arriving Budapest Nyugati at 12:25 . . . and at 0:35(1), arriving Budapest Keleti at 14:23.

Bucharest - Kiev - Moscow

	833	834	834
Dep. Bucharest (Nord)	20:00(1)	20:25(1)	23:14(1)
Arr. Ungeni (Rom. Time)	-0-	4:23(2)	7:15(2)

Set your watch forward 2 hours.

Change trains.

Ungeni is the Russian border station where the trains' wheels are changed to fit the wider Soviet rail gauge.

Dep. Ungeni (Mos. Time)	-0-	7:26(2)	10:25(2)
Arr. Kiev	18:14(2)	20:51(2)	23:05(2)
Arr. Moscow	6:00(3)	9:35(3)	11:00(3)

(1)Train is only sleeping cars. (2)Day 2. (3)Day 3.

Bucharest - Sofia - Istanbul

834

Dep. Bucharest (Nord)	8:00(1)	21:48(2)
Arr. Sofia	19:25	9:26
Arr. Istanbul	10:45	-0-

(1)Runs Wednesday and Friday only. Carries sleeping car. (2)Runs from early June to late September. From mid-June to late August, carries sleeping car daily. Before and after that period, carries sleeping car only on Wednesday.

RUSSIA (U.S.S.R. — SOVIET UNION)

Children under 5 travel free. Half-fare for children 5-9. Children 10 and over must pay full fare.

There are 2 classes of trains in Russia: Soft Class (upholstered seats, which convert to large 4-berth couchette compartments) and Hard Class (plastic or leather seats, which convert to bunks either in 4-berth compartments or open non-compartment coaches). Bedding, including mattresses, is available at an extra charge for both classes.

A few important trains provide a third category of service: Sleeping Cars, with 2-berth compartments which have a folding table at the window, closet and a speaker carrying both recorded music, which can be shut off, and announcements, which cannot be shut off. One car on the Trans Siberian Express is in this category. On these trains, for which reservations are required, conductors in each car serve Russian tea to passengers.

Through sleeping cars going to Western Europe, Scandinavia, Greece, Turkey and Iran have single and double compartments in First Class and 3-berth compartments in Second Class, all with full bedding included in the ticket price.

The only timetables available in Russia are printed in the Cyrillic alphabet. All timetables show Moscow Time, even though Russia has 9 different time zones.

Because Soviet rail tracks are 5 feet wide (along with Finland, whose rail system was constructed while Russians dominated that country), their passenger cars and compartments are considerably roomy. Good road maintenance and excellent engineers make Russian trains smooth-running.

As with all travel in Russia, your rail routes and travel dates must be predetermined and are limited to the provisions of the visa with which you enter the country. Tourists are not permitted to travel on many routes. For example, although the Trans Siberian Express terminates its run in Vladivostock, foreign passengers must leave the train 460 miles earlier, in Khabarovsk.

RUSSIAN HOLIDAYS

January 1	New Year's Day	November 7	Victory Day (World War II)
March 8	Women's Day	May 9	Revolution Day
May 1	Labor Day	November 8	Additional Holiday
May 2	Additional Holiday	December 5	Constitution Day

LONG-DISTANCE TRIPS FROM LENINGRAD

Here are schedules for rail trips from Leningrad to 5 other interesting cities, with notes on what to see at each destination.

Leningrad

Russia's most interesting city. The Hermitage Museum has the world's largest exhibition of fine arts, over 2,500,000 articles. See the 112 columns, gold cupola and priceless paintings and mosaics at St. Isaac's Cathedral. The park and palace at Petrodvorets. The Winter Palace. The 600-ton, 154-foot high Alexandrovskaya Column, marking Russia's victory over Napoleon. The Peter-Paul Fortress and Cathedral. The Summer Gardens. The Museum of the History of Religion and Atheism, in Kazansky Cathedral.

Leningrad - Kiev 867

Dep. Leningrad (Viteb.)	12:05	Dep. Kiev	23:29
Arr. Kiev	16:28(1)	Arr. Leningrad (Viteb.)	5:35(2)

(1)Day 2. (2)Day 3.

Sights in Kiev: The 11th century catacombs at the Pecherskaya Lavra Monastery. The frescos and mosaics at the 11th century St. Sophia Cathedral. The Golden Gate (Zolotiya Vorota) at the intersection of Sverlovskaya and Vladimirskaya. The Museum of Russian Art. The Museum of Western and Oriental Art.

Below are schedules for continuing on from Kiev to Odessa:

Kiev - Odessa 865

Dep. Kiev	8:49(1)	21:43	Dep. Odessa	15:39(1)	22:26
Arr. Odessa	18:27	8:38	Arr. Kiev	1:30	9:00

(1) Meal service.

Sights in Odessa: A sea resort and Russia's second largest port. See the beautiful Opera and Ballet Theater. The Potemkin Stairway, descending 455 feet from Primorsky Boulevard to the waterfront.

Leningrad - Moscow 859

Dep. Leningrad (Mos.)	1:30(1)	10:45(2)	12:52(3)	12:56(4+6)
Arr. Moscow (Len.)	9:52	18:23	18:51	20:46

(1)Second-class only. (2)Runs from early June to late August. Meal service. (3)Runs from early August to late August. (4)Meal service. (5)Carries sleeping car. (6)Plus other departures from Leningrad at 15:41(4), 15:46(2), 21:12(1), 21:48(1), 21:53(1), 23:00, 23:20(4), 23:35, 23:55(5), 23:59 and 0:10(1).

Sights in Moscow: See notes about sightseeing in Moscow under "Long-Distance Trips From Moscow", next in this section.

Leningrad - Murmansk 860

Murmansk is the world's northernmost passenger rail terminus. All arrivals shown below are on Day 2.

Dep. Leningrad (Mosk.)	9:12	18:59	Dep. Murmansk	10:15	21:30
Arr. Murmansk	11:05	21:25	Arr. Leningrad (Mosk.)	12:30	22:55

Sights in Murmansk: The largest city in the world north of the Arctic Circle. Founded in 1915 as a supply post in the First World War. Valuable in World War II as Russia's principal port for receiving war supplies from Britain and the U.S. Its ice-free harbor has made Murmansk a major ship repair center and commercial fishing base.

Leningrad - Tallinn 862

Dep. Leningrad (Var.)	7:00	16:15(1)	Dep. Tallinn	7:08	17:00(2)
Arr. Tallinn	15:44	22:55	Arr. Leningrad (Var.)	16:37	23:27

(1) Another Leningrad dep. at 23:30. (2) Another Tallinn dep. at 22:40.

Sights in Tallinn: A fortified town for more than 2,000 years. Once the capital (1918-1940) of Estonia, before that country was annexed by Russia. In the walled Lower Town, see the 13th century Toom Church. The 13th century Great Guildhall. The 14th century Town Hall. Ruins of the 13th century fort built by invading Danes on Toompea Hill. The Gothic churches, Niguliste and Oleviste. The old castle.

LONG-DISTANCE TRIPS FROM MOSCOW

Here are schedules for rail trips from Moscow to 10 other interesting cities, with notes on what to see at each destination.

Moscow

Red Square, with Lenin's Mausoleum. The 15th century Cathedrals: Uspensky, Blagoveshchensky and Archangelsky. The priceless jewelry, costumes, gold and silver objects, Faberge eggs, carriages and weapons in the Armory Museum (Oruzheinaya Palata). The 16th century gigantic 38-ton canon, Czar Pushka. The Grand Kremlin Palace. The 32-story Moscow University skyscraper. The Saturday and Sunday trading of birds and other pets on Kalitnikovskaya Street.

The Bolshoi Theater. The Tretyakov Gallery, with its more than 50,000 paintings and sculptures. The Lenin State Library, containing over 19 million books, magazines and manuscripts in over 160 different languages. The Zoo. The Lenin Central Museum. The Pushkin Museum of Fine Arts. Dozens of other museums.

Moscow's 9 railstations are: Byelorussian (trips to Warsaw, and on to Western Europe), Kazanski (to Tashkent and Samarkand), Kievski (to the city of Kiev, and on to Eastern Europe), Kurski (to Sochi, and on to the Caspian Sea), Leningradski (to the city of Leningrad, and on to Helsinki), Paveletski (for which Cook's lists no trains), Riga (to the city of Riga and the Baltic area), Savelovski (for which Cook's lists no trains), and Yaroslavski (across Siberia to Russia's Far East area, and to Pekin).

Moscow - Kiev 865

Dep. Moscow (Kiev.)	0:45(1)	9:40(2)	19:30(2+3)	20:15(2+4)
Arr. Kiev	13:14	23:27	7:17	8:39

Sights in Kiev: See notes about sightseeing in Kiev earlier in this section, under "Leningrad-Kiev".

Dep. Kiev	1:44(2)	3:07(2+3)	5:04(2)	11:06(5)
Arr. Moscow (Kiev.)	14:00	14:58	17:23	23:48

(1)Carries sleeping car. (2)Meal service. (3)Runs from mid-May to late September. (4)Plus other departures from Moscow at 21:27(1+2), 22:10(2) and 23:00(1+2). (5)Plus other departures from Kiev at 15:28(2), 18:24(1+2), 21:22(1+2) and 23:15(1+2).

Moscow - Leningrad 859

Dep. Moscow (Len.)	0:36(1)	1:00	11:42(2)	12:30(2+4)
Arr. Leningrad (Mos.)	8:52	9:11	19:55	20:03

(1)Meal service. (2)Runs from early June to late September. (3)Carries sleping car. (4)Plus other departures from Moscow at 13:13, 16:08(1), 20:49, 21:50, 22:20, 23:00 and 23:55(3).

Sights in Leningrad: See notes about sightseeing in Leningrad earlier in this section, under "Long-Distance Trips from Leningrad".

Moscow - Riga 863

Dep. Moscow (Riga)	20:20(1)	21:30(2)
Arr. Riga	10:26	12:15

Dep. Riga	18:01(1)	18:53(2)
Arr. Moscow (Riga)	9:00	10:05

(1)Carries sleeping car. Meal service. (2)Meal service.

Sights in Riga: An important Baltic port. The great pipe organ at the 13th-15th century Cathedral. The 14th century Riga Castle.

Moscow - Sochi - Sukhumi 874

Dep. Moscow (Kurski)	14:46(1)	19:50(1)	23:25(1)	23:59(1)
Arr. Sochi	0:35(2)	4:56(2)	9:21(2)	8:54(2)
Arr. Sukhumi	4:56(2)	8:17(2)	-0-	13:12(2)

* * *

Dep. Sukhumi	2:18(1)	-0-	13:35(1)	23:12(1)
Arr. Sochi	5:54(1)	9:33(4)	16:20(1)	2:10(1+3)
Arr. Moscow (Kurski)	15:05(3)	20:05(3)	4:50(2)	10:25(2)

(1)Carries sleeping car. Meal service. (2)Day 3. (3)Day 2. (4)Meal service.

Sights in Sochi: A popular Black Sea resort. Over 800 species of trees at the Dendrarium. Scenic Lake Ritsa is a 5-hour bus trip away.

Sights in Sukhumi: This is the heart of Russia's subtropical area: citrus fruits, tobacco, etc. See the monkey farm used by Russian scientists in their program of studying human behavior.

Moscow - Tashkent - Samarkand 5031

Dep. Moscow (Kaz.)	13:30	14:00(2)	20:50	22:20(4)
Arr. Tashkent	0:40(1)	5:30(1)	21:47(3)	8:10(3)
Change trains.				
5032				
Dep. Tashkent	6:00(5)	10:40	13:35	16:30(6)
Arr. Samarkand	16:03	18:35	21:13	0:43

(1)Day 5. (2)Runs daily in June, July and August. (3)Day 4. (4)Meal service. (5)Second-class only. (6)Plus another departure from Tashkent at 17:05.

Sights in Tashkent: This has been an important center of trade and handcraft on the major caravan route (the "silk road") between Europe and China and India for nearly 2,000 years. Many 15th and 16th century churches. Heavy Muslim cultural influence here. See: The Academy of Sciences. The Navoi Public Library. The Navoi Theater of Opera and Ballet.

Sights in Samarkand: One of the oldest cities in Central Asia. Alexander the Great captured Samarkand 2300 years ago. Heavy Turkish cultural influence here since the 6th century. Uninhabited from 1720 to 1770 due to an economic decline at that time caused by constant attacks by nomad tribes. The inception of train service in 1896 revived the city. See: The enormous colored domes of the 14th century mausoleums, decorated in marble and gold. The 14th century mosque. The ruins of a 16th century aqueduct.

Moscow - Sevastopol 874

Dep. Moscow (Kur.)	11:55(1)	Dep. Sevastopol	19:21(1)
Arr. Sevastopol	10:56(2)	Arr. Moscow (Kur.)	19:45(2)

(1)Second-class only. Runs daily in June, July and August. Meal service. (2)Day 2.

Sights in Sevastopol: A Russian naval base since 1784. A commercial port since 1808. A railway terminal since 1875. Totally destroyed by Germans in July, 1942. Reconstructed after 1944. See the 377-foot-wide panorama of the 1854 Crimean War siege by English and French forces.

Moscow - Volgograd - Rostov Rostov - Moscow

Here is a great combination train and boat trip: from Moscow to Volgograd by train, and from Volgograd to Rostov by ship on the Volga-Don Canal. Then, return to Moscow by train.

869

Dep. Moscow (Kaz.)	14:30(1)	14:45(1+2)
Arr. Volgograd	10:00	11:14

(1) Carries sleeping car. Meal service. (2) Runs daily in June, July and August.

Change to a ship. Check Intourist for current Volga-Don Canal timetables for this cruise. The complete 2,000 mile ship trip runs from Moscow to Rostov.

874

Dep. Rostov	12:33(1)	13:26(1)	17:49(1)	18:51(1+3)
Arr. Moscow (Kur.)	9:35	10:25	15:05	15:45

(1) Carries sleeping car. Meal service. (2) Meal service. (3) Plus another departure from Rostov at 22:47(2).

Sights in Volgograd: Renamed (from Stalingrad) after being destroyed during a 7-month battle in 1942-43. See: the enormous 63-mile canal. The huge industrial complex, particularly the Tractor Factory.

Sights in Rostov: Another post-World War II metropolis based on heavy industrial manufacturing. See the enormous theater on Teatralnaya Square. Window-shop on Engels Street.

Here is the reverse route for this circle trip:

874

Dep. Moscow (Kur.)	8:50(1)	14:46(1)	19:50(1)	23:25(1+3)
Arr. Rostov	5:11	10:15	16:26	19:28

(1) Carries sleeping car. Meal service. (2) Meal service. (3) Plus another departure from Moscow at 23:54(2).

Change to a ship for the cruise from Rostov to Volgograd. Change to a train in Volgograd.

869

Dep. Volgograd	13:34(1)	14:25(2)
Arr. Moscow (Kaz.)	10:03	11:10

(1) Carries sleeping car. Meal service. (2) Runs daily in June, July and August. Meal service.

INTERNATIONAL ROUTES FROM RUSSIA

Here are the schedules for rail trips from Leningrad to Helsinki (and on to the rest of Scandinavia) and to Warsaw (and on to Western Europe).

Also, from Moscow to Bucharest (and on to the rest of Eastern Europe as well as to Athens and Istanbul), Khabarovsk (and on to Nakhodka, and from there to Yokohama and Hong Kong), Pekin, Tehran and Warsaw (and on to Western Europe).

Leningrad - Helsinki 855

Dep. Leningrad (Finlandski) 11:00 (Second-class only. Meal service.)
Set your watch back one hour.
Arr. Helsinki 17:05

Leningrad - Warsaw 853

Dep. Leningrad (Varshavski) 23:35(1)
Dep. Vilnius 12:05 Day 2
During Poland's Summer Time, set your watch back one hour (2 hours in Winter.)
Arr. Warsaw (Gdanska) 21:20
(1)Carries sleeping car. Meal service.

Moscow - Bucharest

	833	834	834
Dep. Moscow (Kiev.)	0:45(1)	21:27(1)	23:00(1)
Set your watch back 2 hours.			
Arr. Bucharest (Nord)	9:45(2)	7:35(3)	9:20(3)

(1)Train of only sleeping cars. (2)Day 2. (3)Day 3.

Moscow - Pekin 879

Dep. Moscow (Yar.) 21:10(1) | Arr. Pekin 6:20(2)
(1) Fridays only. Carries sleeping car. Both soft and hard cars for seat passengers. Meal service. (2) The following Friday.

Moscow - Pyongyang 5000

Dep. Moscow (Yar.) 21:10(1) | Arr. Pyongyang 15:55(2)
(1) Fridays only. Carries sleeping car. Both soft and hard cars for seat passengers. Meal service. (2) The following Friday.

Moscow - Khabarovsk - Yokohama - Hong Kong

This is the Trans-Siberian rail route.

It is advisable to stopover in Novosibirsk (population 1,500,000) and Irkutsk on the 7½-day Moscow-Khabarovsk trip. The Hotel Novosibirsk has better accommodations than are available in either Irkutsk or Khabarovsk. It is always recommended to bring toilet paper and soap when traveling on Soviet trains, including the Trans-Siberian Express.

878 (Train)		
Dep. Moscow (Yar.)	10:00(1)	
Arr. Novosibirsk	15:50	Day 3
Arr. Irkutsk	0:12	Day 5
Arr. Khabarovsk	0:35	Day 8
Change trains.		
Dep. Khabarovsk	18:25(2+3)	
Arr. Nakhodka	9:25(4)	Day 9
Change to Boat.		
1480		
Dep. Nakhodka	12:00(5)	Day 9
Arr. Yokohama	16:00	Day 11
Dep. Yokohama	11:00(5)	Day 12
Arr. Hong Kong	16:00(6)	Day 16

1480 (Boat)		
Dep. Hong Kong	11:00(5)	
Arr. Yokohama	16:00(6)	Day 5
Dep. Yokohama	11:00(5)	Day 6
Arr. Nakhodka	17:00	Day 8
Change to train.		
878		
Dep. Nakhodka	20:00(3+7)	
Arr. Khabarovsk	11:10	Day 9
Change trains.		
Dep. Khabarovsk	13:55(1)	Day 9
Arr. Irkutsk	1:00	Day 12
Arr. Novosibirsk	9:40	Day 13
Arr. Moscow (Yar.)	15:05	Day 15

(1) Runs daily. Carries sleeping car. Meal service. (2) Runs only on days prior to sailings from Nakhodka to Yokohama. Carries sleeping car. (3) Has only second-class coach cars for seat passengers. Meal service. (4) Day 2 after departure from Khabarovsk. (5) For specific sailing dates, check Cook's Continental Timetable. (6) Fifth day of boat trip. (7) Runs only on days that sailings from Yokohama arrive in Nakhodka. Carries sleeping car.

Sights in **Novosibirsk:** The Theater of Opera and Ballet, which is larger than Moscow's Bolshoi Theater. Take the 18-mile bus ride to Akademgorodok, the "Science Town", located along the Ob Sea, a man-made reservoir.

Sights in **Irkutsk:** A large industrial city with no major tourist attraction. *However,* Irkutsk is the gateway for visiting the most unique place in the Soviet Union: Lake Baykal. Buses take tourists through a virgin forest to the shore of the world's deepest (6,365 feet) lake, 380 miles long and 12 to 50 miles wide, containing one-fifth of the fresh water on the earth's surface (four-fifths of the fresh water in the U.S.S.R.). Its waves sometimes measure over 15 feet.

Formed nearly 30,000,000 years ago by a rupture in the earth's crust,

(Sightseeing notes continue on page 486)

THE TRANS-SIBERIAN TIMETABLE

The times shown here are Moscow Time, considerably different than actual arrival and departure times as this route covers 9 time zones. For example, the real arrival time in Khabarovsk is 8 hours later than the Moscow Time listed. Also, the real departure time from Khabarovsk (for the westward trip to Moscow) is 8 hours later than indicated. The number of travel days is represented by capital letters: A=Day 1, B=Day 2, etc.

Moscow - Khabarovsk	5020			
Dep. Moscow (Yar.)	4:40 **A**	10:00(1) **A**	14:45(2) **A**	19:15 **A**
Dep. Kirov	5:15 **B**	1:08 **B**	9:04 **B**	15:33 **B**
Arr. Sverdlovsk	3:57 **C**	15:02	0:57 **C**	7:17 **C**
Dep. Sverdlovsk	5:06	15:17	1:12	7:32
Arr. Omsk	5:20 **D**	5:10 **C**	17:24	22:19
Dep. Omsk	6:25	5:45	17:39	22:40
Dep. Novosibirsk	21:53	16:12	5:13 **D**	8:56 **D**
Dep. Krasnoyarsk	17:58 **E**	4:45 **D**	19:30	23:06
Arr. Irkutsk	18:54 **F**	0:12 **E**	17:24 **E**	21:05 **E**
Dep. Irkutsk	20:14	0:27	17:39	21:23
Dep. Ulan Ude	7:00 **G**	8:34	3:00 **F**	6:38 **F**
Dep. Chita	20:44	18:37	13:48	18:03
Dep. Skovorodino	22:40 **H**	17:47 **F**	14:05 **G**	20:25
Dep. Belogorsk	11:35 **I**	4:50 **G**	2:15 **H**	19:15 **G**
Arr. Khabarovsk	2:15 **J**	17:35	15:50	22:20 **H**
	*	*	*	
Dep. Khabarovsk	2:00 **A**	3:55 **A**	6:55(1) **A**	20:50(2) **A**
Dep. Belogorsk	19:00	18:20	19:50	10:50 **B**
Dep. Skovorodino	8:40 **B**	6:35 **B**	7:10 **B**	23:20
Dep. Chita	11:48 **C**	8:00 **C**	6:55 **C**	0:30 **D**
Dep. Ulan Ude	0:02 **D**	19:20	17:08	11:48
Arr. Irkutsk	10:35	4:09 **D**	1:00 **D**	20:35
Dep. Irkutsk	12:16	4:27	1:15	10:50
Dep. Krasnoyarsk	14:20 **E**	2:54 **E**	20:50	16:22 **E**
Dep. Novosibirsk	8:32 **F**	17:37	10:00 **E**	9:20 **F**
Arr. Omsk	20:38	4:15 **F**	19:34	19:47
Dep. Omsk	21:38	4:36	19:50	20:05
Arr. Sverdlovsk	21:50 **G**	19:51	9:34 **F**	11:28 **G**
Dep. Sverdlovsk	23:00	20:14	9:48	11:43
Dep. Kirov	22:26 **H**	11:15 **G**	0:15 **G**	3:09 **H**
Arr. Moscow (Yar.)	0:35 **J**	7:20 **H**	15:05	20:50

(1)"Rossia". Carries sleeping car. Meal service. (2)Runs daily in June, July and August.

it is fed by 336 rivers and streams. There are 1,800 species of animals and plants in the lake, about three-quarters of which are found nowhere else in the world.

The day-trip includes a stop at the Limnological Museum, where hundreds of local flora and fauna are exhibited. The excursion to Baykal ends with a 90-minute hydrofoil ride from the Museum, up the Angara River, to Irkutsk.

Moscow - Tehran

These trains carry sleeping cars and have meal service.

5025		4500	
Dep. Moscow (Kurski)	21:35 Sat.	Dep. Djulfa (USSR)	11:30 Tue.
Arr. Djulfa (USSR)	7:26 Tue.	Dep. Djulfa (Iran)	15:00 Tue.
Change trains.		Arr. Tehran	9:45 Wed.

Moscow - Warsaw - Berlin

	854		
Dep. Moscow (Byel.)	12:38(1+2)	17:48(2+3)	19:26(2+4)
Set your watch back 2 hours.			
Arr. Warsaw (Gdanska)	5:50	10:55	13:09
Arr. Berlin (Ost)	16:01	20:06	22:57

(1) Runs from early June to late September. Second-class only. (2) Meal service. (3) Carries sleeping car. Coach cars are second-class only. (4) Carries sleeping car. Has both first and Second-class coach cars.

YUGOSLAVIA

Yugoslavian trains are classified Exspresni (express), Poslovni (rapid), Brzi (fast), and Putnicki (slow). Supplements are charged for internal express trains, except to passengers holding tickets that were issued outside Yugoslavia. Yugoslavia stays on Standard Time all year.

YUGOSLAVIAN HOLIDAYS

January 1	New Year's Day	May 9	Victory Day (World War II)
January 2	Additional Holiday	July 4	Veterans Day
May 1	Labor Day	November 29	Republic Day
May 2	Additional Holiday	November 30	Additional Holiday

ONE-DAY EXCURSIONS AND CITY-SIGHTSEEING

Here are 4 one-day rail trips that can be made comfortably from 3 major cities in Yugoslavia, returning to them in most cases before dinnertime. Notes are provided on what to see at each destination. The number below the name of each route is the Cook's timetable.

The 3 base cities are: Belgrade, Split and Zagreb.

Details on 9 other rail trips recommended for exceptional scenery and schedules for international connections conclude this section.

Belgrade

The collection of monuments to Serbian heroes in the Cathedral of the Holy Archangel Michael. The National Museum. The Kalemegdan fortress. Daman Pasha's Dome. The Museum of Medieval Frescos. The Ethnographic Museum. Many Turkish-style houses.

Split

This is a popular resort. See: The 2220-year old immense (7 acres) Palace of Diocletian, with its 7-foot thick, 72-foot high walls. Sacked in 615, only 3 of its 16 original towers remain. It is considered the largest and best preserved example of Roman palace architecture. Do not miss the fine frescos, marble pulpit and carvings in the Cathedral, which had been a mausoleum until it was converted to a church in 653. The Temple of Jupiter. The Museum of Ethnography in the Venetian Gothic Town Hall. The 12th century belfry at Our Lady of the Belfry Church.

Sarajevo

Turkish houses and mosques. The 16th century arched bridge over the Neretva River. The oriental handicrafts offered along Bascarsija, a row of small shops (silver, copper and other works).

Zagreb

Many medieval palaces. The Modern Gallery. St. Mark's Church. St. Stephen's Cathedral. The cable-car ride to Mount Sljeme.

Belgrade - Zagreb - Belgrade 781

Dep. Belgrade	6:00(1)	6:17(1)	6:34
Arr. Zagreb	11:05	11:26	12:45

Sights in Zagreb: See notes about sightseeing in Zagreb immediately preceding these schedules.

Dep. Zagreb	16:25(1)	16:40(1)	16:57
Arr. Belgrade	22:10	23:15	22:20

(1) Meal service.

Zagreb - Belgrade - Zagreb 781

Dep. Zagreb	5:45(1)	Dep. Belgrade	15:05(1)	15:25(2)	16:50(3)
Arr. Belgrade	11:05	Arr. Zagreb	19:55	21:39	22:10

(1) Reservation required. First-class only. Meal service. (2) Meal service. (3) Plus other departures from Belgrade at 17:42 and 19:25.

Sights in Belgrade: See notes about city-sightseeing in Belgrade at the start of this section.

Zagreb - Ljubljana - Zagreb 781

Dep. Zagreb	7:10(1)	7:30	11:28	11:48	13:00
Arr. Ljubljana	9:30	10:05	13:45	13:57	15:40

Sights in Ljubljana: Sampling (free) hundreds of different Yugoslav wines at the Autumn Wine Fair. Interesting Baroque churches. The Castle. Several good museums.

Dep. Ljubljana	13:30	14:30	16:30(1)	17:10	19:00
Arr. Zagreb	15:46	16:41	18:50	19:30	21:36

(1) Runs from late May to late September.

LONG-DISTANCE RAIL TRIPS IN YUGOSLAVIA

Here are some longer trips in Yugoslavia to interesting destinations:

Belgrade - Split **Split - Belgrade**

788

Dep. Belgrade	17:52(1)	20:30(2)
Arr. Split	7:36	8:00

Sights in Split: See notes about sightseeing in Split at the start of this section.

Dep. Split	19:20(1)	20:00(2)
Arr. Belgrade	9:42	8:04

(1) Carries sleeping car. (2) Carries sleeping car. Also has couchettes.

Split - Zadar **Zadar - Split**

788

Dep. Split	8:50(1)	10:45(3)	15:00(2+5)	
Arr. Knin	11:04	13:02	17:14	
Change trains.				
Dep. Knin	11:32(2)	14:42(4)	19:33(4)	
Arr. Zadar	12:58	16:46	21:30	

* * *

Dep. Zadar	6:50(4)	14:55(2+5)	-0-	20:05
Arr. Knin	8:55	17:04	-0-	21:43
Change trains.				
Dep. Knin	11:06(2+5)	17:16(3)	19:30(2+5)	3:30
Arr. Split	13:03	19:20	21:26	5:54

(1) Runs from late May to late September. Meal service. (2) First-class only. (3) Runs from late September to late May. (4) Second-class only. (5) Meal service.

Sights in Zadar: One of the most beautiful towns on the Adriatic. Many Roman monuments are well-preserved here. See the 9th century St. Donat's Church. The 12th century Cathedral.

Zagreb - Split **Split - Zagreb**

788

Dep. Zagreb	6:00(1+2)	6:30(1+3)	10:25(4)	14:30(1+2+7)
Arr. Split	13:03	15:42	19:20	21:26

Sights in Split: See notes about sightseeing in Split at the start of this section.

Dep. Split	6:15(1+2)	8:50(1+3)	10:45(4)	15:00(1+2+8)
Arr. Zagreb	13:00	17:25	19:14	22:15

(1) Meal service. (2) First-class only. (3) Runs from late May to late September. (4) Runs from late September to late May. (5) Carries sleeping car. Also has couchettes. (6) Carries sleeping car. (7) Plus other departures from Zagreb at 19:23(3+5), 20:10(6) and 21:55(6). (8) Plus other departures from Split at 18:53(3+4), 21:05(6) and 21:40(6).

SCENIC RAIL TRIPS

Belgrade - Bar **Bar - Belgrade**

This is the most scenic rail route in Yugoslavia. Steep canyons, turbulent rivers and mountains. The 325-mile line has 254 tunnels and 234 concrete and steel bridges. The trip climbs from the Danube to heights of 4,000 feet before descending to sea level on the Adriatic coast.

793

Dep. Belgrade	9:15(1)	10:30(2)	14:20(2+3)	20:52(1+4+6)
Arr. Bar	16:50	18:34	21:41	4:16

Sights in Bar: A seaport and popular tourist resort.

Dep. Bar	7:33(1)	9:23(2)	14:01(2+3)	20:22(1+4+7)
Arr. Belgrade	15:42	17:30	21:22	4:32

(1) Runs from mid-June to late August. (2) Meal service. (3) First-class only. (4) Carries sleeping car. Also has couchettes. (5) Carries sleeping car. (6) Plus another departure from Belgrade at 22:00(2+4). (7) Plus another departure from Bar at 22:37(2+4).

Belgrade - Sarajevo **Sarajevo - Belgrade**

This route involves 120 tunnels and many bridges. It gives a view of Ovcar Gorge, the Kablar Mountains and Zapadna River. Many monasteries can be seen on the hillsides. The line from Priboj is narrow-gauge as the train descends to the valley of the Rzav River.

786

Dep. Belgrade	7:10(1)	11:10(2)	15:25(1)	21:45(3+4)
Arr. Sarajevo	12:55	18:20	21:00	4:45

Sights in Sarajevo: See notes about sightseeing in Sarajevo at the start of this section.

Dep. Sarajevo	6:26(1)	10:40(2)	15:15(1)	21:50(3+5)
Arr. Belgrade	12:28	17:35	21:15	5:15

(1) Reservation required. First-class only. Meal service. (2) Meal service. (3) Carries sleeping car. Also has couchettes. Meal service. (4) Plus another departure from Belgrade at 23:30(3). (5) Plus another departure from Sarajevo at 23:00(3).

Belgrade - Skopje **Skopje - Belgrade**

This ride passes along many rivers and ancient Roman towns. The picturesque Juzna Morava Valley can be seen after leaving Nis.

790

Dep. Belgrade	8:30(1)	9:50(2)	13:55(1)	14:30(1)	21:30(3+6)
Dep. Nis	12:16	14:02	17:47	18:05	-0-
Arr. Skopje	15:44	17:44	21:08	21:25	8:38

Sights in Skopje: Daut-Pasha's Bath. St. Spas' Church. The Clock Tower. The 12th century Nerezi Monastery, with its beautiful frescos.

Dep. Skopje	8:36	9:22(2)	10:42	14:30(1)	21:34(3+7)
Dep. Nis	12:20	13:25	14:25	17:58	1:24
Arr. Belgrade	16:12	17:40	18:20	21:58	5:59

(1) Meal service. (2) Runs from mid-June to late August. (3) Carries sleeping car. (4) Has couchettes. (5) Adjustment footnote. (6) Plus other departures from Belgrade at 21:50(3), 22:45(4) and 23:45(3). (7) Plus another departure from Skopje at 22:00(3).

Ljubljana - Postojna - Ljubljana 785

The longest and most beautiful river cave of Europe is near Postojna, where the Pivka River flows through an underground passage. Tourists, traveling through the cave on a small train, are able to see wonderful rows of stalactites and stalagmites, gigantic underground rooms, chasms and little lakes. A 16th century castle is at the entrance to the cave.

Dep. Ljubljana 6:00 10:15 12:00 14:40
Arr. Postojna 60-65 minutes later

* * *

Dep. Postojna 11:10 11:36 15:05 16:05(1) 19:10 20:55(2)
Arr. Ljubljana 60-65 minutes later

(1) Daily, except Sundays and holidays. (2) Plus another departure from Postojna at 21:13.

Ljubljana - Jesenice - Sezana - Ljublana

There are many interesting ski resorts between Ljubljana and Jesenice in this region of the Slovenian Alps. Kranj is noted for fishing, water sports and mountaineering. Lesce-Bled (Lake Bled) is popular both Summer and Winter. All through this area there is fine scenery of evergreen forests and picturesque pastures. The most beautiful region of the Slovenian Alps is the route from Jesenice to Sezana. Here is the one-day circle trip that takes in all this area.

781

Dep. Ljubljana	9:35	12:19
Arr. Kranj	10:05	12:50
Arr. Lesce-Bled	10:29	13:18
Arr. Jesenice	10:43	13:34

Change trains

796

Dep. Jesenice	11:20	14:20
Arr. Nova Gorica	13:15	16:23

Change trains.

796

Dep. Nova Gorcia	15:00	18:40
Arr. Sezana	15:57	19:54

Change trains.

783

Dep. Sezana	18:20	20:00
Arr. Ljubljana	20:15	22:00

Sarajevo - Dubrovnik 786

There is scenery reminiscent of Norway's fjords and one of the most beautiful train rides in Yugoslavia on the Mostar-Kardeljevo portion of the trip from Sarajevo to Dubrovnik.

Dep. Sarajevo	5:15(1)	8:10	13:30	17:10
Dep. Mostar	7:25(1)	10:06	16:01	19:10
Arr. Kardeljevo	8:30	10:55	17:22	20:07

Change to the local bus for the trip from Kardeljevo to Dubrovnik.

Dep. Kardeljevo	10:00(2)	12:15	17:45	20:30(2)
Arr. Dubrovnik	11:50	14:05	19:35	22:20

Sights in Mostar: The Old Quarter is very Turkish, with an open-air market, a mosque and cobblestoned streets. See the arched bridge the Turks built in 1566, using a mortar of eggs, butter and cheese! Dine and drink at the Labyrinth Bar, under the bridge.

Sights in Dubrovnik: One of Europe's most popular beach resorts. See the 4 ancient forts. The 15th century Rector's Palace. Prince's Court. St. Blaise's Cathedral. Sponza Palace. St. Vlah's Church. The Dominican and Franciscan Cloisters. The beautiful 600-year old pharmacy at St. Francis' Monastery. Shop on Stradun (a pedestrian mall) for sheepskin coats, coral jewelry, hand-woven rugs, filigree, lace, embroidery and leather items. Walk on the top of the city walls.

Bus

Dep. Dubrovnik	5:30	8:30(2)	14:50	16:00(2)
Arr. Kardeljevo	7:20	10:20	16:40	17:50

Change to train.

Dep. Kardeljevo	7:35(3)	14:10	16:55(1)	18:14(1)
Dep. Mostar	8:41(3)	15:15	18:15	19:27(1)
Arr. Sarajevo	10:32(3)	17:30	20:08	21:20

(1) Meal service. (2) Runs from late May to late September. (3) One hour later from late September to late March.

Split - Sunja - Zagreb

Between Knin and Sunja, this route passes through gorges and the valley of the Una River. There is excellent scenery of thick forests as the train passes from one bank of the river to the other.

Schedules for this trip appear earlier in this section, under "Long-Distance Trips".

INTERNATIONAL ROUTES FROM YUGOSLAVIA

There are rail connections from Belgrade to Athens (and on to Istanbul), Bucharest (and on to Kiev and Moscow), Budapest (and on to Moscow, Prague, Vienna and Warsaw), Salzburg (and on to the rest of Western Europe and to Scandinavia), Sofia (and on to Athens and Istanbul), and to Venice (and on to the rest of Italy and Southern Europe).

Belgrade - Athens 15 + 891
Dep. Belgrade 8:30(1+2) 13:55(4) 22:45(5)
Set your watch forward 2 hours in Summer, one hour the rest of the year.
Arr. Athens (Larissa) 7:56(3) 14:22(3) 22:56(3)
(1)Meal service from 23:45 on Day 1. (2)Carries sleeping car some days. (3)Day 2. (4)Has couchettes. Meal service from 5:45 on Day 2. (5)Has couchettes. Meal service from 14:55 on Day 2.

Belgrade - Bucharest 795
Dep. Belgrade (Dunav) 17:10 Carries sleeping car.
Set your watch forward 2 hours in Summer, one hour the rest of the year.
Arr. Bucharest (Nord) 8:29

Belgrade - Budapest 791
Dep. Belgrade 6:45 14:15(1) 20:38(2)
Set your watch forward one hour in the Summer.
Arr. Budapest (Keleti) 13:50 21:33 5:55(3)
(1)Reservation required. (2)Carries sleeping car. (3)Arrives at Budapest's Nyugati station.

Belgrade - Sofia 792
Dep. Belgrade 9:05 12:20
Set your watch forward 2 hours in Summer, one hour the rest of the year.
Arr. Sofia 20:00 23:10

Belgrade - Venice 783
Dep. Belgrade 6:00(1) 19:05(2)
Set your watch forward one hour in Summer.
Arr. Venice (S.L.) 21:16 11:06
(1)Meal service 6:00-13:40. (2)Carries sleeping car. Also has couchettes.

Chapter 10

THE MIDDLE-EAST

AFGHANISTAN

There are no passenger railways in Afghanistan.

BAHRAIN

There are no passenger trains in Bahrain.

IRAN

Five rail routes radiate from Tehran: west to Tabriz (and on to both Russia and Turkey), south to Khorramshahr on the Persian Gulf (and on to Iraq), southeast to Zarand (with a spur to Isfahan, a popular tourist resort), and west to both Mashhad and Gorgan. A short line runs from Zahedan into Pakistan.

The country's oldest rail line has been operating only 50 some years. The rail service to Turkey was completed in 1971. Engineering and equipment are both highly modern.

First-class rail fares are nearly double the price for second-class tickets and 3 times the price of third-class. Third-class has only wood or plastic seats. Children under 3 travel free. Half-fare for children 3-13. Children 14 and over must pay full fare. Sleeping cars and couchettes are available on trains to Turkey and to the USSR.

Tehran

See: The museums in the fantastic Shahyad Monument, built to commemorate Iran's 2500th anniversary, only a few years ago. The 6-mile labyrinth of the city's Bazaar. The House of Strength. Gulistan Palace. The 19th century Sepahsalar Mosque. Shah Mosque. The Crown Jewels Museum in Markazi Bank. The Palace.

The gardens and museums of Golestan Palace. The Ethnological Museum. The Archaeological Museum. The Mausoleum of Reza Shah The Great. The Marble Palace. The Decorative Art Museum. The National Art Museum.

Take a one-day excursion to the Shemshak ski resort or to see carpet-washing in the Cheshmeh Ali stream.

Tehran - Tabriz 4500

There is much mountain scenery on this ride. Tabriz is the gateway for rail travel to Turkey (see "International Routes From Iran" later in this section).

All of these trains are air-conditioned in first-class and have meal service.

Dep. Tehran	18:00(1)	Dep. Tabriz	19:00(1)
Arr. Tabriz	8:00	Arr. Tehran	9:30

(1) Meal service. Air-conditioned in first-class. Carries sleeping car on Wednesday from Tehran and Tuesday from Tabriz.

Sights in Tabriz: This is one of the major carpet producing areas in Iran. A popular Summer resort. Do not fail to see the fantastic 15th century Blue Mosque.

Tehran - Khorramshahr 4506

Fine mountain scenery on this journey. Khorramshahr is the gateway for rail travel to Iraq (see "International Routes From Iran" later in this section).

Dep. Tehran	13:00(1)	16:00
Arr. Andimeshk	4:00	5:20
Arr. Karun	7:20	N/A(3)
Arr. Khorramshahr	N/A(2)	N/A(3)

Sights in Khorramshahr: An important port. Many date palm groves in this area.

Dep. Khorramshahr	N/A(2)	N/A(3)
Dep. Karun	11:10(1)	N/A(3)
Dep. Andimeshk	14:25(1)	16:10
Arr. Tehran	5:15	5:55

(1) Air-conditioned in first-class. (2) Service on the 73-mile trip Karun-Khorramshahr and v.v. was temporarily suspended in 1981. (3) Service on the 158-mile trip Andimeshk-Khorramshahr and v.v. was temporarily suspended in 1981.

Tehran - Zarand 4505

Dep. Tehran	17:00(1)	Dep. Zarand	16:10(1)
Arr. Zarand	9:30	Arr. Tehran	9:00

(1) Air-conditioned in first-class.

Tehran - Esfahan 4508

This is the schedule for the spur to Esfahan off the Tehran-Zarand route.

Dep. Tehran	12:45	14:00	19:00	Dep. Esfahan	N/A(1)
Arr. Esfahan	N/A(1)	N/A(1)	N/A(1)	Arr. Tehran	N/A(1)

(1) Time has not been available since 1981.

Sights in Esfahan: A popular tourist resort. See: The blue enameled domes of the mosques. Ali Qapu Palace. The breathtaking frescoes at the Palace of Four Columns. The ancient Friday Mosque. The Theological School. The Bazaar. The tiered bridges. Wonderful textiles, rugs and tiles can be purchased here. Esfahan carpets are magnificent.

Tehran - Neyshabur - Mashhad 4504

Excellent mountain scenery on this trip.

Dep. Tehran	14:30(1)	17:15(2+3)
Dep. Neyshabur	6:20	7:10
Arr. Mashhad	8:50	9:20

Sights in Neyshabur: The birthplace and burial site of Omar Khayyam, Persia's famous astronomer, mathematician and poet.

Sights in Mashhad: The holiest city in Iran. Its great gold-domed shrine contains the Tomb of Imam Reza. Also see: Gowhar Shad Mosque. The Tomb of Nader Shah. Mashhad Museum.

Dep. Mashhad	12:30(1)	16:00(2+4)
Dep. Neyshabur	15:20	18:15
Arr. Tehran	7:00	8:00

(1)Second and third-class space only. (2)Air-conditioned in first-class. (3)Runs Tuesday, Thursday and Sunday. (4)Runs Monday, Wednesday and Friday.

Tehran - Gorgan 4503

Dep. Tehran	7:25(1)	18:00(2)	Dep. Gorgan	5:30(3)	17:45(4)
Arr. Gorgan	19:20	5:00	Arr. Tehran	17:10	5:55

(1)Runs Monday, Wednesday and Saturday. (2)Thursday only. Air-conditioned in first-class. (3)Runs Tuesday, Thursday and Sunday. Friday only. Air-conditioned in first-class.

Sights in Gorgan: This city was rebuilt after being destroyed in an earthquake during the 1930's.

Tabriz - Sufian - Djulfa 4500

Dep. Tabriz	8:00(1)	23:50(3)	Dep. Djulfa	15:00(1)	N/A(4)
Dep. Sufian	N/A(2)	N/A(2)	Dep. Sufian	N/A(2)	N/A(2+5)
Arr. Djulfa	11:45	N/A(4)	Arr. Tabriz	18:30	7:40

(1)Air-conditioned in first-class. (2)Time not available in 1981. (3)Runs Thursday. Has couchettes. (4)Service Sufian-Djulfa and v.v. temporarily suspended in 1981. (5)Runs Saturdays. Has couchettes.

INTERNATIONAL ROUTES FROM IRAN

The gateway for train travel from Iran to both Turkey and Russia is Tabriz. The route to Iraq begins at Khorramshahr. A line starting in Zahedan leads into Pakistan.

Tehran - Tabriz - Haydarpasa - Istanbul 4021

Dep. Tehran N/A(1)
Dep. Tabriz N/A(1)
Set your watch back 30 minutes.
Dep. Kapikoy 7:20(2+3)
Arr. Van Pier 9:37
Change to ferry.
Dep. Van Pier 10:30
Arr. Tatvan Pier 14:30
Change to train.
Dep. Tatvan Pier 15:15(4)
Arr. Ankara 21:00(5)
Dep. Ankara 22:25
Arr. Haydarpasa 9:35(6)

Boat to Istanbul
4025
Dep. Haydarpasa Frequent times from 6:00 to 24:00 for the 20-minute boat trip to Istanbul. When making connections for trains, allow at least 4 hours.

(1) Service "temporarily" suspended in 1979. (2) Runs Monday and Wednesday. Has couchettes. (3) Day 2. (4) Runs Monday and Friday. Carries sleeping car. Also has couchettes. Meal service. (5) Day 3. (6) Day 4.

Tehran - Tabriz - Moscow

4500
Dep. Tehran 18:00(1)
Dep. Tabriz 8:00(2)
Arr. Djulfa (Iran) 11:45(2)
Arr. Djulfa (USSR) 15:00
Change your watch to Moscow time.
5025
Dep. Djulfa (USSR) 21:00(3)
Arr. Moscow 5:45(4)

(1) Air-conditioned in first-class. Carries sleeping car on Wednesdays. (2) Day 2. (3) Fridays only. Carries sleeping car. (4) Day 4 from Djulfa.

Khorramshahr - Abadan - Seeba - Basra - Baghdad 4506+4507+4150

See notes earlier in this section with "Tehran-Khorramshahr schedules. The 14-mile bus service from Khorramshahr to Abadan was suspended in 1981. A motor launch used to make the 15-minute boat trip from Abadan to Seeba, Iraq. From Seeba, there once was bus service for the 25-mile ride to Basra. There is a 4-hour bus service from Basra to Kuwait (for which times have not been available since 1981) and also a boat that operates according to demand, without a regular schedule. The Basra-Baghdad schedules appear in the next section, on Iraq.

Zahedan - Quetta 5942

This is the rail route from Iran into Pakistan. The Zahedan rail-station is 2 miles east of the city.

Dep. Zahedan	7:00	Fridays only. Meal service.
Arr. Quetta	19:15	Day 2

IRAQ

Iraq's 2 rail routes are the standard-gauge line extending south from Baghdad to Basra and north to Mosul, plus a narrow-gauge line running north from Baghdad to Juloua. The latter line forks at Joloula, one tine running further north to Khankin, the other going northwest to Erbil.

Iraqi trains have 3 classes of space: first, tourist and second on standard gauge lines; and first, second and third on metre (narrow) gauge lines. First-class and second-class seats convert into berths for overnight travel. Children under 4 travel free. Half-fare for children 4-9. Children 10 and over must pay full fare.

Baghdad

More than 100 mosques and minarets here, including the spectacular gold-domed Kazimayn Mosque. The 13th century Abbasid Palace and its museum. The 13th century Mustansiriyah law college. The selection of copper, cloth and silver in the many bazaars. The collection of Arabic history and literature at the Library of Waqfs. The Central Library of Baghdad University. The Costumes and Ethnographic Museum. The Iraq Museum. The Iraq Natural History Museum. The Museum of Arab Antiquities. The National Museum of Modern Art. Nearby, the tombs of 2 imams.

Baghdad - Basra 4157

This scenic route follows the Tigris River to the Persian Gulf.

Dep. Baghdad (West)	20:30(1)	21:30(2)
Arr. Basra (Ma'qil)	5:03	6:15

Sights in Basra: This is a prominent river harbor. Many date palm groves in this area.

Dep. Basra (Ma'qil)	20:30(1)	21:30(2)
Arr. Baghdad (West)	5:15	6:15

(1) Air-conditioned space available at extra charge in both first-class and tourist-class. (2) Second-class only.

Baghdad - Mosul 4155

Dep. Baghdad (West)	21:00(1)	22:00(2)	Dep. Mosul	21:00(1)	22:00(2)
Arr. Mosul	5:50	6:35	Arr. Baghdad (West)	5:40	6:50

(1) Air-conditioned space available at extra charge in both first-class and tourist-class. (2) Runs Thursday and Friday. Tourist-class only.

Sights in Mosul: The ruins of ancient Nineveh are near here. The word "muslin" came from the production here once of fine cotton goods. See: The Great Mosque and its leaning minaret. The 13th century Red Mosque.

Baghdad - Kirkuk - Erbil 4156

A very scenic trip through the Iraqi mountains. Tourists are not permitted beyond Kirkuk, as Erbil is a military installation.

Dep. Baghdad (East)	7:35	Dep. Erbil	12:00(1)
Arr. Kirkuk	18:45	Arr. Kirkuk	16:00
Change trains.		Change trains.	
Dep. Kirkuk	5:30(1)	Dep. Kirkuk	7:00
Arr. Erbil	9:30	Arr. Baghdad (East)	17:45

(1) Second and third-class space only.

Sights in Erbil: This area has been inhabited continuously since 3,000 B.C. There is a famous fortress here, on a high mound.

INTERNATIONAL ROUTES FROM IRAQ

There is train service from Iraq to Turkey, Syria and Iran.

Baghdad - Haydarpasa 4020

Dep. Baghdad (West)	21:00(1)	Monday and Friday
Dep. El Yaroubieh	12:26	Tuesday and Saturday
Dep. Gaziantep	8:10(2)	Wednesday and Sunday
Dep. Ankara	8:40	Thursday and Monday
Arr. Haydarpasa	18:25	Same day as Ankara departure

(1) Carries sleeping car. (2) Meal service from Gaziantep to Haydarpasa.

Baghdad - Kamechlie - Aleppo (Halab) 4075

This service was temporarily suspended in 1982.

Dep. Baghdad (West)	21:00	Monday and Friday
Arr. Kamechlie	11:33	Tuesday and Saturday
Arr. Aleppo (Halab)	19:14	Same day as Kamechlie arrival

Baghdad - Basra - Tehran 4157

Dep. Baghdad (West)	20:30(1)	21:30(2)
Arr. Basra (Ma'qil)	5:03	6:15

(1) Air-conditioned space available in both first-class and tourist-class at extra charge. (2) Second-class only.

Sights in Basra: This is a prominent river harbor. Many date palm groves in this area.

From Basra, there once was bus service for the 25-mile ride to Seeba. A motor launch used to make the 15-minute boat trip from Seeba to Abadan. The 14-mile bus service from Abadan to Khorramshahr was suspended in 1981. Fine mountain scenery on the ride from Khorramshahr to Tehran.

4506

Dep. Khorramshahr	N/A(1)
Arr. Tehran	N/A(1)

(1) Service "temporarily" suspended in 1981.

ISRAEL

Plan carefully rail trips in Israel to avoid the crowded conditions on Friday afternoons and the suspension of nearly all transportation service from Friday sunset to Saturday sunset in conformance with the Jewish sabbath, which causes the heavy traffic on Friday afternoons.

The country's principal train route is south from Haifa, to Tel Aviv, Beersheva and Dimona. Its west-east line goes from Tel Aviv to Lod and Jerusalem.

There are no rail connections between Israel and countries adjacent to it.

The heaviest passenger train traffic in Israel is during August. Lightest is in February. Israel Railways urges tourists to make advance seat reservations at all times. Children under 4 travel free. Half-fare for children 4-9. Children 10 and over must pay full fare.

Although Israel is very small in size, there are more than 40 rail-stations on its routes. Summer timetables are in effect from late June to early September. All times given here are Summer schedules.

There are several price reductions on Israeli trains: to organized groups of 20 or more adults (25%), to organized groups of 10 or more children up to the age of 18 (50%), to students having an International Student Card (25%), for women over 60 and men over 65 (25%), and for children from the age of 4 to 9 (50%). Children under 4 years of age travel free.

In order to obtain the various reductions, application must be made in writing at least 3 days in advance of travel date to the Station Master of the starting station or to the office of Traffic and Commercial Manager, Israel Railways, P.O. Box 44, Haifa, Israel.

Seats can be reserved for trips from Haifa, Jerusalem and Tel Aviv.

ISRAELI RAILROVER

Unlimited train travel for one calendar month. Costs $12(US). Can be purchased only outside Israel.

Haifa - Tel Aviv 4001

Dep. Haifa (Merkaz) 5:54(1) 6:24(1) 7:24(1) 8:24(1+5)
Dep. Haifa (Bat Galim) 6 minutes later
Arr. Tel Aviv (Merkaz) 80 minutes after departing Merkaz station

Sights in Haifa: This is Israel's main port. See the Bahai Shrine and Gardens, open 9:00-12:00. The Museum of Prehistory, a Nature Museum and Zoo complex, open Sunday-Thursday 8:00-14:00, Fridays 8:00-12:00,

Saturdays 9:00-14:00. The collection of Islamic folk art and costumes at the Museum of Ethnology, open 10:00-13:00 every day, plus 17:00-19:00 on Mondays and Wednesdays.

Sights in Tel Aviv: One of the oldest cities in the world. See: The Helena Rubenstein Pavillion. The art at the Tel Aviv Museum. The exhibit of coins, folklore, science and technology at the Ha-aretz Museum complex. The view from the observation terrace of the Shalom Building. The fascinating museum of the Jewish underground movement of the 1930's and 1940's, in the Bet Jabotinsky Building on King George Street.

Take a 20-minute bus ride to Jaffa, the ancient port, and browse in the artists' colony there.

One-day bus tours from Tel Aviv go to the occupied Golan Heights (Thursday); the northwestern frontier at Rosh Hanikra, the ruins at Caesarea, and remains of the Crusaders at Acre (Tuesday, Friday and Sunday); Christian holy sites (Monday, Wednesday and Saturday); and to the Dead Sea plus a 1,000-foot ascent by cable car to the Masada fortress (daily, except Fridays).

Dep. Tel Aviv (Merkaz)	6:00(1)	7:00(1)	8:00(1)	9:00(1+6)
Arr. Haifa (Bat Galim)	74 minutes later			
Arr. Haifa (Merkaz)	6 minutes after departing Bat Galim station			

(1)Daily, except Saturday. Meal service. (2)Daily, except Friday and Saturday. Meal service. (3)Daily, except Friday and Saturday. No meal service. (4)Daily, except Friday. (5)Plus other departures from Haifa at 9:45(1), 11:24(1), 12:24(1), 13:24(1), 14:24(1), 15:24(2), 16:24(2), 17:24(2) and 19:24(2). (6)Plus other departures from Tel Aviv at 10:30(1), 12:00(1), 13:00(1), 14:00(4), 15:00(2), 16:00(2), 17:00(2), 18:30(2) and 20:00(2).

Tel Aviv - Beersheva - Dimona 4002

Dep. Tel Aviv (Darom)	N/A(1)
Arr. Beersheva	N/A(1)
Arr. Dimona	N/A(1)

Sights in Beersheva: This modern desert town is the location where Abraham rested on his way south.

Dep. Dimona	N/A(1)
Dep. Beersheva	N/A(1)
Arr. Tel Aviv (Darom)	N/A(1)

(1)Service temporarily suspended in 1981.

Tel Aviv - Lod - Jerusalem 4002

This ride through the Judean wilderness, in operation since 1892, is the most scenic train trip and most exciting travel experience in Israel.

The train winds from the Mediterranean coast past Zor'a and Eshtaol, connected in the Bible with Samson. Next, the route passes through a breach in the wall that the Romans built around Beitar to contain and defeat Bar Kochba, leader of the second rebellion against the Romans.

Dep. Tel Aviv (Darom)	8:18(1+2)	11:30(2+3)	16:00(2+4)
Dep. Lod	9:00(1+2)	11:47(2+3)	16:17(2+4)
Arr. Jerusalam	10:36	13:20	17:45

* * *

Dep. Jerusalam	7:30(2+4)	11:30(2+3)	16:00(2+4)
Dep. Lod	9:05	12:57	17:27
Arr. Tel Aviv (Darom)	9:30	13:38(5)	18:03(5)

(1)Depart from Tel Aviv's Benei Beraq railstation. Runs daily, except Friday and Saturday. (2)Meal service. (3)Runs Fridays only. (4)Daily, except Saturday. (5)Arrives at Tel Aviv's Benei Beraq railstation.

Sights in Jerusalem: The Western (Wailing) Wall of the Temple Mount. The Dome of the Rock (Mosque of Omar). The el-Aska Mosque. The Church of the Holy Sepulchre. The 14 stations of the cross, along Via Dolorosa. Colorful oriental markets.

Mount Zion, with the Tomb of the House of David, Cenacle (the room of the Last Supper), and the Abbey of the Dormition.

The Tombs of the Sanhedrin. En Karem, birthplace of John the Baptist. The Chagall stained-glass windows, depicting the Tribes of Israel, at the Synagogue of the Hadassah Medical Center.

The Bezalel National Art Museum, Samuel Bronfman Biblical and Archaeological Museum, and Billy Rose Art Garden, all in the Israel Museum complex. Alongside it, the Shrine of the Book, housing the Dead Sea Scrolls, open Sundays, Mondays, Wednesdays and Thursdays 10:00-17:00 and Tuesdays 10:00 to sunset.

The Knesset (Israel's Parliament) and the President's Garden, opposite the Israel Museum. The Biblical Zoo. Kennedy Memorial. Yad Vashem Holocaust Memorial, open Sunday-Thursday 9:00-16:45 and Friday 9:00-14:00. The Middle-East archaeology collection in the Rockefeller Museum, open Sunday, Tuesday and Thursday 10:00-17:00 and Saturday 10:00-14:00.

Southwest of the city are the ancient Jewish cemetery at the Mount of Olives and the Christian shrines at the Garden of Gethsemane. Below the Mount of Olives: Absalom's Pillar, the Tomb of Zechariah, and the Tombs of Bnei Hezir.

Northeast of the city are the Tombs of the Kings of Judah, the

Garden Tomb, the Tomb of Simon the Just, the Cave of King Zedekiah (also known as Solomon's Quarries).

Haifa - Lod - Jerusalem	4002		
Dep. Haifa (Merkaz)	6:54(1)	-0-	-0-
Dep. Lod	9:00	11:47(2)	16:17(3)
Arr. Jerusalem	10:32	13:20	17:45
	*	*	*
Dep. Jerusalem	7:30(3)	11:30(2)	16:00(3)
Dep. Lod	9:05	12:57	17:27
Arr. Haifa (Merkaz)	-0-	15:03	19:30

(1)Daily, except Friday and Saturday. Meal service. (2)Runs Fridays and eves of holidays only. Meal service. (3)Daily, except Saturday. Meal service.

KUWAIT

There are no passenger trains in Kuwait.

JORDAN

Jordan's only national railway (Amman to Ma'an), has not operated regularly since British and Arab armies destroyed it in 1917.

There has been Syrian-operated rail service from Amman to Damascus (and on to Beirut, Lebanon). On it, children under 3 travel free. Half-fare for children 3-9. Children 10 and over must pay full fare. There is no other rail connection between Jordan and countries adjacent to it. The rail route from Ma'an to Aqaba is primarily for freight. However, Jordan provides small 8-seat railcars on this line under "charter" arrangements.

Amman

See the remains of the ancient fort. Next to it, the Archaeological Museum and the Roman Amphitheater.

Amman - Damascus - Beirut	4103 (Bus)		
Dep. Amman	N/A(1)	Dep. Beirut	N/A(1)
Arr. Damascus	N/A(1)	Arr. Damascus	N/A(1)
Arr. Beirut	N/A(1)	Arr. Amman	N/A(1)

(1)Time has not been available since 1981.

LEBANON

The 2 Lebanese rail routes are from Beirut: east to Damascus (Syria) and north to Tripoli and on to Aleppo (Syria).

Beirut

Lebanon's major port. There are many art galleries and public gardens here.

Beirut - Damascus 4103

Dep. Beirut	N/A(1)	Dep. Damascus	N/A(1)
Arr. Damascus	N/A	Arr. Beirut	N/A

(1) This service was operated only for freight and local Sunday excursions before being suspended in 1978.

Beirut - Tripoli - Aleppo (Halab) 4076

Dep. Beirut (St. M.)	N/A(1)	Dep. Aleppo (Halab)	11:30(2)
Dep. Tripoli	N/A(1)	Arr. Homs	16:51(2)
Dep. Homs	13:50(2)	Arr. Tripoli	N/A(1)
Arr. Aleppo (Halab)	19:00(2)	Arr. Beirut (St. M.)	N/A(1)

(1)Service was suspended in 1978. (2)Service temporarily suspended in 1982.

Sights in Tripoli: A major port. Popular beach resort. See: The 14th century Teynal Mosque. The 13th century Great Mosque. The 15th century Tower of the Lions.

OMAN

There are no passenger trains in Oman.

PAKISTAN

There are 3 classes of train travel here: air-conditioned, first-class and second-class. The first 2 classes are convertible into sleeping compartments for night travel. Advance application is recommended to reserve bedding rolls in air-conditioned class. Higher fares are charged for second-class space in fast trains than for second-class in ordinary trains. Reservations are recommended for all overnight and long-distance journeys. All of Pakistan's express trains have meal service. Children under 3 travel free. Half-fare for children 3-11. Children 12 and over must pay full fare. Most trains in Pakistan provide "special ladies' accommodation" which both male and female children under 12 may use if they are traveling with a female relative.

Where it is noted that "bedding is available", this includes soap, toilet paper and towel. Private cars can be rented. They are air-conditioned and have a dining-room, kitchen and servants' quarters as well as private bedrooms and drawing rooms.

The 3 major train routes in Pakistan are from Karachi: northeast to Lahore, north to Peshawar, and northwest to Quetta.

Karachi

This is a natural harbor. See: Burns Gardens. The Ghanshyam Art Center. The Zoo in Ghandi Gardens. Good swimming and fishing beaches.

The 270-acre Botanical Garden. The National Museum, with its Greco-Buddhist art, near Cantonment Railstation. Adamji Mosque. The Memorial Museum. Mamon Mosque. The Hindu Temple. Jahangir Park. You will find every thing from mangos to silver anklets in these typical Eastern bazaars: Juna, Khajoor, Jodia, Sarafa and Bahri. See Fire Temple. Islamia College. "Mazaar", the Mausoleum of Quaid-E-Azam Mohammad Ali Jinnah, who guided Pakistan to independence.

Karachi - Hyderabad	5905		
Dep. Karachi (Canton.)	4:30	10:00(1+3)	10:46(1+2+3+5)
Arr. Hyderabad	7:37	12:27	13:38

Sights in Hyderabad: Much lacquerware, ornamented silks and items of gold and silver are made here. See the large 18th century fort. The 1½-mile-long Shahi Bazaar, running from the fort to the Market Tower. The old palaces. The tombs of ancient rulers.

Dep. Hyderabad	3:55(2+3)	5:23(1+2+3)	6:06(1+2+3+5)
Arr. Karachi (Canton.)	7:25	8:55	9:20

(1) Meal service. (2) Air-conditioned space, at an extra charge, can be reserved. (3) Reservation required. (4) Carries air-conditioned Parlor Car. Has only air-conditioned second-class coaches. (5) Plus other departures from Karachi at 11:31(1+2+3), 16:30(1+3+4), 17:00-1+2+3), 17:20, 19:16(1+2+3) and 21:00(2+3). (6) Plus other departures from Hyderabad at 7:12(1+2+3), 9:40(1+3), 13:12(1+3), 13:46(1+3), 15:25 and 16:00(1+2+3).

Karachi - Lahore 5905

Dep. Karachi (Canton.)	6:00(1+2+3+6)	10:00(1+3+8)
Arr. Lahore	22:00	5:15

Sights in Lahore: Pakistan's second-largest city. Often called "the city of gardens". This is a busy rail center, with 10,000,000 passengers handled here every year.

See the complex of 16th-18th century palaces and halls inside Lahore Fort. The Shish Mahal (Palace of Mirrors) with its fretted screens, colored mirrors and marble. The museum of 18th and early 19th century maps, drawings and weapons. The small Moti Masjid Mosque. The royal apartments and throne room. The marble hall, Diwan-i-Khas.

At one of the world's largest places of worship, across from the Fort (on the other side of Hazuri Bagh Square), see the marble ornamentation at the Badshahi (Imperial) Mosque. Its courtyard can hold 100,000 people, and the view of Lahore from its minarets is worth climbing the more than 200 stairs to them.

Take the 2-mile walk from the Fort through many colorful bazaars (jewelry, leather, cooper, brass, cloth). Also see the mirrored ceilings and glass mosaics in the mausoleum of the 18th century playboy, Maharajah Ranjit Singh. The ashes of his 4 wives and 7 concubines, cremated at his death, are also stored there.

The marvelous collection of Gandhara and Greco-Buddhist art (particularly the "starving Buddha") at the Lahore Museum. The many marble ornaments and mosaics of flowers with Arabic and Persian inscriptions at Jahangiri's Tomb, 3 miles north of the city.

Without fail, go 6 miles east of Lahore to the incredibly magnificent 80-acre Shalimar Gardens, one of the greatest gardens in the world. It was designed in the 17th century to rival the one of the same name at Srinigar in Kashmir.

Dep. Lahore	6:00(1+2+3+7)	9:30(1+2+3+5+9)
Arr. Karachi (Canton.)	22:00	7:25

(1) Meal service. (2) Air-conditioned space, at an extra charge, can be reseved. (3) Reservation required. (4) Carries air-conditioned Parlor Car. Has only air-conditioned second-class coaches. (5) Bedding available in air-conditioned class at extra charge. (6) Runs Wednesday and Saturday. (7) Runs Monday and Friday. (8) Plus other departures from Karachi at 10:46(1+2+3+5), 16:30(1+3+4), 17:00(1+2+3) and 21:00(1+2+5). (9) Plus other departures from Lahore at 14:20-(1+2+3+5), 16:30(1+2+3+4), 17:25(1+3), 19:40(1+3) and 21:08-(1+2+3+5).

Karachi - Peshawar Peshawar - Karachi

This is a 1,100-mile journey.

5905

Dep. Karachi (Canton.)
10:00(1+2) 10:16(1+2) 19:16(1+2+4+6) 21:00(1+2+4+6)
Arr. Peshawar (Cent.)
16:35(3) 20:25(3) 9:30(5) 6:10(5)

Sights in Peshawar: Stroll down the ancient Qissah Khwani Bazar (Street of Storytellers), with its stores selling dried fruits, rugs, sheepskin coats and lambskin (karacul) caps. See the 17th century pure white Mahabat Khan Mosque. The 16th century Bala Hisar Fort. The shoes sold at Mochilara Bazaar. The central square, Chowk Yaad Gar. The former Buddhist Monastery, Gor Khatri. The famed Khyber Pass, 10 miles from Peshawar.

Dep. Peshawar (Cent.)
6:29(1+2) 7:29(1+2) 19:09(1+2+4+6) 22:14(1+2+4+6)
Arr. Karachi (Canton.)
12:45(3) 17:10(3) 8:55(5) 7:25(5)

(1) Meal service. (2) Reservation required. (3) Day 2. (4) Air-conditioned space, at an extra charge, can be reserved. (5) Day 3. (6) Bedding available in air-conditioned class at extra charge.

Lahore - Peshawar Peshawar - Lahore

5905

Dep. Lahore	5:45(1)	8:30(1)	19:10(2)	21:10
Arr. Peshawar (Cent.)	16:35	20:25	6:10	8:30

* * *

Dep. Peshawar (Cent.)	6:20(1)	7:20(1)	18:15	22:05(2)
Arr. Lahore	16:55	19:10	5:40	8:55

(1) Reservation required. Meal service. (2) Air-conditioned space, at an extra charge, can be reserved. Bedding available in air-conditioned class at extra charge. Meal service.

Peshawar - Landi Kotal 5922

This route is via the fabled Khyber Pass. The service operates only on Fridays. Landi Kotal is 8 miles east of the Afghan border.

Dep. Peshawar (Cent.)	9:10	Dep. Landi Kotal	14:30
Arr. Landi Kotal	12:45	Arr. Peshawar (Cent.)	17:45

Sights in Landi Kotal: The "smuggler's bazaar", shops that are tucked away in rock caverns and along hilly sidestreets.

Lahore - Quetta 5904

Dep. Lahore	12:00(1)	Dep. Quetta	14:25(1)
Arr. Quetta	12:45(2)	Arr. Lahore	15:15(2)

(1) Reservation advisable. Air-conditioned space, at an extra charge, can be reserved. Bedding available in air-conditioned class at extra charge. Meal service on first day (Lahore-Sibi and v.v.). (2) Day 2.

Sights in Quetta: A popular Summer resort. This town developed around a fort occupied by British troops in 1876. It is a market center for western Afghanistan, eastern Iran and part of Central Asia. See: The Geological Survey of Pakistan (there was severe earthquake damage here in 1935). Sandeman Library.

Karachi - Quetta 5904

Dep. Karachi	11:55(1)	Dep. Quetta	15:50(1)
Arr. Quetta	8:40	Arr. Karachi	13:15

(1) Reservation advisable. Air-conditioned space, at an extra charge, can be reserved. Bedding available in air-conditioned class at extra charge. Meal service.

INTERNATIONAL ROUTES FROM PAKISTAN

The Pakistani rail gateway to Iran is Quetta. Lahore is the departure point for train travel to India.

Quetta - Zahedan
5942

Dep. Quetta	7:50 Wednesday. Meal service.
Arr. Zahedan	15:40 Thursday.

Lahore - Delhi - New Delhi 6026

Dep. Lahore	14:45			
Arr. Amritsar	18:40			
Change trains.	6006 + 6030			
Dep. Amritsar	6:35(1+2+3)	9:40(4)	12:55	16:20(5+7)
Arr. Delhi Junct.	-0-	-0-	-0-	5:25
Arr. New Delhi	14:40	20:05	21:45	-0-

(1) Daily, except Wednesday. (2) Air-conditioned space available at extra charge. (3) Meal service only on Thursday, Friday and Saturday. (4) Meal service. (5) Second-class only. (6) Runs Monday, Wednesday, Friday and Saturday. (7) Plus other departures from Amritsar at 18:45-(2+6), 20:50(2) and 22:25.

Sights in Amritsar: This is the holiest city of the Sikh Religion.

QATAR

There are no passenger trains in Qatar.

SAUDI ARABIA

The only passenger rail route in Saudi Arabia is from the port of Dammam on the Persian Gulf to Riyadh, the inland capital. There are no train connections between Saudi Arabia and countries adjacent to it. The trains are modern air-conditioned diesels. Children under 4 travel free. Half-fare for children 4-11. Children 12 and over must pay full fare.

Dammam - Riyadh

These trains are air-conditioned and provide meal service.

4200

Dep. Dammam	8:45(1)	14:10(2)	Dep. Riyadh	8:10(1)	15:00(2)
Arr. Riyadh	15:39	21:07	Arr. Dammam	15:05	21:58

(1) Runs Monday, Tuesday, Saturday and Sunday. (2) Runs Wednesday and Friday.

Sights in Riyadh: The Museum of Antiquities. The Zoo.

SYRIA

Syria's rail lines are the north-south standard-gauge from Aleppo to Akkari (and on to Lebanon), the north-south special 3′5¼″ gauge Hedjaz Railway from Damascus to Deraa (and on to Jordan), a narrow-gauge from Damascus to Beirut, the west-east route from Aleppo (Halab) to Deir ez Zor and Kamechlie (and on to Baghdad), and 2 short lines running north from Aleppo: one to Karkamis (and on into eastern Turkey), the other to Fevzipasa (and on into central and western Turkey, en route to Ankara and Istanbul). Children under 3 travel free. Half-fare for children 3-9. Children 10 and over must pay full fare.

All of Syria's train routes become international connections.

Passenger train service was once possible from Europe, through Istanbul, via Turkey, Syria and Jordan all the way to Aqaba on the Red Sea. The interruption of service in Jordan from Amman to Ma'an, has made that intercontinental train travel impossible since 1917.

Aleppo (Halab)

Founded before 2,000 B.C. See: The remains of the ancient Cathedral of St. Helena, converted into a mosque in the 12th century A.D. The 11th century minaret on the 8th century Great Umayyad Mosque. The ancient Citadel, built before the 13th century. Fantastic 16th and 17th century bazaars. The archaeological exhibits in the National Museum.

Damascus

"The pearl of the east." Oldest inhabited city in the world, founded about 3,000 B.C. See: Great Umayyad Mosque. Al-Marjah Square, in the center of the city. The National Museum. The Qasr al-'Azm Museum. The Arab Academy, containing the national library. The fabulous orchards of the Ghutah.

Deraa

The ancient Greco-Roman ruins. The 13th century mosque.

Aleppo - Akkari - Tripoli - Beirut 4076

Dep. Aleppo	11:30	Dep. Beirut	N/A(1)
Arr. Homs	16:51	Arr. Tripoli	N/A(1)
Arr. Akkari	N/A(1)	Dep. Tripoli	N/A(1)
Arr. Tripoli	N/A(1)	Arr. Akkari	N/A(1)
Dep. Tripoli	N/A(1)	Dep. Homs	13:50
Arr. Beirut	N/A(1)	Arr. Aleppo	19:00

(1)Service "temporarily" suspended in 1978.

Damascus - Beirut 4103 (Bus)

Dep. Damascus	N/A(1)	Dep. Beirut	N/A(1)
Arr. Beirut	N/A	Arr. Damascus	N/A

(1)Times not available in 1981.

Damascus - Deraa - Amman 4079

Dep. Damascus (Kanawat)	8:10(1)	19:00
Arr. Deraa	11:01	17:54
Arr. Amman	14:17	-0-
*	*	*
Dep. Amman	-0-	8:00(2)
Dep. Deraa	5:40	10:41
Arr. Damascus (Kanawat)	8:35	13:27

(1) Runs Thursday and Sunday. (2) Runs Monday and Friday.

Aleppo (Halab) - Mosul - Baghdad 4075

Dep. Aleppo (Halab)	5:00(1)	6:00(2)	15:00(2)
Arr. Kamechlie	13:05	13:46	22:52
Arr. Mosul	20:25	-0-	-0-
4155			
Dep. Mosul	21:00(3)	22:00(4)	
Dep. Samara	3:14	4:12	
Arr. Baghdad (West)	5:40	6:50	

(1)Service was temporarily suspended in 1982. (2)Second-class only. Air-conditioned. (3)Air-conditioned first-class and tourist-class space available at extra charge. First-class seats convert to sleeping berths. (4)Runs Thursday and Friday. Tourist-class only.

Halab - Ankara - Haydarpasa - Istanbul 4020 + 4055

Dep. Halab	5:45(1)	Wednesday and Sunday
Arr. Ankara	7:50	Thursday and Monday
Arr. Haydarpasa	18:25	Same day as Ankara arrival

(1)Carries sleeping car. Meal service.

When making connections for trains in Istanbul, allow 8 hours from arrival in Haydarpasa even though the boat trip from Haydarpasa to Istanbul is only a 20-minute ride.

Halab - Malataya - Tabriz - Tehran

4055

Dep. Halab	5:45(1)
Arr. Fevzipasa	13:40
Change trains.	
Dep. Fevzipasa	12:00(2)
Arr. Narli	13:28
Change trains.	

4051

Dep. Narli	16:16(2)	
Arr. Malataya	19:33	
Change trains.		
4062		
Dep. Malataya	1:55(3)	
Arr. Tabriz	7:40(4)	
Change trains.		
4500		
Dep. Tabriz	8:10(5)	19:00(2+6)
Arr. Tehran	22:25	9:45

(1)Runs Wednesday and Sunday. (2)Runs daily. (3)Runs Tuesday, Thursday and Saturday. Service was temporarily suspended in 1982. (4)Day 2 from Malataya. (5)Runs Saturday only. Service was temporarily suspended in 1982. (6)Air-conditioned in first-class.

TURKEY

The first-class sleeping cars here have single compartments. Second-class sleeping cars have 2-berth and 3-berth compartments. Named trains also have first class 6-berth couchette cars or first-class reclining-seat cars (designated "Pullman") for which a special fare is charged. Express trains charge higher fares than local or mail trains. Children under 4 travel free. Half-fare for children 4-11. Children 12 and over must pay full fare.

Turkish trains in Asia are liable to cancellation or change.

Most of the train trips in Turkey for which we provide schedules are also the international rail routes to countries adjacent to Turkey. For that reason, we do not show a separate International Route list in this section.

Ankara

Capital of the Turkish Republic. See: The collection of relics from prehistoric times until the present in the magnificent Ataturk Mausoleum, and the view of Ankara from there. The Museum of the National Assembly. The third century Roman Baths. The Columns of Julian. The Temple of Augustus. Haci Bayram Mosque. The Byzantine Citadel. The finest collection of Hittite and pre-Hittite artifacts in Turkey can be seen in the Museum of Anatolian Civilizations. Visit the exhibits of ancient clothing, jewelry, manuscripts, tapestries and wood carving in the Ethnographic Museum. Next to it is the Museum of Modern Art and Sculpture. Ankara has several fine mosques: Alaettin, Ahielvan, Arslanhane and Yeni.

The costumes, carpets, musical instruments and weapons in the Ethnographic Museum. Nearby, the Zoo at Ataturk's Farm.

Istanbul

Colonized 2,600 years ago. First called Byzantium, then Constantinople. The city that links Europe and Asia.

See several exceptional mosques: The 17th century Blue Mosque (Sultanahmet), the rich tiles and stained-glass in the 16th century Suleymaniye, the enormous Fatih, the 15th century Eyup, the extraordinary jasper columns in the 15th century Beyazit, lovely tile decorations in the 17th century Yeni and in the 16th century Rustempasa.

One of the world's richest museums, Topkapi Sarayi, palace of sultans from the 15th to mid 19th century. The turbans, swords and tea cups encrusted with emeralds, rubies and diamonds as well as the satins embroidered with pearls will dazzle you. The kitchens there contain what is said to be the world's finest collection of Chinese porcelain.

The 19th century white marble Palace of Dolmabahce. Two other splendid palaces: Yildiz and Beylerbeyi. The blue and green tiled interior of the 15th century Cinili kiosk.

Istanbul's churches are outstanding: Ayasofia (St. Sophia), first built in 325, reconstructed in 532, later converted to a mosque, now a museum with fine Byzantine mosaics. The 4th century Church of St. Irene. The Byzantine frescoes and mosaics depicting the life of Christ and Old Testament scenes in the ancient Church of St. Saviour, now called Kaariye Mosque. The 14th century beautiful gilded mosaics in the old Church of St. Mary. Penmakaristos, now called Fethiye Mosque.

The Summer open-air folklore performances at Rumeli Castle. The 4th century fortification, The Ramparts. Tour the great underground cistern, Yerebatan Sarayi. This storage facility, connected to the 4th century Aqueduct of Valens, supplied water to the Imperial Palace. It is built with 336 columns that have Corinthian capitals.

Visit the Grand Bazaar. See the ancient Hippodrome of Constantinople, where chariot races took place. One of the 3 tall columns there was taken from the Egyptian Temple of Karnak. Another was removed from the Greek Temple of Apollo at Delphi.

The views of the Bosphorus from the luxury restaurant on Galata Tower and from the top of the Tower of Leander, and the view of Istanbul from the top of the white marble Beyazit Tower.

There are 2 incredibly beautiful fountains: Ahmet II (behind St. Sophia Cathedral) and the marble Tophane.

Istanbul has many excellent museums: The immense Greco-Roman collection at the Archaeological Museum. Next to it, the Assyrian, Babylonian, Sumerian and Hittite treasures in the Museums of the Ancient Orient. The Museum of Mosaics. The Museum of Turkish and Islamic Art. The Municipal Museum.

Istanbul -Haydarpasa (Boat Trip) 4025

The boat departs both piers frequent times from 6:00 to 24:00 for the 20-minute journey. Allow at least 12 hours for making connections with trains.

Istanbul - Athens 900

Dep. Istanbul 19:20
Arr. Athens 6:50 Day 3

Istanbul - Edirne - Svilengrad - Sofia - Belgrade - Munich 901

Dep. Istanbul (Sirkeci)	16:15(1)	19:50(2)	
Arr. Edirne	22:50	1:42	Day 2
Dep. Edirnc	-0-	1:48	
Set your watch back one hour.			
Arr. Svilengrad	-0-	4:53	
821			
Dep. Svilengrad	-0-	6:03	
Arr. Sofia	-0-	10:57	
Arr. Belgrade	-0-	18:00	
Arr. Munich	-0-	12:12	Day 3

(1) Second-class only. Light refreshments. (2) Has couchettes daily. Carries sleeping car on Saturday departure.

Sights in Edirne: There is bus service from the railstation for the 10-minute ride to Hurriyet Square, the center of Edirne. See: The fine blue tiles in Ucserefeli Mosque. The 13-domed Eski (Old) Mosque. Nearby, the fantastic Selimiye Mosque. The 16th century Turkish Bath, still operating and worth using. The Municipal Museum.

Istanbul - Bandirma - Manisa - Izmir

Travel between Istanbul and Bandirma is by boat.

4031		4035	
Dep. Istanbul	8:15	Dep. Izmir (Basmane)	8:20
Arr. Bandirma	12:30	Dep. Manisa	9:54
Change to train.		Arr. Bandirma	15:05
4035		Change to boat.	
Dep. Bandirma	16.00	4031	
Dep. Manisa	21:14	Dep. Bandirma	16:00
Arr. Izmir (Basmane)	22:40	Arr. Istanbul	20:30

Sights in Manisa: The 14th century Ulu Cami (Great Mosque) and the 16th century Muradiye Mosque.

Sights in Izmir: Third largest city in Turkey and its largest Aegean port. Once known as Smyrna. Walk along Ataturk Caddesi on the seafront. See: The elegant Moorish-style clock tower at Konak Meydani. The Bazaar. Three very attractive mosques: Kemeralti, Hisar and Sadirvan. Remains of the second-century Roman Agora. The Archaeological Museum in Culture Park. The magnificent view of the city from Velvet Castle, on Mount Pagos.

Izmir - Balikesir - Ankara	4042	
Dep. Izmir (Basmane)	7:50(1+2)	18:10(2+3)
Dep. Balikesir	12:22	23:00
Arr. Ankara	21:35	8:40
*	*	*
Dep. Ankara	7:30(1+2)	18:05(2+3)
Arr. Balikesir	16:32	3:34
Arr. Izmir (Basmane)	21:00	8:15

(1)First-class only. (2)Meal service. (3)Carries sleeping car.

Izmir - Fevzipasa - Baghdad

4042			4055		
Dep. Izmir (Basmane)	7:50(1)		Dep. Ulukisla	17:28	Day 2
Arr. Kutahya	16:48		Arr. Fevzipasa	2:12	Day 3
Change trains.			Dep. Fevzipasa	2:22	
Dep. Kutahya	0:18	Day 2	Arr. Narli	4:25	
Arr. Ulukisla	17:08		Change trains.		
Change trains.			4060		
			Dep. Narli	17:14(2)	
			Arr. Baghdad	5:40	Day 4

(1)Daily. First-class only. Meal service. (2)Runs Monday and Friday. Supplement charged. Carries sleeping car. Meal service.

Fevzipasa - Halab 4055

Dep. Fevzipasa	15:20(1)		Dep. Halab	5:45(2)
Arr. Halab	17:14		Arr. Fevzipasa	N/A

(1)Runs Monday and Friday. (2)Runs Wednesday and Sunday.

Ankara - Kars - Leninakan - Rostov - Kharkov - Moscow

4056		
Dep. Ankara	9:30(1)	18:55(3)
Dep. Kayseri	17:50	2:36(2)
Dep. Erzurum	10:06(2)	17:25
Arr. Kars	14:45	21:50
Change trains.		
Dep. Kars	9:00(4)	-0-
Arr. Leninakan	14:50(5)	-0-
5025		
Dep. Leninakan	18:31(4)	12:37(1+6)
Dep. Rostov	8:17(8+9)	17:49(7)
Dep. Kharkov	18:47(8)	2:58(8)
Arr. Moscow (Kurski)	5:50(10)	15:05

(1)Carries sleeping car. Meal service. (2)Day 2. (3)Meal service. (4)Runs Tuesday and Friday. Second-class only. (5)Same day. (6)Runs Tuesday and Saturday. (7)Day 2 after departing Leninakan. (8)Day 3 after departing Leninakan. (9)Change trains in Rostov, departing Rostov at 9:58. (10)Day 4 after departing Leninakan.

Sights in Kayseri: Called Caesarea when it was the capital of a Roman province. See: The Byzantine Citadel and, in it, the Faith Mosque. East of the Citadel, the 13th century Huand Mosque and College, and the geometric designs in the Baths of Princess Mahperi. Nearby, the beautifully decorated 13th century Doner Kumbet (Mausoleum). West of the Citadel is the interesting covered market. Also see the Archaeological Museum. The 13th century Koluk Mosque.

Sights in Erzurum: The Seljuk fort. The collonaded courtyard at the 12th century Ulu Cami Mosque. The Cifte Minareli Madrese Museum. The Hatuniye Medrese Mausoleum.

Sights in Kars: The 10th century Church of the Holy Apostles, now a museum. The ancient Georgian fort. The Kumbet Mosque. The 11th century Cathedral. The murals in the Church of St. Gregory. The Evliya Mosque.

Sights in Rostov: A post-World War II Russian metropolis, designed for heavy industrial manufacturing. See the enormous theater on Teatralnaya Square. Window-shop on Engels Street.

Sights in Kharkov: Almost totally reconstructed after World War II with wide streets. Sixth largest city in the USSR. Among the few old treasures that survived Nazi destruction are the 17th century Pokrovsky Cathedral, a belltower commemorating the 1812 victory over Napoleon, the 19th century Patriarchal Cathedral, and an 18th century theater. Modern sights include the large Park of Physical Culture, the Botanical Garden, several museums and a planetarium.

Ankara - Haydarpasa 4040

Dep. Ankara	8:00(1+2)	8:40(2+3)	13:30(1+2+4+5+10)
Arr. Haydarpasa	17:05	18:26	21:00
	*	*	*
Dep. Haydarpasa	9:20(1+2)	10:35(2+7)	13:30(1+2+4+5+11)
Arr. Ankara	19:00	20:18	21:00

(1)First-class only. Has cars with reclining seats. (2)Meal service. (3)Runs Mon., Thurs. and Sat. (4)Reservation required. (5)Supplement charged. (6)Carries sleeping car. (7)Runs Tues., Thurs. and Sun. (8)Runs daily. Notes #2 and #6 apply except Tues. and Sun. (9)Runs daily. Notes #2 and #6 apply except Mon. and Sat. (10)Plus other departures from Ankara at 20:20(2+6), 21:05(1+2+5+6) and 22:25(8). (11)Plus other departures from Haydarpasa at 20:00(9), 21:05-(1+2+5+6), 21:35(2+6) and 23:10.

Haydarpasa - Ankara - Kayseri - Van - Tabriz - Tehran 4021

Dep. Haydarpasa	20:00(1)	Dep. Van (Pier)	19:20(3)
Dep. Ankara	7:20(2)	Arr. Tabriz	N/A(4)
Dep. Kayseri	15:20(2)	Arr. Tehran	N/A(4)

(1)Carries sleeping car on Monday and Saturday. Has couchettes and meal service on Monday, Wednesday and Saturday. (2)Day 2. (3)Day 3. (4)Service "temporarily" suspended in 1981.

Sights in Van: This city is on a lake. See: The old fort. The 2 small Seljuk mosques.

Ankara - Samsun 4059

Dep. Ankara	N/A(1)	Dep. Samsun	N/A(1)
Arr. Samsun	N/A(1)	Arr. Ankara	N/A(1)

(1)Times have not been available since 1980.

Sights in Samsun: Birthplace of the Turkish Republic, in 1919. This is the largest Turkish port on the Black Sea.

Haydarpasa - Ankara - Mersin 4055

Dep. Haydarpasa	10:35(1+2)			Dep. Mersin	16:15(4)	
Arr. Ankara	20:18			Arr. Yenice	17:39	
Dep. Ankara	20:50			Change trains.		
Arr. Yenice	10:07	Day 2		Dep. Yenice	18:10(2+4)	
Change trains.				Arr. Ankara	7:50	Day 2
Dep. Yenice	10:13(3)	Day 2		Dep. Ankara	8:40	Day 2
Arr. Mersin	11:09	Day 2		Arr. Haydarpasa	18:25	Day 2

Mersin - Ankara - Haydarpasa

(1) Runs Sunday, Tuesday and Thursday. (2) Meal service. Carries sleeping car. (3) Runs Monday, Wednesday and Friday. (4) Runs Sunday, Wednesday and Friday.

Sights in Mersin: This is Turkey's principal port on the Mediterranean, surrounded by citrus groves. See: Eski Cami (the Old Mosque) and Yeni Cami (New Mosque). Crusaders' castles. Roman ruins.

Haydarpasa - Ankara - Adana 4055

Dep. Haydarpasa	10:35(1+2)		Dep. Adana	17:35(1+3)
Arr. Ankara	20:40		Arr. Ankara	7:40
Dep. Ankara	20:50(1+3)		Dep. Ankara	7:50(1+2)
Arr. Adana	10:39		Arr. Haydarpasa	18:25

(1) Supplement charged. Carries sleeping car. Meal service. (2) Runs Tuesday, Thursday and Sunday. (3) Daily.

Sights in Adana: This city was founded about 1,000 B.C. See: The second-century stone bridge, Tas Kopru. The 16th century Ulu (Great) Mosque. The 15th century Akca and Ramazanoglu mosques. The Archaeological Museum.

Haydarpasa - Izmit 4040

Dep. Haydarpasa	5:35(1)	8:00(2)	9:20(2+3)	10:35(4+5+7)
Arr. Izmit	7:50	9:15	10:40	11:56

Sights in Izmit: The remains of the ancient Roman walls. The Clock Tower. The Museum. The Pertev Pasha Mosque.

Dep. Izmit	3:15	5:23(4)	6:10(3+4)	6:53(4+8)
Arr. Haydarpasa	5:34	7:15	7:55	8:45

(1) First-class only. (2) Supplement charged. First-class only. Meal service. (3) Has cars with reclining seats. (4) Supplement charged. Has both first and second-class space. Meal service. (5) Runs Tuesday, Thursday and Sunday. (6) Reservation required. (7) Plus other departures from Haydarpasa at 13:30(2+3+6), 15:55(1), 18:25(1), 19:00(4), 20:00(4), 21:05(3+4), 21:30(1), 21:35(1) and 23:10. (8) Plus other departures from Izmit at 7:14(1), 7:50(4), 8:40(1), 14:10(1), 15:22(2+3), 17:48(1), 18:10(2), 19:13(1) and 19:44(2+3+6).

Haydarpasa - Konya 4042

Dep. Haydarpasa	8:00(1)		Dep. Konya	6:45(1)
Arr. Konya	20:39		Arr. Haydarpasa	19:45

(1)Supplement charged. First-class only. Meal service.

Sights in Konya: The 13th century Mevlana Mausoleum, ancient monastery of the Whirling Dervishes, with its greenish-blue tiles, now a museum. The ebony pulpit, 42 Roman columns and sarcophagi of many sultans in the 13th century Alaeddin Mosque. Nearby, the 13th century Karaty College and the interesting ceramics in the ruins of the Seljuk Palace. The 13th century Iplikci Mosque and Sircali College. The 16th century Selimiye Mosque. The Archaeological Museum. The collection of Islamic Art in the Koyunoglu Museum.

Haydarpasa - Ankara - Adana - Aleppo
4055

Dep. Haydarpasa	10:35(1+2)		Arr. Adana	10:39(3)
Arr. Ankara	20:18		Dep. Adana	11:10(2+4)
Dep. Ankara	20:50		Arr. Aleppo	21:25(5)

(1)Runs Tuesday, Thursday and Sunday. (2)Supplement charged. Carries sleeping car. Meal service. (3)Day 2 (Wednesday, Friday or Monday). (4)Runs Friday and Monday. (5)Same day as departure from Adana.

Haydarpasa - Ankara - Mosul - Baghdad 4020

Dep. Haydarpasa	10:35(1+2)	Thursday and Sunday
Dep. Ankara	20:50(1)	Thursday and Sunday
Dep. Gaziantep	21:25(1)	Friday and Monday
Dep. El Yaroubieh	16:30(1)	Saturday and Tuesday
Dep. Mosul	21:00(1)	Saturday and Tuesday
Arr. Baghdad	5:40	Sunday and Wednesday

(1)Carries sleeping car. (2)Meal service to Gaziantep.

UNITED ARAB EMIRATES

There are no passenger trains in the United Arab Emirates.

YEMEN ARAB REPUBLIC

There are no passenger trains in the Yemen Arab Republic.

YEMEN, PEOPLE'S DEMOCRATIC REPUBLIC

There are no passenger trains in the People's Democratic Republic of Yemen.

Chapter 11 AFRICA

ALGERIA

The train lines here are standard-gauge. Algeria's rail system consists of one east-west route (connecting Tunisia with Morocco) from which there are 4 spurs heading north to Mediterranean ports and 3 routes going south from the transcontinental main line.

The 2 principal southern routes, Constantine (via El Gourzi) to Touggourt, and Mohammadia to Colomb Bechar, go through the Atlas Mountains to the Sahara Desert. The third southerly route is the short run from Annaba (via Souk-Ahras) to Tebessa.

The 3 very short spurs heading north are Constantine to Skikda, Boudjellil to Bejaia, and Tlelat to Oran.

Children under 4 travel free. Half-fare for children 4-9. Children 10 and over must pay full fare.

Algiers

See the shops, cafes and unique narrow streets of the Kasbah. The Marechal Franchet d'Esperey Museum. The fabulous palaces (Summer and Winter) of the Governor-General. Many fine mosques. The view of little islands, harbor and city from Notre-Dame d'Afrique Church.

The splendid Jardin d'Essai du Hamma botanical gardens. The view from Saint-Raphael Park. Nearby, several good seashore resorts: Moretti, Zeralda, etc.

Constantine

Located on the eastern edge of the Kabylia mountain area. The ancient section of the city is on top of a steep rock. See: The elaborate Ahmed Bey Palace. Medina, the Moslem Quarter. The Gustav Mercier Museum. Nearby: restored ruins of ancient Roman towns: Tebessa, Timgad, Djemila. Several Berber villages.

There is much good Berber handicraft in this area: pottery, carved furniture, enamel-inlaid jewelry.

Transcontinental Algerian Rail Routes

The 3 services listed below are Algeria's only train connections with countries adjacent to it, Tunisia and Morocco.

Algiers - Constantine - Annaba - Tunis

2540				
Dep. Algiers	8:55(1+2)	12:30(1)	18:00(3)	21:05
Arr. Constantine	16:05	N/A	N/A	5:55
Dep. Constantine	-0-	20:00	2:20(3)	-0-
Arr. Annaba	-0-	22:45	5:17	-0-
Change trains.				
2550				
Dep. Annaba	-0-	-0-	7:10	22:00
Arr. Ghardimaou	-0-	-0-	10:55	1:15
Set your watch forward one hour.				
Dep. Ghardimaou	-0-	-0-	N/A	N/A
Arr. Tunis	-0-	-0-	16:03	4:56

(1) Meal service. (2) Air-conditioned. Supplement charged. (3) Has couchettes. Light refreshments. No train change in Annaba.

Sights in Annaba: This old city was settled by Phoenicians in the 12th century B.C. See: The narrow streets of the old town. The 11th century Sidi Bou Merouan Mosque. (It's columns were taken from Roman ruins.) The Hippo Museum. The 18th century Salah Bey Mosque. The Place d'Armes.

Algiers - Oran

2530					
Dep. Algiers	7:25(1)	10:30(1+2)	12:10(1)	17:45(1)	21:30(3)
Arr. Oran	12:38	15:21	17:28	22:54	6:02

* * *

Dep. Oran	7:15(1)	10:50(1+2)	12:20(1)	17:25(1)	21:20(3)
Arr. Algiers	12:34	15:43	17:36	22:45	6:22

(1) Meal service. (2) Air-conditioned. Supplement charged. (3) Has couchettes. Light refreshments.

Algiers - Rabat - Casablanca - Marrakech

Schedules appear later in this chapter, in the section on Morocco.

Northern Algerian Rail Routes

Here are the schedules for the 4 short spurs heading north from the transcontinental train route.

Constantine - Skikda

2542			
Dep. Constantine	16:50	Dep. Skikda	5:35
Arr. Skikda	18:45	Arr. Constantine	7:37

Sights in Skikda: Ruins of the largest Roman theater in Algeria. Roman antiquities in the City Museum.

Annaba - Skikda

2540			2542		
Dep. Annaba	6:10	18:45	Dep. Skikda	19:40	3:20
Arr. Ramdane Djam	7:27	20:02	Arr. Ramdane Djam	20:00	3:39
Change trains.			Change trains.		
2542			2540		
Dep. Ramdane Djam	18:24	21:30	Dep. Ramdane Djam	21:28	3:50
Arr. Skikda	18:45	21:51	Arr. Annaba	22:45	5:17

Algiers - Bejaia

2540				
Dep. Algiers	6:00	7:15	16:04	17:00
Arr. Bejaia	10:47	12:13	21:11	21:44

* * *

Dep. Bejaia	5:55	7:00	15:15	17:00
Arr. Algiers	10:50	11:52	20:11	21:54

Sights in Bejaia: Many Roman ruins in this area.

Oued Tlelat - Oran

	2530	2525	2530	2525	2530
Dep. Oued Tlelat	5:26	6:48	8:53	9:10	12:20(1)
Arr. Oran	30 minutes later				

* * *

	2525	2530	2525	2530	2525
Dep. Oran	6:45	7:15	10:06	12:20	17:00(2)
Arr. Oued Tlelat	30 minutes later				

(1) Plus other departures from Oued Tlelat at 16:51, 17:03, 20:15 and 22:36. (2) Plus other departures from Oran at 17:25, 18:20, 18:45 and 21:20.

Sights in Oran: This city has 3 sections: La Blanca (the 16th century Spanish city on the hill), La Marine (near the Mediterranean) and La Ville Nouvelle (on the right bank of the Raz el-Ain River).

See: The Turkish Citadel, Santa Cruz. The early 19th century Cathedral of Saint-Louis. The fountain in the 18th century Place Emerat. The 18th century Porte de Canastel. The Great Mosque.

The Sidi al-Hawwari Mosque. Nearby, the Kasbah. Chateau Neuf, once the residence of the rulers and later the headquarters of the French colonial army. The harem of the rulers. The 18th century Jewish cemetery.

The Roman and Punic exhibits at the Municipal Museum. The collection of Islamic art in the Tlemcen Museum. The Aubert Library.

Southern Algerian Rail Routes

The following schedules are for the 3 Algerian train lines going south from the transcontinental route.

Annaba - Souk Ahras - Tebessa 2550

Dep. Annaba	16:44	Dep. Tebessa	4:20
Arr. Souk-Ahras	18:57	Arr. Souk-Ahras	6:41
Change trains.		Change trains.	
Dep. Souk-Ahras	19:22	Dep. Souk-Ahras	6:42
Arr. Tebessa	21:42	Arr. Annaba	8:59

Sights in Tebessa: The walled Byzantine Citadel, with 4 gates and 12 towers. The second century Roman Arch of Caracalla. Only one mile north, the ruins of the Roman Temple of Minerva, thermal baths and an amphitheater at the same site as a beautiful Christian basilica. Much carpet-weaving here.

Constantine - Biskra - Touggourt

2541

Dep. Constantine	5:30	18:50	Dep. Touggourt	7:27	-0-
Arr. Biskra	9:22	22:40	Arr. Biskra	11:15	-0-
Change trains.			Change trains.		
Dep. Biskra	16:22	-0-	Dep. Biskra	17:20	5:30
Arr. Touggourt	20:06	-0-	Arr. Constantine	21:07	9:10

Sights in Biskra: An ancient Roman outpost, now a popular Winter resort. Five miles to the west is the hot sulphur spring famous for medicinal value, Hamman Salahin ("Bath of the Saints"). Many oases here.

Sights in Touggourt: A typical Saharan town. There are many dried mud buildings here. See: The tremendous fortress minaret. The clock tower in the Kasbah. The tombs of the kings. Many date palms in this oasis. Nearby, the tomb of Sidi el-Hadj Ali.

Mohammadia - Bechar

2535

Dep. Mohammadia	7:15(1)	18:45(2)	Dep. Bechar	6:00(1)	17:40(2)
Arr. Bechar	21:41	9:22	Arr. Mohammadia	20:12	7:54

(1)Runs from mid-October to mid-April. (2)Runs from mid-April to mid-October. Meal service.

Sights in Bechar: The city lies at the base of 1,600-foot high Djebel Bechar. Many date palm groves in this area. There are interesting covered narrow streets in the Arab section. Good leatherwork and jewelry are produced here.

ANGOLA

The 3 parallel west-to-east rail lines in Angola start at seaports on the South Atlantic coastline and run inland. One of these, beginning in Benguela, connects at Dilolo with a train service in Zaire and ultimately provides also a train link with Zambia (at Ndola) and then on to Tanzania, Rhodesia, Mozambique, Botswana and South Africa. This route is part of the trans-African railway line.

Children under 3 travel free. Half-fare for children 3-11. Children 12 and over must pay full fare.

Luanda - Malanje 3420

All of these trains have either meal service or light refreshments. This line has 2 short spurs, one to Dondo and another to a hill station, Golungo Alta.

Dep. Luanda	6:00(1)+(2)	6:00(2)+(3)	9:00(4)+(5)
Arr. Malanje	19:10	20:32	16:54

* * *

Dep. Malanje	6:00(2)+(6)	6:00(2)+(7)	9:00(5)+(8)	13:00(5)+(9)
Arr. Luanda	19:14	20:05	17:00	20:18

(1)Runs Monday, Thursday and Friday. (2)Meal service. (3)Runs Tuesday, Wednesday and Saturday. (4)Runs Tuesday and Thursday. (5)Light refreshments. (6)Daily, except Wednesday and Sunday. (7)Runs only Wednesday. (8)Runs only Thursday. (9)Runs only Sun.

Sights in Luanda: The capital of Angola. A major harbor. See the Angola Museum. The Bunda Museum. The old Sao Miguel Fort. The 17th century Chapel of Nazareth. The Zoological Museum.

Sights in Malanje: The 350-foot high Duque de Braganca Falls. The Pungo Andongo stones, enormous black monoliths that figure in tribal legends. To the south, the Game Reserve.

Lobito - Luau - Dilolo

The Benguela Railway is a major segment of Africa's only trans-continental rail line. When operating, there is service from Lobito (on the Atlantic Ocean) to Dilolo on the Zaire border, where the Benguela joins other lines that pass through the copper fields of Zaire and Zambia, terminating at the Indian Ocean cities of Beirain (Mozambique) and Dar es Salaam (Tanzania).

Construction of the Benguela line took from 1903 to 1928.

There is outstanding scenery in the first 40 miles and an ascent from sea level to 6,000 feet in the first 250 miles, after which the train descends to 4,000 feet and goes through eucalyptus forests.

Passenger service over the complete Lobito-Dilolo route was first suspended in 1977 due to anti-government guerrillas attacking the trains by bombing and derailing. A daily service of 3 trains between Lobito and Dilolo was said to be in operation during 1980 "although no fixed schedule is yet in force."

3421

Dep. Lobito	N/A	Dep. Dilolo	N/A
Arr. Luau	N/A	Dep. Luau	N/A
Arr. Dilolo	N/A	Arr. Lobito	N/A

Although daily service was reported in 1982, exact schedules were not available 1979-1982.

Mocamedes - Lubango - Dondo - Menongue 3422

The train ascends from sea level to 5,000 feet on this route. One spur from it goes to Chibia, another spur to Cassinga.

Dep. Mocamedes	7:29(1)	23:05(2)	Dep. Menongue	N/A(4)	-0-
Arr. Lubango	13:08	6:05	Dep. Jamba	6:00(1)	-0-
Dep. Dondo	-0-	N/A(3)	Dep. Dondo	N/A(3)	-0-
Arr. Jamba	-0-	15:20(4)	Dep. Lubango	15:15(1)	9:01(5)
Arr. Menongue	-0-	N/A	Arr. Mocamedes	22:00	14:29

(1)Runs Tuesday and Saturday. (2)Runs Thursday and Sunday. (3)Time has not been available since 1980. (4)Service between Jamba and Menongue was "temporarily" suspended in 1977. (5)Runs Tues. and Fri.

Mocamedes - Lubango - Chibia 3422

Dep. Mocamedes	7:29(1)	Dep. Chibia	N/A(2)
Arr. Lubango	13:08	Arr. Lubango	N/A(2)
Change trains.		Change trains.	
Dep. Lubango	N/A(2)	Dep. Lubango	9:01(3)
Arr. Chibia	N/A(2)	Arr. Mocamedes	14:29

(1)Runs Tuesday and Saturday. (2)Service has been "temporarily" suspended since 1981. (3)Runs Tuesday and Friday.

Mocamedes - Dondo - Cassinga 3422

Dep. Mocamedes	23:05(1)	Dep. Cassinga	N/A(2)
Arr. Dondo	N/A(2)	Arr. Dondo	N/A(2)
Change trains.		Change trains.	
Dep. Dondo	N/A(2)	Dep. Dondo	N/A(2)
Arr. Cassinga	N/A(2)	Arr. Mocamedes	22:00(3)

(1)Runs Thursday and Sunday. (2)Time has not been available since 1979. (3)Runs Tuesday and Saturday.

BENIN

Previously called Dahomey. Children under 4 travel free. Half-fare for children 4-9. Children 10 and over must pay full fare.

Cotonou - Ouidah 3027

Dep. Cotonou	8:04	13:50	17:42
Arr. Ouidah	9:21	15:10	19:08

Sights in Ouidah: This was a European slave trade center in the 18th century. See the 16th century Portuguese fort. The Cathedral. The streets lined with colorful blossoming plants and fruit trees. An interesting temple of the local traditional religion. Nearby coconut and coffee plantations.

Dep. Ouidah	5:52	11:50	17:50
Arr. Cotonou	7:36	13:12	19:12

Cotonou - Parakou 3025

Dep. Cotonou	8:44(1)	13:35(1+2)	17:00(3)
Arr. Parakou	17:12	20:45	8:14
	*	*	*
Dep. Parakou	9:20(1)	13:55(1+4)	17:40(5)
Arr. Cotonou	18:04	21:10	7:54

(1) Light refreshments. (2) Runs Tuesday, Friday and Saturday. (3) Runs Tuesday, Thursday, Friday and Sunday. (4) Runs Wednesday, Saturday and Sunday. (5) Runs Monday, Wednesday, Friday and Sunday.

Sights in **Cotonou:** Many interesting markets. The Supreme Court. The National Assembly. Nearby are Abomey and Ouidah.

Sights in **Abomey:** The 30-foot high walls of the ancient 100-acre fortified palace and the interesting Museum, Jewelry Hall and Statuary Hall in the palace, with good exhibits of weapons, furniture and textiles.

Cotonou - Pobe 3026

Dep Cotonou	17:02	Dep. Pobe	6:00
Arr. Pobe	20:55	Arr. Cotonou	9:54

BOTSWANA

The one rail trip in landlocked Botswana (operated by Rhodesian Railways) leads north from Ramatlhabama near South Africa's border to Plumtree and into Rhodesia. It is one of the 2 routes from Johannesburg (South Africa) to Salisbury (Rhodesia).

Johannesburg - Mafeking - Plumtree - Salisbury

3475

Dep. Johannesburg	12:30(1)	-0-	
Dep. Mafeking	21:00(1)	14:05	
Dep. Ramalthabama	21:30	16:10(3)	
Dep. Plumtree	12:09(2)	10:05(2)	
Arr. Bulawayo	14:10(2)	12:45(2)	

Change to another train or to a bus.

3455

Dep. Bulawayo	19:30(4)	20:00	8:00(5)
Arr. Salisbury	6:00	7:00	16:00

(1)Runs only Thursday from Johannesburg. Runs Tuesday and Thursday from Mafeking. Reservation required. Meal service. (2)Day 2. (3)Meal service. (4)Runs Friday. (5)Bus. Runs Tuesday, Friday and Sunday.

BURUNDI

There are no passenger trains in Burundi.

CAMEROUN

Children under 3 travel free. Half-fare for children 3-9. Children 10 and over must pay full fare.

Douala - Nkongsamba 3128

Dep. Douala	7:10(1)	Dep. Nkongsamba	8:25(1)
Arr. Nkongsamba	14:50	Arr. Douala	15:55

(1) Second-class only.

Sights in Douala: The 13,000-foot high Mount Cameroun, tallest mountain in West Africa. The beautiful view of the enormous bridge over the Wouri River.

Sights in Nkongsamba: Pleasant climate. A popular tourist resort. Many banana, coffee and palm-oil plantations.

Douala - Yaounde 3128

Dep. Douala	8:00	13:30(1)	20:00(2)
Arr. Yaounde	17:58	19:40	5:40

Sights in Yaounde: Capital of Cameroun. Many streams and shaded avenues. Nearby: The cocoa plantations in a very large forest. The Ekom Waterfalls and the Dschang health resort at the 4,000-foot high Bamileke Plateau. Nachtigal Falls. The Grottos of the Pygmies.

Dep. Yaounde	7:30	14:30(3)	21:00(2)
Arr. Douala	17:35	20:40	6:00

(1) Runs Monday, Tuesday, Thursday and Saturday. (2) Runs daily. Has couchettes. (3) Runs Monday, Wednesday, Friday and Saturday.

Yaounde - N'gaoundere 3125

Dep. Yaounde	7:30	20:20(1+2)	Dep. N'gaoundere	7:00	19:00(1+3)
Arr. N'gaoundere	18:42	8:50	Arr. Yaounde	18:40	7:20

(1) Second-class only. (2) Daily. Has first-class couchettes Monday, Wednesday and Friday. (3) Daily. Has first-class couchettes Tuesday, Thursday and Sunday.

Sights in N'gaoundere: Big-game hunting and photography is the attraction here. There are large game reserves nearby.

CENTRAL AFRICAN REPUBLIC

There are no passenger trains in Central African Republic.

CHAD

There are no passenger trains in Chad.

CONGO

The rail system in Congo starts at the South Atlantic seaport of Pointe Noire and runs inland to Loubomo, where it forms the two top arms of a "Y", one fork heading north to M'Binda, the other going east to Brazzaville, the nation's capital. Kinshasa, across the border in Zaire, has a rail line running to Matadi.

Children under 5 travel free. Half-fare for children 5-9. Children 10 and over must pay full fare.

Pointe Noire - Brazzaville

This is the principal Congo-Ocean Railway.

3172

Dep. Pointe Noire	6:25	12:32(1)	18:10(3+4)
Arr. Brazzaville	20:40	15:15(2)	6:10(2)
	*	*	*
Dep. Brazzaville	6:15	11:15(1)	18:50(3+5)
Arr. Pointe Noire	20:03	11:20(2)	6:30(2)

(1) Only third-class space. (2) Day 2. (3) Meal service. (4) Has couchettes on Monday, Thursday and Saturday. (5) Has couchettes on Tuesday, Friday and Sunday.

Pointe Noire - M'Binda 3172

Dep. Pointe Noire	6:25	12:32(1)	18:10(2)
Arr. Loubomo	11:34	21:30	22:37
Change trains.			
Dep. Loubomo	14:46	17:40(1)	-0-
Arr. M'Binda	22:29	8:37	-0-
	*	*	*
Dep. M'Binda	4:40	17:27	-0-
Arr. Loubomo	12:44	11:02	-0-
Change trains.			
Dep. Loubomo	14:54	2:06(3)	3:56(1)
Arr. Pointe Noire	20:03	6:30	11:20

(1) Third-class only. (2) Meal service. (3) Daily. Has couchettes Monday, Wednesday and Saturday.

DJIBOUTI

This was formerly the northwestern corner of Somalia. Its only passenger rail service is the 186-mile portion of the line running from its Gulf of Aden seaport, Djibouti, to Ethiopia's Addis Ababa.

Djibouti - Diredawa - Addis Abeba 3255

Dep. Djibouti	6:15(1)		Dep. Addis Abeba	7:10	
Arr. Diredawa	18:00		Arr. Diredawa	16:45	
Change trains.			Change trains.		
Dep. Diredawa	7:05	Day 2	Dep. Diredawa	6:00(2)	Day 2
Arr. Addis Abeba	17:10		Arr. Djibouti	18:00	

(1)Runs Wednesday, Friday and Sunday. (2)Runs Tuesday, Thursday and Saturday.

Sights in Djibouti: A major seaport. See the Palace, on Menelik Square. The Great Mosque, on Place Rimbaud, where a large camel market is conducted.

EGYPT

Most Westerners prefer to visit Egypt November-March.

Egyptian trains charge a supplement for traveling in air-conditioned cars. First-class sleeping cars have single-berth compartments. Second-class sleeping cars have 2-berth compartments. All sleeping cars are air-conditioned. Passengers in sleeping cars must pay 2 supplemental charges: for the sleeping-car and for air-conditioning.

Children under 4 travel free. Half-fare for children 4-9. Children 10 and over must pay full fare.

From Cairo, there is one rail line south, to Sadd-el-Ali, where a connection can be made for train travel across the desert in Sudan. This is the only international rail route between Egypt and countries adjacent to it.

The 3 other Egyptian rail routes from Cairo are northwest to Alexandria, northeast to Ismailia (and on to Port Said), and east to Suez.

There is also train service along the Suez Canal, from the city of Suez to Ismailia. Egypt's Mediterranean coastline train trip is between Alexandria and Mersa Matruh.

Cairo

See the Egyptian Museum in Tahrir Square, near the Nile Hilton Hotel, the greatest collection in the world of pharaonic treasures. The Coptic Museum. Nearby, the 4th century Church of Abu Serga (St. Sergius). The ancient El Mollaqa Church. The 10th century gate, Bab Zuweilla. Cairo has several hundred mosques, open to visitors except during Friday prayers. Women are not allowed to enter mosques after sunset.

See the ornate Al Azhar Mosque. The Sultan Hassan Mosque, a veritable fortress. The Mohammed Ali Mosque, at the top of the Citadel. El Aqmar Mosque. Al Ghuri Mosque. El Hakim Mosque. The 9th century Ibn Tulun Mosque. King Farouk's tomb, at El Rifai Mosque.

Also visit the Khan al-Khalili Market to see tinsmiths and tentmakers, hand-hammered copper and brass trays, cotton caftans, local inexpensive perfumes. The 17th century house, Bayt El Suhaymi. The museum at Gayer-Anderson House. The Papyrus Institute, which has an interesting exhibit on making the early writing material. The view of Cairo and the Nile from the revolving restaurant on the top of Cairo Tower.

The Sound and Light Pageant (19:30-20:30), in the outdoor theater at the foot of the Sphinx. The English-language commentary at the Pageant (on the history of the pharaohs) is performed Monday, Wednesday and Saturday.

It costs about $10(U.S.) for an hour sailboat ride in the evening on the Nile. The boats leave from the Shepheards and the Meridien hotels.

Visit the Coptic Museum. The Abu Serga Church where, according to legend, the Holy Family stayed when fleeing from Herod. See the Ben Ezra Synagogue.

The Cairo Zoo, in Giza. Several casinos, for non-Egyptians only. Thousands of bazaars.

It is only a 25-minute taxi ride from the center of Cairo to the largest Egyptian pyramid, Cheops in Giza. A visit at sunset is recommended.

Alexandria

Egypt's most important port and second-largest city. Very popular beach resort.

Cairo - Alexandria - Cairo

2660

Those trains which are air-conditioned require reservations.

Dep. Cairo (Main)	Frequent times from 6:05 to 20:25
Arr. Alexandria	3 hours later

* * *

Dep. Alexandria	Frequent times from 5:25 to 19:25
Arr. Cairo	3 hours later

Alexandria - El Alamein

These trains have only second-class and third-class space.

2663

Dep. Alexandria	6:35	10:10	Dep. El Alamein	10:49	15:41
Arr. El Alamein	9:38	13:08	Arr. Alexandria	14:45	19:20

Sights in El Alamein: There is a small museum commemorating General Montgomery's defeat of Field Marshal Rommel in one of the most famous battles of World War II. More than 8,000 soldiers are buried in large cemeteries in this area.

Cairo - Ismailia - Port Said

These trains have only second-class space.

2655

Dep. Cairo (Main)	6:20(1)	11:55	15:25	18:40(2)	21:40(1)
Arr. Ismailia	9:15	14:25	18:25	21:20	0:45
Arr. Port Said	10:55	-0-	-0-	23:00	-0-

* * *

Dep. Port Said	-0-	5:15(2)	12:50(1)	16:50	-0-
Dep. Ismailia	5:10	7:00	14:30	18:38	21:05
Arr. Cairo (Main)	8:40	9:55	17:10	21:25	23:50

(1) Light refreshments. (2) Air-conditioned in second-class.

Sights in Ismailia: Many parks and gardens. The Suez Canal. The Sweet Water Canal, built in 1863 to provide thousands of canal workers with drinking water. There are several ancient ruins 10 miles west of here.

Sights in Port Said: This is Egypt's second most important seaport.

Cairo - Suez

2656

Dep. Cairo (Pont Limoun)	5:50	10:00(1)	15:35	19:35(1)
Arr. Suez	8:35	13:05	18:20	22:40

* * *

Dep. Suez	5:50(1)	9:40	14:50(1)	19:15
Arr. Cairo (Pont Limoun)	9:00	12:25	18:05	22:00

(1)Light refreshments.

Sights in Suez: The Canal and this city's 2 harbors. This is a departure point for pilgrimages to Mecca.

Cairo - Luxor - Aswan 2656

Pyramids, ancient temples and camel trains can be seen on this route.

Dep. Cairo (Main)	7:30(1)	7:40(2)	12:00(1)	12:25(2+3)
Arr. Luxor	18:14	0:50	0:20	1:20
Arr. Aswan	23:20	-0-	-0-	-0-
Dep. Cairo (Main)	16:20(2)	19:00(4)	20:40(2)	22:50(5)
Arr. Luxor	7:04	5:38	14:57	12:35
Arr. Aswan	12:12	10:00	22:35	19:30

* * *

Dep. Aswan	-0-	-0-	-0-	5:15(1)
Dep. Luxor	4:15(3)	4:25(2)	5:15(1)	10:14
Arr. Cairo (Main)	17:30	20:10	16:35	20:55
Dep. Aswan	5:40(2)	-0-	17:45(4)	18:40(2)
Dep. Luxor	12:42	15:10(3)	21:45	23:36
Dep. Cairo (Main)	5:35	6:00	9:50	13:30

(1) Reservation required. Air-conditioned. Meal service. (2) Only second-class and third-class space. (3) Air-conditioned only in second-class. (4) Carries only air-conditioned sleeping cars, both first-class and second-class. Meal service. (5) Third-class only.

Sights in Luxor: In 2133 B.C. this was Thebes, capital of the Egyptian empire, and on the opposite side of the Nile it was Karnak, the "city of the dead", with the kings' mortuary temples. The ruins of the great temples of Karnak, Amon, Mont, Mut and Khons, and the complex of temples called Amon-Re are the interesting places to see here today. Also, the Colossi of Memnon, more than 60 tombs in the Valley of the Tombs of the Kings.

Sights in Aswan: A Winter resort. You can see the ancient quarries from which granite was taken for building the pharaohs' monuments. Four miles north is the Aswan High Dam, completed in 1970, one of the greatest engineering accomplishments in the world. It is 1½ miles long and has 180 sluices.

Nile Cruises

Several cruise firms provide boat service on the Nile. These cruises are so popular that reservations for the high season (September to May) have to be made as much as 3 years in advance.

There are 14-day Nile trips Cairo-Aswan-Cairo, September to April, calling at the principal monuments on the river. There are also 10-day, 14-day and 16-day roundtrip cruises between Luxor and Aswan. One cruise is a one-day (5:15-17:00) hydrofoil service between Aswan and the temple complex at Abu Simbel, operated daily, but generally available only to groups.

The Rail Route to Sudan

Egypt's train connection with Sudan starts with a Nile boat trip from Sadd el Ali to Wadi Halfa.

Sadd el Ali - Wadi Halfa

2690

Dep. Sadd el Ali	16:00(1)	Dep. Wadi Halfa	16:00(2)
Arr. Wadi Halfa	8:00 Day 3	Arr. Sadd el Ali	8:00 Day 3

(1) Runs Monday and Thursday. (2) Runs Tuesday and Friday.

Wadi Halfa - Khartoum

This trip crosses the Nubian Desert.

2700

Dep. Wadi Halfa	16:40(1)	Arr. Khartoum	16:45 Day 2

(1) Runs Wednesday and Saturday. Carries sleeping car. Meal service. Air-conditioned in first-class on Saturdays.

ETHIOPIA

Ethiopia's 2 rail lines are the route between 8,000-foot high Addis Abeba and Dire Daoua (which continues to Djibouti on the Gulf of Aden), and the line from Agordat to Massawa, a port on the Red Sea.

Children under 4 travel free. Half-fare for children 4-9. Children 10 and over must pay full fare.

Addis Abeba - Diredawa - Djibouti 3255

The ride descending from Addis Abeba to Diredawa is very scenic, similar to Colorado mountain scenery.

Dep. Addis Abeba	7:10	Dep. Djibouti	6:15(2)
Arr. Diredawa	16:45	Arr. Diredawa	18:00
Change trains.		Change trains.	
Dep. Diredawa	6:00(1)	Dep. Diredawa	7:05
Arr. Djibouti	18:00	Arr. Addis Abeba	17:10

(1) Runs Tuesday, Thursday and Saturday. (2) Runs Wednesday, Friday and Sunday.

Sights in Addis Abeba: The depiction of Africa's past struggles, present problems and future progress in the magnificent stained-glass window at All Africa Hall. The lavishly decorated National Palace. The mosaics, ceiling carvings and stained-glass at Holy Trinity Cathedral. The obelisk on Miazia 27 Square.

The Natural History Museum. The Imperial Lion House. The handicrafts for sale in the Empress Menen Handicraft School. The view of the city from Mount Entoto. Haile Selassie I Square. The National Museum's archaeology exhibits. The paintings in the Institute of Ethiopian Studies. The Saturday event at Mercato, the large marketplace. Heavy traffic of domestic animals on some of the downtown streets. The imperial lions in the small zoo at Jubilee Palace. St. George's Cathedral. Several palaces.

Sights in Diredawa: The Mosque. The Muslim cemeteries. Prehistoric paintings in the nearby caves. The Palace.

Massawa - Asmara - Agordat 3250

The train makes an amazing climb on this route, similar to some of the steepest gradients in Peru.

Dep. Massawa	N/A(1)	Dep. Agordat	N/A(1)
Dep. Asmara	N/A	Dep. Asmara	N/A
Arr. Agordat	N/A	Arr. Massawa	N/A

(1) This service was suspended in 1977.

Sights in Massawa (also called Mitsiwa): This is one of the hottest places in the world, with an annual average temperature of 87 degrees Fahrenheit (31 degrees Celsius). Despite this, it is an important tourist center. Massawa is a seaport and is used as a naval base. The Ethiopian Orthodox Church is worth seeing. There is an ice factory here.

Sights in Asmara (also called Asmera): The Coptic Church. The Grand Mosque. The Palace. There is good deep-sea fishing off this shore.

GABON

Children under 4 travel free. Half-fare for children 4-11. Children 12 and over must pay full fare.

Owendo (Libreville) - Franceville 3150

Dep. Owendo	7:00(1)	16:00(3)	Dep. Franceville	N/A(2)	N/A(2)
Arr. Ndjole	10:00	19:05	Dep. Ndjole	6:50(3)	16:00(1)
Arr. Franceville	N/A(2)	N/A(2)	Arr. Owendo	10:01	19:03

(1) Air-conditioned. Runs Tuesday, Thursday, Saturday, Sunday and holidays. (2) The track between Ndjole and Franceville, under construction since 1980, has not been completed. (3) Air-conditioned. Runs Saturday, Sunday and holidays.

GAMBIA

There are no passenger trains in Gambia.

GHANA

This country's rail system forms the letter "A", with the western arm running from the Atlantic seaport of Takoradi north to inland Kumasi, the eastern segment going from the port of Accra north to Kumasi, and the cross-arm extending from Tarkwa (on the western route) to the eastern route. The cross-arm is the Takoradi-Accra route.

Each sleeping car has 8 first-class compartments, each with a single bed. Couples can obtain adjoining compartments that have a common door. Second-class sleeping compartments have 8 berths.

Ghana's rail authorities advise travelers that its engines "are old and not wholly reliable" and therefore "breakdowns may occur during the course of travel." They also state: "The situation is being ameliorated but will definitely take some time."

Applicants for visas to travel in Ghana are required to purchase from the Ghana Consulate in their own country travel vouchers for use in purchasing food, lodging and transportation in Ghana. The price varies according to length of stay in Ghana. The price required for 14 days in Ghana is about $305 (U.S.).

Accra

See the port longshoremen carrying crates and bundles on their heads. A spirited nightlife. The Arts Council of Ghana. The Ethnological Museum. The Science Museum. Nearby: The enormous Volta Dam and, behind it, the largest manmade lake in the world, Lake Volta.

Tarkwa

There is much mining here for gold, diamonds, manganese and bauxite. Because of the sand that is found in this area, there is a substantial glass industry here.

Kumasi

The "Garden City of West Africa". The Ashanti kings rule from here. The area is dense forest. See: The Ghana Regiment Museum in the old British fort. The museum, zoo and library at the Ashanti Cultural Center. Good textiles are available here.

Takoradi - Tarkwa - Kumasi 3066

Dep. Takoradi	6:15	21:00(1)	Dep. Kumasi	6:40	21:00(1)
Dep. Tarkwa	9:12	23:21	Dep. Tarkwa	13:15	3:35
Arr. Kumasi	15:45	5:26	Arr. Takoradi	15:31	5:48

(1) Carries sleeping car.

Takoradi - Tarkwa - Accra 3065

Dep. Takoradi	19:30	-0-	Dep. Accra	5:20	19:30
Dep. Tarkwa	21:28	6:00	Dep. Tarkwa	17:00	2:30
Arr. Accra	4:57	17:26	Arr. Takoradi	-0-	4:42

Accra - Kumasi

3061

Dep. Accra	6:20	21:00	Dep. Kumasi	6:20	21:00
Arr. Kumasi	16:25	5:47	Arr. Accra	15:42	5:38

GUINEA

Conakry - Kankan

All of these trains provide light refreshments.

2852

Dep. Conakry	6:30	Tues.	19:47	Fri.
Arr. Kankan	22:25	Tues.	8:43	Sat.
		*	*	*
Dep. Kankan	4:50	Wed.	19:40	Sat.
Arr. Conakry	21:23	Wed.	8:39	Sun.

Sights in Conakry: The Corniche, a lovely promenade along the seashore. The African exhibits at the Museum. Good beaches. The Mosque. The monument to anti-colonial martyrs. The picturesque Boulbinet fishing harbor. Nearby, the Botanical Garden in Camayenne.

Sights in Kankan: This was an 18th century caravan center. The ambience is very Moslem. Many mosques. Much wood, gold and ivory craftsmanship here. A center for trading in reptile skins, sesame, cattle, rice.

IVORY COAST

This country's single passenger rail route is the 725-mile narrow-gauge Abidjan-Niger Line (constructed by France), running from Abidjan on the shore of the Gulf of Guinea to Bobo Dioulasso and then on to Ouagadougou in the grasslands of landlocked Upper Volta.

In 1979, the price of a roundtrip ticket for the 195-mile Abidjan-Bouake portion of this line (5½ hours in each direction) was $21 (U.S.). The cost for a one-way first-class seat from Ouagadougou to Abidjan was then $70(U.S.). Children under 4 travel free. Half-fare for children 4-11. Children 12 and over must pay full fare.

The train's 38 first-class seats are in an air-conditioned section of the turbine-powered locomotive. The back of each seat is fitted with a pull-down meal tray. Food can be purchased near Abidjan's railstation. Sandwiches and beverages are sold in a section of the locomotive. During the trip, a waiter sells a full hot lunch. At several stops, women vendors sell meat snacks, stews and fresh fruit.

People from several different tribes make this trip. Many of the women passengers wear very high-heeled shoes, colorful long dresses and turban-style hats.

The ride is quite smooth due to the modern rails and good roadbed.

After passing through a heavily-foliaged rain forest, the train stops

En route to Ougadougou, the train goes through a heavily-foliaged rain forest before arriving at Dimbokro. After leaving Dimbokro, the train travels alongside a village of dirt streets and many thatched-roof huts. Women can be seen in that village walking with lumber, large packages and trays balanced on their heads.

Next seen on the route are large banana plantations and a jungle with bright flowers.

Adjacent to the Bouake railstation is a 66-room hotel built in 1975, with swimming pool and a restaurant that at least once featured French cuisine in a pleasant dining-room.

Abidjan - Bouake - Bobo Dioulasso - Ouagadougou 3105

Dep. Abidjan	7:53(1)	10:28(2)	12:38(1)	16:28(8)	17:24(3+4)
Arr. Bouake	13:54	15:24	19:00	21:32	24:00
Dep. Bouake	-0-	15:45(2)	-0-	-0-	0:25(3+5)
Arr. Bobo Dioulasso	-0-	0:40(2)	-0-	-0-	12:00(3+5)
Arr. Ougadougou	-0-	5:45	-0-	-0-	18:40
	*	*	*		
Dep. Ougadougou	6:00(1)	10:20(2)	-0-	-0-	13:30(3+7)
Dep. Bobo Dioulasso	13:03	15:40(2)	-0-	-0-	20:30(3+7)
Arr. Bouake	-0-	0:20	-0-	-0-	7:25
Dep. Bouake	-0-	0:35(2)	5:45(1)	7:00(6)	7:50(9)
Arr,. Abidjan	-0-	5:31	13:55	11:59	14:45

(1) Light refreshments. (2) Supplement charged. Air-conditioned train. Carries sleeping car. Meal service. (3) Carries sleeping car. Light refreshments. (4) Runs daily. Has air-conditioned first-class coach, except Wednesday and Saturday. (5) Runs daily. Has air-conditioned first-class coach, except Thursday and Sunday. (6) Supplement charged. Air-conditioned train. Meal service. Runs daily, except Sundays and holidays. Same train departs Bouake on Sundays and holidays at 16:00. (7) Runs daily. Has air-conditioned first-class coach, except Tuesday and Friday.

Carries sleeping car. (8)Supplement charged. Air-conditioned. Meal service. (9)Has air-conditioned first-class coach, except Wednesday and Saturday. Light refreshments. Plus other departures from Bouake at 9:05(1), 11:45(1) and 16:00(8).

Sights in Abidjan: Chief port and largest city in the Republic of Ivory Coast. See: The exhibits of traditional Ivorian art in the National Museum. The handicrafts at Plateau Market in the enormous Square Bressoles. The 2-story bazaar in Treichville, a suburb. The Adme market. The extravagant President's Palace. The wonderful tropical rain forest, Parc National du Banco, north of the city.

Sights in Bouake: Many mosques here. Good textile products for sale. You cannot miss seeing the brilliant-colored clothing worn by the crowds at the open-air market.

KENYA

Kenya's one train line is from Mombasa on the Indian Ocean, inland to Nairobi. From there, the rail route forks, one tine running to Kisumu at Lake Victoria and a second tine going to Tororo on the Kenya-Uganda border, and on into landlocked Uganda.

Children under 3 travel free. Half-fare for children 3-15. Children 16 and over must pay full fare.

Passengers have a view of Tsavo National Park, teeming with African game. After Nairobi, there are extraordinary views of flamingos and of tea and coffee plantations.

Mombasa - Nairobi - Kisumu 3275

Dep. Mombasa	17:00	19:00(4)	Dep. Kisumu	17:30(1)	18:30(5)
Arr. Nairobi	7:50(2)	8:15(2)	Arr. Nairobi	5:30(2)	7:30(2)
Change trains.			Change trains.		
Dep. Nairobi	17:30(1)	18:00(5)	Dep. Nairobi	17:00	19:00(4)
Arr. Kisumu	6:15(3)	8:00(3)	Arr. Mombasa	7:20(6)	8:00(6)

(1)Runs when required. (2)Day 2. (3)Day 3 after departing Mombasa. (4)Carries sleeping car. Meal service. (5)Light refreshments. (6)Day 3 after departing Kisumu.

Sights in Mombasa: The city sits on an offshore island, linked to the mainland by causeway, bridge and ferry. Mombasa was founded by Arab traders in the 11th century and has been an important seaport since then.

See the porcelain and other artifacts in the museum at the 2-acre, 16th century Fort Jesus. The silver door at Lord Shiva Temple. The Moorish-style Anglican Memorial Cathedral, with its silver roof. The exhibit of elephant tusks, hippopotamus teeth and rhinoceros horns in the Game Department Ivory Room, and the semi-annual auctions there.

The stalls of ivory carvers, perfumemakers, goldsmiths, spice merchants and silk dealers in the winding, narrow streets of Old Town. The 16th century Manadhara/Mandhry Mosque. Sheikh Jundani Mosque. The 4 enormous sheet-metal elephant tusks forming an arch over Kilindini Road, the main street. Kilindini Mosque. Take a cruise of Kilindini Harbor.

Sights in Nairobi: This city is almost on the equator. However, it is one mile high, making for temperate climate. See the treasures of Kenya's past and the exhibits of a vast number of birds, insects, mammals, fish, musical instruments, ornaments and tribal weapons in the National Museum of Kenya, a 15-minute walk from the center of Nairobi, open daily 9:30-18:00.

Across the street from it is a large assortment of deadly serpents in the museum at Nairobi Snake Park, also open daily 9:30-18:00. Visit the Sorsbie Art Gallery. Jeevanjee Gardens.

See the trees and flowering plants in the 100-acre Arboretum. Tribal dances performed 14:30-16:00 weekdays and 15:30-17:30 weekends, as well as tribal jewelry, baskets and 16 replicas of tribal villages at the Bomas of Kenya cultural center. Near it, the 44-square-mile Nairobi Game Park. A fantastic collection of African railway relics at the Railway Museum, a 5-minute walk from the railstation.

African and Western contemporary art at Paa-ya-Paa Gallery. The fruit, vegetable, flower and curio stalls in Municipal Market. Jamia Mosque. The African exhibits at McMillan Memorial Library. The fascinating rust-red and white International House.

The tapestries, murals, tribal shields and the conference table made from 33 kinds of Kenya wood, in the National Assembly. The Tuesday morning coffee auction at Kahawa ("coffee")House. City Nurseries, with its enormous number of different species of bougainvillaea.

Mombasa - Nairobi - Nakuru - Eldoret - Tororo - Kampala 3275 + 3286

Carries sleeping cars and has meal service Mombasa-Nairobi and vice versa. Light refreshments are available Nairobi-Kampala and vice versa. The first-class sleeping car was very good quality in 1979. Third-class cars (made in Sweden) had comfortable, padded seats.

Dep. Mombasa	19:00(1)	Dep. Kampala	16:00(5)
Arr. Nairobi	8:15(2)	Arr. Tororo	22:50(3)
Dep. Nairobi	9:30	Dep. Malaba	16:00(1+2)
Dep. Nakuru	15:10	Dep. Eldoret	21:00
Dep. Eldoret	22:28	Dep. Nakuru	3:35(4)
Arr. Malaba	2:50(3+4)	Arr. Nairobi	8:45(4)
Dep. Tororo	6:00(4+5)	Dep. Nairobi	19:00(4)
Arr. Kampala	12:55(4)	Arr. Mombasa	8:00(6)

(1)Carries sleeping car. Has meal service Nairobi-Malaba and v.v. (2)Day 2. (3)Travel 14km by road Tororo-Malaba and v.v. (4)Day 3. (5)Daily, except Monday. (6)Day 4.

Sights in Nakuru: The pelicans on the inland saline Lake Nakuru. Lake Nakuru National Park.

Sights in Eldoret: The temperate climate here is due to the 6,800-foot altitude, which attracted many European settlers in the period this was an English colony.

LESOTHO

There are no passenger trains in Lesotho.

LIBERIA

There are no passenger trains in Liberia.

LIBYA

There are no passenger trains in Libya.

MADAGASCAR

There are 3 short rail lines in north Madagascar: Antananarivo-Moramanga-Tamatave, Moramanga to Ambatosoratra, and Antananarivo to Antsirabe. (Antananarivo is also called Tananarive.)

The southern train route is Finanarantsoa to Manakara.

Children under 4 travel free. Half-fare for children 4-6. Children 7 and over must pay full fare.

Antananarivo - Moramanga - Tamatave 3330

Dep. Antananarivo	6:30(1)	Dep. Tamatave	11:35(1)		
Dep. Moramanga	10:44	Arr. Moramanga	19:30		
Arr. Tamatave	19:00	Change trains.			
		Dep. Moramanga	10:09(2)	14:44(2)	
		Arr. Antananarivo	14:26	19:05	

(1) Air-conditioned in first-class. (2) Day 2.

Sights in Antananarivo: Malagsay's capital. See the 19th century towered palaces of the Imerina kings on the royal estate, above the city. The exhibit of Malagsay culture and archaeology in The Organisation pour la Recherche Scientifique et Technique. The collection of lemurs and other Malagsay animals in the Zoo.

The stupendous Friday outdoor market (called Zoma), on Independence Avenue. Thousands of booths and "blanket shops" offering leather goods, semiprecious stones, woven baskets, etc. This is the place to flex your bargaining muscles. Most items in this market are intended to sell for half the asking price, and buyers are expected to start bidding below that figure.

Sights in Tamatave: This is the country's chief seaport, on the Indian Ocean. Stroll down tree-lined Avenue Poincare.

Moramanga - Ambatosoratra
3330

All of these trains are air-conditioned in first-class.

Dep. Moramanga	11:00	14:53
Arr. Ambatosoratra	16:20	20:24

* * *

Dep. Ambatosoratra	3:40	8:30
Arr. Moramanga	9:17	14:06

Sights in Ambatosoratra: Lake Alaotra.

Antananarivo - Antsirabe 3330

This is a very scenic 92-mile ride to 4,000-foot high Antsirabe. All of these trains are air-conditioned in first-class.

Dep. Antananarivo	5:20	10:55	17:30
Arr. Antsirabe	9:17	14:45	21:22
	*	*	*
Dep. Antsirabe	4:50	12:00	17:06
Arr. Antananarivo	8:28	16:00	21:00

Sights in Antsirabe: This is a thermal springs resort, situated under 8,674-foot high Mt. Tsiafajavona, the top of the Ankaratra volcanic mass.

Fianarantsoa - Ranomena - Manakara

3335

Dep. Fianarantsoa	7:00	13:52(1)	17:20(2)
Arr. Ranomena	8:01	14:53	19:17
Arr. Manakara	11:44	18:37	-0-
	*	*	*
Dep. Manakara	-0-	6:41(4)	13:30
Dep. Ranomena	5:40(3)	11:05	17:58
Arr. Fianarantsoa	6:20	12:10	19:03

(1)Runs Tuesday, Thursday and Saturday. (2)Monday-Friday, except holidays. (3)Daily, except Sundays and holidays. (4)Runs Monday, Wednesday and Friday.

MALAWI

Landlocked Malawi's rail system consists of 2 routes that start at Chipoka on Lake Malawi. The first goes east, across Mozambique, to Nacala on the Indian Ocean. The other runs south through central Mozambique, ending at Beira, another Indian Ocean seaport.

Children under 3 travel free. Half-fare for children 3-13. Children 14 and over must pay full fare.

Chipoka - Nkaya - Nacala

3384
Dep.
Chipoka 6:15(1)
Arr.
Nkaya 12:40
Change trains.
3376
Dep.
Nkaya 9:26(2)
Arr. Entre Lagos 12:00
Change trains.

3345
Dep.
Entre Lagos 21:30(3)
Arr. Cuamba 0:41
Change trains.

Dep. Cuamba	6:00(4)	16:15(5+7)	17:00(6+7)
Arr. Nampula	18:23	3:36	5:21
Change trains.			
Dep. Nampula	-0-	4:00(8)	16:00
Arr. Nacala	-0-	11:58	23:58

(1) Second and third-class space on Thursday and Sunday. Only third-class space the other days of the week. (2) Tuesday and Friday. (3) Third-class only. (4) Runs Thursday. (5) Runs Monday. (6) Runs Wednesday and Saturday. (7) Carries sleeping car. (8) Daily.

Chipoka - Blantyre - Limbe - Sena - Beira

3384	
Dep. Chipoka	6:15(1)
Dep. Blantyre	16:55
Arr. Limbe	17:30
Change trains.	
Dep. Limbe	6:10(2+3)
Arr. V.N. Fronteira	15:50(3)
Change trains.	

3384	
Dep. V.N. Fronteira	13:20(2+4)
Arr. Sena	15:38(4)
Change trains.	
3350	
Dep. Sena	18:35(4+5)
Arr. Beira	7:09

(1) Third-class only, except Thursday and Sunday, when train also has second-class. (2) Third-class only. (3) Day 2. (4) Day 3. (5) Runs Wednesday, Friday and Sunday. Carries first-class sleeping car. Also has second and third-class coach car. (6) Day 4.

Sights in Blantyre: The Museum of Malawi. Jubilee Gardens. Rangely Gardens.

MALI

The 2 rail lines in landlocked Mali are from its capital, Bamako, east to Sikasso and west to Kidira on the Mali-Senegal border (and then on to Dakar). Children under 3 travel free. Half-fare for children 3-9. Children 10 and over must pay full fare.

Bamako - Sikasso 2758

Dep. Bamako	N/A(1)	Dep. Sikasso	N/A(1)
Arr. Sikasso	N/A(1)	Arr. Bamako	N/A(1)

(1)Time not available in 1981.

Bamako - Kayes - Kidira - Dakar 2760

Dep. Bamako	8:00(1+2)	Dep. Dakar	12:00(1+3)
Dep. Kayes	19:10	Dep. Kidira	4:10 Day 2
Arr. Kidira	21:10	Dep. Kayes	7:35
Arr. Dakar	13:17 Day 2	Arr. Bamako	18:15

(1)Runs Wednesday and Saturday. (2)Carries sleeping car. Meal service. (3)Runs Tuesday and Friday.

Sights in Bamako: This city is on the Niger River. See: The fine display of prehistoric-to-modern exhibits in the National Museum. The handicraft (weaving, jewelry, ironwork, sculpture, leatherwork) in Maison des Artisans (Artisans' House). The interesting marketplaces. The excellent Zoo. The Botanical Gardens. Nearby, the forests at Lake Mandingues, La Boule National Game Reserve, Lake Ouegna, the Korounkorokale Grottoes, Oyako Waterfalls.

MAURITANIA

The only passenger rail service in Mauritania is a second-class, limited facility on an overnight iron-ore freight train that runs the 392 miles between Nouadhibou, a West African Atlantic fishing and freight port, and Zouerate, a mining town.

Nouadhibou - Zouerate 2800

Dep. Nouadhibou	15:00	18:20	Dep. Zouerate	12:55	16:55
Arr. Zouerate	5:18	9:04	Arr. Nouadhibou	6:03	10:00

MAURITIUS

There are no passenger trains in Mauritius.

MOROCCO

Moroccan trains are all standard-gauge. A substantial supplement is charged for air-conditioned trains. Sleeping cars are first-class and have single and double compartments. The country's 3 classes of trains are: first-class, second-class and economy. Children under 4 travel free. Half-fare for children 4-11. Children 12 and over must pay full fare.

Its rail system runs east from Marrakech to Casablanca, Rabat and then forks at Sidi Kacem, one tine going to Tangier, the other to Oujda (and on to Algeria).

Tangier

Excellent beaches. Extensive night life. See: Grand Socco, the colorful square in the Old Town, and the market stalls by walking through the twisting alleys to the Petit Socco.

Marrakech

Popular Winter resort. Good skiing at the nearby 8,000-foot Atlas Mountains. This area is a vast 30,000-acre date palm grove. See: Africa's most famous mosque: the 12th century Koutoubia, with its pale green 220-foot high minaret and the thrilling voice of its muezzin. The 16th century Sa'di Mausoleum. The 18th century Dar el-Beida Palace.

The Moorish gardens at the 19th century Bahia Palace. Marvelous fountains: El Mouasine and Eshrob ou Shouf. The fantastic scenes (dancers, acrobats, musicians, snake charmers, costumed water boys) in the tremendous square, Place Djemaa el-F'na. The gardens of the Hotel Mamounia. The casino. The olive orchards of the walled 1,000-acre Agdal gardens and the Menara gardens, at the edge of which the Sahara Desert begins.

The costumes of the mountain and desert people, on a shopping visit. The green and blue tiles on the walls of the central court of the 16th century Medersa of Ben Yussef. The monumental palace, El-Badi, with its small museum and nesting storks. Take a ride around the Old City in a horse-drawn carriage.

Casablanca

Morocco's major seaport. See: The stained-glass at the white Cathedral of the Sacre Coeur. The gardens in the Park of the Arab League. Busy Muhammad V Square. The Municipal College of Fine Arts. Many good beaches.

Rabat

This has been a military post since the 12th century. There are many splendid gardens here: Belvedere, Essai, Udayia, Triangle de Vue. See: The Kasbah. The Museum of Moroccan Art. Tour Hassan, largest Arabian minaret, once part of a now ruined mosque. The collection of Moroccan art in the King Muhammad V Memorial, and the view from its roof.

The Old Town. G'Naoua, the old fort. The Royal Palace, built in the 1950's. The Friday procession of the king, from his palace to Djamaa Abel Fez Mosque. Fine work is done here in carpets, blankets and leather handicrafts.

Nearby, the Roman ruins at Sala Colonia. The 12th century Bab ar-Rouah (Gate of the Wind) and the Archaeological Museum.

Meknes

Founded in the 10th century. See: The 25 miles of 17th century walls that circle the city. The heavily decorated gate, Bab el Mansour. The large Royal Palace. Many big gardens, irrigated by a 10-acre artificial lake, and several other large artificial lakes here. The shops with outstanding rugs.

The exhibit of handicrafts at Dar Jamai, the art museum. The bronze doors of Bou Inania Medersa (school for studying the Koran). Nearby, the ruins of the Roman Volubilis.

Fez

Founded in the 8th century. See: The hundreds of columns in Karaouine Mosque. Dar Batha Museum. The fascinating gate of Andalusian Mosque. The Bon Jelud gardens. Karaouine University. Qarawiyin Mosque, oldest in North Africa, housing a 9th century university and the tomb of Idris II. The Royal Palace and the multi-colored minaret on the Great Mosque, both in the 13th century Fes Jalid complex.

Nearby, the olive groves. The extremely high dam, Bin el Widane.

Marrakech - Casablanca - Rabat - Meknes - Fez - Oujda - Algiers

2510				
Dep. Marrakech	0:15	7:25	17:25(1+2)	
Arr. Casablanca (Voy.)	5:47	11:32	21:07	
Arr. Casablanca (Port)	6:10	11:48	21:28	
Change trains.				
2502				
Dep. Casablanca (Port)	6:33(2+3)	12:20(1+2)	16:35(1+2+8)	
Dep. Rabat (Ville)	8:00(2)	13:48(1+2)	17:46(1+2)	
Dep. Meknes	11:07(2)	17:12(1+2)	21:00(1+2)	
Arr. Fez	11:59	18:07(1+2)	21:51	
Arr. Oujda	-0-	23:59	-0-	
Change trains. Set your watch forward one hour.				
2525				
Dep. Oujda	N/A(6)	N/A(6)		
Arr. Maghnia	N/A(6)	N/A(6)		
Dep. Maghnia	5:45	13:22		
Arr. Oued Tlelat	9:10	16:51		
Change trains.				
2530				
Dep. Oued Tlelat	7:35(7)	12:40(7)	17:45(7)	21:50(2+5)
Arr. Algiers	12:34	17:36	22:45	6:22

(1) Supplement charged. Air-conditioned. (2) Light refreshments. (3) Departs from Cacablanca's Voyageurs station. (4) Carries sleeping car. Also has couchettes. Meal service. (5) Has couchettes. Meal service. (6) Service "temporarily" suspended in 1981. (7) Meal service. (8) Plus other departures from Casablanca (Port) at 20:32(4) arriving Oujda at 7:31, and at 21:53(3+5) arriving Oujda at 9:15.

Algiers - Oujda - Fez - Meknes - Rabat - Casablanca - Marrakech

2530				
Dep. Algiers	7:25(1)	12:10(1)	17:45(1)	21:30(2)
Arr. Oued Tlelat	12:20	17:03	22:36	5:26
Change trains.				
2525				
Dep. Oued Tlelat	-0-	17:30	-0-	7:16
Arr. Maghnia	-0-	21:02	-0-	10:51
Dep. Maghnia	-0-	N/A(3)	-0-	N/A(3)
Arr. Oujda	-0-	N/A(3)	-0-	N/A(3)
Change trains,. Set your watch back one hour.				
2502				
Dep. Oujda	12:13(4)	18:20(2)	21:33(6)	
Dep. Fez	18:20(4)	0:05(2)	3:14(6)	
Dep. Meknes	19:13(4)	1:02(2)	4:11(6)	
Dep. Rabat (Ville)	22:23(4)	4:40(2)	7:05(6)	
Arr. Casablanca (Port)	23:47	6:25(5)	8:27	
Change trains.				
2510				
Dep. Casablanca (Port)	0:20	-0-	8:50(4)	-0-
Dep. Casablanca (Voy.)	0:45	-0-	9:08(4)	18:08
Arr. Marrakech	5:58	-0-	12:48	22:11

(1) Meal service. (2) Has couchettes. Light refreshments or meal service. (3) Service "temporarily" suspended in 1981. (4) Air-conditioned in first and second-class at extra charge. Light refreshments. (5) Arrives at Casablanca's Voyageurs station. (6) Carries sleeping car. Also has couchettes. Meal service.

Casablanca - Rabat - Tangier 2502

Dep. Casablanca (Port)	7:37(1+2)	12:20(1+3)	21:53(4+5)
Dep. Rabat	8:46(1+2)	13:48(1+3)	23:22(4)
Arr. Tangier	13:30	20:41	6:05

* * *

Dep. Tangier	6:10(1+3)	15:50(1+2)	21:00(4)
Dep. Rabat	11:33(1+3)	20:48(1+2)	4:40(4)
Arr. Casablanca (Port)	12:45	22:02	6:25(5)

(1) Air-conditioned. Supplement charged. (2) Meal service. (3) Light refreshments. (4) Has couchettes. Meal service. (5) Departs/Arrives Casablanca's Voyageurs station.

MOZAMBIQUE

This country's 3 major rail terminals are its Indian Ocean seaports: Nacala, Beira and Maputo.

Children under 3 travel free. Half-fare for children 3-9. Children 10 and over must pay full fare.

Nacala - Nkaya - Chipoka

3345		
Dep. Nacala	4:00	15:20
Arr. Nampula	12:04	22:57
Change trains.		
Dep. Nampula	15:30(1+3)	17:10(2+3)
Arr. Cuamba	3:43	3:38
Change trains.		
Dep. Cuamba	16:00(4)	-0-
Arr. Entre Lagos	18:18	-0-
Change trains.		
3376		
Dep. Entre Lagos	12:35(5)	15:00(4)
Arr. Nkaya	15:06	22:30
Change trains.		
3384		
Dep. Nkaya	9:00(4+6)	-0-
Arr. Chipoka	15:04	-0-

(1)Runs Monday, Wednesday and Saturday. (2)Runs Thursday. (3)Carries sleeping car. (4)Third-class only. (5)Runs Tuesday and Friday. (6)Has both second and third-class coach cars on Tuesday and Friday.

Beira - Sena - Limbe - Blantyre - Chipoka

3350	
Dep. Beira	20:00(1)
Arr. Sena	10:23(2)
Change trains.	
3384	
Dep. Sena	10:45(2+4)
Arr. V.N. Fronteira	12:46(2)
Change trains.	
3384	
Dep. V.N. Fronteira	8:10(3+4)
Arr. Limbe	19:34(3)
Change trains.	
Dep. Limbe	4:30(5+6)
Arr. Blantyre	5:05(6)
Arr. Chipoka	15:04(6)

(1)Runs Monday, Wednesday and Friday. Carries first-class sleeping car. Also has second and third-class coach cars. (2)Day 2. (3)Day 3. (4)Third-class only. (5)Third-class daily. Also has second-class coach on Tuesday and Friday. (6)Day 4.

Sights in Beira: The ultra-modern railstation.

Beira - Umtali - Salisbury

3350		3450	
Dep. Beira	7:30	Dep. Umtali	21:00
Arr. Umtali	N/A(1)	Arr. Salisbury	6:00
Change trains.			

(1)Arrive Machipanda (the border) at 20:33. Rail service between Machipanda and Umtali has been suspended since 1977. Travel this 12km trip by taxi or bus.

Maputo - Chicualacuala - Somabula - Salisbury

3355		3455	
Dep. Maputo	6:10(1)	Dep. Somabula	23:36(4)
Arr. Chicualacuala	21:59	Arr. Salisbury	7:00
Change trains.			
3452			
Dep. Chicualacuala	N/A(2)		
Dep. Mbizi	17:08(3)		
Arr. Somabula	4:55		
Change trains.			

(1)Runs Monday, Wednesday and Friday. Second and third-class only. (2)Service was suspended in 1981. Go by road 5km to Mbizi. (3)Third and fourth-class only. (4)Daily.

Maputo - Pretoria - Johannesburg

Both of these trains require reservation.

3510			
Dep. Maputo	**16:35**	Dep. Johannesburg	18:15
Arr. Pretoria	7:45 Day 2	Dep. Pretoria	19:53
Arr. Johannesburg	9:30	Arr. Maputo	11:05 Day 2

NIGER

There are no passenger trains in Niger.

NIGERIA

The 2 classes on Nigerian trains are first and third. Third-class has padded leather seats. Children under 3 travel free. Half-fare for children 4-13. Children 14 and over must pay full fare.

Lagos - Ibadan - Ilorin - Minna - Kaduna - Kano 3005

All of these trains have meal service.

Dep. Lagos (Term.)	8:30	11:00(2)
Dep. Ibadan	13:52	16:42(2)
Dep. Llorin	19:50	22:21(2)
Dep. Minna	6:00(1)	8:25(1+3)
Arr. Kaduna	9:43(1)	12:02(1+3)
Arr. Kano	-0-	17:45(1+3)

* * *

Dep. Kano	8:00(4)	-0-
Dep. Kaduna	13:05(4)	18:30
Dep. Minna	17:00(4)	22:20
Dep. Llorin	2:54(1+5)	8:17(1)
Dep. Ibadan	8:32(1+5)	13:47(1)
Arr. Lagos (Term.)	14:45(1)	20:00(1)

(1)Day 2. (2)Runs daily. Has air-conditioned first-class coach on Wednesday, Friday and Sunday. (3)Runs daily. Has air-conditioned first-class coach on Thursday, Saturday and Monday. (4)Runs daily. Has air-conditioned first-class coach on Monday, Tuesday and Friday. (5)Runs daily. Has air-conditioned first-class coach on Tuesday, Wednesday and Saturday.

Sights in Lagos: Capital of Nigeria. Second largest city in tropical Africa (after Kinshasa, Zaire). Settled more than 300 years ago. It is a complex of lagoons, sandbars and islands. The islands are: Iddo, Lagos, Ikoyi and Victoria. They are connected to each other and to the mainland by bridges. In a population of over 1,000,000 there are about 10,000 who are European, American and Asian.

See: The large harbor. The Zoo. The Iga Idungaran Palace, occupying 10 acres. The Obun Edo and Ebute Ero markets. The exhibit of

Nigerian arts and crafts at the National Museum. Holy Qur'an Mosque. The Government Handicraft Center. The contemporary and historic sculptures in the Orhoghua Art Gallery. The Benin art in the Unikon Museum.

Sights in **Ibadan:** Many streams flow through this ancient city. There are teak forest reserves on the outskirts. Much weaving and pottery here. See: Iba Market. The 130-acre Agodi Garden. Four zoological and botanical gardens. The Central Mosque. Ansar ad-Din Mosque.

Sights in **Ilorin:** The Moorish-style concrete palace and the canopied Mallim Alimi Well, both near the Central Market. Traditional single-story, red-mud houses. The ancient mud wall. Much dyeing of cotton cloth with local indigo, weaving, pottery and leathergoods here. Nearby, the Borgu Game Reserve. There are roads from Ilorin to Ogbomosho, Kabba, Jebba and Kaiama.

Sights in **Minna:** This is a major collecting point for peanuts, cotton, indigo, yams, tobacco, kola nuts, goats and chickens. Much raffia mats and baskets, brassware, pottery and woven and dyed cloth for sale here.

Sights in **Kaduna:** The name of the city is the word for "crocodile". See: The stately Lugard Hall, in Muslim architecture, housing the state legislature. The Geological Survey of Nigeria headquarters. Much manufacturing here: explosives, furniture, soft drinks (kola nut are collected in this area).

Sights in **Kano:** This city has been a tribal capital since the 11th century. A camel caravan center for many centuries. Kano was the greatest commercial power in West Africa in the 1820's, its leather and cotton goods shipped north, across the Sahara, by camel caravan to Morocco, Algeria and Tunisia where its red goatskin products were called "morocco leather".

The Encyclopedia Britannica carries a photo of tall pyramids built from peanuts harvested here. Kano is divided into 100 hamlets, each having its own mosque.

See: The Kurmi Market and Juma'at Mosque, both built in the 15th century. The 15th century Palace. Next to it, the Central Mosque (built in 1951), Nigeria's largest mosque. The collection of Hausa and Fulani artifacts at the museum in Gidan Makama ("Makama's House").

Lagos - Kafanchan - Port Harcourt

3002			3007		
Dep. Lagos	8:30(1)		Dep. Port Harcourt	11:00(1)	
Arr. Kafanchan	15:38	Day 2	Arr. Kafanchan	8:55	Day 2
Change trains.			Change trains.		
3007			3002		
Dep. Kafanchan	22:15(1+2)	Day 2	Dep. Kafanchan	11:50(1)	Day 2
Arr. Port Harcourt	20:45	Day 3	Arr. Lagos	20:00	Day 3

(1) Runs daily. Meal service. (2) Plus another departure from Kafanchan at 19:30 on Tuesday, Thursday, Friday and Sunday.

Sights in Port Harcourt: Nigeria's second largest port. Much manufacturing here: cigarettes, tires, paper. Also offshore oil drilling.

Lagos - Maiduguri 3002

Both of these trains have meal service.

Dep. Lagos (Iddo)	8:00(1)		Dep. Maiduguri	16:30(2)	
Arr. Maiduguri	11:30	Day 3	Arr. Lagos (Iddo)	20:00	Day 3

(1) Runs Monday, Tuesday, Thursday and Saturday. (2) Runs Monday, Wednesday, Thursday and Saturday.

Sights in Maiduguri: This city is on the historic pilgrimage path from Senegal to Mecca and is a major gathering center for many agricultural products. See: The Palace. The Mosque. The very large Monday market and the procession of nomads bringing crocodile skins, cattle hides, goats and sheep as well as finished leather products to the market by donkey and oxen. Chewing-gum and peanut butter are manufactured here, and the tall pyramids of bagged peanuts is something to see.

REUNION

The one rail line on this tiny Indian Ocean island is the 38-mile route along its picturesque seacoast, from Pointe des Galets to St. Benoit. Reunion advised Thomas Cook in 1978 that this service no longer operates regularly.

RWANDA

There are no passenger trains in Rwanda.

SENEGAL

Senegal's 2 rail lines are the short ride from Dakar to St. Louis and the long route from Dakar to Kidira and on to Bamako in landlocked Mali. Children under 3 travel free. Half-fare for children 3-9. Children 10 and over must pay full fare.

Dakar

A major seaport. Capital of Senegal. There are good museums here on the sea, ethnography and archaeology. Also see: The Zoo. The outstanding uniforms of the sentries at the President's Palace. The great Mosque. The beautiful Church of Our Lady of Fatima in the Cathedral du Souvenir Africain. The collection of African art in the National Museum. The array of gold, silver, exotic musical instruments, produce, spices, jewelry and embroidered African garments sewn to order in a few minutes, all at the Sandaga central market. Nearby, the picturesque fishing village, Cayar.

Take the 20-minute ferry ride to Goree Island for a tour of the Slave House Museum. Goree was once the main port for the slave trade. You can see the cells where chained slaves were held before they were moved onto crowded ships.

Dakar - St. Louis 2812

Dep. Dakar	7:25(1)	13:40	Dep. St. Louis	6:20	14:30(1)
Arr. St. Louis	12:00	18:37	Arr. Dakar	11:02	19:10

(1) Runs Monday, Wednesday and Friday.

Dakar - Kidira - Bamako 2815

Dep. Dakar	12:00(1+3)	Dep. Bamako	8:10(2+3)
Arr. Kidira	3:10(4)	Dep. Kidira	22:20
Arr. Bamako	18:15(4)	Arr. Dakar	13:17(4)

(1)Runs Tuesday and Friday. (2)Runs Wednesday and Saturday. (3)Carries sleeping car. Meal service. (4)Day 2.

SIERRA LEONE

There are no passenger trains in Sierra Leone.

SOMALI REPUBLIC

There are no passenger trains in Somali Republic.

SOUTH AFRICA

Summer climate here is November to mid-April. The peak Summer holiday period is December 12 to January 30.

All rail lines in South Africa are narrow-gauge (3′6″) because so much track is over mountain terrain. However, carriages are only slightly narrower than those used on British, European and North American railways.

Reservations can be made up to 6 months in advance, with 2 exceptions: up to 3 months for "Drakensberg" (Johannesburg-Durban), up to 11 months for "Blue Train" (Pretoria-Johannesburg-Cape Town).

First-class coupes carry 2 passengers. First-class compartments carry 4. Second-class coupes carry 3, and second-class compartments accommodate 6. By paying a surcharge, one person can reserve a first-class coupe, and first-class compartments can be reserved for the use of 2 or 3 people.

On night trains, first-class compartments convert to 4 couchette berths and second-class compartments to 6 couchette berths. There is a charge for sterilized bedding, packed in a sealed canvas bag. The seal is broken in the passenger's presence, when the attendant makes up the berth.

Travel is free for children under 7 years old accompanied by an adult who has paid the full advertised ticket price. Half-fare for children under 12 either who are traveling alone or when with an adult who has paid a reduced ticket price. Children 12 and over must pay the full price.

Holders of first-class tickets are permitted up to 100 pounds of free luggage. Passengers arriving by boat may have their baggage collected at the dock and either shipped from there by train to any destination, or delivered to a local address, or placed in the railstation check-room to be collected later.

A similar service is offered for taking luggage from a local address to a railstation or dock. Luggage also can be sent on in advance to await one's arrival at a destination. There is free porterage at all main railstations.

An inexpensive, large timetable published by South African Railways is very useful, containing altitudes, distances and much other interesting information.

The country's extensive rail system connects inland Johannesburg with 5 seaports: Durban, East London, Port Elizabeth, Mossel Bay and Cape Town. There is train service from South Africa to all of the 4 countries adjacent to it: Mozambique, Rhodesia, Botswana and South West Africa (Namibia).

Johannesburg

There are many museums here on archaeology, costumes, transportation, Judaica, geology, medicine and South African history.

See the collection of European and South African paintings at the Art Gallery. The Mosque. The Money Museum. The Zoo. Jan Smuts House. Nearby, the tour of Simmer and Jack gold mine.

Pretoria - Johannesburg - Pietermaritzburg - Durban 3525

Dep. Pretoria	8:35(1)	-0-	17:40	-0-	18:40(6)
Dep. Johannesburg	10:15	17:45(2)	18:30(3)	18:05(4)	20:00(6)
Dep. Pietermaritzburg	4:00	5:58(2)	6:28(3)	7:31(5)	8:50(6)
Arr. Durban	7:00	8:45	9:15	10:15	11:45
	*	*	*		
Dep. Durban	11:45	15:30(6)	17:45(7)	18:00(3)	20:00(4)
Dep. Pietermaritzburg	14:38	18:17(6)	20:04(7)	20:18(3)	22:49(4)
Arr. Johannesburg	5:50	6:20	7:35	8:30(3)	16:00
Arr. Pretoria	6:34	-0-	-0-	9:33	-0-

(1)Runs Mon., Wed., Fri. and Sat. (2)Reservation required. Supplement charged. Air-conditioned. Runs only on Fri. (only on Sat. from Pietermaritzburg). Carries only first-class sleeping car and first-class coach cars. Meal service. (3)Meal service. (4)Runs Tues., Thurs., Fri. and Sun. (5)Runs Mon., Wed., Fri. and Sat. (6)Reservation required. Carries only second and third-class coach cars. (7)Reservation required. Supplement charged. Runs only on Sunday. Carries only first-class sleeping car and first-class coach cars. Meal service.

Sights in Pretoria: The streets lined with jacaranda trees. Paul Kruger's house. The National Cultural History and Open Air Museum. The sunken gardens at Venning Park. The National Zoological Gardens. The Voortrekker Monument.

Sights in Pietermaritzburg: Called "City of Flowers" for its many fine botanical gardens and parks. See the Voortrekker Museum. The Natal Museum. The model native village in nearby Mountain Rise. Many nearby mountain resorts and game preserves.

Sights in Durban: This is South Africa's largest port. See the Botanical Gardens. The Bantu Market. Snake Park. Japanese Water Gardens. The rose gardens in Jameson Park. The Oceanarium. The Indian Market. The nearby game and nature reserves.

Johannesburg - Bloemfontein - East London

			3550	
Dep. Johannesburg	-0-	-0-	14:00(3)	14:20(1+4)
Dep. Bloemfontein	0:15(1+2)	8:15	21:45(3)	22:40(1+4)
Arr. East London	16:15	6:20	12:35	13:40
	*	*	*	
Dep. East London	3:30(1+5)	11:15(6)	13:35(1+8)	21:25
Arr. Bloemfontein	19:59	2:21(7)	4:55(1+9)	17:10
Arr. Johannesburg	-0-	11:15	13:20	-0-

(1)Reservation required. Second and third-class only. (2)Runs Monday and Friday. (3)Reservation required. Meal service. Runs Tuesday, Thursday, Friday and Sunday all year, plus daily from mid-June to mid-July and from late November to early February. (4)Daily, except Saturday. Also on Saturday from early December to mid-January. (5)Runs Wednesday and Thursday. (6)Runs Monday, Wednesday, Friday and Sunday. Also daily from mid-June to mid-July and from late November to early February. Meal service. (7)Runs Tuesday, Thursday, Saturday and Monday. Also daily from mid-June to mid-July and from late November to early February. Meal service. (8)Daily, except Sunday. Also on Sunday from early December to mid-January. Light refreshments. (9)Daily, except Monday. Also on Monday from early December to mid-January. Light refreshments.

Sights in Bloemfontein: The beautiful 300-acre King's Park. The Franklin Game Reserve. Two astronomical observatories: Lamont-Hussey and Boyden Station. The enormous dinosaur and other fossils at the National Museum.

Sights in East London: The 80-acre Queen's Park. This seaport's Museum has a coelacanth, a primeval fish.

Johannesburg - Bloemfontein - Port Elizabeth

3550		3573	
Dep. Johannesburg	14:00(1+2)	Dep. Port Elizabeth	17:10(3+4)
Dep. Bloemfontein	22:25(1+2)	Arr. Noupoort	1:10
Arr. Noupoort	3:55	3550	
3573		Dep. Noupoort	1:35(3+5)
Dep. Noupoort	4:25(3+4)	Arr. Bloemfontein	7:23(3+5)
Arr. Port Elizabeth	13:10	Arr. Johannesburg	15:30

(1)Reservation required. (2)Runs daily from late November to early February. Runs Tuesday, Thursday, Friday and Sunday from early February to late November. (3)Runs daily from late November to early February and also from mid-June to mid-July. (4)Runs Wednesday,

Friday, Saturday and Monday from early February to mid-June and from mid-July to late November. (5)Runs Thurs., Sat., Sun. and Tues. from early February to mid-June and from mid-July to late November.

Sights in Port Elizabeth: Many fine parks, including St. George's Park. The oceanarium in Settler's Park Nature Reserve. Nearby, Addo Elephant National Park.

Port Elizabeth - Mossel Bay - Cape Town 3572

The most scenic train ride in South Africa, called "the Garden Route". This trip offers mountain and seashore scenery. Watch for thousands of ostriches near Oudtshoorn.

Dep. Port Elizabeth	18:40(1)	Dep. Cape Town	15:45(1)
Dep. Oudtshoorn	10:25 Day 2	Arr. Mossel Bay	8:40 Day 2
Dep. Mossel Bay	15:10	Dep. Oudtshoorn	14:15
Arr. Cape Town	8:40 Day 3	Arr. Port Elizabeth	6:15 Day 3

(1) Daily except Saturday (daily from early December to early January). Meal service.

Sights in Mossel Bay: A very nice seashore resort.

Sights in Cape Town: The Malay Quarter. The Municipal Botanic Garden, South African Library, Museum and National Gallery, all at what was once the garden of the East India Company. The Africana collection at both the Library of Parliament and the Castle. The Cultural History Museum. Koopmans de Wet House. Groote Kerk (the "Great Church"). See the marvelous coastal scenery, either by taking the bus tour along Chapman's Peak Drive or the cable car to the top of Table Mountain. Other bus tours go to the many wineries near Stellenbosch.

Pretoria - Johannesburg - Kimberley - Cape Town 3500 + 3570

This is the route of the wonderful, all first-class Blue Train, which provides 4 categories: Super-Luxury (a suite consisting of a bedroom with twin beds, private lounge and a bathroom with tub and toilet), Luxury (compartment with one or 3 berths, with its own bathroom having a tub and toilet), Semi-Luxury (compartment with one or 3 berths, private shower and toilet), and Standard (compartment with one or 2 berths that can be converted to 3 berths). There is only one Super-Luxury compartment. Passengers traveling in a Standard Compartment have use of a shower in the carriage.

Blue Train is so popular that advance seat reservations are nearly always necessary. Due to the heavy demand for travel on this train, space on it can be reserved as much as 11 months in advance of travel date.

Air-conditioning with individual controls. Electrically operated venetian blinds sealed between windows. Suites equipped with refrigerator, wine rack and FM radio reception. Double insulation and advanced construction techniques make this train vibrationless and noiseless. The seats are upholstered in leather.

The schedule provides daytime viewing in both directions of the scenic area between Touws River and Cape Town, during which the line descends or ascends 2,352 feet within one 36-mile section, into or out of De Doorns Valley.

Dep. Pretoria	8:35(1+2)	10:00(1+4)	19:18(5)	20:15(1+2)
Dep. Johannesburg	10:30(1+2)	11:30(1+4)	20:30(5)	22:00(1+2)
Arr. Kimberley	18:32(1+2)	18:46(1+4)	-0-	7:38(1+3)
Arr. Cape Town	14:30(3)	12:00(3)	8:30(3)	8:30(6)

* * *

Dep. Cape Town	9:30(1+2)	12:00(8)	21:00(1+2)
Dep. Kimberley	5:46(1+3+7)	5:19(3+8)	21:00(1+3+7)
Arr. Johannesburg	14:00(1+3+7)	12:30(3+8)	6:07(6)
Arr. Pretoria	15:57(3)	14:00(3)	8:02(6)

(1)Reservation required. Meal service. (2)Daily, except Monday and Wednesday. (3)Day 2. (4)Blue Train. Supplement charged. Air-conditioned. Meal service. Runs Monday all year. Also on Wednesday from mid-August to late April. Also on Friday from early November to late February. Carries only first-class sleeping cars and first-class coach cars. (5)Runs Tuesday, Thursday, Saturday and Sunday. Via Bloemfontein. Meal service. (6)Day 3. (7)Daily, except Tuesday and Thursday. (8)Blue Train. Supplement charged. Air-conditioned. Meal service. Runs Wednesday all year. Also on Monday from late August to early May. Also on Friday from early November to late February. Carries only first-class sleeping cars and first-class coach cars.

Sights in Kimberley: Many diamond mines in this area. See the collection of Bushman artifacts in both the Duggan-Cronin Bantu Gallery and in McGregor Memorial Museum.

Cape Town - Bitterfontein 3577

Dep. Cape Town	20:25(1)	Dep. Bitterfontein	13:45(2)
Arr. Bitterfontein	12:16	Arr. Cape Town	6:03

(1)Runs Tues., Thurs. and Sun. (2)Runs Mon., Wed. and Fri.

Johannesburg - Pretoria - Maputo 3510

The train route to Mozambique.

Dep. Johannesburg	6:45	16:45(1)	18:15
Arr. Pretoria	8:43	18:30	19:53
Arr. Maputo	-0-	-0-	11:05
	*	*	*
Dep. Maputo	-0-	-0-	16:35
Dep. Pretoria	18:10	6:32	7:49
Arr. Johannesburg	20:10	8:15(2)	9:30

(1) Departs at 16:30 on Sunday. (2) Arrives at 9:17 on Sunday.

Johannesburg - Salisbury

The train route through Botswana to Rhodesia.

3475		3455	
Dep. Johannesburg	12:30(1)	Dep. Bulawayo	20:00
Dep. Mafeking	21:00	Arr. Salisbury	7:00(2)
Arr. Bulawayo	14:10(2)		
Change trains.			

(1) Runs Thursday only. Reservation required. Meal service. (2) Day 2.

Johannesburg - De Aar - Windhoek 3570

Dep. Johannesburg	10:30(1)	11:30(2)	20:30(3)	22:00(4)
Arr. De Aar	22:41	22:16	14:05	13:24
Change trains.				
3600				
Dep. De Aar	3:00(5)	19:45(7)	20:20	-0-
Arr. Windhoek	8:25(6)	1:50(8)	6:45(8)	-0-

(1) Daily, except Monday and Wednesday. Reservation required. Meal service. (2) Blue Train. Reservation required. Supplement charged. Air-conditioned. Meal service. Runs Monday all year. Also on Wednesday from mid-August to late April. Also on Friday from early November to late February. Carries only first-class sleeping cars and first-class coach cars. (3) Runs Tues., Thurs., Sat. and Sun. Meal service. (4) Daily, except Mon. and Wed. Meal service. (5) Runs only. Wednesday. Meal service. (6) Day 2 from De Aar. (7) Runs only Friday. Meal service. (8) Day 3 from De Aar.

Cape Town - De Aar - Windhoek 3570

The other train route to South West Africa (Namibia).

Dep. Cape Town	9:30(1)	12:00(2+3)	18:00(4)	18:05(5+9+11)
Arr. De Aar	0:58	1:34	8:45	11:45
Change trains.				
3600				
Dep. De Aar	3:00(6)	19:45(8)	20:20	-0-
Arr. Windhoek	8:25(7)	1:50(9)	6:45	-0-

(1)Reservation required. Runs daily, except Mon. and Wed. Meal service. (2)Blue Train. Supplement charged. Air-conditioned. Meal service. First-class only. (3)Runs Wed. all year. Also on Mon. from late August to early May. Also on Fri. from early November to late February. (4)Runs Mon. and Fri. Reservation required. Meal service. (5)Third-class only. (6)Runs only Wed. Reservation required. Meal service. (7)Runs only Thurs. (8)Runs only Fri. Reservation required. Meal service. (9)Runs only Sun. (10)Daily. Has light refreshments only on Tues., Thurs. and Sun. (11)Plus other departures from Capetown at 18:15(10) and 21:00(1).

SOUTH WEST AFRICA (NAMIBIA)

This country's rail system consists of 3 principal lines: the inland north-south route from Otavi to Keetmanshoop (and on into South Africa), and 2 lines that run east from 3 Atlantic seaports until they connect with the Otavi-Keetmanshoop route.

The northern of these is the rail route from Walvis Bay and Swakopmund to Usakos. The southern path is from Luderitz to Keetmanshoop.

These services are run by South African Railways.

Otavi - Windhoek - Keetmanshoop - De Aar

3603			
Dep.Otavi	11:25(1+2)	-0-	-0-
Arr. Otjiwarongo	15:25	-0-	-0-
Change trains.			
Dep. Otjiwarongo	18:30(1)	-0-	-0-
Arr. Windhoek	8:00(3)	-0-	-0-
Change trains.			
3600			
Dep. Windhoek	7:30(4+5)	17:00(5+7)	20:45(9)
Dep. Keetmanshoop	17:35(4+5)	3:05(5+8)	8:45(5+6+9)
Arr. De Aar	12:15(6)	21:55(6)	8:25(10)
	*	*	*
Dep. De Aar	3:00(5+11)	19:45(4+5)	20:20(9)
Dep. Keetmanshoop	22:00(5+11)	14:50(4+5)	19:00(9+12)
Arr. Windhoek	8:25(12)	1:50(14)	6:45(14)
Change trains.			
3603			
Dep. Windhoek	19:10(1)	-0-	-0-
Arr. Otjiwarongo	8:00(6)	-0-	-0-
Change trains.			
Dep. Otjiwarongo	10:15(2+15)	-0-	-0-
Arr. Otavi	19:00(6)	-0-	-0-

(1)Runs Thurs., Fri. and Sun. (2)Third-class only. (3)Day 2 from Otavi. (4)Sat. only. (5)Meal service. (6)Day 2 from Windhoek. (7)Mon. only. (8)Tues. only. (9)Daily. (10)Day 3 from Windhoek. (11)Wed. only. (12)Day 2 from De Aar. (13)Fri. only. (14)Day 3 from De Aar. (15)Runs Mon., Fri. and Sat.

Sights in Windhoek: The capital of South West Africa (Namibia). Many hot springs in this area. Karakul (Persian lamb) graze here, and the furs are processed in this area. See the State Museum. The lovely gardens around Christus Church.

Walvis Bay - Swakopmund - Windhoek

3602

Dep. Walvis Bay	18:30	Dep. Windhoek	20:15
Dep. Swakopmund	19:40	Dep. Swakopmund	7:07 Day 2
Arr. Windhoek	6:15 Day 2	Arr. Walvis Bay	8:00 Day 2

Sights in Swakopmund: The government moves here from Windhoek, the capital, during the Summer (December and January) because it is cooler here than in Windhoek. This is South West Africa's principal seaside resort. Good fishing. See the exhibits of natural history, marine life and mineralogy in the Swakopmund Museum.

Luderitz - Keetmanshoop

3601

Dep. Luderitz	18:00 Fri. and Sun.	Dep. Keetmanshoop	17:40 Fri. and Sun.
Arr. Keetmanshoop	6:21 Sat. and Mon.	Arr. Luderitz	6:20 Sat. and Mon.

Sights in Luderitz: There is much diamond mining in this area. One cannot enter the prohibited area outside the town without a permit. Rock lobster fishing and processing is extensive here. See the small museum's collection of Bushman tools and other archaeological objects.

SUDAN

Sudan's rail system links Port Sudan on the Red Sea with the inland capital, Khartoum. From Haiya, there are 2 possible train routes to Khartoum. A northern one goes via Atbara, and a southern route runs via Kassala.

There is rail service north from Khartoum to Wadi Halfa and, from there, on to the Nile and to Cairo by a combination of boat and train. This is the only rail connection between Sudan and a country adjacent to it. A short spur from this route goes west to Karima.

Two lines run south from Khartoum, one to Ed Damazine and the other to Kosti (from which there is a slow, 11-day boat trip to Juba) and to Babanousa.

A short spur runs from Kosti northwest to El Obeid. Two spurs continue from Babanousa. One goes northwest to Nyala, another southwest to Wau.

Children under 3 travel free. Half-fare for children 3-11. Children 12 and over must pay full fare. When available, the air-conditioned first-class space is advisable. Routes in Sudan are very dusty.

Little vegetation is seen in Sudan. Grass fires engulf more than half the country every year.

Port Sudan - Khartoum
Via Atbara

2710

Dep.
Port Sudan 13:00(1) 18:00(3)
Arr. Khartoum 16:00(2) 17:45(2)

Dep. Khartoum 7:45(4) 11:15(5)
Arr.
Port Sudan 10:35(2) 10:35(2)

(1)Runs only Thursday. (2)Day 2. (3)Runs Wednesday and Saturday. Air-conditioned in first-class only on Wednesday. Carries sleeping car. Meal service. (4)Runs only Tuesday. Carries sleeping car. Meal service. (5)Runs Thursday and Sunday. Air-conditioned in first-class only on Sunday. Carries sleeping car. Meal service.

Sights in Khartoum: It is very hot here. The temperature reaches more than 100 degrees Fahrenheit every month and goes as high as 117 degrees. The city was founded by Egyptians as an army camp is 1824. See: The Republican Palace. The Sudan Museum. The Ethnographical Museum. The Natural History Museum. The Zoo, along the river. The meeting of the White Nile and Blue Nile, from the White Nile Bridge. Across the bridge is the sister town, Om Durman, with its fabulous Mosque Square that holds 100,000 people. The silver Khalifa's Mosque. The Mahdi-Khalifiana Museum.

Sights in Port Sudan: African Moslems stop here en route on their pilgrimage to Mecca. This is Sudan's principal port.

Port Sudan - Khartoum
Via Kassala

2710

Dep.
Port Sudan 13:00(1) 18:00(2)
Arr. Khartoum 8:45(3) 8:45(3)

Dep. Khartoum 13:30(4) 14:50(5)
Arr.
Port Sudan 9:05(3) 9:05(3)

(1) Runs Wednesday and Sunday. Carries sleeping car. Meal service. (2) Runs only Friday. Air-conditioned in first-class. (3) Day 3. (4) Runs Thursday and Sunday. Carries sleeping car. Meal service. (5) Runs only Tuesday. Air-conditioned in first-class.

Khartoum - Ed Damazine

Both of these trains carry sleeping cars.

2705

Dep. Khartoum	17:00	Mon. and Fri.
Arr. Ed Damazine	11:20	Tues. and Sat.

* * *

Dep. Ed Damazine	8:00	Wed. and Sun.
Arr. Khartoum	3:05	Thurs. and Mon.

Khartoum - Nyala

Both of these trains carry sleeping cars and have meal service.

2705			
Dep. Khartoum	10:30(1)	Dep. Nyala	10:00(2)
Arr. Nyala	13:25 Day 3	Arr. Khartoum	11:15 Day 3

(1)Runs Monday and Friday. Carries sleeping car. Meal service only on Monday. (2)Runs Tuesday and Saturday. Carries sleeping car. Meal service only on Saturday.

Khartoum - Waw 2705

Dep. Khartoum	10:30(1)	Dep. Waw	18:00(3)
Arr. Waw	21:00(2)	Arr. Khartoum	11:15(4)

(1)Runs Wednesday and Saturday. (2)Day 3. (3)Runs Monday and Friday. (4)Day 4.

Khartoum - Kosti - Juba

The Khartoum-Juba trip takes 11 days, the Juba-Khartoum trip 8 days. There are sleeping cars Khartoum-Kosti and v.v.

2705		2707	
Dep. Khartoum	13:30 Tues.	Dep. Juba	5:00 Fri.
Arr. Kosti	3:20 Wed.	Dep. Malakal	20:30 Mon.
Change to boat.		Arr. Kosti	7:00 Thur.
2707		Change to train.	
Dep. Kosti	10:00 Wed.	2705	
Dep. Malakal	16:05 Sat.	Dep. Kosti	17:50 Sat.
Arr. Juba	5:00 Fri.	Arr. Khartoum	5:10 Sun.

Wadi Halfa - Khartoum 2700

This train carries sleeping cars and has meal service.

Dep. Wadi Halfa	16:40(1)	Arr. Khartoum	16:45 Day 2

(1) Runs Wednesday and Saturday. Air-conditioned in first-class on Saturdays.

Sights in Wadi Halfa: This area was the center of archaeological activities in the 1970's to save Egyptian monuments from being covered by the Aswan High Dam reservoir. Egyptian ruins from 2,000 B.C. (the ruins of Buchen) are across the river from Wadi Halfa. An Egyptian colony was here until the Roman invasion.

The Rail Route to Egypt

Sudan's train connection with Egypt from Khartoum involves a Nile boat trip from Wadi Halfa to Sadd el Ali.

Khartoum - Wadi Halfa - Sadd el Ali - Cairo

This trip crosses the vast Nubian Desert. The train runs Wednesday and Sunday, carries sleeping cars and has meal service.

2700

Dep. Khartoum	6:40	Arr. Wadi Halfa	5:40	Day 2

Change to boat, which runs Tuesday and Friday.

2690

Dep. Wadi Halfa	16:00	Arr. Sadd el Ali	8:00	Day 3

Change to train.

2665

Dep. Sadd el Ali	16:00(1)	18:00(2)
Arr. Cairo (Main)	9:20	13:30

(1) Meal service. Air-conditioned. Carries sleeping car. (2) Second and third-class seats only.

SWAZILAND

There are no passenger trains in Swaziland.

TANZANIA

This country's rail system is the modern Tanzam Line that was completed in 1976, running from the seaport of Dar es-Salaam to Tunduma (and on into Zambia), plus 2 routes going north from Dar es-Salaam and 2 that head west from there. One of the northern lines connects another of Tanzania's seaports, Tanga, with Dar es-Salaam.

There is also train-ferry service on Lake Victoria.

Tanzania has many excellent national parks, offering splendid viewing of monkeys, elephants, rhinos, antelopes, lions, zebras and giraffes: Arusha (45 minutes from Dar es-Salaam), Ngorongoro Crater, Lake Manyara, Tarangire, Mikumi, Gombe and the 5,000-square-mile Serengeti.

Children under 3 travel free. Half-fare for children 3-13. Children 14 and over must pay full fare.

Dar es-Salaam - Tunduma - Kapiri Mposhi 3310

During this ride, the train climbs as high as 6,000 feet altitude. If you do not like curry and local maize cuisine, it is advisable to bring your own food for this 37-43 hours of travel.

First-class compartments have seats and sleeping berths for 4 persons. Second-class compartments are for 6 people. Both classes share restaurant car services.

All of the trains on this route have meal service.

Dep. Dar es-Salaam	10.45(1)	Dep. Kapiri Mposhi	16:50(1)
Arr. Nakonde	13:00(2)	Arr. Nakonde	13:00(2)
Change trains.		Change trains.	
Dep. Nakonde	14:20(3)	Dep. Nakonde	16:00(3)
Arr. Kapiri Mposhi	8:42(4)	Arr. Dar es-Salaam	17:22(4)

(1) Runs Wednesday and Saturday. (2) Day 2. (3) Runs Thursday and Sunday. (4) Day 3.

Sights in Dar es-Salaam: Means "Haven of Peace" in Arabic. This is Tanzania's main Indian Ocean seaport. See the 1,700,000 year old skull at the National Museum, as well as abstract Makonde wood carving, Masai weapons, drums and Zanzibar chests and elaborately carved doors. The Botanical Gardens. The Askari Monument. The picturesque boats at Dhow Wharf. The Asian Bazaar, called "Uhindini". Fifteen miles north of here is an extensive complex of seaside resorts.

Dar es-Salaam - Korogwe - Tanga
3300

Dep. Dar es-Salaam	15:00		Dep. Tanga	18:00	
Arr. Korogwe	1:40	Day 2	Arr. Korogwe	20:40	
Change trains.			Change trains.		
Dep. Korogwe	3:00		Dep. Korogwe	23:10	
Arr. Tanga	5:30		Arr. Dar es-Salaam	9:25	Day 2

Dar es-Salaam - Moshi 3300

This train trip goes to the southern foot of Mt. Kilimanjaro, highest mountain (over 19,000 feet) in Africa.

Dep. Dar-es-Salaam	15:00	Dep. Moshi	15:50
Arr. Moshi	8:50	Arr. Dar-es-Salaam	9:25

Tanga - Korogwe - Moshi 3300

Dep. Tanga	18:00	Dep. Moshi	15:30
Arr. Korogwe	20:40	Arr. Korogwe	23:10
Change trains.		Change trains.	
Dep. Korogwe	1:40	Dep. Korogwe	3:00
Arr. Moshi	8:50	Arr. Tanga	5:30

Dar es-Salaam - Tabora - Mwanza 3303

This rail trip goes to Lake Victoria. Both trains have meal service.

Dep. Dar es-Salaam	18:30		Dep. Mwanza	20:00	
Dep. Tabora	20:00	Day 2	Arr. Tabora	5:10	Day 2
Arr. Mwanza	5:10	Day 3	Arr. Dar es-Salaam	8:20	Day 3

Dar es-Salaam - Morogoro - Dodoma - Tabora - Kigoma 3305

Here are the schedules for the train ride to Lake Tanganyika. There is boat service across the lake, from Kigoma to Kalemie (Zaire).

On this 900-mile trip, Dodoma and Tabora are fine stopping places en route, which at least recently had good and picturesque railway hotels near both stations. There is taxi service for the 7-mile trip from Kigoma to Ujiji, the village where Henry Stanley, after many months of ordeal, found Dr. David Livingstone. A small monument marks the site.

Dep. Dar es-Salaam	18:30(1)		Dep. Kigoma	18:45	
Dep. Morogoro	1:35	Day 2	Arr. Tabora	5:40	Day 2
Dep. Dodoma	9:00		Change trains.		
Arr. Tabora	18:15		Dep. Tabora	8:00(1)	
Change trains.			Dep. Dodoma	18:40	
Dep. Tabora	21:00		Dep. Morogoro	2:00	Day 3
Arr. Kigoma	6:45	Day 3	Arr. Dar es-Salaam	8:20	

(1) Meal service.

From Dar es-Salaam to Morogoro is only 7 hours by train. It took Stanley 29 days to walk this 121-mile distance. As at many stations in Africa, here one can buy hard-boiled eggs, peanuts, tea, oranges and samosas (spicy meat knishes)from vendors along the platform.

Sights in Tabora: Long avenues, shaded by mango trees that grew from seeds spitted by endless lines of slaves who were herded down these streets. There is a small Livingstone museum in nearby Kwihara (reached by taxi from Tabora), where Stanley rested many weeks during his 1871 search for Livingstone.

Mpanda - Tabora - Kigoma 3305

This is the train route from Mpanda to Lake Tanganyika.

Dep. Mpanda	13:15(1)		Dep. Kigoma	18:45(2)	
Arr. Tabora	4:10	Day 2	Arr. Tabora	5:40	Day 2
Change trains.			Change trains.		
Dep. Tabora	21:00(2)		Dep. Tabora	19:30(3)	
Arr. Kigoma	6:45	Day 3	Arr. Mpanda	9:55	Day 3

(1)Runs Tues., Thurs. and Sat. (2)Daily. (3)Runs Mon., Wed. and Fri.

TOGO

The 2 classes of trains are first and third. Upholstered seats are available only in first-class. Children under 5 travel free. Half-fare for children 5-9. Children 10 and over must pay full fare. The official language in Togo is French.

Lome - Aneho 3052

Dep. Lome	7:03(1+2)	11:45(1+3)	16:10(1+4)	16:10(1+5)
Arr. Aneho	8:45	13:20	17:46	18:35

* * *

Dep. Aneho	6:00(1+6)	9:00(1+2)	14:05(1+3)	18:00(1+7)
Arr. Lome	8:06	10:35	15:40	19:35

(1)Third-class only. (2)Sat. and Sun. (3)Daily. (4)Mon. and Thurs. (5)Tues. and Fri. (6)Wed. and Sat. (7)Wed., Sat. and Sun.

Sights in Lome: Luxury hotels on the popular resort beach. The German Cathedral. Nearby, Moslems wearing embroidered robes, selling beads, baskets and bracelets. Many stalls stocked with bolts of bright patterned cloth. Many French restaurants. See the fetish market (black roots, crudely carved dolls, iron obects, etc., all used in the local religion).

Lome - Kpalime 3051

Dep. Lome	6:30(1)	15:15	Dep. Kpalime	6:10	14:20(1)
Arr. Kpalime	11:00	19:08	Arr. Lome	10:35	18:45

(1)Daily. Has only third-class space on Tues., Thurs. and Sat.

Sights in Kpalime: The ride from Lome is through many small villages and tropical forest. Experience the Friday night frivolities before each Saturday's market day, where thousands of people from the outlying area come here to do their weekly shopping. Do not fail to see the famous fantastic kente cloth that has irridescent silk and cotton threads woven into geometric patterns.

Lome - Blitta 3050

Dep. Lome	5:45	7:22(1)	13:20(2)
Arr. Blitta	11:49	18:38	19:27

* * *

Dep. Blitta	5:07(3)	6:40(4)	12:30
Arr. Lome	17:14	12:47	18:30

(1)Mon., Wed. and Fri. Third-class only. (2)Sat. only (3)Tues., Thurs. and Sat. Third-class only. (4)Sun. only.

TUNISIA

Because Tunisia is only 2 hours by air from Paris and one hour from Rome, it is a popular vacation place for Europeans.

Tunisia's rail system is 2 lines running west from Tunis (one to Bizerte and the other to Ghardimaou, and on to Algeria) and one heading south from Tunis, to Gabes. An 11-mile spur from Bir-bou-Rekba on this southern line goes to Hammamet and Nabeul.

The 3 classes of seats are first, second and luxury-class. All luxury-class and some first-class space are air-conditioned. Children under 3 travel free. Half-fare for children 3-9. Children 10 and over must pay full fare.

Tunis

There are more than 700 exceptional monuments to see here. The finest and largest collection of Roman mosaics in the world are on exhibit at the National Museum of the Bardo, as well as Punic, Byzantine, Arab and other Roman objects (open daily except Monday 9:00-12:00 and 14:000-17:30).

See the fantastic 9th century Great Mosque Zitouna (Mosque of the Olive Tree). A marvelous collection of illuminated Korans and other Arabic manuscripts in the National Library. The beautiful interior of the Zaouia (temple) of Sidi Mahrez. The marble and sculptured wood in the lovely Dar Ben Abdullah, an example of Tunis' many 19th century "great houses".

The Lapidary Museum of Sidi Bou Krissan. The valuable objects from Egypt, Persia and Turkey at the Dar Hussein Museum of Islamic Art, in an 18th century mansion. The 17th century Mosque of Hamouda Pasha. The 16th century Mosque El Youssefi (Mosque of the Kasbah). The Belvedere Zoo. The many beach resorts south of Tunis.

There are half-day tours to Carthage, Sidi Bou Said and the Bardo Museum. A full-day tour goes to Dougga.

Dougga

It is a short drive from Tunis to Dougga. See the 2nd century B.C. Dougga Mausoleum, a prince's tomb. Many temples and an ancient Market Place, all very well preserved. The Comedie Francaise often performs in the large open-air theater. Dougga is Tunisia's largest archaeological site, one of the best-preserved Roman towns in Tunisia.

Kerkouane

This city is near Tunis. It is the only unmutilated Punic town, the only one that was not built upon by succeeding generations.

Thuburo Majus

Near both Tunis and Sousse. Many fabulous ruins here: temples, a Forum, and public buildings. An excellently-preserved Roman town.

Utica

Near both Tunis and Bizerte. This was a Phoenician port in the 11th century B.C. Some vaults from that period and many fine Roman ruins can be seen here. The Museum has a fine collection of ancient jewels and funeral furniture.

Tunis - Bizerte 2610

All of these trains have light refreshments.

Dep. Tunis (Bizerte)	5:55	14:10	17:28(1)	18:28
Arr. Bizerte	7:48	16:04	19:07	20:39

* * *

Dep. Bizerte	5:35	11:25(1)	12:50	18:20
Arr. Tunis (Bizerte)	7:30	13:05	14:47	20:18

(1) Air-conditioned in first and luxury-class.

Sights in Bizerte: A seaport and naval base. This city has been ruled by Punic, Roman, Byzantine, Arab and Turkish leaders. See: The Er-Rimel beach. The Old Port, with docks for fishing boats. Nearby there are many interesting villages: Tabarka, Utica, Raf-Raf, Ain Draham, Ghar El Melh (Porto Farina), Ras Djebel, Metline, Sounine, Aousdja, Zouaouine, El Alia, Kalaat El Andalous, Sedjenane.

Tunis - Carthage

It is a short ride from Tunis to Carthage on a 1908 wooden train which starts at Place d'Afrique in the center of Tunis and stops at several fashionable seaside resorts.

Get off at Carthage's Hannibal station to visit the birthplace of Hannibal. This city was founded in 814 B.C. There are many outstanding Punic and Roman ruins here. Plays, dances, musical performances and sound and light performances are presented every July and August in both the Roman Theater and in the Baths of Antonin.

See: The very large and beautifully decorated 2nd century Roman baths, nearly 700 feet long. The National Museum of Carthage. The ancient Theater, built in a marble quarry. The pink marble columns and the mosaic floor (depicting birds in the leaves of a tree) at the Villa de la Voliere in the Carthage Antiquarium. The Basilica of St. Cyprian.

Get off at Carthage's Salammbo station to see The Tophet, now an open-air museum, where humans were sacrificed.

2600

Dep. Tunis (Nord)	Frequent times from 3:45 to 23:45
Arr. Carthage	25 minutes later

* * *

Dep. Carthage	Frequent times from 3:20 to 0:05
Arr. Tunis (Nord)	25 minutes later

Tunis - Ghardimaou 2611

Dep. Tunis	5:25(1)	8:03(2+4)	12:28(2+4)	13:33(1+5)
Arr. Ghardimaou	9:26	11:00	15:41	17:28

* * *

Dep. Ghardimaou	1:30(2)	4:10(1)	6:05(1+3)	9:55(1+3+6)
Arr. Tunis	4:56	7:59	9:11	13:05

(1) Light refreshments. (2) Supplement charged. (3) Air-conditioned in first-class. Supplement charged. (4) Meal service. (5) Plus other departures from Tunis at 16:20(1+3), 16:55 (1+3) and 17:55(1). (6) Plus other departures from Ghardimaou at 11:35(1), 12:30(2+4) and 18:05(1).

Ghardimaou - Algiers

2550		2540	
Dep. Ghardimaou	14:55(1)	Dep. Annaba	18:45(1+2)
Arr. Annaba	17:55	Dep. Constantine	22:10
Change trains.		Arr. Algiers	6:35

(1) Light refreshments. (2) Has couchettes.

Tunis - Hammamet - Nabeul 2605

A one-day roundtrip from Tunis to Hammamet and/or Nabeul is possible, as these schedules indicate.

Dep. Tunis (East)	6:05(1+2)	7:10(2)	13:30	16:25(5)
Arr. Bir-bou-Rekba	7:04	8:00	14:26	17:16
Change trains.				
Dep. Bir-bou-Rekba	7:05(3)	8:04(3)	14:29(3)	17:19(3)
Arr. Hammamet	7:12	8:11	14:36	17:26
Arr. Nabeul	7:29	8:28	14:53	17:43

* * *

Dep. Nabeul	5:32(4)	6:11(3)	7:35(3)	13:58(3+6)
Dep. Hammamet	5:50(4)	6:29(3)	7:52(3)	14:16(3)
Arr. Bir-bou-Rekba	5:52(4)	6:35	7:58	14:22
Change trains.				
Dep. Bir-bou-Rekba	5:57(4)	6:40	8:02	14:57
Arr. Tunis	7:16	7:50	8:55	15:56

(1) Light refreshments. (2) Air-conditioned in luxury and first-class. (3) Second-class only. (4) Through train. No change in Bir-bou-Rekba. Second-class only. (5) Plus other departures from Tunis at 18:08(4) and 18:30. (6) Plus other departures from Nabeul at 16:45(3) and 18:50(3).

Sights in Hammamet: A popular seashore resort. See: The medieval fortress. Fantastic gardens of flowers and fruit trees.

Sights in Nabeul: Many fine mosaics. Excellent straw and pottery products are made here.

Tunis - Kairouan	Bus 2602			
Dep. Tunis	5:30	10:00	13:45	
Arr. Kairouan	8:30	13:00	18:30	
		*	*	*
Dep. Kairouan	4:45	10:30	15:15	
Arr. Tunis	8:45	13:30	18:15	

Sights in Kairouan: The unbelievably beautiful carved wood panels of the Minibar (pulpit)and gilded 9th century tiles in the massive 9th century Great Mosque of Okba Ibn Nafaa, the founder of Kairouan. The splendid collection of parchment manusscripts of the Koran, 9th century bookbindings, ceramics and glassware in the Museum of Islamic Art, opposite the Great Mosque.

The 17th century Zaouia of Abou Zamaa El Balaoui (Mosque of the Barber). The 9th century reservoirs, Bassins Aghlabides. Narrow streets that are 1,000 years old. The 9th century facade on the Mosque of the Three Doors. The Museum of Rugs. The ruins of nearby Rakada.

Tunis - Sousse - El Jem - Sfax - Gabes

2605				
Dep. Tunis (East)	6:05(1)	7:10(1+2)	13:05	14:05(1+2+3)
Dep. Sousse	8:12	9:03(1+2)	14:58	16:09(1+2+4)
Dep. El Jem	9:09	9:53(1+2)	15:46	16:57(1+2+5)
Arr. Sfax	9:54	10:37(2)	16:30	17:42(2)
Change trains.				
2615				
Dep. Sfax	-0-	10:42(1)	-0-	21:05(1)
Arr. Gabes	-0-	12:47	-0-	23:10

* * *

2615				
Dep. Gabes	-0-	5:45(1+2)	-0-	15:40(1+2)
Arr. Sfax	-0-	7:45(2)	-0-	17:42(2)
Change trains.				
2605				
Dep. Sfax	6:40(1)	7:50(1)	12:55(1)	17:50(1+6)
Dep. El Jem	7:26(1)	8:36(1)	13:41(1)	18:35(1+7)
Dep. Sousse	8:14(1)	9:35(1)	14:30(1)	19:27(1+8)
Arr. Tunis (East)	10:16	11:23	16:28	21:27

(1) Air-conditioned in luxury and first-class. Light refreshments. (2) Through train. No change in Sfax. (3) Plus other departures from Tunis at 17:30 (1+2) and 18:30(2). (4) Plus other departures from Sousse at 19:28(1+2) and 20:55(1+2). (5) Plus other departures from El Jem at 20:15(1+2) and 21:42(1+2). (6) Plus another departure from Sfax at 5:15. (7) Plus another departure from El Jem at 6:01. (8) Plus another departure from Sousse at 6:50.

Sights in **Sousse:** Exhibits of prehistoric objects as well as Punic, Roman and early Christian mosaics and statues at the Museum, in the Kasbah. The 9th century Ribat (fort), 2 rooms of which are devoted to exhibits of Islamic textiles. ceramics, miniatures, Koran manuscripts, jewelry and glassware. The 9th century Grand Mosque.

Sights in **Maktar:** Near Sousse. Outstanding Roman ruins: the Great Baths and Trajan's Triumphal Arch. Also Punic and Roman marble and bronze statues at the Museum.

Sights in **Mahdia:** Near Sousse. An important vacation resort. The presently restored 10th century Mosque of Mahdia. Fantastic mosaics and Roman architecture. Fine wool embroidery is done here.

Sights in **Sbeitla:** Near Sousse. A truly magnificent ancient capital. See: The Triumphal Arch, Forum, and the mosaics on the floor of an old Christian basilica.

Sights in **Moknine:** Near Sousse. This is a pottery center. Its little museum has ancient gold jewelry, still a specialty of local artisans. Much spectacular weaving is done here.

Sights in **Monastir:** A short ride from Sousse. The remarkably well-preserved 8th century Ribat, one of the largest Arab forts in North Africa, 3 rooms of which have exhibits of Islamic textiles, ceramics, miniatures, Koran manuscripts, jewelry and glassware.

Sights in **El Jem:** A marvelous 3rd century amphitheater, one of the largest and best preserved Roman colosseums. Near it are many statues, mosaics and bronze objects from the Punic, Roman and early Christian periods. Great wool embroidery here.

Sights in **Sfax:** Archaeological collections of mosaics, lamps and glass and bronze objects in the Municipal Museum.

Sights in **Gabes:** This town consists of 2 large villages, Djara and Menzel. It is a 3½-mile long oases at the seashore. There are many date palm groves here. Try the palm wine. Good palm leaf basket-work, jewelry and forged iron are offered in the shops of Djara. See the Sidi Driss Mosque. The Sidi Boulbaba Mosque is on the road to nearby Matmata.

Sights in **Matmata:** Near Gabes. People live here in holes, both to get out of the sun and because of the lack of building materials in this locale. However, the interior of some of these underground homes are beautifully furnished. One hotel, with a bar and restaurant, is completely underground.

Sights in **Zarzis:** Near Gabes. A dense green oasis resort, with a forest of 50-year old olive trees. There is exceptional fishing in nearby Biban Lake.

UGANDA

Landlocked Uganda's rail lines radiate from Tororo: northwest to Pakwach, west to Kasese, and southeast to Nairobi (and on to Mombasa). Children under 3 travel free. Half-fare for children 3-13. Children 14 and over must pay full fare.

Tororo - Gulu - Pakwach 3285

Dep. Tororo	5:00(1)	Dep. Pakwach	14:00(2)
Arr. Gulu	18:00	Arr. Gulu	19:08
Change trains.		Change trains.	
Dep. Gulu	6:00(2)	Dep. Gulu	7:00(3)
Arr. Pakwach	10:15	Arr. Tororo	20:35

(1)Runs Monday, Wednesday and Friday. (2)Runs Saturday. (3)Runs Tuesday, Thursday and Saturday.

Tororo - Jinja - Kampala - Kasese 3286

This line touches the northern shore of Lake Victoria at Kampala.

Dep. Tororo	6:00(1)	Dep. Kampala	16:00(1)
Dep. Jinja	9:32	Dep. Jinja	19:04
Arr. Kampala	12:25	Arr. Tororo	22:50

(1)Daily, except Monday.

Sights in Kampala: The capital of Uganda. See the collection of African musical instruments in the Uganda Museum. Several Hindu temples. Rubaga Cathedral. The white Kibuli Mosque. The "apocalypse" ceiling of St. Francis' Chapel at Makerere University. The Botanical Garden in Entebbe, 20 miles away.

Tororo - Nairobi - Mombasa 3275

Dep. Tororo	N/A(1)	Dep. Mombasa	19:00(2)
Dep. Malaba	16:00(2+3)	Arr. Nairobi	8:15(4)
Arr. Nairobi	8:45(4)	Change trains.	
Change trains.		Dep. Nairobi	9:30(2+6)
Dep. Nairobi	19:00(2)	Arr. Malaba	2:50(1+5)
Arr. Mombasa	8:00(5)	Arr. Tororo	N/A

(1)Travel 14km(8½ miles) by road Tororo-Malaba and v.v. (2)Carries sleeping car. Meal service. (3)Runs Monday, Wednesday and Friday. (4)Day 2. (5)Day 2 from Nairobi. (6)Runs Tuesday, Thursday and Sunday.

UPPER VOLTA

Landlocked Upper Volta has one train route, from Ouagadougou to Bobo Dioulasso, and on into Ivory Coast. Schedules appear earlier in this chapter, under "Ivory Coast".

ZAIRE

This country's rail system is Y-shaped, with Lubumbashi at the bottom of the vertical South-North line and Kamina at the point that one route goes northwest to Ilebo, where there is boat service to Kinshasa and train facility from there to the ports of Banana and Pointe Noire on the coastline of Congo. Another route goes northeast from Kamina to Kalemie (on the west shore of Lake Tanganyika), where there is boat service across the lake to Kigoma in Tanzania, and trains from Kigoma to Dar es-Salaam.

Rail facilities operate south from Lubumbashi to Kapiri Moshi and on through Zambia, Zimbabwe and Botswana into South Africa and all the way to Cape Town. Another major rail line runs west from Tenke (on the Lubumbashi-Kamina route)to Benguela and Lobito on the coastline of Angola.

In Zaire, children under 3 travel free. Half-fare for children 3-9. Children 10 and over must pay full fare.

Lubumbashi - Tenke - Kamina 3225

Dep. Lubumbashi	9:00(1+2)	12:00(2+4)	20:00(5+6)
Dep. Tenke	15:25	21:10(2+4)	13:00(6+7)
Arr. Kamina	2:50(3)	10.00(3)	15:00(8)

* * *

Dep. Kamina	0:15(2+7)	4:50(2+9)	7:15(2+10+12)
Dep. Tenke	13:10(2+7)	16:25(2+9)	20:45(2+10+13)
Arr. Lubumbashi	22:05(3)	22:50(3)	6:00(3)

(1)Runs Mon., Tues. and Thurs. (2)Has couchettes. Meal service. (3)Day 2. (4)Runs Wed. and Sat. (5)Saturday only. (6)Third-class only. (7)Sunday only. (8)Day 3. (9)Thursday only. (10)Tuesday only. (11)Wednesday only. (12)Plus other departures from Kamina at 8:50(2+5), 9:00(6+9) and 22:00(2+10). (13)Plus other departures from Tenke at 20:25(2+5), 15:20(6+9) and 9:35(2+11).

Kamina - Ilebo - Kinshasa - Brazzaville

This route involves a 4-day boat ride from Ilebo to Kinshasa.

3225

Dep. Kamina	11:00(1)	Sat.
Arr. Ilebo	6:00	Tues.

Change to boat.

3209

Dep. Ilebo	15:00	Tues.
Arr. Kinshasa	7:00	Sat.

Change to another boat.

3171

Dep. Kinshasa	N/A(2)
Arr. Brazzaville	20 minutes later

(1)Has couchettes. Meal service. (2)Daytime only. Runs every 30 minutes.

Sights in Kinshasa: The capital of Zaire. Largest city in Black Africa (1,400,000 population). See the Kinshasa Museum.

Kamina - Kalemie - Kigoma - Tabora - Dar es-Salaam

This is the train trip to Like Tanganyika and on into Tanzania.

3220

Dep. Kamina	11:00	Fri.
Arr. Kalemie	6:00	Sat.

Change to boat.

3215

Dep. Kalemie	16:30	Sun.
Arr. Kigoma	7:00	Mon.

Change to train.

3305

Dep. Kigoma	18:45
Arr. Tabora	5:40(1)

Change trains.

Dep. Tabora	8:00(2)
Dep. Dodoma	18:40(2)
Dep. Morogoro	2:00(2+3)
Arr. Dar es-Salaam	8:20(3)

(1)Day 2 from Kigoma. (2)Meal service. (3)Day 3 from Kigoma.

Lubumbashi - Ndola - Kapiri Mposhi

3401

Dep. Lubumbashi	N/A(1)
Arr. Ndola	N/A(1)

Change trains.

3405

Dep. Ndola	21:40(2)
Arr. Kapiri Mposhi	0:25

3405

Dep. Kapiri Mposhi	16:53(2)
Arr. Ndola	22:15

Change trains.

3401

Dep. Ndola	N/A(1)
Arr. Lubumbashi	N/A(1)

(1)Times have not been available since 1980. (2)Carries first-class sleeping car and second-class coach car. Light refreshments.

Lubumbashi - Dilolo - Benguela - Lobito

The rail service to Angola.

3228
Dep. Lubumbashi 17:00(1) Mon.
Arr. Dilolo 15:25 Tues.
Change trains.
3421
Dep. Dilolo N/A(2)
Arr. Benguela N/A(2)
Arr. Lobito N/A(2)

3421
Dep. Lobito N/A(2)
Dep. Benguela N/A(2)
Arr. Dilolo N/A(2)
Change trains.
3228
Dep. Dilolo 9:00(1) Wed.
Arr. Lubumbashi 7:25 Thurs.

(1)Has couchettes. Meal service. (2)Times for this daily service have not been available since 1980.

ZAMBIA

On a map of landlocked Zambia, the outline of its rail system is a sloppy "Y", with Livingstone in the south at the bottom of the "Y". The right-arm runs east from Kapiri Mposhi to Tunduma and on into Tanzania. This is Zambia's portion of the Tanzam Railway, which terminates at the port of Dar es-Salaam.

The left-arm of the "Y" goes from Kapiri Mposhi to Ndola and on into Zaire. A small spur runs off this route, from Ndola to Kitwe.

South of Livingstone is the border with Zimbabwe and a connection to Victoria Falls, and on to Bulawayo, a junction for continuing southwest to South Africa or heading southeast to Mozambique. There is also service from Bulawayo northeast to Salisbury.

First-class seats are upholstered. Second-class seats have leather covering. Children under 3 travel free. Half-fare for children 3-15. Children 16 and over must pay full fare.

Livingstone - Victoria Falls - Bulawayo - Salisbury

3458
Dep. Livingstone N/A(1)
Arr. Victoria Falls N/A(1)
Dep. Victoria Falls 17:30(2)
Arr. Bulawayo 7:15 Day 2
Change trains.
3455
Dep. Bulawayo 20:00 Day 2
Arr. Salisbury 7:00 Day 3

Dep. Bulawayo 19:00(2)
Arr. Victoria Falls 7:30 Day 2
Dep Victoria Falls N/A(1)
Arr. Livingstone N/A(1)

(1)Service was "temporarily" suspended in 1979. (2)Meal service.

Sights in Livingstone: This is the most popular tourist center in Zambia. See the flowers and aviary in Barotse Gardens. The Livingstone

Museum's archaeological, historical and ethnological exhibits. Traditional dances, performed at Maramba Cultural Center.

Nearby, Lake Kariba, Livingstone Game Park, Kafue National Park and Wankie National Park. Take a cruise on the Zambesi River.

The most important sight here is seen by taking an excursion to the nearby majestic Victoria Falls, which are more than 5,500 feet wide and have a minimum drop of 355 feet. The falls are the border between Zambia and Rhodesia. There is a great view from Knife Edge Bridge. However, the best view is from the Rhodesian side, looking at the two-thirds of the falls owned by Zambia.

Livingstone - Lusaka - Kapiri Mposhi - Dar es-Salaam

The Tanzam Railway is the portion from Kapiri Mposhi to Dar es-Salaam. Much wildlife can be seen as the train passes through Mkumi National Park.

The train climbs as high as 6,000 feet altitude during this ride. If you do not like curry and local maize cuisine, it is advisable to bring your own food for this 37-43 hours of travel.

3405		
Dep. Livingstone	8:00(1)	23:40(2)
Dep. Lusaka	17:10(1)	11:40
Arr. Kapiri Mposhi	20:38	16:20
Change trains.		
3310		
Dep. Kapiri Mposhi (New)		16:50(3)
Arr. Tunduma		13:00
Change trains.		
Dep. Tunduma		16:00(4)
Arr. Dar es-Salaam		17:22(5)

3310		
Dep. Dar es-Salaam		10:45(3)
Arr. Nakonde		13:00(6)
Change trains.		
Dep. Nakonde		14:20(4+6)
Arr. Kapiri Mposhi (New)		8:42(7)
Change trains.		
3405		
Dep. Kapiri Mposhi	0:25(2)	12:07(1)
Dep. Lusaka	6:05(2)	15:45(1)
Arr. Livingstone	17:40	0:40

(1)Service temporarily suspended in 1982. (2)Runs daily. Carries first-class sleeping car and second-class coach car. Light refreshments. (3)Runs Wednesday and Saturday. Meal service. (4)Runs Thursday and Sunday. Meal service. (5)Day 2 from Tunduma. (6)Day 2 from Dar es-Salaam. (7)Day 3 from Dar es-Salaam.

Sights in Lusaka: The capital of Zambia. See the large copper cross over the altar in the Anglican Cathedral of the Holy Cross. Luburma Central Market. The Tobacco Auction Floor. The 8-acre Twickenham Road Archaeological Site in Olympia Park, a suburb. Nearby, Munda Wanga Park and Botanical Gardens, Kafue Gorge, the Ayrshire Farm Rock Engravings national monument, and Blue Lagoon National Park.

Kapiri Mposhi - Ndola - Lubumbashi

This is the train route into Zaire.

3405		3401	
Dep. Kapiri Mposhi	16:53(1)	Dep. Lubumbashi	N/A(2)
Arr. Ndola	20:05	Arr. Ndola	N/A(2)
Change trains.		Change trains.	
3401		3405	
Dep. Ndola	N/A(2)	Dep. Ndola	21:40(1)
Arr. Lubumbashi	N/A(2)	Arr. Kapiri Mposhi	0:25

(1)Carries first-class sleeping car and second-class coach car. Light refreshments. (2)Time has not been available since 1980.

Livingstone - Mulobezi 3410

This is a spur off the Victoria Falls-Kapiri Mposhi line.

Dep. Livingstone	9:00(1)	Dep. Mulobezi	8:00(2)
Arr. Mulobezi	17:55	Arr. Livingstone	17:45

(1)Runs Thursday and Sunday. (2)Runs Monday and Friday.

ZIMBABWE (formerly RHODESIA)

There are 4 classes of seats. First-class compartments convert to 4 couchettes at night. Second-class compartments convert to 6 couchettes. There is a charge for bedding. Children under 3 travel free. Half-fare for children 3-11. Children 12 and over must pay full fare.

There are rail connections between Salisbury in landlocked Zimbabwe and Zambia, Mozambique and Botswana.

Salisbury - Bulawayo - Victoria Falls - Livingstone

3455		3458	
Dep. Salisbury	20:00	Dep. Livingstone	N/A(2)
Arr. Bulawayo	7:00	Dep. Victoria Falls	17:30(1)
Change trains.		Dep. Thomson Junction	20:50(1)
3458		Arr. Bulawayo	7:15
Dep. Bulawayo	19:00(1)	Change trains.	
Dep. Thomson Junction	4:35(1)	3455	
Arr. Victoria Falls	7:30	Dep. Bulawayo	20:20
Arr. Livingstone	N/A(2)	Arr. Salisbury	7:00

(1)Meal service. (2)Service between Victoria Falls and Livingstone was "temporarily" suspended in 1979.

Sights in Salisbury: The capital. See the Queen Victoria Memorial Library and Museum. The Rhodes National Gallery.

Sights in Bulawayo: The National Museum. Nearby, Rhodes' Tomb in the Matapo Hills and the Khami Ruins.

Sights in Victoria Falls: These spectacular falls are more than 5,500 feet wide and have a maximum drop of 355 feet. This is the border between Zimbabwe-Rhodesia and Zambia. The best view is from the Zimbabwe-Rhodesia side, looking at the two-thirds of the falls that is in Zambia.

Salisbury - Umtali - Beira

3450			3350		
Dep. Salisbury	21:30	8:10(1)	Dep. Beira	N/A(2)	-0-
Arr. Umtali	6:00	13:05	Arr. Umtali	N/A(2)	-0-
Change trains.			Change trains.		
3350			3450		
Dep. Umtali	N/A(2)	-0-	Dep. Umtali	21:00	7:30(2)
Arr. Beira	N/A(2)	-0-	Arr. Salisbury	6:00	12:25

(1)Bus. (2)Service was "temporarily" suspended in 1977.

Sights in Umtali: The Museum. Nearby, many national parks which attract tourists.

Salisbury - Bulawayo - Mafeking - Johannesburg

3455 (Bus)				
Dep. Salisbury	20:00			
Arr. Bulawayo	7:00			
Change to train.				
3475				
Dep. Bulawayo	11:45(1)	13:30(3)		
Arr. Mafeking	5:30(2)	11:40		
Change trains.				
3545				
Dep. Mafeking	6:15(4)	9:00(5)	10:00(6)	20:30(7)
Arr. Johannesburg	14:10	17:50	16:40	5:44

(1)Reservation required. Runs Tuesday and Thursday. The Tuesday departure is a direct train to Johannesburg with no train change in Mafeking. Meal service 11:45-23:22 on Day 1. (2)Arrives Wednesday and Friday. (3)Meal service. (4)Wednesday only. Reservation required. Meal service. (5)Sunday only. (6)Bus. (7)Daily.

Chapter 12 ASIA

BANGLADESH

Bangladesh offers 6 classes of train space: air-conditioned, first-class, second-express-class, second-ordinary-class, third-mail-class and third-ordinary-class. The first 3 convert to 2-berth or 4-berth compartments at night. Children under 3 travel free. Half-fare for children 3-9. Children 10 and over must pay full fare.

The principal cities in Bangladesh having train service are Chittagong and Dacca.

Chittagong

This is Bangladesh's largest port. See the slab believed to bear the imprint of Mohammed's foot, in the Qadam Mubarik Mosque. The Chandanpura Shahi Jame Mosque. The tortoises at the tomb of Hazrat Bayazid Bostami.

Dacca

This is the nearly 400-year old capital of Bangladesh. See the 17th century Lalbagh Fort and the tomb of Pari Bibi. The 4 bazaars in the Chowk (old market). The 17th century Chowk Mosque. Other notable mosques: The Star, Kar Talab, Baidul Mukarram, and Sat Gumbad. The collection of coins, painting, and stone, wood and metal sculptures in the Museum of Antiquities.

There are many interesting archaeological digs at Mainamati and Lalmai, 5 miles west of Comilla, which is on the Chittagong rail route. Although not on Cook's timetable #2530, Comilla is 50 miles east of Dacca, about a one-hour train ride.

Dacca - Chittagong 6605

Dep. Dacca	10:00(1+2)	11:00(2)	14:30(1+2)	22:30(1+3)
Arr. Chittagong	18:30	20:20	22:20	7:40

* * *

Dep. Chittagong	7:30(1+2)	12:30(1+2)	21:20(2+3)	22:30(1+3)
Arr. Dacca	16:45	20:20	5:40	7:50

(1) Has air-conditioned compartments. (2) Meal service. (3) Seats convert to couchettes.

Dacca - Sylhet 6605

Dep. Dacca	20:30(1)	Dep. Sylhet	20:30(1)
Arr. Sylhet	8:30	Arr. Dacca	8:40

(1) Seats convert into couchettes. Has air-conditioned compartments.

Sights in Sylhet: This is in the tea estates area of the beautiful Surma Valley. Much small-game hunting here.

BURMA

Burma does not publish timetables. Those timetables that are posted at railstations are in Burmese script, including the numerals.

An English-speaking duty officer at the Information Office in Rangoon's railstation will assist foreigners with ticket purchases and will provide information about train connections.

Tickets may be purchased up to 3 days in advance of travel date, and it is usually necessary to make reservations 2 days in advance for First-Class space on the Rangoon-Mandalay ride. Lower class space is very unsatisfactory.

Only tea and soft drinks are served on Burma's trains. Vendors at many stations sell food. This is Burmese food and does not appeal to all Westerners. It is advisable to bring your own food and a container of water. Both Burma Airways and Tourist Burma's office in Rangoon arrange tours of Burma and a 3-hour guided tour of Rangoon.

Children under 3 travel free. Half-fare for children 3-9. Children 10 and over must pay full fare.

Rangoon

The 320-foot high stupa of the enormous 2400-year old Shwe Dagon Pagoda is completely covered with gold leaf. Value of the 8,688 foot-square gold plates on the plantain bud at the top has been computed as over $2,500,000(U.S.). There are 5,448 diamonds and more than 2,000 other precious stones at the top of the bud.

A 25-ton bell is located at one corner of the platform. The British took the bell, as a prize of war, and dropped it into the Rangoon River as they were attempting to load it onto a ship. Unable to raise the bell, the British abandoned it. Burmese workers raised it by tying enough bamboo poles to it until it floated.

In central Rangoon, see: The 2300-year old Sule Pagoda. The National Museum. Burmese students learning their dances at the State School of Music and Drama in Jubilee Hall. Handicrafts at Bogyoke Market. North of the city's center is the contemporary Kaba Aye Pagoda built in 1956.

Rangoon - Mandalay 6700

The 7:00 departures are usually less crowded than the other departures.

Dep. Rangoon	7:00	11:45	18:45(1)
Arr. Mandalay	19:00	5:00	7:45

* * *

Dep. Mandalay	7:00	11:45	18:45(1)
Arr. Rangoon	19:00	5:50	7:45

(1) Carries sleeping car.

Sights in Mandalay: This is one of Burma's youngest cities, existing since only 1857. Great Buddhist carvings here. Fine Burmese timber architecture. Many interesting monasteries, beautiful small pagodas.

Mandalay - Pagan 6702 Bus

Dep. Mandalay	4:00	Dep. Pagan	4:00
Arr. Pagan	14:00	Arr. Mandalay	14:00

Sights in Pagan: Once a fantastic city of many millions and called City of Four Million Pagodas, before Kublai Khan sacked it in the 13th century. Now, there are splendid ruins of more than 5,000 structures to see: great temples and pagodas.

Here are schedules for 3 other possible long train trips from Mandalay:

Mandalay - Lashio 6701

This route has fine scenery.

Dep. Mandalay	5:20	Dep. Lashio	7:00
Arr. Lashio	17:00	Arr. Mandalay	19:25

Mandalay - Myitkyina 6701

Dep. Mandalay	15:00	16:00(1)	Dep. Myitkyina	7:00	8:00(1)
Arr. Myitkyina	14:45(2)	16:05(2)	Arr. Mandalay	6:15(2)	9:10(2)

(1) Carries sleeping car. (2) Day 2.

Mandalay - Thazi - Shwenyaung - Taunggyi 6700

Dep. Mandalay	11:45	18:45(1)	Dep. Shwenyaung	10:05(1)	-0-
Arr. Thazi	15:15	21:21	Arr. Thazi	21:45	-0-
Change trains.			Change trains.		
Dep. Thazi	-0-	4:20(1)	Dep. Thazi	1:37	5:01
Arr. Shwenyaung	-0-	16:35	Arr. Mandalay	5:00	7:45

(1) Carries sleeping car.

It is an 11-mile taxi ride from Shwengaung to Taunggyi, a hill station located at 4712 feet.

HONG KONG

Children under 3 travel free. Half-fare for children 3-9. Children 10 and over must pay full fare.

This country owns the Kowloon-Canton Railway, which operates 40 passenger trains daily between Kowloon and Lo Wu, the border station for rail trips into the People's Republic of China. Nearly 2,000,000 people make this ride every year. There is ferry service from Hong Kong to Kowloon.

Prior to 1979, it had always been necessary to go through customs formalities in Lo Wu and then walk across the bridge spanning the Shum Chun River to the Chinese railstation on the north side of the river before boarding a second train in Shenzhen and proceeding on to Canton.

Since 1979, 2 trains per day make a direct ride from Kowloon to Canton, without requiring passengers to change trains at Lo Wu-Shenzhen.

Kowloon - Lo Wu 5400

Dep. Kowloon	Frequent times from 6:30 to 23:00
Arr. Lo Wu	One hour later.

* * *

Dep. Lo Wu	Frequent times from 5:54 to 21:39
Arr. Kowloon	One hour later.

Kowloon (Hong Kong) - Canton 5400

Dep. Kowloon	7:07	9:09	10:00	12:04	13:00(4+5)
Arr. Lo Wu	8:28(1)	10:20(1)	11:13(1)	13:21(1)	13:54(4)
Change trains.					
Dep. Lo Wu	-0-	-0-	-0-	-0-	13:57
Arr. Shenzhen	-0-	-0-	-0-	-0-	14:06
Dep. Shenzhen	9:54(2)	11:34(2)	13:07(2)	15:00(3)	14:09
Arr. Canton	13:05	14:21	15:04	17:31	15:59

(1)Walk across frontier bridge and board second train in Shenzhen. (2)Second-class only. (3)Relief train. Runs when required. Second-class only. (4)Reservation required. Direct train to Canton. No train change. First-class only. Air-conditioned. Meal service. (5)Plus other departures from Kowloon at 13:18(1+2), arriving Canton at 20:57; and at 14:55(4), arriving Canton at 17:50.

Hong Kong

See the art objects in Fung Ping Shan Museum at the University of Hong Kong. Take the cruise to Yaumati Typhoon Shelter to see the "floating people" who live their entire lives on small boats. Go on the bus tour to Aberdeen and several interesting villages. It also stops at the unique Tiger Balm Gardens.

INDIA

Every day, more than 9,000,000 people ride India's 11,000 trains, connecting 7,085 railstations. This is Asia's largest railway system.

The 5 classes of space on Indian Railways are: air-conditioned, first-class(air-conditioned chair, second-class sleepercoach and second-class. The air-conditioned class converts at night to 2 to 4 berths. First-class converts at night to 4, 5 or 6 berths. Second-class sleepercoaches convert into sleeping berths between 21:00 and 6:00, with 4 or 6 berths in each compartment. The fare for air-conditioned class includes bedding. Passengers in first-class and in sleepercoaches must pay a supplement for bedding.

Foreign tourists can reserve Air Conditioned and First-Class space up to 180 days in advance of travel date. To determine which of the 7 rail offices in India you need contact for advance reservations, first communicate your itinerary to any Government of India Tourist Office. That office will advise you whether to direct your reservation order to the Central, Eastern, North Eastern, Northern, South Central, South Eastern or Western offices of Indian Railway.

Children under 3 travel free. Half-fare for children 3-11. Children 12 and over must pay full fare.

Breaking of a journey at any station en route is permitted with single journey tickets when the entire trip is more than 200 miles, at the rate of one day for every 100 miles. However, the first break of journey cannot be made until the passenger has traveled at least 150 miles from his or her starting station.

There are restaurants at important railstations. The leading passenger trains have restaurant cars which offer both Indian and Western food. India Government Tourist Offices provide a "Tourist Timetable".

INDIA'S TRAIN PASSES

Indrail Pass. Unlimited rail travel. Available to citizens of countries other than India and to those Indians residing outside India who hold valid passports. The bearer is not required to pay for reservations. Indrail Pass must be purchased in India, either at the Tourist Guide Office at a railstation or from a travel agent, and must be paid in the currency of a country other than India. The 1983 prices (in U.S. dollars) are:

	Air-conditioned	First-class	Second-class
7 days	$160	$ 80	$ 35
15 days	200	100	45
21 days	240	120	55
30 days	300	150	65
60 days	450	225	100
90 days	600	300	130

Children 5-12 years old pay half-fare.

Student Discounts. Students of educational institutions and art schools of foreign countries are allowed substantial discounts when traveling for educational purposes or when visiting places of artistic importance. The letter of authority required in order to obtain this concession can be obtained from the Chief Commercial Superintendent in each major city upon presenting a passport and either a Student Identity Card or a letter from one's embassy certifying that the bearer is a student. See the Deputy Superintendent at the railstation in order to obtain the address of the local C.C.I.

India's 4 principal cities (Bombay, Calcutta, Delhi and Madras) are connected by rail routes.

Bombay

This is a fantastic seaport. See: The Zoo and the Victoria and Albert Museum at Victoria Gardens. The Mahatma Phule Market. Jehangir Art Gallery. The collection of Chinese jade and porcelain and the Tata Collection of paintings at The Prince of Wales Museum. The Rajabal Tower.

Calcutta

A major seaport. See: The many alleys with shops called Bara Bazaar. The stone carvings in the India Museum. The large Nakhoda Mosque. The Botanical Gardens. The Kali Temple. The Jain Temple. The white tigers at the Zoo. The assortment of both great art objects and junk in the Marble Palace.

Delhi

See: the 16th century Lodi Tombs. The Great Mosque. Teen Murti's House, once the home of Nehru and his daughter, Indira Gandhi. The Pearl Mosque. The 2200-year old Ashoka Pillar. The 17th century Red Fort. Humayon's Tomb. The view from the top of the 13th century, 238-foot high, red sandstone Qutb Minar tower.

The Zoo. The National Museum. For shopping, stroll Connaught Place and see the marvelous jewelry assortment (emeralds, diamonds, rubies and sapphires) in both the leading stores and at the Sundar Nagar Market. Visit the Central Cottage Industries Emporium on Janpath and the silver and cloth stores on Chandni Chowk.

The 43 locomotives and 17 coaches in New Delhi's enormous Rail Transport Museum, including the world's oldest (1855) and still operational steam locomotive. This museum also has a model train for children and a floating restaurant.

Madras

See: the collection of weapons, chinaware and costumes in the Fort Museum. The view of the harbor from the top of the lighthouse. The fine beach. The Government Museum's archaeological exhibit. The South Indian bronzes at the National Art Gallery. Fort St. George, the oldest Anglican church in the Orient. San Thome Basilica, where the remains of the apostle Thomas are said to lie.

Bombay - Ahmadabad 6066

Dep. Bombay (Central)	5:40	7:45	21:15(1)
Arr. Ahmadabad	15:50	19:41	6:30

Sights in Ahmadabad: The 300 beautifully carved pillars at the lovely 15th century Jama Masjid. The exquisite filligree marble windows at Sidi Said's Mosque. The promenades, boating, gardens and museums at Lake Kankaria.

Dep. Ahmadabad	7:10	7:50	22:00(1)
Arr. Bombay (Central)	16:10	19:30	7:00

(1)Air-conditioned in first-class. Has couchettes in air-conditioned class and in first-class.

Bombay - Allahabad

6080

Dep. Bombay (Victoria)	6:45(1)	16:30(2)	21:15(4)
Arr. Itarsi	20:25(5)	5:50	10:10(5)

Change trains.

6081

Dep. Itarsi	20:55	6:47(3)	10:25(4)
Arr. Allahabad	7:30	15:30	20:45

Sights in Allahabad (City of God): The Pillar of Asoka at the 16th century fort. The Jami Masjid (Great Mosque). The Museum. The beautiful Victorian Nehru House.

Dep. Allahabad	10:05(6)	15:00(7)	17:00
Arr. Itarsi	20:40(5)	0:35(5)	4:50(5)

Change trains.

6080

Dep. Itarsi	21:05(6)	0:55(8)	5:25
Arr. Bombay (Victoria)	11:20	14:05	20:00(1)

(1)Bombay's Dadar station. (2)Air-conditioned. Meal service. (3)Runs Wednesday and Friday. (4)Air-conditioned on Monday, Wednesday and Saturday. (5)Direct train. No train change in Itarsi. (6)Air-conditioned on Monday, Thursday and Saturday. (7)Runs Tuesday and Friday. (8)Runs Wednesday and Saturday.

Bombay - Bangalore

6140		6155	
Dep. Bombay (Victoria)	20:30	Dep. Bangalore	6:10
Arr. Miraj	5:55	Arr. Miraj	22:10
Change trains.		Change trains.	
6155		6140	
Dep. Miraj	6:25	Dep. Miraj	22:40
Arr. Bangalore	22:05	Arr. Bombay (Victoria)	8:10

Sights in Bangalore: The palace of the Maharajah of Mysore. The 18th century Lal Bagh botanic garden. The Mysore Government Museum. The Nandi Hill Station summer resort, 38 miles from here. The nearby Hesaraghatta Lake.

Bombay - Calcutta 6011

Dep. Bombay (Victoria)	6:00(1)	19:15(3)	19:35(5)	21:15(6+10)
Arr. Calcutta (Howrah)	11:35(2)	6:50(4)	19:25(4)	12:25(4)

Sights in Calcutta: See notes about sightseeing in Calcutta at the start of this section.

Dep. Calcutta (Howrah)	10:55(7)	13:00	16:15(8)	19:20(9+11)
Arr. Bombay (Victoria)	13:40(4)	6:25(4)	22:00(2)	11:20(4)

(1) Daily, except Tuesday and Saturday. Meal service. (2) Day 2. (3) Air-conditioned. Has couchettes. (4) Day 3. (5) Runs Tuesday, Friday and Sunday. (6) Has air-conditioned class daily January 1 - June 30, only on Monday, Wednesday and Saturday July 1 - December 31. (7) Runs Monday, Wednesday and Friday. (8) Daily, except Thursday and Sunday. Meal service. (9) Has air-conditioned class daily January 1 - June 30, only on Monday, Thursday and Saturday July 1 - December 31. (10) Plus another departure from Bombay at 21:35, arriving Calcutta 14:15(4). (11) Plus another departure from Calcutta at 20:45(3), arriving Bombay 7:30(4).

Bombay - Madras 6095

Dep. Bombay (Victoria)	7:55(1)	14:30(3+4)	22:10
Arr. Madras (Central)	13:00(2)	16:40(2)	5:10(5)

Sights in Madras: See notes about sightseeing in Madras at the start of this section.

Dep. Madras (Central)	9:30(6)	15:35(1)	22:15
Arr. Bombay (Victoria)	11:45(2+3)	20:55(2)	5:10(5)

(1) Second-class only. (2) Day 2. (3) Bombay's Dadar station. (4) Has air-conditioned compartments on only Saturday. (5) Day 3. (6) Has air-conditioned compartments on only Monday.

Bombay - New Delhi 6070

Dep. Bombay (Central)	6:10(1)	6:45(3)	20:50(4)	15:45(5+6)
Arr. New Delhi	1:47(2)	12:55(2)	10:25(2)	9:20(2)

Sights in Delhi: See notes about sightseeing in Delhi at the start of this section.

Dep. New Delhi	2:56(1)	8:21(4)	14:18(3)	16:05(4+7)
Arr. Bombay (Central)	23:10	8:05(2)	21:30(2)	16:40(2)

(1) Runs Monday and Wednesday from Bombay. Runs Wednesday and Sunday from New Delhi. Air-conditioned. (2) Day 2. (3) Second-class only. (4) Has air-conditioned class. Meal service. (5) Reservation required. Runs Wednesday and Sunday from Bombay. Runs Monday and Thursday from New Delhi. Air-conditioned. Meal service. Carries sleeping car. (6) Plus another departure from Bombay at 20:15(4) arriving New Delhi 19:35(2). (7) Plus another departure from New Delhi at 16:35(5) arriving Bombay 10:42(2).

Bombay - Pune 6095

The first double-deck passenger train in India started operating in 1978 on the 115-mile long Bombay-Pune line. Its coaches seat 148 (versus 90 in ordinary second-class coaches).

Dep. Bombay (Victoria)	6:45	7:55(1)	8:45	12:45	14:30(2+4)
Arr. Pune	11:05	12:10	13:20	17:10	18:35

Sights in Pune: Many ancient palaces and temples. This route involves 25 tunnels and many high bridges and viaducts. Can be made as a one-day roundtrip. The very picturesque narrow-gauge Matheran Hill Railway is near this route and can be visited during the day.

Dep. Pune	0:50	2:10(1)	4:00	6:10(1)	7:10(3+5)
Arr. Bombay (Victoria)	5:10	6:10	8:10	10:10	10:40

(1) Second-class only. (2) Bombay's Dadar station. (3) Meal service. (4) Plus other departures from Bombay at 14:40(1), 17:10(3), 17:50, 20:30, 21:55(1) and 22:10. (5) Plus other departures from Pune at 7:35, 9:35, 15:10, 16:25(1) and 16:45.

Calcutta - Allahabad 6060

Dep. Calcutta (Howrah)	9:45(1+4)	10:55(2)	19:10(4+8)
Arr. Allahabad	0:10	7:20	9:15

Sights in Allahabad: See notes about city sightseeing in Allahabad earlier in this section, under "Bombay-Allahabad".

Dep. Allahabad	2:18(3+4)	6:45(5)	8:45(9)
Arr. Calcutta (Howrah)	16:55	5:20	12:35(6)

(1) Daily, except Monday and Friday. (2) Runs Monday, Wednesday and Friday. Second-class only. (3) Daily, except Wednesday and Saturday. (4) Meal service. Has air-conditioned-class. (5) Second-class only. (6) Arrives at Calcutta's Sealah station. (7) Has air-conditioned-class. (8) Plus another departure from Calcutta at 21:00(7). (9) Plus other departures from Allahabad at 10:25(7), 17:22(4), 21:15(7) and 23:32.

Calcutta - Darjeeling

6120

Dep. Calcutta (Howrah)	12:30(1)	18:55(2)	19:00	21:05
Arr. New Jalpaiguri	5:45	7:45	7:00	19:15

Change trains.

6121

Dep. New Jalpaiguri	7:25	9:00	-0-	-0-
Arr. Darjeeling	14:45	16:30	-0-	-0-

Sights in Darjeeling: At 7,000 feet, this is a cool and beautiful area. Many famous tea plantations. The interesting items to purchase here are jewelry, carvings, colorful fabrics. There is a large population of Tibetans in Darjeeling.

One can walk or take a jeep to Tiger Hill to see the sunrise. There is a hotel at Tiger Hill, and the preferred visit is to spend the night there, see the sunrise the next morning, and then catch the 10:55 train from Darjeeling for the ride back to Calcutta.

Excursions by 4-wheel drive vehicles are made from Darjeeling to Nepal, Sikkim and Bhutan.

6121

Dep. Darjeeling	7:00	11:00	-0-	-0-
Arr. New Jalpaiguri	13:55	17:50	-0-	-0-

Change trains.

6120

Dep. New Jalpaiguri	10:00	15:40(1)	19:45	23:20(2)
Arr. Calcutta (Howrah)	4:40	6:35	8:45	11:52

(1) Second-class only. (2) Has air-conditioned-class. Meal service from Calcutta on Thursday and Sunday only. Meal service from New Jalpaiguri on Wednesday and Saturday only.

Calcutta - Madras 6150

Dep. Calcutta (Howrah)	17:15(1)	20:00(2)	22:40(5)
Arr. Madras (Central)	18:50(3)	4:50(4)	18:15(4)

Sights in Madras: See notes at the start of this section.

Dep. Madras (Central)	8:15(1)	9:00(5)	22:25(6)
Arr. Calcutta (Howrah)	9:30(3)	4:15(4)	6:50(4)

(1)Supplement charged. Meal service. Has air-conditioned coach car. (2)Has air-conditioned-class on Tuesday and Saturday only. Has air-conditioned coach on Saturday only. (3)Day 2. (4)Day 3. (5)Second-class only. (6)Has air-conditioned-class on Monday and Thursday only. Has air-conditioned coach on Monday only.

Calcutta - New Delhi 6060

The train passes through several different regions on this trip. Climate, language and clothing change every few hours.

Dep. Calcutta (Howrah)	9:45(1+2)	17:00(4)	20:40(5)	21:00(6)
Arr. New Delhi	9:35(3)	10:40(3)	-0-	-0-
Arr. Delhi	-0-	-0-	19:40(3)	5:05(7)

Sights in Delhi: See notes about city-sightseeing in Delhi at the start of this section.

Dep. Delhi	7:55(5)	-0-	-0-	22:05(6)
Dep. New Delhi	-0-	16:35(2+8)	17:10(4)	-0-
Arr. Calcutta (Howrah)	6:25(3)	17:10(3)	10:55(3)	6:05(7)

(1)Daily, except Monday and Friday. (2)Has both air-conditioned class and air-conditioned chair coach. Meal service. (3)Day 2. (4)Supplement charged. Reservation required. Runs Monday and Friday from Calcutta. Runs Wednesday and Saturday from New Delhi. Meal service. Carries first-class sleeping car and second-class coach car. (5)Has air-conditioned class. Meal service. (6)Has air-conditioned class. (7)Day 3. (8)Daily, except Wednesday and Saturday.

Delhi - Agra 6073

The 7:10 departure from New Delhi is "Taj Express". It is met on 10:20 arrival in Agra by an air-conditioned government-operated tourist bus and an official guide. Its tour includes the 17th century Taj Mahal and Fatehpur Sikri Fort. Avoid private guides. They do not provide as complete a tour as the government does. Another interesting sight in Agra is the tomb of Hmad-ud-Daulah. The bus brings you back to the Agra station for the 18:55 departure of "Taj Express", arriving New Delhi at 22:15.

As the following schedules indicate, it is not necessary to spend a night in Agra in order to see the Taj by moonlight.

Dep. New Delhi	7:05(1)	7:53(5)	9:20(2+3)	11:45(2+4+10)
Arr. Agra	10:20	11:07	12:28	15:02

(Timetable continues on next page.)

Dep. Agra	15:55	16:45(5)	18:55(1)	20:45(11)
Arr. New Delhi	19:50	20:10	22:15	4:37

(1)Reservation required. Meal service. Has air-conditioned-class and air-conditioned coach. (2)Arrive/Depart at Delhi's Nizamudin station. (3)Daily, except Sunday. Second-class only, except Thursday when train has first and second-class coaches. (4)Runs Monday, Tuesday, Saturday and Sunday. (5)Has air-conditioned coach. (6)Second-class only. (7)Daily. Has air-conditioned-class on Tuesday and Friday only. (8)Daily, except Wednesday and Saturday. (9)Runs Monday, Friday, Saturday and Sunday. (10)Plus other departures from New Delhi at 15:20(6), 19:30(7), 20:35 and 21:30. (11)Plus other departures from Agra at 1:35, 2:15, 4:15(7), 7:00(2), 11:00(2+6+8), 12:00(2+9) and 13:50.

Delhi - Allahabad 6060

Dep. Delhi	-0-	-0-	7:55(3+15)	-0-	-0-
Dep. New Delhi	5:15(1+12)	7:00(2)	-0-	9:40	16:35(4+6+16)
Arr. Allahabad	16:25	15:45	17:12	20:28	2:18

Sights in Allahabad: See notes under "Bombay-Allahabad".

Dep. Allahabad	0:10(5+6)	1:10(7)	2:01(8)	4:00(9)	6:00(17)
Arr. New Delhi	9:35	-0-	-0-	14:35	16:55
Arr. Delhi	-0-	11:15	11:15	-0-	-0-

(1)Runs Tuesday, Thursday, Saturday and Sunday. (2)Runs Tuesday, Thursday and Sunday. Has air-conditioned coach. (3)Has air-conditioned coach. Meal service. (4)Daily, except Wednesday and Saturday. (5)Daily, except Monday and Friday. (6)Has air-conditioned-class and air-conditioned coach. (7)Monday and Friday only. (8)Daily, except Monday and Friday. Second-class only on Wednesday and Saturday. Has first-class and air-conditioned coach only on Tuesday, Thursday and Sunday. (9)Runs Monday, Wednesday and Saturday. Has air-conditioned coach. (10)Daily, Has air-conditioned coach on Monday, Wednesday and Friday only. (12)Has air-conditioned-class. (13)Runs Tuesday, Thursday, Friday and Sunday. (14)Second-class only. (15)Plus other departures from Delhi at 15:55(14), 18:35(10) and 22:05(12). (16)Plus another departure from New Delhi at 22:10(11). (17)Plus other departures from Allahabad at 8:50(6+13), 9:56(12), 12:45(9), 16:20(12), 17:40, 18:15(14), 20:20(11) and 22:35.

Delhi - Jaipur 6061

Pink City Express (one of India's fastest trains)colored pink, departs from a station that is a few miles away from the main Delhi station. Provide extra time to get there.

Dep. Delhi	5:55(1)	9:35	12:30	19:20	22:10
Arr. Jaipur	11:15	17:55	20:47	8:15	5:35

Sights in Jaipur: This city is noted for the unusually colorful clothes worn by its people. See the pink Palace of the Winds.

Dep. Jaipur	0:13	6:25	10:29	17:00(1)	20:32
Arr. Delhi	7:25	14:05	18:50	22:22	8:20

(1)"Pink City Express". Meal service.

Delhi - Madras 6013

Dep. New Delhi	6:55(1)	15:20(3)	19:30(5)
Arr. Madras (Central)	13:10(2)	21:50(4)	8:35(4)

Sights in Madras: See notes about city-sightseeing in Madras at the start of this section.

Dep. Madras (Central)	7:10(6)	14:20(3)	19:20(5)
Arr. New Delhi	13:30(2)	21:40(4)	7:50(4)

(1)Runs Monday, Wednesday and Saturday. Meal service. Has air-conditioned-class and air-conditioned coach. (2)Day 2. (3)Second-class only. (4)Day 3. (5)Has air-conditioned-class from New Delhi on Tuesday and Friday only and from Madras on Wednesday and Sunday only. Meal service. (6)Runs Monday, Thursday and Saturday. Meal service. Has air-conditioned class and air-conditioned chair class.

Madras - Cochin 6170

It is possible to leave the train in Ernakulum, sightsee there, and then later the same day take the trip of a few minutes to Cochin either by ferry boat or by bus across the bridge that connects the 2 cities.

Dep. Madras (Central)	19:20(1)	Dep. Cochin	17:20(1)
Arr. Ernakulam	9:15	Dep. Ernakulam	17:55
Arr. Cochin	9:40	Arr. Madras (Central)	7:50

(1)Has air-conditioned class and air-conditioned chair class.

Sights in Cochin: This is actually a conglomerate of several islands and 3 cities. See the 16th century Santa Cruz Cathedral. The 16th century synagogue. The 16th century tomb of the great Spanish explorer Vasco de Gama. The blue willow-patterned tiles on the floor of a second synagogue. The Dutch Palace. Picturesque palm-lined beaches.

Sights in Ernakulom: The week-long festival at the Siva temple, in January. Performances of the unusual Kathakali dance.

Madras - Pune 6095

Dep. Madras (Central)	9:30(1)	15:35(3)	22:15
Arr. Pune	7:15(2)	16:15(2)	0:40(4)

Sights in Pune: Many ancient palaces and temples.

Dep. Pune	2:55	12:20(3)	18:45(5)
Arr. Madras (Central)	5:10(2)	13:00(2)	16:40(2)

(1)Has air-conditioned-class on Monday only. (2)Day 2. (3)Second-class only. (4)Day 3. (5)Has air-conditioned-class on Saturday only.

INTERNATIONAL ROUTES FROM INDIA

New Delhi is the gateway for train travel to Pakistan. The rail route to Sri Lanka (Ceylon) is via Madras and Rameswaram.

New Delhi - Amritsar - Lahore - Hyderabad - Karachi

6030

Dep. New Delhi	19:18(1+11)
Arr. Amritsar	7:15(2)

Change trains.

6026

Dep. Amritsar	9:15(2)
Arr. Lahore	12:15(2)

5905

Dep. Lahore	9:30(3)	14:20(3)	16:30(5)	17:25(6+12)
Dep. Hyderabad	3:55(3+4)	6:06(3+4)	7:12(4+5)	9:40(4+6)
Arr. Karachi (Cant.)	7:25(4)	9:20(4)	10:00(4)	12:45(4)

(1)Has air-conditioned-class. (2)Day 2 from New Delhi. (3)Reservation required. Has air-conditioned-class. Carries sleeping car. Also has couchettes. (4)Day 2 from Lahore. (5)Coach is second-classs only. Meal service. Has air-conditioned parlor car. (6)Reservation required. Meal service. (7)Meal service. (8)Daily, except Tuesday. Has air-conditioned-class on Sunday and Monday. Meal service on Wednesday, Thursday, Friday and Saturday. (9)Has air-conditioned coach. (10)Runs Tuesday, Thursday, Friday and Sunday. Has air-conditioned-class and air-conditioned coach. (11)Plus other departures from New Delhi at 7:36(7), 11:40(8), 12:40, 19:14(9) and 21:05(10). (12)Plus other departures from Lahore at 19:40(6) and 21:08(3).

Madras - Rameswaram - Talaimannar - Colombo Fort

6182

Dep. Madras (Egmore)	10:45
Arr. Rameswaram	10:00(1)

Change to ferry.

6180

Dep. Rameswaram (Port)	12:00(2)
Arr. Talaimannar (Pier)	15:00

Change to train.

6300

Dep. Talaimannar (Pier)	20:43(3)
Arr. Colombo	8:36(4)

(1)Day 2 from Madras. (2)Runs Monday, Wednesday and Friday. (3)Daily. On Tuesday, Thursday, Saturday and Sunday carries sleeping car. Meal service. On Monday, Wednesday and Friday departs 22:30, carries sleeping car, also has second and third-class couchettes. No meal service. (4)Arrival time every day on Day 3 from Madras.

INDONESIA

Nearly every train ride in Indonesia offers views of extinct volcanoes, mountains, water buffalo and rain forests.

Children under 4 travel free. Half-fare for children 4-11. Children 12 and over must pay full fare.

Jakarta

The main railstation is Kota. See Bali dancing at Gedung Kesenian. The collection of coins, ceramics and archaeological objects at Gedung Artja Museum. Do not miss seeing the morning activity at the Pasar Ikan, a large fish market. The National Mosque. The Museum Kota. The interesting Dutch houses and the canals in Chinatown. Ride out to Bogoru by bus or taxi to see the old Dutch palace (Merdeka Palace) and the fantastic 275-acre Botanical Garden: 10,000 species of trees and more than 500.000 other plants, including more than 100,000 orchid plants. Nothing in the world to compare with these gardens.

Surabaja

There are 3 railstations. Trains for Jakarta depart from Gubeng. Trains for Bandung depart from Kota. Tasar Turi is the third railstation.

This is a major seaport. A 30-minute ferry-boat ride takes you to Madura, where the major attraction is the racing of bulls. Surabaja is a convenient point for visiting Mount Bromo and seeing live animals sacrificed in the boiling volcano crater there.

There are 2 routes from Jakarta to Surabaja.

Jakarta - Surabaja (via Cirebon) 7410

Dep. Jakarta (Kota)	13:00(1+2+3)	16:00(2+4+5+9)
Arr. Surabaja (Kota)	8:15	9:30
	* * *	
Dep. Surabaja (Kota)	13:30(2+3)	16:00(2+4+5+10)
Arr. Jakarta (Kota)	8:30(1)	9:45

(Timetable notes start on the next page.)

(1) Arrive/Depart Jakarta's Gambir railstation. (2) Meal service. (3) Third-class only. (4) Reservation required. Carries sleeping car. (5) Air-conditioned. (6) First-class only. (7) Arrive/Depart Jakarta's Pasarsenen railstation. (8) Arrive/Depart at Surabaja's Pasarturi railstation. (9) Plus other departures from Jakarta at 16:30(2+5+6) and 17:45(2+3+7). (10) Plus other departures from Surabaja at 16:30-(2+5+6+8) and 17:45(2+3+7+8).

Jakarta - Surabaja (via Bandung) 7410

Dep. Jakarta (Kota)	6:15(1)	13:15(3)	15:15(1)	18:35(1+4)
Arr. Bandung	10:05	17:15	19:05	22:10
Change trains.				
Dep. Bandung	17:00(2)	-0-	-0-	5:00(3)
Arr. Surabaja (Kota)	10:45	-0-	-0-	23:40

* * *

Dep. Surabaja (Kota)	5:00(3)	16:50(2)	-0-	-0-
Arr. Bandung	0:05	10:15	-0-	-0-
Change trains.				
Dep. Bandung	5:45(1)	10:45(1)	14:45(1)	17:45(1)
Arr. Jakarta (Kota)	9:35	14:45	18:15(4)	22:00

(1) Second-class only. Meal service. (2) Air-conditioned. Meal service. (3) Second and third-class only. Meal service. (4) Arrive/Depart at Jakarta's Gambir station.

Sights in Bandung: This is a much nicer and cooler city than Jakarta. It is the center of Indonesia's quinine industry, with many cinchona tree plantations here. Quinine is derived from cinchona bark. Numerous tea plantations in this area. See the collection of crocodiles, birds and snakes at the Zoological Garden.

Jakarta - Jogjakarta 7410

Dep. Jakarta (Gambir)	13:00(1+2)	14:00(2+3)	16:00(4+5)	17:00(2+3+6)
Arr. Jogjakarta	1:15	2:11	3:30	5:16

Sights in Jogjakarta: Many ruins in this area. See the dances at the 10th century Roro Djonggrang Temple, 10 miles from Jogjakarta. Also: the gold pillars, gems and sacred weapons in Gadjah Mada University within the Sultan's Palace. Much good batik cloth, silver and buffalo leather items are available here. Nearby is the Mendut Temple with its seated Buddha.

Dep. Jogjakarta	18:00(2+3)	18:42(2+3)	19:30(2+3)	20:30(1+2+7)
Arr. Jakarta (Gambir)	6:25	7:00	7:30	8:30

(1)Third-class only. (2)Meal service. (3)Second and third-class only. (4)Reservation required. Air-conditioned. Meal service. Carries only first and second-class sleeping cars. (5)Departs from Jakarta's Kota railstation. (6)Plus another departure from Jakarta at 19:00(2+3). (7)Plus other departures from Jogjakarta at 21:10(2+3) and 22:27(4).

Jogjakarta - Solo 7410

This is an easy one-day roundtrip.

Dep. Jogjakarta (Gambir)	5:16	6:07	9:30	16:20	
Arr. Solo	6:25	7:22	10:58	17:40	

* * *

Dep. Solo	11:00	15:37	17:00	17:46	18:51(1)
Arr. Jogjakarta (Gambir)	12:30	17:15	18:37	19:25	20:25

(1)Plus other departures from Solo at 19:30, 20:55 and 22:30.

Sights in Solo: A quite attractive village. Famous for its good batik cloth and its Sriwedai Amusement Park, which has a fine Zoological Garden.

The one rail route on Sumatra is across the bay from Penang. A one-day roundtrip from Medan to Tanjong Balai is possible. There are large oil palm and rubber-tree plantations near Medan.

Medan - Rantau Prapet - Tanjon Balai 7400

All of these trains serve light refreshments and are second and third-class only.

Dep. Medan	7:00	9:30	14:50
Arr. Rantau Prapet	-0-	16:54	-0-
Arr. Tanjong Balai	11:25	-0-	19:14

* * *

Dep. Tanjong Balai	6:35	-0-	13:45
Dep. Rantau Prapet	-0-	8:00	-0-
Arr. Medan	11:09	15:36	18:19

JAPAN

Those magical 2 elements that are necessary for top quality rail service both exist in Japan: high population density and short distances.

Japan enacted in 1970 its "Law for Construction of Nationwide High-Speed Railways". This program calls for speeds up to 150 miles per hour on many routes when the entire system is completed, about 1985. Some of the links are already in operation.

When completed, the 22-mile long undersea Seikan Tunnel will connect Tappi and Yoshioka.

Japanese National Railways surpasses all other rail systems in the world as to speed, service and size. It operates more than 26,000 trains a day.

Express trains between Tokyo and Osaka (345 miles) usually run at 125mph, sometimes going as fast as 137mph. Passengers can follow the trains' speed on speedometers located throughout the trains. On the stretch from Tokyo to Kyush, some trains reach a speed of 156mph.

The most famous Japanese trains are its Shinkansen "bullet trains". The great "Hikari", leaving Tokyo every 15 or 20 minutes, runs the 345 miles from Tokyo to Osaka in 3 hours 10 minutes. The 455-mile run from Tokyo to Okayama is made in 4 hours 10 minutes. From Tokyo to Hakata (735 miles), it is only 6 hours 40 minutes.

Bullet trains have telephone service, while traveling, to 26 cities.

When we rode a bullet train both from Tokyo to Kyoto, and then the next day back to Tokyo, the speed was so great that it was difficult to focus on scenery or objects within 1,000 feet from the train. The interior was immaculately clean. It is one of the world's best travel experiences.

And the bullet trains are very safe. To guard against natural disasters, the Japanese installed seismoscopes, anemometers and rain gauges along the entire line. In case of an earthquake exceeding a certain intensity, the electrical current that runs the trains in the area concerned will automatically cut off.

If there are excessive rains or winds, the running speed of the train is restricted or the train is stopped. Each train window is made of double-layer glass with a dry air space between so as to minimize noise, wind pressure and moisture condensation, as well as to guard against flying stones.

Tickets for all Japanese trains which require reservation go on sale one month before travel day and can be purchased at JNR railstations and at major travel agencies throughout Japan.

Children under 6 travel free. Half-fare for children 6-11. Children 12 and over must pay full fare.

Passengers are permitted to take 2 suitcases weighing a total of 44 pounds into their car and may also check 3 additional suitcases at a small fee for transit in the baggage car. Also, for little cost, arrangements can be made either to have baggage delivered from the train to one's residence or to be stored at a railstation. Porters are available at all main stations.

Principal trains have restaurant cars. There are refreshment vendors on almost all other long-distance trains. Both Japanese and Western food are provided.

There are 4 classes of trains in Japan: Super-Express (Hikari and Kodama), Limited Express, Ordinary Express and Local. A surcharge is required for all types of express trains. When any express train arrives 2 hours or more late, the express surcharge is refunded at the destination.

Each express train has one or more "Green Cars". Seat reservations, at an additional charge, are required for space in a Green Car.

Sleeping cars have roomettes (for one person) and double compartments in Class "A" cars. Class "B" cars provide 2-berth and 3-berth compartments.

Combination tickets (for both hotel rooms and seats on bullet trains) can be purchased from either Japanese National Railways or from Japan Travel Bureau.

All of Japan's many privately-owned trains are single-class and require seat reservations. Many of these trains serve resort areas.

JAPAN'S TRAIN PASSES

Japan Tour Tickets. These cover a variety of routes listed by Japanese National Railways. Offering reduced-rate excursions, they can be obtained at principal Japanese railstations, or at the Kobe, Kyoto and Tokyo offices of Japan Travel Bureau, and also at all offices of Kinki Nippon Tourist.

Japan Railpass. Unlimited travel on the trains, buses and ferries of the Japanese National Railways System. Does not cover travel on private lines. Vouchers are sold only outside Japan, at offices of Japan Air Lines and Japan Travel Bureau. After arriving in Japan, the voucher is exchanged for the pass at JNR ticket counters at the New Tokyo International Airport (Narita) and at JNR offices in Hakata, Hiroshima, Kumamoto, Kyoto, Nagoya, Niigata, Osaka, Sapporo, Sendai, Tokyo, West Kagoshima and Yokohama. The 1982 prices for first-class were: Y30,000 for 7 days, Y48.000 for 15 days, and Y64,000 for 21 days. Second-class prices: Y21,000, Y33,000 and Y44,000.

In planning a tour of Japan, keep in mind that the country is 3 major islands: Honshu (Tokyo and Kyoto), Kyushu (Nagasaki) to the south, and Hokkaido (the wild northern land of Japan).

Hiroshima

Rebuilt since 1955. See the monuments at Peace Memorial Park. The interesting exhibits in the Peace Memorial Museum.

Kyoto

You will not see all worth seeing here in a few days. There are more than 600 shrines, over 1400 temples, plus 9 museums, 3 palaces and an imposing castle in Kyoto.

The 17th century Nijo Castle is first on everyone's list. Beautiful gold ceilings, wood sculptures, and murals to see at this complex.

Other sights in Kyoto: the 13th century 393-foot long Sanjusangendo (Hall of 33 Bays). The incredible halls at Nishi Hongan-ji. The 200-acre park in the center of Kyoto, with the Imperial Palace. The 3 large gardens of the 68-acre Shugaku-in. The 22 subtemples at Daitoku-ji, one of the city's many Zen temples. The Library, Zoo, Art Gallery and Heian Jingu Shrine, all in Okazaki Park. Hundreds of narrow streets, each with interesting shops, food stores and inns.

Kinkaku-ji (Temple of the Golden Pavilion). Ryoan-ji (Temple of the Peaceful Dragon). Kokedera (The Moss Temple), with many different types of moss in its lovely garden. The 17th century Kiyomizu (Clear Spring Temple).

Osaka

The 16th century Osaka Castle, and its fine museum. Shitenno-ji Temple. Nishi Temple. Higashi Hongan-ji Temple. The Kabuki Theater. The view from the top of 338-foot high Tsutenkaku (Tower Leading to Heaven). The view from the top of the 340-foot high observation platform on Osaka Tower. Sumiyoshi Taisha Shrine.

Temmangu Shrine. The Bunraku puppet theater. The dozen different farmhouses with hundreds of utensils in the Museum of Japanese Farmhouses. The Japan Handicraft Museum. Ancient and modern art at the Municipal Art Museum in Tennoji Park, where the Zoo and Botanical Garden are also located.

The Electric Science Museum. The Transportation Museum. The Natural Science Museum. The Fujita Art Museum. A tourist specialty in Osaka is visiting factories: clothing, beverages, ice cream, chocolate, cameras, autos, bread, etc.

Tokyo

Schedules for the 60-minute train ride between Tokyo's Ueno Keisei station and Narita Airport appear later in this section, under "Tokyo-Narita".

There is monorail and bus service between Haneda Airport and the center of Tokyo. A special train goes non-stop between Narita Airport Station (a 6-minutes bus ride from the terminal) and Tokyo.

Several English-language daily newspapers list entertainment events.

Any tour of Tokyo must focus on visiting the massive park surrounding the Palace, in the center of the city. Then see: The gardens at the Meiji Shrine. The enormous Zoo, the National Museum of Western Art, and the Tokyo National Museum, all in Ueno Park, next to Ueno Railstation. The tremendous assortment of sealife at the wholesale fish market at Tsukiji, very early in the morning.

Stroll the Ginza, particularly after dark. See the elegant lobby of the Imperial Hotel. The Iris Garden (Shobu-en). The gardens at Shinjuku Gyoen. Kiyosumi Garden. The 60-acre Hama Rikyu Park. Buddhist art at Goto Museum. The collection of ancient Japanese and Chinese art in the Nezu Museum. Koishikawa Botanical Garden.

The city's largest department stores have amusement parks on their roofs and many restaurants. Several have underground malls connected to Tokyo Railstation.

Hiroshima - Kokura - Beppu 8070

Dep. Hiroshima	8:06(1)	10:16(2)	11:34(1)
Arr. Kokura	9:23	11:44	13:02

Change trains.
8120

Dep. Kokura	9:39	12:00	13:35
Arr. Beppu	11:37	13:43	15:18

Sights in Beppu: Noted for its curative mineral baths.

Dep. Beppu	14:53	16:31	17:57	18:27	20:00
Arr. Kokura	16:44	18:29	19:44	20:15	21:53

Change trains.
8060

Dep. Kokura	16:59(1)	19:04(1)	20:00(1)	20:59(2)	21:59(2)
Arr. Hiroshima	18:12	20:17	21:19	22:28	23:26

(1)Res. required. Meal service. (2)Res. required. Light refreshments.

Hiroshima - Hakata 8060

Most of the trains on this route require reservations. All serve either light refreshments or meals.

Dep. Hiroshima	Frequent times from 6:34 to 22:08
Arr. Hakata (Fukuoka)	2 hours later

Sights in Hakata: (Hakata is the railstation for Fukuoka.) This twin-city is famous for Hakata dolls. Much night-life here. There is cormorant fishing only a few miles from here, at Harazuru.

Dep. Hakata (Fukuoka)	Frequent times from 6:00 to 21:30
Arr. Hiroshima	2 hours later

Hiroshima - Kagoshima

Most of the trains on the Hiroshima-Hakata route require reservations. All serve light refreshments or meals.

8070

Dep. Hiroshima	Frequent times from 6:34 to 22:08
Arr. Hakata (Fukuoka)	2 hours later

Change trains.

8111

Dep. Hakata (Fukuoka)	9:05	9:22(1)	11:05	13:05(3)
Arr. Kagoshima	13:35	14:49	16:07	17:57

Sights in Kagoshima: A good base for visiting the beautiful crater lake, many live volcanoes and thick forests of Kirishima National Park.

Dep. Kagoshima	6:30	7:45	8:18	9:29(4)
Arr. Hakata (Fukuoka)	11:21	12:15	13:13	14:15

(1)Meal service. (2)Carries sleeping car. (3)Plus other departures from Hakata at 14:06, 15:05, 17:05, 18:05, 0:05(2), 4:29(2), 7:05 and 8:05. (4)Plus other departures from Kagoshima at 11:08, 12:22(1), 13:35, 15:04, 16:16, 16:43, 17:49, 19:34 and 22:08(2).

Change trains. 8070

Dep. Hakata (Fukuoka)	Frequent times from 6:00 to 21:30
Arr. Hiroshima	2 hours later

Hiroshima - Kumamoto

Most trains on the Hiroshima-Hakata route require reservations. All serve either light refreshments or meals.

8070

Dep. Hiroshima	Frequent times from 6:34 to 22:08
Arr. Hakata (Fukuoka)	2 hours later

Change trains.

8111

Dep. Hakata (Fukuoka)	9:05	9:22	9:34	10:05	11:05(1)
Arr. Kumamoto	10:33	11:08	11:20	11:45	12:41

Sights in Kumamoto: It is a short drive from here to marvelous Suizenji Park.

Dep. Kumamoto	9:39	10:45	11:31	12:40	13:27(2)
Arr. Hakata (Fukuoka)	11:21	12:15	13:13	14:15	15:14

(1)Plus other departures from Hakata at frequent times from 12:05 to 18:58 plus 21:10, 0:05, 4:29, 7:05 and 8:05. (2)Plus other departures from Kumamoto at frequent times from 14:34 to 22:50 plus 2:45, 6:27, 7:44 and 8:27.

Change trains. 8070

Dep. Hakata (Fukuoka)	Frequent times from 6:00 to 21:30
Arr. Hiroshima	2 hours later

Hiroshima - Nagasaki

Most trains on the Hiroshima-Hakata route require reservations. All serve either light refreshments or meals.

8070

Dep. Hiroshima	Frequent times from 6:17 to 22:10
Arr. Hakata (Fukuoka)	2 hours later

Change trains.

There is great scenery of Omura Bay on the ride from Hakata to Nagasaki. Sit on the right-hand side.

8110

Dep. Hakata (Fukuoka)	9:08	9:34	10:01	10:56	11:58(1)
Arr. Nagasaki	11:49	12:15	12:51	13:25	14:41
	*	*	*		
Dep. Nagasaki	4:50	6:49	7:48	8:44	9:20(2)
Arr. Hakata (Fukuoka)	8:20	9:23	10:22	11:25	12:11

Change trains. 8070

Dep. Hakata (Fukuoka)	Frequent times from 6:00 to 21:30
Arr. Hiroshima	2 hours later

(1) Plus other departures from Hakata at frequent times from 12:58 to 20:13, plus 4:43, 6:16, 7:00 and 7:43. (2) Plus other departures from Nagasaki at frequent times from 10:42 to 19:57.

Sights in Nagasaki: Japan's first contact with the Western world was here, as well as the country's early traffic with China. That explains both the Chinese and Catholic influence on this area. The local tradition is flying the huge kites that were first flown in China. Two other Chinese influences seen here even now are the annual June racing of large row-boats to the tempo of a drum that is beaten amidship and an annual October festival featuring Chinese-style costumes, floats and dragons.

See: The Catholic Cathedral. (Nearly half of Japan's small Catholic population lives in this area.) The view of the city and harbor from Glover House, the place where Madame Butterfly (in Puccini's imagination) waited for Pinkerton to return. The 17th century Chinese temple (Sofukuji). The 33-foot high bronze torii at the Suwa Shrine. Much marvelous seacoast scenery in this area.

Kyoto - Gifu

All trains on the Kyoto-Nagoya route require reservations.

8070

Dep. Kyoto	7:29	9:17	11:29
Arr. Nagoya	8:17	10:22	12:17

Change trains.

8082

Dep. Nagoya	8:35	10:40	13:00
Arr. Gifu	9:05	11:08	13:29

8082

Dep. Gifu	14:21	18:37	19:26
Arr. Nagoya	14:46	19:02	19:51

Change trains.

8070

Dep. Nagoya	15:03	19:32	20:15
Arr. Kyoto	15:51	20:34	21:06

Sights in Gifu: There is large production of lovely paper lanterns and paper umbrellas here. Numerous hot springs resorts in this area. See the cormorant fishing, almost every night from mid-May to mid-October.

Kyoto - Kobe 8070

These trains require reservations and serve either light refreshments or meals.

Dep. Kyoto	Frequent times from 7:42 to 21:53
Arr. Kobe	35 minutes later

Sights in Kobe: This is Japan's largest seaport. See: Ikuta Shrine. Take a bus tour to Minatogawa Shrine and the ancient Temple in Sumadera. Great cherry tree blossoms there every Spring. Equally beautiful maple tree foliage, every Autumn, at Zenshoji Temple. See the Hakutsuru Gallery of Oriental Art, near Mikage station. Visit the Zoo, Botanical Garden and all-girl opera at nearby Takarazuka.

Dep. Kobe	Frequent times from 7:03 to 21:38
Arr. Kyoto	35 minutes later

Kyoto - Matsuyama

All trains on the Kyoto-Okayama route require reservations and serve light refreshments or meals.

8070		
Dep. Kyoto	7:53	10:17
Arr. Okayama	9:10	11:54
Change trains		
8138		
Dep. Okayama	9:13	12:13
Arr. Uno	9:46	12:46
Change to boat.		
8138		
Dep. Uno	9:56	12:54
Arr. Takamatsu	10:56	13:54
Change to train.		
8139		
Dep. Takamatsu	11:14	14:08
Arr. Matsuyama	14:07	17:33

Sights in Matsuyama: This is a popular hot springs resort. See the lovely maple trees in nearby Omogo Valley. There is a fine castle here. Local sport is bullfighting.

8139		
Dep. Matsuyama	9:13	14:26
Arr. Takamatsu	12:09	17:14
Change to boat.		
8138		
Dep. Takamatsu	12:25	17:28
Arr. Uno	13:25	18:28
Change to train.		
8138		
Dep. Uno	13:37	18:34
Arr. Okayama	14:11	19:08
Change trains.		
8070		
Dep. Okayama	14:21	19:23
Arr. Kyoto	15:39	20:51

Kyoto - Nagoya 8070

These trains require reservation and serve either light refreshments or meals.

Dep. Kyoto Frequent times from 6:19 to 22:16
Arr. Nagoya 40-50 minutes later

Sights in Nagoya: The art objects in the recently re-built 5-story 17th century castle. The view of Nagoya from the top of the 350-foot high television tower. The modern Nittaiji Temple, a gift from Thailand. The 1700-year old Atsuta Shrine. The Tokugawa Art Museum. Shop for fine Noritake chinaware and Ando cloisonne. It is only a 45-minute train ride to Inuyama to see the 16th century castle and the Kiso rapids there.

There is bus service every 20 minutes at the Nagoya station for the 1½-hour ride to the marvelous preservation park at Meiji, a 172-acre mountain village that has reproduced the lifestyle that existed in Japan at the end of the 19th century. Among the many monuments from the 1868-1912 era are: the railroad coach of the Meiji Emperor, the lobby of the original Frank Lloyd Wright Imperial Hotel (a Tokyo landmark for almost 50 years until it was demolished in the 1960's), a public bath, a merchant's townhouse, a teahouse, a Kabuki theater, antique railway machines, a hand-printing press, and textile spinning, weaving and threading machines. The village is open 10:00-17:00 March-October and 10:00-16:00 November-February.

Dep. Nagoya Frequent times from 6:40 to 22:27
Arr. Kyoto 40-50 minutes later

Kyoto - Nara 8088

Dep. Kyoto Frequent local service
Arr. Nara 12 minutes later

Sights in Nara: This is a very crowded tourist town. Weekends should be avoided. See the 1250-acre Nara Park and its temples.

Dep. Nara Frequent local service
Arr. Kyoto 12 minutes later

Kyoto - Okayama 8070

These trains require reservation and serve either light refreshments. or meals.

Dep. Kyoto Frequent times from 6:00 to 21:53
Arr. Okayama 90 minutes later

Sights in Okayama: The bamboo groves, tea plantation, streams and ponds in the 28.5-acre Korakuen Park, one of Japan's finest gardens, established in 1700. Nearby, the lovely Kibitsu Shrine and the Saidaiji Temple. There is much extraordinary fruit in this area: white peaches, muscat grapes and unusual pears.

Dep. Okayama Frequent times from 6:03 to 20:38
Arr. Kyoto 90 minutes later

Kyoto - Takamatsu

All trains on the Kyoto-Okayama route require reservation and serve either light refreshments or meals.

8070				8138			
Dep. Kyoto	9:45	10:36	14:17	Dep. Uno	11:54	12:54	16:54
Arr. Okayama	10:56	11:54	15:52	Arr. Takamatsu	12:54	13:54	17:54
Change trains.							
8138							
Dep. Okayama	11:13	12:13	16:13				
Arr. Uno	11:46	12:46	16:46				
Change to boat.							

Sights in Takamatsu: The museum of 12th century battle relics in Yashima Temple, 5 miles away. The outstanding Ritsurin Park and Zoo. The Kompira Shrines, only an hour ride by electric train to Kotohira. Nearby Kotobiki Park.

8138			
Dep. Takamatsu	12:25	17:28	19:37
Arr. Uno	13:25	18:28	20:37
Change to train.			
Dep. Uno	13:31	18:34	21:04
Arr. Okayama	14:06	19:09	21:39
Change trains.			
8070			
Dep. Okayama	14:21	19:23	22:26
Arr. Kyoto	15:51	20:52	23:25

Kyoto - Toba

0000 (Kinki Nippon Rly. Not shown in Cook's.)

Dep. Kyoto	Every 20 minutes	Dep. Toba	Every 20 minutes
Arr. Toba	35 minutes later	Arr. Kyoto	35 minutes later

Sights in Toba: See women divers gathering oysters into which an irritant is inserted which starts the process of pearl formation. A program is presented at Pearl Island, near the waterfront. Then continue on to Kashikojima, where you will want to visit the Cultured Pearl Institute to see the exhibition there.

Kyoto - Tottori 8095

Dep. Kyoto	4:26	9:20	16:33
Arr. Tottori	8:48	13:10	20:38

Sights in Tottori: Many hotsprings here. See the sand dunes on the nearby shore.

Dep. Tottori	8:27	14:58	18:02	19:49
Arr. Kyoto	12:22	18:53	22:24	0:06

Osaka - Himeji 8080

Dep. Osaka Frequent local service.
Arr. Himeji 1½ hours later

Sights in Himeji: The 5-story White Herron Castle.

Dep. Himeji Frequent local service.
Arr. Osaka 1½ hours later

Osaka - Kanazawa 8035

All of these trains have meal service.

Dep. Osaka Frequent times from 7:05 to 20:15
Arr. Kanazawa 3 hours 10 minutes later

Sights in Kanazawa: A lovely castle city on Japan's seacoast. See Kenroken, the beautiful garden with ponds and waterfalls, next to the castle. Mountain-climbing trips start from here.

Dep. Kanazawa Frequent times from 7:00 to 19:07
Arr. Osaka 3 hours 20 minutes later

Osaka - Kobe 8070

All of these trains require reservation.

Dep. Osaka (1) Frequent times from 6:06 to 22:13
Arr. Kobe 17 minutes later

Sights in Kobe: See notes under "Kyoto-Kobe".

Dep. Kobe Frequent times from 7:02 to 23:19
Arr. Osaka (1) 17 minutes later

(1) Shin-Osaka, a commuter station.

Osaka - Nagoya 8070

These trains require reservation and serve either light refreshments or meals.

Dep. Osaka (1) Frequent times each hour from 6:00 to 21:57
Arr. Nagoya 90 minutes later

Sights in Nagoya: See notes under "Kyoto-Nagoya".

Dep. Nagoya Frequent times each hour from 6:40 to 22:27
Arr. Osaka (1) 90 minutes later

(1) Shin Osaka, a commuter station.

Osaka - Okayama 8070

These trains require reservation and serve either light refreshments or meals.

Dep. Osaka (1) Frequent times from 6:00 to 22:13
Arr. Okayama 60-90 minutes later

Sights in Okayama: See notes under "Kyoto-Okayama".

Dep. Okayama Frequent times from 6:00 to 22:23
Arr. Osaka (1) 60-90 minutes later

(1)Shin-Osaka, a commuter station.

Osaka - Tottori 8095

Dep. Osaka	8:00(1)	9:30	12:10	18:00	21:32(2)
Arr. Tottori	12:13	13:45	16:29	22:24	3:32

Sights in Tottori: See notes about city-sightseeing in Tottori earlier in this section, under "Kyoto-Tottori".

Dep. Tottori	0:26(2)	6:21	9:30	12:42	15:54(3)
Arr. Osaka	6:36	10:49	14:38	17:09	20:11

(1)Meal service. (2)Reservation required. Carries sleeping car. (3)Plus another departures from Tottori at 17:01(1).

Osaka - Toyama 8035

All trains on this route have meal service.

Dep. Osaka Frequent times from 7:05 to 20:15
Arr. Toyama 4 hours later

Sights in Toyama: Famous since the 17th century for its medical powders, pills, drugs and other pharmaceutical items.

Dep. Toyama Frequent times from 6:04 to 18:20
Arr. Osaka 4 hours later

Tokyo - Kanazawa 8072

Dep. Tokyo (Ueno)	8:19	9:16	11:16	14:46	20:53(1+3)
Arr. Kanazawa	15:04	16:11	18:10	21:38	5:59

Sights in Kanazawa: See notes about city-sightseeing in Kanazawa earlier in this section, under "Osaka-Kanazawa".

Dep. Kanazawa	6:56	9:55	13:53	15:46	21:00(2+4)
Arr. Tokyo (Ueno)	14:00	17:00	20:59	22:33	5:45

(1) Carries sleeping car. (2) Sleeping cars only. (3) Plus other departures from Tokyo at 21:17(2) and 21:49(1). (4) Plus other departures from Kanazawa at 21:30(1) and 21:44(1).

Tokyo - Lake Hakone 8048

Dep. Tokyo (Shinjuku)
7:30 plus every 30 minutes from 9:30 to 17:00 + 18:00 and 18:30.
Sundays: plus 8:00, 8:30, 9:00, 17:30 and 19:00
Arr. Hakone-Yumoto 90 minutes later

Take a taxi or bus from Yumoto to the lake.

Sights: Beautiful scenery on this easy one-day roundtrip.

Dep. Hakone-Yumoto
9:12 plus every 30 minutes from 10:42 to 18:42 + 20:12
Sundays: plus 9:42, 10:12, 19:12, 19:42 and 20:42
Arr. Tokyo (Shinjuku) 90 minutes later

Tokyo - Kofu - Matsumoto
8050

Dep. Tokyo (Shinjuku)	6:45	8:00	9:00	10:00	13:00	14:00(1)
Arr. Kofu	8:42	9:51	10:55	11:54	14:53	15:53
Arr. Matsumoto	2 hours after arriving Kofu					

(1) Plus other departures from Tokyo at 15:00, 16:00, 17:00, 18:00 and 19:00.

Sights in Kofu: Good views of the Japanese Alps. Fine Summer and Winter sports facilities. From Kofu, there are connections to Lake Suwa.

Sights in Matsumoto: Great mountain scenery. Gateway to the Japanese Alps.

Dep. Matsumoto	5:53	8:00	9:55	11:00	11:38	13:40(1)
Dep. Kofu	7:50	9:46	11:48	12:46	13:35	15:27
Arr. Tokyo (Shinjuku)	9:54	11:30	13:33	14:33	15:36	17:13

(1) Plus other departures from Matsumoto at 14:18, 14:40, 15:40, 17:15 and 18:16.

Tokyo - Mito 8019

Dep. Tokyo (Ueno)	8:00	13:00	14:48	19:50	20:50(1+2)
Arr. Mito	9:32	14:31	16:11	21:13	22:28

Sights in Mito: Visit Kairaku-en Park, noted for its plum blossoms, about one mile west of the railstation. The special flowering season is late February to mid-March.

Dep. Mito	5:01	5:40	10:00	12:37	19:46(3)
Arr. Tokyo (Ueno)	6:35	7:24	11:20	13:55	21:16

(1) Reservation required. (2) Plus other departures from Tokyo at 21:40. 21:53, 23:00, 23:05 and 23:20. (3) Plus other departures from Mito at 3:36, 4:17, 5:01, 5:10 and 5:40.

Tokyo - Narita 8021

Here are the connections with the international jet airport that serves Tokyo.

Dep. Tokyo (Ueno Keisei)	Frequent times from 5:00 to 22:10
Arr. Narita	60-90 minutes later

Sights in Narita: Located 40 miles from Tokyo and only 15 minutes by taxi from the international airport. Many Buddhist temples here. Be sure to visit the 10th century Shinshoji Temple and see the daily Goma ceremony there. Also: Issaikyodo Temple. The Historical Museum, located behind Naitasan Temple, and the nearby 45-acre park with flowering trees and plants, waterfalls and reflecting ponds. There are many country-inn restaurants on Monzen-Dori, Narita's narrow main street.

Dep. Narita	Frequent times from 6:07 to 22:33
Arr. Tokyo (Ueno Keisei)	60-90 minutes later

Tokyo - Niigata 8045

These timetables will change when 120 mph trains start operating on this route in 1982 through the 22.3km-long Daishimizu Tunnel, completed in 1979. It is the world's longest tunnel, followed by Switzerland's 19.8km-long Simplon Tunnel. The "bullet train" will clear the Daishimizu in 7 minutes at a speed of 200km per hour.

Dep. Tokyo (Ueno) Frequent times from 6:49 to 16:49, plus 18:19, 18:23, 19:19, 22:38(1) and 23:20(2).
Arr. Niigata About 4 hours later.

Sights in Niigata: The leading Sea of Japan seaport.

Dep. Niigata Frequent times from 6:48 to 18:48, plus 23:00(3) and 23:12(4).
Arr. Tokyo (Ueno) About 4 hours later.

(1) Carries sleeping car. Arrives Niigata 5:07. (2) Arrives Niigata 5:15. (3) Arrives Tokyo 5:06. (4) Carries sleeping car. Arrives Tokyo 5:55.

Tokyo - Nikko 8047

These trains are first-class only.

Dep. Tokyo (Asakusa)	7:20	8:00	8:40	9:00	11:00(1+2)
Arr. Nikko	2 hours later				

Sights in Nikko: A cool retreat from hot Tokyo in Summer. Beautiful foliage in Autumn. Fine Winter sports. Many mountain lakes in this area.

Dep. Nikko	8:41(1)	9:08(1)	10:14(1)	12:01(1)	13:42(1+3)
Arr. Tokyo (Asakusa)	2 hours later				

(1)Change trains in Shimoimaichi. (2)Plus other departures from Tokyo at 11:30(1), 12:30(1), 13:30(1), 14:30(1), 16:00(1), 17:00(1), 19:40(1) and 20:10. (3)Plus other departures from Nikko at 14:42(1), 16:00, 16:08(1), 16:40, 17:00, 17:40 and 19:40(1).

Tokyo - Sendai 8020

Dep. Tokyo (Ueno) Frequent times from 6:33 to 19:50
Arr. Sendai 4 hours later

Sights in Sendai: The Osaki Hachiman Shrine. The Star Festival (early August) is the most splendid display of color in Japan. Each year at this time, Sendai's streets are decorated with brilliant paper streamers. The celebration goes 24 hours. Also see the nearby Matsushima National Park. Nearly every night in August, you can see the Summer Dance Festival, illuminated by lanterns painted by school children. Only a 30-minute bus ride from Sendai are many pinetree mountain hot springs resorts with inns. Much beautiful foliage there. Skiing at nearby Mt. Zao.

Dep. Sendai Frequent times from 6:40 to 20:33
Arr. Tokyo (Ueno) Dep. Tokyo

Tokyo - Karuizawa 8072

Dep. Tokyo (Ueno)	Frequent times from 6:23 to 20:53
Arr. Karuizawa	2½ hours later

Sights: Japanese Alps scenery. There are connections in Karuizawa for Lake Nojiri and Akakura, where there is good skiing.

Dep. Karuizawa	Frequent times from 7:28 to 20:50
Arr. Tokyo (Ueno)	2½ hours later

Tokyo - Toyama 8072

Dep. Tokyo (Ueno)	8:19	9:16	11:16	14:46	20:53(1+3)
Arr. Toyama	14:14	15:24	17:21	20:51	4:50

Sights in Toyama: See notes about city-sightseeing in Toyama earlier in this section, under "Osaka-Toyama".

Dep. Toyama	7:44	10:44	14:40	16:32	21:55(2+4)
Arr. Tokyo (Ueno)	14:00	17:00	20:59	22:33	5:45

(1) Carries sleeping car. (2) Sleeping cars only. (3) Plus other departures from Tokyo at 21:17(2) and 21:49(1). (4) Plus other departures from Toyama at 22:35(1) and 22:50(1).

Tokyo - Yokohama 0000

Dep. Tokyo	By suburban train, at frequent times.
Arr. Yokohama	30 minutes later.

Sights in Yokohama: The Chinatown area. The boutiques in the Motomachi section. The 19th century garden, Sankei-en. A stroll outside Myohoji Temple. The thousands of Buddhas in the Taya Caves. The history written on the tombstones in the Foreign Cemetery.

Dep. Yokohama	By suburban train, at frequent times.
Arr. Tokyo	30 minutes later.

HOKKAIDO TRAIN TRIPS

What Hokkaido offers tourists is wild, primitive scenery: great lakes, fierce animals, aborigines, large herds of cattle, a severe northern climate, fine Winter sports, scenic mountains and forests. The 2 train routes on Hokkaido are: Hakodate-Kushiro and Hakodate-Abashiri.

Hakodate

This is the starting point for rail trips to Japan's northernmost frontier. See the only Western castle in Japan: Goryokaku fortress, constructed in the form of a 5-pointed star.

Sapporo

Marvelous skiing here. Hot springs resorts. The snow sculptures at the annual February Snow Festival. Visit the Shikotsu-Toya National Park and the Akan National Park, with its Ainu aborigines.

Kushiro

One of the bases for visiting Akan National Park.

Hakodate - Sapporo - Kushiro 8002

Unless otherwise designated, a supplement is charged.

Dep. Hakodate	4:50(1)	9:40(2)	11:45	14:32(5)
Arr. Sapporo	9:22	13:50(2)	16:27	20:07
Change trains.				
Dep. Sapporo	12:20(1)	13:56(2)	17:15	22:10(3+6)
Arr. Kushiro	18:53	19:15	22:14	6:15
	*	*	*	
Dep. Kushiro	7:20(2)	11:55	22:35(3)	-0-
Arr. Sapporo	12:19(2)	18:14	6:25	-0-
Change trains.				
Dep. Sapporo	12:25(2)	19:20	10:20	-0-
Arr. Hakodate	16:40	23:55	16:08	-0-

(1) Meal service daily. (2) Direct train. No train change in Sapporo. Meal service on alternate days. (3) Carries sleeping car. (4) Second-class only. No supplement. (5) Plus another departure from Hakodate at 23:51(4). (6) Plus another departure from Sapporo at 7:05.

Hakodate - Sapporo - Asahigawa - Abashiri

Unless otherwise designated, a supplement is charged.

8000 + 8002

Dep. Hakodate	-0-	4:45(1)	7:40(1)	11:40(3+6)
Arr. Sapporo	-0-	8:57	11:59	15:55(3)

Change trains.

8007

Dep. Sapporo	7:00(1)	9:28(1)	13:40(2)	16:00(3+7)
Dep. Asahigawa	8:48(1)	11:16(1)	15:40(2)	17:51(3)
Arr. Abashiri	12:48	15:39	23:04	21:57

Sights in Asahigawa: The aborigine Ainu village at Chikabumi, a few minutes away. Instead of stopping in Asahigawa, many tourists drive by rental car to hot spring resorts a few hours away (Shirogane and Sounkyo), where there are good inns, skiing and beautiful mountain scenery. This is in the excellent Daisetsuzan National Park. Good fishing

8007

Dep. Abashiri	5:40	8:58(3)	13:54(1)	17:02(1+8)
Arr. Asahigawa	9:56	13:07(3)	17:57(1)	21:15(1)
Arr. Sapporo	12:10	14:59(3)	19:53	23:04

Change trains.

8000 + 8002

Dep. Sapporo	12:25(5)	15:05(1)	20:00(1+9)	-0-
Arr. Hakodate	16:40	19:24	0:20	-0-

(1) Meal service. (2) Second-class only. No supplement. (3) Direct train. No train change in Sapporo. Meal service. (4) Carries second-class sleeping car. (5) Meal service on alternate days. (6) Plus another departure from Hakodate at 14:55(1), connecting with departure from Sapporo at 22:15(4). (7) Plus other departures from Sapporo at 17:10 and 22:15(4). (8) Plus another departure from Abashiri at 21:14(4). (9) Plus other departures from Sapporo to Hakodate: see preceding table.

DISTANCE TRAIN TRIPS FROM TOKYO

Tokyo - Kyoto and Osaka

These trains require reservation and serve either light refreshments or meals.

8070

Dep. Tokyo	Frequent times from 6:00 to 20:24
Arr. Kyoto	3 hours later
Arr. Osaka	18 minutes after departing Kyoto

* * *

Dep. Osaka	Frequent times from 6:00 to 20:37
Dep. Kyoto	18 minutes later
Arr. Tokyo	3 hours 15 minutes after departing Osaka

Tokyo - Aomori (via Niigata)

8045

Dep. Tokyo (Ueno)	8:49	12:49
Arr. Niigata	13:00	17:00

Change trains.

8035

Dep. Niigata	14:37	17:30(1)
Arr. Aomori	22:18	23:50

* * *

Dep. Aomori	4:50(1)	6:50	12:55
Arr. Niigata	11:15	14:26	21:22

Change trains.

8045

Dep. Niigata	11:48	14:48	23:00	23:12(2)
Arr. Tokyo (Ueno)	16:03	19:03	5:06	5:55

(1) Meal service. (2) Carries sleeping car.

Tokyo - Aomori (via Sendai)

Unless oherwise designated, a supplement is charged.

8019

Dep. Tokyo (Ueno)	7:33(1)	8:33(1)	10:03(1)	12:33(1)	13:33(1+8)
Arr. Aomori	16:22	17:25	19:04	21:25	22:25

* * *

Dep. Aomori	4:50(1)	8:20(1)	9:20(1)	11:20(1)	12:55(1+9)
Arr. Tokyo (Ueno)	13:55	17:10	18:09	20:09	21:42

(1) Meal service. (2) Second-class coach car only. (3) Carries first and second-class sleeping car and second-class coach. (4) Carries second-class sleeping car and first-class coach car. (5) Reservation required. (6) Carries only sleeping cars (first and second-class). (7) Carries only

second-class sleeping cars. (8) Plus other departures from Tokyo at 14:48(1), 15:30(1), 19:08(2), 19:31(3), 19:50(4), 20:50(3+5), 21:40(4), 21:53(7), 22:00(6), 22:21(3), 23:00(7) and 23:20(2). (9) Plus other departures from Aomori at 14:25(1), 15:50(3), 16:35(2), 18:09(6), 18:40(7), 19:15(7), 19:52(3), 20:35(3), 21:10(4), 23:58(4) and 0:02(2).

Tokyo - Aomori (via Akita)

8038					
Dep. Tokyo (Ueno)	8:03(1)	12:03(1)	19:31(2)	22:00(2)	22:41(2)
Arr. Akita	15:55	19:55	5:40(2)	7:00(2)	8:53(2)
Change trains.					
8035					
Dep. Akita	19:04(1)	21:19(1)	5:49(3)	7:16	9:08(3)
Arr. Aomori	21:45	23:50	9:10	10:16	12:10

* * *

Dep. Aomori	8:07(1)	15:50(2)	18:09(2)	20:35(2)
Arr. Akita	10:42	19:02(2)	21:05(2)	23:42(2)
Change trains.				
8038				
Dep. Akita	11:48(1)	19:21(2)	21:14(2)	23:50(2)
Arr. Tokyo (Ueno)	19:40	6:05	6:30	10:06

(1) Meal service. (2) Carries sleeping car. No train change in Akita. (3) Second-class only.

THE TRANS-SIBERIAN RAIL TRIP

This is the westward ride on the Trans-Siberian Express.

Yokohama - Khabarovsk - Moscow

5050		
Dep. Yokohama	11:00(1)	Day 1
Arr. Nakhodka	17:00	Day 3
Change to train.		
5045		
Dep. Nakhodka	N/A(2)	Day 3
Arr. Khabarovsk	4:10	Day 4
Change trains.		
5020		
Dep. Khabarovsk	6:55(3)	Day 4
Arr. Moscow (Yar.)	15:05	Day 10

(1) For specific sailing dates, check a current Cook's International Timetable. (2) Runs only on arrival days of ships from Yokohama. Carries sleeping car. Only hard cars for seat passengers. Meal service. (3) Runs daily. Soft and hard cars. Carries sleeping car. Meal service.

KAMPUCHEA

(formerly called Khmer Republic and Cambodia)

The one rail route in Kampuchea links the seaport of Kompong Sam with the capital, Phnom Penh, and then extends westward from there to Aranyaprathet, just inside Thailand's border, and on to Bangkok.

Phnom Penh - Kompong Sam 7101

Dep. Phnom Penh	N/A(1)	Dep. Kompong Sam	N/A(1)
Arr. Kompong Sam	N/A(1)	Arr. Phnom Penh	N/A(1)

(1) Service has been suspended since the closing of the frontier in 1976.

Sights in Phnom Penh: The diamond encrusted black derby at the Royal Museum in the Royal Palace. Also there: The Throne Hall, Silver Pagoda (with its solid silver floors and Golden Buddha), Pavilion of the Holy Sword, and the open-air Chanchhaya Hall, where royal ballets once were performed. Also see, nearby, The National Museum and the Khmer Art School, with its arts and handicrafts (silk sarongs, small figures of dancers and musicians, and silver carriages).

Phnom Penh - Aranyaprathet - Bangkok 7100

Dep. Phnom Penh	N/A(1)		
Arr. Aranyaprathet	N/A(1)		
Change trains.			
7059			
Dep. Aranyaprathet	5:35(3)	7:10(2)	13:15(3)
Arr. Bangkok	10:55	12:40	18:35

(1)Service has been suspended since the frontier closed in 1977. (2)Second-class only. (3)Third-class only.

LAO PEOPLE'S DEMOCRATIC REPUBLIC

There is no passenger train service in Lao.

MALAYSIA

Children under 4 travel free. Half-fare for children 4-11. Children 12 and over must pay full fare.

There is passenger rail service from Kuala Lumpur to 4 Malayan seaports: Penang and Padang Besar on its westcoast, and to Tumpat and Kuantan on its eastcoast. Kota Bahru, 8 miles inland from the South China Sea, is also served by trains from Kuala Lumpur.

There is also train service from Kuala Lumpur south to Singapore.

The views through Malaysia include pepper-vine farms, rice paddies, colorfully clothed people at small railstations, water buffalo, and many different tree farms: rubber, banana, tapioca, coconut and palm oil nut, used in making soap and margarine.

Malayan Railway Pass

Unlimited train travel on all classes of coach on all rail lines within Peninsular Malaysia, including travel to and from Singapore. The 1983 prices are: M$70 for 10 days, M$150 for 30 days. Space in first-class air-conditioned coaches must be reserved. (The single air-conditioned coach operated between Kuala Lumpur and Singapore has seats for only 22 people.) Reservations for first-class space can be made up to 3 months in advance of travel date from: Director of Commerce, Malayan Railway, Jalan Sultan Hishamuddin, Kuala Lumpur. This pass is sold at stations in Kuala Lumpur, Penang, Padang Besar, Johore Baru, Butterworth, Pelabuhan Kelang, Rantau Panjang, Wakaf Bharu and Singapore.

Kuala Lumpur

See the marvelous collection of dioramas portraying primitive Malay life, costumes, ancient vehicles, silver, brass and weapons in the National Museum (Muzium Negara). Parliament House. Rubber and pewter factories, Tin mines. The old Central Mosque. The National Art Gallery. The Zoo. The Batu Caves, a Hindu shrine, 8 miles away. The breathtaking modern Majid Negara (National Mosque). The Chan See Shu Yuen Society Temple.

The Sunday Market (to be visited Saturday night) on Jalan Raja Muda Musa, to sample Malay food. The antiques and art in Wisma Loke, formerly the residence of a wealthy Chinese merchant, on Jalan Medan Tuanku.

Kuala Lumpur - Butterworth (Penang) - Padang Besar

7005				
Dep. Kuala Lumpur	7:30(1)	9:00(1)	15:00(1+2)	20:10(3+8)
Arr. Butterworth	13:25	17:30	21:25	5:40
Change trains.				
7016				
Dep. Butterworth	6:50(3)	7:55(4)	9:55(5)	
Arr. Padang Besar	10:20	11:30	14:49	
	*	*	*	
Dep. Padang Besar	14:00(3)	15:00(6)	16:30(5)	
Arr. Butterworth	18:10	18:45	22:40	
Change trains.				
7005				
Dep. Butterworth	20:35(3)	22:00(1+7)	8:15(1+2)	8:45(1+9)
Arr. Kuala Lumpur	5:55	7:00	14:35	17:25

(1) Air-conditioned in first-class. Meal service. (2) Reservation required. (3) Second and third-class only. (4) Runs Monday, Wednesday and Friday. Meal service. (5) Third-class only. (6) Runs Tuesday, Thursday

and Sunday. Meal service. (7)Carries first and second-class sleeping car. Has only second and third-class coach car. (8)Plus another departure from Kuala Lumpur at 22:00(7). (9)Plus another departure from Butterworth at 13:55(1).

Sights in Penang: An island, just off Butterworth. See the Snake Temple. Ayer Hitami Temple. Khoo Kongsi Temple. The view of the island from the top (2500 feet) of Penang Hill, reached by a funicular. Siva Temple. Goddess of Mercy Temple. The sociable monkeys at the Botanical Gardens. The shops on Campbell Street. The pagoda at Kek Lok Si Temple. Kapitan Kling Mosque.

Kuala Lumpur - Mentakab - Kuantan - Kota Bahru 7015

Dep. Kuala Lumpur	8:00	19:30	Dep. Kota Bahru	8:00	19:30
Dep. Mentakab	N/A(1)	N/A(1)	Dep. Kuantan	N/A(1)	N/A(1)
Dep. Kuantan	N/A(1)	N/A(1)	Dep. Mentakab	N/A(1)	N/A(1)
Arr. Kota Bahru	18:00	7:30	Arr. Kuala Lumpur	18:00	7:30

(1)Time has not been available since 1980.

Kuala Lumpur - Mentakab - Tumpat

7015		7006	
Dep. Kuala Lumpur	15:00	Dep. Tumpat	10:00(2)
Arr. Mentakab	17:00(1)	Arr. Mentakab	20:29
Change trains.		Change trains.	
7006		7015	
Dep. Mentakab	6:33(2)	Dep. Mentakab	5:30(1)
Arr. Tumpat	18:00	Arr. Kuala Lumpur	7:30

(1)Estimated. (2)Meal service.

INTERNATIONAL ROUTES FROM MALAYSIA

Butterworth is Malaysia's train gateway to Thailand. Kuala Lumpur is the starting point for rail trips to Singapore.

Butterworth - Bangkok 7050

Dep. Butterworth	7:55(1)	Arr. Bangkok	6:45	Day 2

(1)Runs Monday, Wednesday and Friday. Carries sleeping car. Meal service.

Kuala Lumpur - Singapore 7005

Dep. Kuala Lumpur	7:30	9:00(1)	15:05(1+2)	20:15(3)	22:00(4)
Arr. Singapore	13:35	17:30	21:35	5:55	7:25

(1)Air-conditioned in first-class. Meal service. (2)Reservation required. (3)Second and third-class only. (4)Air-conditioned in first-class. Carries sleeping car.

NORTH KOREA

In overnight trains, the first-class seats convert to berths with complete bedding; second-class seats convert to couchettes. Children under 3 travel free. Half-fare for children 3-9. Children 10 and over must pay full fare.

The 16-car train from Pyonyang to Pekin is pulled by an electric engine. About half of the cars have sleeping facilities. These are occupied mainly by non-Koreans. The other cars have 4-seat benches. Passage between the 2 classes of cars is prevented by locked doors.

A restaurant car is accessible to the first-class sleeping cars. In it, passengers can buy food, beer and Pullosul, a yellow liqueur containing an alcohol-preserved pit viper snake.

The scenery on this route is mostly rice paddies.

Before reaching the Chinese border, the train crosses the Yalu River. On the other side of the Yalu, a steam engine replaces the electric Korean locomotive. Chinese immigration officers board the train when it stops in Dandong, where a Chinese restaurant car replaces the Korean one.

After reaching Pekin, there are connections by train from there to both Moscow and to Hanoi (and on from there to Ho Chi Minh City, formerly called Saigon).

Chongjin - Pyongyang

5205

Dep. Chongjin	N/A(1)
Arr. Pyongyang	N/A(1)

* * *

Dep. Pyongyang	N/A(1)
Arr. Chongjin	N/A(1)

(1)Timetables have not been available since 1977.

Pyongyang - Pekin

5200

Dep. Pyongyang	12:00	Wed. and Sat.
Arr. Dandong	16:23	

5306

Dep. Dandong	17:54	Wed. and Sat.
Arr. Shenyang	22:15	

5307

Dep. Shenyang	22:30	Wed. and Sat.
Arr. Pekin	8:40	Thurs. and Sun.

PEOPLE'S REPUBLIC OF CHINA

In overnight trains, the first-class seats convert to berths with complete bedding; second-class seats convert to couchettes. Children under 3 travel free. Half-fare for children 3-9. Children 10 and over must pay full fare.

The 3 categories of Chinese National Railways trains are Express, Fast and Ordinary. Short-distance trains have soft and hard seat accommodations. Long-distance trains provide soft-class compartment berths and hard-class sleeping berths. We learned on our 1980 rail trips (Shanghai-Changsha, Changsha-Guilin and Canton-Hong Kong) that Chinese trains do not provide drinking water, toilet paper, or soap, although each sleeping compartment is supplied with a thermos of hot water, tea and cups. There is enough storage space in each 4-person compartment for 6 large suitcases. Each berth has a reading lamp.

You can count on 2 things when touring China: the government will keep you on the go 10-14 hours every day, and you will be placed in a Friendship Store from one to 3 hours almost every day. These emporiums sell every possible souvenir you could want to bring home from China: jade, ivory, fabrics, furniture, porcelain, clothing, lacquerware, jewelry, books, etc.

Canton (Guangzhou, pronounced "Kwang-chow")

In the 64-acre Memorial Garden to the Martyrs (also called Red Uprising (the 1927 massacre of many Chinese Communist Party members by government soldiers), holding more than 5,000 bodies. Also: The Pavillion of Sino-Korean Friendship and the Memorial Pavillion. The Tomb of the 72 Martyrs, honoring leaders of the unsuccessful 1911 revolution, located at Huanghuagang (Yellow Flower Hill Park). The Sun Yat-sen Memorial Hall.

At the enormous Yuexiu Park, go to the top of the 600-year-old Zhen Hai Tower (also called Five-Storied Building) for a view of all of the city. Also located in this park are the Museum of Liberation and many other museums: prehistory, Ming Dynasty, the Manchu era, the Opium Wars, and one on the industrialization of Canton.

At the west side of Yuexiu Park, there is an excellent Chinese Orchid Garden. The 82-acre Zoo, with more than 200 varieties of birds and animals, is considered one of the best in Asia and is famous for its Panda bears.

Other notable sights: the 6th century Lu Yung Temple (Temple of the Six Banyan Trees). The 7th century Huaisheng Mosque. The 4th century(B.C.) Kwang Shiao Temple. Many parks and lakes. The view from White Cloud Mountain. The Monument to the Struggle Against the British Invasion, at Sanyuanli, north of the city.

Pekin (Beijing)

It is said that everyone starts a tour of Pekin from the enormous Tian'anmen Square (nearly 100 acres), where Chairman Mao Zedong first raised the flag of the People's Republic of China and initiated the contemporary era of China.

At the north side of the Square is Tian'anmen (Gate of Heavenly Peace), the entrance to the fabled Forbidden City, a 250-acre compound containing many palaces, museums, pavillions and gardens.

You walk first through the Upright Gate, then down Sightseer's Route to Meridian Gate and then through Gate of Supreme Harmony, next reaching the exhibits inside Hall of Supreme Harmony, followed by Hall of Complete Harmony, Hall of Preserving Harmony, Gate of Heavenly Purity, Palace of Heavenly Purity, Hall of Union, Hall of Earthly Peace, Gate of Earthly Peace, and finally reach Hall of Imperial Peace, surrounded by the Imperial Garden.

East of Tian'anmen Square are the Chinese History Museum and the Museum of the Chinese Revolution. West of the Square is the Great Hall of the People. Its banquet room seats 5,000 people. A theater near it holds 10,000. At the south side of the Square is the magnificent Chairman Mao Memorial Hall and the Monument to the People's Heroes.

Other important sights in Pekin are: The large Zoo, featuring Giant Pandas. The 770-foot long white marble Marco Polo Bridge, spanning the Yungting River. The National Art Gallery. The fantastic 15th century Temple of Heaven, located in a complex measuring 16 square miles.

It is a 90-minute bus ride from Pekin to the Great Wall, the mightiest human construction in history. Although a special excursion train departs Pekin daily at 7:03 (arriving back in Pekin at 13:30), the train leaves passengers about ¼-mile from the Great Wall. Buses from Pekin take you directly to the section of the Great Wall at Badaling that was restored in 1957 for visitors.

Most of the 3,600-mile long wall was built 476-221(B.C.), with more than another 100 years of work performed to restore and reinforce it in the 14th-15th century(A.D.).

Seven miles from Pekin is the Summer Palace, set in a 700-acre park that includes the lovely Kunming Lake and many museums. The walk down the beautifully decorated "Long Corridor", along the lakeshore, is memorable.

Thirty miles from Pekin, the Ming Tombs cover an area of several square miles. The sculptured animals along the road leading to the exhibit tomb are very interesting.

Canton - Kowloon - Hong Kong 5400

Prior to 1979, it was always necessary to walk from Shenzhen across the bridge spanning the Shum Chun River, to the Lo Wu rail-station on the south side of the river before boarding a second train in Lo Wu and proceeding on to Kowloon and Hong Kong.

Since 1979, 2 trains per day make a direct ride from Canton to Kowloon, without requiring passengers to change trains at Shenzhen-Lo Wu.

Departures for the short ferry-boat ride from Kowloon to Hong Kong are frequent.

Dep. Canton	6:30(1)	7:25(1)	8:30(3)	9:14(1)	10:10(3)
Arr. Shenzhen	8:36(2)	9:16(2)	10:20	11:30(2)	12:00
Dep. Shenzhen	-0-	-0-	10:23	-0-	12:03
Arr. Lo Wu	-0-	-0-	10:28(3)	-0-	12:08(3)
Change trains.					
Dep. Lo Wu	9:34	10:46	10:31	13:09	12:11(3)
Arr. Kowloon	10:47	12:08	11:26	14:24	13:07

(1) Second-class only. (2) Walk across the frontier bridge. (3) First-class only. Reservation required. Meal service. Direct train to Kowloon. No change of trains in Lo Wu.

Canton - Shanghai 5330

Dep. Canton (Guangzhou)	14:25	Dep. Shanghai	9:18
Arr. Shanghai	23:10 Day 2	Arr. Canton (Guangzhou)	18:05 Day 2

Sights in Shanghai: This is the largest city in the world (more than 11,000,000 population). See Chung Shan Lu Street, on the waterfront, called "the Bund", with its European-style buildings, from the period when foreigners controlled the city. You will want to visit the Number One Department Store while strolling this famous street.

Also see People's Park, once a race track. The enormous People's Square. The goods displayed at the Industrial Exhibit, everything from jade to ship-building.

Next to the City God Temple are the Yueyuan Gardens and the Temple of the Town Gods and the Garden of the Purple Clouds of Autumn.

Do not miss the 3rd century pagoda, rebuilt in the 10th century, located in Lung Hua Park. The laughing Buddha in the temple there is a major attraction.

Visit the large natural exhibit Zoo in Si Jiao Park and the smaller Zoo in Fu Hsing Park. The vast collection of artwork in the Museum of Shanghai. The white jade Buddha in the Jade Buddha Temple. The antiques for sale at the Antique and Curio Branch of Shanghai Friendship Store. The Children's Palace. Swan Lake in West Suburb Park.

Shanghai - Pekin

Stops are made at Nanking, Tsinan, Tientsin and many towns not on the Cooks timetable: Soochow, Wusih, Pengpu, etc. At most stops, passengers alight to buy local food items sold along the platforms. At Tientsin, the favorite is meat-filled dumplings that the Chinese regard as the best in their country.

The route actually originates in Foochow. This is a critical military area and, as the case of Vladivostok with the Soviets, is closed to most foreigners.

Compartments are fitted with loudspeakers from which pour a steady combination of propaganda and music, the same as we experienced on the "Trans Siberia Express".

However, where the Soviet off-switch is in plain sight, the Chinese have placed theirs more obscurely under a small reading table.

The compartments on the Shanghai-Peking Express have a fin de siecle elegance: potted plants, porcelain cups, and tea bags. An acupuncturist is available for anyone requiring that service. As on all Chinese express trains, women workers are constantly scrubbing and mopping the interior. Boiling water is provided free in large thermos containers.

Each compartment has 4 berths. However, foreigners traveling in pairs are usually given the entire space. Early in the trip the train goes along the Grand Canal that was being used before Marco Polo saw it 6 centuries ago. It still has heavy boat traffic. Arrivals below are on Day 2.

5330				
Dep. Shanghai	9:16	11:59	14:55	19:09
Arr. Pekin	5:35	11:03	10:04	14:25
	*	*	*	
Dep. Pekin	12:50	17:12	19:10	21:08
Arr. Shanghai	7:50	13:48	18:04	16:19

Pekin - Guilin 5320

Dep. Pekin (Beijing)	23:59		Dep. Guilin	1:26
Arr. Guilin	7:12 Day 3		Arr. Pekin (Beijing)	9:10 Day 2

Sights in Guilin: The most magnificent scenery in China. Green fields or rice and sugar cane. Hundreds of weird shart karst peaks. Take the popular half-day boat ride down the meandering Li Jiang River. Visit Huanchu Cave, Seven Star Cave, Reed Flute Cave, Banyan Lake, Pagoda Hill. See the incredible view from the top of Tuhsiu Peak.

INTERNATIONAL ROUTES FROM PEOPLE'S REPUBLIC OF CHINA

Here are the routes from Pekin to Russia, Vietnam and North Korea.

Pekin - Moscow 5100

Dep. Pekin	7:40	Wednesday
Arr. Moscow	19:50	Monday (Day 6)

Carries sleeping car. Meal service from Naushki (USSR border) to Moscow.

Pekin - Hanoi 5320

Dep. Pekin	23:59		Dep. Nanning	N/A(1)
Arr. Nanning	14:43	Day 3	Arr. Hanoi	N/A(1)

(1) Service "temporarily" suspended in 1980.

Pekin - Pyonyang - Chongjin

In Dandong, a Korean restaurant car replaces the Chinese one. It is accessible to the first-class sleeping cars. Passengers can buy food, beer and Pullosul, a yellow liqueur containing an alcohol preserved pit viper snake. An electric Korean locomotive replaces the Chinese steam engine, and the train crosses the Yalu River.

About half of the cars have sleeping facilities. These are occupied mainly by non-Koreans. The other cars have 4-seat benches. Passage between the 2 classes of cars is prevented by locked doors.

5307		
Dep. Pekin	16:51(1)	
Arr. Shenyang	3:31	Day 2
5306		
Dep. Shenyang	3:46(2+3)	
Arr. Dandong*	8:02	
5200		
Dep. Dandong	9:35(2+3)	
Arr. Pyongyang	15:55	

5205	
Dep. Pyongyang	N/A(4)
Arr. Chongjin	N/A(4)

(1) Monday and Thursday. (2) Tuesday and Friday. (3) Carries sleeping car on Friday only. (4) Timetable not available since 1977.

*The revised spelling of Antung.

PHILIPPINES

The rail system on Luzon is 2 lines, north from Manila to San Fernando and south from Manila to Camalig.

Children under 3 travel free. Half-fare for children 3-9. Children 10 and over must pay full fare.

Manila

See: Representations of the country's major regions(Visayas, Mindanao, Vigan and the Mountain Provinces) at the Philippine Village, next to the airport. Excellent souvenirs are sold there. Visit the complex of Cultural Center, Folks Art Theater and Convention Center. The sidewalk cafes, Chinese and Japanese gardens, planetarium and the lagoon with "dancing" fountains, all in Rizal Park. Fort Santiago, San Augustine Church (which has artifacts from the era of Spanish rule) and Manila Cathedral, all in the 16th century walled city called Intramuros. Near it, Chinatown and the marble tombs in the Chinese cemetery. The Zoological and Botanical Garden. Take a hydrofoil for the short trip to see the ruins of Corregidor, the famous World War II fort. The 18th century 12-foot wide Bamboo Organ of Las Pinas is only a few miles from Manila.

Manila - San Fernando 7700

Dep. Manila (Tutuban)	12:45(1)	Dep. San Fernando	7:00(1)
Arr. San Fernando	20:25	Arr. Manila (Tutuban)	14:45

(1)Second and third-class only.

Manila - Camalig 7700

There are great views of Mayon Volcano from Camalig to Naga and of Pagsanjan Falls and Rapids if you take the 15:00 departure from Camalig.

Dep. Manila	15:00(1)	19:00(2)	Dep. Camalig	15:00(1)	17:10(2)
Dep. Naga	7:00(1)	11:25(2)	Dep. Naga	18:53(1)	20:00(2)
Arr. Camalig	9:35	14:05	Arr. Manila	9:45	11:25

(1)Has third-class couchette. First and third-class coach car. Meal service. (2)Second and third-class coach cars only.

REPUBLIC OF CHINA (TAIWAN)

The special tourist trains in Taiwan are called Chu Kuang and Tze-Ciang.

Nearly the entire length of the western side of Taiwan can be traveled by train. Rail service is also available for a considerable portion of the island's east coast.

Express service starts at the northern top of Taiwan, at Kee-Lung, and extends south along western Taiwan to Pingtung. From there, local trains run to a fork at Chen-an. From Chen-an, one local spur goes to Tung-chiang and another to Fanh-liao. Another rail line runs from Kee-Lung along the eastern side of the island, south to Hualien and Tai-tung Hai-an.

Taipei

Among the leading sights to see in Taipei are the fabulous art treasures from mainland China in the National Palace Museum. Also see: The Monument of the Martyrs. The Memorial to Dr. Sun Yat Sen. Luan Shen Temple, and the street of food stores across from the Temple. The lobby and halls of the world's most extravagant and most beautiful hotel, The Grand Hotel, atop a hill that overlooks all of Taipei.

Taipei - Taichung - Kaohsiung 7800

Dep. Taipei	6:20	7:00(1)	7:30	8:00(1)	8:45	9:30(3+5)
Arr. Taichung	9:00	9:31	10:07	9:57	-0-	11:48
Arr. Kaohsiung	11:47	12:12	12:53	12:16	14:40	14:33

* * *

Dep. Kaohsiung	6:20	7:00	8:00(1)	8:30(2)	9:30(2)	10:30(6)
Dep. Taichung	9:04	-0-	10:09	11:16	12:27	-0-
Arr. Taipei	12:15	11:44	12:16	14:03	15:05	16:39

(1) Air-conditioned train. (2) Air-conditioned train. Meal service. (3) Meal service. (4) Carries sleeping car. (5) Plus other departures from Taipei at 10:00(1), 11:00(1), 12:00(1), 12:30, 14:00(1), 15:00(1), 16:00(2), 17:00, 17:30(1), 18:00, 19:49(1), 22:00(1+4), 23:00 and 23:30(1). (6) Plus other departures from Kaohsiung at 11:30, 12:20, 13:00(1), 13:20(1), 14:30(1), 14:57(1), 15:10, 15:55, 16:30(1), 17:00(2), 18:00(1), 18:20, 19:40(1), 22:00(1), 22:30(1+4) and 23:00.

We had the advantage of being escorted for 9 days in the Republic of China by the prominent Taiwan engineer and orchid expert, Mr. L. F. King, whose comments and knowledge illuminated everything we saw.

His kindnesses made our travels in Taiwan the most idyllic touring we have ever had in our travel throughout the world.

Taiwan's railstations and other of its public places have enormous mirrors. Personal appearance is very important to the Taiwanese, who like to inspect themselves when starting and ending a journey.

No one could become mussed on the air-conditioned, non-stop ride we made from Taipei to Taichung. A few minutes after leaving Taipei, Chinese-language newspapers are given to each passenger without charge. Next, an attendant brings hot, damp wash-cloths, and everyone washes face and hands. Meanwhile, recorded Western and Chinese music is played over the train's public address system. Other train employees place tea bags and hot water into large glasses that fit into holders along the wall, next to where one is sitting and within easy reach. More hot water is served frequently during the trip.

Mr. King, whose taste in art, orchids and food is impeccable, carries with him when he travels a special blend of tea, which he brought on our trip in sufficient quantity for us so that we might have it to enjoy in place of the tea that the train serves.

During the ride, he alerted us to various brick and ceramic factories, the construction of a new super-highway which his company was then building, and other interesting sights. Halfway to Taichung, the train goes along the Formosa Strait.

Vendors come through the train with sandwiches, candies and cigarettes. An hour before arriving in Taichung, a hot meal of beef, rice and a hardboiled egg flavored with tea can be purchased at one's seat for $1.00 (U.S.).

This train has airplane style seating, all passengers facing forward. Each car has separate lavatories for men and women. The price for that journey from Taipei to Taichung on that all first-class express train is $7.00 (U.S.).

Taichung - Sun Moon Lake

One of Taiwan's 2 most famous tourist attractions is the incredibly beautiful Sun Moon Lake, visited by a short bus trip from Taichung.

Government Timetable

Dep. Taichung	7:30	8:30	9:50	13:30	15:30
Arr. Sun Moon Lake	9:20	10:30	11:40	15:20	17:20
	*	* *			
Dep. Sun Moon Lake	10:30	12:30		16:00	18:00
Arr. Taichung	12:20	14:'20		17:50	19:50

Here is an easy stopover in Taichung, en route from Taipei to Kaohsiung or vice versa, with a side-trip to Sun Moon Lake.

Dep. Taipei	10:00	Dep. Kaohsiung	9:30
Arr. Taichung	12:19	Arr. Taichung	12:30
Take bus to Sun Moon Lake.		Take bus to Sun Moon Lake.	
Dep. Taichung	13:30	Dep. Taichung	13:30
Arr. Sun Moon Lake	15:20	Arr. Sun Moon Lake	15:20
Dep. Sun Moon Lake	16:00	Dep. Sun Moon Lake	16:00
Arr. Taichung	17:50	Arr. Taichung	17:50
Continue on train.		Continue on train.	
Dep. Taichung	18:16	Dep. Taichung	18:47
Arr. Kaohsiung	20:47	Arr. Taipei	21:37

Chia I - Alishan 7800

This spur off the Kaohsiung-Taipei line has great mountain scenery. The station at Alishan (7,461 feet) is the highest railstation in East Asia.

Dep. Kaohsiung	6:20	Dep. Chia I	8:00
Arr. Chia I	7:41	Arr. Alishan	12:00
Change trains.		Dep. Alishan	13:30
		Arr. Chia I	17:15

* * *

Dep. Chia I	18:25	Dep. Chia I	19:10
Arr. Taipei	22:29	Arr. Kaohsiung	20:39

Taipei - Hualien 7801

Dep. Taipei	7:00	9:35	13:06
Arr. New Hualien	10:16	13:45	17:29

* * *

Dep. New Hualien	12:45	19:40
Arr. Taipei	17:15	22:54

Only a 20-minute auto ride from Hualien is the eastern end of Taiwan's most fantastic scenic subject, Taroko Gorge. Spectacular marble mountains and, in the river along which you drive, marble boulders of various colors and patterns larger than a sightseeing bus. Within an hour, the road comes to a carved marble bridge. Do not drive over it. Instead, be sure you get out of your car and walk across this bridge in order to get a good view under the bridge of a raging waterfall and the massive boulders that have been polished by the extremely heavy and fast-falling watercourse.

There are many marble factories on the outskirts of Hualien. We went through the largest, RSEA Marble Plant. It is well worth visiting. You can watch blocks of unpolished raw marble the size of a large automobile being sawed into smaller pieces and then see the smaller pieces being carved and buffed into ornamental vases, urns, tables, chairs, ash trays, wine glasses, lamps, chessboards, dragons, etc.

The other great attraction in Hualien is the marvelous show presented 2 times during the day and once at night that features dancing and singing by very attractive, beautifully-costumed aborigine Taiwanese.

Hualien - Taitung 7801

This is a very scenic ride.

Dep. Hualien	11:40	17:17	19:25	Dep. Taitung	7:50	11:45	19:35
Arr. Taitung	15:05	20:42	22:50	Arr. Hualien	11:15	15:10	23:00

Taipei - Su Ao 7801

Here is a short train route along Taiwan's northeastern seacoast.

Dep. Taipei	10:07	Dep. Su Ao	7:49	16:43
Arr. Su Ao	12:43	Arr. Taipei	10:38	19:19

SABAH

Children under 4 travel free. Half-fare for children 4-11. Children 12 and over must pay full fare.

Extraordinary scenery of dense jungles, wild animals and high mountains is seen on the short rail trips in Sabah, one north from Beaufort and the other south from Beaufort.

Beaufort - Kota Kinabalu 7500

Dep. Beaufort	5:45(1+3)	7:30(2+3)	8:12(1+4)	9:02(2+4+5)
Arr. Kota Kinabalu	8:21	10:16	9:55	11:01

Sights in Kota Kinabalu: The small museum on Gaya Street. Visit nearby Kinabalu National Park. The marvelous beach resort at Tanjong Aru.

Dep. Kota Kinabalu	6:30(1+4)	7:20(2+4)	7:30(1+3)	7:59(2+3+6)
Arr. Beaufort	8:13	9:10	10:06	10:50

(1)Daily, except Sundays and holidays. (2)Sundays and holidays only. (3)Third-class only. (4)First-class only. (5)Plus other departures from Beaufort at 9:23(1+3), 10:50(1+3), 11:00(2+3), 13:40(1+3), 14:30(2+3), 14:56(1+3), 15:36(2+4)and 16:24(1+4). (6)Plus other departures from Kota Kinabalu at 7:45(1+3), 11:00(1+3), 11:24(2+3), 13:30(1+3), 13:44(2+3), 14:40(1+4), 14:54(2+3)and 16:35(1+3).

Beaufort - Tenom 7500

Dep. Beaufort	6:45(1+3)	8:13(2+4)	9:10(1+4)	12:15(2+3+5)
Arr. Tenom	8:45	9:45	10:45	14:54

* * *

Dep. Tenom	6:40(2+4)	7:20(1+4)	7:50(2+3)	7:55(1+3+6)
Arr. Beaufort	8:12	9:02	10:50	10:10

(1)Sundays and holidays only. (2)Daily, except Sundays and holidays. (3)Third-class only. (4)First-class only. (5)Plus other departures from Beaufort at 13:38(2+3), 14:30(1+3), 15:40(1+4)and 16:26(2+4). (6)Plus other departures from Tenom at 12:50(2+3), 13:55(1+4) and 14:55(2+4).

SINGAPORE

The long train ride from Singapore is to Kuala Lumpur, and on to Butterworth (Penang) and Bangkok. The short trip from Singapore is to Johore Bahru.

Singapore

A great seaport and the most modern city in Asia. See: the excellent exhibit of Malay culture at the National Museum. The food markets in Chinatown, soon to be relegated to oblivion as this section is demolished in order to make way for modern high-rise apartment buildings. The view of the city and harbor from the top of Fort Canning Hill.

The 50-foot tall, 300-ton statue of Buddha and other wonders in the Temple of 1,000 Lights in the Indian section, near Serangoon Road. The Thian Hock Keng Taoist temple. The ornately-carved Sri Mariammon Hindu Temple. The wood and marble carvings in Sian Lim Sian Si temple.

The orchids (some of which we contributed) and the monkeys at the excellent Botanical Garden. The Chettiar Hindu temple. The Sultan Mosque. Twin Grove temple. Sakya Muni Gaya temple.

Take a one-hour cruise to see the hundreds of ships anchored in the world's fourth busiest harbor, only 77 miles north of the Equator. The cable car or ferry trip to Sentosa Island, to see its beaches, the museum of corals and shells, and the 18-hole golf course. A 3-hour out-of-town tour, visiting the nearby Malay villages, rubber and coconut plantations, temples and a crocodile farm.

Participate in the open-air eating that starts at 17:00 at the dozens of food stalls and pushcarts which vend Chinese, Indonesian and Malaysian delicacies at the Ras Singapura Food Centre (next door to the Singapore Arts and Crafts Centre) and also at Car Park on Orchard Road, near many hotels. There are similar food facilities at Newton Eating Stalla, Albert Street, Hokkien Street and Bugis Street. Prawn fritters, fried pork, satay, beef curry, fish-head fried rice, carrot cake, exotic fruits, a rice dish called Nasi Goreng, and on and on. The gourmet can find in Singapore 9 styles of Chinese cuisine plus Thai, Indian, Malay, Italian, German, French and Japanese food.

See the many Chinese and Indian shops on narrow, twisting Change Alley. The more than 7,000 birds of 350 species in aviaries (some so large that visitors can walk through them) in Jurong Bird Park. Near it, the elaborately landscaped Chinese and Japanese Gardens.

Also see the tremendous collection of jade from every important Chinese dynasty, in the House of Jade. The daily cultural show at Instant Asia. The exhibit of more than 3,000 fish and the many corals at Van Kleef Aquarium. Over 600 animals in the 70-acre Zoological Garden. Souvenirs and antiques in the stalls at Thieves' Market.

Singapore - Kuala Lumpur - Butterworth (Penang) - Bangkok 7005

Dep. Singapore	8:00(1)	8:45(2+3)	13:55	22:00(2+5)
Arr. Kuala Lumpur	14:30(1)	17:20	19:55	6:05
Change trains.				
Dep. Kuala Lumpur	15:00(1)	21:10(4)	22:00(2+3+5)	7:30(2+3)
Arr. Butterworth (Penang)	21:25	5:40	7:15	13:25
Change trains. 7050				
Dep. Butterworth	-0-	-0-	7:55(3+6)	-0-
Arr. Bangkok	-0-	-0-	6:45(7)	-0-

(1)Direct train. No train change in K.L. Air-conditioned in first-class. Meal service. (2)Air-conditioned in first-class. (3)Meal service. (4)Second and third-class only. Has air-conditioned first-class on Thursday only. (5)Carries sleeping car. (6)Runs daily. Carries sleeping car on Monday, Wednesday and Friday only. (7)Day 2 from Butterworth.

Singapore - Johor - Bahru Bus 7008

Dep. Singapore	Frequent times from 6:00 to 23:00
Arr. Johore Bahru	30 minutes later

* * *

Dep. Johore Bahru	Frequent times from 6:00 to 23:00
Arr. Singapore	30 minutes later

Sights in Johore Bahru: Do not forget to bring your passport. This short trip takes you from the Republic of Singapore to Malaysia. See: The Hindu Mariamman Temple. The Sultan Suleiman Mosque. The Chinese Goddess of Mercy Temple. The National Museum collection of arts, crafts and Malaysian culture.

SOUTH KOREA

First-class sleeping compartments have one berth. Second-class sleeping compartments have 2 berths. A supplement is charged for all of the many categories of express trains, refundable if the train's arrival is more than one hour later than scheduled. Children under 3 travel free. Half-fare for children 3-11. Children 12 and over must pay full fare.

Seoul is the focal point for rail trips in South Korea, to 3 different seaports: Gangreung, Mokpo and Pusan.

Seoul

See: The Kyonghweru Banquet Hall and the Throne Hall in the 14th century Kyongbok (Great Happiness) Palace, rebuilt in 1867 after a 16th century Japanese invasion destroyed it. Nearby, the beautiful Pagoda, the Folklore Museum and Kwanghwa Gate. The collection of metal craft, pottery, paintings and sculpture in the National Museum.

The fantastic 78-acre Secret Garden in the 17th century Changdok (Illustrious Virtue) Palace, with its museum. Nearby, the Yun Kyung Dang residence, Changyong-won (Garden of Bright Happiness), the Zoo and the Chong Myo Royal Shrine.

In the center of Seoul, the Duksoo (Virtuous Longevity) Palace. The view from the 763-foot high hill in the park on Namsan. The exhibits of music, dance, architecture and art at Korea House. The colorful Chogye-sa Buddhist Temple. Tong Myo Shrine. The great silks on sale at the Great East Market.

Seoul - Jeonju - Yeosu	5502			
Dep. Seoul (Main)	9:45	12:10(1)	13:45	21:00(2)
Dep. Jeonju	13:45	15:57(1)	17:44	1:54(2)
Arr. Yeosu	17:10	19:10	21:10	5:30

Sights in Jeonju: The Tourist Information Office is in front of the railstation. This city is also spelled "Kyonju" and "Gyeongiu". It is South Korea's most popular tourist resort and has been called "a museum without walls" because of the number of historical attractions here, including 20 ancient tombs in Tumuli Park. See the gold and jade Silla crown in the National Museum. On the outskirts of Jeonju are many interesting sculptures, temples and royal tombs. The hotels have rental cars for driving to many such nearby places of interest.

Dep. Yeosu	7:45	10:15(1)	13:00	19:35(2)
Dep. Jeonju	11:15	13:32(1)	16:33	23:29(2)
Arr. Seoul (Main)	15:20	17:30	20:50	4:35

(1) Air-conditioned. Meal service. (2) Carries first-class sleeping car and second-class coach car.

Seoul - Mogpo 5500

Dep. Seoul	7:30	11:10(1)	12:30	14:30	17:10(1+3)
Arr. Mogpo	13:55	17:15	18:55	20:55	22:45

* * *

Dep. Mogpo	8:20(1)	9:20	10:55(1)	13:55	14:55(4)
Arr. Seoul	13:55	16:00	17:10	20:30	21:35

(1) Air-conditioned. Meal service . (2) Carries sleeping car. (3) Plus another Seoul departure at 21:30(2). (4) Plus another Mogpo departure at 20:35(2).

Seoul - Pusan (via Andong) 5505

Dep. Seoul (Cheon.)	10:30	21:30(1)
Arr. Andong	15:57	2:59(1)
Change trains.		
Dep. Andong	16:30	3:09(1)
Arr. Pusan	21:05	8:00

Dep. Pusan	8:40	20:55(1)
Arr. Andong	13:07	1:34(1)
Change trains.		
Dep. Andong	15:00(2)	1:44(1)
Arr. Seoul (Cheon.)	20:10	7:15

(1) Direct train. No train change in Andong. Carries first-class sleeping car and second-class coach car. (2) Air-conditioned. Meal service.

Sights in Pusan: This is South Korea's principal seaport. Many beaches, monasteries and hot springs resorts a few miles from here. See the museums and temple at the Chung-Yol Shrine (open during daylight hours), where brightly-costumed dancers, singers and musicians perform. Visit Boma-Sa (15 miles north of Pusan), a temple complex with 30 buildings.

Seoul - Pusan (via Daejeon) 5501

Most of these trains are air-conditioned and have meal service. Some overnight trains carry sleeping cars.

Dep. Seoul (Main)	Frequent times from 7:40 to 17:00 and 22:00 to 23:20
Arr. Pusan	5-7 hours later

* * *

Dep. Pusan	Frequent times from 7:40 to 17:00 and 22:00 to 23:40
Arr. Seoul (Main)	5-7 hours later

Seoul - Onyang 5502

Dep. Seoul (Main)	8:05(1)	10:05(2)	13:05(1)	16:05(1)	18:00(3)
Arr. Onyang	9:30	11:27	14:31	17:39	19:25
	*	*	*		
Dep. Onyang	10:23(1)	11:32(3)	15:25(1)	17:30(2)	20:28(1)
Arr. Seoul (Main)	12:00	13:05	17:00	19:05	22:05

(1)Second-class only. (2)Air-conditioned. Meal service. (3)Meal service. Second-class only.

Sights in Onyang: A major hot springs resort, surrounded by beautiful scenery.

SRI LANKA (CEYLON)

Rail travel cannot be much more exotic than the 32 package tours that Sri Lanka Government Railways offers year-round in its air-conditioned trains throughout the tiny (270-mile by 140-mile) island off the southern tip of India. Among the sights to see in Sri Lanka are ancient palaces, shrines, temples, libraries and pleasure-gardens.

The tours range from one to 3 days and include bus transportation between hotel and railstation, all meals, hotel rooms, guides and sightseeing.

Origin points are Alutgama, Bentota, Colombo Fort, Hendala, Miragama, Mount Lavinia and Negombo.

Children under 3 travel free. Half-fare for children 3-13. Children 14 and over must pay full fare.

Colombo

See: the exhibit of stone and bronze sculptures at the Museum. Nearby, the performing elephants at the Zoo. Also a short distance away, the Buddhist murals in Kelaniya, at Raja Maha Vihara Temple.

Bentota, Mount Lavinia and Negombo are beach resorts a short distance from Colombo.

Colombo - Colombo Airport 6302

All of these trains are third-class only.

Dep. Colombo	5:10	5:26	13:40	15:20
Arr. Colombo Airport	6:69	7:26	15:10	16:54
	*	*	*	
Dep. Colombo Airport	7:56	8:30	16:32	17:20
Arr. Colombo	9:16	9:48	17:47	18:54

Colombo - Badulla 6304

Dep. Colombo Fort	6:35(1)	9:30(1)	20:15(2)
Dep. Nanu Oya	14:00(1)	15:31(1)	3:56(1)
Arr. Badulla	17:40	18:51	7:53

This extremely scenic rail trip is through mountains and tea plantations. The area at Nanu Oya (6,000 feet) is cool and green. Badulla is 5,000-foot altitude.

Dep. Badulla	5:55(1)	10:05(1)	18:15(2)
Dep. Nanu Oya	9:45(1)	14:15(1)	22:36(2)
Arr. Colombo Fort	15:15	21:26	6:15

(1)Caries observation car. Has second and third-class coach cars. (2)Carries sleeping car. Also has third-class couchettes and both first and second-class coach cars.

Colombo - Polonnaruwa - Batticaloa 6301

Dep. Colombo Fort	6:05(1+2)	12:45(1)	20:00(1+2+3)
Dep. Polonnaruwa	11:47(1+2)	19:06(1)	3:12(1+2+3)
Arr. Batticaloa	13:36	21:08	5:20

* * *

Dep. Batticaloa	5:00(1)	14:00(1+2)	19:40(1+2+3)
Dep. Polonnaruwa	6:51(1)	15:51(1+2)	22:12(1+2+3)
Arr. Colombo Fort	13:18	22:06	5:50

(1)Second and third-class coach cars. (2)Meal service. (3)Carries sleeping car.

Sights in Polonnaruwa: The ruins from this city's greatest era, in the 10th century.

Sights in Batticaloa: The singing fish.

Colombo - Kandy 6304

For the best views on this ride, sit on the right-hand side en route to Kandy, on the left-hand side when going to Colombo. These trains have second and third-class coach cars.

Dep. Colombo Fort	5:55	6:35	10:15	13:35	17:10	20:15
Arr. Kandy	3-3½ hours later					

* * *

Dep. Kandy	2:10	6:45	9:37	14:57	17:00	18:03
Arr. Colombo Fort	3-3½ hours later					

Sights in Kandy: The praying and ceremonies at the pink-domed Dalada Maligawa (Temple of the Tooth), so-named because it claims to have an authentic tooth of Buddha. See wonderful orchids displayed at the 147-acre Botanical Gardens in nearby Peradeniya. The Tea Factory. Elephants taking baths, nearly all afternoon.

Colombo - Galle - Matara 6305

This very scenic train ride, along Sri Lanka's coastline, offers many miles of palm-fringed beaches washed by turquoise ocean. These trains have second and third-class coach cars.

Dep. Colombo Fort	6:20	8:40	13:35	15:45
Dep. Galle	9:33	11:14	16:20	18:05
Arr. Matara	11:02	13:00	17:28	19:15

* * *

Dep. Matara	5:50	6:40	12:10	15:15
Dep. Galle	6:56	7:46	13:35	16:18
Arr. Colombo Fort	9:15	10:40	16:25	19:45

Sights in Galle: A Portuguese seaport before the Dutch seized it and then Sri Lanka's chief port until Colombo was developed in the 1880's.

Sights in Matara: An ancient fort town. See the old Dutch Reformed Church. Swim and snorkel at nearby Polhena.

Colombo - Trincomalee 6301

The coach cars on these trains are second and third-class.

Dep. Colombo Fort	6:05(1)	12:45	21:20(1+2)
Arr. Trincomalee	12:50	20:22	5:15

Sights in Trincomalee: One of the world's finest natural harbors. The 17th century fort constructed by Portuguese invaders from the ancient Temple of a Thousand Columns.

Dep. Trincomalee	6:00	14:05(1)	20:00(1+2)
Arr. Colombo Fort	13:18	22:06	5:00

(1) Meal service. (2) Carries sleeping car and coach car.

INTERNATIONAL ROUTE FROM SRI LANKA

There is ferry service from Talaimannar to Rameswaram in southern India. (Rail service is provided from Rameswaram to both Bombay and Calcutta, via Madras.)

Colombo - Talaimannar	6300
Dep. Colombo Fort	18:50(1)
Arr. Talaimannar	4:30
Arr. Talaimannar Pier	4:45

(1) Daily. Departs 19:25 on Tues., Thurs., Sat. and Sun. Carries first and second-class sleeping cars. Also second and third-class coach. Meal service.

6180		6182	
Dep. Talaimannar Pier	9:00(1)	Dep. Rameswaram	13:55(2)
Arr. Rameswaram	12:00	Arr. Madras (Egmore)	8:10

(1) Runs Tuesday, Thursday and Saturday. (2) Daily.

THAILAND

Children under 4 travel free. Half-fare for children 4-11. Children 12 and over must pay full fare. In 1981, the State Railway of Thailand began replacing first-class coach cars with new air-conditioned second-class cars.

Reservations in Thailand can be made only in person (or by a local travel agent) and no more than 10 days before travel date. A supplement is charged for fast trains, sleeping berths and air-conditioned coaches.

The rail lines from Bangkok to Chiang Mai and to Nam Tok come close to Burma's border. The routes to Nong Khai and to Ubon Ratchathani go to Laos' border. The ride to Aranyaprathet is on the border of Kampuchea (Cambodia, Khmer)and extended to Phnom Penh prior to the closing of that frontier in 1976.

Thailand's sixth rail route is to Butterworth (Penang) and then through the length of Malaysia to Singapore.

Bangkok

A boat ride on the klongs (canals) to a floating market and a visit to the Royal Palace are the 2 major tourist attractions in Bangkok. The best place to hire a boat is at the pier in back of the Oriental Hotel. Cruises on the Chao Phya River also start from there.

In the Royal Palace complex, see: Chakri Palace, the gold thrones in the Amarin, Dusit Hall, the Chapel of the Emerald Buddha. Nearby, the Temple of the Reclining Buddha.

Also in Bangkok: The Weekend Market at Pramane Ground. The carrara Marble Wat. The Pasteur Institute Snake Farm. The collection of Thai paintings and pottery at James Thompson's House. Another collection of Thai art at Kamthiang House. Suan Pakkad Palace.

Bangkok - Chiang Mai 7060

Dep. Bangkok	15:45(1)	18:00(2)	Dep. Chiang Mai	14:45(1)	16:50(2)
Arr. Chiang Mai	6:20	7:50	Arr. Bangkok	5:40	6:30

(1)Second and third-class. Air-conditioned in second-class. Meal service.
(2)Carries sleeping car. Also has air-conditioned second-class coach car. Meal service.

Sights in Chiang Mai: An abundance of Thai handicrafts are available here: lacquerware, woodcarving, pottery, weaving, batik cloth, silk and pottery. See: the 14th century temple, Wat Chiang Man. The porcelain decorated 17th century Wat Koo Tao. The 14th century Wat Phra Singh. The beautiful bronze Buddha in Wat Kao Tue. The view from the mountain-top Wat Doi Sutep, 3500 feet above Chiang Mai. The Zoo. The Botanical Garden. Take a tour to see the tribesmen. Another to see an exhibition of working elephants.

Bangkok - Thon Buri - River Khwae Bridge - Nam Tok 7057

Take the 5-minute ferry from Bangkok to Thon Buri, a suburb.

The bridge, rebuilt after World War II, is a plate girder bridge. To see timber bridges such as the one in the famous motion picture, continue the ride through the jungle, past the River Kwae Bridge, all the way to Nam Tok. This is an easy one-day roundtrip.

Dep. Thon Buri	8:00	Dep. Nam Tok	12:35
Arr. River Khwae Bridge	10:33	Arr. River Khwae Bridge	14:24
Arr. Nam Tok	12:20	Arr. Thon Buri	16:55

Bangkok - Ubon Ratchathani 7065

Dep. Bangkok	6:50(1)	7:15(1)	15:25(1)	18:45(1+3)
Arr. Ubon Ratcha.	17:35	19:55	3:35	5:25

* * *

Dep. Ubon Ratcha.	6:35(1)	7:00(1)	15:30(1)	18:25(1+4)
Arr. Bangkok	17:20	19:20	4:20	5:15

(1)Second and third-class coach cars. (2)Carries first and second-class sleeping cars. (3)Plus other departures from Bangkok at 20:30(1+2) and 23:20(1). (4)Plus other departures from Ubon Ratchathani at 19:35(1+2) and 23:20(1).

Bangkok - Aranyaprathet 7059

Dep. Bangkok	6:00(1)	13:10(1)	14:25(1)
Arr. Aranyaprathet	11:20	18:40	19:40

* * *

Dep. Aranyaprathet	5:35(1)	7:10(2)	13:15(1)
Arr. Bangkok	10:55	12:40	18:35

(1)Third-class only. (2)Second-class only.

Bangkok - Butterworth (Penang) - Kuala Lumpur - Singapore

7050

Dep. Bangkok	16:10(1)
Arr. Butterworth	18:45 Day 2

Change trains.

7005

Dep. Butterworth	22:00(2)
Arr. Kuala Lumpur	7:00 Day 3

Change trains.

7005

Dep. Kuala Lumpur	7:30	9:00(3)
Arr. Singapore	13:25	17:30

(1)Runs Mon., Wed. and Sat. Carries sleeping car. Meal service. (2)Air-conditioned in first-class coach. Carries sleeping car. (3)Air-conditioned in first-class coach. Meal service.

VIETNAM

Children under 3 travel free. Half-fare for children 3-9. Children 10 and over must pay full fare.

The single rail route in Vietnam is from Hanoi to Ho Chi Minh City (formerly Saigon). This train's name is "Reunification Train".

Hanoi - Hue - Da Nang - Ho Chi Minh City 7305

Dep. Hanoi	21:20		Dep. Ho Chi Minh Cy.	20:23	
Arr. Hue	3:16	Day 3	Arr. Da Nang	3:55	Day 3
Arr. Da Nang	8:22		Arr. Hue	8:30	Day 3
Arr. Ho Chi Minh Cy.	19:27	Day 4	Arr. Hanoi	11:31	Day 4

This trip involves an overnight stop in Hue and in Da Nang in both directions.

Sights in Ho Chi Minh City: Chinese, Japanese, Vietnamese, Cham and Khmer art objects in the National Museum. The Zoo. The Cho Ben Thanh Market. The Botanical Garden. The Flower Market. The Chinese temples in Cholon, the city's Chinatown suburb.

Sights in Danang: The Buddhist monastery at Marble Mountain.

Sights in Hue: Thai Hoa (Palace of the Full Peace). Dien Tho (Everlasting Longevity) Palace. The-Mieu Temple. Ngu Phung (Five Phoenix Building). Tin Tam (Serenity of Heart) Lake. The 7-story Phuoc Duyen Tower. The imperial tombs of the Nguyen emperors.

INTERNATIONAL ROUTE FROM VIETNAM

The Vietnam gateway for rail travel to the People's Republic of China is Hanoi.

Hanoi - Pekin 5320

Dep. Hanoi	N/A(1)	N/A(1)	N/A(1)	N/A(1)
Dep. Hankou*	13:59	16:39	17:45	21:35
Arr. Pekin	6:01	9:10	10:32	17:00

*The revised spelling of Hankow.

(1) Service was temporarily suspended in 1980 between Hanoi and the Chinese border at Nanning.

Chapter 13

AUSTRALIA

Summer here is December 21 to March 20. Winter is June 21 to September 20.

To make advance reservations, write to: The Booking Officer, P.T.C. Travel & Tours Centre, 11 York Street, Sydney, N.S.W. 2000, Australia.

Children under 4 travel free. Half-fare for children 4-15. Children 16 and over must pay full fare.

The State Rail Authority of New South Wales offers more than 20 different special one-day train tours that leave Sydney between 7:40 and 9:20, arriving back in Sydney between 16:30 and 21:45.

Typical of a day's outing is the "Wine Tasting Tour" that has been offered every year. The air-conditioned train takes a scenic route to Broadmeadow, where passengers transfer to a motorcoach which drives through the wine-producing area of Pokolbin. At the Wyndham Estate Winery, passengers are given a wine-tasting with a barbecue lunch. After lunch, the bus continues through scenic countryside to Newcastle, where the tourists board the train for the return ride to Sydney.

Other one-day tours go to lakes, seashores, mountains, caves and sheep stations.

The 2 most outstanding train rides in Australia are luxurious and long.

"Indian Pacific", Australia's most elegant train, makes a 63-hour run between Sydney and Perth, a 2,461-mile journey from Australia's East Coast to its West Coast, and return. This trip involves 3 nights on board.

Fully air-conditioned and sound-proofed, the train carries 144 sleeping-berth passengers (88 first-class and 56 economy-class). Sleeping berths, all meals and morning as well as afternoon tea are included in the fares.

Two types of sleeping accommodations are available to first-class. Twinette cabins (2 berths) have private shower and toilet, wash basin, refrigerated water dispenser, and choice of radio or taped music. Roomettes (for one person) have all this, except they lack the private shower. However, there are shower rooms at both ends of the Roomette carriage.

This train has one deluxe compartment, a luxurious bed-sitting room with armchairs.

"Indian Pacific" carries a restaurant car, lounge car (with piano, taped music and bar service), and a cafeteria club car that serves morning and afternoon teas, ice cream sandwiches and liquor.

All food served on this train is prepared on board. The "Indian

Pacific" is famous for its lavish breakfast: fruit juice, cereal, bacon and eggs, steak or sausages, potatoes, toast and beverage.

On this route, temperatures outside the train average 109 degrees Fahrenheit in February.

Overseas tourists are allowed up to 336 pounds of free luggage for first-class, 224 pounds if traveling economy-class.

Reservations can and should be made one year in advance. Stops may be made at any station en route and journey resumed later at no extra cost provided that the whole journey is completed within 3 months.

The other sensational train ride in Australia (covering part of the same route as "Indian Pacific" does) is on the air-conditioned "Trans-Australian Railway Express", making a 35-hour run between Port Pirie and Perth, a trip of 1,464 miles. Reservations should be and can be made as much as one year in advance of travel date on this train.

This train carries a lounge car for first-class passengers that is divided into 2 sections: a smoking area and a music salon with piano.

Music, news and announcements are piped into each compartment's individually-controlled speakers. Among many other amenities, each car has showers. First-class passengers receive a breakfast tray in their "cabin". Economy passengers are served a Continental breakfast in the restaurant car. Afternoon tea is served to all passengers in their cabin. Sleeping berths, meals and teas are included in the fares.

AUSTRALIAN TRAIN PASS

Austrailpass. Unlimited first class travel on all Australian railways, including suburban and metropolitan lines (except in Adelaide). Use of this pass must begin within 6 months of the date it is issued (within 12 months when issued in New Zealand).

Cannot be purchased in Australia. (Exception: a 7-day extension to the 14-day pass can be purchased after arriving in Australia.)

Austrailpass is sold worldwide by travel agents and Tour Pacific/ Australian Travel Service (phone for all U.S.A. except California: 800-423-2880 . . . for Cal.: 800-232-2121). The prices from April 1, 1983 through March 31, 1984 are: 14 days A$290, 7-day extension A$130, 21 days A$365, one month A$465, 2 months A$650, and 3 months A$750. Although sleeping berths and meals are included in the price of some Australian tickets, they are not covered by Austrailpass.

The state railways of New South Wales, Victoria and Western Australia offer separate train passes, valid for travel within their state borders.

Sydney

See the view from the observation deck on the 48th floor of one of Australia's tallest buildings, Australia Square on George Street. Take the guided tour of Sydney Opera House. Go on a walking tour around The Rocks, the oldest part of Sydney, after obtaining information from the Visitors' Centre in George St. North.

Visit the collection of Australian and European art at the Art Gallery of New South Wales. The exhibit of Aboriginal artifacts and relics in Australia Museum, College Street. The planetarium at the Museum of Applied Arts and Sciences, Harris Street.

The collection of Australian and European art at the Art Gallery of New South Wales. The exhibit of Aboriginal artifacts and relics in Australian Museum, College Street, open Tuesday-Saturday 10:00-17:00 and on Sunday and Monday 12:00-17:00. The planetarium at the Museum of Applied Arts and Sciences, Harris Street. The craft, gift and curio shops at Argyle Arts Center, open daily 10:00-18:00. Lush tropical plants and exotic trees at Royal Botanic Gardens, open daily 8:00 to sunset. The changing of the guard every Thursday at 13:30 at the ANZAC Memorial in beautiful Hyde Park. Take a day tour to visit nearby sheep and cattle stations.

The sharks and other Australian fish at Marineland. Take the ferry or hydrofoil from Circular Quay, also the departure point for visits to Taronga Zoo Park. There are many excellent beaches, easy to reach from the center of Sydney.

Rail tours operate to Old Sydney Town, 44 miles to the north, where the settlement of 1810 has been re-created complete with convict dwellings, jail, church, shops and 2 old ships.

Sydney - Port Pirie - Kalgoorlie - Perth 9000

This is the all-sleeping car "Indian Pacific". Reservation required. Air-conditioned train. Meal service.

Dep. Sydney (Cent.)	15:15(1)	Dep. Perth (Term.)	21:00(2)
Set watch back one hour.		Dep. Kalgoorlie	7:00 Day 2
Arr. Broken Hill	9:05 Day 2	Arr. Cook	19:30
Dep. Broken Hill	9:30	Set watch forward 1½ hours.	
Arr. Port Pirie	15:16	Dep. Cook	21:30
Dep. Port Pirie	17:00	Arr. Port Pirie	13:00 Day 3
Arr. Cook	8:35 Day 3	Dep. Port Pirie	13:40
Set watch back 1½ hours.		Set watch forward one hour.	
Dep. Cook	7:45	Arr. Broken Hill	19:54
Dep. Kalgoorlie	20:30	Dep. Broken Hill	20:24
Arr. Perth (Term.)	7:00 Day 4	Arr. Sydney (Cent.)	15:50 Day 4

(1) Runs Monday, Wednesday, Thursday and Saturday. (2) Runs Tuesday, Thursday, Saturday and Sunday.

Sights in **Broken Hill:** This is the area of the dry, sunburnt "outback". The city is built over huge silver, lead and zinc deposits. Visits to mines can be arranged. Also see the collection of coins, minerals, shells and Aboriginal artifacts at Carlton Gardens and Art Gallery. The restored Afghan Mosque, once used by the camel drivers imported to carry supplies through the region.

Scenic air tours operate from here to various nearby points of interest such as the diggings of the world's only source of black opals at White Cliffs, plus trips to Kinchega National Park, Menindee Lakes and several outback stations. Only 82 miles northeast are ancient Aboriginal rock carvings, at Mootwingee. The restored Silverton ghost town is also nearby.

Sights in **Kalgoorlie:** This famous goldrush town is still Australia's largest producer of gold. Tours of a mine can be arranged.

Sights in **Perth:** Wide sandy beaches on the Indian Ocean, with good surfing. Tours to wildflower and forest areas nearby from August to November, when it is Spring here. See: The marvelous display of wildflowers in the 1,000-acre King's Park. London Court, a shopping area re-created as a 16th century English street. The folk museum of early pioneering days, Old Mill.

The exhibit of the large Blue Whale sekeltons, meteorites, Aborigine culture and paintings in the Western Australian Art Gallery. The lovely Georgian-style Old Court House, in Stirling Gardens.

The marvelous horses 37 miles away at El Caballo Blanco, where Andalusian dancing horses are bred. Skin-diving off Rottnest Island, 12 miles offshore. (Ferries operate 5 days a week, daily in Summer.) The 6,000-acre Yanchep Park, only 37 miles away, with its koalas, black swans, limestone caves and profusion of wildflowers.

The Maritime Museum and Art Center in nearby Fremantle, and the great views of the city and harbor from the Round House there. The popular Rottnest Island resort, 12 miles off the coast of Perth.

* * *

Adelaide

The coin collection and paintings at the Art Gallery of South Australia. The Australian birds and animals in the South Australian Museum. The spectacular water-lilies at the Botanic Gardens. The view of Adelaide from Light's Vision. The sealife at Marineland. Australian native animals in nearby Cleland Wildlife Reserve.

Winery tours in the nearby McLaren Vale and Southern Wine District. Coach and 4-wheel drive vehicle tours go from Adelaide to the Andamooka and Coober Pedy opal fields, often visiting Alice Springs and Ayers Rock.

Adelaide - Port Pirie - Kalgoorlie - Perth

The "Trans-Australian Railway Express". All sleeping car Port Pirie-Perth and v.v. Reservation required. Meal service. Air-conditioned train.

9001

Dep. Adelaide	12:50	Dep. Perth (Term.)	21:00
Arr. Port Pirie	16:00	Dep. Kalgoorlie	7:00 Day 2
Change trains.		Arr. Cook	19:30
Dep. Port Pirie	17:00	Set watch forward 1½ hours.	
Arr. Cook	8:35 Day 2	Dep. Cook	21:30
Set watch back 1½ hours.		Arr. Port Pirie	13:00 Day 3
Dep. Cook	7:45	Change trains.	
Dep. Kalgoorlie	20:30	Dep. Port Pirie	13:50
Arr. Perth (Term.)	7:00 Day 3	Arr. Adelaide	17:23

Adelaide - Mount Gambier

9080

Dep. Adelaide	8:00(1)	21:15(2)
Arr. Mount Gambier	15:56	8:00

* * *

Dep. Mount Gambier	8:05(1)	20:35(3)
Arr. Adelaide	16:05	7:30

(1) Daily, except Sundays and holidays. Light refreshments. Air-conditioned. (2) Runs Tuesday, Thursday and Sunday. (3) Runs Monday, Wednesday and Friday.

Sights at Mount Gambier: The remarkable Blue Lake. Australia's largest pine forests. Skin-diving in Little Blue Lake.

Eastern Australia Rail Routes

An extensive rail system in eastern Australia radiates west and north from Melbourne.

Melbourne

The view from the top of the ICI Building, Nicholas Street, with a guide there pointing out the main features of the area. Also see: The largest plant collection in the Southern Hemisphere, at the Royal Botanic Gardens. The Zoological Gardens in Royal Park. Treasury Gardens, near Parliament House. The superb collection of Australian trees, shrubs and plants at Maranoa Gardens.

Australia's largest art collection, at National Gallery, St. Kilda Road. Old Melbourne Gaol and Penal Museum, Russell Street. Institute of Applied Science Museum, Swanston Street. Australian birds, animals and minerals, as well as Aborigine artifacts, at the National Museum, Russell Street. The exhibit of Australian ceramics, weaving and hand-made jewelry in the Galaxy of Handicrafts, 99 Cardigan Street.

Captain Cook's Cottage, in Fitzroy Gardens, honoring the discoverer of eastern Australia. The kangaroos, koalas, emus, wombats and platypuses at Healesville Sanctuary, 39 miles east of Melbourne. Take a ride on one of Melbourne's old-fashioned trams. See the Rhododendron garden at 100-acre Olinda. The demonstrations of sheep dogs working, sheep shearing, wool classing and freeze branding of cattle at Grevisfield, 24 miles from Melbourne.

Take the bus to Philip Island to see the "Penguin Parade", a large number of Penguins coming onto the shore to feed their young.

Suburban electric trains run frequently from Melbourne's Flinders Street station for the 70-minute ride to Belgrave. Several different 2-hour roundtrip steam-train excursions on "Puffing Billy" offer fine mountain scenery on the 8-mile ride between Belgrave and beautiful Emerald Lake Reserve. A collection of early steam locomotives can be seen at the Steam Museum in Menzies Creek, one of the stops on that line.

Melbourne - Adelaide 9080

Both trains require reservations, are air-conditioned, carry sleeping cars and a club car, and have meal service.

Dep. Melbourne (Spencer St.)	20:55	Dep. Adelaide	19:10
Arr. Adelaide	9:35	Arr. Melbourne (Spencer St.)	9:30

Melbourne - Sydney 9070

All of these trains are air-conditioned, require reservation and have meal service.

Dep. Melbourne (Spencer St.)	9:00(1)	18:45(2)	20:00(3)
Arr. Sydney (Central)	21:47	8:45	9:00
	*	*	*
Dep. Sydney (Central)	7:45(1)	20:00(3)	20:10(2)
Arr. Melbourne (Spencer St.)	20:20	9:00	9:55

(1)Daily from late December to late January. Daily except Sundays and holidays from late January to late December. (2)Carries sleeping car. Also has coach car. (3)Carries only sleeping cars. Has Club Car. Restaurant Car opens at 19:00, reservation recommended.

Syndey - Canberra - Cooma 9065

It is an easy one-day roundtrip to visit Canberra.

Dep. Sydney (Cent.)	7:30(1)	17:23(2)	20:30(3)
Arr. Canberra	12:19	23:00	-0-
Arr. Cooma	14:28	-0-	5:50

Sights in Canberra: The modern art exhibit at National Library. The 6 tons of water jetting 450 feet into the air by the Captain Cook Memorial Water Jet on Lake Burley Griffin (10:00-12:00 and 14:00-16:00). The Sunday afternoon (14:45-15:30) concerts of the 53-bell carillon on Aspen Island. The daily exhibits at the Indonesian Pavilion.

The view of the marvelous surroundings of Canberra from Mt. Ainslie, Mt. Pleasant or Red Hill Lookout. All Saints' Anglican Church in a railway station that was built in 1868. Its bell is from a locomotive. The Tidbinbilla Nature reserve collection of kangaroos, emus and Koalas, 24 miles away.

Dep. Cooma	-0-	15:15(1)	-0-
Dep. Canberra	6:55(4)	17:25(1)	17:25(5)
Arr. Sydney (Cent.)	11:48	22:17	22:53

(1) Daily, except Sundays and holidays. Reservation required. Air-conditioned train. Light refreshments. (2) Daily. (3) Runs Monday, Wednesday, Friday and Saturday. (4) Daily, except Sundays and holidays. (5) Sundays and holidays only.

Melbourne - Bendigo - Swan Hill 9078

All of these trains require reservation and are air-conditioned.

Dep. Melbourne (Spen.)	9:35(1)	17:40(2+3)	18:05(3+4)
Dep. Bendigo	12:15	20:00	20:20
Arr. Swan Hill	14:30	22:15	22:35

Sights in Bendigo: Central Deborah Gold Mine. Pottery Centre. Joss House. The Historical Museum and Art Gallery at nearby Castlemaine.

Sights in Swan Hill: The re-creation of pioneer days at the Folk Museum.

Dep. Swan Hill	6:40(3+5)	16:30(1)
Dep. Bendigo	9:00	19:00
Arr. Melbourne (Spen.)	11:05	21:20

(1) Sundays and holidays only. (2) Monday-Friday, except holidays. (3) Light refreshments. (4) Saturday only. (5) Daily, except Sundays and holidays.

Sydney - Brisbane 9050

Watch for the outstanding forest and river scenery between Gosford and Sydney en route from Brisbane. This area comes in view about 90 minutes before arriving Sydney. The best way to see this area is by taking a ride on a suburban train from Sydney, returning to Sydney the same day.

Both of these trains require reservation, are air-conditioned, carry sleeping cars, and have meal service.

Dep. Sydney (Cent.)	18:30	Dep. South Brisbane	15:20(1)
Arr. South Brisbane	10:14(1)	Arr. Sydney (Cent.)	7:32

(1) One hour earlier from early November to early April.

Sights in Brisbane: The view from the observation platform of the clock tower at City Hall. Sub-tropical flowers and shrubs in the 50-acre Botanic Gardens. The Queensland Museum. Queensland Art Gallery. The lovely lake and the native animals and plants at Alma Park Zoo and Tropical Palm Gardens. The 12,000 rose trees in bloom from September through November in New Farm Park, along Brisbane River. The Miegunyah Folk Museum.

You can hold a koala and watch the kangaroos and wallabies at the Lone Pine Koala Sanctuary. Take the 2½-hour boat trip to Moreton Island, or a day cruise to Stradbroke Island.

Sydney - Lithgow - Sydney

Marvelous Blue Mountain scenery on this easy one-day roundtrip by frequent suburban service.

Interurban trains depart from Sydney's Terminal railstation frequently for the 3-hour trip to Lithgow.

Sydney - Murwillumbah 9050

Both trains require reservations, carry sleeping cars, are air-conditioned, haul autos and have meal service.

Dep. Sydney (Central)	18:40	Dep. Murwillumbah	15:25
Arr. Murwillumbah	11:05	Arr. Sydney (Central)	9:08

Sights in Murwillumbah: This is Australia's "Gold Coast" land development, similar to the USA's Florida coastline resort area.

Sydney - Newcastle - Sydney 9045

It is an easy one-day roundtrip to take Australia's most scenic rail route. This line travels through the Ku-ring-gai National Park, the Hawkesbury River estuary (famous for its oyster farms), Australia's longest rail tunnel and the Lake McQuarie district.

Dep. Sydney (Cent.)	6:28(1)	7:35(2+3)	8:12(1)	8:50(4+7)
Arr. Newcastle	2½-3½ hours later			

* * *

Dep. Newcastle	6:55(2+3)	7:36(1)	8:55(4)	12:50(1+2+8)
Arr. Sydney (Cent.)	2½-3½ hours later			

(1) Monday-Friday, except holidays. (2) Reservation required. Air-conditioned. (3) Daily, except Sundays and holidays. (4) Saturday only. (5) Daily, except Saturday. (6) Sunday only. (7) Plus other departures from Sydney at 9:00(2+5), 12:50(2+3), 13:40(1), 14:10(6) and 15:50(4). (8) Plus other departures from Newcastle at 13:10(1), 13:15(6), 13:45(2+4), 15:45(1) and 16:40(2+6).

Brisbane - Rockhampton - Townsville - Cairns

All of these trains require reservations, are air-conditioned, carry sleeping cars and have meal service.

9040

Dep. Brisbane (Roma St.)	7:15(1)	16:00(3)
Arr. Rockhampton	20:53	5:31(2)
Arr. Townsville	12:45(2)	21:25(2)
Arr. Cairns	20:55(2)	6:15(4)

* * *

Dep. Cairns	6:45(5)	15:00(6)
Dep. Townsville	14:30	23:15
Dep. Rockhampton	6:00(2)	15:25(2)
Arr. Brisbane (Roma St.)	19:40(2)	5:45(4)

(1) Runs Monday, Tuesday, Wednesday and Thursday. (2) Day 2. (3) Runs Friday and Saturday. (4) Day 3. (5) Runs Wednesday, Thursday, Friday and Saturday. (6) Runs Sunday and Monday.

Sights in Cairns: Visitors can study coral gardens and colorful marine life from the Underwater Observatory or from a glass-bottomed boat at Green Island, only 17 miles from Cairns. The Atherton Tableland Rainforest, teeming with birdlife, is to the west of cairns. Aerial tours of the Great Barrier Reef take tourists from Cairns along the jungle coastline and over many cattle stations.

Brisbane - Toowoomba 9031

The ascent through the Great Dividing Range offers outstanding scenery on this easy one-day roundtrip.

Dep. Brisbane (Roma St.)	6:46(1)	7:02(2)	8:13(3)	9:02(2+6)
Arr. Toowoomba	9:00	9:10	10:25	11:10

Sights in Toowoomba: This is a garden city in the center of the very rich 8,500,000-acre Darling Downs agricultural area. A week-long Carnival of Flowers takes place here every September. The dense rainforest with many species of birds in Ravensbourne National Park is 28 miles from here.

Dep. Toowoomba	6:25(1)	6:45(3)	7:45(2)	8:40(1+7)
Arr. Brisbane (Roma St.)	8:43	9:00	10:00	11:00

(1) Monday-Friday, except holidays. (2) Sunday and holidays only. (3) Saturday only. (4) Daily. (5) Daily, except Sundays and holidays. (6) Plus other departures from Brisbane at 9:32(1), 12:13(3), 12:32(1), 16:02(2), 16:54(1), 17:02(3), 18:02(4) and 20:02(2). (7) Plus other departures from Toowoomba at 10:40(5), 12:40(3), 15:05(1), 15:45(2), 16:45(2), 17:40(5) and 18:45(2).

Rockhampton - Winton

All of these trains require reservation, are air-conditioned, carry sleeping cars and have meal service.

9025				
Dep. Rockhampton	17:55(1)	Dep. Winton	14:00(2)	17:00(3)
Arr. Winton	14:06	Arr. Rockhampton	10:10	13:10

(1) Runs Tuesday and Friday. (2) Runs only Thursday. (3) Runs only Saturday.

Townsville - Mount Isa 9020

Dep. Townsville	10:30(1)	12:00(2)	16:30(3)	16:45(4+5)
Arr. Mount Isa	3:10(6)	15:01(7)	1:15(6)	13:45(7)

Sights in Mount Isa: Visitors may inspect one of the world's richest copper, silver-lead and zinc mines.

Dep. Mount Isa	11:45(8)	14:00(5+9)	16:00(10)	22:00(5+10)
Arr. Townsville	2:58(6)	10:30(7)	8:48(6)	18:30(7)

(1) Daily. Departs 13:35 on Monday and Friday. (2) Wednesday and Thursday. (3) Saturday only. (4) Tuesday and Friday. (5) Reservation required. Carries sleeping car. Meal service. Air-conditioned. (6) Day 3. (7) Day 2. (8) Daily, except Saturday. Departs 12:30 on Thursday and Friday, at 16:00 on Sunday. (9) Thursday only. (10) Saturday only.

Cairns - Kuranda - Cairns 9010

Excellent scenery on this easy one-day roundtrip. The 9:00 departure from Cairns is a special tourist train, making stops along the way for passengers to take photos and enjoy waterfall scenes. People going on this special excursion may either return to Cairns on the same train or go back to Cairns on a special bus tour.

Dep. Cairns	5:15(1)	9:00(2)	9:30(3)	13:45(4)	15:40(2)
Arr. Kuranda	7:00	10:28	11:06	15:13	16:58

* * *

Dep. Kuranda	7:05(2)	11:00(2)	16:05(4)	16:53(5)	19:12(2)
Arr. Cairns	8:23	12:40	17:25	18:38	20:30

(1) Wednesday only. (2) Daily, except Sundays and holidays. (3) Monday-Friday, except holidays. (4) Sundays and holidays only. (5) Thursday only.

The Central Australian Rail Route

Adelaide - Port Pirie - Alice Springs 9004

Called "The Ghan", this standard-gauge train is the successor to the original narrow-gauge operation of the same name that ran from Port Pirie to Alice Springs from 1930 to 1980. The name is in tribute to the Afghan traders who in the 19th century carried passengers and goods on camels between Port Pirie and Oodnatta, the end of the original rail line.

This train is air-conditioned. Carries sleeping car. Also has second-class coach car. Meal service for sleeping car passengers. Light refreshments for coach car passengers. Carries motor vehicles.

Dep. Adelaide	10:40(1)		Dep. Alice Springs	15:30(2)	
Arr. Port Pirie	13:47		Arr. Port Pirie	11:55	Day 2
Dep. Port Pirie	14:30		Dep. Port Pirie	13:50	
Arr. Alice Springs	10:30	Day 2	Arr. Adelaide	17:15	

(1)Thursday only. (2)Saturday only.

Sights in Alice Springs: This is the ideal base for tours to the "Great Outback". It is a frontier town with modern homes and wide, tree-lined streets. Alice Springs is the headquarters for both the Royal Flying Doctor Service and the unique School of the Air, the sole means of education for those living in the deserted areas of Australia.

Visitors can listen to the children and the teachers, and visit the Flying Doctor facility.

See the museum in the Old Telegraph Station. Many art galleries and souvenir shops. The Pitchi-Richi Bird Sanctuary, 2 miles from Alice Springs, has a collection of Aboriginal sculptures and implements, also Australian gemstones.

Take a tour to awe-inspiring Ayers Rock to see it change color at sunset and sunrise.

Adelaide - Port Pirie

Here is the complete list of schedules for train services between these 2 cities. All of these trains are air-conditioned.

9107

Dep. Adelaide	10:40(1)	12:50(2)	18:05(3)
Arr. Port Pirie	13:47	16:00	21:22
	*	*	*
Dep. Port Pirie	7:55(4)	14:00(2)	17:45(5)
Arr. Adelaide	11:10	17:35	21:19

(1)Thursday only. (2)Reservation required. Runs daily. (3)Daily, except Saturday. (4)Daily, except Sundays and holidays. (5)Fridays only.

Western Australian Routes

Perth - Albany 9138 (Bus)

All of these buses require reservation.

Dep. Perth (Term.)	9:00(1)	9:00(2)	15:30(4)	18:00(5)
Arr. Albany	15:25	16:15(3)	21:20	23:50

Sights in Albany: A magificent harbor. This is the starting point for tours through the Porongurup and Stirling mountain ranges for scenic walks and viewing marvelous wildflowers August-November.

Dep. Albany	9:00(6)	9:00(7)	15:00(4)	17:30(5)
Arr. Perth (Term.)	15:20	17:30	22:45	23:00

(1)Monday-Friday, except holidays. Via Kojunup. (2)Runs Monday, Thursday, Friday and Saturday. Via Katanning. (3)Arrives Albany 16:55 on Friday, at 17:35 on Monday and Thursday. (4)Sundays and holidays only. Via Kojunup. (5)Fridays only. Via Kojunup. (6)Daily, except Sundays and holidays. Via Kojunup. (7)Runs Thursday and Friday.

Perth - Bunbury

This is an easy one-day roundtrip.

9131

Dep. Perth	9:30(1)	Dep. Bunbury	15:00(1)
Arr. Bunbury	12:40	Arr. Perth	18:10

(1) Daily except Sundays and holidays. Meal service.

Sights in Bunbury: An important port. Good fishing and surfiing here.

Perth - Fremantle

9145 (Bus)

Dep. Perth	Frequent departures Mon-Sat 5:20-23:20, Sun 9:15-19:30
Arr. Fremantle	35 minutes later

* * *

Dep. Fremantle	Frequent departures Mon-Sat 5:50-23:20, Sun 7:55-19:15
Arr. Perth	35 minutes later

Sights in Fremantle: This is Western Australia's principal port. See: The Maritime Museum and Art Center. The great views of the city and harbor from The Round House.

Perth - Kalgoorlie 9130

The fully air-conditioned "Prospector" (all the schedules listed below) is Australia's fastest train, making its 395-mile (655km) trip in 7 hours 45 minutes. Reservations are required. Stewardesses bring hot meals to the passengers' seats: lunches at 12:30, dinners at 18:30.

Dep. Perth (Term.)	9:00(1)	15:00(2)	16:15(3)
Arr. Kalgoorlie	16:35	22:35	23:45

Sights in Kalgoorlie. See notes about sightseeing in Kalgoorlie earlier in this chapter, under "Sydney-Port Pirie-Kalgoorlie-Perth".

Dep. Kalgoorlie	8:15(4)	14:25(5)	15:30(3)
Arr. Perth (Term.)	15:55	22:05	23:15

(1)Tuesday and Thursday. (2)Monday, Wednesday and Sunday. (3)Friday. (4)Monday and Thursday. (5)Tuesday, Wednesday and Sunday.

Tasmania

Australia's island state, 150 miles south of mainland Victoria, measures 190 miles from east to west and 180 miles from north to south. Visitors can inspect historic homes and folk museums, stay at old inns, see the ruins of old penal colonies, enjoy fine beaches, swimming and excellent mountain and rural scenery.

Tasmania's one rail route ceased operating in 1978. It ran north from Hobart to Launceston and then west to Devonport and Wynyard.

Chapter 14

NEW ZEALAND

Sleeping cars have 2-berth compartments. Children under 4 travel free. Half-fare for children 4-14. Children 15 and over must pay full fare.

The country is 2 islands: North Island and South Island. There is ferry service between the 2 islands, connecting Wellington (at the southern tip of North Island) with Picton (the north tip of South Island).

NEW ZEALAND'S TRAIN PASS

New Zealand Railways/Road Service Tourist Pass. Unlimited travel for 14 consecutive days on all trains, buses (except suburban ones) and inter-island ferries. Can be extended to a maximum of 28 days. Not transferable or refundable. Available from bus and train depots in New Zealand and from any New Zealand Government Tourist Bureau or accredited travel agent in New Zealand. Valid only from February 1 to December 14.

The 1983 prices are: NZ$120 for 8 days, NZ$180 for 15 days, NZ$240 for 22 days, and NZ$15 for each additional day up to a maximum of 28 days. Half-fare for children 4-14 years old. Children under 4 travel free.

North Island Rail Routes

The rail system on North Island is 3 lines running south until they terminate in Wellington, plus a short route from New Plymouth that goes east half-way across the island to Taumarunui, where it connects with the Auckland-Wellington line.

Auckland

See: Westhaven Marina. The view of the city from Mt. Eden, a dormant volcano. The collection of Maori artifacts at the War Memorial Museum. Auckland Kiwi House. The Waitakere Scenic Reserve. Parnell Rose Gardens. The Cathedral of the Holy Trinity.

The views of Hauraki Gulf from Musick Point. The Emily Nixon Garden of Memories. The Pioneer Village at the Museum of Transport and Technology.

Take a swim in the thermal hot pools at nearby Waiwera. A tour of the Earth Satellite Tracking Station. A 2-day motorcoach tour to Rotorua and Waitomo.

Auckland - Hamilton - Wellington

This scenic trip includes the Raurimu Spiral and 3 high volcanoes: Ngaurahoe (7,515 feet), Ruapehu (9,175) and Tongariro (6,517).

The morning departure from both Auckland and Wellington is "Silver Fern". On it, light refreshments are served to the passengers at their seats, airline style. Lunch is available during a stop at Taihape. Announcements as to points of interest are made en route. Air-conditioned.

The night departures from both Auckland and Wellington are "Northerner", carrying 5 day cars and one sleeping car that has both single and 2-berth compartments. Dinner is served in the restaurant car 19:30-21:30. Light refreshments are available throughout the night.

Both "Silver Fern" and "Northerner" require reservations.

9760

Dep. Auckland	8:00(1)	19:30(2)
Dep. Hamilton	9:55	21:45
Arr. Wellington	18:55	8:30

* * *

Dep. Wellington	8:20(1)	19:30(2)
Dep. Hamilton	17:31	6:13
Arr. Auckland	19:25	8:35

(1) Daily, except Sundays and holidays. Light refreshments. Air-conditioned. (2) Carries sleeping car. Meal service.

Sights in Hamilton: This is only 68 miles from **Rotorua,** an interesting place with thermal swimming pools, the beautiful Government Gardens, the Maori Arts and Crafts Institute, trout fishing, St. Faith's Maori Church, TeWairoa (an excavated Maori village), the exhibits at Agrodome, and the overall Polynesian ambience.

Sights in Wellington: The view of the city, harbor and Hutt Valley from the 648-foot high Mount Victoria. The 62-acre Botanical Gardens. Lady Norwood Rose Gardens. The Zoological Gardens. The crafts at the New Zealand Display Center. Conducted tours of the marble-faced House of Parliament.

Government Building, one of the largest wood structures in the Southern Hemisphere. The collection of Maori exhibits at Dominion Museum and National Art Gallery. Nearby, the Carillon and Hall of Memories. The Carter Observatory. Many fine beaches. Freyberg Tepid Pool.

Napier - Gisborne

This route includes the shoreline of Hawkes Bay.

9760			
Dep. Napier	13:55(1)	Dep. Gisborne	9:55(1)
Arr. Gisborne	18:30	Arr. Napier	14:45

(1) Reservation required. Meal service.

Napier - Wellington 9760

Dep. Napier	14:45(1)	Dep. Wellington	7:45(1)
Arr. Wellington	20:40	Arr. Napier	13:45

(1) Reservation required. Meal service.

Sights in Napier: The exhibit of dolphins, sea lions, sea leopards, penquins and other animals and sea birds at Marineland. The assortment of birds in the Botanic Gardens. The fine swimming and fishing beaches. The beautiful Sunken Garden and lovely Golden Mile Park, along the shore.

Taumarunui - New Plymouth

This route is a spur off the Auckland-Wellington line.

9760		9766	
Dep. Auckland	8:00(1)	Dep. New Plymouth	8:40
Arr. Taumarunui	12:11	Arr. Taumarunui	12:30
Change trains.		Change trains.	
9766		9760	
Dep. Taumarunui	15:20	Dep. Taumarunui	15:14(1)
Arr. New Plymouth	19:10	Arr. Auckland	19:25

Here are schedules for the Wellington-New Plymouth route:

9761		9766	
Dep. Wellington	8:20(1)	Dep. New Plymouth	8:40
Arr. Taumarunui	15:14	Arr. Taumarunui	12:30
Change trains.		Change trains.	
9766		9760	
Dep. Taumarunui	15:20	Dep. Taumarunui	0:30(1+2)
Arr. New Plymouth	19:10	Arr. Wellington	8:30

(1) Reservation required. (2) Carries sleeping car. Meal service.

Wellington - Picton

This is ferry service, connecting North Island and South Island. These ships carry both automobiles and passengers. They have food and beverage service. Bus and taxi service is available between Wellington's railstation and the pier there.

9780

Dep. Wellington	7:20(1)	10:00	14:20(2)	16:00(1)	18:40(6)
Arr. Picton	10:40	13:20	17:40	19:20	22:00
	*	*	*		
Dep. Picton	10:00(4)	11:40(1)	14:20	18:40(2)	20:00(1+7)
Arr. Wellington	13:20	15:00	17:40	22:00	23:20

(1) Daily, except Thursday. (2) Daily, except Tuesday. (3) Daily, except Monday and Tuesday. (4) Daily, except Tuesday and Wednesday. (5) Daily. (6) Plus another departure from Wellington at 22:40(3). (7) Plus another departure from Picton at 22:40(5).

South Island Rail Routes

The rail system on South Island is one route along the South Pacific shoreline due south from Picton via Christchurch and terminating in Invercargill, plus a single cross-island line running from Christchurch to Greymouth.

Wellington - Picton - Christchurch   Christchurch - Picton - Wellington

A daylight journey from Wellington to Christchurch (and v.v.) is possible with the following schedule. The good scenery on this ride includes views of many attractive beaches and the Kaikoura mountain range.

9780 (Boat)		9800 (Train)	
Dep. Wellington	10:00	Dep. Christchurch	7:00
Arr. Picton	13:20	Arr. Picton	13:40
Change to train.		Change to boat.	
9800		9780	
Dep. Picton	14:10	Dep. Picton	14:20
Arr. Christchurch	20:45	Arr. Wellington	17:40

Sights in Christchurch: Takahe, the carved Maori meeting house. The Botanical Gardens. Cathedral Square. Beautiful Hagley Park. The view from Summit Road. The mementoes from Captain Cook's 3 voyages, displays on Antarctica explorations, and the exhibit of Maori articles (including a 47-foot wood war canoe) in the Canterbury Museum on the side of Hagley Park.

Christchurch - Timaru - Dunedin - Invercargill

There is fine scenery of the South Pacific coastline and the Canterbury Plains on this ride. Looking to the west, one can see the New Zealand Alps. The Dunedin-Invercargill portion of this route is the most southerly train ride in the world (latitude 46 degrees south).

The schedules below are for "Southerner", a luxury train with meal service. Reservation is required. Seats can be reserved up to 6 months prior to travel date. As you board, you are given a folder about the journey, with a map and notes on points of interest en route. This service operates daily, except Sundays and holidays.

A hostess will serve morning and afternoon teas and light meals to anyone who is physically unable to eat in the buffet car and to mothers traveling with young children. Arrangements can be made to have a rental car or taxi waiting for one's arrival. In the smoking carriage, passengers are served wine, cocktails and liquor at their seat.

9800

Dep. Christchurch	8:40	Dep. Invercargill	8:40
Dep. Timaru	11:02	Arr. Dunedin	12:16
Arr. Dunedin	15:00	Dep. Dunedin	12:21
Dep. Dunedin	15:05	Dep. Timaru	16:19
Arr. Invercargill	18:45	Arr. Christchurch	18:35

Sights in Timaru: A large port. A great beach. Good fishing in this area. Nearby, the National Park with its many mile-high mountains.

Sights in Dunedin: Attractive old stone buildings such as the Railstation. The Larnach Castle on Otago Peninsula. Nearby, Mount Aspiring National Park and several lovely lakes: Manapouri, Te Anau, Ohau, Pukaki and Tepako. Visit nearby Larnach Castle. Enjoy miles of beaches.

Sights in Invercargill: The view of the city from the seventh floor of the Kelvin Hotel. The collection of Maori exhibits and art gallery at the Southland Centennial Museum in the 200-acre Queen's Park, located in the center of Invercargill. The park features a display of native and exotic trees and plants, a group of statues for children, a large sunken rose garden surrounded by flowering prunus and cherry trees, and a special iris garden.

At the eastern side of this park is a wide variety of tropical plants, a large pond containing aquatic plants and fish, a large lily pond, and a well-stocked aviary, all in the Steans Memorial Winter Garden.

Also see the City Gardens, along the Otepuni stream that runs through the center of Invercargill. The 85-acre Waihopai Scenic Reserve. The City Art Gallery in the 60-acre Anderson Park. The 25-mile long sandy Oreti Beach, fine for swimming.

Christchurch - Arthur's Pass - Greymouth

This is the most scenic rail trip in New Zealand. After departing Christchurch, the train climbs to 2,500 feet at Arthur's Pass before going through the 5½-mile Otira Tunnel. Some grades are as great as 4% on this steep ride. On the approach to Greymouth, there are splendid views of the Tasman Coast.

9800

Dep. Christchurch	9:40(1)	18:40(2)	19:20(3)
Dep. Arthur's Pass	12:32	21:36	22:15
Arr. Greymouth	14:35	23:35	0:05
	*	*	*
Dep. Greymouth	6:00(3)	8:00(4)	18:15
Dep. Arthur's Pass	8:03	10:21	20:37
Arr. Christchurch	10:25	13:00	23:05

(1) Daily except Sundays and holidays. (2) Daily except Saturday. (3) Runs Saturday only. (4) Monday-Friday, except holidays.

Sights in Greymouth: Visit a coal mine. Take a jet-boat ride up the Taramakau River to the Kaniere gold dredge and see the little museum of the gold-rush days at Hokitaka. Trout fishing at nearby Brunner.

Lumsden - Kingston

This 42-mile steam train trip on "Kingston Flyer" to the south shore of Lake Wakatipu is a very popular special excursion that runs only from mid-December to Easter Monday. Advance reservations are advisable. The service between Invercargill and Lumsden is by bus.

9806

Dep. Invercargill	10:45(1)	Dep. Kingston	10:15(2)
Arr. Lumsden	12:25	Arr. Lumsden	11:40(2)
Change to train.		Change to bus.	
Dep. Lumsden	13:00(2)	Dep. Lumsden	13:10(1)
Arr. Kingston	14:20(2)	Arr. Invercargill	14:30

(1) Daily, from November 1 to April 30. Daily except Sundays and holidays, from May 1 to October 31. (2) Estimated.

Chapter 15 NORTH AMERICA

Winter in North America is from December 21 to March 20. Summer is from June 21 to September 20.

CANADA

First-class includes use of a Club Car on day trains or any sleeping accommodation (berth, roomette, bedroom, etc. for which there is an extra charge) on a night train. Bedrooms have 2 berths, toilet and wash basin. Second-class is use of a seat in a coach car, day or night. On major trains, coach seats recline and food is provided both in restaurant cars and by tray meals served to the passengers' seats, airline style.

Children under 5 travel free when first-class space has *not* been reserved for them. Children 5-11 pay half of the second-class fare but must pay all of the charge for any sleeping accommodation. Children 12 and over must pay full fare.

The major Canadian passenger train operation functions under the name "VIA Rail Canada".

Canada's other train systems are: Algoma Central Railway, British Columbia Railway, Ontario Northland Railway, Quebec North Shore & Labrador Railways, and Toronto Hamilton & Buffalo Railway.

The Canrailpass described below is valid only on VIA routes.

Three Canadian cities have 2 or more railstations: Edmonton, Montreal and Saint John.

In order to cross all of Canada by rail, one need change trains only once, in Montreal.

Reservation agents of Amtrak in the U.S.A. and of VIA Rail Canada make reservations and issue tickets on each other's lines. Amtrak operates trains to and from Montreal and Vancouver. VIA Rail Canada has service to Windsor, which connects by taxi with Amtrak's Detroit railstation.

CANADA'S TRAIN PASS

Canrailpass. Unlimited train travel in Standard Coaches on VIA trains. The pass can be purchased both in Canada and worldwide. It is issued for 5 different areas: (1) Entire System (coast-to-coast), (2) Winnipeg and east of Winnipeg, (3) Winnipeg and west of Winnipeg, (4) the Quebec City-Toronto-Windsor Corridor, and (5) Edmonton-Calgary and the rail lines west of those cities.

The 1982 prices in Canadian dollars for travel June 1 to September 30 were:

AREA	8 days	15 days	22 days	30 days
(1)			$345	$395
(2)		$225	$260	
(3)		$225	$260	
(4)	$100	$130		
(5)	$130	$155		

The 1982 prices in Canadian dollars for travel any day October 1 to December 14 and January 5 to May 31 (except the Thursday before Easter and the Monday after Easter) were:

AREA	8 days	15 days	22 days	30 days
(1)			$240	$280
(2)		$160	$200	
(3)		$160	$200	
(4)	$95	$120		
(5)	$95	$120		

Children 5-11 years old travel at half the rates above.

Holders of the Canrailpass can obtain accommodations higher than Standard Coach on any ride by paying a supplement.

Group Fare Reduction. Available every day (except from December 15 through January 4) when the ride is at least $4.00(Can.). Groups of 3 or more persons are allowed the following discounts on ticket prices, including sleeping car space: Groups of 3-6 adults 15%, 7-29 receive 20% discount, 30 or more receive 30% discount. For group fare computation, 2 children each paying half-fare qualify as one adult. Advance reservations are essential for groups of 7 or more. Group discounts are not given for sleeping space from June 1 through September 30.

65 Plus. Available every day of the year when the ride is at least $4.00(Can.). People 65 and over can purchase tickets at a 33% discount.

Under 5. One child under 5, accompanied by a parent or guardian who has purchased a ticket (is not using Canrailpass or some other discount), travel free in Standard Coach. Each additional child under 5, accompanied by the same parent or guardian, can travel in Standard Coach at one-half the ticket price.

CANADIAN RAIL TOURS

VIA Rail Canada offers many tour packages, available through travel agents or VIA Passenger Sales Offices.

"Explorer Tours" are escorted and include: sleeping car accommodations on overnight trains, luxury seats on daylight runs, the best available hotels, some meals on and off trains, city sightseeing and narrated bus trips with selected stops for photography. These tours are available only to groups of 20 or more passengers.

"Discoverer Tours" are independent, are for one or more persons, and are not escorted. They are available in 2 qualities: deluxe and economy.

The tour packages range from the 2-day, 1-night "Opera Train Tour" (roundtrip train Montreal-Toronto-Montreal, one night at a hotel in Toronto, and a choice seat at the opera) to the 19-day, 20-night "Transcontinental Discoverer" (a cruise from Vancouver City to Vancouver Island and return, then train to Jasper, bus to Banff, train to Montreal, train to Quebec City, and train to Toronto, including 17 nights in hotels and sightseeing in all cities).

Montreal

Take this walking tour that starts and ends at Place d'Armes: The Sulpician Seminary, built in 1685, the oldest building in Montreal. The oldest wood clock in North America is exhibited there. Then to see the 10-ton bell ("Le Gros Bourdon") and marvelous stained-glass windows in the Notre Dame Cathedral, completed in 1829. It resembles Westminster Abbey. See the gifts from Louis XIV in the tiny museum next to the Chapel.

Other sights: the Chateau de Ramezay, the most interesting museum in Montreal. St. Joseph's Oratory. The Place des Arts complex of concert and theater halls. The vast underground shopping malls in the ultramodern center of the city, called Place Ville-Marie. Take the short trip to Mount Royal.

Ottawa

See: The Parliament buildings, particularly the 53-bell carillon in the 291-foot high Peace Tower. The National Arts Center. The Arboretum at the Central Experimental Farm. The Governor General's Residence. Hog's Back Falls, located in the city. The Royal Canadian Mint. The Canadian War Museum. The Indian Burial Grounds. The Centennial Cabin Museum. The Old Depot Museum. Superb art dating back to the 13th century, in the National Gallery of Canada.

Quebec City

See: The Plains of Abraham. Parliament buildings. The old gates and fortifications of the walled city, The Citadel. The ancient narrow streets. Place Royale. The 25-minute son-et-lumiere recreation of the 6 sieges to which Quebec City has been subjected, in the Musee du Fort at 10 Rue Ste. Anne. The collection of antique furniture in Chevalier House at Place Champlain. The 3-week Winter Carnival, ending on the night of Mardi Gras. Take the 4-hour cruise on the St. Lawrence Seaway.

Toronto

A major port. See: The astounding view from the top of Canadian National's Tower, the tallest (1,800 feet) free-standing structure in the world. City Hall. The Art Gallery of Ontario. The Marine Museum of Upper Canada. Fort York. Casa Loma Castle. Ontario Science Center. The 19th century MacKenzie House, home of Toronto's first mayor. The Royal Ontario Museum and McLaughlin Planetarium. Black Creek Pioneer Village. The Ontario Place recreation complex, at the waterfront.

The Hockey Museum. Ride the special train through the 710-acre Metro Zoo for a view of the 4,000 animals exhibited there. Visit The Islands, a 612-acre complex of amusement ride, bike paths, parks, beaches and lagoons. Go on one of the boats that tour the harbor, departing from next to the Hilton Hotel. Some of these have dinner-dancing cruises.

Vancouver

See: The Zoo and the killer whales in 1,000-acre Stanley Park. The view while walking across Capilano Suspension Bridge. The exhibit of the history of British Columbia from the ice age to today, at the Centennial Museum. The Shakespearean Gardens. Nitobe Gardens. Chinatown. The Maritime Museum.

Nearby, the shows in the MacMillan Planetarium. The Museum of Anthropology at the University of British Columbia.

Halifax - Montreal 3

All of these trains carry sleeping cars, have meal service and are air-conditioned.

Dep. Halifax	13:30	Dep. Montreal (Cent.)	20:50
Dep. Truro	15:10	Set watch forward 2 hours.	
Dep. Moncton	18:30	Dep. Moncton	14:00
Set watch back 2 hours.		Dep. Truro	17:30
Arr. Montreal (Cent.)	9:15	Arr. Halifax	18:40

Moncton - Saint John 92

Dep. Moncton	14:10(1)	Dep. Saint John	16:10(1)
Arr. Saint John	16:00	Arr. Moncton	18:00

(1) Second-class only. Air-conditioned. Light refreshments.

Montreal - Toronto - Winnipeg - Calgary - Lake Louise - Vancouver 1

The "Canadian". Reservation required. Meal service. Air-conditioned. Carries sleeping car. Has dome car Winnipeg-Vancouver and v.v.

During the 2-hour layover in Winnipeg, travelers can bathe in a

"Fresh-Up Room" in the old Hotel Fort Gary. The charge for 2 hours is about $15(U.S.) for one person, $22 for 2 people. During the 2 hours in Calgary (en route to Vancouver), it is a nice diversion to visit the 3-story-high hanging gardens in the Devonian.

West of Calgary, the train travels through the stunning scenery of the Rocky Mountains and the Selkirk Mountains, glaciers near Lake Louise, the Spiral Tunnels at Yoho, across Stoney Creek Bridge, and through the 5-mile Connaught Tunnel.

An Amtrak bus provides transfer between the Vancouver and Seattle railstations.

Dep. Montreal (Central)	16:30	
Arr. Toronto (Union)	22:10	
Dep. Toronto (Union)	23:59	
Set watch back one hour.		
Arr. Winnipeg	11:00	Day 3
Dep. Winnipeg	13:30	
Dep. Regina	22:15	
Set wach back one hour.		
Arr. Calgary	8:10	Day 4
Dep. Calgary	10:30	
Dep. Banff	12:50	
Dep. Lake Louise	13:35	
Set watch back one hour.		
Arr. Vancouver	7:00	Day 5

Dep. Vancouver	21:45	
Set watch forward one hour.		
Dep. Lake Louise	17:40	Day 2
Dep. Banff	18:35	
Arr. Calgary	20:40	
Dep. Calgary	21:50	
Set watch forward one hour.		
Dep. Regina	9:20	Day 3
Set watch forward one hour.		
Arr. Winnipeg	18:00	
Dep. Winnipeg	20:10	
Arr. Toronto (Union)	7:00	Day 5
Dep. Toronto (Union)	9:00	
Arr. Montreal (Central)	15:10	

Rail Routes From Toronto

Train travel to both Canada's eastern and western frontiers can originate from Toronto, which is also the major gateway for rail connections to northeastern U.S. cities (Buffalo, and on to New York or Cleveland; or to Detroit, and on to Chicago . . . see "International Routes From Canada" later in this section).

Toronto - Montreal 85

All of these trains are air-conditioned.

Dep. Toronto (Union)	7:10(1)	10:45(2)	13:00(3)	15:45(2+6)
Arr. Montreal (Cent.)	11:35	15:50	17:40	20:10

* * *

Dep. Montreal (Cent.)	7:20(1)	10:45(2)	13:00(3)	15:45(2+7)
Arr. Toronto (Union)	11:45	15:00	17:40	20:10

(1) Reservation required. Runs daily, except Sundays and holidays. Light refreshments. (2) Reservation required. Runs daily. Light refreshments.

(3)Runs daily. Light refreshments. (4)Reservation required. Runs daily, except Saturday. Light refreshments. (5)Reservation required. Carries sleeping car and club car. (6)Plus other departures from Toronto at 16:30(3), 17:50(4) and 23:35(5). (7)Plus other departures from Montreal at 16:30(2), 17:50(4) and 23:35(5).

Toronto - Ottawa 85

All of these trains are air-conditioned.

Dep. Toronto (Union)	9:00(1)	17:10(2)	22:35(3)
Arr. Ottawa (Union)	15:00	22:35	6:30
	*	*	*
Dep. Ottawa (Union)	8:30(2)	16:25(2)	23:35(3)
Arr. Toronto (Union)	14:40	21:45	7:30

(1)Reservation required. Light refreshments. (2)Light refreshments. (3)Runs daily, except Saturday. Carries sleeping car. Also has second-class coach car. Light refreshments.

Toronto - Winnipeg - Saskatoon - Edmonton - Jasper - Vancouver

Between Edmonton and Vancouver, this route crosses 3 spectacular mountain ranges: the Rockies, Selkirks and Coast mountains. You will see ancient glaciers, large lakes and waterfalls. For the best views, sit on the right-hand side when going West, on the left-hand side when traveling East.

An Amtrak bus provides transfer between the Vancouver and Seattle railstations.

1		
Dep. Toronto (Union)	23:59(1)	
Set watch back one hour.		
Arr. Winnipeg	10:00	Day 3
Change trains.		
30		
Dep. Winnipeg	20:00(2)	
Arr. Saskatoon	5:40	Day 4
Dep. Saskatoon	6:00	
Set watch back one hour.		
Arr. Edmonton	12:45	
Dep. Edmonton	13:30	
Dep. Jasper	18:50	
Set watch back one hour.		
Arr. Vancouver	6:45	Day 5

30		
Dep. Vancouver	12:15(3)	
Set watch forward one hour.		
Dep. Jasper	2:50	Day 2
Arr. Edmonton	7:15	
Dep. Edmonton	8:00	
Set watch forward one hour.		
Arr. Saskatoon	15:45	Day 3
Dep. Saskatoon	17:00	
Arr. Winnipeg	5:30	Day 4
Change trains.		
1		
Dep. Winnipeg	20:10(1)	
Set watch forward one hour.		
Arr. Toronto (Union)	15:10	Day 5

(1)Reservation required. Carries sleeping car and second-class coach car. Air-conditioned. Meal service. (2)No sleeping car for balance of trip to Vancouver. (3)No sleeping car to Winnipeg.

Northern Canadian Rail Routes

In addition to train service in Nova Scotia, to be covered later in this section, there are 17 rail routes on the mainland extending north from Canada's transcontinental lines.

Moncton - Matapedia - Gaspe 92

All of these trains are air-conditioned and have meal service.

Dep. Moncton	18:30(1)	-0-
Arr. Matapedia	22:30	-0-
Change trains.		
Dep. Matapedia	7:35(1)	9:25
Arr. Gaspe	14:30	16:20

Dep. Gaspe	13:20	15:50(1)
Arr. Matapedia	20:43	22:35
Change trains.		
Dep. Matapedia	7:35(1)	-0-
Arr. Moncton	13:43	-0-

(1) Reservation required.

Sept Iles - Schefferville

There is meal service on all these trains.

96

Dep. Sept Iles	8:00(1)	8:00(2)
Arr. Schefferville	19:15	21:00

Dep. Schefferville	8:00(3)
Arr. Sept Iles	19:15

(1) Friday only. (2) Tuesday only. (3) Wednesday and Saturday.

Montreal - Quebec City 91

All of these trains are air-conditioned.

Dep. Montreal (Central)	8:00(1)	-0-	12:30(1)	-0-	17:00(1)
Dep. Montreal (Windsor)	-0-	8:40(2)	-0-	13:10(3)	-0-
Arr. Quebec (Ste. Foy)	10:45	12:10	15:30	16:40	19:40
	*	*	*		
Dep. Quebec (Ste. Foy)	7:20(1)	8:30(2)	12:05(1)	13:00	17:30(1+4)
Arr. Montreal (Windsor)	-0-	12:10	-0-	16:40	-0-
Arr. Montreal (Central)	9:59	-0-	15:00	-0-	20:45

(1) Light refreshments. (2) Daily, except Sundays and holidays. (3) Plus another departure from Montreal (Windsor) at 19:40. (4) Plus another departure from Quebec at 19:30.

Quebec - Hervey - Senneterre - Cochrane 88

All of these trains are air-conditioned.

Dep. Quebec (Ste. Foy)	N/A(1)	Dep. Cochrane	16:25(6)
Arr. Hervey	N/A(1)	Arr. Senneterre	22:00
Change trains.		Change trains.	
Dep. Hervey	22:19(2+3)	Dep. Senneterre	22:35(3+6)
Arr. Senneterre	8:50(4)	Arr. Hervey	8:17(7)
Change trains.		Change trains.	
Dep. Senneterre	9:15(5)	Dep. Hervey	N/A(1)
Arr. Cochrane	14:50	Arr. Quebec (Ste. Foy)	N/A(1)

(1)Train service discontinued in 1982. (2)Runs Mon., Wed. and Fri. (3)Carries sleeping car. Light refreshments. (4)Arrives Tues., Thurs. and Sat. (5)Runs Tues., Thurs. and Sat. (6)Runs Tues., Thurs. and Sun. (7)Arrives Wed., Fri. and Mon.

Montreal - Hervey - Chicoutimi 88

These trains are air-conditioned and have light refreshments.

Dep. Montreal (Cent.)	12:30(1)	Dep. Chicoutimi	9:05(1)
Dep. Hervey	15:40	Dep. Hervey	15:05
Arr. Chicoutimi	21:40	Arr. Montreal (Cent.)	18:15

(1)Runs Monday, Wednesday and Friday. (2)Runs Tuesday, Thursday and Saturday.

Montreal - Hervey - Senneterre - Cochrane 88

Dep. Montreal (Cent.)	18:50(1+2)	Dep. Cochrane	16:25(5)
Arr. Hervey	22:19	Arr. Senneterre	22:00
Arr. Senneterre	8:50(3)	Change trains.	
Change trains.		Dep. Senneterre	22:35(1+5)
Dep. Senneterre	9:15(4)	Dep. Hervey	8:17(6)
Arr. Cochrane	14:50	Arr. Montreal (Cent.)	11:35

(1)Light refreshments. Carries sleeping car. (2)Runs Mon., Wed. and Fri. (3)Arrives Tues., Thurs. and Sat. (4)Runs Tues., Thurs. and Sat. (5)Runs Tues., Thurs. and Sun. (6)Runs Wed., Fri. and Mon.

Toronto - North Bay - Cochrane - Moosonee 63

"Polar Bear Express" makes one-day excursion roundtrips into the Canadian wildernesss daily except Friday, from late June to early September, to Moosonee, a trading post since 1673. There are 2 hotels in Moosonee for travelers wishing to stay overnight. For further information regarding this excursion, contact Ontario Northwest Railway, 195 Regina Street, North Bay, Ontario, Canada.

All of these trains are air-conditioned and have meal service.

Dep. Toronto (Union)	21:25(1)	-0-
Dep. North Bay (C.N.)	2:50(1)	-0-
Arr. Cochrane	9:40	-0-
Change trains.		
Dep. Cochrane	10:40(2)	8:30(3)
Arr. Moosonee	16:15	12:50

Dep. Moosonee	9:00(4)	17:15(3)
Arr. Cochrane	14:30	21:20
Change trains.		
Dep. Cochrane	20:05(1)	-0-
Arr. North Bay (C.N.)	2:50(1)	-0-
Arr. Toronto (Union)	8:10	-0-

(1) Carries sleeping car. Air-conditioned. (2) Runs Monday, Wednesday and Friday. (3) Polar Bear Express. Runs from late June to early September daily except Friday. (4) Runs Tuesday, Thursday and Saturday.

Cochrane - Kapuskasing 63

This is a short spur off the North Bay-Moosonee line. These trains are air-conditioned.

Dep. Cochrane	9:30
Arr. Kapuskasing	11:30

Dep. Kapuskasing	17:55
Arr. Cochrane	20:05

Sault Ste. Marie - Hearst 58

These trains are air-conditioned and have meal service.

Dep. Sault Ste. Marie	8:30(1)
Arr. Hearst	17:50

Dep. Hearst	7:15(2)
Arr. Sault Ste. Marie	16:30

(1) Runs Friday, Saturday and Sunday from late March to early January. Only on Saturday and Sunday from early January to late March. (2) Runs Saturday, Sunday and Monday from late March to early January. Only on Saturday and Sunday from early January to late March.

Sights in Sault Ste. Marie: The marvelous scenery on the one-day (8:00-17:00) Agawa Canyon sightseeing excursion train operated by Algoma Central Railway. Fall foliage is particularly outstanding, attracting up to 1,500 people daily. About 86,000 passengers make the ride during the late May to mid-October operation. The view of the Montreal River from a 130-foot high and 1,550-foot long bridge and of hundreds of lakes are some of the interesting sights on this ride. Comments are broadcast on the train's public address system. Before making the return ride to Sault Ste. Marie, passengers have time to climb to lookout points above the canyon and walk into the canyon. Hot lunches are sold on the train. The Canadian meat pie and strawberry shortcake are favorites.

Winnipeg - Hudson Bay - Churchill

This is a mind-boggling train trip, 992 miles from Winnipeg to the chilly, distant Churchill. VIA Rail Canada offers an escorted 6-day "Hudson Bay Explorer Tour", a package that includes rail fare, berth and all meals.

Passengers are provided sightseeing in 2 mining communities (Flin Flon and Thompson), a night in Churchill, then sightseeing in The Pas (one of the oldest outposts in Manitoba) on the return trip.

These trains require reservation, carry sleeping cars, are air-conditioned and have meal service.

52					
Dep. Winnipeg (C.N.)	17:50(1)		Dep. Churchill	18:00(2)	
Dep. Dauphin	22:05		Dep. Gillam	2:40	Day 2
Arr. Hudson Bay	4:30	Day 2	Dep. Thompson	9:15	
Dep. Hudson Bay	4:50		Arr. The Pas	16:30	
Arr. The Pas	7:00		Dep. The Pas	18:15	
Dep. The Pas	8:30		Arr. Hudson Bay	20:10	
Dep. Thompson	17:15		Dep. Hudson Bay	20:30	
Dep. Gillam	0:01	Day 3	Dep. Dauphin	3:15	Day 3
Arr. Churchill	7:00		Arr. Winnipeg (C.N.)	7:30	

(1) Runs Tuesday, Thursday and Sunday. (2) Runs Tuesday, Thursday and Saturday.

Sights in **Churchill:** This is the only town in the world that is located on a polar bear migratory route. They can be seen here during September and October. Seals can be viewed here May-June and white beluga whales from mid-June to mid-September. The grain elevator in Churchill fills ships from all over the world. See the 18th century Fort Prince of Wales and the Eskimo Museum.

Sights in **Thompson:** The huge International Nickel Company mining complex.

Sights in **Flin Flon:** The beautiful scenery at Beaver Lake.

Hudson Bay - Prince Albert - Saskatoon - Regina

When going west across Canada and detouring north to Churchill, it is not necessary to return to Winnipeg in order to rejoin the transcontinental line. One can return from Churchill to the cross-country line on a different route than that taken to Churchill by changing to a bus at Hudson Bay and proceeding from there to Prince Albert, Saskatoon and Regina. The train from Prince Albert to Saskatoon was discontinued in 1982, and the train departure from Saskatoon to Regina is not matched with the bus arrival in Saskatoon.

When going east across Canada, the detour to Churchill can start at Regina, and one can return from Churchill by continuing from Hudson Bay on to Winnipeg, rather than returning to Regina.

38 (Bus)				
Dep. Hudson Bay	-0-	-0-	6:05	-0-
Arr. Prince Albert	-0-	-0-	11:00	-0-
Change buses.				
Dep. Prince Albert	-0-	10:30	14:00	18:00
Arr. Saskatoon	-0-	12:35	15:50	19:55
Change buses.				
42				
Dep. Saskatoon	8:00	13:30	17:30	20:00
Arr. Regina	10:50	16:25	20:20	22:50
	*	*	*	
Dep. Regina	8:00	13:30	17:30	20:00
Arr. Saskatoon	10:50	16:20	20:20	22:50
Change buses.				
38				
Dep. Saskatoon	14:00	17:25	18:00	9:00
Arr. Prince Albert	15:50	20:40	20:05	10:55
Change buses.				
Dep. Prince Albert	19:30	-0-	-0-	-0-
Arr. Hudson Bay	0:35	-0-	-0-	-0-

Saskatoon - Regina - Winnipeg 25

Here are the schedules for the air-conditioned train service.

Dep. Saskatoon	8:00	Dep. Winnipeg	11:00
Arr. Regina	11:55	Dep. Regina	18:20
Arr. Winnipeg	19:15	Arr. Saskatoon	22:15

Winnipeg - Hudson Bay - The Pas - Lynn Lake

Bring food with you on these rides. These trains, which are air-conditioned, have no food service. The days in early April when we made the trip, the temperature was below zero Fahrenheit. The area north of Winnipeg was under 4 feet of snow.

A good place to rest and eat in The Pas is the Wescana Inn, a few blocks from the railstation. On our trip, they had a good restaurant and treated travelers considerately.

52		50	
Dep. Winnipeg (C.N.)	17:50(1+2)	Dep. Lynn Lake	7:30(4)
Dep. Dauphin	22:05	Arr. The Pas	17:50(4)
Arr. Hudson Bay	4:30 Day 2	Change trains.	
Dep. Hudson Bay	4:50	52	
Arr. The Pas	7:00	Dep. The Pas	18:15(2+5) Day 2
Change trains.		Arr. Hudson Bay	20:10
50		Dep. Hudson Bay	20:30(2+5)
Dep. The Pas	10:00(3)	Dep. Dauphin	3:15 Day 3
Arr. Lynn Lake	20:15	Arr. Winnipeg (C.N.)	7:30

(1) Runs Tuesday, Thursday and Sunday. (2) Reservation required. Carries sleeping car. Meal service. Air-conditioned. (3) Runs Wednesday, Friday and Monday. (4) Runs Tuesday, Thursday and Saturday. Requires staying overnight in The Pas before taking train next day to Hudson Bay. (5) Runs Wednesday, Friday and Sunday.

Sights in The Pas: The hand-carved pews and the Ten Commandments in the Cree Indian language. The Museum. The Cathedral of Our Lady of the Sacred Heart. The Pas, and most of the land north of it, is a massive reservation for Indians, a few of whom trap for furs.

The train from The Pas to Lynn Lake will stop at any point to let passengers board or get off. On our ride, it stopped in a completely deserted area so that a very old Indian man whose house could be seen on a hill a mile away from the track could get off. As the train started, we could see him beginning his long walk from the track to his house, on the other side of a frozen lake.

Our train for the 233-mile ride from The Pas to Lynn Lake was 23 freight cars, 2 passenger cars, and a caboose, hauled by 4 locomotives. Only a few of the seats were filled, mostly by Indians.

The track goes alongside more than 20 very large lakes after the 11:25 stop in Cranberry Portage, and nearly all of this route is heavily forested. Much ore is transported out of here in open gondola freight cars.

Some cabins of fur trappers are only a few feet from the rail track.

In Winter, you can also see the snowmobile paths leading from the train track into the forest, to trapper cabins located away from the rail line.

From October to May, while there is snow on the ground, footprints of moose, deer, lynx, foxes and rabbits can be seen for hundreds of miles, only a few feet from the railway track.

In June, July and August, the splendid fishing and wilderness camping in this area attract many tourists. It is possible to camp and hike only a short distance from either the rail track or the well-traveled highway running between Lynn Lake and Pukatawagan.

Calgary - Edmonton 37

These trains are air-conditioned.

Dep. Calgary (C.P.)	8:30(1)	17:30(2)
Arr. South Edmonton	12:00	21:00

* * *

Dep. South Edmonton	8:00(1)	17:25(2)
Arr. Calgary (C.P.)	11:25	20:50

(1) Daily, except Sundays and holidays. (2) Daily, except Saturdays.

Edmonton - Jasper - Prince George - Prince Rupert 15

These trains require reservation, carry sleeping car and coach car, have meal service and are air-conditioned. There is very beautiful scenery between Burns Lake and Prince Rupert.

Dep. Edmonton	16:30(1)	Dep. Prince Rupert	8:30(1)
Dep. Jasper	22:30(1)	Arr. Prince George (VIA)	20:45
Arr. Prince George (VIA)	5:30(2+3)	Dep. Prince George (VIA)	21:10
Dep. Prince George (VIA)	6:10(3)	Arr. Jasper	6:30(2+3)
Arr. Prince Rupert	18:30	Arr. Edmonton	12:00

(1) Runs Wednesday, Friday and Sunday. (2) Day 2. (3) Runs Thursday, Saturday and Monday.

Vancouver - Squamish - Lillooet - Prince George 16

All of these trains are air-conditioned.

This is one of the most scenic rail trips in Canada. The train travels the entire length of Lord Howe Sound before climbing the steep and heavily-timbered Cheakamus Valley to Alta Lake. After Pemberton, it passes through wilderness along the shore of fjord-like Anderson and Seton Lakes. Then, it drops down to Lillooet in the Fraser River Valley.

Dep. North Vancouver	7:30(1)	7:30(2)	Dep. Prince George (BCR)	7:30(3)	-0-
Dep. Squamish	8:44(1)	8:44(2)	Dep. Lillooet	15:25(3)	15:25(4)
Dep. Pemberton	10:27(1)	10:27(2)	Dep. Pemberton	17:30(3)	17:30(4)
Arr. Lillooet	12:35	12:35(2)	Dep. Squamish	19:11(3)	19:11(4)
Arr. Prince George (BCR)	-0-	20:30	Arr. North Vancouver	20:30	20:30

(1)Runs Tues., Wed., Fri. and Sun. (2)Runs Mon., Thurs. and Sat. (3)Runs Tues., Fri. and Sun. (4)Runs Mon., Wed., Thurs. and Sat.

Nova Scotia Rail Routes

The rail route southwest from Halifax connects in Digby with ferry service to and from Saint John, New Brunswick.

Halifax - Yarmouth 92

All of these trains are air-conditioned and have light refreshments.

Dep. Halifax (C.N.)	17:30(1)	19:00(2)
Dep. Kentville	19:30	21:00
Dep. Digby	21:24	22:54
Arr. Yarmouth	22:50	0:20

* * *

Dep. Yarmouth	7:00(1)	13:00(2)
Dep. Digby	8:26	14:26
Dep. Kentville	10:30	16:30
Arr. Halifax (C.N.)	12:20	18:20

(1) Daily, except Sundays and holidays. (2) Sundays and holidays only.

Digby - Saint John 113

Ferry service.

Dep. Digby	4:45(1)	5:00(2+3)	12:30(4)	14:30(5+9)
Arr. Saint John	3 hours later			
Dep. Saint John	0:01(2+3)	0:15(1)	8:45(4)	10:30(6+10)
Arr. Digby	3 hours later			

(1)Tuesday-Saturday from early May to mid-June. Monday-Saturday from mid-June to early October. (2)Tuesday-Saturday. (3)Daily, Runs late October to early May. (4)Daily. Runs mid-June to early October. (5)Saturday and Sunday only. Runs mid-May to mid-June and most of October. (6)Daily from early May to mid-June and most of October. Also Monday-Saturday from late October to early May. (7)Monday-Friday from early May to mid-June and most of October. Monday-Saturday from late October to early May. (8)Sunday only. (9)Plus other departures from Digby at 15:30(7), 17:00(3+8), 20:00(4)and 21:30(5). (10)Plus other departures from St. John at 12:30(3+8), 16:15(4) and 18:00(5).

Halifax - Truro - Sydney 92

The rail route north from Halifax connects in North Sydney with the ferry service to Port aux Basques, Newfoundland.

These trains have light refreshments and are air-conditioned.

Dep. Halifax	9:40	16:00(1)	Dep. Sydney	8:30(1)	15:00
Arr. Truro	11:05	17:25	Dep. No. Sydney	8:59	15:28
Change trains.			Arr. Truro	14:20	21:00
Dep. Truro	11:20	19:35	Change trains.		
Arr. No. Sydney	16:45	22:53	Dep. Truro	14:30	21:20
Arr. Sydney	17:20	23:25	Arr. Halifax	16:00	22:50

(1)Direct train. No train change in Truro.

North Sydney - Port aux Basques 114 (Ferry Boat)

Dep. North Sydney	9:00(1)	11:00(2)	11:45(1)	23:30(3)
Set your wach forward one hour.				
Arr. Port aux Basques	15:00	17:00	17:45	6:30

* * *

Dep. Port aux Basques	10:30(1)	11:00(2)	17:45(1)	23:55(3)
Set your watch back one hour.				
Arr. North Sydney	16:30	17:00	23:45	6:30

(1)Runs from mid-June to late August. (2)Runs from early January to mid-June and from early September to late December. (3)Reservation required.

Glace Bay - Port Morien

The Cape Breton Steam Railway offers visitors a 10-mile trip from Glace Bay, a mining town, to Port Morien, a small fishing village. Passengers can visit the Miner's Museum at Glace Bay.

0000

Dep. Glace Bay	N/A	Dep. Port Morien	N/A
Arr. Port Morien	N/A	Arr. Glace Bay	N/A

Bus Service in Newfoundland

There is cross-island bus service, connecting with the arrival of the ferry from Nova Scotia, and its return trip.

130

Dep. Port aux Basques	8:30	Dep. St. John's	8:00
Arr. Gander Airport	17:20	Dep. Gander Airport	13:15
Arr. St. John's	22:30	Arr. Port aux Basques	22:10

Special Canadian Train Excursions

Here are schedules for 3 special rail trips featuring steam locomotives.

North Vancouver - Squamish - North Vanvouver 16

This is an easy one-day roundtrip (27 miles each way), featuring a steam locomotive tour of scenic Howe Sound. Runs daily except Saturday from May to early September.

Dep. North Vancouver	7:30	Dep. Squamish	19:11
Arr. Squamish	8:44	Arr. North Vancouver	20:30

Toronto - Niagara Falls 67

Dep. Toronto (Union)	9:05(1)	10:00(2)	17:35	23:05
Arr. Niagara Falls	11:10	12:35	19:30	0:50

* * *

Dep. Niagara Falls	6:40	13:10	17:00(2)	18:35(1)
Arr. Toronto (Union)	8:35	15:05	19:30	20:30

(1) Meal service. (2) Steam train for special roundtrip excursion. including sightseeing at Niagara Falls. Runs Wednesday and Saturday, July 1 to August 30. For those who do not want to linger at the Falls, the train makes a trip from there to Yager and back to the Falls (12:40-16:55) before returning to Toronto.

Ottawa - Wakefield

Another steam locomotive one-day excursion. The 25-mile scenic trip starts at Ottawa's National Museum of Science and Technology, goes across the Ottawa River and then follows the Gateneau River to Wakefield, where the locomotive is manually turned on a turntable. Passengers picnic until it is time for the ride back to Ottawa.

0000

Dep. Ottawa	N/A	Dep. Wakefield	N/A
Arr. Wakefield	N/A	Arr. Ottawa	N/A

INTERNATIONAL ROUTES FROM CANADA

The gateways for train travel from Canada to the United States are: Montreal (to Boston, New York and south along the eastern U.S. seaboard), Toronto (to Buffalo and on to New York City or Cleveland, also to Detroit and on to Chicago), and Vancouver (to Seattle).

Montreal - New York City - Philadelphia - Baltimore - Washington

Both of these trains have meal service and are air-conditioned.

	180	181
Dep. Montreal (Windsor)	-0-	10:15
Dep. Montreal (Central)	18:55(1)	-0-
Arr. New York (Grand Central)	-0-	19:09
Arr. New York (Penn.)	6:45	-0-
Arr. Philadelphia (30th St.)	8:36	-0-
Arr. Baltimore (Penn.)	10:03	-0-
Arr. Washington (Union)	10:46	-0-

(1)Carries sleeping car. Also has couchettes.

Toronto - Buffalo - New York (or Cleveland) 67

Dep. Toronto (Union)	9:05(1)
Arr. Buffalo (Depew)	12:50
Arr. New York (Grand Central)	20:50

	240
Dep. Buffalo (Depew)	3:55(2)
Arr. Cleveland (Lakefront)	7:17

(1)Meal service. (2)Reservation required. Carries sleeping car. Also has coach car.

Toronto - London - Windsor - Detroit 67

All of these trains are air-conditioned.

Dep. Toronto (Union)	7:00	9:30	12:30	15:30(2+3)
Arr. London (C.N.)	9:10	11:40	14:40	17:45
Arr. Windsor (Walkerville)	11:05	13:35	16:35	19:40

(1)Light refreshments. (2)Daily, except Saturday. (3)Plus other departures from Toronto at 17:30 and 19:30(1).

Take a taxi from Windsor through the International Tunnel to Detroit.

Toronto - Brantford - Toronto 67

Dep. Toronto (Union)	8:30	14:00	17:30	19:30	20:45	23:15
Arr. Brantford	9:40	15:08	18:41	20:42	21:50	0:25

Sights in Brantford: The home of Alexander Graham Bell, with the world's first telephone business office. The history of Brant County, from Paleo-Indian culture to the days of the Six Nations Indians and Canadian pioneers, in the Brant Historical Museum. The exhibit of Woodland Indian artifacts at the Wood and Indian Museum.

Dep. Brantford	13:12	15:25	15:50	17:51	20:38	21:05
Arr. Toronto (Union)	14:30	16:45	17:00	19:10	21:50	22:25

Vancouver - Seattle

In 1981, this train service was replaced by bus transportation between VIA Rail Canada's terminal in Vancouver and Amtrak's station in Seattle, allowing for connection between the Montreal-Vancouver train and the Seattle-Los Angeles train.

MEXICO

Mexico's passenger railroads are operated by these 5 companies: Ferrocarril Chihuahua al Pacifico (CH-P), Ferrocarriles Nacionales de Mexico (NdeM), Ferrocarril del Pacifico (FCP), Ferrocarril Unidos del Sureste (FUS), and Ferrocarril Sonora-Baja California (S-BC).

Nacionales de Mexico is the principal line, with routes along the U.S. border from Juarez (El Paso), Piedras Negras, Nuevo Laredo (Laredo), and Matamoros (Brownsville), all of these providing service to Mexico City. Other N de M gateways to Mexico City are Tampico, Veracruz, Coatzacoalos, Oaxaca, Uruapan, Durango, Manzanillo and Guadalajara.

All Mexican railway schedules use the same time as U.S. Central Standard Time (same as Chicago). Children under 5 travel free when accompanied by a parent. Half-fare for children 5-11. Children 12 and over must pay full fare.

Several U.S. and Mexican tour operators offer escorted private train tours of Mexico. Check your travel agent for details. Because Mexican railways do not pay travel agents a commission, an agent who assists you in obtaining train reservations is entitled to a fee of 15% of the ticket price. Advance reservations are advisable.

Mexico City

Altitude of 7,350 feet (2,240 meters) limits activity for many tourists. Cool and dry weather except during the May-September rainy season. Railways link Mexico City with 5 Gulf of Mexico seaports (Matamoros, Tampico, Veracruz, Coatzacoalcos and Campeche) and 4 Pacific ports (Los Mochis, Mazatlan, Manzanillo and Ciudad Hidalgo).

The art, sculpture, movies and scale models of ancient cities at the National Museum of Anthropology and History in Chapultepec Park are the major attractions. You will see the results of more than 15,000 discovery sites, including the 167-ton statue of Tlatloc, the Aztec rain god, and a 30-ton Aztec calendar stone.

All the major Indian tribes of Mexico are represented at this fabulous museum (jewelry, paintings, furniture, sculpture). Guided tours are conducted in many languages, including English.

Also see: The Museum of Modern Art. The 16th century Basilica de Guadalupe, most sacred shrine in Mexico. The mariachi bands in Plaza de Garibaldi. The daily markets Centro de Abastos and San Juan). Window-shop the displays of silver jewelry on Juarez and Madero streets. The shops in Zona Rosa. The textiles at the Londres Street Market.

Visit Zocalo (or Plaza Mayor), the main square. The Cathedral, oldest and largest church in Latin America. The National Pawnshop

(Monte de Piedad). Palacio Nacional. The Palace of Fine Arts. The fine collection of European paintings at the School of Fine Arts. Plaza Mexico, largest bullfighting ring in the world. Jai-Alai at Fronton Mexico. The largest of many parks here (almost 1,000 acres) is Bosque de Chapultepec.

There are several splendid one-day excursions from Mexico City. It is only 40 miles to the pre-Aztec pyramids at Teotihuacan. Take the short ride to Cuernavaca and the Popocatepetl and Ixtaccihuati national parks. Do not miss seeing the floating gardens at Xochimilco.

Information about many special one-day train excursions from Mexico City can be obtained from Club Amigos del Ferrocarril, Apartado Postal 7-1373, Mexico 7, D.F., Mexico.

Unless indicated otherwise, Mexico City departure and arrival times are for its Buenavista railstation.

U. S. RAIL GATEWAYS TO MEXICO

Brownsville - Matamoros - Monterrey - Mexico City 1056

Take a taxi from Brownsville, Tex. to Matamoros.

Dep. Matamoros	6:50	Dep. Monterrey	6:00
Arr. Monterrey	13:55	Arr. Matamoros	13:05

Sights in Matamoros: The Mexican Museum. The cannon, walls and turrets of old Fort Mata. The Cathedral. The leather, jewelry and souvenirs for sale in the city's 2 street markets. The handwork of Tamaulipas artisans on sale at the Arts and Crafts Center.

Sights in Monterrey: The collection of rare books in Indian languages and more than 2,000 editions of Don Quixote in many languages. Sampling free cerveza at the Carta Blanca brewery. The 18th century Cathedral in Plaza Zaragosa, where band concerts are performed. El Obispado (the Bishop's Palace), once occupied by pancho Villa. Visit nearby Horseshoe Falls, scenic Huasteca Canyon, the subterranean lake at Garcia Caves, and the pine-covered slopes of Chipinique Mesa.

Monterrey was founded in 1579.

Monterrey - Mexico City 1065

Dep. Monterrey	9:08	18:00(1)	0:01(2)
Arr. Mexico City	6:23	9:00	20:04
	*	*	*
Dep. Mexico City	8:00(2)	18:00(1)	21:15
Arr. Monterrey	2:20	9:00	17:59

(1) Air-conditioned. Carries sleeping cars only. Observation car. Meal service. (2) Air-conditioned. Carries sleeping cars and coaches. Meal service.

Laredo - Mexico City 1065

Many package tours of Mexico (transportation, hotels, sightseeing, entertainment and meals) start and end in Laredo. Check your travel agent for details. Several connections can be made from Monterrey.

Dep. Neuvo Laredo	18:55(1)	Dep. Mexico City	8:00(1)
Arr. Monterrey	23:30	Dep. San Luis Potosi	17:38
Dep. Monterrey	0:01	Arr. Monterrey	2:20
Dep. San Luis Potosi	10:35	Dep. Monterrey	2:50
Arr. Mexico City	20:04	Arr. Nuevo Laredo	7:20

(1) Air-conditioned. Carries sleeping car. Meal service.

Monterrey - Torreon - Durango

1040		1043	
Dep. Monterrey	8:10	Dep. Durango	7:00
Arr. Torreon	14:42	Arr. Torreon	11:30
Change trains.		Change trains.	
1043		1040	
Dep. Torreon	15:10	Dep. Torreon	12:05
Arr. Durango	20:10	Arr. Monterrey	18:50

Attractions in Torreon: Many wineries. The famous Willie's ice cream.

Sights in Durango: Very popular for hunting game (wolves, bears, deer, ducks). The 17th century Cathedral. The iron-water spring.

San Luis Potosi - Tampico 1080

Between Cardenas and Valles, the track follows a small stream that widens into a rushing river. Watch to the left for the spectacular Micos Waterfall.

Dep. San Luis Potosi	7:50	Dep. Tampico	6:30
Arr. Tampico	20:45	Arr. San Luis Potosi	20:20

Sights in San Luis Potosi: The frescoes at the modern railstation. The Cathedral. The ornate tower of San Agustin Church. The suspended glass boat and the beautiful white and blue tiled dome of San Francisco Church. The Capilla de Aranzazu in the museum behind San Francisco Church. The lovely altar and pulpit of Carmen Church, as well as its tiled dome.

Sights in Tampico: Great sea and river fishing here. Playa de Miramar, nearby, is a popular beach resort.

El Paso - Ciudad Juarez - Mexico City 1023

Passengers transferring from or to Amtrak in El Paso have to make their own provision for crossing the border. There is taxi service. At Chihuahua, there is a connection for taking the "Copper Canyon Ride" to Los Mochis. At Torreon, a feeder line runs to Durango. At Irapuato, there is a connection for Guadalajara.

Dep. Ciudad Juarez	18:25(1)	Dep. Mexico City	19:50(1)
Arr. Chihuahua	23:25	Arr. Irapuato	3:10 Day 2
Dep. Chihuahua	23:55	Dep. Zacatecas	10:33
Arr. Torreon	8:00 Day 2	Arr. Torreon	17:20
Dep. Torreon	8:30	Dep. Torreon	17:50
Dep. Zacatecas	15:55	Arr. Chihuahua	1:47 Day 3
Arr. Irapuato	23:20	Dep. Chihuahua	2:17
Arr. Mexico City	6:55 Day 3	Arr. Ciudad Juarez	7:20

(1) Air-conditioned. Meal service. Carries sleeping car.

Sights in **Chihuahua City:** The dungeon of Miguel Hidalgo, Mexico's George Washington, at the Federal Palace. The Cathedral, built from 1724 to 1826 because Indian wars interrupted its construction. The museum at Quinta Gameros, an old private residence. Quinta Luz, Pancho Villa's home, now a museum about him and his exploits. The 18th century Chihuahua Aqueduct. The murals in Government Palace, depicting the history of Chihuahua. Plaza de la Constitucion.

Sights in **Zacatecas:** The images of St. Peter and St. Francis, made from hummingbird feathers, in the Church de Nuestra Senora Guadalupe, and the hundreds of paintings there as well as the Christ on the Cross made of cornstalks and the porcelain Virgin Mary. The outstanding wrought-iron in Pension Tacuba. The marvelous Cathedral. You can visit the tremendous El Bote Silver Mine by obtaining a permit and guide at the Tourist Office. It is only a 30-mile drive south to La Quemada to see the prehistoric Chicomoztoc Ruins.

These are the schedules for making a detour from Torreon to Durango en route from Ciudad Juarez to Mexico City.

Torreon - Durango

1023		1043	
Dep. Ciudad Juarez	18:25(1)	Dep. Durango	7:00
Arr. Torreon	8:00(2)	Arr. Torreon	11:30
Change trains.		Spend night in Torreon.	
1043		1023	
Dep. Torreon	15:10(2)	Dep. Torreon	8:30(1+2)
Arr. Durango	20:10(2)	Arr. Mexico City	6:55(3)

(1) Air-conditioned. Meal service. Carries sleeping car. (2) Day 2. (3) Day 3.

Sights in Durango: See notes earlier in this section, under "Monterrey-Durango".

Durango - Regocijo 1045

Considered by many to be the most beautiful rail trip in Mexico. An easy one-day excursion that provides great mountain scenery. Be sure to see the last 3 miles going into Regocijo from the rear of the last car.

Dep. Durango	6:30(1)	Dep. Regocijo	11:55(1)
Arr. Regocijo	11:30	Arr. Durango	16:37

(1) Runs Tuesday, Wednesday, Friday and Saturday.

Chihuahua - Los Mochis

This is the Copper Canyon scenic ride. One of the most exciting train trips in the world. A veritable roller coaster. Highest point of the journey is 8,071 feet at Los Ojitos.

Both 8:20 departures carry a Vistadome car and an observation-restaurant car. They have broad windows for picture taking.

Completed only in 1962, the rail line to Los Mochis crosses 39 very tall bridges and passes through 8½ miles of 73 tunnels. The bridge over Septentron River is 335 feet high. At several points, the route is so rugged that the track must double back in a complete circle.

Scenery includes spectacular deserts, mountains and subtropical landscape. What is regarded as the most impressive part of the journey begins as the line leaves the plateau west of Chihuahua City and climbs into the Sierra Madres. Upon reaching Creel, the aborigine Tarahumara Indians can be observed.

Halfway between Chihuahua and Los Mochis, the train comes into Divisadero. Meaning "look-out point", Divisadero stands on the rim of Urique Canyon. The train stops here for 20 minutes of viewing down 6,000 feet into the canyon.

Then the train proceeds into a mile-long tunnel, making a 180-degree turn inside the mountain so that when it emerges it is heading back in the direction from which it came as it passes a 400-foot waterfall.

The next large town is El Fuerte, once a very rich mining town. Another 50 miles, and the destination of Los Mochis is reached.

1035

Dep. Chihuahua	8:00(1+2)	8:20(3+4)	22:30(1+5)
Dep. Creel	12:58	13:37	4:25
Arr. Divisadero	13:45	14:32	-0-
Arr. Los Mochis	20:00	21:51	13:00

* * *

Dep. Los Mochis	8:00(2+6)	8:00(5+7)	8:00(4+8)
Arr. Divisadero	13:47	-0-	14:40
Dep. Creel	15:40	17:15	16:34
Arr. Chihuahua	20:30	22:55	21:50

(1)Runs Tuesday and Friday. (2)Second-class coach cars plus first-class parlor car. Meal service. (3)Runs Monday, Thursday, Saturday and Sunday. (4)"Vista Train". Second-class coach cars plus first-class dome car and parlor car. Meal service. (5)Train of only sleeping cars. Meal service. (6)Runs Wednesday and Saturday. (7)Runs Monday and Thursday. (8)Runs Tuesday, Friday and Sunday.

Ciudad Juarez - Irapuato - Mexico City

Here are the schedules for making a detour from Irapuato to Guadalajara en route from Ciudad Juarez to Mexico City.

1023

Dep. Ciudad Juarez	18:25(1)	
Arr. Irapuato	23:00	Day 2

Change trains.

1024

Dep. Irapuato	3:59(1)
Arr. Guadalajara	8:10

1070

Dep. Guadalajara	20:55(1)
Dep. Irapuato	1:37
Arr. Mexico City	8:45

(1)Air-conditioned. Carries sleeping car. Meal service.

Nogales - Mazatlan - Guadalajara - Mexico City 1024

Dep. Nogales	16:30(1)	Dep.Mexico City	20:30(1)
Arr. Mazatlan	8:25(2)	Arr. Guadalajara	8:10(2)
Dep. Mazatlan	8:35	Dep. Guadalajara	8:50
Arr. Guadalajara	19:00	Arr. Mazatlan	18:30
Dep. Guadalajara	20:55	Dep. Mazatlan	18:40
Arr. Mexico City	8:45(3)	Arr. Nogales	10:20(3)

(1)Air-conditioned. Carries sleeping car. Meal service. (2)Day 2. (3)Day 3.

Sights in Mazatlan: A marvelous seashore resort. Ride a 3-wheel "pneumonia" past the hotels, boutiques and shopping centers that line the seaside Avenida de Mar. This is home port for Mexico's largest shrimp fleet. Prize billfish are caught here. Much hunting for wild boar, deer, rabbit, ducks, quail and pheasant in the nearby mountains.

Sights in Guadalajara: The Cathedral, surrounded by 4 plazas in the shape of a cross. The Orozco murals at Government Palace and at El Hospico Cabanas Orphanage. The Orozco Museum. Santa Monica Church. Municipal Palace. Plaza de Toros. San Juan de Dios Church. The State Museum. The Library.

Guadalajara - Manzanillo 1061

This sensational ride down the steep sides of the Sierra Madre is very uncomfortable, dusty and hot (no air-conditioning).

Dep. Guadalajara	10:00	Dep. Manzanillo	8:00
Arr. Manzanillo	18:16	Arr. Guadalajara	16:45

Sights in Manzanillo: Mexico's principal Pacific seaport. Excellent beaches and great deep-sea fishing here. Much hunting in the nearby hills. The fabulous Las Hadas resort complex.

The California connection with rail travel to Mexico City begins by walking or driving from Calexico across the border to Mexicali and taking Sonora Baja California Railways' short line from there to Benjamin Hill, where a connection can be made with the Nogales-Mexico City line operated by Ferrocarril Nacionales de Mexico.

Mexicali - Benjamin Hill - Mazatlan - Guadalajara - Mexico City 1024

Dep. Mexicali	8:00(1+2)	Dep. Mexico City	20:30(1+4)
Arr. Benjamin Hill	17:30	Arr. Guadalajara	8:10(3)
Through cars switched here.		Dep. Guadalajara	8:50(1)
Dep. Benjamin Hill	18:46(1)	Arr. Mazatlan	18:30
Arr. Mazatlan	8:25(3)	Dep. Mazatlan	18:40(1)
Dep. Mazatlan	8:35(1)	Arr. Benjamin Hill	7:25(5)
Arr. Guadalajara	19:00	Through cars switched here.	
Dep. Guadalajara	20:55(1+4)	Dep. Benjamin Hill	7:40(1+2)
Arr. Mexico City	8:45(5)	Arr. Mexicali	13:35

(1) Air-conditioned. Carries sleeping car. (2) Meal service only Mexicali-Benjamin Hill and v.v. (3) Day 2. (4) Meal service only Guadalajara-Mexico City and v.v. (5) Day 3.

Mexico City - Morelia 1086

Excellent Michoacan farm scenery is viewed on this ride.

Dep. Mexico City (Buenavista)	6:55	21:29(1)	Dep. Morelia	10:33	23:12(1)
Arr. Morelia	17:30	6:20	Arr. Mexico City (Buenavista)	20:50	7:50

(1) Air-conditioned. Carries sleeping car.

Monterrey - Tampico 1055

These trains are second-class only.

Dep. Monterrey	8:00	Dep. Tampico	7:48
Arr. Tampico	18:45	Arr. Monterrey	18:40

Sights in Tampico: Great sea and river fishing here. Nearby Playa de Miramar is a popular beach resort.

Routes South of Mexico City

There are 4 principal train routes south from Mexico City: to Veracruz, Oaxaca, Merida and Ciudad Hidalgo.

Mexico City - Veracruz 1101 and 1105

The excellent scenery on this route, including Orizaba Volcano (Mexico's tallest), warrants taking this trip during daylight. It is necessary to bring your own food. Box lunches can be purchased on the lower level of Mexico City's Buenavista Railstation.

Dep. Mexico City	7:18	7:34	21:32(1)
Arr. Veracruz	19:25	19:00	7:00

Sights in Veracruz: A very picturesque resort. See the excellent 17th century Palacio Municipal. Look for the silver-decorated tortoiseshell jewelry that is a specialty here. The beautiful Isla de Sacrificios beach. Take the bus marked "Ulua" to see the 16th century San Juan de Ulua Castle on Gallega Island (reached by a road).

Dep. Veracruz	7:25	8:00	21:30(1)
Arr. Mexico City	19:45	19:12	7:37

(1) Air-conditioned. Carries sleeping car.

Mexico City - Puebla - Oaxaca 1095

Dep. Mexico City	17:32(1)	Dep. Oaxaca	18:20(1)
Arr. Puebla	22:15	Arr. Puebla	3:30
Arr. Oaxaca	8:05	Arr. Mexico City	8:46

(1) Air-conditioned. Carries sleeping car.

Sights in Puebla: The beautiful tiles at the Patio de los Azulejos. The great view of many snow-capped volcanoes from the top of Avenida Internacional, and a similar view from the Cathedral's bell-tower.

The marvelous onyx and marble statues, marble floors and gold leaf decor in the Cathedral. Nearby, Casa del Alfenique (Sugar Candy House). The outstanding museum of Mexican history near the forts of Guadalupe and Loreto. The sensational 16th century Talavera tiles in the Museo de Santa Rosa. The 17th century Church of San Critobal.

The fascinating architecture, Indian statues in Santa Maria de Tonantzintla Church, and the excavated pyramid at nearby Cholula. The courtyard and tiled entrance at the Consejo de Justicia. The Cinco de Mayo civic center. The 16th century Theater, oldest in the western hemisphere.

The collection of Talavera pottery and Chinese porcelain in the Museo de Bello. The onyx and souvenir stores on Plaza Parian.

Sights in Oaxaca: The arcaded Zocalo Plaza, with the 17th century Cathedral and, nearby, the fantastic gold leaf and the national museum in Santo Domingo Church. The Saturday Indian market. Do not miss seeing the sculpture and ironwork in the 17th century La Soledad Church. See the view from the monument to Juarez on Cerro de Fortin. Shop for woolen zarapes, gold and silver jewelry, blankets made from cane, green and black pottery, embroidered blankets and clothing, rugs, etc.

Mexico City - Merida 1115

Stopovers en route at Palenque and Campeche (to see Mayan ruins) can be arranged. Short excursions from Merida to Uxmal and Chichen-Itza are recommended. A first-class bus to Uxmal leaves Merida at 8:00, returning there at 15:00. Uxmal is an hour drive southwest from Merida. Chichen-Itza is a 2-hour drive east.

Dep. Mexico City	20:10(1)		Dep. Merida	20:00(1)	
Arr. Palenque	22:00	Day 2	Arr. Campeche	23:20	
Arr. Campeche	6:02	Day 3	Arr. Palenque	8:06	Day 2
Arr. Merida	9:05		Arr. Mexico City	9:15	Day 3

(1) Air-conditioned. Carries sleeping car. Meal service.

Sights in **Palenque:** Interesting ruins of stone buildings from the 7th and 8th centuries are located only 5 miles from this lovely orchard village. One of these, the pyramid-like Temple of the Inscriptions, was built into the side of a hill. Visitors can descend 65 feet below the entrance to the tomb of a Mayan ruler and see the 12½-foot long carved stone slab that covered a sarcaphagous. The fireflies in this area are so large that a newspaper can be read by the light of a few captured ones.

Sights in **Campeche:** A fortified city, walled in the 17th century for protection from marauding pirates. See the white and vermillion painted wood altars in the 16th century San Francisquito Church. The excellent museum. The rocky seacoast. The museums at the 18th century San Miquel Fort. About 25 miles by road, the Edzna pyramid.

Sights in **Merida:** It is great to sightsee here in a horse-drawn carriage (about $3.00 U.S. per hour). See: The marvelous wrought-iron on the mansions on Paseo de Reforma. The massive Monument of the Flags, the entire history of Mexico in bas-relief. Casa Montejo, home of the man who founded this city.

The 16th century Cathedral. Buy souvenirs at the tremendous public market (traditional Yucatan costumes, embroidered cotton smocks, huaraches, hammocks, mountains of fruit). Maps and advice can be obtained from the English-speaking employees of the Tourist Office on Zocalo Plaza. Take the short bus ride to Progreso Beach to swim and to eat fish, turtle and shrimp. Try the mild regional Yucatan cuisine.

Sights in **Uxmal:** Ruins of the 11th century Mayan complex. One week here might be adequate.

Mexico City - Tapachula - Ciudad Hidalgo 1105

Dep. Mexico City (Buenavista)	21:32(1)	Dep. Ciudad Hidalgo	8:30
Arr. Veracruz	7:00(2)	Arr. Tapachula	9:50
Change trains.		Change trains.	
Dep. Veracruz	9:05	Dep. Tapachula	18:10
Arr. Tapachula	8:20(3)	Arr. Veracruz	17:20(2)
Change trains.		Change trains.	
Dep. Tapachula	13:15	Dep. Veracruz	21:30(1)
Arr. Ciudad Hidalgo	14:35	Arr. Mexico City (Buenavista)	7:37(3)

(1) Air-conditioned. Carries sleeping car. (2) Day 2. (3) Day 3.

Sights in Tapachula: The extinct volcano that towers above the city: The beach resort at nearby Puerto Madero.

INTERNATIONAL CONNECTIONS FROM MEXICO

The only train service from Mexico to countries south of Mexico was the line from Ciudad Hidalgo, via Tecun Uman. Although that service has been suspended since 1980, there is bus transportation for that route.

When trains were operating, it was a very difficult trip, and we advised against attempting it. There is no acceptable lodging in either primitive Ciudad Hidalgo or in similarly primitive Tecun Uman, the Guatemalan city on the other side of the border. Further, there was an overnight interval of more than 17 hours (from 14:35 until 8:00 the next morning) between arriving in Ciudad Hidalgo from Mexico City and departing from Tecun Uman for Ciudad Guatemala. Passengers had to walk more than one mile in very hot temperature and great dust from the Mexican terminal to the Guatemalan railstation, and a substantial toll was charged for crossing the border bridge.

Mexico City - Ciudad Hidalgo - Tecun Uman - Ciudad Guatemala

1105	
Dep. Mexico City (Buenavista)	21:32(1)
Arr. Ciudad Hidalgo	14:35(2)
Change to bus.	
1155	
Dep. Ciudad Hidalgo	N/A(3)
Arr. Tecun Uman	N/A(3)
Change buses.	
Dep. Tecun Uman	N/A(3)
Arr. Ciudad Guatemala	N/A(3)

(1)Air-conditioned. Carries sleeping car. (2)Day 3. (3)Time has not been available since 1980.

* * *

All the schedules for rail travel between Mexico and United States gateways appear at the start of this section, under "U.S. Rail Gateways to Mexico".

Information and Reservations

Because few travel agents book Mexican train travel, you will find the following sources of information and reservations helpful.

LARADO
Ferrocarril Nacionales de Mexico
P.O. Box 595
Laredo, Tex.

EL PASO
Ferrocarril Nacionales de Mexico
P.O. Box 2200
El Paso, Tex. 79951

NOGALES
Ferrocarril del Pacifico
Calle Internacional No. 10
Nogales, Sonora
Mexico

CALEXICO
Sonora-Baja California Ry.
P.O. Box 3-182
Mexicali, B.C.
Mexico (TEL: 7-21-63 7-21-01)

CHIHUAHUA - LOS MOCHIS
Ferrocarril Chihuahua al Pacifico
P.O. Box 46
Chihuahua, Chih.
Mexico (TEL: 2-22-84)

For return reservations from Mexico City to the U.S., contact: Passenger Traffic Dept., Ferrocarril Nacionales de Mexico, Buenavista Central Station, Mexico 3, D.F., Mexico (TEL: 547-31-90).

UNITED STATES OF AMERICA

There are 2 classes of trains in the U.S.A.: first-class and coach class. Children under 2 travel free. Half-fare for children 2-11 in coach class only. Children over 12 must pay full fare.

On some day trains, first-class service consists of reserved-seat club cars with 2 seats on one side of the aisle and one seat on the other side.

Night trains have variable sleeping accommodations. Most are complete with private wash and toilet facilities. All have doors that can be locked. All sleeping spaces must be reserved in advance.

Roomettes are for one person. The seat used during the day folds over at night, making room for a bed that is lowered from a recess in the wall.

Bedroom is available in 2 different daytime styles, one with a 2-person divan, the other with 2 chairs. At night, the porter makes up one upper bed and one lower bed.

Bedroom Suite results when the dividing partition between 2 adjoining bedrooms is removed. Accommodations up to 4 persons and has 2 wash basins and 2 toilets.

Slumbercoach costs much less than other sleeping spaces. Rooms for one or 2 persons are available. Much smaller than other sleeper spaces. Has full-length beds and private lavatory.

New 2-level Superliner sleeping cars have deluxe, economy, family and special bedrooms. Deluxe sleeps 2 persons and has private wash and toilet facilities. Some have a shower. Economy accommodates one or 2 persons but does not have either private wash or toilet. Family bedroom sleeps 3 adults and 2 children. Special bedrooms with private bath and toilet are available for handicapped persons.

Coaches have 2 seats on each side of the aisle. These seats are adjustable to a semi-reclining position, similar to airplane reclining seats. Certain long-distance trains have reserved-seat coaches with reclining seats and leg rests for overnight journeys.

All Amtrak trains are air-conditioned. Most long-distance trains carry a restaurant car. Some short-distance trains have a snack bar or lounge car with counter food service. Most Amtrak long-distance trains operating west of Chicago carry 2-level Superliner observation-lounge cars with large wrap-around windows for viewing the scenery.

Amtrak's fares are shown in its free timetables, available by writing to: Timetable Dept., Amtrak Distribution Center, Western Folder, 850 W. Fullerton Ave., Addison, Ill. 60101.

Trains in the U.S.A. run through 4 time zones: Eastern, Central, Mountain and Pacific. There is a one-hour difference between each adjacent time zone. Summer schedules are in effect from late April to late October.

U.S.A. TRAIN PASSES

Both U.S.A. National Railpass and U.S.A. Regional Railpasses are sold only outside North America. Residents of North America are *not* eligible to buy them. These passes offer unlimited coach travel on all Amtrak trains other than Metroliners. Coach seats can be upgraded by paying an additional fee for reserved-seat club car or for sleeping car space. For more information, write to: Amtrak International Sales, 400 No. Capitol St., N.W., Washington, D.C. 20001, U.S.A.

U.S.A. National Railpass. 7 days $250(U.S.), 14 days $375, 21 days $500, 30 days $625. Children under 2 not occupying a separate seat travel free. Half-fare for children 2-11. Children 12 and over must pay full fare.

U.S.A. Regional Railpass. Unlimited travel for 14 days, allowing unlimited stopovers. One adult pays full price. His or her spouse and Children 12-21 pay 50% of the pass price. Children 2-11 pay 25%. The eastern pass is priced at $115. The price for the western, central and southern passes is $200 each.

Family U.S.A. Rail Pass. The head of household pays full fare for tickets. The spouse and children 12-21 years old pay half-fare. Children 2-11 pay $85 each regardless of ticket price. A child under 2 not occupying a separate seat travels free.

Senior Citizens and Handicapped Persons Roundtrip Discount. A 25% discount on rountrip ticket prices for those who prove they are 65 or older and those who offer certification from a physician, a government agency or an organization of handicapped persons that the applicant is handicapped.

Packaged Tours. Amtrak offers 150 different packaged tours (some escorted, some independent), ranging from an independent $25 San Diego "Zoofari" ($12.25 for a child) that includes the Los Angeles-San Diego roundtrip and admission to the San Diego Zoo, to its 22-day $2,500-$3,000 escorted "Majestic Americana" tour by deluxe rail roundtrip from New York City to U.S. and Canadian national parks such as Grand Teton, Yellowstone, Glacier, Banff and Lake Louise, and including many nights in luxury hotels.

Amtrak tour books can be obtained from travel agents or by writing to: Amtrak Distribution Center, P.O. Box 311, Addison, Ill. 60101, U.S.A.

Notes for city-sightseeing in 9 principal U.S. cities are provided below.

Boston

The collection of Oriental and Egyptian art at the Museum of Fine Arts. The splendid Italian Renaissance paintings in the Isabella Stewart

Gardner Museum. The many outstanding museums of science and industry at Harvard University. The elegant 19th century architecture of the Boston Public Library, which has many fine murals. The New England Aquarium. Arnold Arboretum. The Massachusetts Institute of Technology. The Museum of Science and Hayden Planetarium, both in Science Park. The Christian Science Mother Church. Take the Bay Cruise.

The many historic places: Boston Massacre Site. Old South Church. Bunker Hill. The Tea Party Site. Boston Common. Haymarket Square. The Paul Revere House. The ship "Old Ironsides". Old South Meeting House. King's Chapel. Benjamin Franklin's birthplace.

Chicago

The Field Museum of Natural History. Shedd Aquarium, world's largest collection of sealife. Adler Planetarium. The collection of Near East art at Chicago University's Oriental Institute and, near it, the enormous Museum of Science. Lincoln Park Zoo. The Picasso statue at Civic Center Plaza. The Chagall mosaic at First National Bank Plaza. The Museum of Contemporary Art. The exhibit of impressionist art at the splendid Art Institute of Chicago.

Los Angeles

You cannot depend on public transportation to sightsee in Los Angeles. To do so by taxi is extremely expensive. Car rental is the solution. See: Olvera Street, across from the railstation. This is where the city began. The incomparable Music Center complex of 3 outstanding theaters and the City Mall, leading from it to City Hall and the Civic Center of city, county, state of California and Federal buildings.

The marvelous interior of the 19th century Bradbury Building. The Coliseum. Site of the 1932 Olympics and also where the 1984 games will be held. Near it, a splendid Natural History Museum. Heading west on Wilshire Boulevard toward the Pacific Ocean, the Los Angeles County Museum of Art and, a 2-minute walk from it, the Page Museum of prehistoric mammals and birds at the La Brea Tar Pits. Nearby, Farmers' Market for the finest fruits, vegetables, meats and seafood in the world, also restaurants serving Mexican, Chinese, Italian and American food.

In the Hollywood area: The interesting forecourt at the Chinese Theater, with footprints and handprints of Hollywood's greatest stars from Mary Pickford to Marilyn Monroe. The great musical events at the Hollywood Bowl all Summer.

The many wealthy residential estates in Beverly Hills, Bel Air, Westwood and Brentwood. The Alcoa "Century City" complex, between Beverly Hills and Westwood. Window-shopping the row of high-priced stores on Rodeo Drive in Beverly Hills. The University of California at Los Angeles campus, in Westwood.

The expanse of great beaches on the Pacific Ocean shoreline, from

Santa Monica north to Malibu and Oxnard and south to Newport Beach, Laguna and San Diego. Marineland. The spectacular collection of private yachts at both Marina Del Rey (near Los Angeles International Airport) and at Balboa.

For the best chocolate candy in the world, stop at The Nutty Chocolatier, 17200 Ventura Blvd., Encino (in the Town & Country Shopping Center). Take the guided tours nearby of both Universal Studios (Universal City) and the National Broadcasting Company (Burbank).

Visit the Rose Bowl Stadium, Norton Simon Museum of Art, and Huntington Art Museum, all in Pasadena. Hearst's Castle in San Simeon is a 2½-hour drive by auto from Los Angeles. Disneyland, in Anaheim, is a one-hour drive by auto.

New Orleans

Jazz on Bourbon Street and the Spanish-French architecture in the French Quarter. Absinthe House. Audubon's Little House. Boat tours of the harbor. The view from the top of the 400-foot high International Trade Mart, at the foot of Canal Street. Mardi Gras.

New York City

The Statue of Liberty. The United Nations complex. The view from the top of the Empire State Building. The New York Stock Exchange. The Rockefeller Center complex. The Metropolitan Museum of Art, greatest art museum in the United States. The Whitney Museum of American Art. The Solomon R. Guggenheim Museum. The American Museum of Natural History.

The International Center of Photography. Central Park, but never after dark. The Museum of the City of New York. The Cathedral of St. John the Divine, far more interesting than St. Patrick's, but often neglected by tourists. The exhibition rooms and movies at the country's first capitol, at 26 Wall Street. The museum of Revolutionary War relics and Washington memorabilia at Fraunces Tavern. Guided tours at the Federal Reserve Bank. Chinatown. The Bronx Zoo and Botanical Garden.

Philadelphia

The Liberty Bell and Independence Hall, on Independence Square. Stroll down Elfreth's Alley, one of America's oldest streets, to the Betsy Ross House. Nearby, the grave of Benjamin Franklin. See the hundreds of fine portraits at The Historical Society of Pennsylvania.

The War Library and Museum. Rosenbach Museum. The Pennsylvania Academy of Fine Arts. The Academy of Natural Sciences. The Rodin Museum, largest collection of Rodin sculptures outside Paris. The Philadelphia Museum of Art. The 388-acre food industry park (stores, warehouses, processing plants) called Food Distribution Center.

Performances of the Philadelphia Orchestra at the Academy of Music. The Civic Center Museum. The Franklin Institute of Science

Museum. The University Museum.

San Francisco

Fisherman's Wharf. Watch them making chocolate at nearby Ghirardelli Square. The Maritime Museum. The Chinese Museum. The treasures for sale at Gump's store. Chinatown. North Beach. The cable cars. The Presidio. Golden Gate Bridge. The Arboretum and the spectacular exhibits of Far Eastern art at the de Young Memorial Museum, both in the 1,017-acre Golden Gate Park. Fleischacker Zoo, one of the world's best zoos.

The pyramidal Transamerica Building. San Francisco Museum of Art. Nob Hill, and the cable car ride from there, down California Street.

Seattle

The monorail ride to the 605-foot high tripod Space Needle tower. The Aquarium at Waterfront Park. The 200-acre Arboretum. A tour of Boeing's 747 assembly plant (phone 206-342-4801 for reservations and directions).

The Seattle Art Museum. The more than 1,000,000 used books for sale at Shorey Bookstore. The granite sculptures at Myrtle Edwards Park. The crafts in the specialty shops at Pioneer Square. The pleasure boats anchored along Shilshole Bay Marina.

Take the 2½-hour sightseeing cruise of Puget Sound, from Pier 51 at 10:30 and 13:00. Or go on the ferry-boat ride, starting at the foot of Marion Street.

Washington, D.C.

There is rail service between Washington's Union Station and its National Airport. Take the "Red Line" Subway from the railstation to Metro Center (heart of the city's business district). At Metro Center, transfer to the "Blue Line" Subway, in the direction which services both the Pentagon and the National Airport.

For subway service from Union Station to the Smithsonian complex and to RFK Stadium, take the "Blue Line" at Metro Center, in the opposite direction from the "Blue Line" route to National Airport.

Sights in Washington: The many great museums in the Smithsonian Institution complex: The exhibit of balloons, dirigibles, primitive propellor airplanes and on to the Apollo II space ship in the Air & Space wing. The many displays (dinosaurs, Hope Diamond and other gems, etc.) in the Natural History Museum. The many old machines and clothing in the Museum of History & Technology. The marvelous French Impressionist and Italian Renaissance paintings at the National Gallery of Art. The sculptures and mobiles in the circular Hirschorn Museum. The collection of art in the Freer Gallery. Most of the museums are open 10:00-17:30.

See Congress in session. Tours of the House of Representatives and the Senate operate every 15 minutes from 9:00 to 15:45 daily, starting from the Rotunda. Walk up the 897 steps to the top of the 555-foot high Washington Monument obelisk, open 9:00-17:00 daily (also 20:00-24:00 in the Summer). The Reflecting Pool in West Potomac Park. The Jefferson Memorial, open 24 hours. The Lincoln Memorial, always open. (There are guided bus tours of all the monuments.)

The National Zoo. The National Arboretum, with its azaleas, daffodils and magnolias. The eternal-flame tomb of John F. Kennedy, the Greek Revival Arlington House, and the Tomb of the Unknowns, all in Arlington National Cemetery.

The largest collection of books, maps, newspapers, documents and manuscripts in the world, at the Library of Congress. Guided tours are conducted Monday-Friday, 9:00-16:00.

See the art collections at Corcoran Gallery, Phillips Collection, the National Portrait Gallery and the National Collection of Fine Arts. Take a tour of the F.B.I., every 15 minutes (9:15-16:15, Monday-Friday) at 13th Street and Pennsylvania Avenue. There is a 25-minute tour of the Bureau of Engraving & Printing (where money is not printed as fast as it is spent) Monday-Friday 8:00-11:30 and 12:30-14:00 at 14th and "C" Streets, SW.

Visit the White House for a 40-minute tour Tuesday-Saturday, 10:00-12:00. Tour the Supreme Court when the Court is not in session, Monday-Friday 9:00-16:30 and, when it is in session, 10:00-14:30. Take the short guided bus trip to Mt. Vernon.

MAJOR U.S. RAILSTATIONS

Reservation and Information Telephone Numbers

Albany	(518) 465-9971	Kansas City (Mo.)	(816) 421-4725
Albuquerque	(505) 242-7816	Las Vegas	(800) 421-8320
Atlanta	(404) 688-4417	Los Angeles	(213) 624-0171
Baltimore	(301) 539-2112	Miami	(305) 371-7738
Boston	(617) 482-3660	Milwaukee	(414) 933-3081
Buffalo	(716) 856-1229	Minneapolis	(612) 339-2382
Chicago	(312) 556-1075	New Orleans	(504) 525-1179
Cincinnati	(513) 579-8506	New York City	(212) 736-4545
Cleveland	(216) 861-0105	Oklahoma City	(405) 943-5337
Dallas	(800) 421-8320	Orlando	(305) 843-8460
Denver	(303) 893-3911	Philadelphia	(215) 824-1600
Detroit	(313) 963-7396	Reno	(702) 323-4375
Fort Worth	(817) 336-1010	St. Louis	(314) 241-8806
Houston	(713) 757-1713	San Francisco	(415) 982-8512
Indianapolis	(317) 632-1905	Seattle	(206) 464-1930
Jacksonville	(904) 731-1600	Washington, D.C.	(202) 484-7540

TRANSCONTINENTAL RAIL ROUTES

There is a rail route from New York City to Chicago. From Chicago, there are 4 different train routes to the West Coast of the United States.

Another route to the West is from New York City, the long ride via New Orleans.

NEW YORK ROUTES WEST

New York - Albany - Buffalo - Cleveland - Chicago

This route can also be started in Boston, by connecting in Albany.

These trains require reservations, are air-conditioned, have meal service, and carry sleeping cars, Slumbercoach and ordinary coach.

240			
Dep. New York (Gr. Cent.)	18:45	Dep. Chicago (Union)	16:40
Dep. Albany	22:10	Dep. Cleveland (Lakefront)	0:35
Dep. Buffalo (Depew)	3:35	Set your watch forward one hour.	
Set your watch back one hour.		Dep. Buffalo (Depew)	4:15
Dep. Cleveland (Lakefront)	7:15	Dep. Albany	10:15
Arr. Chicago (Union)	13:35	Arr. New York (Gr. Cent.)	13:05

Boston - Albany 240

These trains require reservations.

Dep. Boston (South)	16:40	Dep. Albany	10:20
Arr. Albany	21:35	Arr. Boston (South)	15:20

Detroit - Chicago 300

All of these trains have a club car and serve light refreshments.

Dep. Detroit (Mich. Ave.)	8:30	12:30	16:50
Arr. Chicago (Union)	13:05	17:15	21:25

* * *

Dep. Chicago (Union)	8:30	12:50	17:15
Arr. Detroit (Mich. Ave.)	15:00	19:23	23:43

New York - Pittsburgh - Chicago 310

This route can be started in Washington, with a connection in Philadelphia.

These trains require reservations, are air-conditioned, have meal service, and carry sleeping car, Slumbercoach and ordinary coach.

Dep. New York (Penn.)	14:15	Dep. Chicago (Union)	20:00
Dep. Philadelphia (30th St.)	16:05	Set watch forward one hour.	
Dep. Pittsburgh (Penn.)	23:52	Dep. Pittsburgh (Penn.)	7:23
Set your watch back one hour.		Dep. Philadelphia (30th St.)	14:46
Arr. Chicago (Union)	9:00	Arr. New York (Penn.)	16:37

Washington Philadelphia 260

These trains require reservation, are air-conditioned and serve light refreshments.

Dep. Washington (Union)	6:00(1)	7:00(1)	7:30(3)	8:00(2+4)
Arr. Philadelphia (30th St.)	7:56	8:47	9:28	9:56

* * *

Dep. Philadelphia (30th St.)	5:24(3)	6:50(1)	7:52(1)	8:41(2+5)
Arr. Washington (Union)	8:12	9:14	9:44	10:50

(1) Monday-Friday, except holidays. (2) Daily, except Sunday. (3) Daily.
(4) Plus frequent other departures from Washington from 8:30 to 22:30.
(5) Plus frequent other departures from Philadelphia from 9:36 to 22:27.

New York - New Orleans - Houston - Los Angeles

A long (3,417 miles) but interesting route from New York to the West Coast is via New Orleans, where there is a 19-hour layover on the trip West and 12 hours when going from Los Angeles to New York. Passengers were once allowed to occupy sleeping space on the train during each overnight stop, but now must make other provision.

These trains carry sleeping cars and have meal service.

Between Phoenix and Los Angeles, "Sunset Limited" rides at the lowest altitude of the Amtrak system: 231 feet (70 meters) *below* sea level, near Niland, California.

190		
Dep. New York (Penn.)	14:00(1)	
Dep. Philadelphia (30th St.)	15:49(1)	
Arr. Washington (Union)	18:15	
Dep. Washington (Union)	18:45(1)	
Dep. Atlanta (Peachtree St.)	8:00(1)	Day 2
Set your watch back one hour.		
Arr. New Orleans	18:35	
193		
Dep. New Orleans	13:50(2)	Day 3
Dep. Houston	22:55(2)	
Dep. San Antonio (East Com. St.)	4:15(3)	Day 4
Dep. El Paso	15:30(3)	
Set your watch back one hour.		
Dep. Phoenix	22:50(3)	
Set your watch back one hour.		
Arr. Los Angeles	7:40	Day 5

193		
Dep. Los Angeles	22:30(4)	
Set watch forward one hour.		
Dep. Phoenix	6:45(5)	Day 2
Set watch forward one hour.		
Dep. El Paso	16:45(5)	
Dep. San Antonio (East Com. St.)	5:55(6)	Day 3
Dep. Houston	10:40(6)	
Arr. New Orleans	20:10	
190		
Dep. New Orleans	8:15(1)	Day 4
Set watch forward one hour.		
Dep. Atlanta (Peachtree St.)	20:15(1)	
Arr. Washington (Union)	10:00	Day 5
Dep. Washington (Union)	10:30(1)	
Arr. Philadelphia (30th St.)	12:54	
Arr. New York (Penn.)	14:38	

(1) Daily. (2) Monday, Wednesday and Friday. (3) Tuesday, Thursday and Saturday. (4) Tuesday, Friday and Sunday. (5) Wednesday, Saturday and Monday. (6) Thursday, Sunday and Tuesday.

CHICAGO ROUTES WEST

Here are the schedules for the 5 train services west from Chicago.

Chicago - Minneapolis - Glacier Park - Spokane - Seattle 412

These trains require reservations, carry sleeping car and coaches, have meal service, and are air-conditioned.

Dep. Chicago (Union)	14:30	
Dep. Milwaukee	16:05	
Dep. Minneapolis	23:05	
Dep. Fargo	3:30	Day 2
Set your watch back one hour.		
Dep. Glacier Park	17:45(1)	
Set your watch back one hour.		
Arr. Spokane	0:35	Day 3
Arr. Seattle (King St.)	9:15	

Dep. Seattle (King St.)	16:15	
Dep. Spokane	0:05	Day 2
Set watch forward one hour.		
Dep. Glacier Park	8:25(1)	
Set watch forward one hour.		
Dep. Fargo	1:00	Day 3
Dep. Minneapolis	6:50	
Arr. Milwaukee	13:45	
Arr. Chicago (Union)	15:15	

(1) Stops only from late May to mid-September.

Chicago - Denver - Reno - Oakland (San Francisco) 189 + 501

These trains require reservations, carry sleeping car and coaches, have meal service, and are air-conditioned.

Between Denver and Ogden, "Zephyr" rides at the highest altitude of the Amtrak system: 8,013 feet (2,442 meters), at Sherman Hill, Wyoming.

Dep. Chicago (Union)	18:50	
Dep. Omaha	3:16	Day 2
Set your watch back one hour.		
Dep. Denver (Union)	12:10	
Dep. Ogden	23:50	
Set your watch back one hour.		
Arr. Reno	8:10	Day 3
Arr. Oakland	15:40(1)	
Arr. San Francisco	16:10	

Dep. San Francisco	11:40(1)	
Dep. Oakland	13:05	
Dep. Reno	19:22	
Set watch forward one hour.		
Dep. Ogden	7:20	Day 2
Dep. Denver (Union)	18:35	
Set watch forward one hour.		
Dep. Omaha	4:21	Day 3
Arr. Chicago (Union)	13:05	

(1) Bus service Oakland to San Francisco and v.v.

Chicago - St. Louis - Dallas - San Antonio - Los Angeles 187

These trains require reservations, carry sleeping car and coaches, have meal service, and are air-conditioned.

Dep. Chicago (Union)	17:20	
Dep. St. Louis	23:05	
Dep. Dallas	13:30	Day 2
Dep. Fort Worth	15:10	
Arr. San Antonio	21:55	
Dep. San Antonio	4:15	Day 3
Dep. El Paso	15:30	
Set your watch back one hour.		
Dep. Phoenix	22:50	
Set your watch back one hour.		
Arr. Los Angeles	7:40	Day 4

Dep. Los Angeles	22:30	
Set watch forward one hour.		
Dep. Phoenix	6:45	Day 2
Set watch forward one hour.		
Dep. El Paso	16:45	
Arr. San Antonio	5:25	Day 3
Dep. San Antonio	8:30	
Dep. Fort Worth	15:40	
Dep. Dallas	16:45	
Dep. St. Louis	7:50	Day 4
Arr. Chicago (Union)	13:00	

Chicago - Kansas City - Albuquerque - Los Angeles 188 + 470

At Flagstaff, there is bus service to the Grand Canyon (see last page of this section).

These trains require reservations, carry sleeping car and coaches, have meal service and are air-conditioned.

Dep. Chicago (Union)	15:45	
Dep. Kansas City	23:35	
Dep. Dodge City	5:53	Day 2
Set your watch back one hour.		
Dep. Albuquerque	15:35	
Dep. Flagstaff	20:05	
Set your watch back one hour.		
Arr. Los Angeles	7:20	Day 3

Dep. Los Angeles	19:40	
Set watch forward one hour.		
Dep. Flagstaff	6:30	Day 2
Dep. Albuquerque	13:10	
Set watch forward one hour.		
Dep. Dodge City	0:20	Day 3
Dep. Kansas City	6:45	
Arr. Chicago (Union)	15:15	

Chicago - New Orleans 367

These trains require reservations, carry sleeping car and coaches, have meal service, and are air-conditioned.

Dep. Chicago (Union)	18:10	
Dep. Memphis	4:40	Day 2
Arr. New Orleans	12:15	

Dep. New Orleans	14:55	
Dep. Memphis	22:16	
Arr. Chicago (Union)	9:00	Day 2

Eastern Seaboard Train Routes

The train route in the United States with the heaviest traffic is the Boston-Washington corridor.

Boston - New York City - Philadelphia - Washington 220

Note: There are departures not listed here (Cook's Table 260) on the hour and half-hour from New York City to Washington 6:30-21:00 and from Washington to New York City 6:00-20:30.

Unless designated otherwise, all of the trains listed below have light refreshments.

Additional New York-Boston schedules appear immediately after the following list.

Dep. Boston (South)	5:53(1)	7:00(2)	7:50(1)	9:40(3+9)
Dep. New York (Penn.)	10:50(1)	11:45(2)	12:45(1)	14:50(3+10)
Dep. Philadelphia (30th St.)	12:22(1)	13:25(2)	14:21(1)	16:31(3+11)
Arr. Washington (Union)	14:39	15:24	16:40	18:47

* * *

Dep. Washington (Union)	6:30(4)	7:30(5)	9:30(3)	11:30(2+12)
Dep. Philadelphia (30th St.)	8:37(4)	9:43(5)	11:35(3)	13:40(2+13)
Arr. New York (Penn.)	10:20(4)	11:30(5)	13:07(3)	15:25(2+14)
Arr. Boston (South)	15:10	16:12	17:50	20:13

(1) Daily, except Sundays and holidays. Carries club car. (2) Daily. (3) Daily. Carries club car. (4) Monday-Friday, except holidays. Carries club car. (5) Saturdays, Sundays and holidays only. (6) Carries sleeping car. (7) Daily, except Sundays and holidays. (8) Sundays and holidays only. (9) Plus other departures from Boston at 12:59(2), 14:40(2) and 22:15(2+6). (10) Plus other departures from New York at 17:50(2), 19:45(2) and 3:17(2+6). (11) Plus other departures from Philadelphia at 19:23(2), 21:30(2) and 5:24(2+6). (12) Plus other departures from Washington at 12:30(3), 13:30(7), 14:30(8), 15:30(3) and 22:30(2+6). (13) Plus other departures from Philadelphia at 14:35(3), 15:33(7), 16:39(8), 17:34(3) and 0:55(2+6) (14) Plus other departures from New York at 16:10(3), 17:40(7), 18:30(8), 19:08(3) and 3:14(2+6).

New York - Boston 220

These are schedules in addition to those appearing in the preceding list.

Dep. New York (Penn.)	7:25(1)	9:10(1)
Arr. Boston (South)	12:00	13:58

* * *

Dep. Boston (South)	16:50	18:00
Arr. New York (Penn.)	21:45	22:46

(1) Carries club car. Light refreshments.

New York - Philadelphia - Washington - Miami 182 + 183

These trains require reservations, carry sleeping car and coaches, have meal service, and are air-conditioned.

	183	182
Dep. New York (Penn.)	9:25	15:35
Dep. Philadelphia (30th St.)	11:05(1)	17:18(1)
Dep. Washington (Union)	14:00(1)	20:05(1)
Arr. Miami	13:13(2)	17:25(2)

* * *

	182	183
Dep. Miami	8:47	13:28
Arr. Washington (Union)	6:05(2+3)	13:10(2+3)
Arr. Philadelphia (30th St.)	7:22(3)	16:03(3)
Arr. New York (Penn.)	10:40	17:47

(1) Stops only to take boarding passengers. (2) Day 2. (3) Stops only to allow passengers off train.

West Coast Train Routes

Los Angeles - Las Vegas - Salt Lake City - Ogden 535

Connects in Ogden with both the "Zephyr" to San Francisco and the "Zephyr" to Denver and Chicago (Cook's Table 501).

These trains require reservation, carry sleeping cars, have meal service and are air-conditioned.

Dep. Los Angeles	12:40	
Arr. Las Vegas	19:45	
Set watch forward one hour.		
Arr. Salt Lake City	5:20	Day 2
Arr. Ogden	6:35	

Dep. Ogden	23:59	
Dep. Salt Lake City	1:05	Day 2
Set watch back one hour.		
Arr. Las Vegas	9:00	
Arr. Los Angeles	16:05	

Los Angeles - San Diego 571

Amtrak has a one-day independent tour package from Los Angeles to San Diego and return, which includes rail fare, transfers between the San Diego railstation and the exceptional San Diego Zoo, admission to the Zoo, a 40-minute guided bus tour of the 100-acre facility, and a ride on the Zoo's aerial tram. Another San Diego attraction: Sea World.

These trains are air-conditioned and have light refreshments.

Dep. Los Angeles	8:00	9:50	11:55	13:50	17:00(3)
Arr. San Diego	10:45	12:35	14:40	16:35	19:45

* * *

Dep. San Diego	5:15(1)	7:00	8:50	12:10	15:00(4)
Arr. Los Angeles	7:55	9:40	11:35	14:55	17:45

(1) Monday-Friday, except holidays. (2) Saturdays, Sundays and holidays only. (3) Plus other departures from Los Angeles at 17:55(1),

18:35(2) and 20:20(1). (4)Plus other departures from San Diego at 16:20, 18:10(2) and 19:40.

Los Angeles - Oakland (San Francisco) - Portland - Seattle 192

A very scenic route: seacoast, forests, snow-capped mountains. These trains carry sleeping cars and have meal service.

Dep. Los Angeles	10:15	Dep. Seattle (King St.)	11:00
Arr. Oakland	20:25(1)	Arr. Portland	15:00
Dep. Oakland	20:50	Dep. Portland	15:15
Arr. Portland	14:15(2)	Arr. Oakland	7:55(1+2)
Dep. Portland	14:30	Dep. Oakland	8:30
Arr. Seattle (King St.)	18:30	Arr. Los Angeles	19:15

(1) Bus service to/from San Francisco connects with Oakland arrival/departures. (2) Day 2.

Portland - Seattle 585

Here are all the schedules for this route. These trains are air-conditioned.

Dep. Portland	8:00(1)	14:30(2)	17:40(3)
Arr. Seattle (King St.)	11:55	18:30	21:30
	*	*	*
Dep. Seattle (King St.)	8:00(3)	11:00(2)	17:30(1)
Arr. Portland	11:50	15:00	21:20

OTHER U.S. RAIL TRIPS

Additional U.S. train routes appear in the following schedules:

Salt Lake City - Denver **Denver - Salt Lake City**

Many regard this to be the most scenic train ride in the U.S.A. This route reaches a height of more than 9,000 feet and provides marvelous views of the Rocky Mountains.

This is not an Amtrak service. It is operated by Denver & Rio Grande Western Railroad.

These trains have domecars and meal service. There is limousine service Salt Lake City-Ogden and v.v.

500

Dep. Salt Lake City (D&RGW)	7:30(1)	Dep. Denver (Union)	7:30(3)
Dep. Glenwood Springs	13:10(2)	Dep. Glenwood Springs	15:40(2)
Arr. Denver (Union)	21:30	Arr. Salt Lake City (D&RGW)	21:30

(1)Runs Monday, Thursday and Saturday. (2)Connection for Aspen. (3)Runs Tuesday, Friday and Sunday.

Salt Lake City - Boise - Portland - Seattle 195 + 530

These trains carry sleeping cars, have meal service and are air-conditioned.

Dep. Salt Lake City (Amtrak)	22:50	Dep. Seattle (King St.)	8:00
Dep. Ogden	0:10	Dep. Portland	12:00
Dep. Boise	7:00	Set watch forward one hour.	
Set your watch back one hour.		Dep. Boise	23:40
Dep. Portland	17:40	Dep. Ogden	7:00
Arr. Seattle (King St.)	21:30	Arr. Salt Lake City (Amtrak)	8:10

Philadelphia - Atlantic City 265

These trains run Monday-Friday, except holidays.

Dep. Philadelphia (16th St.)	16:29	17:04
Arr. Atlantic City	18:00	18:32

Sights in Atlantic City: Many large gambling casino hotels. The boardwalk.

Dep. Atlantic City	5:45	6:50
Arr. Philadelphia (16th St.)	7:18	8:14

New York - Atlantic City 269 (Bus)

Dep. New York (Port Auth. Term.)	0:01	1:00	7:00	8:00	8:30(1)
Arr. Atlantic City	3:09	4:00	9:20	10:20	10:50
	*	*	*		
Dep. Atlantic City	0:01	1:30	2:00	4:15	4:45(2)
Arr. New York (Port Auth. Term.)	2:21	4:35	4:20	6:35	7:05

(1) Plus frequent other departures from New York from 9:00 to 22:00.
(2) Plus frequent other departures from Atlantic City from 6:00 to 23:00.

San Francisco - Oakland - Reno 501

Bus		Train	
Dep. San Francisco (Transbay Term.)	11:40	Dep. Reno	8:10
Arr. Oakland	12:00	Arr. Oakland	15:40
Change to train.		Change to bus.	
Dep. Oakland	13:05	Dep. Oakland	15:50
Arr. Reno	19:12	Arr. San Francisco (Transbay Term.)	16:10

Sights in Reno: Many gambling casinos. Nearby are gold-mining ghost towns and beautiful Lake Tahoe.

SCENIC RAIL TRIPS

The schedules for these 8 scenic train rides appear earlier in this section.

Salt Lake City - Denver (500)

This route reaches a height of more than 9,000 feet and provides marvelous views of the Rocky Mountains.

Salt Lake City - Seattle (530)

This route goes through 2 of the most scenic river valleys in North America: the Snake River Valley in southern Idaho and the Columbia River Valley through Oregon and Washington State.

Reno - Oakland - San Francisco (501)

Excellent mountain scenery of the High Sierra can be seen on this portion of the Ogden-San Francisco ride.

Los Angeles - Seattle (192)

Very fine views of the Pacific seacoast, forests and snow-capped mountains.

Raton Pass (470)

Crossing the Colorado-New Mexico state line (Chicago-Albuquerque-Los Angeles route), the train goes over the 7,588-foot high Raton Pass.

Glacier National Park (412)

Fifty-six miles of glaciers and soaring peaks can be seen as the Chicago-Havre-Seattle route passes through Glacier National Park.

New York City - Albany (228 + 240)

The train follows the beautiful Hudson River for 142 miles on this trip. You also travel along Lake Champlain.

Washington - Cincinnati (276)

Beautiful mountain scenery on the West Virginia portion of this ride.

Two Alaskan Scenic Rail Trips

One of the most scenic rail trips in the U.S. and Canada requires a bit of doing to get on board. It is the Skagway-Lake Bennett portion of the White Pass Railway's route in Alaska and British Columbia, which connects Whitehorse on the Alcan Highway with the port of Skagway.

The scenery equals many of the most glorious train trips in Europe.

A special roundtrip excursion train operates daily from early June to late September.

We made this 41-mile, narrow-gauge ride by taking a cruise ship from Vancouver, B.C. up the West Coast of Canada and then north to Ketchikan and Juneau, before reaching Skagway.

Cruise ships dock in Skagway in early morning so that passengers can connect with the train's 10:00 departure. After arriving in Bennett, there is adequate time to visit the old Gold Rush church and take pictures of the lakeshore. Included in the tour fee is a prospector's lunch of beef stew, baked beans, apple pie and beverage served in the large Bennett station restaurant, which can accommodate 900 persons.

The train, varying from 5 to 10 cars long depending on the day's passenger volume, arrives back in Skagway early enough to allow a few hours for wandering Skagway's dismal streets, haunting its "frontier" bars, and selecting cheap souvenirs before one's ship pulls anchor.

A few minutes after leaving Skagway, watch out the right-hand side of the train for the very small goldrush graveyard, only a few feet to the side of the track. The train climbs along the edge of mountains for an hour before reaching a plateau at the summit. This ascent of 2,885 feet is made in only 21 miles, with a grade of 4% at one point. During the ascent, there is a great view looking down at Skagway and up at the snow-topped mountains.

The final stretch, into Bennett, has excellent scenery, including many cold-blue indigo ponds and dwarfed pine trees. Other sights en route are the 100-ton granite Black Cross Rock, Bridal Veil Falls, Dead Horse Gulch (where 3,000 pack animals died while carrying the prospectors' supplies) and Beaver Lake.

Now deserted, except for a few railstation employees, Bennett was where more than 10,000 men built rafts and crude boats in 1898 to get themselves and their equipment up the Yukon River to the Klondike gold fields. Highest point on the complete Skagway-Whitehorse route is 2,916 feet, at Log Cabin, B.C.

Because Alaska coastal ferries carry vehicles, tourists can reach the White Pass Railway without being on an Inland Passage cruise as we were—either by auto, auto plus trailer, or camper.

Vehicles must be delivered to the railway station in Skagway before 7:30 and in Whitehorse no later than 6:00 on the day of travel on the railroad, and passengers must travel on the same train. Advance reservations are mandatory. Write to: White Pass & Yukon Route, P.O. Box 2147, Seattle, WA. 98111, U.S.A.

Vehicles are not accepted for transportation that are over 30 feet long, or over 11′ 6″ high, or over 7′ 6″ wide. Also unacceptable are Fifth Wheel trailer units and motorcycles, canoes or boats that are not attached to a vehicle.

This service allows motoring up the Alcan Highway to Whitehorse, traveling to Skagway by train, and then continuing from Skagway by ferry south to Juneau, Sitka, Petersburg, Wrangell, Ketchikan or Prince Rupert.

Or, one can first ferry to Skagway, train to Whitehorse, and then proceed by auto or camper either north to Mayo, Dawson, Tok, Fairbanks and Anchorage . . . or south to Prince George and Vancouver.

Ferry and train space for vehicles is far less than the demand. Arrangements should be made far in advance through a travel agent.

After gold was discovered in the Klondike Valley, early prospectors landed at Skagway and carried their outfits the 40-mile walk (mostly uphill) to Lake Bennett, proceeding from there to the gold fields by boat on the Yukon River. It soon became impossible to provide the growing population in the Klondike with adequate supplies.

Construction of the White Pass and Yukon Route started on May 27, 1898. The summit was reached on February 18, 1899, and transportation from Skagway to Bennett was completed on July 6 of that year, the first train to run in Alaska. Rail service from Bennett to Whitehorse began on July 29, 1900.

This was one of the most difficult railroad constructions ever engineered. Supplies had to be brought 1,000 miles, from Seattle, on small coastal steamships. There was no heavy construction equipment. Workers had only horses, shovels and black powder to cut through barriers of solid rock.

Skagway - Bennett - Whitehorse

Trains have a 60-minute meal stop in Bennett.

905			
Dep. Skagway	8:00(1+3)	10:00(2+3)	19:45(2)
Arr. Bennett	11:20	12:45	22:55
Dep. Bennett	12:20	13:45	23:55
Arr. Whitehorse	15:30	17:00	3:30

(Timetable continues on next page)

Dep. Whitehorse	8:00(1+3)	9:45(2+3)	19:45(2)
Arr. Bennett	11:30	12:50	22:55
Dep. Bennett	12:30	13:50	23:55
Arr. Skagway	15:30	16:15	3:30

(1) Monday-Friday, except holidays. Runs from early October to late May. (2) Daily. Runs from early June to late September. (3) Has parlor car. Carries passengers' vehicles (autos, campers, trailers, etc.), which may not exceed 7'6" in width, 30' in length and 11'6" in height.

All persons with the vehicle must travel on the same train that transports the vehicle. Space for vehicles must be reserved in advance of travel date. Vehicles must be delivered to the railstation before 8:00 and are not carried on Sundays.

Mt. McKinley Park Rail Route

Completed in 1923, the Alaska Railroad's 356-mile line from Anchorage to Fairbanks with Vistadome cars ranks among the world's most exotic train journeys.

This railway, first surveyed in 1914, provides access to North America's highest mountain, Mt. McKinley (20,320 feet). Construction began in 1915. The temperature on this route ranges from 100(F) in Summer to −70(F) in Winter.

Connected with this line is another that proceeds south from Anchorage to Portage, running east from Portage to Whittier. Only freight service is operated Anchorage-Seward, with the exception of special charter passenger trains. The shuttle service between Portage and Whittier is run for the State of Alaska.

The Anchorage-Fairbanks line affords many interesting travel possibilities: an easy one-day roundtrip Anchorage-McKinley Park-Anchorage, another easy one-day roundtrip Fairbanks-McKinley Park-Fairbanks, the complete ride from Anchorage to Fairbanks (and vice versa), and the complete Anchorage-Fairbanks or Fairbanks-Anchorage ride with a stopover at the McKinley Park resort.

Inside the 3,030 square mile national park are 3 other prominent mountains: Mt. Foraker (17,000 feet), Mt. Hunter (14,960 feet) and Mt. Russell (11,500 feet). On Summer days, Mt. McKinley and Mt. Foraker are clearly visible from Anchorage, more than 150 miles to the South.

Headquarters for park activities is the McKinley Park Station Hotel, built in 1972 and operated by a private firm, with accommodations for 275 guests. The hotel is open from late May to late September. A highway links the hotel with such points of interest as Sable Pass, Polychrome Pass, Caribou Pass, Toklat Creek, Igloo Creek, Camp Eielson, Wonder Lake, Camp Denali and Richardson Highway.

If making hotel reservations prior to April 15, write to: Outdoor World Ltd., 451 Park View Dr., Suite 9, Sacramento, CA. 95825, U.S.A. If making reservations after April 15, write to: McKinley Park, Alaska 99755, U.S.A.

Caribou, giant Alaska moose, 33 other mammals and 112 kinds of birds comprise the animal life in the park. There are grizzly bears and 200-pound mountain sheep to be seen there. Salmon and trout abound in the nearby lakes, streams and rivers.

The hotel offers 2 guided tours. One starts at 6:00, so as to have maximum opportunity to observe wildlife. For late sleepers, a second tour starts at 15:00.

Both McKinley Park Station Hotel and McKinley Village provide free transportation from the train station to the free shuttle bus, which runs through the park on an hourly basis.

A 2-hour "Hills of Fire Tour" leaves McKinley Park Station Hotel at 16:30. Pack trips in and around the park are also available.

Some of the interesting points along the route from Fairbanks to Anchorage are: College, where the northernmost institution of higher education in the world is located, the University of Alaska. Dunbar, from which trails lead to a goldmining district. (It is 70 degrees below zero here in the Winter.) Clear, a military post. Mountain sheep, between Healy and McKinley Park. Honolulu, with many beaver dams, on the western side of the track. Hurricane Gulch, which the train crosses on a bridge that is 296 feet above the creek. From Mt. McKinley Station to Chulitna, there are splendid views of Mt. McKinley, and then such views again from Curry to Nancy.

Anchorage

Alaska's largest city (200,000 population). Named for Captain Cook having anchored his ships here in 1778. See the National Park Service movies 12:15 and 14:30 at the NPS Information Center at 540 West Fifth Ave. Subjects covered in the film are park lands, Alaskan history and the northern environment (Canada and Alaska).

Also see the traditional prospector's log cabin, which houses the Visitor Information Center at Fourth Ave. and "F" Street. The 139-foot high Sitka spruce flagpole at the City Hall. Eskimo, Aleut and Athabascan Indian artifacts at the Historical and Fine Arts Museum, 121 West Seventh Ave.

There are good buys here in fox, mink, seal, beaver, muskrat, wolf and coyote furs. Also Eskimo carvings (scrimshaw) in whalebone, walrus ivory, jade and soapstone.

Anchorage - McKinley Park - Fairbanks

All of these trains have domecars, meal service, and carry autos. Sixty thousand people ride this route every year.

900

Dep. Anchorage	8:30(1+2)	9:00(2+3+4)	9:45(1+5)
Dep. McKinley Park	14:30(1+2)	16:45(2+3+4)	16:25(1+5)
Arr. Fairbanks	18:15	20:55	20:15

* * *

Dep. Fairbanks	9:00(2+3+6)	10:30(1+2)	11:30(1+7)
Dep. McKinley Park	13:00(2+3+6)	14:10(1+2)	15:00(1+7)
Arr. Anchorage	20:40	20:10	22:15

(1)Runs from mid-May to mid-September. (2)Has dome car. (3)Runs from late September to mid-May. (4)Saturday only. (5)Runs Monday, Thursday and Saturday. (6)Sunday only. (7)Runs Tuesday, Friday and Sunday.

Anchorage - Portage - Whittier 902

All of these trains run only Wednesday, Friday and Sunday, have light refreshments and carry autos.

About 100,000 people ride this route every year, along the Portage Glacier.

Dep. Anchorage	13:00	-0-	Dep. Whittier	17:10	19:30
Dep. Portage	15:20	18:20	Dep. Portage	17:45	20:10
Arr. Whittier	15:55	18:55	Arr. Anchorage	-0-	21:40

INTERNATIONAL ROUTES FROM THE UNITED STATES

U.S. gateways for train trips from the United States to Canada are: Boston, New York, Detroit and Seattle.

Boston - Springfield - Montreal

214		215	
Dep. Boston (South)	16:35(1)	Dep. Springfield	0:27(2)
Arr. Springfield	19:00	Arr. Montreal (Cent.)	9:20
Change trains.			

(1) Reservation required. Meal service. Air-conditioned. (2) Carries sleeping car. Air-conditioned.

New York - Montreal

Both trains have meal service and are air-conditioned.

	229	215
Dep. New York (Grand Central)	10:25	-0-
Dep. New York (Penn.)	-0-	20:48(1)
Arr. Montreal (Windsor)	19:13	-0-
Arr. Montreal (Central)	-0-	9:20

(1)Carries sleeping car. Also has couchettes.

New York - Toronto 240

There is excellent Hudson River scenery for 142 miles after leaving New York City. You also travel along Lake Champlain. Sit on the left side of the train when going to Toronto, on the right side when going to New York City. The train crosses the gorge below Niagara Falls.

These trains have meal service.

Dep. New York (G.C.)	8:45	Dep. Toronto	9:05
Arr. Niagara Falls (USA)	17:43	Dep. Niagara Falls (USA)	11:50
Arr. Toronto	20:30	Arr. New York (G.C.)	20:49

Detroit - Windsor - Toronto

Take a taxi from Detroit through the International Tunnel to Windsor.

67			
Dep. Windsor (Walkerville)	7:00(1)	8:30	10:10(2+3)
Arr. Toronto (Union)	11:15	12:35	14:30

(1)Daily, except Sundays and holidays. (2)Light refreshments. (3)Plus other departures at 12:50(2), 14:50 and 18:00(2).

Seattle - Vancouver

In 1981, this train service was replaced by bus transportation between Amtrak's Seattle terminal and VIA Rail Canada's station in Vancouver, allowing for connection between the Vancouver-Montreal train.

U.S. gateways for train trips from the United States to Mexico are: Brownsville, Laredo, El Paso, Nogales and Calexico (Mexicali). All of these schedules appear earlier in this chapter in the section on "Mexico".

ADDENDUM

Earlier in this section, schedules appear for the Chicago-Albuquerque-Los Angeles route, including a stop at Flagstaff. Here are the bus services between Flagstaff and the Grand Canyon.

There are guided tours at Grand Canyon.

Flagstaff - Grand Canyon (Bus) 542

Dep. Flagstaff	7:30(1)	9:00	14:30(1)	Dep. Grand Canyon	9:45(1)	17:00
Arr. Grand Canyon	9:20	10:50	16:20	Arr. Flagstaff	11:35	18:50

(1)Runs from late April to late October.

Chapter 16

CENTRAL AMERICA and WEST INDIES

COSTA RICA

Children under 3 travel free. Half-fare for children 3-10. Children 11 and over must pay full fare.

There are no train connections from Costa Rica to adjacent countries. It is possible to travel by train in Costa Rica from the Caribbean (Limon) to the Pacific Ocean (Puntarenas). This is the only rail route in Costa Rica for which reliable timetables are available. En route, the train passes through Cartago and San Jose, the country's capital. All tracks in Costa Rica are narrow-gauge.

Cartago

See the tiny (under 6 inches tall) statue of La Negrita, the legendary Indian Virgin, in the Basilica of Our Lady of the Angels. This is the location where a primitive structure was built in 1715 on the place where the Virgin Mary is believed to have appeared to a peasant girl. Pilgrims come from all over Central America to see "La Negrita". The Sunday market in Cartago is an interesting event. Take the short bus trip to see the crater of Irazu Volcano.

Limon

Millions of bunches of bananas are exported from this seaport every year. See the gardens in Vargas Park.

San Jose

The capital of Costa Rica. See: The National Theater, with its statues, gold-decorated foyer and marble staircases. The excellent collection of pre-Columbian (as far back as 10,000 B.C.) ceramic and stone vases, figurines, tools and other antiques in the National Museum, open daily except Monday, 9:00-17:00. Thousands of pre-Columbian jade birds, ornaments, musical instruments and human figures at the Jade Museum (in the Insurance Building on Calle 17), open daily except Monday, 10:00-16:00. The National Liquor Factory, in Parque Espana. Frescoes of Costa Rican life in the Salon Dorado at the old La Sabana Airport, now an enormous park.

See the colored glassware and carved wood pieces sold at the government craft center, next to Soledad Church. The leather goods for sale at Caballo Blanco on Moravia Church Plaza.

San Jose - Cartago - Limon 1402

(NOTE: This trip leaves from the San Jose railstation that is located on the northeast side of Parque Nacional!)

There is extraordinary scenery on this 102-mile train trip, which takes about 7 hours partly because of the nature of the route (scores of tunnels, bridges and hairpin curves as you descend 5,000 feet to sea level) and partly due to the fact that there are 52 scheduled stops in addition to some unscheduled ones.

It cost thousands of lives (yellow fever, dysentery, beriberi) to build this line between 1871 and 1890. In the area of the 20 miles leading into Limon, it has rained as much as 35 inches in a 30-hour period.

Tres Rios, the first stop on the ride from San Jose, is in the heart of the coffee country. Then come dense rain forest jungles, swamps, waterfalls, hibiscus, poinciana trees, sugar cane, the rampaging Reventazon River, coconut trees, orchids and many other wildflowers. The train makes one 3,000-foot descent in 30 minutes.

You can visit a Chinese general store during a 5-minute stop in Bataan, a Chinese community. White, sandy beaches along the Caribbean come into view during the last 12 miles, before arriving in Limon.

En route, Indian vendors offer hot coffee, watermelon slices, cashews, corn on the cob, mangoes, hard-boiled eggs, cold chicken and guava juice. There is a 26-minute airplane flight (about $10 U.S.) you can take for the return to San Jose.

Dep. San Jose (Atlantico)	8:10	12:20	17:30(1)
Dep. Cartago	9:15	13:15	18:20
Arr. Limon	14:55	17:40	23:15
	*	*	*
Dep. Limon	6:10	8:15	18:25(1)
Dep. Cartago	11:15	14:06	23:46
Arr. San Jose (Atlantico)	12:00	15:00	0:35

(1) Runs Friday, Saturday and Sunday.

San Jose - Puntarenas 1400

NOTE: This train departs from the San Jose railstation that is located at the south end of the city!

Dep. San Jose	6:00	9:15	15:15	17:15
Arr. Puntarenas	9:00	13:15	19:15	20:15

Sights in Puntarenas: Good sea bathing and fishing (shark and tuna) here. An inexpensive boat ride ($1.00 U.S.) takes you on Sunday mornings to San Lucas Island, with its great El Coro beach. Because it is a penal colony, your guide on San Lucas will be an English-speaking prisoner!

Dep. Puntarenas	6:00	10:00	15:00	18:00
Arr. San Jose	9:00	14:00	19:00	21:00

CUBA

Children under 6 travel free. Half-fare for children 6-11. Children 12 and over must pay full fare.

The 4 rail trips from Habana are west to Pinar del Rio and Guane, a short trip east to Matanzas, and the route southeast to both Cienfuegos and to Santiago de Cuba.

Habana

This is the largest, most cosmopolitan and most beautiful city in the Caribbean.

See: El Morro Castle. The view from the tower of the city's oldest fort, La Fuerza. Marvelous gardens in Parque Central. Vermay paintings in El Templete on Plaza Carlos Manuel Cespedes. The patio at the former palace of the Captain's General, on the west side of the Plaza Cespedes.

The lovely interior of La Merced Church. The view from the east tower of the Cathedral. The National Museum in Palacio de Bellas Artes. The Botanical Gardens on Avenida Allende. The Museum of Natural Sciences, in the Capitol building. The Museum of the Revolution, in the Presidential Palace. The statues and mausoleums in the outstanding Colon Cemetery. Ernest Hemingway's home, maintained as it was when he lived there in 1960. The art gallery, carnival rides, equestrian center and restaurants in the enormous Lenin Park. The tremendous monument to Jose Marti, a leader of the last century's revolution against Spain, in the Plaza of the Revolution, competing with the enormous picture on a government building of Che Guevara, who helped Fidel Castro overthrow Batista in this century.

Santiago de Cuba

See The Colonial Museum.

Habana - Pinar del Rio - Guane 1511

Dep. Habana (Central)	-0-	5:50(2)	-0-	-0-
Dep. Habana (Tulipan)	4:55(1)	-0-	10:00(1)	15:20(1+4)
Arr. Pinar del Rio	8:50	12:40(2)	13:50	19:20
Change trains.				
Dep. Pinar del Rio	10:20(3)	12:50	17:20(3)	19:45(3)
Arr. Guane	11:47	15:09	18:47	22:04
* * *				
Dep. Guane	4:30(1+2)	5:00(2)	8:00(3)	13:20(3+5)
Arr. Pinar del Rio	6:08(2)	7:38(2)	9:27	14:47
Change trains.				
Dep. Pinar del Rio	6:18(1)	7:48	10:00(1)	15:30(1)
Arr. Habana (Tulipan)	10:03	-0-	14:03	19:25
Arr. Habana (Central)	-0-	15:14	-0-	-0-

(1) Air-conditioned. Light refreshments. (2) Direct train. No train change in Pinar del Rio. (3) Service subject to confirmation. (4) Plus another departure from Habana (Tulipan) at 20:50(1+2). (5) Plus another departure from Guane at 16:20(3).

Habana - Matanzas	1510					
Dep. Habana (S.C.)	4:50	8:00	11:35	14:55	18:12	21:25
Arr. Matanzas	7:30	10:41	14:20	17:41	20:53	0:05
	*	*	*			
Dep. Matanzas	4:45	7:57	11:35	14:51	18:09	21:20
Arr. Habana (S.C.)	7:27	10:40	14:20	17:39	21:51	0:03

Habana - Cienfuegos	1515			
Dep. Habana (Tulipan)	6:00(1)	-0-	12:25(1)	22:30(1)
Dep. Habana (Central)	-0-	7:00	-0-	-0-
Arr. Cienfuegos	12:22	17:10	18:59	4:52
	*	*	*	
Dep. Cienfuegos	7:45(1)	8:30	15:38(1)	23:05(1)
Arr. Habana (Central)	-0-	18:45	-0-	-0-
Arr. Habana (Tulipan)	14:21	-0-	22:15	5:40

(1) Air-conditioned. Light refreshments.

Habana - Santiago de Cuba	1520		
Dep. Habana (Central)	23:53		
Arr. Santiago de Cuba	18:46		
	*	*	*
Dep. Santiago de Cuba	12:15	18:30(1)	
Arr. Habana (Central)	6:26	9:20	

(1) Air-conditioned.

EL SALVADOR

Children under 3 travel free. Half-fare for children 3-9. Children 10 and over must pay full fare.

The principal train line in El Salvador is from Cutuco, a seaport on the Pacific Ocean, to inland San Salvador. The only international rail route from El Salvador is a continuation of the Cutuco-San Salvador line into Guatemala. Because El Salvador is largely 2 rows of volcanoes, many volcanoes can be seen on the trips listed here.

Cutuco

This is a popular resort for swimming and fishing.

San Salvador

See: The Zoo. Many beautiful parks. Casa Presidencial. The view from the top of Mount Chulul, looking through 2 tremendous vertical rocks called Puerta del Diablo (Devil's Door). Recommended short excursions: to Panchimalco and Lake Ilopango, the crater of San Salvador Volcano, Izalco Volcano and Atecosol Park, Ichanmichen Park, Lake Coatepeque, and Cerro Verde.

Cutuco - San Salvador 1200

Dep. Cutuco	6:30	Dep. San Salvador	6:45
Arr. San Miguel	8:43(1)	Arr. San Vicente	8:55(1)
Dep. San Miguel	8:53	Dep. San Vicente	9:05
Arr. Zacatecoluca	11:35(1)	Arr. Zacatecoluca	9:47(1)
Dep. Zacatecoluca	11:45	Dep. Zacatecoluca	9:57
Arr. San Vicente	12:33(1)	Arr. San Miguel	12:35(1)
Dep. San Vicente	12:43	Dep. San Miguel	12:45
Arr. San Salvador	15:10	Arr. Cutuco	14:50

(1) Estimated arrival time.

Sights in **San Miguel:** Fine parks. The statues and fountains at Chinameca Church.

Sights in **Zacatecoluca:** Inchanmichen, the garden park.

Sights in **San Vicente:** El Pilar, the most unique church in El Salvador.

Three other rail routes in El Salvador are: San Salvador-San Jeronimo, San Salvador-Ahuachapan, and San Salvador-Sonsonate.

San Salvador - San Jeronimo 1200

Dep. San Salvador	6:15	Dep. San Jeronimo	12:55
Arr. San Jeronimo	12:20	Arr. San Salvador	18:50

San Salvador - Ahuachapan 1200

Dep. San Salvador	6:15	Dep. Ahuachapan	12:45
Arr. Texis Junction	9:35	Arr. Texis Junction	15:20
Change trains.		Change trains.	
Dep. Texis Junction	9:45	Dep. Texis Junction	15:25
Arr. Ahuachapan	12:20	Arr. San Salvador	18:50

Sights in Ahuachapan: The Atehuezian waterfalls. Many geysers. Two lakes draw visitors: Laguna Verde and Apaneca.

San Salvador - Sonsonate 1200

Dep. San Salvador	6:25	14:20	Dep. Sonsonate	6:00	14:00
Arr. Sonsonate	9:55	17:50	Arr. San Salvador	9:40	17:40

Sights in Sonsonate: The Sunday market (dairy products, tropical fruits, hides). El Pilar Church. The white porcelain cupola on the Cathedral. It is a 30-minute bus ride from Sonsonate to the fine beaches at Acajutla, El Salvador's main seaport.

INTERNATIONAL ROUTE FROM EL SALVADOR

Here is the route from El Salvador to western Guatemala.

San Salvador - San Jeronimo - Anguiatu - Zacapa - Guatemala City

1200	
Dep. San Salvador	6:15
Arr. San Jeronimo	12:20(1)
Change trains.	
1154	
Dep. Anguiatu	13:00(2)
Arr. Zacapa	17:40
Stay overnight in Zacapa.	
1152	
Dep. Zacapa	13:35(3)
Arr. Guatemala City	19:30

(1)Walk or take bus or taxi ½-mile to Anguiatu. (2)Runs Monday, Wednesday and Friday. (3)Runs Tuesday, Thursday and Saturday.

GUATEMALA

Children under 3 travel free. Half-fare for children 3-11. Children 12 and over must pay full fare.

It is possible to travel in Guatemala by train from the Caribbean (Puerto Barrios) to the Pacific Ocean (Tecun Uman).

Guatemala City

See: Mayan treasures in the Archaeolgical Museum in La Aurora Park, open daily except Monday. A very large collection of Mayan figurines, masks and pottery at Popol Vuh Museum (9 Calle 3-62), open daily except Sunday. Museo Ixchel (4 Avenue 6-27) has a good exhibit of Indian textiles and clothing, open daily except Monday.

The murals, stained-glass and tiled patios and fountains in the National Palace, near Central Park. Next door is the Metropolitan Cathedral. The gold and mahogany altar at Cerro del Carmen Church, and the splendid view of the city from the gardens there.

The marvelous assortment of fabrics at the Central Market. The Botanical Gardens. The Zoo. The National Museum of History and Fine Arts. A display of products made in Guatemala, at the Popular Arts and Handicrafts Center (10 Avenue and 11 Calle). The fish-shaped Templo de la Expiacion. These churches: La Merced, San Francisco, Santo Domingo, Las Capuchinas, and Santa Rosa.

The slide lecture on Mayan archaeology, every night at 19:00 Camino Real Hotel, 9 Calle 4-69.

Take a local bus to the western side of the city to see the Mayan ruins of Kaminal Juyu (Valley of Death). It is a short bus ride to see these nearby Indian villages: Chinautla, San Pedro Sacatepequez and San Juan Sacatepequez.

Visit nearby (28 miles) **Antigua** to see many colonial churches, plazas, fountains and walled palaces where 70,000 people lived before Antigua was destroyed by earthquake in the 18th century. One of the many giant volcanos here is still very active.

Visit nearby (90 miles) **Chichicastenango** for fabulous bargains in strawgoods, fabrics (tablecloths, napkins, etc.) and pottery at the extraordinary Thursday and Sunday markets.

Visit nearby (134 miles) **Quirigua** to see excellent remains of the Mayan Old Empire.

Visit nearby 50-square-mile **Lake Atitlan** to see its beautiful setting amid mountains and volcanos. The lake's color changes constantly.

Puerto Barrios

Nearby beaches are very popular: Escabas and Santo Tomas de

Guatemala City - Puerto Barrios 1152

This route goes through many banana plantations and dense jungles. Watch for 3 volcano cones, a short distance from Guatemala City.

Dep. Guatemala City	7:00(1)	Dep. Puerto Barrios	7:00(1)
Dep. Jalapa	9:57	Dep. Zacapa	13:35
Dep. Zacapa	13:25	Dep. Jalapa	16:32
Arr. Puerto Barrios	19:30	Arr. Guatemala City	19:30

(1) Runs Tuesday, Thursday and Saturday.

Sights in **Jalapa:** The Valley of Monjas, one of the country's most fertile valleys, is near Jalapa.

Sights in **Zacapa:** En route from Guatemala City, a stop is made here for dining at the railstation. This is the junction for the train service to and from El Salvador.

Guatemala City - Esquintla - Mazatenango - Tecun Uman 1151

Dep. Guatemala City	N/A(1)	Dep. Tecun Uman	N/A(1)
Dep. Escuintla	N/A	Dep. Mazatenango	N/A
Dep. Mazatenango	N/A	Dep. Escuintla	N/A
Arr. Tecun Uman	N/A	Arr. Guatemala City	N/A

(1) Service was "temporarily" suspended in 1981.

Sights in **Escuintla:** Famous for fruits and medicinal baths. Nearby are giant sculptures in La Democracia (an archaeological park) and the 13th century ruins at Mixco Viejo.

Sights in **Mazatenango:** The production of tropical fruits, coffee, sugar and cacao.

INTERNATIONAL ROUTES FROM GUATEMALA

There are train connections from Guatemala to El Salvador and Mexico.

Guatemala City - Zacapa - Anguiatu - San Jeronimo - San Salvador

1152
Dep. Guatemala City 7:00(1)
Arr. Zacapa 13:15
Stay overnight in Zacapa.

1154
Dep. Zacapa 6:30(2)
Arr. Anguiatu 11:25(3)
Change trains.
1200
Dep. San Jeronimo 12:55
Arr. San Salvador 18:50

(1) Runs Tuesday, Thursday and Saturday. (2) Runs Monday, Wednesday Friday. (3) Walk or take bus or taxi ½-mile to San Jeronimo.

Guatemala City - Tecun Uman - Cuidad Hidalgo - Mexico City

1151
Dep. Guatemala City   Service "temporarily" suspended in 1981.
Arr. Tecun Uman
Change trains.

It is possible, although very difficult, to travel by train from Guatemala City into Mexico. The reasons we advise against attempting this trip until the conditions improve are:

There is no acceptable lodging in either primitive Tecun Uman or in primitive Cuidad Hidalgo, the 2 border cities where a transfer is necessary.

Further, there is an overnight interval of nearly 14 hours (from 18:45 until 8:30 the next morning) between arriving in Tecun Uman and departing from Ciudad Hidalgo for Mexico City.

The final obstacle is that passengers attempting this transfer must walk more than a mile in great heat and mucho dust from the Guatemalan terminal to the Mexican railstation, and pay a substantial toll charge to cross the border bridge.

1105
Dep. Ciudad Hidalgo 8:30
Arr. Tapachula 9:50
Change trains.
Dep. Tapachula 18:10
Arr. Vera Cruz 17:20(2)
Change trains.

Dep. Vera Cruz 21:30(1)
Arr. Mexico City (Buenavista) 7:37(3)

(1) Air-conditioned. Carries sleeping car. (2) Day 2. (3) Day 3 from Ciudad Hidalgo.

HONDURAS

The country's rail lines serve banana plantations and 2 seaports.

Children under 3 travel free. Half-fare for children 3-11. Children 12 and over must pay full fare.

Puerto Cortes

Honduras' main port. Very hot climate here. Take the bus ride to see the castle at Omoa.

San Pedro Sula

This is the gateway (by air or bus) for travel to Tegucigalpa. Terribly hot here. The population is cosmopolitan: North American, Irish, Cuban, Russian. Fabulous Mayan ruins are located at Copan, 112 miles by road from San Pedro Sula.

Tela

This seaport ships mountains of bananas. See United Fruit Company's experimental farm in nearby Lancetilla.

San Pedro Sula - Baracoa - Puerto Cortes

1250

Dep. San Pedro Sula	7:00	Dep. Puerto Cortes	15:15
Dep. Baracoa	8:15	Dep. Baracoa	16:15
Arr. Puerto Cortes	9:15	Arr. San Pedro Sula	17:30

San Pedro Sula - Baracoa - Tela

1250

Dep. San Pedro Sula	15:00	Dep. Tela	6:00
Arr. Baracoa	16:05	Arr. Baracoa	7:40
Change trains.		Change trains.	
Dep. Baracoa	16:15	Dep. Baracoa	7:45
Arr. Tela	18:00	Arr. San Pedro Sula	9:00

Tela - Baracoa - Puerto Cortes

1250

Dep. Tela	13:45	Dep. Puerto Cortes	7:00
Dep. Baracoa	16:15	Dep. Baracoa	8:15
Arr. Puerto Cortes	17:15	Arr. Tela	10:30

JAMAICA

Jamaica has 3 rail lines: one from Kingston to Port Antonio, one from Kingston to Montego Bay, and a short line for one-day excursions from Montego Bay to the Appleton Rum Distillery.

Children under 4 travel free. Half-fare for children 4-13. Children 14 and over must pay full fare.

Kingston

The capital and commercial center of Jamaica. Shopping for duty-free items is the key tourist attraction here. See: The carvings and historical items at the Institute of Jamaica. The Royal Botanical Gardens at Hope, only a few minutes away, a fine collection of tropical plants, including many orchids.

Montego Bay

Also popular for its duty-free goods. Take the glass-bottom boat to see the beautiful coral gardens. Much deep-sea fishing, sailing, water skiing, golf and tennis here.

Kingston - Spanish Town - Port Antonio

1550

Dep. Kingston	8:20(1)	13:30(2)	16:15
Dep. Spanish Town	9:02(1)	14:25(2)	16:42
Arr. Port Antonio	12:30	18:45	20:15

Sights in Spanish Town: The Cathedral. A broad canvas of Jamaican history and good ethnic exhibits at the Museum. Much fine 18th century English architecture.

Sights in Port Antonio: Every ocean sport is excellent here. Try a ride on a bamboo raft, down the Rio Grande, to see lush jungle scenery.

Dep. Port Antonio	5:30	6:20(2)	16:00(1)
Dep. Spanish Town	9:00	11:12(2)	19:40(1)
Arr. Kingston	9:30	11:45	20:20

(1) Saturdays, Sundays and holidays only. (2) Daily, except Sundays and holidays.

Kingston - Montego Bay

1550

Dep. Kingston	7:10	10:40(1)	15:40
Dep. Spanish Town	7:43	11:21(1)	16:14
Arr. Montego Bay	13:00	18:10	21:24

Sights in Spanish Town: See notes above, under "Kingston-Spanish Town-Port Antonio".

Dep. Montego Bay	6:45	8:15(1)	15:30
Dep. Spanish Town	12:18	14:55(1)	20:42
Arr. Kingston	12:50	15:30	21:15

(1) Daily, except Sundays and holidays.

Montego Bay - Appleton Rum Distillery 1550

The one-day excursion to Appleton and the rum distillery there is very popular. Although there are 3 morning departures from Montego Bay, be sure to take the 9:30 "Catapuda Choo-Choo", for which it is advisable to reserve seats well in advance through either hotels or travel agents in Montego Bay.

This tour package includes the only train on the 34-mile route that has a bar, a guide and calypso band on board, and a layover en route of nearly 2 hours in Catapuda for souvenir shopping. The full-day outing also features a tour of the Appleton Distillery, rum drinks and lunch, plus transportation from your Montego Bay hotel to the railstation and, at end of day, from the railstation back to hotels.

Dep. Montego Bay	6:45	8:15(1)	9:30(2)	15:30
Arr. Catapuda	7:53	9:36	10:15	16:37
Dep. Catapuda	7:56	9:39(1)	12:06(2)	16:40
Arr. Appleton	8:53	10:54	13:55	17:27
	*	*	*	
Dep. Appleton	10:57	14:10(3)	15:31(1)	19:21
Arr. Catapuda	11:54	15:14	16:43	20:18
Dep. Catapuda	11:57	15:17(3)	16:46(1)	20:21
Arr. Montego Bay	13:00	16:20	18:10	21:25

(1) Daily, except Sundays and holidays. (2) Catapuda Choo-Choo special excursion train. (3) Light refreshments.

NICARAGUA

The one rail route in Nicaragua goes from Corinto on the Pacific Ocean to Managua, and then to Granada on the shore of Lake Nicaragua. There are no rail connections between Nicaragua and adjacent countries.

Children under 3 travel free. Half-fare for children 3-11. Children 12 and over must pay full fare.

Corinto

Nicaragua's main seaport.

Leon

See: The largest Cathedral in Central America. Ancient streets and buildings. The 16th century Subtiava Church. Do not miss the iron cannon at the old colonial bridge, Guadalupe. En route from Leon to Managua, there is a short spur to El Sauce, for which timetables are not available.

Managua

Most of this city was totally destroyed in the 1972 earthquake and has been in the process of being rebuilt since then. Be sure to stroll through the beautiful Parque Central (fountains, statues, stately trees). See the Cathedral and the nearby National Palace.

Masaya

Much Indian handicrafts here. Between Managua and Masaya there is a short spur to Jinotepe and Diriamba, for which timetables are not available.

Granada

This city is at the end of the 114-mile rail line that starts in Corinto. Boats leave from the center of Granada for excursions to islands on Lake Nicaragua, one of the world's most unique phenomenon.

The area of this lake was once part of the Pacific Ocean. Volcano lava formed a fill, separating this area from the ocean, but not until after salt-water species of fish had been cut off from the ocean. Over millions of years, the water changed slowly from salt-water to fresh-water, allowing the sea life time to adapt to the new environment. The only fresh-water sharks in the world inhabit this lake.

Sights to see in Granada: The Jalteva and San Francisco churches. The turtles and baby crocodiles in the fountains at Parque Central. A very interesting cemetery. Ride in a horse-drawn carriage.

Corinto - Managua - Granada

1300			
Dep. Corinto	11:50	Dep. Granada	5:00
Dep. Leon	13:30	Dep. Masaya	5:50
Arr. Managua	15:50	Dep. Managua	7:20
Change trains.		Dep. Leon	10:50
Dep. Managua	16:30	Arr. Corinto	13:25
Dep. Masaya	17:45		
Arr. Granada	18:35		

PANAMA

It is possible to travel by train from the Caribbean (Colon) to the Pacific Ocean (Panama City) in 90 minutes. There are on this trip excellent views of the jungle, the canal and the ships passing through the Canal. Try to sit on the left side for the best view. There are no rail connections between Panama and adjacent countries.

Children under 5 travel free. Half-fare for children 5-14. Children 15 and over must pay full fare. A supplement is charged both children and adults for air-conditioned space.

Panama City

Stroll down Paseo de las Bovedas and see the view from there of the Bay of Panama and the islands offshore (Flamenco, Naos and Perico). See: The President's Palace, called Palacio de las Garzas. The egrets there are worth the visit. The gold altar and famous organ in San Jose Church. The view of the bay from the top of La Cresta. Inca and Spanish treasures in the National Museum. The monument dedicated to the Canal, at Plaza de Francia. Instituto Bolivar. The 17th century Cathedral, facing Plaza de la Independencia.

Panama City - Colon

All of these trains have both air-conditioned class and second-class.

1500

Dep. Panama City
5:00(1) 6:45(1) 8:30(2) 9:50(1) 11:40(1) 12:35(2)
15:20(1) 17:05(1) 17:50(2) 21:50(1)

Arr. Colon 90 minutes later

Sights in Colon: This is one of the world's busiest ports. See: The old Spanish ruins of Portobelo. The statues on Paseo Centenario. The Cathedral. The Casino. Many nightclubs. Shop for English bone china, ivory, furniture and perfume on Front Street. There are 3 good excursions from Colon: To Gatun Locks and the nearby jungle. To Fort San Lorenzo, at the mouth of the Chagres River. And a boat trip to the San Blas archipelago.

Dep. Colon 4:50(1) 6:40(2) 6:55(1) 9:40(1) 10:45(2) 11:50(1)
15:10(1) 16:00(2) 17:15(1) 21:00(2)

Arr. Panama City 90 minutes later

(1)Runs Monday-Friday, except holidays. (2)Runs Saturdays, Sundays and holidays only.

Concepcion - Puerto Armuelles

0000 (LTR)

Dep. Concepcion	N/A	Dep. Puerto Amuelles	N/A
Arr. Puerto Armuelles	N/A	Arr. Concepcion	N/A

Chapter 17

SOUTH AMERICA

Winter in South America (south of Colombia and Venezula)is from June 21 to September 20. Summer is from December 21 to March 20.

AMERAILPASS

Much like the Eurailpass that is valid for 16 countries in Europe, the Amerailpass provides unlimited train travel on first-class, second-class and one-class passenger trains in the 6 countries which are members of The Association of Latin American Railways: Argentina, Bolivia, Brazil, Chile, Paraguay and Uruguay.

The Association recommends 2 major "circuits" that offer extensive variety. Complete details on each leg of these appear in this chapter.

The first circle rail trip includes Buenos Aires, the fantastic Transandine route to Santiago and Valparaiso, then south to Puerto Mont, from which the balance of the journey is the southern transcontinental trip to Bariloche and on to Bahia Blanca, and then north to Buenos Aires.

The second "circuit" consists of Buenos Aires to La Paz, then the transcontinental trip to Sao Paulo and Rio de Janeiro, completed by proceeding south from Sao Paulo to Montevideo and Buenos Aires.

Amerailpass becomes valid on the first day it is used, must be used for the first time within 6 months after the day it is issued, and it stops being valid at Midnight the last day of the validity period. It can be purchased from any of the 6-nation member railroads.

If one's rail itinerary involves a relatively short train ride on the first day and a fairly long ride on the day after the pass ceases to be valid (or vice versa), it can be worthwhile to purchase a ticket for the short ride.

There is no refund if the pass is lost or stolen. An unused pass can be returned to the office where it was purchased for a refund of 85% of the price.

The 1982 prices were: $120(U.S.) for 16 days, $140 for 23 days, $175 for 30 days, and $260 for 60 days. Children 3 to under 12 (based on age as of the first day of using the pass) pay half-fare but can travel only when accompanied by an adult. Children under 3 travel free if they are held and do not occupy a separate seat.

Information about Amerailpass can be obtained from the offices listed on the next page.

ARGENTINA

Centro Informaciones de
Ferrocarriles Argentinos
Florida 753
Buenos Aires

ALAF
Av. Cordoba, 883
6 Piso
Buenos Aires 1054

BOLIVIA

Empresa Nacional de Ferrocarriles, Estacion Central, La Paz

BRASIL

Red Ferroviaria Federal S.A.
Plaza Procopio Ferreira, 86
Rio de Janeiro

Red Ferroviaria Federal S.A.
Plaza de Luz 1
San Pablo

CHILE

Ferrocarriles del Estado de Chile
Subdepartamento de Comercio
Balmaceda 1215 = 2 Piso
Santiago

Ferrocarriles de Antofagas a Bolivia
Gerencia de Trafico
Antofagasta

PARAGUAY

F.C. "Pte Carlos A. Lopez"
Eligio Ayala y Mexico
Asuncion

URUGUAY

Secretaria de Prensa,
Publicidad y Turismo
La Paz 1057
Montevideo

In planning trips based on information in this chapter, readers are advised to consider the fact that throughout Eastern Europe, Asia, Africa and Latin America, second-class space is usually primitive and almost always extremely crowded. It is best to reserve first-class space when traveling these areas by train.

As is true of countries in Western Europe, train schedules and ticket prices are always subject to change. **All over the world, departure and arrival times should be re-checked at each leg of a trip.** Where changes have occurred, usually the changes will be slight and have little effect on one's itinerary. Re-checking will help you avoid arriving at a rail-station after your train has departed.

Another point that has been repeated throughout this book is that many cities all over the world have 2 or more railstations.

In this book, we have taken pains to tell you the name of the railstation in parenthesis immediately after the name of a city, when that city has more than one railstation, so you will not miss a connection by going to the wrong station.

ARGENTINA

There are 27,000 miles of rail service in Argentina, radiating out from Buenos Aires.

The 6 major rail routes from Buenos Aires are to Rosario (from where one branch continues to Tucuman and Jujuy, via Cordoba, and a second goes to Tucuman and Jujuy via La Banda), the transcontinental route to Mendoza (and on to Valparaiso, Chile, the most exciting rail trip in South America), and the lines to Santa Rosa, Bahia Blanca (from where one branch continues to Zapala and a second branch goes to Viedma and from there on to San Carlos de Bariloche, gateway to the Lake District), Mar del Plata, and to Posadas.

The connection with Uruguay (and on to Brazil) involves using hydrofoil boat service from Buenos Aires to Colonia and then bus service from Colonia to Montevideo, from where rail service resumes.

There is also connection by rail from Buenos Aires to Asuncion Paraguay.

Children under 3 travel free. Half-fare for children 3-11. Children 12 and over must pay full fare.

ARGENTINA'S DISCOUNT RAIL PASS

Boletos de Libre Circulacion. Not transferable. Unlimited first-class train travel. Can be upgraded for sleeping car accommodation by paying the supplemental charge for sleeper space. The validity period begins on the first day the pass is used and ends at 24:00 on the final day.

There is a very small charge for obtaining a refund before starting to use the pass. When a 60-day or 90-day pass has been used any part of the first 30 days, it can be returned to the Argentine Railways for a refund that results in the passenger paying only for a 30-day pass. Similarly, if the 90-day pass is used 31-60 days, it can be returned for a refund that results in paying only the price for a 60-day pass.

The prices for this pass have increased frequently since the end of 1978, as they are indexed to Argentina's inflation. The prices charged in September of 1979 were: 30 days 215,600 Argentine Pesos, 60 days 360,000(AP), and 90 days 505,700(AP). In November of 1979, those prices in U.S. dollars were: $140, $234 and $328.

Buenos Aires

The railstations here and the routes they serve are: Constitucion (southern), Lacroze (northeastern Paraguay), Once (western), Puente

Alsina, Retiro (Chile and Bolivia), and Velez Sarsfield (northwestern).

Sights in Buenos Aires: The magnificent Avenida 9 Julio. Colon Opera House. Museum of Modern Art. Palermo Park and the nearby Zoological and Botanical Gardens. The statues and paintings in the Cathedral. The Museum of Fine Arts. See and hear the tango in the oldest section of the city, San Telmo, where a fair takes place every Sunday. Eva Peron's mausoleum, in Recoleta Cemetery.

The collection of gaucho artifacts, silver and iron objects, musical instruments and tapestries in the Museo de Motivos de Jose Hernandez (Avenida de Libertador 2373). The tapestries and antiques at the Museum of Decorative Arts and the National Museum of Oriental Art (both at Ave. de Libertador 1902). The Museo de Bellas Artes (Ave. de Libertador 1473), open Tuesday-Saturday 9:00-13:00 and 15:00-19:00.

The Natural Sciences Museum (Avenida Angel Gallardo 470). The Isaac Fernandez Blanco Museum of Spanish-American Art (Suipacha 1422). El Pilar Church (Junin 1904). The Municipal Museum. The Numismatic Museum at the Banco Central.

Buenos Aires - Rosario 2270

Dep. B. A. (Retiro)	7:30(1)	10:00(2)	13:00(1)	16:00(3)	17:00(2+6)
Arr. Rosario Norte	11:50	14:45	17:45	20:15	21:45

Sights in Rosario: The Juan B. Castagnino Municipal Museum and the Provincial Historical Museum, both in Parque Independencia. The Cathedral (Calle 25 de Mayo). Stroll on Boulevard Orono. The Monument of The Flag, along the river bank.

Dep. Rosario Norte	4:25(4)	6:20(5)	7:30(1)	9:25(1)	10:00(2+7)
Arr. B. A. (Retiro)	9:00	11:00	12:15	14:10	15:05

(1) Meal service. (2) Light refreshments. (3) Tuesday and Friday. Meal service. (4) Carries sleeping car. (5) Wednesday and Sunday. Meal service. (6) Plus other departures from Buenos Aires at 18:00(1), 19:00(1) and 21:00(1). (7) Plus other departures from Rosario at 13:00(1), 17:00(2) and 19:00(1).

Buenos Aires - Rosario - Tucuman - Guemes - Salta or Jujuy 2257

Dep. Buenos Aires (Ret.)	22:00(1)	Dep. Jujuy	22:45(4)
Dep. Rosario	3:35(2)	Dep. Salta	22:35
Dep. Tucuman (Norte)	22:11(2)	Dep. Guemes	0:40(2)
Arr. Guemes	4:32(3)	Arr. Tucuman (Norte)	6:19(2)
Arr. Salta	6:45(3)	Dep. Rosario	0:45(3)
Arr. Jujuy	6:45(3)	Arr. Buenos Aires (Ret.)	6:10(3)

(1) Monday and Thursday. Train is divided into 2 sections. At Guemes, one section goes to Salta, the other goes to Jujuy. (2) Day 2. (3) Day 3. (4) Tuesday and Friday. Train is divided into 2 sections. One starts in

Jujuy, the other starts in Salta. The 2 sections combine in Guemes.

Sights in **Alta Cordoba:** The Cathedral. The Jesuit church. The College of Monserrat. The 17th century university. The Historical and Colonial Museum in the Viceroy's House, on Calle Rosario. The lovely doorway at the Church and Convent of Santa Teresa, on Calle Independencia. The cedar vault and cupola in the 17th century La Merced Church, on Calle Rivadavia. The serpent collection at the excellent Zoological Garden, and the view of Alta Cordoba from there. The Museum of Fine Arts at the Plaza Centenario. The Academy of Fine Arts, near the Plaza Velez Sarsfield. Sacred Heart Church.

Sights in **Tucuman:** Government Palace. At Plaza Independencia: The Church of San Francisco, the Cathedral, Government Palace, and the statue of Liberty, surrounded by orange and palm trees. The Museum at Casa Historica, on Calle Congresso, and the "son et lumiere" programs presented there every night. The menhir stone in beautiful Parque 9 de Julio. The herbarium, animals and insects in the Instituto Miguel Lillo. The lovely Parque Avellaneda and Parque Quebrada de Lules. The Folklore Museum. The Anthropological Museum at 25 de Mayo 492. Nearby: the outstanding Villa Nougues residential area.

Sights in **Salta:** The 16th century images of Cristo del Milagro and the Virgin Mary, in the Cathedral. The Museum of Colonial History and Fine Arts, at Caseros 575. The historical museum, Cabildo, at Caseros 549. Shopping for handicraft, particularly onyx. The view of Salta from Cerro San Bernardo, a short walk or drive. There is train service from Salta to Resistencia, Posadas, La Paz and Antofagasta.

Sights in **Jujuy:** The superb wood pulpit in the Cathedral at Plaza Belgrano. The Palacio de Tribunales. Parque San Martin. Nearby: numerous ancient Franciscan, Dominican and Jesuit churches.

Here is the second route between Rosario and Tucuman.

Buenos Aires - Rosario Norte - Tucuman (via La Banda) 2270

Dep. Buenos Aires (Ret.)	10:00(1)	16:00(3+4+5)	18:00(3)
Arr. Rosario (Norte)	14:45	20:15(3)	22:20(3)
Change trains.			
Dep. Rosario (Norte)	15:45(2)	20:30(3+4+5)	22:35(3)
Arr. Tucuman (GM)	8:45	9:30	13:45
Dep. Tucuman (GM)	17:15(3+4+6)	18:45(3)	22:45(8)
Arr. Rosario (Norte)	6:05(3)	9:10(3)	15:30
Change trains.			
Dep. Rosario (Norte)	6:20(3+7)	9:25(3)	17:00(1+2)
Arr. Tucuman (GM)	11:00	14:10	22:05

(1) Light refreshments. (2) Tuesday, Thursday and Sunday. (3) Direct train. No train change in Rosario. Meal service. (4) Carries sleeping car.

Has Club Car. (5)Tuesday and Friday. (6)Wednesday and Sunday. (7)Monday and Thursday. (8)Monday, Wednesday and Friday.

Buenos Aires - Santa Fe - Resistencia 2266

All of these trains have meal service.

Dep. B.A. (Ret.)	8:45(1)	8:45(2)	Dep. Resistencia	9:55(3)	19:20(4)
Dep. Santa Fe	18:30(1)	18:59(2)	Arr. Santa Fe	8:01(2)	8:37(5)
Arr. Resistencia	7:10	17:30	Arr. B.A. (Ret.)	17:50	17:50

(1)Wed. only. (2)Tues., Thurs. and Sat. (3)Mon., Wed. and Fri. (4)Thurs. only. (5)Fri. only.

Sights in **Santa Fe:** The 17th century La Merced Church on Plaza Mayo. Nearby, Casa de Gobierno. The marvelous 17th century San Francisco Church. Across from it, the Provincial Historical Museum. The Rosa Galisteo de Rodriguez Museum of Fine Arts on Calle General.

Buenos Aires - Santa Rosa 2300

Dep. Buenos Aires (Once)	21:05(1)	Dep. Santa Rosa	20:35(1)
Arr. Santa Rosa	8:32	Arr. Buenos Aires (Once)	8:10

(1)Daily, except Saturday. Meal service. Has Club Car.

Buenos Aires - Bahia Blanca 2305

Dep. B.A. (P. Con.)	8:20(1+2)	12:30(2)	21:45(3)
Arr. Bahia Blanca	18:06	22:45	8:30(4)

Sights in Bahia Blanca: The statues and lakes in Parque de Mayo. The Zoological Garden in Parque Independencia.

Dep. Bahia Blanca	9:25(2)	21:05(2+3+5)
Arr. B.A. (P. Con.)	20:15	8:13

(1)Runs Wed. and Sun. (2)Meal service. (3)Daily. Carries sleeping car on Tues., Thurs., Sat. and Sun. (4)Arrives 10:40 on Wed. and Fri. (5)Departs at 18:55 on Tues. and Thurs.

Buenos Aires - Bahia Blanca - Zapala 2308

Dep. B.A. (P. Con.)	12:30(1)	Dep. Zapala	18:35(1)
Dep. Bahia Blanca	23:10	Arr. Bahia Blanca	9:00
Arr. Zapala	14:00	Arr. B.A. (P. Con.)	20:15

(1) Carries air-conditioned sleeping car. Meal service.

Sights near Zapala: The Copahue Volcano and mineral baths in Copahue National Reservation, at the Chilean border, which can be visited by bus. The animal and bird sanctuary in Laguna Blanca National Park. Lake Huechulafquen, a long bus ride from Zapala.

Buenos Aires - Bahia Blanca - San Carlos de Bariloche 2325

All arrivals shown are on Day 2.

Dep. B.A. (P. Con.)	8:20(1+2)	Dep. San Carlos de B.	13:30(1+4)
Dep. Bahia Blanca	18:54	Arr. Bahia Blanca	12:48
Arr. San Carlos de B.	14:20(3)	Arr. B.A. (P. Con.)	23:30

(1)Carries air-conditioned sleeping car. Meal service. Has Club Car. (2)Runs on Sun. all year. Runs Wed. only from mid-Dec. to mid-March. (3)Wed. departure from B.A. arrives at 17:40 Thurs. (4)Runs on Fri. all year. Runs Mon. (17:30 departure) all year. Runs Tues. (14:15 departure) only from mid-Dec. to mid-March.

Sights in San Carlos de Bariloche: This is the biggest ski area in South America (7 different chairlifts). Similar to an Alpine village. Much mountain climbing here, also. See the collection of Indian artifacts in the Nahuel Huapi Museum. Take the cable car from Cerro Cathedral. Many tours of Argentina's Lake District originate in Bariloche.

THE PATAGONIAN EXPRESS

The southernmost rail trip in the Western Hemisphere is this spur from the Bariloche-Buenos Aires line, the ride from Ing. Jacobacci to Esquel, a ranch town that attracts skiers in September and October. There are 70mph cyclones here in July and August. During harvest period, that train operates at different times and on different days than the schedule published by Argentina.

San Carlos de Bariloche - Buenos Aires 2325 + 2331

Dep. San Carlos de B.	13:30(1+2+3)	14:15(1+4+5)	17:30(1+6)
Arr. Ing. Jacobacci	18:25	19:12	21:45
Change trains.			
Dep. Ing. Jacobacci	11:00(3+6)	13:30(5+7)	
Arr. Esquel	1:05	3:35	
* * *			
Dep. Esquel	2:50(2+3)	3:50(5+8)	
Arr. Ing. Jacobacci	17:05	18:05	
Change trains.			
Dep. Ing. Jacobacci	18:30(1+2+3)	19:17(1+4+5)	21:50(1+6)
Arr. Buenos Aires (P.Con.)	23:30(9)	23:30(9)	23:30(9)

(1)Meal service. Carries sleeping car. (2)Fri. only. (3)Runs mid-March to mid-Dec. (4)Wed. and Fri. (5)Runs mid-Dec. to mid-March. (6)Mon. only. (7)Sat. only. (8)Wed. only. (9)Day 2.

Buenos Aires - San Carlos de Bariloche 2325 + 2331

Dep. Buenos Aires (P. Con.)	8:20(1+2)	8:20(1+4+5)	8:20(1+6+7)
Arr. Ing. Jacobacci	9:54(3)	12:45(3)	13:40(3)
Change trains.			
Dep. Ing. Jacobacci	11:00(7+8)	13:30(5+9)	
Arr. Esquel	1:05(3)	3:35(3)	
* * *			
Dep. Esquel	2:50(7+10)	3:50(5+6)	
Arr. Ing. Jacobacci	17:05	18:05	
Change trains.			
Dep. Ing. Jacobacci	9:59(1+8)	12:50(1+5+11)	13:45(1+7+12)
Arr. San Carlos de Bariloche	14:20	17:40	18:35

(1) Meal service. Carries sleeping car. (2) Sun. only. (3) Day 2. (4) Wed. and Sun. (5) Runs mid-Dec. to mid-March. (6) Wed. only. (7) Runs mid-March to mid-Dec. (8) Mon. only. (9) Sat. only. (10) Fri. only. (11) Mon. and Thurs. (12) Thurs. only.

Lake District Bus Connections

Bariloche - Puerto Montt 2334

Dep. Bariloche	8:00(1)	8:30(2)
Dep. Osorno	14:30(1)	15:00(2)
Arr. Puerto Montt	16:30	17:00

Dep. Puerto Montt	8:00(3)
Dep. Osorno	10:00(3)
Arr. Bariloche	17:30

(1) Tuesday and Thursday. (2) Daily. (3) Daily, except Monday and Saturday.

The interesting lakes in this area are: Argentino, Nahuel Huapi, Correntoso, Espejo, Traful, Gutierrez, Mascardi, Futulafquen, Meliquina, Falkner, Villarino, Epulafquen and Tromen. There is much outstanding trout fishing in many of these lakes.

Buenos Aires - Mar del Plata 2320

All of these trains have meal service, unless designated otherwise.

Dep. B.A. (P. Con.)	7:00(1)	8:00(2)	9:15(1)	10:35(1+3+12)
Arr. Mar del Plata	11:35	12:55	13:50	15:03

Sights in Mar del Plata: Five miles of attractive sandy beaches. A very large casino.

Dep. Mar del Plata	7:00(1)	8:45(1)	9:50(4)	9:55(1+7+13)
Arr. B.A. (P. Con.)	12:20	14:03	14:55	17:50

(1) Runs mid-Dec. to mid-March. (2) Runs all year. (3) Daily, except Sundays and holidays. (4) Runs mid-March to mid-Dec. (5) Fri. only. (6) Daily, except Sat. (7) Second-class only. No meal service. (8) Tues.

and Fri. (9)Sundays and holidays only. (10)Wed., Sun. and holidays. (11)Sun. only. (12)Plus other departures from Buenos Aires at 11:50(1), 15:25(2), 16:55(4+5), 18:35(4+5), 18:35(1+6), 19:00(1+7), 20:30-(4+7+8), 23:00(1+5), 23:55(2), 1:00(1) and 1:45(1). (13)Plus other departures from Mar del Plata at 15:20(1), 16:05(4+9), 17:10(4), 17:20(1), 17:50(4+9), 17:55(1), 20:25(4+7+10), 20:40(1+6), 21:35-(1+11), 23:45(2) and 1:35(1+3).

INTERNATIONAL ROUTES FROM ARGENTINA

Argentina's gateways for rail travel to Bolivia, central Brazil, northern Chile and southern Peru are Tucuman and Salta.

From Tucuman, there is rail service to La Paz (with spurs to Potosi, Sucre and Cochabamba), to Santa Cruz (and on across Brazil to Sao Paulo, Brasilia and Rio de Janeiro), and also a beautiful valley ride to Antofagasta.

The starting point for 2 train trips to southern Chile, Paraguay and Uruguay (and on to southern Brazil) is Buenos Aires.

Tucuman - La Paz 1910

Dep. Tucuman (GM)	14:50	Monday and Friday. Meal service.
Arr. La Quiaca	5:05	Tuesday and Saturday.
Walk 3km across border to Villazon.		
Dep. Villazon	13:25	Daily, except Mon. and Thurs. Meal service.
Arr. La Paz	9:34	Day 2.

Salta - Yacuiba - Santa Cruz

2255	
Dep. Salta	8:00(1)
Arr. Yacuiba	N/A(2)
Change trains.	

1915			
Dep. Yacuiba	6:15(3)	17:00(4)	22:00(5)
Arr. Santa Cruz	18:59	11:34	6:32

(1)Sat. only. Light refreshments. (2)Time not available in 1982. (3)Wed., Fri. and Sun. Meal service. (4)Wed. and Sun. Second-class only. (5)Supplement charged. First-class only. Meal service.

Tucuman - Antofagasta

This is a very scenic valley train ride.

2257	
Dep. Tucuman (Norte)	22:11(1)
Arr. Guemes	4:32(2)
Dep. Guemes	5:07(3)
Arr. Salta	6:45
Change to bus.	

2256 Bus	
Dep. Salta	16:40(4)
Arr. Socompa	12:15(2)
Arr. Antofagasta	N/A(5)

(1)Mid-December to early March: runs Tues., Thurs., Fri. and Sun. Early March to mid-December: runs Tues. and Fri. (2)Day 2. (3)Daily. (4)Wed. only. (5)Time has not been available since 1980.

Buenos Aires - Mendoza - Valparaiso (Santiago)

Before it was discontinued in 1980, the Mendoza-Los Andes portion of this rail trip was the most exciting train ride in South America.

Altitudes (in feet) En Route

ASCENT		DESCENT	
Mendoza	2,518	Caracoles (tunnel exit)	10,420
Paso de los Andes	3,069	El Portillo	9,408
Blanco Encalda	3,502	El Juncal	7,321
Cacheuta	4,080	Guardia Vieja	5,397
Portrerillos	4,443	Rio Blanco	4,764
Guido	4,957	Salta del Soldado	4,141
Uspallata	5,741	San Pablo	3,174
Rio Blanco	7,000	Los Andes	2,669
Zanjon Amarillo	7,236	Valparaiso	-0-
Punta de las Vacas	7,852		
Puente del Inca	8,915		
Las Cuevas	10,331		
Tunnel Entrance	10,452	(The summit is 13,082.)	

Breakfast was served at the railstation in Mendoza before boarding a narrow-gauge train that went through a scenic valley to Paso de Los Andes. There is much snow in this area from May to November. The ride from Puente del Inca to Las Cuevas was by rack railway. It is a deep descent from Las Cuevas to Portillo. At Llay Llay there is a fork, and one branch of the train route went to Santiago, the other to Valparaiso.

Here is the current train + bus schedule:

2290 Train					
Dep. Buenos Aires (Ret.)	18:30(1)	20:30(3)			
Arr. Mendoza	8:20(2)	13:20(2)			
Change to bus.					
2423					
Dep. Mendoza	8:00	8:00	8:30	11:00	12:00
Dep. Puente del Inca	N/A(4)	N/A(4)	-0-	N/A(4)	N/A(4)
Dep. Los Andes	N/A(4)	N/A(4)	-0-	N/A(4)	N/A(4)
Set your watch back one hour.					
Arr. Santiago	N/A(4)	N/A(4)	15:30	18:00	22:00
Arr. Valparaiso	15:30	19:00	-0-	-0-	-0-

(1) First-class only. Carries air-conditioned parlor car. Meal service. Daily, except Thurs. and Sun. Runs from mid-Dec. to mid-March. (2) Day 2. (3) Carries sleeping car and air-conditioned parlor car. Meal service. (4) Time has not been available since 1980.

Sights En Route

Mendoza is a large, modern city, having been completely rebuilt after it was destroyed by earthquake and fire in 1861. Its proliferation of gardens make the city extremely beautiful. A 24-hour stopover here is well worthwhile Do not miss seeing the public park with the splendid monument to Jose de San Martin, the liberator of Chile and Peru. It has an incredible collection of statues and bas-reliefs. Then walk to the lake and streams in the nearby Zoological Gardens.

Also see: The San Martin Museum (Av. General San Martin). The exhibit of Argentine animals and plants in the Moyano Museum of Natural History (Calle Belgrano). The beautiful Romanesque Law Courts building. Window-shop on Calle Las Heras.

There is a splendid all-day bus trip to see the famous Christ the Redeemer statue, which cannot be seen on the train trip. Great scenery on this ride, with a stop for lunch at **Las Cuevas.** Particularly recommended for those not making the complete train trip to Chile.

From **Cacheuta,** the train follows an old Spanish trail called Camino de los Andes. After **Uspallata,** a desolate and vast plain comes into view. There are many rushing mountain streams in the area of **Rio Blanco.** Next in sight is Aconcagua, highest (22,834 feet) mountain in the Western hemisphere.

Puente del Inca is a popular Winter sports resort, attracting the largest crowds of visitors from November to May. It is named for the natural stone bridge spanning the Mendoza River and is one of South America's most marvelous sights. This city is also popular as a base for excursions by foot and horseback to many high valleys in the Andes.

Next in sight is the Horcones River, before arriving at **Las Cuevas** on the Chilean border. This is another popular ski resort.

Extremely good rock scenery can be seen after emerging from the tunnel at **Caracoles.** Next, you will see the Aconcagua River. Here, on the Pacific side of the Andes, the ground is covered by foliage, including many flowers.

Portillo, another Andean ski resort, has many attractive lodges and hotels. The views from the ski lefts and at the 10,824-foot peak are so superb, it's worthwhile visiting here even if you don't ski. The best ski weather is from mid-August to mid-September. Only 4,000 people are allowed to use this facility each season. Of these, there are 3,000 who have permanent privilege. The few hundred newcomers are culled from over 8,000 applicants, permitting entry only to those who come here on a package tour (check the tour desk of Braniff International). There is much farming in the valley that continues from Portillo to Valparaiso.

Buenos Aires - Puerto Montt

For this transcontinental train trip across southern Argentina, please refer to separate schedules earlier in this section for (1) Buenos Aires-Bahia Blanca, (2) Bahia Blanca-San Carlos de Bariloche, and (3) Bariloche-Puerto Montt.

Buenos Aires - Posadas - Villa Encarnacion - Asuncion 2230

The 40-hour trip from Buenos Aires to Asuncion is a very rough ride, 930 miles through dense brush and jungle. The inconveniences include hard wood seats, stifling heat, swarms of mosquitoes and much dust.

From Encarnacion to Asuncion at night the station platforms at villages along the route are lined with people who, sitting at tables while eating and singing, enjoy watching the train pass by. The locomotive on this portion of the route was built in 1912. The train is said to be the oldest train in South America.

Be sure to have an inexpensive (about $1.00 U.S.) "through ticket" before departing Buenos Aires. Passengers without it are required to leave the train at Posadas, carry their luggage to the auto ferry pier, take the auto ferry across the river, and re-board the train on the other side of the river, in Encarnacion. With a "through ticket", passengers can remain on the train as it is carried across the river.

Dep.		
Buenos Aires (F. La Croze)	12:00	Tuesday and Thursday
Dep. Posadas (Train Ferry)	9:30	Day 2 (Wednesday and Friday)
Set your watch back one hour from April 1 to September 30.		
Arr. Encarnacion	12:00	
Dep. Encarnacion	12:35(1)	
Arr. Asuncion	4:30	Day 3 (Thursday and Saturday)

(1) Meal service.

Sights in Posadas: Make the 210-mile bus trip to see one of South America's most impressive sights, Iguazu Falls, much grander than Victoria Falls or Niagara Falls. The biggest flow is August to November.

Buenos Aires - Corrientes 2263

These trains carry sleeping cars and have meal service.

Dep. B.A. (F. LaCroze)	8:40(1)	Dep. Corrientes	12:15(3)
Arr. Corrientes	6:00(2)	Arr. B.A. (F. LaCroze)	9:30(2)

(1) Mon., Wed. and Fri. all year. Also Sat. from mid-Dec. to late March. (2) Day 2. (3) Tues., Thurs. and Sat. all year. Also Sun. from mid-Dec. to late March.

Sights in Corrientes: The Colonial Historical and Fine Arts Museum. The Church of La Cruz. Government Palace on Plaza 25 de Mayo. The Cathedral.

Buenos Aires - Montevideo
2217

Dep. Buenos Aires	8:00	10:00	11:00	14:15(1)	16:00(2+6)
Arr. Colonia	9:00	11:00	12:00	15:15	17:00
Change to bus.					
Dep. Colonia	9:10	11:10	12:10	15:25	17:10
Arr. Montevideo	11:45	14:00	14:45	18:15	19:45

(1) Mon., Tues., Wed. and Thurs. (2) Daily, except Fri. and Sun. (3) Sat. and Sun. (4) Daily, except Sat. (5) Fri., Sat. and Sun. (6) Plus other departures from Buenos Aires at 16:30(3), 17:30(4) and 20:15(5).

Buenos Aires - Rio de Janeiro 2125 Bus

Dep. Buenos Aires	16:30	
Arr. Rio de Janeiro	16:30	Day 3

BOLIVIA

Children under 3 travel free. Half-fare for children 3-11. Children 12 and over must pay full fare.

All of Bolivia's scant 1,400 miles of railway are narrow-gauge, one metre wide.

La Paz

This is the world's highest capital (11,735-foot altitude). See: The National Art Museum, across from the Cathedral, in the Palace of the Condes de Arana. Window-shop on Calle Comercio. See the Central Food Market, largest one in South America. Stroll Calle Sagarnaga, called "Street of the Indians" to examine the assortment of handicrafts sold there. The view of La Paz from Monticulo Park. Walk on The Prado and on Avenida Buenos Aires. See ancient Indian arts and crafts in The National Museum (Calle Don Bosco 93). The furniture and paintings exhibited at Casa de Murillo. Visit The House of Culture. Go to the Tiahuanco ruins, 49 miles from La Paz.

La Paz - Cochabamba 1910

Dep. La Paz	8:20(1)	Dep. Cochabamba	8:00(1)
Arr. Cochabamba	19:25	Arr. La Paz	19:13

(1) Meal service.

Sights in Cochabamba: This is the most comfortable area in Bolivia, a mere 8,500 feet altitude. See: The former home of tin baron Simon Patino, now a museum. The several museums in the Palace of Culture. Colorful stalls in the Municipal Market.

La Paz - Potosi - Sucre 1900

This train ride over the Andes is both the highest meter-gauge track in the world (15,705 feet at El Condor, between Rio Mulato and Potosi), and it is also the world's highest passenger train run on any gauge.

Dep. La Paz	18:00(1)		Dep. Sucre	15:40(2)
Arr. Potosi	8:14	Day 2	Dep. Potosi	21:25(2)
Arr. Sucre	13:54		Arr. La Paz	11:50 Day 2

(1) Wednesday and Sunday. (2) Monday and Thursday.

Sights in Potosi: The silver and silk statue of Christ in San Francisco Cathedral. The silver altar in San Lorenzo Church. Half-day tours of the tin mine are offered weekdays at 9:00, starting at the headquarters of COMIBOL. The mine can be reached by taxi or by taking the 7:45 bus from Plaza 10 de Noviembre. After the tin mine tour, you can see the nearby ancient Inca hot springs. Do not fail to visit the Royal House of Money, built in 1773, for a 2-hour tour of this ancient mint. See the small shops near the mint, on Calle Bustillos.

Sights in Sucre: This city is 10,300 feet high. See the marvelous 16th and 17th century architecture. Many interesting palaces, museums and churches. The ancient University of San Francisco Xavier. The Palace of Justice. The Monastery of La Recoleta.

La Paz - Puno 1826

Dep. La Paz	14:40	Friday	Boat		
Arr. Guaqui	17:49	Friday	Dep. Puno	21:00	Wednesday
Change to boat.			Arr. Guaqui	9:30	Thursday
Dep. Guaqui	20:00	Friday	Change to train.		
Arr. Puno	7:00	Saturday	Dep. Guaqui	10:45	Thursday
			Arr. La Paz	13:45	Thursday

Sights on Lake Titicaca: Trout fishing. Many hydrofoil tours. Watch Indians building reed boats on Suriqui Island.

INTERNATIONAL ROUTES FROM BOLIVIA

La Paz - La Quiaca - Jujuy - Tucuman - Buenos Aires 1910 + 2257

On this 1500-mile route to Argentina, there is an approximately 13-hour wait at La Quiaca, involving a search for drugs by Argentine customs officials before they allow the train to proceed to Tucuman. A Monday departure from La Paz brings you into Buenos Aires on Friday. If you leave La Paz on Friday, you arrive Buenos Aires the next Tuesday.

(Timetable notes appear on next page.)

Dep. La Paz	16:00(1)	
Set your watch forward 2 hours.		
Arr. Villazon	12:20	Day 2
Walk 3km across border to La Quiaca.		
Dep. La Quiaca	2:40(2)	Day 3
Arr. Jujuy	9:22	
Dep. Jujuy	9:37(2)	
Arr. Tucuman (G.M.)	16:30	
Arr. Rosario	9:10(3)	Day 4
Arr. Buenos Aires	14:10	

(1)Daily, except Wed. and Sun. Meal service. (2)Wed. and Sun. (3)Thurs. and Mon.

The route to Peru is via Cuzco.

La Paz - Cuzco - Lima

1815 Bus	
Dep. La Paz	8:00(1)
Arr. Puno	20:00
Change to train.	
1825	
Dep. Puno	20:30(2)
Arr. Juliaca	21:45
Change trains.	
1810	
Dep. Juliaca	8:25(3)
Arr. Cuzco	17:35
Change to bus.	

1814 Bus	
Dep. Cuzco	7:30(4)
Arr. Huancavelica	N/A(5)
Change to train.	
1816	
Dep. Huancavelica	7:00(6)
Arr. Huancayo	10:10
Change trains.	
1821	
Dep. Huancayo	7:00(6)
Arr. Lima (Des.)	N/A(7)

(1)Tues., Thurs. and Sat. (2)Daily. (3)Mon-Fri, except holidays. (4)Mon. and Fri. (5)Time has not been available since 1980. (6)Daily, except Sun. and holidays. (7)Train service from La Oroya (arrival at 10:06) to Lima was by 5-hour bus in 1982 due to damaged bridge near Matucana.

There are 2 rail routes from La Paz to Chile.

La Paz - Charana - Arica 1901

You travel on 30 miles of rack and pinion track during this 270-mile trip. The highest place on this route is 14,000 feet at General Lagos. The best scenery is during the descent from La Paz, at the start of the trip.

Dep. La Paz	12:00 Tuesday
Arr. Charana	19:46
Change trains.	
Dep. Charana	22:50 second and fourth Tues. of each month
Arr. Arica	8:05

La Paz - Antofagasta 1910

From La Paz to Ollague, for more than 22 hours, the train is constantly at more than 12,000-feet altitude.

Dep. La Paz	12:10(1)	Fri.	Dep. Calama	17:00 Sat.
Dep. Ollague	10:30	Sat.	Arr. Antofagasta	20:00 Sat.
Arr. Calama	16:10	Sat.		
Change to bus.				

(1) Meal service.

Santa Cruz - Sao Paulo - Rio de Janeiro

There is great jungle scenery on the Santa Cruz-Corumba portion of this train trip to Brazil.

1915				
Dep. Santa Cruz	18:20(1)	14:40(2)		
Arr. Corumba	6:28	8:17		
Change trains.				
2068				
Dep. Corumba	8:00(3)			
Arr. Bauru	13:05	Day 2 from Corumba		
Change trains.				
2085				
Dep. Bauru	13:49(4)	22:48(3)	4:22(4)	8:00(4)
Arr. Sao Paulo (Luz)	20:01	6:00(5)	10:45	14:53
Change trains.				
2075				
Dep. Sao Paulo (Luz)	23:20(6+7)	8:00(7)	-0-	-0-
Arr. Rio de Jan. (D. Ped.)	8:27	17:03	-0-	-0-

(1) Thurs. only. First-class only. Supplement charged. Meal service. (2) Daily, except Thurs. Meal service. (3) Carries sleeping car. Meal service. (4) Meal service. (5) Day 2 from Bauru. (6) First-class only. Carries sleeping car. Also has couchettes. (7) Air-conditioned. Meal service.

Santa Cruz - Yacuiba - Salta

1915				2255	
Dep. Santa Cruz	11:55(1)	14:30(2)	16:40(3)	Dep. Yacuiba	N/A(4)
Arr. Yacuiba	20:25	3:11	11:03	Arr. Salta	21:25

(1) First-class only. Supplement charged. Meal service. Runs Mon., Wed., Fri. and Sun. (2) Runs Tues., Thurs. and Sat. Meal service. (3) Second-class only. Runs Wed. and Sun. (4) Time, not available since 1981, is a short time prior to 9:30. Runs Tues. only. Light refreshments.

BRAZIL

Children under 3 travel free. Half-fare for children 3-9. Children 10 and over must pay full fare.

Nearly all (91%) of Brazil's 23,000 miles of rail lines are located within 300 miles of its shoreline on the Atlantic Ocean. Brazil employs 5 different rail gauges. However, most of its tracks are one metre. The only practical route for train travel to the unique capital, Brasilia, is from Sao Paulo.

Belo Horizonte

See the odd-shaped church at Pampulha, on the edge of the city. Palacio de Liberdade, in Praca de Liberdade. The City Museum. The collection of lamps, photographs, tools, maps and crystal in the Tassini Museum. The Chapel of Sao Francisco. The gardens in the Municipal Park. The marble and glass Museum of Modern Art. The fantastic rock shapes in the 22-million-year-old Lapinha Cavern.

Brasilia

In existence only since 1960, this has been Brazil's capital since then. See: The lovely water gardens at the Ministry of Foreign Affairs, the most beautiful structure in Brazil. Across from it, the Palacio de Justica. The blue glass Church of Dom Bosco. Great sculptures throughout the city. The view at night of the white marble federal buildings, sparkling in the glow of spotlights.

The unique housing units, each containing expensive apartments, buildings for middle-income workers, and a complete shopping center. The National Cathedral. Nearby, the 18 buildings that are each for a different government department. Plenalto Palace, where the President's office is located. Alvorada Palace, residence of the President. Arcos Palace. The Metropolitan Cathedral. The 600-foot-long Gallery of States shopping mall, featuring handicrafts from each of Brazil's 22 states. Take the 50-mile drive around Paranoá.

The Museum. The Hall of Mirrors, scene of formal state receptions. The exquisite interior of Alvorada Palace. The National Theater.

Rio de Janeiro

Perhaps the most beautiful city in the world. See: Copacabana Beach. Take the funicular from Rua Cosme Velho 513 to see the incredible 100-foot-high 700-ton statue, Christ The Redeemer, at the 2400-foot-high top of Corcovado. It is a short walk from the Cosme Velho station to the 5 marvelous colonial-style houses in the little square called Largo do Boticário.

Ride the cablecar to the top of Sugar Loaf for the fine view from there. See the concrete and steel Candelária Cathedral (styled after Mayan temples). Next to the Cathedral is a stop for the city's last streetcar. Ride it for a one-hour roundtrip on its route through the hilly Santa Teresa residential area.

Take bus #206 from Largo da Carioca to Silvestre. Visit Ipanema, Barra da Tijuca and Leblon beaches. Sao Bento Monastery. The Church of Penha. Gloria Church. The Museum of Modern Art on Avenida Presidente Vargas. The Museum of Fine Arts (Avenida Rio Branco 100). The collection of movie theaters, called Cinelandia. The photos, jewels and costumes of the great Brazilian entertainer of the 1930's, at the Carmen Miranda Museum. The collection of weaving, stone works, leather and ceramics in the Indian Museum (Rua Mata Machado).

Gems and precious stones at the Museum of Geology and Mineralogy (Avenida Pasteur 404). The Museum of Villa-Lobos (Rua da Imprensa 16). The Museum of the Republic (Rua do Catete 153) in the granite and rose-colored marble Catete Palace. The Museum of Sacred Arts. The Museum of Pictures and Sound. The Municipal Theater.

The enormous collection of plants and trees at the Botanical Gardens (Rua Jardim Botanico). The National Library (Avenida Rio Branco). Fine colonial art in the Convent of Santo Antonio. The Church of Candelaria. Quinta da Boa Vista Museum, with one of the world's best collections of birds, reptiles and insects. Nearby, the Zoo.

Salvador

Called "Bahia" by Brazilians. English-speaking guides are available at the Tourist Office at Praca da Se. To its left is the 18th century Archbishop's Palace. On the other side of the Tourist Office is the 18th century Holy House of Mary Church.

See: The Sao Damaso Seminary. The absolutely beautiful Church of Sao Francisco Convent, filled with gold-leaf decorations. The picturesque market near Praca Cairu. Take the ride on the Lacerda elevator, from Praca Cairu to Praca Municipal to see the Government Palace and Municipal Library, and to window-shop on Rua Chile.

The 17th century furniture in Sao Bento Church. The Instituto Geografico e Historico. Sao Pedro Fort. The Zoo, in the Botanical Gardens at Ondina. The view from Ondina Hill.

The 16th century Basilica Cathedral and the church of St. Peter of the Clerics, in the square of Terreiro de Jesus. The silver altar and the tiles in the Museum of Sacred Art in the 17th century Santa Teresa Church. Do not miss seeing Largo do Pelourinho, Alfredo de Brito Street. The 17th century Convent of the Desterro, most beautiful of all of Brazil's convents.

Dique, the 17th century artificial lake below the Tororo steps. The blue tiles inside University Rectory, en route to Lagoa do Abaete. The beach at Itaparica. The lofty coconut trees at Itapoa Beach. The forts of Santa Maria and Sao Diogo. Igreja da Graco, Salvador's first church.

The stalls of fish, pork, beef and tropical fruits at the Agua de Meninos market.

See the Fratelli Vita glassblowing factory. The Fort of Mont Serrat, and the nearby Mont Serrat Church. The Cacao Institute, for a look at the processing of chocolate from seed to candy.

Sao Paulo

Largest city in Latin America. See the view while standing on the bridge that spans Avenida Anhangabau. The Municipal Theater, across from Praca Ramos de Azevedo. Instituto Butantan, South America's largest snake farm. Nearby, the collection of antique pottery and furniture in Casa do Bandeirante.

Stroll through Ibirapuera Park, with its statues, Japanese Pavillion (an exact copy of Japan's Katura Palace), the various museums (Science, Aeronautics and Technical Arts) in the History Pavillion, contemporary art in the Pavillion Pereira, and the Planetarium. Visit Praca de la Republica. Window-shop on Rua Augusta.

The Zoological Park (Avenida Miguel Estefeno), considered to be the world's largest. Nearby, the world-famed orchid collection (over 35,000 species). To visit the orchids and Zoo, take Bus #546 from Praca da Liberdade or from Anhangabau. The Art Museum (Avenida Paulista 1578), an outstanding collection of Renoir, Lautrec, Rembrandt, Frans Hals, and many modern Brazilian painters. The Sound and Image Museum (Avenida Europa 158). South America's largest cathedral, in Cathedral Plaza. Liberdade, the city's oriental district (rock gardens, herb stores and many restaurants).

The Museum of Brazilian Art (Rua Alagoas 903), with its collection of copies of all the statues and monuments in the buildings and parks of Brazil. The Museum of Sacred Art in Convento da Luz. The State Art Collection (Avenida Tiradentes 141). The collection of Indian artifacts at Casa do Sertanista (Avenida Francisco Morato 2200).

If you want to learn to dance the samba, there are 44 samba schools here, and Sao Paulo's annual Carnival features their students.

Routes in Northern Brazil

The principal seaports north of Salvador (Sao Luiz, Parnaiba, Fortaleza, Natal and Recife) are connected by train service.

There is also rail service from Rio de Janeiro, north to the ports of Campos and Vitoria as well as from Rio, south to Santos, Paranagua, Porto Alegre, Pelotas and Rio Grande do Sul.

The southernmost rail connections are to Quaraio and to Santana do Livramento, both at the border with Uruguay.

Rio de Janeiro - Salvador 2039 + 2042 + 2043

Bus service.

Dep. Rio de Janeiro	N/A(1)
Arr. Salvador	N/A(1)

Sights in Salvador: See notes about sightseeing in Salvador earlier in this section.

Dep. Salvador	N/A(1)
Arr. Rio de Janeiro	N/A(1)

(1)Time has not been available since 1980.

Salvador - Recife 2039

Bus service.

Dep. Salvador	N/A(1)	Dep. Recife	N/A(1)
Arr. Recife	N/A(1)	Arr. Salvador	N/A(1)

(1)Time has not been available since 1980.

Sights in Recife: Named for the reefs along its coastline. Called "the Venice of Brazil" because it is on 3 rivers. The churches to see here are: the 17th century Capela Dourada (with its gold carved altar), the 17th century Santo Antonio, the 18th century Sao Pedro dos Clerigos, Convento de Sao Francisco, Madre de Deus, and Conceicao dos Militares.

Visit the Museum of Sugar and Alcohol. The Anthropological Museum of Insituto Joaquim Nabuco. Olinda, 5 miles away, is the arts and crafts capital of this region. Attracting many tourists is the faithful reproduction of Jerusalem at Nova Jerusalem, 115 miles to the west.

Recife - Caruaru - Salgueiro 2035

Dep. Recife	7:45(1)	Dep. Salgueiro	5:00(2)
Dep. Caruaru	11:35(1)	Dep. Caruaru	17:05(2)
Arr. Salgueiro	23:32	Arr. Recife	20:49

(1)Tuesday and Saturday. Meal service. (2)Wednesday and Sunday. Meal service.

Sights in Caruaru: Great leather, straw articles and pottery bargains at the Wednesday and Saturday market.

Recife - Fortaleza

2027 Bus		2026	
Dep. Recife	N/A(1)	Dep. Fortaleza (Felipe)	17:05(2)
Arr. Lavras	N/A(1)	Arr. Lavras	5:30
Change to train.		Change to bus.	
Dep. Lavras	16:42(2)	Dep. Lavras	N/A(1)
Arr. Fortaleza (Felipe)	5:10	Arr. Recife	N/A(1)

(1) Service was suspended in 1981, and time was not available in 1982.
(2) Meal service.

Sights in Fortaleza: The best lobsters in Brazil. The museum and shops in the Tourist Center. Excellent beaches. Good textiles, including exquisite hand-made laces.

Fortaleza - Teresina 2005

This is a very scenic rail trip.

Dep. Fortaleza (Felipe)	19:45(1)	Dep. Teresina	10:05(2)
Arr. Teresina	13:25	Arr. Fortaleza (Felipe)	4:05

(1) Monday and Friday. Meal service. (2) Thursday and Sunday. Meal service.

Sights in Teresina: See the washed clothing laid out to dry on the river bank. The open market.

Teresina - Sao Luiz 2007

This freight train has limited passenger accommodation.

Dep. Teresina	4:00(1)	Dep. Sao Luiz	4:00(2)
Arr. Sao Luiz	20:17	Arr. Teresina	20:17

(1) Tuesday, Thursday and Saturday. (2) Monday, Wednesday and Friday.

Rio de Janeiro - Niteroi

2050 Train		2043 Bus	
Dep. Rio de Janeiro (B. de Maua)	23:00(1)	Dep. Niteroi	N/A(3)
Arr. Campos	6:30(2)	Arr. Cachoeira do Itapemirim	N/A(3)
Arr. Cachoeira do Itapemirim	N/A(2)	Change to train. 2050	
Change to bus. 2043		Dep. Cachoeira do Itapemirim	N/A(2)
Dep. Cachoeira do Itapemirim	N/A(3)	Dep. Campos	22:30(1)
Arr. Niteroi	N/A(3)	Arr. Rio de Janeiro (B. de Maua)	6:00

(1)Daily. First-class only. Carries sleeping car. Meal service. (2)Service temporarily suspended in 1982 between Campos and Cachoeira. (3)Time has not been available since 1980.

Sights in Niteroi: The 17th century Boa Viagem Church. The Antonio Parreira Museum. Take the very pretty ride on bus #33 to the Icarai, Sao Francisco and Jurujuba beaches.

Rio de Janeiro - Vitoria 2050

Dep. Rio de Janeiro (B. de Maua)	23:00(1)	Dep. Vitoria	4:40(4)
Arr. Campos	6:30(2)	Arr. C. do Itapemirim	12:35(2)
Arr. C. do Itapemirim	N/A(2)	Arr. Campos	N/A(2)
Change trains.		Change trains.	
Dep. C. do Itapemirim	5:20(3)	Dep. Campos	22:30(1)
Arr. Vitoria (RFFSA)	13:25	Arr. Rio de Janeiro (B. de Maua)	6:00

(1)First-class only. Carries sleeping car. Meal service. (2)Service between Campos and Cachoeira temporarily suspended in 1982. (3)Tues., Thurs. and Sat. (4)Mon., Wed. and Fri.

Sights in Vitoria: A beautiful seaport. Marvelous beaches.

Rio de Janeiro - Belo Horizonte 2072

Dep. Rio de Janeiro (D. Pedro)	20:15(1)	Dep. Belo Horizonte	20:15(1)
Arr. Belo Horizonte	8:45	Arr. Rio de Janeiro (D. Pedro)	8:45

(1)Friday and Sunday. First-class only. Carries sleeping car. Air-conditioned. Meal service. Has Club Car.

Sights in Belo Horizonte: The Governor's Palace. Three outstanding churches: Nossa Senhora de Lourdes, Nossa Senhora de Boa Viagem, and Igreja de San Francisco de Assis. The large (110,000 seats) soccer stadium. The 2,000 varieties of trees in the Municipal Park.

Belo Horizonte - Brasilia Bus 2060

Dep. Belo Horizonte	7:00	8:00	17:00	19:00	20:00	21:45
Arr. Brasilia	18:00	N/A(1)	N/A(1)	N/A(1)	N/A(1)	8:45
		*	*	*		
Dep. Brasilia	7:00	19:00	20:00	21:45	22:00	22:30
Arr. Belo Horizonte	18:00	N/A(1)	N/A(1)	8:45	N/A(1)	N/A(1)

(1)Time has not been available since 1980.

Routes in Southern Brazil

Sao Paulo - Curitiba - Paranagua

The ride from Curitiba to the coastal town of Paranagua is down a steep mountainside.

Bus service.
2100

Dep. Sao Paulo	22:25(1)	24:00(1)
Arr. Curitiba	5:25	7:00

Change to train.
2102

Dep. Curitiba	7:00	8:10(2)
Arr. Paranagua	10:30	11:00

Train.
2102

Dep. Paranagua	15:30(2)	16:30
Arr. Curitiba	18:05	20:20

Change to bus.
2100

Dep. Curitiba	21:00	22:25(1)
Arr. Sao Paulo	4:00	5:25

(1)Sleeper bus. Has couchettes. (2)First-class only. Air-conditioned.

Sights in Curitiba: This is Brazil's melting-pot: Italian, Polish, German, Slav, Japanese and Syrian settlers galore. See: The Cathedral, patterned after the one in Barcelona. The Civic Center. The tropical fish collection at the Aquarium in Passeio Publico, a public park in the center of the city. The Coronel David Carneiro Museum. The Paranaense Museum, in the old city hall. Trips to Iguassu Falls originate from here.

Sights in Paranagua: Much of Brazil's coffee is shipped from this seaport. See: The Museum of Archaeology and Popular Art in the wonderful Colegio dos Jesuitas building. The fascinating market near the waterfront. The Church of Sao Benedito. The 17th century fountain. Nearby, the Nossa Senhora do Rocio shrine. Take the one-hour boat trip to see the 18th century Nossa Senhora dos Orazeres Prazeres fort.

Sao Paulo - Curitiba - Porto Alegre Bus 2100

Dep. Sao Paulo	8:00(1)	Dep. Porto Alegre	8:00(3)
Arr. Curitiba	N/A(2)	Arr. Curitiba	N/A(2)
Dep. Curitiba	N/A(2)	Dep. Curitiba	N/A(2)
Arr. Porto Alegre	N/A(2)	Arr. Sao Paulo	N/A(2)

(1)Frequent additional departures 14:00-21:00. (2)Time has not been available since 1980. (3)Frequent additional departures 13:00-20:00.

Sights in Porto Alegre: A marvelous modern seaport city, at the junction of 5 rivers. Very Germanic here. See: Farroupilha Park. The Zoological Gardens. The Julio de Castilhos Museum. Rua dos Andradas, a strolling street.

Santa Maria - Porto Alegre 2112

Dep. Santa Maria	1:56(1)	9:00(2)	22:15(3)
Arr. Porto Alegre	7:15	16:55	5:45
	*	*	*
Dep. Porto Alegre	8:15(2)	19:00(2)	22:30(3)
Arr. Santa Maria	16:05	0:19	6:05

(1)First-class only. Air-conditioned. Meal service. (2)Meal service. (3)Carries sleeping car. Has parlor car. Meal service.

Porto Alegre - Santa Maria - Uruguaiana 2112

All of these trains have meal service.

Dep. P. Alegre	19:00(1)	22:30(2)	Dep. Uruguaiana	11:45(4)	19:20(1)
Arr. Santa Maria	0:18(1)	6:02	Arr. Santa Maria	21:13	1:50(1)
Change trains.			Change trains.		
Dep. Santa Maria	0:26(1)	7:00(3)	Dep. Santa Maria	22:15(2)	1:56(1)
Arr. Uruguaiana	7:00	17:12	Arr. P. Alegre	5:45	7.15

(1)Direct train. No train change in Santa Maria. First-class only. Air-conditioned. (2)Carries sleeping car. (3)Tues., Thurs. and Sat. (4)Mon., Wed. and Fri.

Rio Grande - Cacequi 2113

Both of these trains have light refreshments.

Dep. Rio Grande	7:30(1)	Dep. Cacequi	11:30(2)
Arr. Cacequi	17:55	Arr. Rio Grande	22:00

(1) Runs Monday, Wednesday and Friday. (2) Runs Tuesday, Thursday and Saturday.

SCENIC RAIL TRIPS IN BRAZIL

There is a spectacular 67-mile rail trip from Paranagua to Curitiba. The train ascends in 4 hours from sea level to 3,000 feet. Along the way. there is great mountain, gorge, waterfall and jungle scenery.

Paranagua - Curitiba 2102

Dep. Paranagua	15:30(1)	16:30
Arr. Curitiba	18:05	20:20

Sights in Curitiba and Paranagua: See notes about city-sightseeing in Curitiba and Paranagua earlier in this section, under "Sao Paulo-Curitiba-Paranagua". (See: "Routes in Southern Brazil".)

Dep. Curitiba	7:00	8:10(1)	13:30(2)
Arr. Paranagua	10:30	11:00	17:20

(1) First-class only. Air-conditioned. (2) Saturday only.

Santos - Sao Paulo 2095

One of the rail wonders of the world can be experienced on the 50-mile trip from Santos to Sao Paulo. At 5 separate locations, the entire train is lifted by wire cables from one elevation to another until the train reaches the top of the 2300-foot high Serra do Mar escarpment.

Dep. Santos	5:40(1)	6:50(2)	15:50(1)	18:15(2)
Arr. Sao Paulo (Luz)	7:27	8:37	17:40	19:55

* * *

Dep. Sao Paulo (Luz)	6:00	16:10(1)	18:20(2)
Arr. Santos	7:57	18:05	20:16

(1) Daily, except Sundays and holidays. (2) Sundays and holidays only.

Sights in Santos: A very popular holiday resort and Brazil's most active seaport. Many monuments in the various parks: Praca da Republica, Praca Rui Barbosa, Praca Jose Bonifacio. Night-life activities in the Gonzaga area.

INTERNATIONAL ROUTES FROM BRAZIL

Brazil's international train routes are from Rio de Janeiro south to Uruguay and Argentina, and from Sao Paulo west to Bolivia and Chile.

Rio de Janeiro - Sao Paulo - Buenos Aires 2125 Bus

Dep. Rio de Janeiro	18:00	
Dep. Sao Paulo	0:15	Day 2
Dep. Curitiba	6:30	Day 2
Dep. Porto Alegre	19:00	Day 2
Arr. Uruguaiana	N/A(1)	
Dep. Uruguaiana	N/A	Day 3
Dep. Paso de los Libres	4:40	Day 3
Dep. Santa Fe	11:10	Day 3
Arr. Buenos Aires	18:00	Day 4

(1) Time has not been available since 1980.

Rio de Janeiro - Sao Paulo - Montevideo 2075

Dep. Rio de Janeiro (D. Pedro)	8:00(1)	23:00(1+2)	
Arr. Sao Paulo	16:27	8:05	
Change to bus.			
2100			
Dep. Sao Paulo	8:00	14:00	16:00(5)
Arr. Porto Alegre	N/A(3)	N/A(3)	N/A(3)
Change buses			
2120			
Dep. Porto Alegre	20:00	21:00	22:00
Arr. Montevideo	9:15	9:35	10:00

(1)First-class only. Air-conditioned. Meal service. (2)Carries sleeping car. Also has couchettes. (3)Time has not been available since 1980. (4)Direct bus. No bus change in Porto Alegre. (5)Plus other departures from Sao Paulo at 18:00, 18:30, 20:00 and 22:00(4).

Sao Paulo - Corumba - Santa Cruz - La Paz

2085

Dep. Sao Paulo (Luz)	9:00(1)	12:05(1)	19:25(1)	22:25(2)
Arr. Bauru	15:05(3)	18:50(3)	1:43(3)	5:00(3)

(1)Meal service. (2)Carries sleeping car. Meal service. (3)Estimated.

Change trains. You cross the Mato Grosso mountain range going from Bauru to Corumba.

2068

Dep. Bauru	15:45(1)
Arr. Corumba	19:17 Day 2

(1)Carries sleeping car. Meal service.

Change trains.

1915

Dep. Corumba	11:20(1)	13:00(2)	20:00(3)
Arr. Santa Cruz	23:19	7:00	19:48

CHANGE TO BUS.

1911

Dep. Santa Cruz	6:00
Arr. Cochabamba	12 hours later

CHANGE TO TRAIN.

1910

Dep. Cochabamba	8:00(4)
Arr. La Paz	19:13

(1)Fri. only. Meal service. (2)Daily, except Fri. Meal service. (3)Second-class only. Wed. and Sun. only. (4)Daily. Meal service.

Sao Paulo - Antofagasta

1915			
Arr. Santa Cruz from Sao Paulo (see preceding timetable)	23:19(1)	7:00(2)	19:48(3)
Change trains			
Dep. Santa Cruz	11:55(4)	14:30(5)	16:40(6)
Arr. Yacuiba	20:25	3:11	11:03
Change trains			
2255			
Dep. Yacuiba	N/A(7)		
Arr. Salta	21:25		
Change to bus.			
2256			
Dep. Salta	7:30(8)		
Arr. Antofagasta	N/A(9)		

(1)Fri. only. (2)Daily, except Sat. (3)Mon. and Thurs. only. (4)Mon., Wed., Fri. and Sun. First-class only. Meal service. (5)Tues., Thurs. and Sat. Meal service. (6)Wed. and Sun. only. Second-class only. (7)Tues. only. Sometime before 9:30. Second-class only. Light refreshments. (8)Tourist Train. Second-class only. (9)Time has not been available since 1980.

CHILE

Children under 3 travel free. Half-fare for children 3-9. Children 10 and over must pay full fare.

From September to March, first-class train tickets in Chile are difficult to obtain. It is advisable to reserve space far in advance of travel date through a prominent travel agency in Santiago or Antofagasta.

Train service runs from Antofagasta to Puerto Montt, on the shore of the Gulf of Ancud. Feeder lines branch off the main north-south line, eastward to great resorts at Lake Villarrica, Lake Panguipulli, Lake Ranco, Lake Puyehul and Lake Llanquihue. The Lake District is the area east of the rail line from Temuco to Puerto Montt. The connecting point is Puerto Varas.

The average width of Chile is a scant 120 miles, ranging from 312 miles at its widest to 56 miles where it is the most narrow.

Antofagasta

There are many beautiful beaches, parks and plazas in this city.

Santiago

See: The Presidential Palace. The view of the city from the terrace of Castillo Gonzalez on Santa Lucia Hill. The Popular Arts Museum in Castillo Hidalgo. The Cathedral, near Plaza de Armas, with its fine painting of The Last Supper. These churches: Santo Domingo, San Francisco, San Augustin, La Merced, Santa Ana, Recoleta Dominica and Recoleta Franciscana.

The foods and souvenirs (saddles, baskets, ceramics, dolls, rugs) in the central market. The Palace of Fine Arts at Parque Forestal. The National Library and the Historical Museum, both in the same building at Alameda, between Miraflores and McIver streets. The Natural History Museum and Modern Art Museum, both in the Quinta Normal.

Take the funicular to the top of San Cristobal Hill for a spectacular view of Santiago, stopping on the ascent to see the Zoo that is about one-third of the way up.

Valparaiso

See: The Beaux Arts Museum. Severin Public Library. The view from Miradero O'Higgins, in Alto del Puerto. Take the 20-minute ride to the beaches at Vina del Mar, called "The Pearl of the Pacific" and "The Garden City". Also in Vina: The Academy and Museum of Fine Arts in the Quinta Vergara, the Naval History Museum, and the Municipal Casino.

Valparaiso - Santiago - Concepcion

Marvelous scenery: fertile farms (first colonized by Germans in the early 19th century), snow-capped mountains, shimmering lakes, mile after mile of wildflowers, vineyards and pine forests.

2426

Dep. Valparaiso (Puerto)	7:20(1)	14:30(1)	18:30(1)
Dep. Vina del Mar	7:34	14:44	18:44
Arr. Santiago (Mapocho)	10:35	17:40	21:40

Change trains . . . and change railstations.

2430

Dep. Santiago (Alameda)	14:30(2)	22:00(3)	23:00(2+4)	8:30(1)	9:00(2+5)
Arr. Concepcion	22:05	8:00	7:00	17:30	16:35

* * *

Dep. Concepcion	9:00	9:30	14:00	22:00	23:00
Arr. Santiago (Alameda)	16:40	18:15	21:30	8:15	7:00

Change trains . . . and change railstations.

2426

Dep. Santiago (Mapocho)	8:30(1)	12:30(1+6)	14:30(1)	19:10(1)
Arr. Vina del Mar	11:27	15:27	17:27	22:07
Arr. Valparaiso (Puerto)	13 minutes later			

(1) First-class only. (2) Train consists of only first-class parlor car. Meal service. (3) Carries sleeping car. Meal service. (4) Fri. and Sun. only. (5) Air-conditioned. (6) Mon.-Fri., except holidays.

Sights in Concepcion: The Pedro del Rio Zanartu Museum. The view of the city from Cerro Amarillo. A lovely view of valleys and Bio-Bio, Chile's largest river, from Cerro Caracol.

Arica - Antofagasta - Santiago Bus 2425

Rail passenger service for this 1,300-mile trip, basically a freight train with limited passenger accommodation, is considered to be so appalling that the state railway refuses to publish information about the journey. Here is the schedule for a 2-day bus trip.

Dep. Arica	9:00	10:30(2)	Dep. Santiago	9:00
Arr. Antofagasta	N/A(1)	N/A(1)	Arr. Antofagasta	N/A(1)
Dep. Antofagasta	N/A(1)	N/A(1)	Dep. Antofagasta	N/A(1)
Arr. Santiago	N/A(1)	N/A(1)	Arr. Arica	N/A(1)

(1)Time has not been available since 1980. (2)Plus other departures at 22:00 and 22:35.

Antofagasta - Santiago Bus 2425

Schedules in addition to those shown on the Arica-Antofagasta-Santiago table.

Dep. Antofagasta	17:00(1)	Dep. Santiago	10:00(2)
Arr. Santiago	13:10	Arr. Antofagasta	6:40(3)

(1)Daily, except Sun. Departs 16:00 on Wed. (2)Daily, except Sundays and holidays. (3)Arrives 7:40 on Fri.

Antofagasta - Arica Bus 2425

Schedules in addition to those shown on the Arica-Antofagasta-Santiago table.

Dep. Antofagasta	N/A(1)	Dep. Arica	N/A(1)
Arr. Arica	N/A(1)	Arr. Antofagasta	N/A(1)

(1)Time has not been available since 1980.

Santiago - Puerto Montt 2430

Dep. Santiago (Alameda)	18:30(1)	Dep. Puerto Montt	15:30(1)
Arr. Puerto Montt	12:20	Arr. Santiago (Alameda)	9:25

(1) First-class only. Carries sleeping car. Meal service.

LAKE DISTRICT BUS CONNECTIONS

Puerto Montt - Bariloche 2334

Dep. Puerto Montt	8:00(1)
Arr. Bariloche	17:30

* * *

Dep. Bariloche	8:00(2)	8:30(3)	8:30(4)
Arr. Puerto Montt	16:30	N/A(5)	17:00

(1)Daily, except Monday and Saturday. (2)Tuesday and Thursday. (3)Tuesday, Thursday, Friday and Saturday. (4)Monday, Wednesday and Saturday. (5)Time has not been available since 1980.

SPECIAL ONE-DAY ANDEAN SCENIC TRAIN TRIP

Prior to 1980, schedules permitted an exciting one-day glimpse at the overwhelming Andes range, both from Valparaiso and Santiago. Changes in 1980 made a one-day roundtrip from Valparaiso impossible. Check to see if the old schedules have been resumed.

Valparaiso - Los Andes 2422

Dep. Valparaiso (Puerto)	9:30(1)	18:00(2)
Dep. Llay Llay	11:11(1)	19:38(2)
Arr. Los Andes	12:10	20:40

Dep. Los Andes	8:00(3)	19:05(4)
Arr. Llay Llay	8:54	20:02
Arr. Valparaiso (Puerto)	10:40	21:45

(1)Saturday only. (2)Daily, except Saturday. (3)Daily, except Sunday. (4)Sunday only.

Santiago - Llay Llay 2426

Dep. Santiago (Mapocho)	8:30	12:30(1)	14:30	19:10
Arr. Llay Llay	1½ hours later			

* * *

Dep. Llay Llay	7:26(1)	9:01	16:10	20:10
Arr. Santiago (Mapocho)	1½ hours later			

(1)Monday-Friday, except holidays.

INTERNATIONAL ROUTES FROM CHILE

There is train service from both Arica and Antofagasta to La Paz. One can cross the continent by rail from Antofagasta, to either Rio de Janeiro or Buenos Aires. Until 1980, there was transcontinental train service from Valparaiso to Buenos Aires.

Valparaiso (Santiago) - Mendoza - Buenos Aires

The Los Andes-Mendoza portion of this rail trip was the most exciting train ride in South America before the train was replaced by bus.

Altitudes (in feet) En Route

ASCENT	
Valparaiso	-0-
Los Andes	2,669
San Pablo	3,174
Salto del Soldado	4,141
Rio Blanco	4,764
Guardia Vieja	5,397
El Juncal	7,321
El Portillo	9,408
Caracoles (tunnel entrance)	10,420

(The summit is 13,082.)

DESCENT	
Tunnel Exit	10,452
Las Cuevas	10,331
Puente del Inca	8,915
Punta de las Vacas	7,852
Zanjon Amarillo	7,236
Rio Blanco	7,000
Uspallata	5,741
Guido	4,957
Portrerillos	4,443
Cacheuta	4,080
Blanco Encalda	3,502
Paso de los Andes	3,069
Mendoza	2,518

On the original train ride, there were great amounts of snow Los Andes-Mendoza from May to November. It was a steep descent from Portillo (a Winter sports resort) to Las Cuevas, another ski resort. Then, it was a rack railway from Las Cuevas to Puente del Inca. The ride from there to Mendoza was by narrow-gauge, through a scenic valley.

2423 Bus

Dep. Valparaiso	7:30	-0-	8:30	-0-
Dep. Santiago	-0-	8:30	-0-	9:00
Set your watch forward one hour.				
Dep. Los Andes	N/A(1)	N/A(1)	N/A(1)	N/A(1)
Dep. Puente del Inca	N/A(1)	N/A(1)	N/A(1)	N/A(1)
Arr. Mendoza	16:00	16:00	18:00	18:00

Change to train.

2290

Dep. Mendoza	16:20(2)	21:15(4)
Arr. Buenos Aires (Ret.)	9:00(3)	11:00(3)

(1)Time has not been available since 1980. (2)Daily. Carries air-conditioned sleeping car. Also has parlor car. Meal service. (3)Day 2 after departing Mendoza. (4)Monday and Friday only. Runs all year. First-class only. Carries air-conditioned sleeping car. Also has parlor car and cinema car. An additional first-class only train that has parlor car but no sleeping car operates daily except Monday and Friday from mid-December to mid-March at same 21:15 departure time.

Sights En Route

The train travels through a fertile valley until beginning the ascent to **Portillo,** a popular ski resort with many hotels. Mountain slopes on the Pacific side of the Andes are covered with foliage, including many flowers. You see the Aconcagua River and excellent rock scenery before entering the tunnel at Caracoles. See notes about skiing at Portillo, earlier in this chapter under "Buenos Aires-Valparaiso".

The next arrival is at **Las Cuevas,** another popular ski resort. After leaving Las Cuevas, you have a view of the Horcones River before arriving at **Puente del Inca,** a popular Winter sports resort area, attracting the greatest crowds from November to May. It is named for its natural stone bridge spanning the Mendoza River and is one of South America's most marvelous sights. This city is also popular as a base for excursions by foot and horseback to many high valleys in the Andes: Los Penitentes, Laguna de los Horcones, etc.

After leaving Puente del Inca, Aconcagua is next in sight. It is the highest (22,834 feet) mountain in the western hemisphere. Many rushing mountain streams can be seen in the area of Rio Blanco. Then, a desolate and vast plain comes into view before reaching **Uspallata.** The train follows an old Spanish trail called Camino de los Andes between Uspallata and **Cacheuta.**

The next stop is **Mendoza.** If you left Valparaiso or Santiago on a Saturday, a 48-hour stopover here is well worthwhile, continuing on to Buenos Aires the following Monday. Completely rebuilt after it was destroyed by earthquake and fire in 1861, Mendoza is a large, modern city. Its proliferation of gardens makes the city extremely beautiful. Do not miss seeing the public park with the splendid monument to Jose de San Martin, the liberator of Chile and Peru. It is an incredible collection of statues and bas-reliefs. Then walk to the lake and streams in the nearby Zoological Gardens.

Also see: The San Martin Museum (Av. General San Martin). The exhibit of Argentine animals and plants in the Moyano Museum of Natural History (Calle Belgrano). The beautiful Romanesque Law Courts building. Window-shop on Calle Las Heras.

There is a splendid all-day bus trip from Mendoza to see the famous Christ the Redeemer statue, which cannot be seen on the train trip. Great scenery on this ride, with a stop for lunch at Las Cuevas.

There are 4 rail routes from Chile to Bolivia. The first we list includes the great Transandine ride from Valparaiso (or Santiago) to Mendoza. Instead of going from Mendoza east to Buenos Aires, however, you proceed from Mendoza north to Tucuman and then on from there to either La Paz or Santa Cruz. The one rail route from Chile to Brazil is from Antofagasta to Sao Paulo.

Mendoza - Tucuman

2423

Arr. Mendoza 16:00 and 18:00 (by bus from Valparaiso or Santiago)

Change buses.

2267

Dep. Mendoza	13:00	14:00(2)
Arr. Tucuman	9:05	8:19

(1)Time has not been available since 1980. (2)Mon. and Fri. only.

Tucuman - La Paz

1910

Dep. Tucuman	14:50(1)	Dep. Villazon	13:25(2)
Arr. La Quiaca	5:05	Arr. La Paz	9:34
Walk 3km across border.			

(1)Mon. and Fri. only. Meal service. (2)Daily, except Mon. and Thurs. Meal service.

Tucuman - Salta - Yacuiba - Santa Cruz

2257	
Dep. Tucuman (Norte)	22:13(1)
Arr. Guemes	4:32
Change trains.	
Dep. Guemes	5:25
Arr. Salta	6:45

2257			
Dep. Salta	8:00(2)	-0-	-0-
Arr. Yacuiba	N/A(3)	-0-	-0-
Change trains.			
1915			
Dep. Yacuiba	6:15(4)	17:00(5)	22:00(6)
Arr. Santa Cruz	18:59	11:34	6:32

(1)Tues. and Fri. all year. Also Thurs. and Sun. from mid-Dec. to mid-March. (2)Sat. only. Light refreshments. (3)Time not available in 1982. (4)Wed., Fri. and Sun. Meal service. (5)Second-class only. Runs only Wed. and Sun. (6)Mon., Wed., Fri. and Sun. Supplement charged. First-class only. Meal service.

Arica - La Paz 1901

There are 30 miles of rack and pinion track during this 270-mile rail trip. The highest place on this route is 14,000 feet, at General Lagos. The best scenery is during the last portion of the trip, on the descent into La Paz. During the last 6 miles, a series of loops traveled very slowly, there is excellent scenery of 3 tremendous Andean peaks: Illampu (21,490 feet), Illiman (21,315 feet) and Huayna-Potosi (20,407 feet).

Dep. Arica	11:00(1+2)	11:30(1+3)
Arr. Charana	20:10	20:30
Change trains.		
Dep. Charana	17:00(4)	22:00(5)
Arr. La Paz	0:22	6:15

(1)2nd and 4th Tues. of each month only. (2)Runs mid-March to mid-Oct. (3)Runs mid-Oct. to mid-March. (4)Fri. only. (5)Tues. only.

Antofagasta - La Paz 1910

Bus		
Dep. Antofagasta	9:00	Wed.
Arr. Calama	12:00	Wed.
Change to train.		

Train		
Dep. Calama	12:55(1)	Wed.
Arr. La Paz	14:40	Thurs.

(1)Meal service.

It is easy to understand why this train trip of 705 miles takes 36 hours. The first 18 miles out of Antofagasta, there is an ascent of 1,800 feet as the route crosses the Atacama Desert. In the next 211 miles, the train climbs to the summit of the Chilean section of the ride: 13,000 feet above sea level, at Ascotan. There is generally a 3 to 4-hour wait at the Chile-Bolivia border (Ollague) while Bolivian customs officers go through the train to check passports and inspect baggage.

One of the most unusual sights on this trip occurs on the second day, just before reaching Poopo. Thousands of flamingos can be seen on a lake that is 12,000 feet above sea level. Also to be seen are the snow-covered peaks of the tremendous Cordillera Real mountain range. The top of 21,000-foot Illimani can be seen if there are no clouds or fog.

The train descends 1,000 feet to the highest capital in the world. La Paz is nearly 12,000 feet above sea level.

Antofagasta - Salta - Yacuiba - Bauru - Sao Paulo

2256 Bus		1915	
Dep. Antofagasta	13:00(1)	Dep. Santa Cruz	18:20(5+8)
Arr. Salta	8:00(2)	Arr. Corumba	6:28
Change to train.		Change trains.	
1915		2068	
Dep. Salta	8:00(2+3)	Dep. Corumba	8:00(9)
Arr. Yacuiba	N/A(2+4)	Arr. Bauru	13:05(10)
Change trains.			
Dep. Yacuiba	22:00(5+6)		
Arr. Santa Cruz	6:32(7)		

(1)Fri. only. (2)Sat. only. (3)Light refreshments. (4)Time not available in 1982. Estimated arrival: 20:00. (5)First-class only. Supplement charged. Meal service. (6)Runs only Mon., Wed., Fri. and Sun. (7)Arrives day after departing Yacuiba. (8)Thurs. only. (9)Daily. Carries sleeping car. Meal service. (10)Arrives day after departing Corumba.

2286				
Dep. Bauru	4:22(1)	8:00(2)	13:49(2)	22:48(1)
Arr. Sao Paulo (Luz)	10:45	14:53	20:01	6:00

(1) Carries sleeping car. Meal service. (2) Meal service.

COLOMBIA

Children under 3 travel free. Half-fare for children 3-11. Children 12 and over must pay full fare.

This is the only South American country with a coast on both the Atlantic and Pacific oceans. There is no train service between Colombia and adjacent countries, only a few short internal narrow-gauge rail routes.

Bogota

Capital of Colombia. Founded in 1538 at 8,460-feet altitude. Population is nearly 5,000,000. See the 20,000 pre-Columbian gold items and the world's largest emerald in the Museo del Oro in Santander Park on Carrera 7. It is an indescribable thrill to stand in the totally dark room on the Gold Museum's third floor and instantly see more than 10,000 gold objects when the lights are switched on.

Of the city's more than 300 churches, be sure to see the ceiling of Islamic designs in La Concepcion, Bogota's oldest church (late 16th century). The panelled ceiling and the main altar in the very beautiful

Moorish-style 17th century San Francisco Church. The carved oak-and-cedar altar in the 18th century La Tercera Church. The colonial paintings by Vasquez and the columns inlaid with tourquoise in the lovely El Sagrario Chapel, next door to the Cathedral. The outstanding stained-glass in the Church of Maria del Carmen. The 16th century Veracruz Church. Also visit San Diego, San Augustin, San Ignacio and Santa Ines churches.

See exceptional art and history collections at the National Museum. The Museum of Natural History and the sidereal projection room, both in the City Planetarium. Take the cable car to the top of Montserrate, 2000 feet above the city, for a spectacular view of Bogota. Seeing the pilgrims climb the mountain on their knees during Holy Week is a fantastic spectacle. Nearby is Yequendama Falls, set in lush jungle foliage. Quinta de Bolivar, the villa given to the liberator by a wealthy man, now a museum of Napoleonic-style furniture and Bolivar relics. The gardens there are decorated with busts of heroes and heavy bronze cannons used in the country's War of Independence (1810).

The Palace of San Carlos. The Municipal Palace. The coin presses and wood balconies in the Mint House Museum. The pre-Columbian pottery in the mansion of the Marques de Jan Jorge. The incredible carved ceiling in the Presidential Palace. The Museum of July 20, 1810 (Independence Day). The Musum of Folk Art. The excellent collection of paintings in the Museum of Colonia Art. Teatro Colon. Luis Angel Arango Library.

Exceptional art and history collections at the National Museum. Many rare coins at Casa de la Moneda. Rare manuscripts at Hierba Buena Literary Museum. The craftwork at the Handicrafts and Traditional Arts Museum. Religious art at the Theological Seminary Museum. The elegant police uniforms. The ramshackle huts in the suburbs.

Shop for emeralds, reptile leatherwork (alligator, crocodile, snake) and beautiful linen shirts. The handicrafts of more than 1,000,000 artisans are sold at Artesanias de Colombia. Stroll the cobbled streets of the La Candelaria area to see the 17th century colonial homes with red tile roofs, overhanging balconies and interior patios. Celebrate the tradition of afternoon "Chocolate Santaferreno".

Bogota - Barrancabermeja - Santa Marta 1710

Some meal stops are made during this trip. Most of the journey offers great jungle, river and mountain scenery. Particularly scenic is the descent at Puerto Salgar to the Magdalena River.

Dep. Bogota	13:00(1+2)	13:00(2+3)
Dep. Barrancabermeja	1:52	2:22
Arr. Santa Marta	13:06	14:33

Dep. Santa Marta	6:00(2+4)	17:30(2+5)
Dep. Barancabermeja	17:53	4:53
Arr. Bogota	8:22	18:07

(1)Runs from Dec. 1 through Jan. 31, on Monday and Friday. Carries sleeping car. (2)Meal service. (3)Runs all year, on Tuesday and Saturday. (4)Runs all year, on Monday and Thursday. (5)Runs from Dec. 1 through Jan. 31, on Tuesday and Saturday. Carries sleeping car.

Sights in Barrancabermeja: The Cathedral of the Sacred Heart of Jesus.

Sights in Santa Marta: This was the first European city in South America. It is now a banana center. Founded in 1525, it is Colombia's important commercial Atlantic seaport. Simon Bolivar, South America's great liberator, died here. You can visit the plantation where he lived his last days, 3 miles southeast of the city. Also see: The Gaira and Rodadero beaches. The Cathedral. The Church of San Francisco. Two nearby fishing villages: Taganga and La Concha. The marine biology institute at Punta de Betin.

Bogota - Grecia - Medellin

1710			
Dep. Bogota	13:00(1+2+3+4)	13:00(4+5+6)	13:00(2+4+7)
Arr. Grecia	23:02(1)	22:42	23:02
Change trains.			
1715			
Dep. Grecia	23:03(1+2+3+4)	10:56(2+8)	21:26(2+4+9)
Arr. Medellin	5:54	18:40	3:49

* * *

Dep. Medellin	15:00(1+2+4+9)	16:00(2+3+4)	17:10(2+8)
Arr. Grecia	21:04(1)	22:13	14:38
Change trains.			
1710			
Dep. Grecia	21:05(1+2+4+9)	21:25(2+4+10)	7:55(4+5+7)
Arr. Bogota	8:22	8:22	18:07

(1)Direct train. No train change in Grecia. (2)Runs all year. (3)Saturday only. (4)Meal service. (5)Runs Dec. 1 - Jan. 31. Carries sleeping car. (6)Monday and Friday. (7)Tuesday and Saturday. (8)Daily. Second-class only. (9)Monday only. (10)Monday and Thursday.

Sights in Medellin: The 17th century churches: San Benito, La Veracruz, San Jose and the Old Cathedral. The cattle auctions on Tuesday and Thursday. The South American animals and birds in the Zoo. The Museum of Folk Art. The Museo Zea. The Botanical Garden, with its world-famous collection of orchids.

Cauca Valley Scenic Train Rides

There are 3 beautiful short rail trips in the scenic Cauca Valley.

Cali - Armenia 1730

Dep. Cali	7:00(1)	13:30	Dep. Armenia	6:30	14:15(1)
Arr. Armenia	11:42	18:56	Arr. Cali	11:57	18:57

(1) Monday, Wednesday and Friday.

Sights in Cali: See relics of the city's last Royal Sheriff in the colonial ranchhouse called Canasgordas. The Museum of Natural History. Plaza de Caicedo, with the Cathedral and National Palace. There are great views of Cali from San Fernando Mountain. See the 3,000 different types of orchids at "El Orquideal". There is excellent deep-sea fishing at Buenaventura, a 2-hour ride from Cali.

Sights in Armenia: A modern city. See Quindio University.

Cali - Cartago 1730

Dep. Cali	5:40	7:40	8:25	9:15	11:25	16:15	18:35
Arr. Cartago	9:03	11:19	12:01	13:19	15:00	19:50	22:44

Sights in Cartago: Many fine colonial buildings. See Casa de Los Virreyes (House of the Viceroys).

Dep. Cartago	4:50	6:30	9:30	12:10	13:30	13:55	16:25
Arr. Cali	8:56	10:12	13:05	15:37	17:10	18:10	19:57

Cali - Suarez 1730

Dep. Cali	6:30	13:00	Dep. Suarez	9:30	17:45
Arr. Suarez	8:59	16:30	Arr. Cali	11:59	20:50

ECUADOR

Children under 3 travel free. Half-fare for children 3-11. Children 12 and over must pay full fare. There is no train service between Ecuador and adjacent countries.

The 288-mile ride from Guayaquil (Duran Alfaro) is one of the world's most thrilling train trips — and advance reservations are essential. The former antique bus on rail wheels that provided 30 uncomfortable wood seats was replaced in 1980 by a new autoferro that has 43 upholstered seats. No food is sold en route. There is time for breakfast in a restaurant at the first of many stops where food and beverages can be purchased.

The ride begins with a 20-minute ferryboat trip from Guayaquil to Duran. You ascend a 5.5 percent gradient, climbing in one 50-mile stretch (Bucay-Palmira) from 975 feet to 10,600 feet. At a point called "Devil's Nose", there is a double switchback zig-zag, carved out of a rock mountain.

Highest point on the route is 11,841 feet, at Urbina. Watch for Mt. Chimborazo, rising an additional 8,000 feet above the train. This trip involves hundreds of bridges and tunnels. You can make the return trip by airplane in 35 minutes. A popular stopover is at Riobamba.

Here are the stations and their altitudes:

MILES FROM GUAYAQUIL		ALTITUDE IN FEET	MILES FROM GUAYAQUIL		ALTITUDE IN FEET
	Guayaquil	15	142	Luisa	10,379
14	Yaguachi	20	150	Riobamba	9,020
21	Milagro	42	170	Urbina	11,841
31	Naranjito	100	178	Mocha	10,346
43	Barranganeta	300	186	Cevallos	9,100
54	Bucay	975	196	Ambato	8,435
72	Huigra	4,000	219	San Miguel	8,645
76	Chunchi	4,875	227	Latacunga	9,055
81	Sibambe	5,925	239	Lasso	10,375
89	Alausi	8,553	250	Cotopaxi	11,653
95	Tixan	9,200	263	Machachi	10,118
103	Palmira	10,626	266	Aloag	9,090
112	Guamote	10,000	273	Tambillo	9,891
132	Cajabamba	10,388	288	Quito	9,375

Guayaquil - Quito 1755

Dep. Guayaquil (Duran)	6:20(1+2)	Dep. Quito	6:00(1+3)
Dep. Milagro	6:58	Dep. Latacunga	8:05
Dep. Sibambe	9:08	Dep. Ambato	8:57
Dep. Alausi	9:32	Dep. Riobamba	11:05
Dep. Riobamba	11:55	Dep. Alausi	13:01
Dep. Ambato	13:30	Dep. Sibambe	13:21
Dep. Latacunga	14:23	Dep. Milagro	15:29
Arr. Quito	16:30	Arr. Guayaquil (Duran)	16:10

(1) Reservation required. (2) Mon., Wed. and Fri. (3) Tues., Thurs. and Sat.

On the route from Guayaquil to Quito, Indian women meet the train's arrival in Milagro, hawking fruits and native bread. Lush foliage can be seen after leaving Bucay. Then the train ascends the Chanchan River gorge as it approaches Huigra and finally climbs 1,000 feet above the river, up the Devil's Nose (Nariz del Diablo).

Many small Indian mountain villages line the track en route to Sibambe. In Alausi, a resort village, bus connections to Quito are available. At Palmira, there is a view of many high mountain peaks: Altar, Carihuairazo, Chimborazo, Sangay, Tungurahua.

Next, the train skirts the shoreline of Lake Colta before coming into Riobamba. Highest point of the trip (11,841 feet) is shortly after leaving Riobamba, at Urbina Pass. The Indian market at Ambato is worth seeing. Nine volcanoes can be seen from Latacunga.

Guayaquil

This is the largest city (800,000 population) in Ecuador as well as the country's financial and commercial center. See: The City Museum. La Rotunda. Government Palace. San Carlos Fort. The Municipal Tower. The tombs and monuments at "White City", the major cemetery. Santo Domingo Church. Colon Park. Do not miss the view of the city from El Mirador, or a visit to the world's largest balsa wood factory.

Riobamba

There are wonderful views from here of the peaks of Altar, Chimborazo and Tungurahua. See: The Saturday fair, in 9 different plazas (leather articles, rope sandals, embroidered belts, etc.). Nearby, see the carpets in Guano.

Quito

Ecuador's capital. See: The marvelous sculptures at the San Francisco Convent. The gold leaf in La Compania Church. Fine art in the Cathedral. The campus at the Central University. The National Palace. The view of Quito from the top of the 600-foot high Panecillo Hill. Colonial homes along La Ronda. Some of Ecuador's best art, in the Municipal Art and History Museum at the Real de Lima. Stroll in 2 suburbs: Guapulo and San Roque. You can stand on the equator by taking a 15-mile auto trip north of Quito, where you can place one foot in the northern hemisphere and the other in the southern hemisphere.

Take the very scenic 2½-hour $1.20 bus ride to Otalvo, particularly on Friday in order to see the early-morning opening of the Saturday market with its many concessions (merchandise, food, beverages) and the colorful Indian costumes worn there.

Sibambe - Cuenca 1761

Dep. Sibambe	12:30	Dep. Cuenca	4:35
Arr. Cuenca	17:30	Arr. Sibambe	9:40

Sights in Cuenca: Founded by Spaniards in the 16th century on the ruins of the residence of a former Inca ruler. The major tourist attraction here is the Indian market. See the 16th century La Concepcion Convent and the 17th century Las Carmelitas Descalzas Convent. The Municipal Museum.

Quito - San Lorenzo 1750

Dep. Quito	N/A(1)	-0-	Dep. San Lorenzo	7:00(2)	12:20(3)
Arr. Ibarra	N/A(1)	-0-	Arr. Ibarra	13:00	18:30
Change trains.			Overnight in Ibarra.		
Dep. Ibarra	7:00(2)	12:20(3)	Dep. Ibarra	N/A(1)	-0-
Arr. San Lorenzo	13:00	18:30	Arr. Quito	N/A(1)	-0-

(1)Service temporarily suspended in 1982. (2)Second-class only. (3)First-class only.

Sights in San Lorenzo: Ecuador's second rail-connected seaport, linked by train service (via Quito) with the other port, Guayaquil.

GUYANA

There is no train service between Guyana and adjacent countries. The 2 rail lines in Guyana have been replaced by bus service.

Georgetown

See the collection of orchids, palms and birds at the 120-acre Botanic Gardens. Local animals at the Zoo. Guyanese objects in the Natural History Museum. The world's tallest wood building, the Anglican Cathedral. The assortment of sundries at the Stabroek Market. The tiny, 216-seat Playhouse Theater.

Georgetown - Rosignol 1643 Bus

Dep. Georgetown	Frequent times	Dep. Rosignol	Frequent times
Arr. Rosignol	3 hours later	Arr. Georgetown	3 hours later

Vreed-en-Hoop - Parika 1642 Bus

Dep. Vreed-en-Hoop	Frequent times	Dep. Parika	Frequent times
Arr. Parika	60 minutes later	Arr. Vreed-en-Hoop	60 minutes later

GUYANE (French Guiana)

There are no passenger trains in Guyane.

PARAGUAY

Children under 3 travel free. Half-fare for children 3-9. Children 10 and over must pay full fare. Paraguay's only rail route is from Asuncion to Encarnacion. Its only passenger train service to an adjacent country is the extension from Encarncion to Argentina.

Asuncion

The capital of Paraguay. Linked by rail (via Encarnacion) with Buenos Aires. See: Government Palace, on Calle El Paraguayo Independiente. The Pantheon of Heroes, the national shrine designed to emulate the Invalides in Paris. The Gran Hotel del Paraguay. The view of Asuncion from Parque Carlos Antonio Lopez. The Botanical and Zoological Garden, location of the Museum of Natural Science.

Window-shop on Calle Palma. Take a ride on one of the old trolleys, maintained for tourists as San Francisco, California's cable cars are.

Encarnacion

A busy river port. This is a base for taking auto or airplane trips to see the Iguazu Falls, most spectacular from August to November.

Asuncion - Encarnacion 2230

This route is through dense brush and jungle. The inconveniences include hard wood seats, stifling heat, swarms of mosquitoes and much dust. The locomotive was built in 1912, and the train is said to be the oldest in South America.

At night, the station platforms at villages along the route are lined with people who, sitting at tables while eating and singing, enjoy watching the train pass by.

Dep. Asuncion	20:00(1)	Dep.			
Arr. Encarnacion	12:00(2)	Encarnacion	5:00(3)	12:35(4)
		Arr. Asuncion	21:00	4:30(2)

(1)Tues., Thurs. and Fri. Meal service. (2)Day 2. (3)Sun. only. Meal service. (4)Wed. and Fri. Meal service.

Encarnacion - Posadas - Buenos Aires

Be sure to have an inexpensive (about $1.00 U.S.) "through ticket" before departing Asuncion for Encarnacion. Passengers from Asuncion who do not have a "through ticket" are required to leave the train at Encarnacion, carry their luggage to the auto ferry pier, take the auto ferry across the river, and re-board the train on the other side of the river, in Posadas.

Passengers with a "through ticket" can remain on the train as the train is ferried across the river.

2230

Dep. Encarnacion	14:30(1)
Dep. Pacu Cua (Train Ferry)	17:30(1)
Arr. Posadas	18:20(1)
Arr. Buenos Aires (F. LaCroze)	14:10(2)

(1)Wed. and Fri. Meal service. (2)Day 2.

PERU

Children under 4 travel free. Half-fare for children 4-11. Children 12 and over must pay full fare.

Many rail routes in Peru are at such high altitudes that several trains provide passengers with free oxygen. Details on trips follow a description of interesting sights in 6 cities which can be visited by train.

Arequipa

This is called "The White City" because it is built mostly of white volcanic rock. It lies at the foot of 19,200-foot high El Misti Volcano. See: The beautiful furniture in the 17th century Santa Catalina Convent, reflecting medieval architecture and life. The flowery Plaza de Armas. The colonial residences: Casa del Moral, Casa Ricketts and Casa Gibbs. Leatherwork is a specialty here. At an altitude of 7,500 feet, much lower than Cuzco, Arequipa has a splendid climate.

Cuzco

November to March is the rainy season. The rest of the year, this is the popular tourist spot in Peru. At 11,400 feet altitude, it is often cold here in what was once the capital of the Inca Empire. Many Inca remains in this area. See: The Palace of Manco Capac, the first Inca ruler and founder of Cuzco. The famous stone of Twelve Anles, in the walls of the Palace of Inca Roca. Main Square, where Incas held their celebrations and ceremonies. Stroll Callejon Loreto, a perfectly preserved Inca street. Visit the unusually quiet Indian market.

The base of the ancient Temple of the Sun, now in the foundation of the Church of Santo Domingo. The gold and bejeweled pulpit in the 17th century Cathedral. The House of the Chosen Women, now the Convent of Santa Catalina. Five colonial churches: El Triunfo, La Merced, Santo Domingo, Jesuite and Jesus and Maria.

The excellent murals, carved altars and paintings in La Compania de Jesus, Cuzco's most beautiful church. The magnificent main altar in Belen de los Reyes Church, outside the city. The Inca stonework throughout the city's streets. The prominent colonial residences: La Casa de Garcilaso de la Vega Inca, La Casa de los Marqueses de Buenavista, La Casa de Diego Maldonado, and La Casa de Concha.

The museums: Art, Anthropological and Archaeological, Culture, Larco Heriera and Viceregal. Two ancient forts nearby: Puca Pucara (the "red fort") and the enormous Sacsayhuaman (pronounced "sexy woman") with its 3 tremendous parallel walls. The ruins of Quenko, Tambomachay and Pucara.

The great excursion from Cuzco is the trip to Machu-Picchu, the large ancient Inca city-fortress. Details for this train ride appear later in this section.

Huancayo

Located where an Inca highway once existed, in a wide valley at 10,696 feet altitude. Sunday fairs are the big tourist event here (herbs, fruits, embroidered skirts and petticoats, vegetables, furs, silver jewelry, gourds, etc.). This is the most famous market in Peru, attracting both Peruvian and Bolivian Indians.

Juliaca

Great woolen goods, leather items and alpaca knits are offered in the Sunday and Monday markets in the enormous Plaza Melgar.

Lima

In Summer, stores and offices here are closed from 12:30 to 16:00 so that local people can go to the beaches. Shopping for silver and gold jewelry, alpaca and llama furs, and colonial antiques is a key tourist activity in Lima.

See: Much fine 16th and 17th century colonial architecture. Torre Tagle Palace and these churches: Santo Domingo (one block west of Government Palace), La Merced (on Jiron de la Union, 2 blocks from Plaza de Armas), San Francisco (one block east of Government Palace), San Augustin (2 blocks from Plaza de Armas), and San Pedro (2 blocks east and one block south of Plaza de Armas).

The curved mahogany ceiling in the main hall at the Court of the Inquisition. The city's famous bullring. Plaza San Martin, a lovely park. The centuries-old, 15-minute ritual of Changing of the Guard at Government Palace, daily except Sunday at 13:00.

The Museum of Art (5,000 years of Peruvian culture) in the 1868 Exposition Palace on Paseo Colon. Pre-Hispanic relics (back to 500 B.C.) in the Museum of Anthropology and Archaeology, and the adjoining Museum of the Republic, both at Plaza Bolivar. The Museum of Peruvian Culture at 650 Alfonso Ugarte Ave.

Colonial paintings, furniture and costumes in the Museum of Viceroyalty in the Quinta de Presa mansion. The Museum of Italian Art on Paseo de la Republica. The gold and silver collection at the Rafael Larco Herrera Museum. The Gold of Peru collection at the residence of Sr. Mujica Callo in nearby Monterrico. The mosaic tiles at La Punta, along the beach. The Military Museum at Fort Felipe Real.

The fantastic gold and silver items in the Gold Museum at Monterrico, a suburb. The 3½-hour tour (operated every day by Lima Tours, located near Hotel Bolivar) to the nearby Pachacamac ruins. Sunday afternoon fights in the Plaza de Acho bullring.

Puno (and Lake Titicaca)

It is cold and windy here, at 12,648 feet. The legend is that the Sun God created the first Inca king and his queen on the Island of the Sun in Lake Titicaca, on Peru's western border with Bolivia. Today, 37-pound trout are the monarchs of the lake that is 2 miles above sea level, 35 miles wide and 95 miles long. There are boat excursions to small "floating islands" of reeds, populated by Uru Indians.

Lima - Huancayo 1821

The Lima-La Oroya portion of this train journey is the highest standard gauge rail trip in the world (built in 1893 and reaching a height of 15,681 feet) and carries a staff doctor. The descent to 10,696-foot high Huancayo becomes a relief ! The altitude is so debilitating that most passengers sleep or take oxygen inhalation.

For optimum experience, depart Lima on Saturday morning, spend that night in Huancayo, see the weekly Indian market there on Sunday (silver, llama wool blankets, hides, etc.), and return to Lima on Monday morning.

At the early part of the trip is Chosica, a popular Winter resort. Then, the train goes through scenic valleys and passes Indian farmhouses and rustic railstations where Indian women sell fruits and flowers. The track follows the Rimac River as it crosses 59 bridges, goes through 66 tunnels and makes 22 switchbacks. The "descent" into Huancayo is along small wheat farms.

Dep. Lima (Desamparados)	N/A(1)	Dep. Huancayo	7:00(2)
Dep. La Oroya	13:40(2)	Arr. La Oroya	10:06(1)
Arr. Huancayo	16:38	Arr. Lima (Desamparados)	N/A(1)

(1)Train service suspended in 1982 due to damaged bridge near Matucana. There is 5-hour bus service Lima-La Oroya and v.v. (2)Daily, except Sundays and holidays. Meal service.

La Oroya - Cerro de Pasco 1817

Dep. La Oroya	14:00(1)	Dep. Cerro de Pasco	6:30(1)
Arr. Cerro de Pasco	17:42	Arr. La Oroya	9:35

(1)Daily, except Sundays and holidays. Meal service.

Sights in Cerro de Pasco: At 14,232-foot altitude, this is one of the world's highest towns. There are many metal mines here (copper, gold, zinc, lead). The town was rebuilt in the early 1970's.

Huancayo - Huancavelica 1816

All of these trains run daily, except Sundays and holidays.

Dep. Huancayo	7:00(1)	7:30(2)	13:00(1)
Arr. Huancavelica	10:10	13:55	16:10
	*	*	*
Dep. Huancavelica	7:00(1)	7:30(2)	13:00(1)
Arr. Huancayo	10:10	13:50	16:10

Cuzco to Machu Picchu and Inca City 1810

One of the most popular train journeys in Peru is from Cuzco to Machu-Picchu, paralleling the turbulent Urubamba River. The 5,000-foot descent from Cuzco through the verdant jungle is considered by many as one of the most scenic rail trips in the world. The other attraction, of course, is seeing the incredible 15th century Inca ruins at Machu-Picchu, an 8,000-foot high plateau surrounded by snow-covered mountains, not discovered until the early 20th century by Hiram Bingham, a Yale University professor.

Bingham, in his book "The Lost City of the Incas", wrote: "I know of no other place in the world that can compare to this sight."

At some train stops, native women go through the train, selling tortillas. En route, the train goes through a fertile valley at Ollantaytambo. A bus provides transportation from the Machu-Picchu railstation 1,000 feet up to the ruins. The small (14 rooms) Hotel Turista accommodates visitors who want to stay overnight before returning to Cuzco.

Dep. Cuzco (S. Pedro)	6:00	7:00(1)	14:25	22:15
Arr. Machu-Picchu	9:33	-0-	18:17	1:29
Arr. Pte. Ruinos	-0-	10:25	-0-	-0-
	*	*	*	
Dep. Pte. Ruinos	-0-	-0-	15:20(1)	-0-
Dep. Machu-Picchu	1:31	8:22	-0-	15:51
Arr. Cuzco (S. Pedro)	5:25	12:25	19:00	19:50

All of these trains carry parlor cars. (1)Special tourist train. Supplement charged. There is bus service for the 8km trip Pte. Ruinos-Inca City and v.v.

Cuzco - Juliaca 1810

This extremely scenic route is along the heights of the Andes. Indian women sell colorful knitted garments at the Juliaca railstation.

These trains may be replaced in 1983 by new equipment, with departures from Cuzco at 14:00 and from Juliaca at 22:30.

All of these trains have meal service.

Dep. Cuzco	8:10(1)	Dep. Juliaca	8:25(2)	10:45(3)
Arr. Juliaca	17:35	Arr. Cuzco	17:35	19:50

(1) Daily, except Sundays and holidays. (2) Monday-Friday, except holidays. (3) Runs Saturday only.

Juliaca - Arequipa 1825

The train passes along many grain fields. Highest place on the route is 14,688-foot high Crucero Alto, after which point all water flows toward the Pacific Ocean. Many tall mountains can be seen as well as vicunas, sheep, llamas and alpacas grazing. The train descends in 189 miles from Juliaca (12,500 feet) to Arequipa (7,500 feet).

These trains may be replaced in 1983 by new equipment, with departures from Arequipa at 14:00 and from Juliaca at 21:00.

All of these trains have meal service.

Dep. Juliaca	8:35(1)	10:55(2)	21:55(3)
Arr. Arequipa	16:50	19:00	6:00

* * *

Dep. Arequipa	8:45(4)	22:00(3)
Arr. Juliaca	19:00	8:40

(1)Tuesday and Thursday. (2)Saturdays only. (3)Carries sleeping car. Meal service. (4)Monday, Wednesday and Friday.

Chimbote - Huallanca 0000

This is an 88-mile ride up Santa Valley to the del Pato canyon.

Dep. Chimbote	N/A	Dep. Huallanca	N/A
Arr. Huallanca	N/A	Arr. Chimbote	N/A

INTERNATIONAL ROUTES FROM PERU

Rail connections are available from both Cuzco and Arequipa to both Bolivia and Chile. Puno, on the shore of Lake Titicaca, is 12,648 feet high. These trains may be replaced in 1983 by new equipment, with departures from Cuzco at 14:00, Juliaca 22:30, Arequipa 14:00 and Puno 21:00.

Cuzco-Puno
1810

Dep. Cuzco	7:00(1)
Arr. Juliaca	17:35

Change trains.
1825

Dep. Juliaca	17:55(1)
Arr. Puno	19:00

Arequipa-Puno
1825

Dep. Arequipa	8:45(2)	22:00(3)
Dep. Juliaca	17:55	7:33
Arr. Puno	19:00	8:40

(1)Daily, except Sun. and holidays. Meal service. (2)Mon., Wed. and Fri. Meal service. (3)Carries sleeping car. Meal service.

Puno - Guaqui - La Paz 1826

Boat trip.

Dep. Puno	21:00	Wed.
Arr. Guaqui	9:30	Thurs.

Change to bus.

Dep. Guaqui	10:45	Thurs.
Arr. La Paz	13:45	Thurs.

Arequipa - Guaqui - Viacha . . . and on to Arica or Antofagasta 1826

Arr. Guaqui from Puno 9:30 Thursday

(See preceding schedules: "Puno-Guaqui-La Paz".)

Change from boat to Bus.

1815

This was a 2-hour daytime train ride in 1977.

Dep. Guapui	N/A(1)
Arr. Viacha	2 hours later

(1)Time has not been available since 1977.

Viacha - Arica 1901

Dep. Viacha	13:46(1)
Arr. Charana	19:46
Change trains.	
Dep. Charana	22:50(2)
Arr. Arica	8:05

Viacha - Antofagasta 1910

Dep. Viacha	13:33(3)
Arr. Calama	16:10(4)
Change to bus.	
Dep. Calama	17:00(5)
Arr. Antofagasta	20:00

(1)Tues. only. (2)2nd and 4th Tues. of each month only. (3)Fri. only. (4)Sat. (5)Sat. only.

SURINAM

Children under 3 travel free. Half-fare for children 3-14. Children 15 and over must pay full fare. The only passenger rail line in Surinam is Onverwacht-Brownsweg. There is good forest and mountain scenery on that route.

Paramaribo

See the lovely 18th and 19th century Dutch building on Oranjeplein. The Museum in Fort Zeelandia. The Zoo in Cultuurtuin Park. The picturesque waterfront.

Paramaribo - Onverwacht - Brownsweg 1635

Bus

Dep. Paramaribo	6:30(1)
Arr. Beekhuizen	6:59
Change buses.	
Dep. Beekhuizen	7:00
Arr. Onverwacht	7:30
Change to train.	
Dep. Onverwacht	8:00
Arr. Brownsweg	12:30

Train

Dep. Brownsweg	13:00(2)
Arr. Onverwacht	17:00
Change to bus.	
Dep. Onverwacht	17:30
Arr. Beekhuizen	17:59
Change buses.	
Dep. Beekhuizen	18:00
Arr. Paramaribo	18:30

(1)Friday only. (2)Saturday only.

URUGUAY

Children under 3 travel free. Half-fare for children 3-9. Children 10 and over must pay full fare.

Montevideo is the hub for Uruguay's 1,874 miles of rail service. The 4 lines from there are to Colonia, Mercedes, Rio Branco and Rivera. A branch off the line to Rivera leads to Salto and Artigas.

Colonia

See: The Municipal Museum. The Mansion of the Viceroy. The beautiful plaza. The Parochial Church.

Montevideo

Peak tourist season here is January and February. The major attraction is the city's big beaches. See: The enormous marble Legislative Palace. The National Historical Museum (Rincom 437). Plaza Independencia and the nearby Natural History Museum (Buenos Aries 652). The large lake and National Fine Arts Museum in Rodo Park.

The Oceanography and Fish Museum (Rambla Republica de Chile 4215). The Zoo on Avenida de Rivera. The Military Museum (Montevideo Hill), and the view from there. The Pre-Columbian Museum (Mateo Vidal 3249). The collection of paintings and sculptures at the Joaguin Torres Garcia Museum (Constitujente 1467). The outstanding Rose Garden (850 varities) and Municipal Museum of Fine Arts and History, both in El Prado Park. The Sunday morning flea market on Calle Tristen Narvaja, across from the University's statue of David.

The many fine statues in Batlle y Ordonez Park. The Cathedral, on Plaza Constitucion. Stroll down Avenida 18 de Julio. East of Plaza Zabala, see the Customs House, the Bolsa (Stock Exchange) and Banco de la Republica. Lunch at the stand-up bars (barbecued meats, fruits, soups, sandwiches, fish) at Mercado del Puerto, at the waterfront. Then walk to the breakwater at Punta Santa Teresa to see ships coming into port, or walk along the beaches bordered by Rio de Plata.

The nearby Punta del Este beach resort, during the peak season (mid-December to mid-March). The Casa Pueblo Museum, featuring the work of Uruguayan painter Carlos Paez Vilaro, the Picasso of South America. Night life centers at the local gambling casino. Stroll Avenida Gorlero to see its antique shops, notable for American and European Art Nouveau items from the early years of this century. Take a boat to Isla de Lobos to see the seal colony there.

Rivera

See: Canapiru Dam. Plaza Internacional. Stroll the street which is the border with Brazil. On the other side of the street is the Brazilian city Santa Ana do Livramento.

Salto

See: Lovely Solari Park. The walkway along the Uruguay River.

Montevideo - Colonia 2213

Dep. Montevideo (Gen. Artigas)	6:25(1)	Dep. Colonia	16:00(1)
Arr. Colonia	11:52	Arr. Montevideo (Gen. Artigas)	21:37

(1) Runs Monday, Wednesday and Friday.

Montevideo - Mercedes 2213

Dep. Montevideo (Gen. Artigas)	16:15(1)	Dep. Mercedes	5:05(1)
Arr. Mercedes	23:05	Arr. Montevideo (Gen. Artigas)	11:50

(1) Daily, except Sundays and holidays. Meal service.

Montevideo - Rio Branco 2203

Dep. Montevideo (Gen. Artigas)	5:40(1)	Dep. Rio Branco	15:45(1)
Arr. Rio Branco	13:40	Arr. Montevideo (Gen. Artigas)	23:53

(1) Supplement charged. Meal service.

Montevideo - Rivera 2205

Dep. Montevideo (Gen. Artigas)	6:45(1)	23:25(2)	Dep. Rivera	5:10(3)	22:00(2)
Arr. Rivera	20:30	8:55	Arr. Montevideo (Gen. Artigas)	19:07	7:56

(1) Friday only. Light refreshments. (2) Supplement charged. Meal service. (3) Saturday only. Light refreshments.

Montevideo - Salto - Artigas 2210

Dep. Montevideo (Gen. Artigas)	6:45(1)	19:50(3)	Dep. Artigas	8:00(5)	13:10(6)
Arr. Salto	23:10	11:15(4)	Arr. Salto	17:05	19:40
Change trains.			Change trains.		
Dep. Salto	13:10(2)	11:45(4)	Dep. Salto	17:40	3:30(7)
Arr. Artigas	19:35	21:10(4)	Arr. Montevideo (Gen. Artigas)	9:34(4)	19:07

(1) Fri. only. Light refreshments. (2) Thurs. and Sat. only. (3) Direct train. No train change in Salto. Runs Sun. only. Carries sleeping car. Meal service. (4) Day 2. (5) Direct train. No train change in Salto. Runs Tues. only. Carries sleeping car. Meal service. (6) Fri. and Sat. all year. Also Sun. during school terms. (7) Sat. only. Light refreshments.

INTERNATIONAL ROUTES FROM URUGUAY

Montevideo - Buenos Aires 2217

Dep. Montevideo by Bus	5:30	6:30	9:30(1)	10:15	11:45(2+5)
Arr. Colonia	8:30	9:15	12:30	13:00	14:45
Dep. Colonia by Hydrofoil	8:45	9:30	12:45	13:15	15:00
Arr. Buenos Aires	60 minutes later				

(1)Mon., Tues., Wed. and Thurs. (2)Fri., Sat. and Sun. (3)Daily, except Fri. and Sun. (4)Fri. and Sun. only. (5)Plus other departures from Montevideo at 12:45(1), 14:15(3), 15:50(4) and 15:45(2).

Montevideo - Sao Paulo

2120 Bus				
Dep. Montevideo	20:00	21:00	22:00	23:30(2)
Arr. Porto Alegre	8:00(1)	9:20(1)	11:10(1)	11:35(1+2)
Change buses.				
2100				
Dep. Porto Alegre	8:00	13:00	15:00(5)	N/A(2+3)
Arr. Sao Paulo	N/A(3+4)	N/A(3+4)	N/A(3+4)	6:55(4)

(1)Day 3. (2)Direct bus to Sao Paulo. No bus change in Porto Alegre. (3)Time has not been available since 1980. (4)Day 5 from Montevideo. (5)Plus other departures from Porto Alegre at 16:00, 18:00, 18:30 and 20:00.

VENEZUELA

Children under 3 travel free. Half-fare for children 3-11. Children 12 and over must pay full fare.

There is no train service between Venezuela and adjacent countries. The only rail service for which timetables are available is the 105-mile route from Puerto Cabello to Barquisimeto. Puerto Cabello is a heavily industrialized city. Barquisimeto is a collecting point for sugar, cacao, cereals, coffee and cattle.

Puerto Cabello - Barquisimeto 1655

Dep. Puerto Cabello	6:12	9:00	13:12	17:42
Arr. Barquisimeto	8:57	11:45	15:57	20:27
	*	*	*	
Dep. Barquisimeto	6:00	9:00	13:00	17:45
Arr. Puerto Cabello	8:45	11:45	15:45	20:30

Chapter 18

EURAIL® GUIDE ROUTE CHART

In view of the fact that there are over 100,000 miles of railroad lines in just the 16 Eurailpass countries, it would be impossible to list every conceivable trip one could make by train in Western Europe. We do provide you in this chapter a list of 734 trips that most people touring Europe might make, giving the travel time and first-class fare for each.

We have condensed route descriptions by listing them only in alphabetical priority. For example, the first route is Aix-en-Provence to Marseilles. If you were looking for the trip from Marseilles to Aix-en-Provence, you would refer to the name that has alphabetical priority: Aix-en-Provence. Similarly, the trip Rome-Paris will be found as Paris-Rome, etc.

The rates listed are first-class fares, in U.S. dollars. To compute second-class fares, figure 66% of the first-class fare shown. While this will not always be the exact second-class fare, it will be very close to it. Also remember that European train fares, like all other European goods and services, are subject to change relative to dollar devaluation. On the other hand, once a Eurailpass has been issued to you, you are spared the possibility of further dollar devaluation increasing the cost of your train transportation—another hidden plus to having a Eurailpass.

All the fares listed in this chapter are subject to a seat reservation fee of $2.00 per person (if you want to be sure of having a seat). This charge is made whether traveling with a ticket or with Eurailpass. However, a Eurailpass holder does *not* have to pay the supplement that is charged in addition to the ticket price when riding on a Trans Europ Express, International Inter-City or TGV train, ranging from $3 to $18.

We have listed a few TEE and IIC ticket prices to illustrate that cost and to show how much is saved when traveling with a Eurailpass. Many TEE, IIC and TGV prices are not included here. The complete list of those special trains and their routes appear in Chapter 7.

Keep in mind that trips to or from Eurailpass countries and non-Eurailpass countries are only partly covered by Eurailpass. A passenger holding a Eurailpass has to pay the non-Eurailpass portion of such a fare.

Because Paris has 6 different railstations, we indicate in parenthesis after the name "Paris" the name of the Paris railstation at which a train is arriving.

EURAIL® GUIDE ROUTE CHART

1983 first-class train fares, not including seat reservation fee.

	Travel Time	Fare
AIX-EN-PROVENCE		
Marseille	½	6.00
ALBORG		
Copenhagen	6	34.00
ALGECIRAS		
Cordoba	5½	22.00
Granada	6½	21.00
Madrid	10	51.00
Malaga	5	17.00
Seville	7½	24.00
ALICANTE		
Valencia	3	14.00
ALKMAAR		
Amsterdam	½	5.00
AMSTERDAM		
Antwerp	2½	23.00
Basle (via Roosendaal)	9½	101.00
Berlin	8½	82.00
Bremen	4	45.00
Brussels	3½	28.00
TEE	2½	35.00
Cologne (Koln)	3	33.00
Copenhagen (Kobenhavn)	12	109.00
Dusseldorf	2½	29.00
Frankfurt	6	62.00
Hamburg	6	60.00
Hannover	5½	47.00
Heidelberg	6½	70.00
Hoek Van Holland	2	13.00

Luxembourg (via Roosendaal)	5	51.00
Munich (Munchen)	12	110.00
Paris (Nord)	5½	63.00
TEE	5	75.00
Rotterdam	1	11.00
Salzburg	13	130.00
Utrecht	½	5.00
Vienna (Wien)		
(via Passau)	15	142.00
Wiesbaden	6	57.00
Zurich	11	116.00
ANDALSNES		
Oslo	8	68.00
Trondheim	5½	49.00
ANDERMATT		
Brig	2	16.00
Chur	2½	22.00
Lugano	2	23.00
Luzern	2	19.00
Zurich	2	23.00
ANTWERP		
Brussels	1	5.00
Paris (Nord)	3½	40.00
Rotterdam	1½	14.00
AOSTA		
Milan	3½	16.00
Turin (Torino)	1½	9.00
ARHUS		
Copenhagen (Kobenhavn)	5	29.00
ARLES		
Marseille	1	11.00
Nimes	½	6.00
AROSA		
Chur	1	6.00
Zurich	3	26.00

ASSISI		
Florence (Firenze)	3	13.00
Rome	2½	13.00
ATHENS		
Patras	3	14.00
Thessaloniki	9	26.00
AVIGNON		
Barcelona	6½	46.00
Cannes	3½	35.00
Carcassone	2½	29.00
Geneva	4½	45.00
Lourdes	7	58.00
Lyon	2½	27.00
Marseille	1	15.00
Nice	4	39.00
Nimes	1	7.00
Paris (Lyon)	7	82.00
Port Bou	4	34.00
BARCELONA		
Bilboa	9½	47.00
Carcassone	6	32.00
Geneva	12	89.00
IIC	9½	99.00
Genoa	13½	93.00
Lourdes	10	60.00
Lyon	10	71.00
Madrid	8	50.00
Marseille	8	55.00
Nice	10	78.00
Paris (Austerlitz)	12	117.00
Rome	20	128.00
Seville	22	69.00
Toulouse	7	41.00
Valencia	5	26.00
Vigo	27	77.00
Zaragoza	4½	27.00

BARI		
Bologna	7½	45.00
Brindisi	1½	8.00
Messina	9	43.00
Milan	10	57.00
Naples	4	23.00
Pescara	3½	21.00
Rome	6	37.00
Taranto	1½	8.00
Turin (Torino)	13	62.00
Venice	13	54.00
BASEL		
Bern	1½	20.00
Brig	3½	35.00
Brussels	7	65.00
Bucharest (Partly covered by Eurailpass)	29	161.00
Budapest (Partly covered by Eurailpass)	16	105.00
Cologne (Koln)	6	66.00
Copenhagen (Kobenhavn)	15	154.00
Florence (Firenze)	10	66.00
Frankfurt	3½	45.00
Geneva	3½	35.00
Genoa	9	55.00
Hamburg	9	108.00
Hannover	7½	88.00
Heidelberg	3	34.00
Innsbruck	6	46.00
Interlaken	2½	29.00
Lausanne	2½	30.00
Locarno	4½	37.00
Lugano	4½	38.00
Luxembourg	4	41.00
Luzern	1½	16.00
Milan	6	44.00
TEE	5	54.00
Montreux	3	31.00
Paris (Est)	6	58.00
Rome	14½	88.00
Rotterdam (via Brussels)	8½	83.00
Salzburg	9	66.00
Strasbourg	1	17.00
Venice	10	62.00
Vienna (Wien)	12	83.00
Wiesbaden	4	47.00
Zurich	1	15.00

BAYONNE		
Hendaye	1	6.00
Madrid	6½	51.00
BAYREUTH		
Nurnberg	1½	13.00
BERGEN		
Bodo	26½	163.00
Flam	3½	23.00
Goteborg	12	107.00
Myrdal	2½	22.00
Oslo	7	69.00
Trondheim	14½	110.00
Voss	1½	14.00
BERLIN		
Bremen	5½	52.00
Brussels	10	98.00
Cologne (Koln)	7	75.00
Copenhagen (Kobenhavn)	8	48.00
Dusseldorf	6½	69.00
Frankfurt	7	61.00
Hamburg	3½	35.00
Hannover	4	35.00
Leipzig	1½	20.00
Luxembourg	11	101.00
Malmo	8½	48.00
Munich (Munchen)	9	81.00
Nurnburg	7	55.00
Oslo	19½	126.00
Paris (Nord)	14	129.00
Rotterdam	10	83.00
Stockholm	15½	107.00
Vienna (Wien) (Sudbf.) via Prague	14	72.00
BERN		
Brig	2	26.00
Geneva	2	26.00
Interlaken	1	13.00
Lausanne	1	17.00
Lugano	4½	38.00
Luzern	1½	20.00
Milan (via Lotschberg)	4½	37.00

Montreux	3½	29.00
Paris		
(Est) via Grenchen	7	72.00
(Lyon) via Verrieres	6	68.00
Zurich	1½	22.00

BILBAO		
Hendaye	4	20.00
Madrid	5½	37.00
Vigo	12	55.00
Zaragoza	5	24.00
BODEN		
Stockholm	16	81.00
BODO		
Goteborg		
via Stockholm	34	176.00
via Oslo	24½	165.00
Oslo	19½	130.00
Trondheim	12	89.00
BOLOGNA		
Florence (Firenze)	1½	7.00
TEE	1½	13.00
Genoa	4½	21.00
Innsbruck	6½	31.00
Milan	2½	15.00
TEE	2	23.00
Naples	6½	44.00
TEE	6	58.00
Paris (Lyon)	12½	108.00
Ravenna	1½	6.00
Rimini	1½	8.00
Rome	4	29.00
TEE	4	40.00
Turin (Torino)	4½	23.00
Venice	2	11.00
Verona	1½	8.00
BONN		
Cologne (Koln)	½	5.00
Frankfurt	2	23.00
Koblenz	1	8.00

BORDEAUX		
Geneva	10	88.00
Hendaye	3	27.00
Lourdes	3½	31.00
Lyon	9	70.00
Marseille	7	75.00
Nice	12	99.00
Paris (Austerlitz)	5	64.00
TEE	4	79.00
Toulouse	3½	29.00
Tours	3½	39.00
BREMEN		
Budapest (Partly covered by Eurailpass)	19½	146.00
Cologne (Koln)	3	43.00
Copenhagen (Kobenhavn)	7	64.00
Dusseldorf	3	37.00
Essen	2½	32.00
Frankfurt	6	61.00
Hamburg	2	16.00
Hannover	1	16.00
Heidelberg	7	71.00
Munich (Munchen)	8½	95.00
Stuttgart	8½	82.00
Vienna (Wien)	14	125.00
BRIG		
Chur	4½	38.00
Interlaken	1½	22.00
Lausanne	1½	26.00
Zermatt	1½	20.00
BRUGGE		
Brussels	1½	10.00
BRUSSELS		
Budapest (Partly covered by Eurailpass)	20½	155.00
Calais	3	25.00
Cologne (Koln)	2½	25.00
Copenhagen (Kobenhavn)	13½	129.00
Frankfurt	5½	55.00
Ghent	½	6.00
Hamburg	8	83.00
Liege	1	11.00
Luxembourg	3	24.00

Munich (Munchen)	10	104.00
Paris (Nord)	3	35.00
TEE	2½	44.00
Rotterdam	2	19.00
Vienna (Wien) (via Frankfurt)	15	134.00
Zurich	13	80.00
BUCHS		
Innsbruck	3	17.00
Zurich	1½	20.00
BUDAPEST		
These trips are only partly covered by Eurailpass.		
Cologne (Koln)	18	133.00
Frankfurt	15½	104.00
Hamburg	19½	153.00
Milan	16½	90.00
Munich (Munchen)	11	69.00
Paris (Est)		
via Nancy	21	177.00
via Basel	25	163.00
Rome	25½	110.00
Trieste	15	69.00
Venice	13	72.00
Vienna (Wien)	4	26.00
Zurich	18	96.00
CADIZ		
Madrid	8	50.00
Seville	2	11.00
CALAIS		
Paris (Nord)	4	35.00
Strasbourg	9½	69.00
CANNES		
Florence (Firenze)	11	36.00
Geneva	9	78.00
Genoa	3	19.00
Marseille	2	22.00
Milan	7½	30.00
Nice	1	5.00
Paris (Lyon)	11	115.00
Rome	13	54.00
San Remo	3	10.00

CARCASSONE		
Lourdes	4	31.00
Marseille	4	38.00
Nice	7	61.00
Paris (Austerlitz)	8	88.00
Port Bou	2½	20.00
Toulouse	1	12.00
CHAMONIX-MONT BLANC		
Geneva	2½	14.00
Grenoble	2¼	28.00
Martigny (Second-class only)	3	10.00
Paris (Lyon)	8	78.00
CHARTRES		
Paris (Montparnasse)	1	11.00
CHERBOURG		
Paris (St. Lazare)	3½	42.00
CHUR		
St. Moritz	2½	21.00
Zurich	1½	20.00
COLOGNE (KOLN)		
Copenhagen (Kobenhavn)	11	103.00
Dortmund	1	16.00
Dusseldorf	½	6.00
Essen	1	11.00
Frankfurt	2½	30.00
Hamburg	5	61.00
Hannover	3	40.00
Heidelberg	3	37.00
Koblenz	1	13.00
Luxembourg	3½	31.00
Luzern	7½	82.00
Mainz	2	23.00
Mannheim	3	32.00
Milan	12	109.00
Munich (Munchen)	7	79.00
Paris (Nord)	7	56.00
Rotterdam	3½	31.00
Salzburg	8½	95.00

Stuttgart	4½	50.00
Vienna (Wien)	12	112.00
Wiesbaden	2	23.00
Zurich	7½	81.00

COIMBRA

Lisbon	2½	13.00

COMO

Lugano	½	5.00
Luzern	4	32.00
Milan	1	4.00
Venice	4	22.00
Zurich	4	37.00

COPENHAGEN (KOBENHAVN)

Frankfurt	11½	110.00
Fredrickshavn	7	36.00
Hamburg (via Puttgarden)	5	48.00
Helsinki	24	108.00
Kristiansand	15	57.00
Luxembourg	14½	131.00
Malmo (Hydrofoil)	½	7.00
Milan	22½	197.00
Munich (Munchen) (via Berlin)	19	122.00
Narvik	32½	118.00
Odense	3	16.00
Oslo (via Goteberg)	10	81.00
Paris (Nord)	14	160.00
Rome	31½	241.00
Rotterdam	13	110.00
Stockholm (via Hassleholm)	8	66.00
Trondheim (via Goteborg)	18	144.00
Venice	26	194.00
Vienna (Wien)	21	178.00
Wiesbaden	13	127.00

CORDOBA

Granada	4½	17.00
Madrid	5½	31.00
Malaga	3	14.00
Seville	1½	10.00

DAVOS

Zurich	3	27.00

DIJON		
Lausanne	3	25.00
Lyon	2	23.00
Paris (Lyon)	2½	35.00
Strasbourg (via Belfort)	4	39.00
DORTMUND		
Paris (Nord)	7	71.00
DUNKERQUE		
Lille	1½	13.00
Paris (Nord)	3½	33.00
Strasbourg	8	68.00
DUSSELDORF		
Essen	½	5.00
Frankfurt	3	34.00
Hamburg	4	53.00
Hannover	3	37.00
Munich (Munchen)	11	86.00
Paris (Nord)	6	62.00
ESSEN		
Hamburg	4	50.00
FLAM		
Myrdal (2nd class fare)	1	3.00
Oslo	7	53.00
FLORENCE (FIRENZE)		
Geneva	10	63.00
Genoa	4	17.00
Innsbruck	8	37.00
Lausanne	9	59.00
Leghorn (Livorno)	1½	8.00
Luzern	9	57.00
Marseille	12	57.00
Milan	3	22.00
TEE	3	31.00
Munich (Munchen)	10	55.00
Naples	6	37.00
TEE	5	50.00
Nice	5	33.00
Paris		
(Est) via Chiasso	18	124.00
(Lyon) via Iselle	15	114.00
(Lyon) via Pisa	18	110.00
(Lyon) via Turin (Torino)	18	112.00

Perugia	2½	12.00
Pisa	1½	6.00
Ravenna	3	11.00
Rome	3	22.00
TEE	2½	31.00
Siena	2½	7.00
Turin (Torino)	6	29.00
Venice	3	18.00
Vienna (Wien)	13	67.00
FRANKFURT		
Hamburg	5½	68.00
Hannover	3½	45.00
Heidelberg	1	13.00
Innsbruck	7½	78.00
Luxembourg	4½	36.00
Mainz	½	5.00
Mannheim	1	11.00
Munich (Munchen)	5	53.00
Nurnberg	2½	30.00
Paris (Est)	7	74.00
Rotterdam	6	60.00
Salzburg	7	71.00
Stuttgart	2½	27.00
Vienna (Wien)	9	83.00
Wiesbaden	½	6.00
Zurich	5	60.00
FREDRICKSHAVN		
Hamburg	8½	55.00
Oslo	10	59.00
Stockholm	11½	59.00
GARMISCH-PARTENKIRCHEN		
Innsbruck	1½	10.00
Munich (Munchen)	1½	14.00
GAVLE		
Stockholm	2	22.00

GENEVA		
Genoa		
via Milan	7½	52.00
via Turin (Torino)	7	43.00
Grenoble	3½	20.00
Gstaad	2½	26.00
Interlaken (via Bern)	3	31.00
Lausanne	½	10.00
Locarno	4½	42.00
Lourdes	10	101.00
Luzern	3½	35.00
Lyon	3	20.00
Marseille (via Lyon)	6½	58.00
Milan	6	41.00
IIC	4	44.00
Montreux	1	15.00
Nice (via Lyon)	10½	82.00
Paris (Lyon) (via Lausanne)	6	66.00
Rome	10	83.00
Turin (Torino)	5	32.00
Venice	8	60.00
Zurich	3	36.00
GENOA		
Lausanne	7	48.00
Luzern	7½	45.00
Marseille	7½	40.00
Milan	2	11.00
IIC	1½	14.00
Monaco-Monte Carlo	3	13.00
Munich (Munchen)	11½	61.00
Naples	8½	49.00
Nice	3½	16.00
Paris (Lyon) (via Torino)	12	93.00
Pisa	2½	12.00
Rome	7	35.00
Salzburg	14	63.00
San Remo	2	10.00
Turin (Torino)	2½	12.00
Venice	7	29.00

GOTEBORG		
Copehagen (Kobenhavn)	4½	34.00
Hamburg	10	79.00
Helsingborg	3	29.00
Kalmar	7	42.00
Oslo	5	50.00
Stockholm	4½	50.00
Trondheim	21	99.00
GRANADA		
Madrid	6½	34.00
Malaga	3½	14.00
Seville	5½	20.00
Valencia	12½	42.00
GRANVIN		
Voss (Second-class only)	1	3.00
GRAZ		
Vienna (Wien)	3½	19.00
GRENOBLE		
Marseille	5½	35.00
GRINDELWALD		
Interlaken (Not covered by Eurailpass)	1	5.00
Zurich (Only partially covered by Eurailpass)	3	35.00
HAMBURG		
Hannover	2	23.00
Heidelberg	7	79.00
Helsinki	33	153.00
Luxembourg	8½	90.00
Malmo (via Travemunde)	7	52.00
Munich (Munchen)	8½	99.00
Oslo	15	126.00
Paris (Nord)	11	114.00
Rotterdam	6½	61.00
Salzburg	10	117.00
Stockholm	14½	111.00
Stuttgart	8	89.00
Vienna (Wien)	13	132.00

HANNOVER		
Munich (Munchen)	6	79.00
Paris (Nord)	10	96.00
Rotterdam	5	48.00
Wurzburg	4	47.00
HAPARANDA		
Helsinki	12	50.00
Narvik	11	62.00
Stockholm	19	84.00
HEIDELBERG		
Koblenz	2	23.00
Luzern	4½	50.00
Mainz	1	13.00
Munich (Munchen)	4	45.00
Nurnberg	4	34.00
Paris (Est)	7	67.00
Rothenburg	3	30.00
Stuttgart	1	16.00
Wiesbaden	1½	14.00
HELSINKI		
Kuopio	6	33.00
Oslo	22	113.00
Oulu	7½	44.00
Stockholm	12½	42.00
Turku	3	16.00
HENDAYE		
Lisbon	17	68.00
Lourdes	3½	21.00
Madrid	7	45.00
Paris (Austerlitz)	8	89.00
Zaragoza	5½	24.00
HOEK VAN HOLLAND		
Rotterdam	½	5.00

INNSBRUCK		
Kitzbuhel	1	11.00
Luzern	6	41.00
Milan	6½	33.00
Munich (Munchen)	4	23.00
Paris (Est)	21	104.00
Rome	12½	58.00
Salzburg	4	22.00
Venice	5	31.00
Verona	5	23.00
Vienna (Wien)	8	47.00
Zurich	5	37.00
INTERLAKEN		
Jungfraujoch (Not covered by Eurailpass.)	2	40.00
Kleine Scheidegg (Not covered by Eurailpass.)	1½	18.00
Lausanne	2	29.00
Luzern	2	13.00
Milan	5	36.00
Montreux	3	27.00
Paris (Lyon) via Verrieres	8½	79.00
Paris (Est) via Grenchen	8	81.00
Schilthorn (Not covered by Eurailpass.)	2	19.00
Zurich	2¾	30.00
KARLSTAD		
Oslo	3	36.00
Stockholm	3½	39.00
KLAGENFURT		
Salzburg	4	21.00
Venice	4½	24.00
Vienna (Wien)	6	28.00
KLOSTERS		
Zurich	2½	26.00
KOBLENZ		
Luxembourg	2½	20.00
KONSTANZ		
Zurich	1	16.00
KRISTIANSAND		
Oslo	5	54.00
Stavanger	3½	36.00

LAUSANNE		
Locarno	4	38.00
Luzern	3	31.00
Milan	4½	37.00
Montreux	½	4.00
Paris (Lyon)	6	60.00
Rome	14	79.00
Venice	8½	56.00
Zurich	2½	31.00
LEGHORN (LIVORNO)		
Pisa	½	2.00
Rome	3	22.00
LE HAVRE		
Paris (St. Lazare)	2½	26.00
LIEGE		
Luxembourg	3	16.00
Paris (Nord)	4	41.00
LINZ		
Salzburg	2	13.00
Vienna (Wien)	2	17.00
LISBON		
Madrid (Atocha)	9	44.00
Paris (Austerlitz)	25	157.00
Porto	4	19.00
Santiago de Compostela	9	33.00
Seville	12	38.00
Vigo	9	27.00
LOCARNO		
Lugano	1	8.00
Luzern	3	29.00
Milan	1	17.00
Zurich	3½	30.00
LOURDES		
Madrid	12	66.00
Nice	12	90.00
Paris (Austerlitz)	8½	93.00
Toulouse	2½	21.00

LUGANO		
Luzern	3	29.00
Milan	1½	8.00
Venice	6	26.00
Zurich	3½	30.00

LUXEMBOURG		
Marseille	10	96.00
Metz	1	9.00
Munich (Munchen)	9	83.00
Nurnberg	7	68.00
Paris (Est) via Bettembourg	4	48.00
Salzburg (via Strasbourg)	11	98.00
Strasbourg	3	26.00
Stuttgart	6	49.00
Vienna (Wien)	13	119.00
Zurich	5	56.00

LUZERN		
Milan	4½	35.00
Montreux	5½	32.00
Munich (Munchen)	6½	61.00
Paris (Est)	10	74.00
Pilatus	1½	17.00
Rigi	1½	15.00
Rome	13	79.00
Venice	8	53.00
Vienna (Wien)	13	78.00
Zurich	1	10.00

LYON		
Marseille	4	40.00
Milan	4½	46.00
Nice	5	63.00
Paris (Lyon)	4	57.00
Strasbourg	6	53.00
Turin (Torino)	4½	36.00
Tours	7	50.00

MADRID		
Pamplona	7	31.00
Paris (Austerlitz)	16	134.00
Port Bou	19	59.00
Rome	34	175.00
San Sebastian	7	44.00
Santiago de Compostela	9	55.00
Seville	6	40.00
Toledo	2	7.00
Valencia	5½	29.00
Vigo	9	47.00
Zaragoza	4	24.00
MAINZ		
Munich (Munchen)	5	57.00
MALAGA		
Seville	4	17.00
MALMO		
Stockholm	6	61.00
MARSEILLE		
Milan	11	51.00
Nice	3	26.00
Paris (Lyon)	8	94.00
Port Bou	4½	43.00
Rome	15	75.00
Toulouse	5	47.00
Venice	17	70.00
MILAN		
Montreux	4	35.00
Munich (Munchen)	8½	51.00
TEE	6¾	65.00
Naples	8	56.00
TEE	8	74.00
Nice	6	27.00
Padua	3	16.00
Paris (Est) via Basel	13	102.00
Paris (Lyon) via Vallorbe	10	92.00
TEE	8	110.00
Rome	7	44.00
TEE	6	59.00

Stuttgart	9	69.00
Turin (Torino)	2	11.00
Trieste	6	30.00
Venice	3	19.00
Verona	1½	10.00
Vienna	15½	67.00
Zurich	4½	40.00
TEE	4	49.00

MONTREUX

Paris (Lyon)	6½	65.00
Zurich	3¼	34.00

MOSJOEN

Oslo	14	109.00

MUNICH (MUNCHEN)

Nurnberg	1½	25.00
Oberammergau	2	13.00
Paris (Est)	10	110.00
Rome	14	76.00
Rotterdam	11	108.00
Salzburg	2	20.00
Stockholm	20	183.00
Stuttgart	3	30.00
Venice (via Innsbruck)	9	49.00
Vienna (Wien)	6	47.00
Wiesbaden	5	57.00
Wurzburg	3	37.00
Zurich	5	54.00

MYRDAL

Oslo	5½	50.00

NANCY

Paris (Est)	3	40.00

NAPLES

Nice	14	62.00
Paris (Lyon)		
via Rome-Florence	21	144.00
via Rome-Genoa	23½	136.00
Reggio Calabria	5½	33.00
Rome	2	15.00

Taranto	5	22.00
Turin (Torino)	10	57.00
Venice	9	53.00
Vienna (Wien)	19	99.00
NARVIK		
Oslo	33	132.00
Stockholm	22	100.00
NICE		
Paris (Lyon)	11½	118.00
Rome	11½	51.00
Turin (Torino)	4½	23.00
Venice	11½	46.00
OSLO		
Stavanger	9	81.00
Stockholm	6½	71.00
Trondheim	8	78.00
Voss	5½	57.00
PALERMO		
Paris (Lyon)	32	145.00
Rome	13	58.00
PARIS		
(Parentheses indicate Paris station)		
Port Bou (Austerlitz)	12	105.00
Reims (Est)	2	19.00
Rome (Lyon) via Culoz	17	127.00
Salzburg (Est)		
(via Nancy)	11½	128.00
(via Basel)	16	124.00
San Sebastian (Austerlitz)	9½	90.00
Stockholm (Nord)	24	219.00
Strasbourg (Est)	4½	56.00
TEE	4	69.00
Stuttgart (Est)	7½	79.00
Toulouse (Austerlitz)	7	78.00
TEE	6	97.00
Trieste (Lyon)	15½	121.00
Turin (Torino) - (Lyon)	11	82.00
Venice (Est) via Basel	15	120.00
Venice (Lyon) via Vallorbe	13	111.00
Vienna (Wien) - (Est)	15	155.00
Zurich (Est)	7½	73.00

PERUGIA		
Rome	3	15.00
PISA		
Rome	3½	24.00
Siena	2½	8.00
RATTVIK		
Stockholm	4	34.00
RAVENNA		
Venice	3	13.00
ROME		
Siena	4½	18.00
Trieste	8	50.00
Turin (Torino)	7	46.00
Venice	6	40.00
Vienna (Wien)	20	87.00
Zurich	10	84.00
ROTTERDAM		
Vienna (Wien)	19	140.00
SALZBURG		
Trieste	7½	32.00
Venice	7½	35.00
Vienna (Wien)	4	27.00
Villach	3	17.00
Zurich	8½	57.00
STOCKHOLM		
Trondheim	12½	83.00
Turku (boat)	12½	25.00
Uppsala	1	9.00
STUTTGART		
Vienna (Wien)	9	77.00
Zurich	4	33.00

TRIESTE		
Venice	2½	11.00
Vienna (Wien)	10	46.00
TURIN (TORINO)		
Venice	5	29.00
VENICE		
Verona	2	9.00
Vienna (Wien)	10	49.00
Zurich	7	58.00
VIENNA (WIEN)		
Zurich	12	74.00

INDEX OF CITIES

NOTES

NOTES

NOTES

1983

January 1983

S	M	T	W	T	F	S
						1
2	3	4	5	6	7	8
9	10	11	12	13	14	15
16	17	18	19	20	21	22
23	24	25	26	27	28	29
30	31					

February 1983

S	M	T	W	T	F	S
		1	2	3	4	5
6	7	8	9	10	11	12
13	14	15	16	17	18	19
20	21	22	23	24	25	26
27	28					

March 1983

S	M	T	W	T	F	S
		1	2	3	4	5
6	7	8	9	10	11	12
13	14	15	16	17	18	19
20	21	22	23	24	25	26
27	28	29	30	31		

April 1983

S	M	T	W	T	F	S
					1	2
3	4	5	6	7	8	9
10	11	12	13	14	15	16
17	18	19	20	21	22	23
24	25	26	27	28	29	30

May 1983

S	M	T	W	T	F	S
1	2	3	4	5	6	7
8	9	10	11	12	13	14
15	16	17	18	19	20	21
22	23	24	25	26	27	28
29	30	31				

June 1983

S	M	T	W	T	F	S
			1	2	3	4
5	6	7	8	9	10	11
12	13	14	15	16	17	18
19	20	21	22	23	24	25
26	27	28	29	30		

July 1983

S	M	T	W	T	F	S
					1	2
3	4	5	6	7	8	9
10	11	12	13	14	15	16
17	18	19	20	21	22	23
24	25	26	27	28	29	30
31						

August 1983

S	M	T	W	T	F	S
	1	2	3	4	5	6
7	8	9	10	11	12	13
14	15	16	17	18	19	20
21	22	23	24	25	26	27
28	29	30	31			

September 1983

S	M	T	W	T	F	S
				1	2	3
4	5	6	7	8	9	10
11	12	13	14	15	16	17
18	19	20	21	22	23	24
25	26	27	28	29	30	

October 1983

S	M	T	W	T	F	S
						1
2	3	4	5	6	7	8
9	10	11	12	13	14	15
16	17	18	19	20	21	22
23	24	25	26	27	28	29
30	31					

November 1983

S	M	T	W	T	F	S
		1	2	3	4	5
6	7	8	9	10	11	12
13	14	15	16	17	18	19
20	21	22	23	24	25	26
27	28	29	30			

December 1983

S	M	T	W	T	F	S
				1	2	3
4	5	6	7	8	9	10
11	12	13	14	15	16	17
18	19	20	21	22	23	24
25	26	27	28	29	30	31

1984

January 1984

S	M	T	W	T	F	S
1	2	3	4	5	6	7
8	9	10	11	12	13	14
15	16	17	18	19	20	21
22	23	24	25	26	27	28
29	30	31				

February 1984

S	M	T	W	T	F	S
			1	2	3	4
5	6	7	8	9	10	11
12	13	14	15	16	17	18
19	20	21	22	23	24	25
26	27	28	29			

March 1984

S	M	T	W	T	F	S
				1	2	3
4	5	6	7	8	9	10
11	12	13	14	15	16	17
18	19	20	21	22	23	24
25	26	27	28	29	30	31

April 1984

S	M	T	W	T	F	S
1	2	3	4	5	6	7
8	9	10	11	12	13	14
15	16	17	18	19	20	21
22	23	24	25	26	27	28
29	30					

May 1984

S	M	T	W	T	F	S
		1	2	3	4	5
6	7	8	9	10	11	12
13	14	15	16	17	18	19
20	21	22	23	24	25	26
27	28	29	30	31		

June 1984

S	M	T	W	T	F	S
					1	2
3	4	5	6	7	8	9
10	11	12	13	14	15	16
17	18	19	20	21	22	23
24	25	26	27	28	29	30

July 1984

S	M	T	W	T	F	S
1	2	3	4	5	6	7
8	9	10	11	12	13	14
15	16	17	18	19	20	21
22	23	24	25	26	27	28
29	30	31				

August 1984

S	M	T	W	T	F	S
			1	2	3	4
5	6	7	8	9	10	11
12	13	14	15	16	17	18
19	20	21	22	23	24	25
26	27	28	29	30	31	

September 1984

S	M	T	W	T	F	S
						1
2	3	4	5	6	7	8
9	10	11	12	13	14	15
16	17	18	19	20	21	22
23	24	25	26	27	28	29
30						

October 1984

S	M	T	W	T	F	S
	1	2	3	4	5	6
7	8	9	10	11	12	13
14	15	16	17	18	19	20
21	22	23	24	25	26	27
28	29	30	31			

November 1984

S	M	T	W	T	F	S
				1	2	3
4	5	6	7	8	9	10
11	12	13	14	15	16	17
18	19	20	21	22	23	24
25	26	27	28	29	30	

December 1984

S	M	T	W	T	F	S
						1
2	3	4	5	6	7	8
9	10	11	12	13	14	15
16	17	18	19	20	21	22
23	24	25	26	27	28	29
30	31					